MW01256322

Intricacy, Design, & Cunning
In the Book of Judges

E. T. A. Davidson

Copyright © 2008 by E. T. A. Davidson.
Rubens' *Samson and Delilah* on the cover is used with permission of the National
Gallery, London.

Library of Congress Control Number: 2005910124
ISBN: Hardcover   978-1-4257-0078-2
                       Softcover   978-1-4257-0077-5

All rights reserved. No part of this book may be reproduced or transmitted in any
form or by any means, electronic or mechanical, including photocopying, recording,
or by any information storage and retrieval system, without permission in writing
from the copyright owner.

This book was printed in the United States of America.

To order additional copies of this book, contact:
Xlibris Corporation
1-888-795-4274
www.Xlibris.com
Orders@Xlibris.com
30027

To the storyteller

Preface

We possess art lest we should perish from the truth. —Nietzsche

The struggle to reach the top is itself enough to fulfill the heart of man. One must believe that Sisyphus is happy. —Camus, *The Myth of Sisyphus* (1942)

Of all the books in the Hebrew Scriptures, *Judges*, despite its apparent simplicity, is the most difficult to comprehend. Containing many curious anomalies, non sequiturs, and other ostensibly irrelevant details, it seems crude, chaotic, and close to being nihilistic. At first sight, it is an anthology of folktales about male and female heroes of Israel—probably composed by storytellers long before Israel became a nation. But what odd heroes these characters turn out to be—undisciplined and heartless caricatures, compared with noble Achilles and Hector—defying the reader's expectations about sacred history and how heroes ought to behave. Readers have always found these stories difficult to understand and deeply disturbing.

The stories, however, were regarded as part of Israelite history. According to this history, the tribes escaped from oppression in Egypt, and after wandering forty years in the Sinai, entered Canaan under Joshua in about 1250 BCE, annihilated the towns and inhabitants of the land they believed Yhwh had given them, and settled down in the respective territories Joshua had allotted to them. *Judges* supposedly recounts actual events in the period 1250-1020 BCE, which took place right after the Conquest, before the Israelites finally persuaded Samuel to anoint a king. The Jewish tradition emanating from Josephus was that the scriptures had been transmitted orally and accurately through the ages—not a jot nor a tittle of it altered. Despite the discrepancies between the Septuagint, the MT, and the Dead Sea Scrolls, this seemed in the main true. With the example of how the Homeric epics were passed along orally for hundreds of years before finally being written down, the accuracy of oral transmission of the Bible seemed possible, too, and this possibility lent authority to its witness as history.

Although *Judges* tells us many things we expect only from fiction and almost none of the things we expect from history, pressure from biblical scholarship has always kept even skeptical readers in a straightjacket, preventing them from seeing what was really going on in the stories.

This was because most of the biblical scholarship on *Judges* before 1980 was done by the believing community, and it concerned history, religion, and language, but next to nothing about the style and the literary quality of the book by literary critics. Interpreters either assumed it was written in much the same manner as the "historical" books of the Bible, or else ignored its style completely. Even when literary critics tackled the book beginning in the 1980s and continuing until now, none of them—to my knowledge—analyzed this author's style. Believing that the author of *Judges* was mainly a chronicler blinds the reader to perceiving *Judges* as literature, and a very creative work of literature at that. This present study is an attempt to explore and demonstrate its greatness.

Chapter 1. Introduction

To the literary critic, everything about a text contributes to its meaning and value. Without an understanding of the author's method, the structures he created, and the literary games that he played and without comprehending the *book as a whole* instead of merely piecemeal, we cannot completely decipher its meaning.

Although at first bewildering, the plots can be made out well by a careful reader either through using the numerous commentaries or through using the method of the "hermeneutical circle," whereby one reads the book in the usual fashion—from top to bottom—numerous times, and then at subsequent readings applies what one has previously learned, gradually accumulating and using all possible information.

But there is another way of reading the book: one lays the stories down side by side, and reads *across* the stories, also numerous times, to find out how *each* word and/or idea is related to *all* other appearances of the word and/or idea. Instead of concentrating on a certain topic or a particular character or a particular custom or belief, we begin looking at the book in its entirety, at all the characters simultaneously, as it were, and switch back and forth between them at will. We are like viewers in an airship gazing down at the landscape of Israel below us and watching those figures as if they are all living and acting contemporaneously. What we see is a vast network of relationships like the neural network of the human brain, producing a multidimensional, multivalent text. With 10,000 words in this text, there are innumerable relationships to crunch, incalculable ideas to ponder, and countless conclusions to reach. Our enterprise is to comprehend all these relationships, no matter how arduous the enterprise, for understanding this complexity makes all the difference in how we interpret the stories and how we evaluate them as art.

The book was carefully designed to consist of a structure of many parallels of stories with comparable and contrasting situations and people, its parts almost perfectly symmetrical. The correspondences and contrasts, besides being useful, are also aesthetically pleasing, symmetry being a highly prized constituent of art, as it is indeed of life forms (the design of the snowflake or the chambered nautilus, for example). The design also demonstrates the ingenuity and skill of the writer.

This symmetrical device is exemplified in the Deborah and Samson stories, which are almost the same length and are intricately intertwined, causing us to compare, among other possibilities, Jael's subduing of the enemy with Delilah's, Sisera's mother with Samson's, and Barak's method of warfare with Samson's. Another example would be the many parallel stories about parents and children—five stories about Fathers and Daughters (Achsah, Jephthah's daughter, the

Timnite, and the Concubine, as well as the fathers of the daughters of Shiloh); two stories about Mothers and Sons (Sisera and Micah); and one story with two incidents concerning Fathers and Sons (Joash/Gideon and Gideon/Jether) as well as a third relationship, Jerubbaal/Abimelech. In literature as in life, it is only through comparisons and contrasts that we can determine which actions or people or things are preferable, or even what anything means. We learn that something is good or bad only because it is either better or worse than something else. This is the basic reason, other than design, for the many parallels in this book.

In the best of the modern Twentieth Century literary-artistic fashion, the author never "tells" us anything, but "shows" all. Though this method is found in other narratives of the Bible, it is a defining characteristic of style here. The author himself does not interpret the comparisons for us but makes readers analyze them and hypothesize about what the differences mean. And here is a major difficulty: to assimilate so many details and make choices about them is too laborious for the reader. But since the author has set up this problem for us to solve, *not* to do so is to miss completely what the book intends to teach.

These correspondences are a form of intertextuality. Intertextuality is one of the ways meaning is established in all language systems. Every text in a language is ultimately involved with all other texts—i.e., language is always referring to other words and texts; it is the contexts of *all* texts that define the meaning of any particular word. No text stands alone. Once writing systems are developed, intertextuality happens naturally and pervasively. But it can also be a consciously-contrived artistic device, as in Eliot's *The Waste Land*. Likewise, the intertextuality of *Judges* is deliberate and consists in both an *inner* intertextuality like the examples above, and an *outer* one, with parallels and references to many stories and passages from *Genesis* through *2 Kings*. Intentional intertextuality is one of the secrets of how the author gains multiple meanings from his otherwise simple stories.

Keywords belonging to more than fifty different categories have been sprinkled throughout the text. Among other functions of these keywords is that they serve as signposts, pointing out where the comparisons are to be made.

Another part of the design is that the book is highly "iconic"—every story containing dramatic tableaux, in which the characters are as if frozen in memorable postures. It is a picture book, of sorts. Also tucked into the design here and there is a variety of curious little word patterns, each with its own special import.

Because of the perfection of the design, I assume a single authorship. Or possibly, if the book was altered by a later redactor, the fact that the symmetry and proportions of the book were preserved means that the redactor understood the structure and followed the rules of the games that the author played.

The fact that the designs were so precise means that not a lot of tampering was done by later editors.

To aid the reader in determining the extent of the author's design, I have supplied a number of tables in this chapter—among them, 1) a comparison of the Deborah and Samson stories, 2) the father-daughter, mother-son, father-son stories, 3) the references and allusions to other stories in the Bible, and 4) the author's ingenious chiastic structure, at least of the beginning of the book with its end.

Chapter 2. The Comedy of Horrors

One reason for the difficulty in understanding these stories may be that readers fail to recognize them as being simultaneously both horrific and comic. The horrific elements have the effect of nullifying the comic, and vice versa.

A census of the casualties and deaths reveals an astonishing amount of violence, usually ignored by commentators. There are 88 cases of violence in which the victims (those with names) are killed. 267,860 nameless people are slaughtered in battle, as well as "great slaughter" (no count made) in a large number of other battles. At least 9 named cities are destroyed as well as a large number of unnamed cities, including "all" the Benjaminite towns. In addition, many kinds of fraud and violence are committed, such as Samson catching 300 foxes, lighting torches attached to their tails, and sending them into the fields of the Philistines to burn them up. Instances of terrorism like these mark the cunning of underdogs, the weakest triumphing over the strongest. The mood of the Israelites toward the Canaanites and Philistines throughout seems to be: "Exterminate all the brutes." The land is a heart of darkness.[1]

What is so strange is that this devastation, destruction, slaughter, and carnage have largely been ignored by interpreters. J. Cheryl Exum, a well-known critic who has written many excellent articles and books on *Judges*, admits that the gouging out of Samson's eyes did not disturb her until very recently when she saw a painting by Lovis Corinth of the blinded Samson, which brought out its horror to her for the first time.[2] Milton did not make that mistake. The author meant for the violence to be noticed, for it is strongly stressed and is a definite part of the design. My analysis of the words of violence may surprise the reader in that they are so many and yet so unremarked.

Why has this carnage been slighted by almost every modern critic? Possibly critics are so single-minded—so preoccupied with their own topics, whether characters, plot, or history—that they do not think about it, or else regard the violence and ferocity as mere "background." Oddly enough, despite his almost excessive attention to the details of slaughter, the author himself does not mention pain or suffering or bloodshed. Mutilations abound, but there are no gory descriptions. This also keeps the reader in a state of denial and ignorance.

One reason for the denial of pain in literature and in life that Elaine Scarry suggests in *The Body in Pain* is its "inexpressibility." Unless one is the sufferer, one *cannot* enter into the other person's suffering: "Even with effort, one may remain in doubt about its existence, or may retain the astonishing freedom of denying its existence."[3] Of course, pain could be, and probably was, expressed by the storyteller to his live audience.

Thus the author has achieved a kind of "alienation effect," for the book has hundreds of instances of various kinds of comedy which counteract its horrors. These include slapstick, farce, irony, satire, parody, riddles, games and puzzles, out-of-the-ordinary heterogeneity, exaggeration, people (the "folk") in all kinds of relationships, women as destructive of men, women as foils, disguises and masks, strange uses of bodily parts, degradations of all kinds, food, wine, and banquets, weddings, topsy-turvy world (e.g., woman on top, the wrong person as king), bizarre use of common objects such as the use of strange objects for weapons, etc., as well as numerous instances of humor for which no adequate classification can be found—

funny situations which in a film would evoke laughter, but because they are in the Bible, produce bewilderment and only a guilty pleasure, if that. The characters engage in all kinds of "preposterous acts" (like Samson with his foxes), which cause us to stop in our tracks and try to figure out how—in reality—such crazy acts could have been perpetrated. The list of these is long and amusing, once the reader begins to view them in this way.

"The site of comedy is the body," says Seth Lerer.[4] Mikhail Bakhtin makes this clear in his classic study of grotesque humor in Rabelais.[5] And the body—especially mutilations, dismemberments, and references to what Bakhtin calls the "material bodily lower stratum" (such as bowels and bowel movements)—is the site of some of the comedy in *Judges*. With the help of Bakhtin's analysis of Rabelais, the comedy can be defined as "carnivalesque-grotesque"—or in modern terminology, "black comedy." We also find abundant use of the Trickster, a well-known underdog figure. Samson is the Trickster par excellence.

The whole book is ironical, moreover, and at the end, the Israelites seem oblivious that they are now committing, and thus condoning, the very atrocity that they had originally condemned when they aided and abetted those very Benjaminites (whom they are punishing for the crime of rape) to abduct (and rape) the virgins of Jabesh-Gilead and Shiloh! (Is this comic, or is this horrifying?)

Tragedies end with violent premature death and wanton destruction, while comedies end with marriage, and *Judges* ends not merely with one or two or three or four marriages, as in Shakespeare, but with mass weddings: the 600 remnants of the Benjaminites have carried off 600 brides. From what we imagine to be the male point of view, then, *Judges* ends with a huge *revel*, which is the Greek word for *comedy*. If critics have failed to see this comedy, it may be because it has been counter-weighted with horror. We do not see what we have not been taught to see. Art is something we have to learn to understand.

Chapter 3. Hidden Objects: Wrestling with Anomalies, Solving the Enigma

Into this horror/comedy/folktale mix, the author has planted hundreds of "hidden objects," in the form of keywords belonging to a large number of categories. Discovering them is like digging in an archaeological site. I have attempted to list most of the keywords, put them in their proper categories, and show how plentifully, and perhaps playfully, they are distributed, and what each of the categories signifies; they include People and Kinship Relations; Animals and Agriculture; Buildings and Building Parts (including Doors, Entrances, Gates, and the words Open/Shut and Inside/Outside); and Bodies, Body Parts, and Dismemberments, with a special category for Hands; Fabrics; Food and Drink; Containers; Invitations and Hospitality; and Tools, Instruments, and Vehicles, to mention only a few. Unlike the use of keywords in the Ugaritic myths, *Judges* has many more categories, and each of the categories represents an important theme in the narrative.

The census of the People and Kinship Relations, for example, uncovers an amazing variety of kinship relations and occupations. The author wants us to keep the whole society and its communities and families in mind. The impression one gets is of a dense, active, thriving, bustling population, belying the population estimates given by archaeologists for any of the early periods in which the stories might have originated. Examination of the hospitality, food, and drink categories—to mention one example—takes us inside the private spheres of the characters, revealing certain manners and customs, and violations of them. Hospitality figures in each one of the narratives and helps to unify them.

Like Homer's use of epic similes, the keywords afford us glimpses of society apart from the terrible deeds of war that are being recorded. From these words and objects we are enabled to reconstruct the society and the historical period into which this author placed his fictional characters. The tales depict life in an agricultural and pre-political, pre-technological society, an age of very small towns, isolated from each other, before the development of skilled crafts, commerce, government, and law, and before the rise of an aristocracy. Except for the Canaanite chariots drawn by horses and the Midianite camels mentioned in the Deborah and Gideon stories, the book contains no trace of Israel's later developments as a civilization.

Related to keywords are the "binary opposites," which are integral both to the design and to meaning. To some extent, this chapter is a careful linguistic study on which Semitic scholars may correct, add, or build. No doubt many "objects" still remain to be dug up by other readers—for they are truly hidden. Although these objects and binaries are ornamental, they also comprise a system for increasing the density of information in the text.

One of the literary games played by critics of this book is searching out the hundreds of ironies in it and classifying them.[6] In a table at the end of this chapter, I have listed and explained the "rules of the game" that I was able to uncover.

What formerly seemed to be anomalies and irrelevant details are now revealed to be building blocks of an information system.

Chapter 4. Hidden Objects: Case Law

One of the most common approaches of both the biblical scholar and the literary critic is to examine the morals and ethics of the society and the behavior of the characters depicted. Although *Judges* is not usually considered "philosophical," the incidents pose three serious philosophical questions that all societies grapple with: "What kind of knowledge do we have about our world? what is 'right' conduct? and how should we be governed?"[7] The stories provide clues to the answers. Through a careful analysis of the many ethical dilemmas faced by the characters, and with the help of information gleaned in earlier chapters, we can now speculate about how such stories may have functioned in the evolution of a legal system.

One of the most important keyword categories is Concealment and Hidden Things (deviousness, deception, treachery; hiders, spies, ambushes; traps; secrets and riddles). The *characters* (underdogs) exercise cunning in their strategies to defeat the enemy; likewise, the *author* uses cunning in his strategies to hide all kinds of information from plain view (one of the "games"). People are hiding—like Sisera in Jael's tent and the Israelites in the caves and dens at the beginning of the Gideon story (to mention two examples), and there are many ambushes in the various battles.

Cryptic messages have to be decoded (Ehud's message to Eglon and Samson's riddle); and secrets have to be discovered (like the secret of Samson's strength). The author, in fact, plants clues that the whole book has a hidden meaning when Ehud tells Eglon: "I have a secret message for you,

O king" (3.19) and, when the Levite, at the end of the book, asks: "And now, you Israelites, give your decision and advice" (20.3), messages, in both cases, directed obliquely to the reader. And Gideon asks the angel-messenger: "If the LORD is with us, why has all this happened to us?" (6.13). The main secret to be ferreted out of *Judges* is the author's answer to Gideon's question.

Categories of good and evil that are fruitful to study include the many references to anger; vows, oaths, and promises; and finally punishment and reward, retribution, requital, and revenge, which are exemplified over and over again in all of the stories.

Judges does not refer even once to the laws of Moses. If the laws already existed at the time the stories reached its present form, the stories may be a matching test for students in a law class, in which they were to find which laws to apply to which story. Or if the laws did not exist, the listeners were to propose possibilities.

Most of this chapter is devoted to a discussion of the evils portrayed in the stories, followed by an adjudication of the worst cases—like Jephthah's and Samson's. I have considered all the ramifications of each case, extenuating nothing that might have a possible bearing on it, weighing other parallel instances to make sure that what is considered right or wrong, or just or unjust, in one case will get the same evaluation in another, and in this way building up our knowledge of right and wrong. For example, Jael and Delilah both eliminate an enemy, but with significant differences. Is Delilah's act worse than Jael's? If so, why?

When the stories are viewed as law cases, then the readers become the judges of them. By thinking of themselves as judges, they are gradually shown (if they have eyes to see) what role their own personal schemas and belief systems have played, how they have been tricked into rationalizing about, and approving of, behavior that they would condemn in one case but not in another, and how readers may phase out or twist information that does not conform to what they expect, or want to see, or been told that the case (or book) is about.

Thus they gradually learn how every single detail in each of the cases impacts on their verdict, how one's perspective matters, and how a system of law is built up by memory of its cases. Another thing they learn is how difficult it is to make legal decisions.

Finally, as Aeschylus shows in the *Oresteia*, we must conclude that in order for the Israelites to escape the chaos of an endless cycle of revenges, they need a body of laws and a strong ruling authority so that they do not have to continue inventing laws for every occasion as it arises—a Hobbesian conclusion.

Judges is the author's oblique explanation of how the country came to be divided, why the kingdoms of Yhwh's chosen people were annihilated, how Yhwh had tried to save them, but how the people, in the author's eyes, persisted in going their own ruthless and selfish ways. *Judges* implies what reforms were needed (or what the priestly redactors thought were needed) so that the reconstituted Yehud (Judah) could survive after the return from the Babylonian Captivity in the sixth century BCE.

Chapter 5. Submerged Ugaritic Myths

One common approach of the literary critic is to investigate the possible sources of a text not only to determine how authors use their sources but also to gain insight about the author's creative methods.

As this chapter shows, the folktales of *Judges* may be of Ugaritic or Canaanite origin, and date from a time when the inhabitants of the land had a common religion of El and his pantheon (including Athirat, Baal, Anat, Yam, and Mot), and before the Israelites branched off to develop their own version of this religion and transform the polytheistic religion into a monotheistic one. The characters of the Israelite stories may be the gods of a polytheistic pantheon, who have been brought down to earth and are now viewed as human beings.

The only extant examples of "Canaanite" literature are the Ugaritic myths. Because traces of the Ugaritic myths are found in numerous places in the Bible, it seems reasonable to suppose that traces might also be found in *Judges*. I have discovered many.

In order to help the reader understand the comparisons, I have identified all the characters of the myths and briefly summarized the plots, reviewed the evidence of the myths in other parts of the Bible, and summarized some of the more recent theories about Israelite history and the development of its religion. The rest of the chapter discusses how the myths—especially those about Baal—were demythologized and adapted to Israelite scenes and circumstances in the story of Deborah, Barak, and Jael, and to a lesser degree in some of the other stories. At the end of this chapter I supply a table of how the myths and the folktales are different from, and similar to, each other. It is another kind of "intertextuality."

Chapter 6. Conclusion

Finally, I list the many characteristics of style and performance that together are evidence that this book, though small in compass, is a great literary work. I also develop both an information theory and a narrative theory and hypothesize about how the author contrived such an intricate literary system in a preliterate age.

The proliferation of binary opposites forces the reader to shift continually back and forth between possibilities, like good or evil, strong or weak, male or female, father or mother, Yhwh or other gods, etc. This off/on (1/0) system is like the binary computer language in use today.

Once we perceive the system as dialectical, we find ourselves swimming in a sea of indetermination. But as human beings longing for closure, we instinctively try to take sides and reach definitive conclusions. Since the details can be added up in many different ways, the reader ends up with multiplicities of meanings. The text is not, however, anarchical; for in setting up parallels between episodes within *Judges* and between episodes in *Judges* and the historical books of the Bible, the author is providing his readers with a gloss. An example of this gloss is a comparison of the attempted threatened rape of the angels in *Genesis* 19 with the actual rape of the Levite's Concubine in *Judges* 19 and the daughters of Shiloh in Ch. 21. What we have to figure out is how the latter cases differ from the former. In the end we will not arrive at a definitive interpretation, but at a choice among interpretations.

In dissecting the whole book and trying to perceive the relationship of each tiny part to every other tiny part and from thence to the whole book, I have engaged throughout this study in what is called the process of "deconstruction," the postmodern theory of literature that was first proposed by Jacques Derrida. And I have discovered numerous examples of this theory—for example, that meaning is obtained through "différance," including a system of binary opposites;

that reading involves the free play of signification; that intertextuality produces meaning, while aporias (impasses and gaps) blur meaning; that there is a surplus of meaning and a deferral of meaning; and that these all result in a certain amount of indeterminacy and undecidability.

One of the vexing problems to be dealt with in a literary study of the Bible is how to deal with God—1) as the Yhwh of *Judges*; 2) as the God of the universe; 3) as but another character in the stories; *or* 4) as not there at all. I have tried to keep focused on *the author's* Yhwh and not allow any other interpretations of God, including my own, to creep into my study. Although the accumulated biblical scholarship up to this time has been most useful and necessary, I have tried to elicit all my information *from the text of Judges itself.* Relevant information from other scholars and differences of opinions are usually relegated to the endnotes.

Through oral transmission of the well-known stories over and over again, one of the storytellers would have made modifications in each telling over possibly many years, incorporating all the intricacies into the text one by one, trying them out, and either deleting them or retaining them subsequently in his own personal text. The text was fluid until someone set down his final version and fixed the text.

The scant plots in *Judges* were merely scenarios, which we can imagine that the ancient storyteller, like storytellers of all time, embellished and acted out as his spirit impelled. Storytelling could have been a dynamic performance art, perhaps involving costumes, acting, music, and sound effects, beloved by the audience, who would hoot and roar with laughter and cry and thump and become silent in turn as they responded to each dramatic event. At the end they might have their say in determining the verdicts: thumbs up, thumbs down. We can imagine whose side they were on.

The surface meaning of the book extols great heroes of the tribal wars after the alleged Conquest, while the sub-surface (or subversive) meaning questions each one of them. *Judges* seems to have one meaning for the masses: that it is about the heroes—but another for the inner circle, those who have been initiated into its deeper meaning (its dark matter)—that it is a savage black comedy that attacks pride, cowardice, megalomania, tyranny, brutality, and lust and in the process makes serious philosophical and political comments about Israel. Most important, it is a story about the downfall of the tribes.

The author of *Judges* was a miniaturist, with a small canvas on which to paint. Whereas most writers can say very little in only thirty pages of space in an English text, this author was able to portray a vast network of meaning, perhaps indeed an "infinity" of meaning in that small compass.

A Note about My Text

A scholarly book, my book was written with lay readers in mind. Why should nonscholarly readers who have no investment in the Bible or in religion or in *Judges* want to read my book? Because *Judges* is an important foundational book of western culture, helping us to understand in part how we came to be as we are today, and because, as I try to show throughout, it is *a singular masterpiece of literature.*

The greatest problem for me as a writer was to try to make its overarching complexity accessible to readers who are not closely familiar with *Judges* and who might not have the endurance for the depth analyses and close logical reasoning that are essential in order to enter into the artist's imagination and elicit the many insights which await discovery there. These insights could have been summarized and generalized, but in my opinion, the author's achievement could not be fully appreciated without the accumulated mass of evidence. I have tried to make that appreciation possible for everyone. Readers are invited to "join the team" and send corrections and additions to the author.

While each chapter is independent of all the other chapters, each one is carefully cross-referenced with them. Because of the different methodologies used in different chapters, I had to discuss most of the stories several different times, but each time, it was with a different perspective and different conclusions. A certain amount of repetition was inevitable. I tried to limit that as much as possible.

The many charts, tables, and appendices given throughout help prove the extent to which the author went in order to fashion his intricate design. I also hope they will be of use to anyone entangled in the web of *Judges* as I have been, who wants to pursue this project further. Much more still remains to be learned.

Having spent many years of my wonderful life on this book, I can corroborate Camus' insight, that Sisyphus was happy.

Acknowledgments

My gratitude goes to the State University of New York at Oneonta, for grants in the early 1980s to attend conferences both on the computer and on the Bible-and-the-computer and for work on this project, including a Walter B. Ford Professional Development Grant and a Faculty Research Fellowship in the 1981-1982 University Awards Series and also for the financing of my many trips to annual and regional meetings of the Society of Biblical Literature and other related conferences.

I also thank the National Endowment for the Humanities for the grant to attend the eight-week Bible as Literature Institute at the University of Indiana in 1979, administered by Dr. Jim Ackerman, Dr. Ken Gros Louis, and Mr. Thayer Warshaw, during which half of the participants (biblical scholars) were given instruction in literary criticism and the other half (we literary critics) were given a thorough and stimulating introduction to biblical scholarship and the basics of biblical Hebrew. We all heard lectures by a number of leading biblical scholars, including James Crenshaw, Robert Alter, and Michael Fishbane. Looking over my notes from that institute, after years of engaging in biblical scholarship myself, I am appreciative of how well that seminar was organized, how much we learned, and how much fun it was.

My thanks go to the Pittsburgh Theological Seminary (and their helpful librarians), which generously allowed me to use their wonderful Barbour Library for many years. Thanks also to my son, Scott Davidson, who solved all (or most of) the mysteries of my present computer software, helped me in purchasing, updating, and installing my computers and software, constructed all of the tables in this book, designed the cover of this book, and gave me many other services too numerous to list. Thanks to that best of literary critics of the Bible, Dr. Robert Alter, Professor of Comparative Literature at the University of California at Berkeley, who graciously read and commented on my chapter "The Comedy of Horrors." I also wish to thank Rachel Carson, a student of Professor Keith Bodner's, at Tyndale College, Toronto, Ontario, Canada, who read my manuscript thoughtfully and offered many helpful remarks.

I am grateful as well to Dr. Suzette Henke, whose graduate course in Feminist Criticism I audited at SUNY/Binghamton in 1989; and to Dr. Helen Reguerio Elam, Assistant Professor of English, four of whose courses on contemporary literary theory I audited in 1991-1992 at Albany University, Albany, New York.

Also thanks to my husband Loren, to my beautiful children Tina, Eva, Scott, Lâle, and Loren, Jr., to relatives, staunch friends, and younger and older students at the State University College of Oneonta and elsewhere, my thanks for never evincing boredom when hearing about my project and for telling me, eagerly, that they wanted to read my book when it was published.

In particular, my everlasting thanks to Mr. Arnon, the retired Superintendent of Schools in Tel Aviv, Israel, who benevolently tutored me in Hebrew for my entire year in Israel (1971-1972) and taught me much else about the Bible, the history of the Jews, and Israel. Such kindness must never be forgotten.

E. T. A. Davidson
Oneonta, New York

Contents

Tables

Chapter One

Chapter Two

Chapter Five

Foreword

Now

In an article in *The Atlantic*, Ron Rosenbaum compares the evil of the Holocaust with the evil of the destruction of the World Trade Center and partial destruction of the Pentagon on September 11, 2001, *in which 3,000 people were killed.* Trever-Roper had argued that because Hitler was sincerely convinced of his own rectitude, he could not be called truly "evil." This "True-Believer hypothesis," says Rosenbaum, makes it difficult to determine just how evil bin Laden's act is,

> because it suggests a lesser degree of culpability, a lesser degree of evil than if Hitler and bin Laden had been convinced of their criminality . . . . In the sometimes paradoxical-seeming hierarchy of evil that philosophers have adumbrated, such willingness to sanction mass murder openly, as a mission from God, might consign bin Laden to a lesser category of evil than the one to which Hitler's somewhat surreptitious and self-protective approach to mass murder consigns him.
>
> . . . According to some accounts, bin Laden, a wealthy heir to a billion-dollar Saudi contracting fortune, spent time as a player in every sense of the word—from womanizer to actor—before entering into *jihad* in behalf of the Afghan *mujahideen* . . . .

Rosenbaum reminds us that in bin Laden's tape of December 13, he laughed privately about the overwhelming success of his plot against the Twin Towers.

> It's not impossible to imagine that bin Laden brought some of a player's love for the game to the game of international terrorism. He may well have become a true believer, but the consummate shrewdness of his operations suggests . . . the cynicism of the operator. *

Then

In the book of *Judges* in the Bible, Samson, too, was turned on by women—enemy women: the Timnite, whom he temporarily married, the harlot of Gaza, and Delilah. He terrorized the Philistines until Delilah set a trap for him and enabled the Philistines to seize him, gouge out his eyes, and set him to grinding grain in prison. He was then "eyeless in Gaza, at the mill with slaves," as Milton puts it.

His last act was a suicide mission, *in which he killed 3,000 men and women,* who

---

*   "Degrees of Evil: Some thoughts on Hitler, bin Laden, and the Hierarchy of Wickedness," *The Atlantic*, 289 (February 2002): 65, 66.

tumbled from the roof of the temple of Dagon, and also killed an untold number in the congregation below:

> Now the lords of the Philistines gathered to offer a great sacrifice to their god Dagon, and to rejoice; for they said, "Our god has given Samson our enemy into our hand." When the people saw [Samson], they praised their god; for they said, "Our god has given our enemy into our hand, the ravager of our country, who has killed many of us." And when their hearts were merry, they said, "Call Samson, and let him entertain us." So they called Samson out of the prison, and he performed for them. They made him stand between the pillars; and Samson said to the lad who held him by the hand, "Let me feel the pillars on which the house rests, so that I may lean on them." Now the house was full of men and women; all the lords of the Philistines were there, and on the roof there were about *three thousand men and women*, who looked on while Samson performed. Then Samson called to Yhwh and said, "O Adoni Yhwh, remember me, and I pray thee, strengthen me, I pray thee, only this once, O Elohim, so that with this one act of revenge, I may pay back the Philistines for my two eyes." And Samson grasped the two middle pillars upon which the house rested, and he leaned his weight against them, his right hand on the one and his left hand on the other. Then Samson said, "*Let me die with the Philistines*." Then he strained with all his might; and the house fell upon the lords and all the people that were in it. So the dead he killed at his death were more than those whom he had killed during his life (*Judges* 16.23-30, NRS with my modifications).

This was Samson's last neat trick. Readers of the Bible have gone away laughing ever since. What a difference perspective makes.

Identification of Characters, Tribes, Locations, Foreign Peoples, and Gods

Abimelech, son of Gideon, killed his brothers and became king in Shechem with the help of the Shechemites. He was killed attacking Shechem after 3 years of rule (Ch. 9)

Achsah, daughter of Caleb, married Othniel (1.12)

Adoni-Bezek, Canaanite king defeated by Israelites (1.5)

Barak, commander of the Israelite army, defeated Sisera's army but lost the honor of killing Sisera (Chs. 4-5). From Naphtali

Caleb (1.12), helped Joshua conquer the promised land. From Judah. His daughter Achsah married Othniel

Deborah, a prophetess and judge, went to battle with Barak against Sisera (Chs. 4-5). From Ephraim

Delilah, a Philistine woman of Sorek (probably near Gaza), helped the Philistines capture Samson

Eglon, king of Moab, conquered by Ehud (3.12ff.)

Ehud, a Benjaminite, assassinated Eglon of Moab with the help of the Ephraimites (3.12-30)

Gael, an outsider, moved into Shechem and incited an insurrection against Abimelech (Ch. 9)

Gideon, of the clan of Abiezer, of the tribe of Manasseh, defeated the Midianites, Amalekites, and peoples of the East (Chs. 6-8). Gideon was clothed with the spirit of Yhwh. His other name, Jerubbaal, is used throughout Ch. 9

Heber, a Kenite and the husband of Jael

Jabin, king of the Canaanites; his commander was Sisera (4.1)

Jael, wife of Heber, murdered Sisera (4.18 ff.) (Chs. 4-5)

Jephthah, a Gileadite, an outlaw bribed by the elders to deliver them from their enemy. He tried to negotiate with the Ammonites and then conquered over them. He sacrificed his daughter in order to fulfill a vow. He served 6 years (Ch. 11-12)

Jerubbaal, see Gideon

Jether, Gideon's firstborn son, who refused to kill Zebah and Zalmunna

Joash, father of Gideon (Ch. 6)

Jotham, son of Gideon, told a fable against his brother Abimelech (Ch. 9); he was the only survivor after Abimelech killed his 70 brothers

Levite from Judah, became Micah's priest, then deserted him to join the Danites in their migration (Ch. 17-18)

Levite from Ephraim, who pushed his Concubine out to a gang of Benjaminite rapists; he incited the Israelites to make war against Benjamin (Ch. 19-20)

the Levite's Concubine, originally from Judah, concubine of the Levite from Ephraim, gang-raped by Benjaminites in Gibeah

Manoah, a Danite, father of Samson (Ch. 13, 14)

Micah, an Ephraimite, whose idols were stolen by the Danites (Ch. 17-18)

Micah's mother, whose money Micah stole; after he returned it, she had idols made of a portion of the money

Oreb and Zeeb, Midianite captains slain by the Ephraimites in the story of Gideon

Othniel, a Calebite, married Caleb's daughter (1.13); was raised by Yhwh to conquer Cushan-rishathaim, king of Aram (3.12)

Purah, Gideon's servant, probably an armor-bearer; went down to the Midianite camp in the middle of the night with Gideon (7.11)

Samson, a Danite (Chs. 13-16); his mother vowed that he would be a Nazirite (holy man); he married a Philistine from Timnah; he visited a Philistine prostitute; he had a relationship with Delilah, a Philistine; was finally captured by the Philistines, had his eyes gouged out; but he conquered over them by pulling down their Temple of Dagon. Served as judge 20 years

Samson's mother (Ch. 13, 14)

Shamgar ben Anath, killed 600 Philistines with an ox-goad (3.31) and "delivered" Israel

Sihon, king of the Amorites, who in an earlier time prevented the Israelites from passing through his country on their way to Canaan; the Israelites fought against him and defeated him, and the tribes of Reuben, Gad, and half of Manasseh settled in this territory. In Jephthah's time, the Ammonites tried to seize this territory

Sisera, a Canaanite warrior, defeated by Deborah and Barak. He was killed by Jael (Ch. 4-5). He had 900 chariots of iron

Sisera's mother, waited in vain for her son to return home from battle

the Timnite, a Philistine woman of the city of Timnah who married Samson (Ch. 14-15); she revealed the secret of the riddle to the Philistine guests; later she was given away by her father to another man, and in retaliation against Samson, the Philistines burned up the Timnite and her father's house

Yhwh (Yahweh), the name of God throughout most of *Judges*; also called Elohim (plural for *gods*) but not frequently

Zebah and Zalmunna, Midianite kings slain by Gideon

Zebul, Abimelech's deputy (Ch. 9)

Minor Judges

Abdon, a minor judge of Pirathon, land of Ephraim. Served 8 years (Ch. 12)

Elon, a minor judge of Zebulun. Served 10 years (Ch. 12)

Ibzan, a minor judge of Bethlehem (Judah). Served 7 years (Ch. 12)

Jair, a minor judge from Gilead. Served 22 years (Ch. 10)

Tola, a minor judge of Issachar. Served 23 years (Ch. 10)

Israelite Tribes

Twelve tribes of Israel: the most important in this book are Judah, Benjamin, Dan, Gilead (Gad), Manasseh (also called Machir), and Ephraim. (Ephraim and Manasseh together are called the House of Joseph). Others: Simeon, Asher, Issachar, Zebulun, Naphtali, Reuben, Levi (no land allotted to this tribe).

Simeon (almost nonexistent) and Judah are southern tribes. The rest are northern. When the kingdom of David split into two parts, the northern kingdom was called Israel, the southern Judah. The name "Israel" usually refers to the 10 northern tribes

Asher, a tribe which sat still by the coast and did not go to battle with Barak and Deborah but fought under Gideon against the Midianites and Amalekites

Benjamin: Ehud's tribe, which probably fought against the Moabites under him; went to battle with Deborah and Barak. Gibeah, in the tribe of Benjamin, is where the Levite's Concubine was gang-raped and murdered. When the tribe of Benjamin did not give up the rapists for punishment, all-Israel went to war against them. The book ends with its near destruction and the ruses by which the Israelites got wives for the remnant of the Benjaminites.

Dan, a tribe which abided by its ships and did not go to battle with Barak and Deborah. Samson was of this tribe. The Danites migrated from a central location, near the tribe of Benjamin, and settled in the north; on their way north, they stole Micah's idols and persuaded his Levite priest to come along with them; Micah was prevented from attacking them because they were heavily armed

Ephraim: Deborah's tribe. Ephraim went to battle with Deborah and Barak; defeated Oreb and Zeeb (captains) in the battle against the Midianites, but accused Gideon of not having called them out (he had); accused Jephthah of not having called them out (he claimed he had); 42,000 of them were slaughtered by Jephthah. The man in the Benjaminite town of Gibeah who invited the Levite and his Concubine in for the night was an Ephraimite

Gilead, land east of the Jordan where the Israelite tribe of Gilead (Gad) settled; Gilead stayed beyond the Jordan and did not go to battle with Barak and Deborah; the Gileadites under Jephthah defeated the Ammonites

Issachar, a tribe in the Transjordan which went to battle with Deborah and Barak; did not fight under Gideon

xxx   Intricacy, Design, & Cunning in the Book of Judges

Judah, a southern tribe. 3000 men of Judah took Samson prisoner and handed him over to the Philistines. When the Israelites "inquired" of Yhwh, twice they were designated to "go up first"

Levi (a tribe without an allotment). Two Levites are important characters in Chs. 17-20

Manasseh, Gideon's tribe, fought under Gideon against the Midianites and Amalekites

Naphtali, a tribe which went to battle with Barak and Deborah and also fought under Gideon against the Midianites and Amalekites; Barak was from Naphtali

Reuben, a tribe which refused to go to battle with Barak and Deborah

Zebulun, a tribe which went to battle with Barak and Deborah and also fought under Gideon against the Midianites and Amalekites

Places, Foreign People

Abiezer, a clan of Manasseh, to which Gideon belonged

Amalekites, ancient enemies of the Israelites, joined with the Midianites to attack Israel, defeated by Gideon

Ammonites, a nation east of the Jordan, defeated by Jephthah

Ashdod, one of the 5 Philistine cities

Ashkelon, one of the 5 Philistine cities; Samson killed 30 Ashkelonites for their clothing

Bethel, a religious site in Ephraim where the Israelites "inquired" of Yhwh in their war against Benjamin, formerly called Luz (Chs. 20-21)

Canaan, "the Promised Land"; ancient Palestine; the name given to the land by the Israelites before they occupied it. "It is not possible to define an ethnic group as the 'Canaanites,' but a social entity recognized in the Bible as the 'inhabitants of Canaan' (Exod. 15;15) is distinct from the Philistine and the Transjordanian Edomites and Moabites."[8] Very likely the inhabitants of that land did not know themselves as "Canaanites"

Edom, a nation east of the Jordan, enemy of Israel

Ekron, one of the 5 Philistine cities

Gath, one of the 5 Philistine cities

Gaza, one of the 5 Philistine cities; Samson visited a prostitute there; was put in prison there; pulled down the temple of Dagon there

Gibeah, a Benjaminite city where the Levite decided to stay overnight (Ch. 19)

Jabesh-Gilead, town which did not come to fight against the Benjaminites; it was razed and everyone killed except 400 virgins who were given to the Benjaminites as wives. It was a town devoted to Saul in 1-2 Samuel

Jerusalem, city where the Levite decided not to spend the night because the inhabitants were Jebusites, not Israelites (Ch. 19)

Kenites, a Midianite tribe (not one of the 12 tribes), thought to be descended from Cain

Machir, another name for Manasseh

Meroz, an unknown city in the north of Israel, did not go to battle with Deborah and Barak, and was cursed

Midian, an Arabian people coming from southeast of the Jordan and invading Israel

Midianites, formidable enemies of Israel, defeated by Gideon

Mizpah, Jephthah's home village in Gilead, where Jephthah made his vow; the Israelites assembled before Yhwh in Mizpah to decide to fight against the offending tribe of Benjamin (20.1)

Moab, a nation east of the Jordan, enemy of Israel. Eglon in *Judges* was a Moabite tyrant extracting tribute from the Israelites

Penuel, city east of the Jordan, refused to give food to Gideon, later was punished by Gideon

Philistines, enemy of the Israelites, lived on the seacoast and had 5 important cities: Ashkelon, Gaza, Ekron, Ashdod, Gath

Shechem, city from which Abimelech ruled, temple of Baal-Berith and El-Berith (probably names for the same temple) located there, thus a city with polytheistic leanings

Shiloh, a religious city where the ark was kept and from which the daughters came out to dance and were abducted by the Benjaminites (21.19-23)

Succoth, city east of the Jordan which refused to give food to Gideon, later punished by Gideon

Tower of Shechem, burned down by Abimelech

Tower of Thebez, attacked by Abimelech; Abimelech killed there by a millstone dropped by a woman in the tower

Foreign Gods

Asherah (Athirat in Ugarit mythology) consort of El, mother of 77-88 children, including Yam and Mot. At some point in Israelite history was thought to be the consort of Yahweh. In the Bible she was the consort of Baal

Baal, rain and storm god in Ugarit mythology, son of Dagon, but a member of El's court, patron of the city of Ugarit

Dagon, god of grain in Ugarit mythology, father of Baal. Ugarit myths have no stories about him.

El, head god in Ugarit mythology, possibly the god of the Israelites before he was identified as Yhwh

Mot, god of death in Ugarit mythology, son of El and Athirat

Yam, god of the sea in Ugarit mythology, son of El and Athirat

Dates to Remember

Dates of events in the Bible are the traditional ones given or implied in the Bible itself. Further discussion of dating is given in the rest of the book. There is very little historical corroboration for the events of the Hebrew Bible (Old Testament) or the New Testament. The indented information is about the Bible; the rest is about Middle Eastern events and ancient literature. New abbreviations adopted by the Society of Biblical Literature: BCE = B.C. and CE = A.D.

2000	BCE migration of the Greeks to Greece
1900-1850	Abraham
1700	Joseph in Egypt
1600-600	Gilgamesh Epic (tablets from many different time periods) (Akkadian, Assyrian, Sumerian)
1400-1200	the Amarna Letters written
	flourishing of the city of Ugarit
ca. 1350	the Ugaritic Myths (written and) preserved
1280-1250	The Exodus
1150	settlement of the Philistines in Palestine
1250-1020	Period of the Judges
1207	Merneptah stele erected in which the Pharaoh announces victory over Israel: "its seed is not"
1100	*Enuma Elish* (Babylonian)
1020-1000	reign of Saul
1000-961	reign of David
961-922	reign of Solomon
922	division of the Kingdom into 2 parts: Israel (north), Judah (south)
842-814	reign of Jehu of Israel
835	Tel Dan inscription in which Hazael, king of Damascus (Syria), boasts of having conquered two kings of the "house of David"
859	Black Obelisk erected in which Jehu, King of Israel, is depicted as groveling before Assyria
830	Moabite Stone erected in which Mesha of Moab boasts of breaking away from Israel
700s	Kuntillet 'Ajrud inscriptions about Yhwh and his Asherah

ca. 750	Homer
722/721	fall of Israel (conquered by Assyrians)
621	discovery of the Book of Deuteronomy (Josiah's reform)
598, 587	conquest of Judah by Babylon
598, 586-539	Babylonian Captivity
538	return of the "remnant" to Jerusalem
520-515	building of the 2nd Temple (Wailing Wall)
500-400	Golden Age of Greece (Aeschylus, Sophocles, Euripides)
399	death of Socrates
332	capture of Jerusalem by Alexander
323	death of Alexander
323-167	Hellenistic Period: Ptolemys and Seleucids
167-64	Maccabean Revolt
142-63	Jewish rule of Israel (Hasmoneans)
63	coming of Pompey (the Romans)
63-4	Herodian period
19	death of Virgil
4 BCE-29 CE	life of Jesus
66-73 CE	Jewish Revolt against the Romans.
70 CE	destruction of Jerusalem and the 2nd Temple
73 CE	fall of Masada
90 CE	Council of Jamnia (traditional date of fixing of the Hebrew canon by the Rabbis)
200-300s	Hebrew canon further defined

Chapter One

INTRODUCTION:
STRUCTURE, PARALLELS, AND PATTERNS

The artist's task is "to find a form that accommodates the mess."   —Samuel Beckett

Only connect.   —E. M. Forster

I. Introduction

Judges may be the least liked book of the Bible. Except for the story of Samson, virtually none of the many characters in this book is familiar to readers unless it is Gideon—and for many, he is known only by name. Because this book was apparently the only information about Israel for the period 1250-1020 BCE, it was mined in the past chiefly by historians and theologians, by editors and translators of the Bible, by Semitic scholars, and by textual critics, but avoided or disliked by the average reader. Why this is true must be determined, since this book is, in my opinion, one of the most fascinating books, small or large, ever written.

The Bible, and *Judges* in particular, were written for ancient readers, not for our contemporary world, and readers today tend to go to it with the wrong expectations. Few of us have been taught how to decode the Bible.

Problems of style. First, these stories do not follow the narrative conventions in which readers have been educated. Although the style seems to be similar to that of *Genesis* and *1* and *2 Samuel*, the book is filled with strange details, which may be misconstrued as mere touches of realism and therefore put in brackets or dismissed, without our realizing that to ignore anything is fatal to understanding the book.

Second, most readers find very little that they can connect with, limited use of sense impressions except sight and sound—taste (none), smell (the "dirt" in the Ehud story), touch (blind Samson feeling the pillars)—the kind that help readers live vicariously the lives of the characters, no colors, no weather, no heat or cold (except one reference to rain), no passing of the seasons, no nuclear families, no emotion or romantic passion (à la Ruth), no normal everyday calamities, no hunger, no illness, no weak old age, no outstanding virtue or goodness, no suggestion that creation is amazingly wonderful (à la Job), no sense of beauty, no striving for success (except in war), no drop of kindness or generosity, no philosophical reflections. Though it is a book about war, there are no wounds, no disabilities, no suffering, and no compassion for the afflicted except Yhwh's occasional compassion for the misery of the Israelites when they fall into error.

Third, readers expect authorial interpretation to keep them informed about what conclusions to draw. But this book does not interpret itself, and its shocking ending is baffling and dismaying. Readers must reach conclusions themselves.

Fourth, they do not realize that *Judges* must be read as a whole, not piecemeal. It's an information system—like reading Hegel. To make sense of the book, its entire structure must be grasped.

Problems with the characters. It is hard to keep these characters straight.[*] The stories are so short, that hardly do readers grasp onto the meaning of one of them, than a new set of characters is encountered and the preceding ones promptly erased. Surprises, sudden bursts of violence, cruelty interspersed with laughable actions, one's reason telling one something is bad while one's intuition tells one it is funny—this causes a dreadful and unallayable cognitive dissonance within the uninitiated.

The characters are such bizarre men and women! What are readers to make of them?

1. Ehud, bearing a message from Yhwh, who suddenly stabs Eglon
2. Deborah, presented in two somewhat contradictory versions, in which she, the main character, disappears halfway through the story, to be immediately replaced by a lone woman in her tent viciously hammering a tent peg into a warrior's skull
3. Gideon, defying the connotations of his name of heroism ("Hacker"), more like a cowardly caricature than a hero
4. Gideon's evil son Abimelech, his story wrapped in complexities of which one can scarcely make out who is fighting against whom and for what reasons
5. Jephthah, whose story begins with a long seemingly irrelevant digression and then is terminated twice, once with his cruel sacrifice of his only child and the second time with a non sequitur about his ruthless slaughter of a fellow tribe
6. Samson, with his unruly passions, duped by dangerous foreign women

---

[*]   A cast of characters has been supplied in the Foreword.

7. Insignificant little Micah, stealing a huge amount of money from his mother and worshiping idols, which the bullies in the tribe of Dan without any conscience steal

8. The Levite's Concubine,** scandalously gang-raped by thugs, the book continuing with a chaotic series of ambushes and battles between the tribes—hard for the reader to negotiate—and closing with the defeated decimated tribe of Benjaminites hiding in a vineyard, seizing young girls as they troop out to dance, and running off with them, bringing this shocking book of the Bible to an abrupt and abhorrent (or is it funny?) conclusion.

Wrong expectations. First, the book is supposedly studded with heroes and heroines. But it is hard for most people to conceive of emulating any of these characters. Only by ignoring gory details can one turn these stories into something befitting the reputation that the *Epistle to the Hebrews* gives to Gideon, Barak, Samson, and Jephthah, "who through faith conquered kingdoms, enforced justice, received promises, stopped the mouths of lions, quenched raging fire, escaped the edge of the sword, won strength out of weakness, became mighty in war, put foreign armies to flight" (11.32-34). In order to fit the entire cast of characters into this template of saviors of Israel, readers must ignore the many repulsive details which render this task impossible.

Second, after *Joshua,* readers expect to find the Israelites peacefully settled in their allotted territory, but *Judges* presents a conflicting version of the Israelites' conquest of Canaan. The book begins with chaos and the failure of the "chosen" people, whose defeats are inexplicably greater than their victories, and who fail to settle down properly into their allotments.

Third, under the false impression that the country is "Israel," that the twelve tribes are united, and that the behavior of the tribes is commendable, the reader may fail to realize that the stories are mainly about the ten northern tribes, not about Judah (which is located south of Benjamin) or Simeon, which disappears almost immediately after its first mention. Judah is not yet part of "Israel" in this book, and plays only a minor role in the Samson story.

Fourth, the word "Israelites" does not refer to *all* the people of all the twelve tribes, but may refer to the people of one tribe or the few tribes active in a particular story, and less frequently, to all the ten northern tribes. Not realizing how important the tribes are to this book, readers think them unimportant and disregard vital information about the individual tribes. Because of this important gap in information, readers fail to understand that the aim of the book is to show how the tribes went wrong.

** Because the Levite's Concubine is nameless, the word "concubine" is capitalized each time it refers to her.

Fifth, they expect some religious information, yet God is peculiarly absent.*** What little information readers learn about God in this book does not coincide with their own beliefs. Or putting their own beliefs about God into that word when it appears on the page, they completely miss the author's god and what his god demands or expects. Though it is supposed to be a sacred text, it has little to say about religion. It seems to lack "spirituality."

Only with a great deal of perseverance, do readers come to realize that this is not a history book or a book of theology, or a book of wisdom. It is a little book of horrors—something that, until they understand this, they are unwilling to accept. They cannot imagine that the Bible would contain horror stories, nor why.

Judges transgresses our expectations in all kinds of ways. Centuries of scholars and readers, perhaps unconsciously, have tried to purify these stories—usually by ignoring some events and magnifying others—because they did not know what else to do with them. If one starts by believing the characters are heroes, then one has to twist the evidence to fit that mold. Expecting that the tribes are "good," readers therefore cannot fathom the tribes' respective failures, one by one, or realize that the aim of the book is to show the ten northern tribes' trajectory of suicide. Even the best scholarly introductions do not make this clear.

From time to time conscience-stricken historians have also expressed their abhorrence for certain of the behaviors of the main characters. Phillips P. Elliott, in the *Interpreter's Bible* (1973), for example, wrote:

> By even the most elementary standards of ethics [Ehud's] deception and murder of Eglon stand condemned. Passages like this, when encountered by the untutored reader of the Scriptures, cause consternation and questioning. One must see the situation in the light of the times, when the important matter was to help Israel, and the means of doing it were not examined or questioned. All through our Jewish-Christian history there has been this temptation to put so high a value upon the end that any means are justified to achieve it. Conversations at the point of the sword are not unknown to our modern world. So Ehud's deceit and murder of Israel's foe received praise and honor.[1]

In the same vein is his comment about Jael:

> The event is like the deceit and murder of Eglon by Ehud (Ch. 3). These are rough times of which we are reading, when "human flesh is cheap" [S. A. Studdert-Kennedy's "Indifference"]. Such evil deeds cannot be justified or defended; they can only be

---

*** Throughout this book, God is referred to with the name used in the Hebrew text, either Yhwh or Elohim, so as not to confuse contemporary conceptions of God with the author's understanding of the god in *Judges*.

    In my study, Yhwh is always regarded *not* as God, but as an expression of the ancient author's belief.

understood, and that dimly, on the basis of a ruthless age and [with] so intense a concern for Israel's life and faith that whatever contributed to that end was condoned. Yet even the ancient writers did not regard this act as inspired by God . . . (716-717).

The omission of Jael and Ehud from its list of Judges in *Hebrews* is interpreted by Elliott to mean that the author of the Epistle shared Elliott's revulsion toward the behavior of such as Jael and Ehud.

Another modern scholar dismayed by this kind of morality is John L. McKenzie, *The World of the Judges* (1967), who wrote:

The moral level of the stories of Samson is appalling . . . . The murderous career of Samson exceeds even what the reader of the history of early Israel must teach himself to expect . . . an amoral giant with uninhibited passions, particularly the passions of anger and lust. That such a man should be presented as a charismatic hero, impelled by the spirit of Yahweh to deliver Israel, has always been a shock to readers of the Bible.[2]

So great is McKenzie's impatience with the last story of *Judges* (Chs. 20 and 21) that he dismisses the massacre of the inhabitants of Jabesh-Gilead as "so intrinsically improbable that it needs no further consideration" (167). (We in the 21st Century, who have seen frequent destruction of cities, do not consider it so improbable.) As for the story of the Levite's Concubine (Ch. 19), Julius Wellhausen regarded it as "merely a late imitation of the story of Lot" (Gen. 19) and "arbitrarily dismissed it as having no positive value."[3]

In her brilliant recent commentary on *Judges* (2000), Cheryl A. Brown finds it difficult to reconcile *Judges* with her Christian ideas of what the Scriptures ought to contain:

. . . the OT, especially books such as Judges, contains material that flies in the face of everything we identify as biblical morality. We do not know what to do with the rape, murder, genocide, sexual immorality, child sacrifice, lying, idolatry, and stealing. While "all Scripture is God-breathed [inspired] and is useful for teaching, rebuking, correcting and training in righteousness" (2 Tim 3.16), some parts of Judges do not readily appear "useful." A significant body of Christian interpreters have solved the problem by allegorizing it, reading a message into the text rather than out of it, in essence, making it say whatever they wanted, often with the help of ingenious hermeneutical gymnastics. Others have ignored the problematic or embarrassing passages. But these are no solutions for those who take the whole of Scripture seriously.[4]

Of Samson, she writes:

Samson is admittedly the most problematic of all Israel's judges. Any honest interpreter would have to acknowledge that he or she would rather skip over some parts of his story; evidence that most do ignore it is the fact that few sermons are preached on every verse in Judges 13-16. Small wonder, Samson does not conform to our idea of how a biblical hero should act. This arrogant, duplicitous, womanizing trickster is hardly an exemplary model of biblical morality (239).[5]

Of the story of the Levite's Concubine, she writes:

These chapters have not found their way into many Sunday school books or sermons or onto the "top ten Christian books" list. They are difficult to read and more difficult to interpret. They portray human nature at its worst, and even worse than worst, because the main players were God's covenant people. They did the unthinkable, and they did it to each other (271).

But one of the important aims of the book, as I will subsequently show, was just that: to give us examples of human behavior for us to learn from (see Chapter 4). Obviously, we need bad examples to judge, not only good ones. Then we have no problem in dealing with disagreeable material.

Comparison with other ancient literature

Unlike the Ugaritic myths, the *Gilgamesh Epic*, the *Iliad* and the *Odyssey*, this book at first glance does not seem like "great" literature. The exception, perhaps, is *The Song of Deborah*. Despite the difficulties of the text, the poem has great power and is masterfully wrought, but its power is offset, even nullified, by the ruthlessness, cruelty, curse, and hatred which the Israelites in the poem harbor for their enemies, a hatred matched in the Bible only by *Psalm 137* ("By the waters of Babylon").

Judges, or course, is a book about wars, and war is hell. But the greatest ancient Greek and Middle Eastern literature about war is not simply cruel and ferocious, as this book is, but contains messages that we can live by. The *Iliad* (ca. 750 BCE) depicts "grace under pressure"; the enemy is not hated but respected, and noble Priam is able to appeal to the hardened heart of Achilles and receive magnanimous mercy. Even more ancient than *Judges*, the Ugaritic poems (ca. 1350 BCE) are short, brisk beautiful tales, descriptive and sensuous, written with a charmingly comic tone. Dialogues are ample and leisurely. Whereas the Israelites in *Judges* are abrupt and unmannerly, the Ugaritic gods by comparison are gracious, and the more evil ones are merely doing their duty. And *Gilgamesh*, another ancient tale (as early as c. 2000 BCE), tells of a profound bond of friendship, of deep unconsolable grief at the loss of that friend, and of Gilgamesh's inability to attain to immortal life, so nearly in his grasp. In contrast to *Judges*, these books are treasuries of human wisdom and glimmer with beauty. Thus the antiquity of *Judges* cannot explain away its apparently primitive character.

Apparent unevenness and ineptness

These ancient stories have all the earmarks of having originated as folktales about bizarre heroes, which were handed down over generations from one storyteller to another like the ballads of Robin Hood.[6] That the stories were probably transmitted orally over centuries might account not only for some of the apparent unevenness and coarseness found in the book but also for the many anomalies. Everywhere there seem to be rough edges, non sequiturs, irrelevant information and overall a poor sense of pacing. The action moves by fits and starts. The author sometimes lingers too long on what seem to be irrelevant details, and he races over what is important. His many repetitions, especially of words, seem so inept that if a word is repeated 5 times in a certain passage, the translator may render it 5 different ways, trying to improve on the original. There is no unity of mood, so desirable to Aristotle, for just when the story is most tragic, the reader feels like bursting into laughter. And the text sometimes seems to be corrupt, thus making it difficult to translate. J. Alberto Soggin maintains that about one-quarter of *The Song of Deborah* is completely obscure, so that much of the translated versions are largely guesses about meanings.[7] (See section on patterns and anomalies below.)

Disunity and Editing

Thus the author[8] has been regarded as inept and the text defective for one reason or another. One theory advanced to explain his lack of skill is that the original text was heavily edited by later editors, who did not merge the parts seamlessly. Richter summarized the theories of composition and posited at least three redactors, who had different ideological agenda.[9] This kind of dissection continues to be done today. Some critics hold that the last three chapters of the book were tacked onto an existing collection of stories. Boling calls Chs. 19-21 a "Postview" and a "supplement" and conjectures that it, as well as Ch. 1, was added by a Deuteronomic editor during the Exile (37). Soggin sets off Chs. 17-21 as an "Appendix on Various Themes" (261). And Marc Brettler carries on the tradition and in my opinion, spends too much energy piecing the book together from different imagined sources. After dismantling it, he does not tell us what it all adds up to. And after stating a number of times that there is no unity in the book and that there was no single author, he grudgingly comes around to concede that there is unity, but only because of the "framework."[10]

A number of scholars including Barry G. Webb and Lillian R. Klein, however, have claimed unity of *Judges*, and Tammi J. Schneider in her recent commentary on *Judges* finds it a "unified document," focusing on the "degenerative progression" of the Israelites, particularly toward leadership, tension among the tribes, and relation to the deity.[11]

Nevertheless, the idea that the prologue and epilogue are "additions" survives, as we see in the recently published *Eerdmans Dictionary of the Bible* (2000) which claims that the fact that the tribes are disunited in some parts of the book but not in others is evidence that the book lacks unity,[12] an idea which I will refute.

Such opinions amount to an apology that the book is unsatisfactory. When one understands the literary strategies of the author, however, these theories fade into insignificance.

Bible as literature

Examining the Bible as "literature" was a new development in Biblical criticism in the 1970s. At first, *Judges* was largely avoided by the new biblical-literary critics, who may have found other parts of the Bible more fruitful for new theories than *Judges*. Or perhaps like others before them, they were perplexed by it and found it unsavory. In recent years, hundreds of excellent articles have appeared, but most of the critics have been biblical scholars first—concerned with history and theology—and literary critics only second.

Most of these interpreters could not detach themselves from the idea that the Bible is history, so that although they might focus on characterization, for example, they would be bent on fitting the stories into a historical frame. Thus they would neglect other features of the work, features which, without their realizing it, actually affected all the other topics addressed. Most of these scholars came out of seminaries and divinity schools. Many were understandably inhibited by their theological concerns and constrained by inherited perspectives. Sometimes showing considerable interest in new literary theories like structuralism and semiotics, they found it hard to break loose from the traditional ways of looking at the Bible; and lacking the technical skills acquired by long experience analyzing all kinds of literatures, many did not fully understand literary devices and techniques nor were aware of all the other possibilities involved in literary criticism.

The best of them, however, are those who are equally at home with Biblical scholarship, the Hebrew language, and literary criticism. The outstanding example of this type of critic is Robert Alter. His first three books of literary criticism of the Bible are *The Art of Biblical Narrative* (1981); *The Literary Guide to the Bible* (1987), edited by Alter and Frank Kermode, in which Alter wrote the Introduction[13] and the chapters on *Psalms* and Hebrew poetry; and *The World of Biblical Literature* (1992).[14]

Unlike many critics, who hone one topic, one book, or even one character, without placing this in the context of the rest of the Bible, Alter has a profound grasp of both the whole Bible and of literary criticism and thus can make generalizations about the style that are hard to fault. He can discuss narrative or dialogue with ease or the biblical use of repetition or puns with great authority, and we can trust him because he is so well informed about the two disciplines. He is unsurpassable on the nuances of Hebrew words and how they interact with one another. And his own mastery of the English language, which in my opinion comes only from lifelong experience with centuries of great literature, enables him to express these insights tellingly. For example, he calls contrasting parallels of stories or sentences "dissonant allusions" and identifies three classes of them: "local allusion for the definition of [the ideas], allusion dictated by actual continuity and narrative re-enactment, allusion to models as part of an ideological argument . . . ."[15]

He always opens our eyes to the artistry of the Biblical writers:

> The masters of ancient Hebrew narrative were clearly writers who delighted in an art of
> indirection, in the possibilities of intimating depths through the mere hint of a surface

feature, or through a few words of dialogue fraught with implication. Their attraction to narrative minimalism was reinforced by their sense that stories should be told in a way that would move efficiently to the heart of the matter, never pausing to elaborate mimetic effects for their own sake. (65-6)

One must have a firm grasp of literary skills to be able to perceive this.

Best of all, he argues for *a multiplicity of meanings*, rather than trying to arrive at one definitive meaning for any one story:

The Bible as a whole is conceived as an intricate edifice of *puzzlement*—philological, compositional, historical—that one by one require solutions and with a combination of ingenuity and serendipity will get them. (143)

What critics do not understand, says Alter, is that *the Bible may have been written "precisely not to yield a solution, but to yield multiple and contradictory solutions,* and that this might be the very hallmark of its greatness"* (144, my emphasis). And he recognizes that what produces the multiplicity of meanings are *the techniques of "indeterminacy"* of the Hebrew writers:

Meaning . . . was conceived as a *process*, requiring continual revision—both in the ordinary sense and in the etymological sense of seeing-again—continual suspension of judgment, weighing of multiple possibilities, brooding over gaps in the information provided.[16]

His way of looking at situations in the stories is kindly, humane, and philosophical—the thoughts of a person who has been in touch with the insights of the greatest writers on the human condition.

Finally, his is not a clinical approach: we are supposed to have emotional reactions to the stories, and Alter is not afraid to express them. For example, he writes that the Bible is

a literature that speaks to us urgently, with the power to "draw us out" of ourselves. It is able to do this in part because it scrutinizes the human condition with such a probing, unblinking gaze that is conveyed in the most subtle narrative vehicle, whatever its evolution and its composite character. But it is also able to do this by the boldness with which it represents human figures confronted, challenged, confounded by a reality beyond human ken. (23)

The Bible draws us out not because it is religious, but because it is well-written.

. . . the literary analyst, though he should be aware of the differences of ancient mind-set and ancient literary procedures, presupposes a deep continuity of human experience that makes the concerns of the ancient text directly accessible to him. These millennia-old expressions of fear, anguish, passion, perplexity, and exultation speak to us because they issue from human predicaments in some respects quite like our own and are cast in the molds of plot, character, dialogue, scene, imagery, wordplay, and sound play that are recognizable analogues to the modalities of literary texts more easily familiar to us, closer to us in time and space. (205)

We are in the hands of an expert. He is a proven literary critic with his work on Stendhal, for example, and he is as well versed in the Bible as the novelist Nabokov is a recognized expert on butterflies.

His one weakness, in my opinion, is that although he calls the characters "fictional," his religious belief—that this is a "real" God acting in history—slips into this otherwise fictitious story from time to time. At bottom, he thinks of the characters as "constructs," but he does not think of God as one. Admittedly, handling God in literary criticism is extremely difficult. Is God merely a literary device used to explain the exigencies of any situation, or is he a real force to the author, and/or is he a real force to the reader? And if so, is he a God of the ancient world or a God of the present time? The boundaries between these representations are difficult to determine, and difficult to stick to. A critic is entitled to his own decision on how to deal with this problem. But is Alter not inconsistent, applying a double standard in dealing with the details of the story?

As for history, Alter wants Biblical scholars to see that it is no crime to challenge the historical interpretation of the Bible, and acknowledges that he has called "ideological assumptions into question" (44):

> . . . it is clear from the way the text is organized that the writer has exercised considerable freedom in shaping his materials to exert subtle interpretive pressure on the figures and events. In such writing, it is increasingly difficult to distinguish sharply between history and fiction, whatever the historical intentions of the writers. (59)

And

> Ideology tends to draw lines, insist on norms, in the interests of a particular system of governance and social relations. *Literary invention,* to a large extent because *it involves the kind of free play of the imagination* with a verbal and fictional medium that we have been following, often has the effect of calling ideological assumptions into question, or qualifying them ironically, or at any rate raising certain teasing possibilities counter to the accepted ideology (44, my emphasis).

On the other hand, he admits that he has vexed Biblical scholars "by applying the term *fiction* to biblical narrative," and immediately apologizes for doing this, "though I did try to make clear that at least in my usage there was no contradiction between fiction and the intent effort of historical truth telling" (39). He is hedging his bets here, doing a bit of damage control. He does not want to offend the religious establishment (and I do not think he does), yet is trying to remain true to his literary-critical principles as well as to his own belief. He walks a delicate line, carefully and diplomatically.

It is a difficult problem for any critic of the Bible, whether believer or nonbeliever. Overall, Alter is trying to appreciate the author's art, and this means he cannot ignore the importance of God,

> for the Hebrew writers do, of course, keep in steady focus God and Israel, creation, covenant, and commandments (though not very noticeably in Esther), and from moment to moment all their subtleties of their literary art are exploited to make palpable their

God-driven vision of reality, together with the individual and collective obligations
dictated by it. (34)

Since the 1970s, critics have come to accept the literary challenges of the Bible,
and a great deal of excellent work has emerged, especially by feminists. But no one,
in my opinion, surpasses Alter.

The religio-historical approach, and the study of redactions, though fine for
their objectives, are narrow approaches. It is only through literary-critical
methodologies that we can finally come to understand the multiplicities and
complexities of *Judges* and appreciate it as the great work of art that it is. Alter's
ground-breaking studies—and in particular, the passages I have quoted—are very
important to an understanding of *Judges*.

Feminist criticism

More than any other interpreters of the last twenty years, feminist critics have
opened up this book for readers. Despite there being many different kinds of
feminisms, certain generalizations about feminist interpretations of the narratives
can be made. Most important, it is a liberation criticism, for feminists regard the
figure of "woman" in the Bible as a male "construct," which excludes or marginalizes
women, silences them, subjugates them, and even more important, fails to reveal
what women were really like. As Phyllis Bird writes,

> The Old Testament is a collection of writings by males from a society dominated by
> males. These writings portray a man's world. They speak of events and activities engaged
> in primarily or exclusively by males (war, cult, and government) and of a jealously
> singular God, who is described and addressed in terms normally used for males.

Women in the Hebrew Bible, she says, despite their variety of roles, are in general
treated as inferiors.[17] The male perspective, moreover, teaches distrust of women:
"Patriarchal literature, and thus the Bible in general," writes J. Cheryl Exum, "reflects
the underlying attitude that women's sexuality is to be feared and thus carefully
regulated."[18] Adele Reinhartz lists other woman-related issues tackled by feminists:
"writing women into biblical history, society and cult; examining the representation
of women in canonical and non-canonical texts; searching for evidence of women's
hands in material artifacts; addressing androcentrism and patriarchy in texts as well
as in scholarship, and exploring the relationship between biblical texts and women's
lives in all their complexity."[19]

While literary critics of the mid-twentieth century and after taught that readers
had to understand the author's intention and interpret from the author's point of
view, feminists such as Judith Fetterley teach them to be "resisting readers" and to
bring women from the margins into the center. One way they do this is to replace the
male perspective with a "feminist perspective," by which the feminist critics uncover
the hierarchical relationships which perpetuated, and still perpetuate, existing
power relationships between the genders. The greatest achievement of feminist

critics may be that they reveal that all texts have a hidden political agenda and that the biblical agenda concerning women continues to be a cultural restraint on women's freedom. This is what they found necessary to uncover.

But this is not exactly literary criticism. Despite the otherwise notable achievements of feminist critics,[20] their approach to *Judges* is essentially theological, sociological, and historical. Their approach is helpful, but for literary criticism, it is not completely satisfactory. To be fair, most of them probably did not imagine themselves as literary critics.

From the point of view of literary criticism (and only from this point of view), feminist criticism has several weaknesses. First, sometimes feminists concentrate on the social position of women and try to reconstruct what the "real" society consisted of, instead of concentrating on the story itself. It is one thing if women were treated by the society in a certain way, and another if they are fictional characters, created by their author to serve a narrative purpose, as will be shown in this book. Some feminist writers also apply modern standards about women to an ancient world.

Second, by focusing on women, the feminists downplay or neglect the rest of the picture and do not always evaluate the action judiciously. For example, they are appalled by the treatment of women (such as Jephthah's daughter and the women in the story of the Levite's Concubine), but they are not appalled by the treatment of males. The author of *Judges* is not condemning women *only*; most of his condemnation of behavior, in fact, is of men. And men are also victims in this book. Feminists largely ignore this. Balance is needed. To get the intrinsic meaning of the book, it must be seen as a whole.

What is rather odd is that most feminists give no more than a passing glance to the slaughter throughout the stories. They focus on the violence to women but seem unconcerned about the excessive violence throughout. Perhaps it is because our contemporary world is so violent that critics and readers scarcely raise an eyebrow to the horrors that shocked Elliott and McKenzie. Or perhaps it is that most critics, whether regarding *Judges* either as fiction or history, take the perspective that the Conquest was divinely motivated and thus the warfare a divine consequence, so to speak, and not to be questioned.

Third, despite some disclaimers to the contrary,[21] most feminist interpreters, like other critics, usually try to discover the *definitive* meaning, apparently not recognizing that the book is deliberately polysemous, that there are "infinite" meanings and that the other possible meanings should not be eliminated.

Fourth, most feminist scholars of the Bible have an investment in some religious institution, and what they are mainly interested in is changing the institution. Their primary interest is not art.

Finally, they do not seem to be interested in how the book has been wrought, nor of what the art consists. What they have in common with most other biblical critics of

Judges is that they do not realize that until we become aware of the artistic patterns of the book, we cannot begin to judge any of the characters—not merely the women—properly. This holistic method is different from isolating them to analyze their individual behavior.

Literary critics in general commonly single out a specific theme or character or passage or stylistic peculiarity to discuss. But after doing so, the critic must put the theme or character or passage or stylistic peculiarity or whatever *back into the text* and show what this new understanding does to the text, how it elicits new meanings. This is often where feminist critics fail. By extracting women from the text of *Judges*, and focusing on the author's bias or the bias of that society, feminist critics divert attention from the complex meaning of the whole.

Perhaps it is impossible to do otherwise, for when critics have uncovered what is wrong with the male depiction of women, the women cannot then be fitted back in, as the story *depends* upon the male perspective. It may also be impossible for our human brains to process two different things simultaneously—in this case, women and the art. In the following chapter, I tried to deal with the horror and the humor simultaneously, but found that focusing on the humor of the stories impaired my ability to experience the horror at the same time. Luckily, a genre has been created for this type of literature, called "black humor," a genre common in the contemporary media. Nothing like this exists so far for feminist criticism.

After critics have taken a work apart, their focus on a single topic—whether feminism, history, or theology—makes it difficult to put the whole book back together again. In a way, "we murder to dissect," as Wordsworth put it. Most critics, including the feminists, leave it up to the reader to do this restoration and reach conclusions about it.

Nevertheless, the feminists have plunged into *Judges*, and made outstanding contributions to our understanding of the females in the ancient world. Their "radical rethinking and re-evaluation of the norms and canons of biblical criticism" must be acknowledged (Reinhartz 232.) Our debt to them cannot be overestimated.

II. The Art

What I am concentrating on in this study is the author's art. One of the first things a literary critic looks at is imagery. Paradoxically, the language of *Judges* is not descriptive nor imagistic nor is it connotative nor emotional. What the author does, however, is to provide us with innumerable tableaux—pictures, one after another, which I call *icons* because of the energy and the meanings that they supply to the text.

Writers of both the Hebrew Bible and the New Testament commonly place characters in dramatic and memorable positions. Take, for example, the picture of Absalom, hanging by his hair in a terebinth tree, three darts stuck into his breast by Joab (2 Sam 18.9, 14). What is so unusual about *Judges* is that there are so many pictures. These are not just any old pictures as we might snap of our family's events with our camcorder, but dynamic and memorable ones, full of import. They seem to strike powerfully at something deep within our human beingness. They are memorable in the way that the picture of the little naked terrified sobbing girl fleeing the napalm attack in Vietnam is memorable, or the blast-to-the-head closeup execution of a Viet-Cong traitor by the Vietnamese captain, or the Raising of the Flag on Iwo Jima, or the wreckage at ground zero of the World Trade Center. We do not tire of these pictures. We are deeply affected by them no matter how often we look. The pictures in *Judges* are suitable for adaptation for a dramatic presentation like the Passion Play at Oberammergau, each tableau in its own unique unforgettable mise en scène.

The author of *Judges* does not use loaded words to gain effect, but achieves emotional effect through the juxtaposition and arrangement of pictures. What must be stressed is that the emotion is not in the pictures. It is in us, the readers or listeners or viewers. If we do not mentally construct the pictures in our minds, if we do not react, or if we do not even notice them, there will be no emotion. But if a picture is worth ten thousand words, for the reader who really *looks*, the book of *Judges* is dense indeed. The drama is in the pictures.

Iconicity

This remarkable skill of the author of *Judges* can be quickly exemplified by examining the positions of the bodies of the characters who have fallen to the ground, most of them dead. Notice how the following tableaux fall into a nearly perfect chiasmus (except for C′) (see **Chiasmus of Iconic Poses**, next page). As one reads through the following list, one should read each pair together (e. g., A with A′ , B with B′) in order to understand the point of the chiasmus, which is now presented in chronological order:

The corpse of Eglon is exactly symmetrical to the corpse of the Concubine, one inside, one outside, of a locked door. Notice also the symmetry of Jael and Delilah: both women are *working on a man's head,* Jael using a hammer (a man's work) and Delilah weaving the man's hair into a loom (a woman's work). Both are using the same tool (יתד). Gideon chasing the Midianites is symmetrical with Micah chasing the Danites. In Gideon's case, it is an Israelite with a few men chasing after hostile *enemies* (*outsiders* invading *insiders* [*Israel*]), while in Micah's case, it is an Israelite with a very few men chasing after a large number of hostile *Israelites* who are themselves *insiders* marching away to invade *outsiders.* Another symmetry is Abimelech's slaying of his 70 brothers on *one* stone and Jephthah slaying 42,000 Ephraimites (i.e., a brother tribe) for mispronouncing *one* word (12.6). Representing things symmetrically is part of the design, the art of the book, and it is also an aspect of game (humor). There are many other symmetries. It is from analyzing the differences in a given symmetry that we elicit significant meanings.

Chiasmus of Iconic Poses

A. Achsah, newly married, alighting from her ass (1.4). (She is not dead, but very much active and alive in contrast to her counterpart at A′, the Concubine, who is dead.)

    B. Eglon, sword stuck through his belly, lying *inside a room with a locked door* (3.25);

        C. Sisera, tent peg (יתד) through his temple, lying in bed covered with a blanket (4.22; 5.26-7);

            D. Joash (with Gideon perhaps cringing behind him) being threatened by a mob of angry men (6.30);

                E. The decapitation of the two Midianite princes by the Ephraimites: Oreb on the rock and Zeeb at the wine press (7.26) and the slicing up of the Midianite kings, Zebah and Zalmunna, by Gideon (8.21);[****]

                    F. Gideon and a small army of 300 men chasing after an army of 15,000 Midianites;

                        G. Abimelech slaughtering his 70 brothers on one stone;

                            H. Abimelech, skull crushed by a millstone (one stone), sword through his body (9.54);

                        G′. Jephthah slaughtering 42,000 Ephraimites for one word as they crossed the river;

                    F′. Micah and a handful of neighbors chasing after an army of 600 men (18.22)

                E′. Samson fallen beneath the rubble of the collapsed temple amid a tangle of corpses (16.30);[*****] (this is also parallel to H above, as both Samson and Abimelech were killed by falling objects);

            C′. Samson lying prone, asleep, his hair being woven with a weaving pin (יתד) into the fabric of a loom (16.14); [the item is out of place in the chiasmus];

        D′. The Ephraimite host trying to negotiate with the base Benjaminites surrounding his house (the Levite, perhaps, cringing behind him) (19.22-24);

    B′. The Concubine fallen dead *outside a locked door*, with her hands on the threshold (19.27);

A′. The corpse of the Concubine, thrown over an ass, ready to be transported home (19.28).

[****] 2 + 2 Midianite enemies of the Israelites are killed here, while only one is killed in E′ (an important Israelite enemy of the Philistines).

[*****] E′ is not an exact mirror image of E, however, except that the fallen Midianites were princes and kings and Samson was the reigning Israelite champion.

Add to these the pictures of animals being killed or used by Samson:

the lion being torn apart by Samson, bare-handedly (14.6), and later seen as a decomposing carcass (14.8);

the ass—a skeleton (carcass with the flesh removed)—from which Samson takes a jawbone and kills a thousand Philistines (15.15);

and the foxes—300 of them, tied by their tails together in pairs, a torch tied to each pair, soon to be charred carcasses (15.4-5).

The great variety and number of these images assures us that the method is intentional and done for a reason. The following is a selection of the other powerful images in the book:

Adoni-Bezek, minus his big toes and thumbs, crawling under a table to pick up crumbs (1.7);

Achsah alighting from her ass (1.14);

Ehud thrusting his sword through Eglon's obese belly, and the dirt coming out at the back (3.22);

Sisera's mother, with her wise women, peering out the window for her son's return (5.28-29);

Gideon beating out wheat in a wine press (6.11);

Gideon's men at the river, some kneeling and drinking water out of their hands, some crouching and lapping from the stream (7.5-6);

the loaf of barley bread in the Midianite's dream, rolling into a tent and knocking it down (7.13);

Gideon's men juggling the trumpets, torches, drums, and swords in the middle of the night, followed by the pandemonium of the Midianites (7.19-20);

Gideon threshing the elders of Succoth with thorns and briers and tearing down the tower of Penuel, slaying all its occupants (8.16-17);

Jotham orating his fable from the top of a mountain (9.7);

Abimelech and his men with branches on their shoulders approaching the tower of Shechem to burn it down (9.48-49);

Abimelech fatally injured by an upper millstone dropped from the tower by a woman (9.53-54);

an armor bearer running Abimelech through the middle with his sword, like Ehud with Eglon (9.54);

Jephthah's shock at seeing his daughter come out of the door, with timbrels and dancing (11.34);

the Levite, Concubine, and servant lad waiting desperately in the square at Gibeah for someone to invite them in for the night (19.17);

the young Concubine being pushed out the door to the ravening sex maniacs (19.25);

the corpse of the Concubine being slung over the back of the ass by the Levite (19.28);

the Levite hacking the body of his concubine into 12 parts (19.29);

the daughters of Shiloh coming out at night to dance in the vineyards (a pretty picture), oblivious to the predatory Samsonlike Benjaminites lurking in ambush underneath the vines (21.21, 23);

200 Benjaminites seizing and carrying off their prey, the daughters of Shiloh (21.23).

The many pictures of Samson are dynamic and amusing (including the three already mentioned above):

tearing the lion apart with his bare hands (14.6);

eating honey out of his hands, giving honey to his parents, the three of them walking slowly along licking up the gooey honey (no mention of how they cleaned off their hands) (14.9);

feasting with the 30 wedding companions for seven days (14.10-11);

slaughtering the 30 Ashkelonites and stripping their corpses of their garments (14.19);

tying the tails of 300 foxes together, setting fire to them, and letting them run off to burn the fields, orchards, and vineyards of the Philistines (15.5);

killing 1,000 Philistines with the jawbone of an ass (15.15);

ripping out the gate of Gaza and carrying it up the hill to Hebron on his shoulders (16.3)

being bound first by the Judahites and later twice by Delilah and breaking his bonds each time (15.13-14; 16.6, 12);

having his hair woven into the fabric on Delilah's loom (16.13-14);

having his seven locks shaved off by Delilah's man (16.19);

having his eyes gouged out (16.21);

blinded, in brass fetters, grinding grain at the mill in Gaza (16.21);

pushing out the pillars that supported the temple of Dagon (16.29-30); and

being crushed when the 3,000 Philistines come tumbling down from the roof onto the people below (16.27, 30).

Just listing and sketching some of the pictures is a delight and pleasure. Each one contains an important message. Notice the verbs in the above lists, dynamic verbs playing an essential part to the whole.

The book is a feast for such artists as Rubens (*Samson and Delilah*), Rembrandt (*Samson at his Father-in-law's Window*), Doré (*Deborah telling Barak that Sisera will fall into the hands of a woman*), Léon Bonnat's wonderful painting of the muscular nude Samson prying open the jaws of a fierce lion with his bare hands, Lovis Corinth's *Samson Blinded*. Also brought to mind are paintings like Poussin's *Rape of the Sabine Women* (reminding us of the daughters of Shiloh) and Michelangelo's *Last Judgment* in the Sistine Chapel (reminding us of the mass of people falling down from the temple roof onto others below in the Samson story). If I could hire an artist to illustrate a book of *Judges*, I would try to get Goya, the Goya of the etchings in "Los desastres de la guerra." Not Doré; he is too pious, too melodramatic. Or if not Goya, then Brueghel or Bosch. Or the Picasso of *Guernica*.

Temple Grandin, an autist scholar studied by Oliver Sachs, writes in her book *Thinking in Pictures*, "Animals and autistic people don't see their ideas of things; they see the actual things themselves. We [autistic people] see the actual things themselves, into their general concept of this world, while normal people blur all those details together into their general concept of the world."[22]

In an age when the technology had not been developed for drawing and disseminating pictures widely, the author of *Judges* devised a way to do it. He thinks in pictures.[23]

Patterns and anomalies

One of the techniques writers and artists use to keep us entertained is the alienation technique, or, in Tolstoy's words, "making it strange." This whole book is full of strangeness.

Strange things, like the combination of horror and humor, contribute to the notion of the disunity of the book as do the many intricate patterns; the strange little designs planted here and there; odd words embedded in the fabric, which appear to have no reason for existence, repetitions of words that by today's standards seem indications of lack of vocabulary; and anomalies—funny little details which do not match the critic's notion of the gravity of the stories, and which are assumed to have no bearing on the narrative, and regarded as exemplifying the ineptness of the author or of the text's transmission.

As for these anomalies, most Biblical critics ignore them completely. If they pay attention to them, it is to find some historical justification for their presence, or to conclude that they meant something to ancient audiences, but not to us now, or to argue that the gaps and discontinuities are the result of long process of oral transmission of the stories.

One such anomaly that they routinely ignore is the "weaponless weapon" (discussed in detail in Chapter 2). A number of peculiar weapons are used to conquer the enemy. To give but two examples: Jael and Delilah use a יתד (tent peg or weaving pin) on their victims; and Samson does not wield a sword, but uses his fists, the jawbone of an ass, the lighted tails of foxes, and the pillars of a pagan temple. These methods are important.

Another example of the odd detail is the author's showing us Achsah "alighting from her ass" (חמור) when she comes to her father after marrying Othniel (1.14). Considering the supposed time and place in history, it is a reasonable form of transportation but completely gratuitous to the narrative, especially in such a short, short story. If we scrutinize the entire book carefully, however, we shall discover why the ass is important. Achsah, a woman on an ass, is being contrasted with another woman on an ass at the end of the book. And the contrast tells volumes, for the second woman is a rape victim, a corpse.

To give a few other examples of anomalies:

> Why did Achsah ask for "springs of water" for her "present"?
> Why is it at the "images" that Ehud turns around to attack Eglon?
> Why does Gideon use trumpets, pitchers, and torches to intimidate the Midianites?
> Why are we told that some of his men lap "with their tongues like dogs"—instead of simply "lap with their tongues"?
> Why is it a "loaf of barley bread" that knocks down the tent in the Midianite's dream?
> Why does Gideon have two names?
> Why does Abimelech murder his half brothers "on one stone"?

And many more. A literary critic is accountable for the presence of every word. Whether these anomalies got there by accident or design is irrelevant from a poststructuralist point of view, but they affect the text in one way or another, and the literary critic should show how.

But as we shall discover, the many anomalies and patterns are not pure baroque, nor careless attempts to provide realism, they are structural devices, part of the design.

Importance of every detail

Nor are the anomalies to be considered abnormalities, irregularities, or discrepancies, but important keys to events, without which the system cannot be deciphered. Understanding this principle causes the old paradigm to dissolve, and an entirely new one to emerge. As Kuhn noticed in science, so it is in *Judges*:

> Discovery commences with the awareness of anomaly . . . . But after the subject has begun [to bring these anomalies into the system and] to learn to deal with his new world, his entire visual field flips over . . . . [24]

A Hegelian idea: a dialectic. When we finally begin to resolve the meaning of these oddities in *Judges*, we suddenly find ourselves in a new dimension, like Alice on the other side of the looking-glass, and we become aware that the author is telling much more than what was previously regarded as simple folktales sprung spontaneously from a primitive pre-literate society. We will appreciate all the more that *Judges* is an artistic creation in which every word is there for a purpose.

"Judges" as a postmodernist work

A curious thing about this work is that it can be so well used to illustrate certain twentieth century literary theories, especially those of reader-response, intertextuality, and deconstruction. In fact, the author "invented" them. He was a craftsman who knew what he was doing when he matched the intrigue, machinations, and slyness of his characters with the intricacy, design, and cunning of the style and structure of his book. A new information theory evolved in the process. This will be demonstrated throughout the book and explored further in Chapter 6.

III. Structure and Design

Judges has an artistic structure, and it is so clear-cut that we may assume that it was shaped deliberately. **Table I** shows the proportion of space devoted to each story and reveals a remarkable symmetry except for the fact that in Position A (present structure), the Introduction occupies approximately 14.2% of the whole, while its counterpart, the story of the Levite's Concubine, occupies 17.5%. That is, the introductory material is 3.3% shorter than its corresponding part at the end. Because of the exactness of everything else, it seems possible that 3.3% of the information had been removed or displaced.

The symmetry is perfect in Position B (hypothetical original structure), where the material before Deborah is 17.5%, matching that of the Concubine story. The likely candidate for removal is the group of minor judges (10.1-16 and 12.8-1),[25] which occupy 3.3% of the whole. Shamgar stays in position before the Deborah story. **Table II** represents this symmetry graphically.

The minor judges are thought to have been a list which included a short mention of Jephthah. When the long version of the Jephthah story was put in its present position, with the minor judges flanking it, the shorter mention of the Jephthah story was eliminated. So the theory goes.

Table I. Symmetry of Parts

Position A. Minor judges in present position in the book:

Intro. + Ehud + Shamgar		14.20%
Deborah		9.00%
Gideon		16.00%
Abimelech		8.70%
Minor Judges		2.30%
Jephthah		7.80%
Minor Judges		1.00%
Samson		16.50%
Micah		7.00%
Levite's Concubine & punishment of Benjamin		17.50%

Position B. Minor Judges in their hypothetical original position:

Intro.+ Ehud + minor judges + Shamgar		17.50%
Deborah		9.00%
Gideon		16.00%
Abimelech	8.7%}	–
plus	equals	16.50%
Jephthah	7.8%}	–
Samson		16.50%
Micah		7.00%
Levite's Concubine & punishment of Benjamin		17.50%

To repeat, when the minor judges flank Jephthah (Position A), the desirable symmetry is destroyed. When they are at the beginning of the book (hypothetical Position B), the symmetry is perfect. (The percentages are similar no matter what text is used.) The question is: why the change?

Table II. Overall Structure by Amount of Space

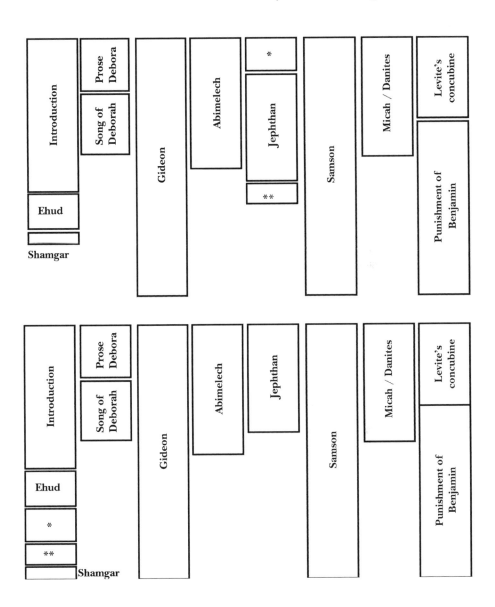

*   two minor judges and divine speech

** three minor judges

In Table II, the upper diagram shows the present position of the minor judges.
The lower diagram shows where they might have been in their original position and
the symmetry created by the blocks.

Table III. Offspring of Minor Judges and Jephthah

Name	Patronymic?	Progeny	Number of Children	Children Married?	Number of People
Tola	yes	0	0	no	0
Jair	no	30 sons riding 30 asses with 30 cities	30	probably	90
Jephthah	yes (but mother a harlot)	0 (kills his only daughter)	0	no	0
Ibzan	no	30 sons married 30 outsiders; 30 dtrs married 30 outsiders	60	yes	120
Elon	no	0 children	0	no	0
Abdon	yes	40 sons with 30 grandsons on 70 asses	40	yes	140

Table III. Offspring of Minor Judges and Jephthah shows that the present position of the minor judges sets up a contrast of the number of children Jephthah had with the number of children and possessions that the minor judges had. The judges having many progeny and many possessions alternate with those who have none. Jephthah has none.

In **Table III**, the numbers increase as we go down the list. We are to understand that progeny is good (the promise oft the covenant) and *lack* of progeny is bad. Being denied progeny is thought to be a consequence of bad behavior (i.e., disobedience to Yhwh), an idea contested much later in *Job*. Thus this table is evidence not only of the magnitude of Jephthah's loss of his daughter through his regrettable vow, but also of his foolishness.[26] (See later discussion of Jephthah's ethical problems.)

Having Shamgar follow the minor judges in their present position in Position B (**Table I**) would have fulfilled the demand of the alternating pattern shown in **Table III** in that the number of Shamgar's progeny is not given and therefore, like Jephthah's, is zero. But Shamgar cannot be moved from Position A because although he "served" Israel, he is not a judge, and with his Canaanite patronymic, he may not be an Israelite, while the others are called judges and are Israelites. Also because of a reference to "the days of Shamgar" in *The Song of Deborah*, he cannot come *after* Deborah. Incidentally, he is one of the clues that there is Canaanite material in the stories (see Chapter 5).

The minor judges are not active characters, and therefore three of them do not show the typical "decline" of people and tribes mentioned above. Perhaps they are intended to show that there had always been some good people for Israel to rely on, with the possible exception of Ibzan, whose sons and daughters married outsiders.

The structure of the book

Though the size and shape of the scroll may have had something to do with the shapes and proportions of the symmetrical blocks, the author was thinking in terms of a visible design—something like a mosaic of words, incidents, and meanings—and the proportions are deliberate, as we will see when we study the keywords in Chapters 3 and 4.

As already mentioned, the last two parts of the book—the story of Micah and the story of the Levite's Concubine with the Punishment of Benjamin (Chs. 17-21)—are often regarded as "appendices" tacked on to the story of the *Judges* in an artificial and incomprehensible way. As *Eerdmans Dictionary* puts it:

> At a final stage of development, the prologue (1:1-2.5) and epilogue (17.1-21.25) were added. That these sections were added at a later stage is clear from the fact that *the prologue and the epilogue intrude into a story line* that runs continuous from Joshua to Judges and Judges to Samuel. Moreover, in the rest of Judges the tribes are presented as *united under the judge, but in the prologue and epilogue the tribes act independently* (752). (Emphasis mine.)

But these explanations do not hold water.

First, the stories do not concern "all the tribes," until possibly the last story, and even then, we cannot be sure who are included. Usually the stories are about one tribe, acting independently, which may collaborate with one or possibly two or three others. The Ehud story mentions only that he was a Benjaminite, that he blew his trumpet in the region of Ephraim, and that "Israelites" followed him (3.27). The name "Israelites" here probably refers only to those who followed him, not all the Israelites together. Or the word could refer only to the Ephraimites. We cannot tell if any other Benjaminites besides himself were in the battle. In Ch. 4, only Ephraim, Zebulun, and Naphtali combine against the enemy. In Ch. 5, six tribes cooperate. *The Song* laments the failure of three other tribes to join in, and three tribes are not even mentioned. Except for Deborah herself, who dwelt in the hill country of Ephraim, the Ephraimites as a tribe, who fought gallantly under Ehud, are not mentioned or singled out for glorious action in either Ch. 4 or 5. Contentions and divisions among the tribes continually occur throughout the rest of the book until a serious civil war erupts near the end.

Second, the tribes are not being "held together" by a judge except possibly after a victory, and not even then, as we do not really know what the judge did. Third, all the judges (except possibly Deborah) are seriously flawed, becoming progressively worse throughout the book. The last stories are an explanation for the decline and disappearance of the judges as well as the *continuing* deterioration of the principles of the Conquest. True, the tribes are somewhat "united" at the end (as far as we can tell), but not against a common enemy. They are united against one of their own tribes. The book is about *why* this happened.

Finally, the themes are announced one by one in the prologue (Ch. 1-2), and the stories from beginning to end carry out the plan. And the fact that the language (except for *The Song*) is remarkably consistent from beginning to end, as is the author's use of parallels,[27] symmetries (seen in the above tables), and keywords—all these things signify that the last chapters are not an "afterthought" but part of the unit.

Some hypotheses about patterns and authorship

As one studies the many patterns in the book, the question arises sooner or later whether or not this was the work of one author alone or a team, and whether later editors altered it.

Because the patterns are largely intact and because of the author's consistent sprinkling and linking of keywords throughout (discussed in Chapters 3 and 4), it would seem that the book is the work of only one author, though it could have been done by a team who knew and followed the rules of the game. It is hard to imagine that much editing was done, since drastic tampering by editors ignorant of the design would have destroyed the patterns. The single exception to consistency of style is *The Song of Deborah*. (A theory of how the work was created is developed in Chapters 5 and 6.)

If we extrapolate from the complexity of the structure of the whole book, the most likely scenario would be that the author started with one story, then erected a second structure, and added the other structures one by one to fit in with his scheme. The language, style, and structure of *The Song* are so different from anything else in the book that it seems likely that it was the first composition to be used, and all the other stories contrived afterwards to "fit" into its pattern.

In a later chapter, the hypothesis will be posed that both Deborah and Samson are "fallen gods" from some other Canaanite literature (like the Ugaritic tales), which the author preempted and modified for his own purposes. If the original language of *The Song* was another Semitic language like Ugaritic (Northwest Semitic instead of Biblical Hebrew), this might account for the strangeness of *The Song's* vocabulary with its problems of translation, unintelligible details about locations of the action, odd unexplained relationships of the characters, and other anomalies.[28] The story may have been well-known to the original (Canaanite) audience and the background material, common knowledge.

This theory would account for the duplication of the story in a prose version. The prose version might be the author's "translation" of what, because of its antiquity and possible foreign origin, may have been a difficult poem for later Israelites to understand. The prose version, despite discrepancies, has helped scholars in the distant past, as well as today, in deciphering the poem. The prose version, however, increases the number of parallels with the Samson story. And finally the "doubleness" of the story might have some connection with the doubleness in the Gideon story, which may be a code for the duplicity in Gideon's character (see Chapter 2). In like manner, the dual stories of Deborah may be a signal that the Deborah story also has dual meanings.

Because of the Deborah story's close relationship with the Samson story, Samson was likely the second story to be inserted. Once these two stories were in place, the others could be added to fit into the scheme: to show the deterioration of the characters and situations from rather good situations at the beginning to a terrible one at the end. (See **Table VI** below listing the parallels between Deborah and Samson.)

Possibly the Deborah/Samson pair of stories were linked from antiquity, the Samson story having many characteristics which can be identified as "Canaanite" (see Chapter 5).

Because of the intricate relationship of the Gideon and Samson stories as well, the Gideon story would have to be the third to be composed. It would hardly be possible for the author to *find* a tale with all the needed comparisons and contrasts. Gideon with his cowardice, caution, and irresolution, at the beginning, is such a perfect opposite to Samson's courage, strength, and impetuosity that one can imagine Gideon as being a story created for this specific purpose. Any simply "found" story would either not fit into the scheme, or would contain many elements that would disturb the existing parallels between the three stories. Because of the symmetry and balance of the artifice, it seems likely that while the author might not have created the Deborah or Samson stories from whole cloth, he might have more or less invented the Gideon story as well as all the other stories—deriving his basic material from known myths and folktales, most likely of Canaanite origin (see Chapter 5). Afterwards, the author would add the other stories and continue shaping all the materials so as to provide all the other parallels. This would not be possible to do from historical materials alone without considerable fabrication.

Religious formulae

The divine speeches with their Deuteronomic "formulae" of apostasy, hardship, moaning, and rescue (cf. Boling, 74) are in stark contrast to the folkloristic aspect of the stories. The formulae claim that the Israelites served the Baals and the Ashtaroth. Since the stories do not show the Israelites doing this—except in the case of Gideon's ephod and Micah's idols—the formulae do not "fit" very well. They and the prophecy in 6.7-12 were perhaps not in the original folktales but were inserted to satisfy later theological needs and to rationalize the contradiction between the success of the conquest in *Joshua* and its failure in *Judges*

Because of their affinity with the Deuteronomic writings, source critics speculate that these passages are a later interpolation of the seventh or sixth centuries BCE by Deuteronomic editors in order to lend the tales religious authority and to bring them into conformity with the later religion of Israel. That the religious formulae do not interfere with the symmetries of the book suggests that the redactor was careful not to displace the symmetries when he inserted them.

Throughout all the history of Israel, however, the Canaanite gods, with El as their head, continued to be worshiped along with Yhwh. A contest was being held about which god was to prevail. The decision may not have been made until the Exile and after. The religious formulae are the evidence of this effort to extirpate Baal. But of course, the storytellers themselves doubtless had supernatural explanations for extraordinary events, and these the Deuteronomist adapters adjusted to their own needs. (For the possible Canaanite, polytheistic origin of these tales, see Chapter 5.)

Chiasmus

A complex chiasmic arrangement not only of the iconic parallels already mentioned, but of all the materials seems evident, but it is so complex that a full discussion is beyond the scope of this book. (See **Appendix 1** to this chapter.) What purpose this chiasmus serves is not clear, unless it is simply to exhibit the author's skill in being able to devise such patterns, not resorting to anything clumsy or artificial but making everything seem perfectly natural. It might also have been a mnemonic aid or an ancient convention that was expected of the best artists. We know that Homer's *Iliad* contains an elaborate chiastic frame.[29]

Introduction and Themes (1.1-3.11)

The Introduction supplies us with information about the size and extent of Israel, the locations of the indigenous inhabitants, where the tribes settled, and the kinds of troubles that arose when two objects (Israelites and Canaanites) tried to occupy the same place at the same time. The author's camera seems to pan across all this shuffling and jostling of the tribes and the inhabitants, but now and then zooms in on a close-up in which we are allowed glimpses of tiny dramatic scenes, characteristic of what is occurring. These scenes alternate in a regular pattern with interludes of larger skirmishes and battles, and each one announces one of the central themes:

(a) Skirmishes
  (1) Adoni-Bezek (1.5-7).
(b) Skirmishes
  (2) Achsah (1.12-15).
(c) Skirmishes
  (3) destruction of the city of Luz (1.24-26).
(d) Skirmishes
  (4) appearance of the messenger-angel who speaks of the covenant (2.1-4).
(e) The misery of the people
  (5) the death of Joshua (2.8).
(f) Skirmishes of the people with the Baalim
  (6) appearance of Yhwh, his anger kindled (2.20-23).
(g) Skirmishes, and finally
  (7) Othniel's victory over Cushan-rishathiam (3.1-11).

The first tale of the collection of the eight longer tales which follow is the tale of Ehud (3.12-30). Variation of the structural scheme should be noticed in parts *e* and *f* above.

As **Tables II** and **III** show, the Introduction (1.1 up to the story of Ehud at 3.12) is balanced with the story of the Punishment of Benjamin (Civil War) (Chs. 20, 21), while Ehud and the Minor Judges are roughly equivalent in length to the story of the Levite's Concubine (Ch. 19).The Introduction amounts to a table of contents:

> Adoni-Bezek introduces the themes of Mutilation and Retribution (1.5-7).
>
> Achsah introduces the themes of Fathers and Daughters, and of Reward and Marriage (1.12-15).
>
> The story of Bethel/Luz introduces the themes of Hospitality, Spying, Deception, and the Destruction of Cities (1.23-26).
>
> The messenger-angel introduces the themes of the Covenant, Obedience, and the Need for Law (2.1-5).
>
> The death of Joshua introduces the theme of Governance and the Lack of a Great Leader (2.8-9).
>
> The appearance of the messenger of Yhwh introduces the theme of Apostasy and the Testing of the Tribes through Warfare (2.14-23).
>
> And the final skirmishes introduce the theme of Obtaining Wives—Wives from the Tribes vs. Foreign Wives (3.1-6).

These short pericopes preview the entire book.

The following passage is an example of one of smaller structures. Here we have a *tribe*, five *cities* and surrounding *suburbs*, as well as three references to *inhabitants* (1.27). The author omitted two parts of the pattern, perhaps aware that too precise or symmetrical a formula is not as interesting as one with variation:

Manasseh did not drive out Beth-shean	and its villages,
Tanaach	and its villages,
the inhabitants of Dor	and its villages,
the inhabitants of Ibleam	and its villages,
the inhabitants of Megiddo	and its villages;

but the Canaanites continued to live in that land.[30]

A number of the other tribes, though not all, are introduced in the Introduction, as well as their difficulties settling the land. Other designs can be found throughout the book.

The "downward slope," ethics, and the principle of arrangement

The author had apparently one guiding principle in arranging the stories: every list—or nearly every list—has a "downward slope" (to use Bakhtin's term in his study of Rabelais). *The New Interpreter's Bible* also mentions the "downward political and religious spiral."[31] Daniel I. Block notes that the characters are not "noble," but are seriously flawed.[32]

When we carefully analyze each of these characters—according to law and ethics—we shall see that our author was like an ancient Dante, arranging the creatures of his Inferno from the first circle down to the bottom of the pit. One can distinguish four categories of characters, though it is quite possible that the author of *Judges*, like Dante, had more levels in mind.

On the *first* level, the characters have no discernibly outright defects.

On the *second* level, character flaws like cowardice can be found as well as violations of custom and expectation.

On the *third* level, the characters are much worse than those preceding them, and they break many "conditional" laws.

On the *fourth*, the characters are completely out of control and commit crimes involving violation of more important, sometimes apodictic, or absolute, laws.

Early in *Judges* the characters have ideals, but gradually ideals are being lost, and the concept of warfare begins to deteriorate. If the author is discussing a list of women (e.g., the women in Samson's life), the first woman will be fairly good, the second will be bad, but the third will be so bad that in retrospect the second seems better than we had previously thought, etc.

Table IV. Inferno

First {Adoni-Bezek
Level (good)   {Achsah
                  {Othniel

Second   {Ehud
Level (bad)   {Jael and Sisera (Deborah)
                     {Gideon

Third   {Abimelech
Level (evil)   {Jephthah
                        {Samson

Fourth   {Micah & the Danites
Level (vicious)   {Levite's Concubine
                             {All-Israel vs. the Benjaminites

On the *first* level, Adoni-Bezek seems to be merely an enemy who receives strange and unusual punishment. Only later in the book—and only by comparison and contrast with the other characters—do we perceive in him an ethical awareness that all the others lack. Achsah, Caleb, and Othniel are apparently blameless, though the informer in the Bethel-Luz story (a non-Israelite) is not. When we have finished the book, however, we begin to recognize that these early characters are more flawed than we first realized, but still better than those following them.

On the *second* level, the actions of the characters are surprisingly disturbing, because our instincts tell us that although they "saved" Israel, these people are defective. No matter if Eglon and Sisera (the enemy) are tyrants and villains, Ehud and Jael (their Israelite slayers) are cunning, ruthless, and vicious, and both of them defy the ancient laws of hospitality.

In the Deborah story and *The Song* (2nd level), Barak—especially in contrast with Sisera—behaves like a coward. Though some of the Israelite tribes fight valiantly, others are cowardly and self-serving. Sisera may be a worthy enemy leader (despite the unfair advantage of his chariots of iron), but Sisera's mother and her ladies are gloating in advance over booty that they expect the victory will provide: luxuries for themselves and captive Israelites maidens for their men. Barak loses his opportunity for honor, for Sisera puts himself into the power of a woman. This clues us into how serious was Abimelech's loss of honor (3rd level) (*what* honor? you might ask), when he tried to avoid being killed by a woman, and the nadir to which Samson sank when he also put himself in the power of a woman. But Abimelech's gesture is futile, for he *was* felled by a woman. The coup de grâce given by his servant actually does not change the ignominy of his fate.

Gideon is an outright coward (much more of a coward than Barak—and this alone justifies placing him below Barak), while the flaw of the Ephraimites is that they are uncooperative troublemakers. Neither Gideon nor the Ephraimites, however, is "evil."

With Abimelech, the son of Gideon, we descend to the *third* level, those who are truly evil. Abimelech hired "worthless and violent fellows,"[33] slew his own half brothers, and broke his father's promise that neither Gideon nor any of his sons would become king (see discussion of Abimelech and his brothers in Chapter 4). He is a study in the abuse of power. But he was not exactly a usurper: the Shechemites chose him, and only when they turned on him, did he become a tyrant. Nevertheless he was not so bad as the drunken Gaal, who violated the laws of hospitality and loyalty when he fomented an insurrection against Abimelech, thus betraying his host. Betrayal being the worst sin to Dante, Gaal is worse than Abimelech. Or is he? Is Abimelech not also a betrayer?

Dante puts murderers in the seventh circle, not at the bottom. That Abimelech murdered his half-brothers makes him a candidate for Dante's ninth circle—those treacherous to kin. But in that case, Ehud and Jael would also belong there—those treacherous to host (Ehud) and guest (Jael). Gaal would be in the lowest ring, treachery to one's master being worse than treachery to kin. The author, of course, did not know Dante. But his mind seems to be working in the same way.

Jephthah is usually regarded as morally superior to Abimelech, but the author may not share this interpretation. In the first place, Jephthah comes from a sordid background. Whereas Abimelech's mother was a concubine (not a full wife), Jephthah's mother was a harlot (not even a concubine) (11.1). (And the Levite's Concubine "played the harlot," which is no doubt even worse.) (Note again the "downward" pattern: the second woman is a step lower than the first.) In the story of Jephthah, it might be argued, however, that the author is trying to prove that good people can come from bad parents. We have to wait to see how Jephthah turned out.

Jephthah keeps bad company with "worthless fellows" (אנשים ריקים), the same phrase used to describe the followers of Abimelech. Jephthah and his gang did not, however, slay Jephthah's brothers. Consequently, our first impression is that he is on a higher level than Abimelech. However, Jephthah slays his daughter; and then he slays many Ephraimites. Is it worse to slay one's only child than one's 70 brothers? And are we not to understand from Genesis that the tribes are "brothers"? Whereas Abimelech slew 70 brothers, Jephthah slew 42,000 Ephraimite "brothers." Abimelech did not slay his own child, but Jephthah did, and in doing so, might be construed as slaying the future of Israel.

As we are going to discover when we analyze the Deborah/Samson parallels, the author is playing games with points of view. He has tricked us into regarding Jephthah as superior to Abimelech, leaving us to discover for ourselves that he may actually be worse.

As the last character on the *third level*, Samson is irrational and violent and brings serious trouble upon both the Danites and the Israelites. Samson's dangerous and abusive behavior was also unwise, making it so hot for the Danites in their allotted territory that they were forced to move (Chs. 17-18). Samson has many defects—lust for Philistine women and the breaking of a religious vow, to mention two of them, and he violated the *lex talionis* (an eye for an eye) in his feud with the Philistines.

If we now look back at Adoni-Bezek at the beginning of the book, here was a man (the enemy at that) who understood the meaning of just retribution. Not so Samson.

On the *fourth level*, the last two stories (Ch. 17-21) show that evil is not being committed by one or two, but by practically everyone, including two Levites, the Danites, the Benjaminites, and ultimately, all the tribes. Micah and his mother not only are idolaters but also violators of other commandments and laws—if not the Deuteronomic ones, then the "natural" laws, the Homeric concept called *themis*, defined by Alisdaire MacIntyre as "the concept of customary law shared by all civilized peoples."[34] The Danites break the commandment against stealing when they steal both the idols and the priest and become idolaters. The Levite violates hospitality, he is an accomplice in the theft of Micah's images, and he is an idolater. But as the downward pattern teaches us, the first Levite is not so bad as the Levite in the story that follows.

The second Levite's treatment of his Concubine—putting her out to the rapists (יצא אליהם החוץ, 19.25)—is on the level of the base actions of first, the Benjaminite men who raped and murdered her and second, the entire tribe of Benjamin, which committed obstruction of justice by protecting the felons. Finally, the Benjaminites may not be the most unworthy group of all, for one can argue that "all Israel" may be even worse—because they come close to annihilating a whole tribe (which is worse than Jephthah's killing of 42,000 Ephraimites); because they were ruthless toward Jabesh-Gilead and the daughters of Shiloh; and because they forswore their vow not to give their daughters to the Benjaminites (21.1).

Actually, the author is playing highly sophisticated psychological games with us. It is as if he has constructed a set of pictures which at a glance look accurate. Underneath each frame, however, is the direction: "Discover what is wrong with the picture." If we have an understanding of law and ethics, we will see the errors in each of the stories. If we have not learned our lesson, we will never understand the meaning of the book.

Like Aristotle in *Nicomachean Ethics* and Dante much later, this author has shown concern for degrees of viciousness by placing the vices in a significant order.

IV. Parallels

All of the stories have intricate parallels and contrasts with all the other stories of the book.

Table V. Chiasmus of Correspondences

A. Introduction
  B. Ehud, brave
    C. Deborah and Jael
      D. Gideon, good leader in battle
        E. Abimelech, bad leader
      D′. Jephthah, good leader in battle
    C′. Samson
  B′. Micah, coward, and the Danites
A′. Levite's Concubine & aftermath

But it is not so simple as one-to-one correspondences, for a story may be similar to, and different from, more than one other story and in diverse ways. And the parallels are not always easy to detect at first, though once spotted, they become obvious. (Chapter 3 is largely about the parallels signaled by keywords.)

The importance of the parallels cannot be overestimated. They have a serious bearing on the way we judge the actions in any story. We may reach a judgment in one story, only to have the details of another story correct our decision because the details of the second story give us a new perspective from which to judge and new ideas to think about. We get these differences in perspectives through comparing and contrasting the stories in various ways. One of the best examples is in a comparison of the deeds of Jael and Delilah. Though they commit almost identical crimes, one is "the most blessed of tent dwelling women," while the other is a villainess. The way the author has manipulated our perceptions and paralyzed our power of judgment is worthy of the most sophisticated kind of narrative technique of our own century.

The readers are the judges, or שפטים, of the events in this book. As good judges, we should be objective and impartial. What is amazing is that this author, writing at least 2,500 years ago, had such a grasp of the function of *point of view* in narratives.

Introduction vs. conclusion

The introduction to *Judges* shows how the tribes coordinated their efforts at the beginning of the settlement. A specific example of friendly cooperation between tribes is given in the incident with Judah and Simeon (1.3, 17). The battles and skirmishes at the beginning of the book seem to be like those of *Joshua*—the traditional and accepted "holy war"—but at the end of the book, the whole land is in turmoil. Conflict is now directed not toward the enemy but toward a fellow tribe. Civil war has broken out. True, the tribes of "all-Israel" are still capable of cooperation, but to a bad end, to annihilate one of their brother tribes, Benjamin. (See "Stages of War" in Chapter 2.)

Ehud vs. Micah. Micah's Images

One way to look at the correspondences between the stories of Ehud and Micah is through their use of keywords referring to *images* or *idols*. (Keywords as an artistic device are discussed in Chapter 3.)

Images (פסילים) (idols) are found twice (2x) in the Ehud story (3.19, 26) and seem to serve only as a geographical landmark, the author perhaps counting on the reader's knowing what and where these images are, in order to make the tale seem more "factual." In addition, they may be a signal that something is wrong with Israel from the beginning: the Israelites have *images*.

They also signal an important correspondence with the Micah story, where images are found as religious objects that Micah's mother had had smelt for her son, mentioned 8x (17.3, 4; 18.14, 17, 18, 20, 30, 31). Micah also has *molten images* (מסכה), mentioned 5x (17.3, 4; 18.14, 17, 18), an *ephod* (אפוד), mentioned 5x (17.5; 18.14, 17, 18, 20), and *teraphim* (תרפים), mentioned 5x (17.5; 18.14, 17, 18, 20)—a total of 23x.****** It is the author's fortississimo. No other set of keywords receives as much emphasis in the book as this. The images are also evidence of Micah's idea of super piety, although by the standards of the time, they are questionable objects.[35]

Ehud is good in that he represents direct confrontation with a foreign enemy who has oppressed his people and exacted tribute for 18 years. He is active and fearless and removes the tyrant who has invaded and occupied his land. A model of strength and courage, we can use him as a way of measuring the courage of Zebah and Zalmunna, Jephthah, and Samson.

In contrast, Micah is bad in that he does not confront a foreign enemy or an oppressor. Instead he is confronted by a brother tribe, the Danites, who are en route

---

****** I use the arithmetic expression "2x" instead of "two times" throughout and also cite numbers as numerals, rather than as words, for statistical purposes.

to invade another land and who steal his images and his Levite priest in passing. He is brave in running in protest after them, but ridiculous in losing courage when the Danites intimidate him. He turns and flees in shame. Micah's weakness and self-indulgence are in contrast to Ehud's strength, courage, and selflessness. His *cowardice* can be compared with that of Barak (who refuses to go to battle without Deborah), Sisera (who flees when defeated instead of going down with his men), and Gideon (who uses all kinds of pretexts to avoid combat as long as possible). He can be contrasted with Jael, who although a woman, gave a (dastardly) blow to a heavily armed (though sleeping) soldier. But can Micah in fact be said to be a coward? After all, he is being threatened by "six hundred men armed with weapons of war," a phrase which is repeated 3x, lest we miss the odds against him (18.11, 16, 17). He acknowledges that the Danites are "too strong" for him (כִּי־חֲזָקִים הֵמָּה מִמֶּנּוּ, 18.26), a sensible conclusion. "Coward" is too strong a word, though he is perhaps negligent in being unprepared to defend himself and his house. He wins his place at the bottom of the downward slope because of his idolatry.

Gideon vs. Jephthah

Stories are linked in various ways. An important link between the Gideon and Jephthah stories is how they deal with the Ephraimites. Whereas Gideon propitiates them, Jephthah slaughters them. An even more interesting contrast may be that whereas *Yhwh* ordered Gideon to reduce *his own army* and he did so—from 32,000 to 300—by sending the extras peacefully "home to their own place," Jephthah *himself reduced* the Ephraimite tribe by 42,000 men, slaughtering them as they were crossing over the Jordan toward home. The difference in why and how the two armies were reduced is what we are supposed to notice.

Two other links: the enemy invades Gideon's land, then Gideon chases after them, though he does not leave Israel. While an enemy also invades Jephthah's land, Jephthah, in contrast to Gideon, may have *left his land to invade another* when he crossed (עבר) over to the Ammonites to fight against them (11.29). Another parallel, though with a difference, is that the Danites, whom Micah chases after, actually leave their land to invade, and settle in, another.

A wonderful parallel is the following: Gideon invites his son Jether to kill the enemy kings Zebah and Zalmunna, while in contrast, Jephthah kills his own daughter. Jether, lacking confidence because he is very young, is cowardly; but Jephthah's daughter, also young, is courageous. She, also a child, is as courageous as the male Midianite kings, Zebah and Zalmunna, when they told Gideon to play the man and slay them himself.

Succoth and Thebez, the two cities which Gideon chastises, are another link with Jephthah; they lie in Gilead, the territory Jephthah was eventually to rule.

Abimelech vs. Jephthah

Of the main Israelite characters, Abimelech is the only one of the main characters who is killed by another (Samson kills himself). Certain elements in the story show the

Abimelech story to be a counterpart of both the Gideon and Jephthah stories. Abimelech's outlaw associates and the inferior status of his mother (a concubine), making him a poor candidate to rule, are a connection with Jephthah, who also consorts with outlaws and whose mother is inferior (a prostitute). We do not know how well Jephthah rules. Abimelech's slaying of his own brothers is comparable to Jephthah's slaying of his daughter and 42,000 Ephraimites. He rules badly. The question we are being asked is: which is worse?

Gideon vs. Abimelech

Gideon was vindictive toward *two cities*: he pulled down the *tower* of Penuel and killed the men in it, and he chastised the elders in the city of Succoth. Abimelech also struck against *two cities*: he burned down the *tower* of Shechem and razed the city. He tried, but failed, to burn down another *tower* in the city of Thebez. Which is worse? Jephthah, however, does not chastise any cities.

Adrien Janis Bledstein lists some of the contrasts between Abimelech and his father, Gideon, which can be given in a table:

Gideon	Abimelech
called by Yhwh to liberate Israel	designates himself king
Gideon slays a bull to sacrifice on an altar	slays his 70 brothers
is energized by the spirit of Yhwh	is given a spirit of discord by Yhwh
liberates Israel from the Midianites, but uses brutality against scoffers, dismantles a tower, massacres the inhabitants	is brutal against his foes, burns them in a tower, and destroys his own city
Yhwh was with Gideon and his 300 men against the Midianites	Yhwh fought against Abimelech
refused kingship	seized kingship and worshiped Baal
kept the peace for 40 years and died an old man	died after 3 years
a hero	not a hero[*******]

[*******]Most of this table is quoted from Bledstein, "Is Judges a Woman's Satire of Men Who Play God?" in *A Feminist Companion to Judges* (ed. Althalya Brenner; Sheffield: JSOT Press, 1993), 44-45.

We see immediately which is worse and why. These oppositions, though they are a "play" element of the art, are set up for a purpose, and it is up to us to find out what that is.

Destruction of cities by Gideon, Abimelech, Danites, and all-Israel.

The destruction of the Tower of Penuel (by Gideon) and the Tower and city of Shechem (by Abimelech) was introduced as a theme at the beginning of the book by the destruction of the enemy city Bethel-Luz by the Joseph tribes (1.23). This is compared with the destruction of Succoth (by Gideon), Shechem (by Abimelech), Laish (by the Danites), and Jabesh-Gilead (by all-Israel minus Benjamin). All of these are friendly cities (Laish, though non-Israelite, has shown no hostility). Destruction of enemy cities in Canaan is very different from destruction of friendly cities or of unprotected cities beyond the pale, which may have been illegal action according to the rules of holy war.

Gideon/Samson

The similarity of the theophany of the Gideon prologue (6.11-23) to that of Samson's parents (Ch. 13) is undoubtedly a clue that the Gideon and Samson materials are counterparts. The messenger-angels in each story help two entirely different kinds of persons. Gideon is a producer and protector of food (see Chapter 3), while Samson is a consumer and destroyer of food. Gideon is a coward, but once having proved himself, grows brave and arrogant, while Samson is a bully from first to last.

V. More Complex Correspondences

Correspondences exist not between any two stories alone, but between one story and many others. Three sets of correspondences will be discussed: those between (1) the Deborah and the Samson stories; (2) Jephthah with Sisera's mother; and (3) the "Father-Daughter, Mother-Son Stories," starting with the story of Achsah and continuing though a number of other stories in the book.

Deborah vs. Samson

So numerous are the correspondences between the two stories of Deborah and Samson that it is impossible to imagine that the writer did not create them for a specific purpose.[36] The correspondences between the Deborah and Samson stories stretch back and forth, lacing the stories together and inviting us to appraise, evaluate, and judge what we are observing.

Table VI. Comparison & Contrast of Deborah and Samson

Deborah	Samson
1. Flowing locks (5.2)	1. Samson's hair
2. Sisera, strong man	2. Samson, strong man
3. Sisera: 900 chariots of iron; "no shield or spear in Israel"	3. Bare hands; jawbone of an ass
4. Sisera "oppressed the people of Israel cruelly for twenty years" (4.3)	4. Philistines call Samson "the ravager of our country who has slain many of us" (16.24); he judged Israel twenty years
5. Barak needs a woman's help. He loses his honor for this. Sisera falls prey to a woman	5. Samson needs women. He consorts with three foreign women, losing his honor, and falls prey to one of them
6. Three + several women: Jael (a Kenite), a wife, an enemy to Sisera, though Sisera does not know this; Jael possibly disloyal to her people but loyal to the Israelites; Deborah, a wife Sisera's mother wise women	6. Four women: Delilah, possibly a harlot (apparently a Philistine), lover of Samson, but unbeknownst to him, an enemy. Delilah loyal to her people; Samson's wife (the Timnite) Samson's mother harlot of Gaza
7. Israelites demolish an army no information on how many Israelites were killed	7. Philistines kill only the Timnite and her father; Samson kills many
8. Jael's name means *female goat*	8. Samson's father prepares a goat for the angel-messenger; "Samson tore the lion . . . as he might have torn a young goat" (14.6); Samson takes a young goat when he goes to visit his wife
9. Deborah's name means *honey bee*	9. Samson finds *bees* and *honey* in the lion's carcass (דבורים . . . ודבש עדת) (14.8)
10. Deborah's husband's name is Lappidoth (*torches,* לפידות)	10. Samson uses torches (לפידים) on the foxes' tails

Deborah	Samson
11. Jael lures Sisera in, as a prostitute would do (cf. *Proverbs*); perhaps he seduces (rapes?) her	11. The Timnite entices Samson; Samson visits a prostitute; Delilah probably sleeps with him. Delilah entices him to tell his secret
12. Jael pretends to like Sisera, but really hates him Jael is foreign (a Kenite) to Sisera (a Canaanite)	12. Delilah pretends to love Samson, but really hates him–this is what she has accused him of doing toward her. Delilah is foreign (a Philistine) to Samson (an Israelite)
13. Sisera says: "I am thirsty. Please give me some water." milk is supplied by Jael; he dies after his drink	13. Samson cries to Yhwh: "Must I now die of thirst?" water is supplied by Yhwh; he revives after his drink
14. Sisera hides in Jael's tent from the Israelites; tells her not to reveal his hiding place	14. Samson is in Delilah's room; the Philistines are hiding in an inner room. Samson hides in the cleft of the Rock of Etam
15. Jael betrays a sleeping man; violation of hospitality	15. Delilah betrays a sleeping man; violation of hospitality
16. Jael's weapon is a tent peg (יתד); Jael also uses a hammer	16. Delilah's weapon is a weaving pin (יתד); Delilah also uses a razor
17. Sisera's brain is crushed; mutilation	17. Samson's eyes gouged out; mutilation
18. Sisera falls down dead; innumerable Canaanites killed	18. Thousands of Philistines literally "fall down" and die in the temple
19. Canaanite hero killed	19. Israelite hero killed
20. "Awake, awake, Deborah" Sisera sleeps	20. With the prostitute in Gaza, at midnight he arose; with Delilah, Samson sleeps
21. Sisera is sold "into the hand of a woman" (4.9)	21. Samson is sold by a woman into the hands of the Philistines (for 1,100 pieces of silver)
22. Yhwh "sells Sisera"	22. Dagon "has given Samson our enemy into our hand" (16.23)

23. Jael says to Barak: "Come, I will show you the man whom you are seeking" (4.22)	23. Delilah said to the Philistine lords: "Come back once more, for he has told me everything"
24. The kings took no spoil (5.19); Sisera's mother and the wise women are waiting (in vain) for spoil (mentioned 4x); they get none	24. "The Lords of the Philistines came up to [Delilah] and brought the money in their hands" (16.18); Philistines are waiting to make sport of Samson; they get none
25. Sisera's mother is waiting for "colorful garments" (mentioned 3x), but gets none (NIV, 5.30)	25. Samson seizes 30 linen garments and 30 sets of clothes for his "companions"
26. Sisera's mother materialistic and arrogant	26. Samson's mother innocent and possibly spiritual
27. Reference to woven things (*rich carpets* and *dyed stuffs*)	27. Samson's hair is woven into a web on the loom
28. His mother thinks Sisera will bring home captive women (*wombs*); he doesn't	28. Samson's mother's *womb* is mentioned 6x; Samson gets three women, but we do not know how many "*wombs*"
29. Sisera is captured and killed by a woman; he dies in his tent– ignominiously for him	29. Samson is captured by a woman; he dies amid a multitude people on the roof of, and in, the temple of Dagon–ignominiously for the Philistines
30. "Most blessed of women is Jael" (to the Israelites)	30. Delilah must be a heroine to *her* people (the enemy)
31. Triumph for Israel	31. Triumph for Israel
32. Poem ends with the hope that those who love Yhwh will "be like the sun as he rises in his might."	32. Samson rises in the night at Gaza (16.3); שמש (*sun*) = שמשו (Samson); also he rises from slavery
33. Deborah judged	33. Samson judged

The only chapter of the Samson story which does not figure significantly in the above set of correspondences (except for the reference to Samson's mother) is the theophany of Ch. 13.[37] Thus one may suspect that Ch. 13 was a later addition, perhaps to give emphasis to the Nazirite vow that the mother takes, or to provide a correspondence with the theophany in the Gideon story (6.11).

The most obvious pairs of characters to compare and contrast are (a) Jael/Delilah and (b) Sisera/Samson (perhaps also Samson/Barak). An analysis of **Table VI** follows.

Jael vs. Delilah

Despite the differences between them, Jael (a Kenite) and Delilah (a Philistine) are remarkably similar in behavior. When we first read the story of Jael's triumph over Sisera and Delilah's over Samson, we very likely identify with the Israelite point of view, but after scrutinizing the two stories closely, we may change our minds.

Both women defeat a man who has trusted them. They differ in that Jael does her deed for no reward, while Delilah does hers for money. She is a gold-digger, always considered a reprehensible role. Jael entices her victim into her tent: "Turn aside, my lord, turn aside to me; have no fear" (4.18). Samson, however, comes of his own free will to Delilah's room, but afterwards allows himself to be enticed. Both women use their female wiles to give false confidence to the male in their power. Both women are alone with a sleeping man. As females, both are symbols of sexuality and defenselessness. Both males are symbols of enormous power and experience in battle or single combat against their enemies, but both become as defenseless as women, and under the spell cast by their mistresses are trapped in their webs. It is an elaborate paradox.

The use of the same keywords in both stories is a signal that the characters are meant to be compared and contrasted. Both women wield a tool (יתד) translated *tent peg* in the first story and *weaving pin* in the second. Both of them *drive* it (תקע, 4.21; 16.14), just as Ehud *drove* his sword into Eglon's belly (3.21) and as Joab *drove* his darts into Absalom's heart (2 Sam 18.14). But there is a difference: while Jael *drives* the tool into her victim's *head*, Delilah *drives* it into her victim's *hair*, weaving his hair into the web of the loom. Jael's tool was described as a *tool of the tent* (האהל יתד) to emphasize that she was a tent-dweller. The KJV, NIV and NRS fail to catch the meaning of תקע (drive) in the Delilah story when they translate it as *fastened*, *tightened* and *wove*, respectively, instead of as *drove*, the best word to emphasize Delilah's forcefulness.

Jael's deed is ferocious. She is compared to a workman in the way she wields her mallet and her tool and crushes Sisera's skull. In contrast, Delilah uses a womanly tool in a womanly way—to weave. That availing nothing, she uses a second tool, a *razor*, but instead of cutting her victim's *throat*, she simply has his *hair* cut off. She does not herself physically harm Samson. Nevertheless, she captures him. Whereas

Jael performs the mutilation, Delilah is not responsible for the gouging out of Samson's eyes. Is not Delilah then ethically superior to Jael—contrary to the usual interpretation of the story?

Both Jael and Delilah wield a weapon against someone who considered himself a friend, lover, or ally. Both murder a man to whom they have offered hospitality and who, at their enticement, lies prostrate, asleep, and completely vulnerable. Can we call them cowardly? But as weak women, they have to use cunning and deception.

Both Jael and Delilah have divided loyalties. Jael's husband is a friend of the Canaanites: "There was peace (שלום) at that time between King Jabin of Hazor and the clan [house] of Heber the Kenite" (4.17). So why does Jael help the Israelites? No bit of information is insignificant. The answer may be that she helps them because she is a Kenite, not a Canaanite. The Kenites were supposedly descended from Cain; and Cain was an Israelite. Consequently, her first loyalty may not be to the Canaanites but to her ancestors' nationality. She is a descendant of the first murderer. A murderer herself, she is a chip off the old block.

What did Sisera have in mind when he came to Jael's tent? Was it because he knew her and expected protection from her? But maybe Sisera was actually a stranger. Under the circumstances, it would not be surprising that he raped her, as we might decide from the fact that he immediately fell into such a profound sleep. Sexual intercourse and rape are certainly an important theme in the book.

Though Sisera had a good reason to be exhausted—he had just fought a terrific battle—the evidence also suggests that it was sexual intercourse that weakened him. The author works through comparisons. If Samson slept with Delilah, then Sisera probably slept with Jael. (Does it make a difference to the story, whether he did or did not?)

Jael is to be compared with all the women: with Achsah, the bride (having an appropriate relationship with a man); Jephthah's daughter (the only one who remains a virgin); Delilah, the seductress; and the Concubine and the daughters of Jabesh-Gilead and Shiloh, who are raped. Victor H. Matthews and Don C. Benjamin think that Jael killed Sisera in order to protect herself against rape.[38] Sex is important in this story, but specific information about it is not given. Perhaps the ancient listener or reader knew the story, just as the Greeks knew which gods raped which mortal women. And perhaps the oral storyteller embellished the scenario and improvised to fill in the gaps as he narrated it.

On the other hand, the author works with contrasts. Jael may be an example of the virtuous woman, which is likely, as she appears in the first half of the book where the characters are more or less proper. In this interpretation, she had no sexual intercourse. Or in order to save her chosen country, she may have seduced Sisera herself.[39] Then she might be a Mata Hari. We are left with a mystery, a riddle. The issue is moot.

Delilah is a Philistine, or at least a friend of the Philistines. On the other hand, Samson is not a stranger, but her lover. To whom should she have the greater loyalty? Samson falls asleep, possibly also after sexual intercourse, as many believe. If she is only feigning to be a lover in order to get him into her power, then *she* is a Mata Hari.

From the perspective of the Israelites, Jael is a heroine and Delilah a villain. From the perspective of the Canaanites and Philistines, Delilah is a heroine and Jael a villain. Or switch the victims: had Jael's victim been Samson, she would be a villain to the Israelites, while if Delilah's had been Sisera, she would be a heroine to them. Right and wrong consists in whose side one is on and who is killed. "Most blessed of women be Jael, the wife of Heber the Kenite, of tent-dwelling women most blessed" (5.24).

Jael may be more treacherous than Delilah, however, because she was *disloyal* to her adopted country (her husband's lord), while Delilah (assuming that she was a Philistine) was *loyal* to *her* country. In Dante's *Inferno*, both of them would be in the bottom circle among the betrayers. But since betrayal of one's lord is worse than betrayal of a lover, Jael would be lower than Delilah.

The riddle of their ethics is more intricately wrought than Samson's riddle, and we must apply ingenuity to solving it. Because of the complexity of these relationships, the case is difficult to adjudicate between the two women. But given the information we have, it would seem that the scales of Justice are evenly balanced between them.

Jael and Delilah vs. other women

We are being shown that women have all kinds of potential, not only for good, but also for evil; but it is not always easy to distinguish between the two kinds. Compare Jael and Delilah with the woman in the tower who drops the upper millstone on Abimelech's head (9.53). Is there such a thing as an unethical way of killing your enemy, especially if you are a weak woman and your country's destiny lies in your hands? Feminists claim that this book is reinforcing the traditional male belief that women cannot be trusted. But another way to look at this is that women who are dealing with enemies do not have to be "trustworthy," provided they remain loyal to their own country. Sex can be very dangerous. Foreigners can be dangerous. Men have to be on their guard. Caveat emptor.

Should our judgment of a person be influenced by that person's social status? Delilah, like the harlot in Gaza, probably is a prostitute. Do we judge prostitutes differently from their lovers? How does she, who apparently is not married, compare with the Timnite (a wife, but a Philistine), with Abimelech's mother (a concubine and a Shechemite, probably not an Israelite), with Jephthah's mother (a harlot of unknown nationality, though probably a Gileadite) and with the Levite's Concubine (a pure Israelite)?

In the case of the Levite's Concubine, the Concubine was not just a victim. She was also an agent, for we are told that 1) she played the harlot (should we take this phrase literally?) and that 2) she ran away from her husband. Neither of these acts can be construed as "good" in that society, no matter what these acts mean nor why they happened. Thus her victimization by the gang-rapists may be seen as a kind of "frontier justice": she was repaid in kind. Retribution.

The reader who does not agree with any of these conclusions, must at least consider them. The above discussion also shows how the Deborah/Samson connections multiply when set beside other patterns in the book. Each story leads to other actions in other stories in the network of the book. The fabric on Delilah's loom is not the only web in *Judges*, and Delilah is not the only spider. There are no easy answers to any of these questions. No case is clear-cut black or white.

(The Jael/Delilah material will be discussed in Chapter 2, to show how the combination of horror and humor affects our judgment further. Though not all the details of the story are repeated there, some overlapping is necessary. Chapter 4 is about ethics, law, and judgment. The Jael/Delilah and Samson/Sisera comparisons here would normally belong there as a "law case," but have been omitted in Chapter 4 because of the lengthy discussion here.)

Barak vs. Sisera vs. Samson

Barak is dependent upon a woman when he should have been courageous and self-reliant. He feared to go to battle without Deborah; nevertheless, though he did not personally kill the enemy leader, he fought and triumphed. Sisera rode at the head of his troops, was overwhelmed in battle, fled to save himself, and fell ignominiously into the hands of a woman. Thus Barak is superior to Sisera, though both needed a woman.

Heavily armed with 900 iron chariots (mentioned 5x in Ch. 4) in an unequal fight against a people who had no shields or spears, Sisera can be compared with the 600 heavily armed Danites against poor Micah. But was he not, like Micah, also craven? The odds were suddenly reversed, and all his chariots were disabled and his army thrown into a panic by Yhwh himself; he had no choice but to alight from his chariot and flee for his life. (Is there a faint echo of Achsah alighting from her ass here?) Suffering a reverse with no possibility of succor— for who can withstand Yhwh?—he behaves the way anyone would under the circumstances, and we would have no reason to despise him, had he withstood the blandishments of a woman. Like Samson, he finds himself alone and defenseless, sleeping in a woman's room. What a come-down. "For low they fall whose fall is from the sky." In this, he is better than Samson because Sisera desperately needed rest and a place to hide, and he supposed that Jael was a friend of his country.

Samson, by comparison, is a troublemaker. Samson does not lead any troops. He only stirs up the enemy and kills a good number of them; he seems to do no harm to the enemy as a whole except to make them angry and vengeful. Some of his fellow Israelites (the men of Judah) are so disquieted with his intransigence and propensity for getting the Israelites into trouble that they, even they, hand him over to the enemy. Had he consorted with decent Israelite women and kept his Nazirite vows, all might have been otherwise. But because he, like Sisera, was trapped by women and did what was "right in his own eyes," instead of what might have been right in Yhwh's eyes, Samson brought only trouble on himself and on his tribe, the Danites, who in the next story, migrate out of their territory, ostensibly to find a better "allotment," possibly because of the trouble Samson fomented with the Philistines.

Though Samson ultimately triumphed over his captors, his behavior with women, his violence, and his abuse of innocent bystanders—animals (the lion and the foxes), property (the fields, orchards, and vineyards), and people (the 30 Ashkelonites, among many others)—are what place him beneath Sisera in nobility.

Captive women at the end of *The Song of Deborah*—"A girl or two for every man"—emphasizes the fact that instead of *women* being taken captive by fighting *men*, the male hero *Sisera* has been taken captive—by a *woman*. Samson also was taken captive by a woman. "Captive women" (רחם רחמתים *wombs, two wombs*, 5.30) is a link with the Levite's Concubine and with the daughters of Jabesh-Gilead and Shiloh, all of whom become captive wombs seized by men in gang and mass rapes at the end of the book.

The second most important set of parallels after the Deborah/Samson set, is a rather large and complex set of Father-Daughter Stories. At this point, it would be useful to study the parallels and read across the grid in **Table VII** to become familiar with the complexity of the narrative scheme.

VI. Father-Daughter, Mother-Son Stories. Father-Son Relationships

The Story of Achsah

The Achsah story is swiftly told:

> Then Caleb said, "Whoever attacks Kiriath-sepher and takes it, I will give him my daughter Achsah as wife." And Othniel son of Kenaz, Caleb's younger brother, took it; and he gave him his daughter Achsah as wife. When she came to him, she urged him to ask her father for a field; as she dismounted from her donkey, Caleb said to her, "What do you wish?" She said to him, "Give me a present; since you have set me in the land of the Negeb, give me also Gulloth-Mayim [springs of water]." And Caleb gave her Upper Gulloth [upper springs] and Lower Gulloth [lower springs] (1.12-15).

It is a fairy tale. The hero will win the princess and the throne if he conquers the enemy. He conquers and wins. Othniel seems to be suitable: he is the son of Kenaz, Caleb's nephew (also called "younger brother"). The Kenizzites were absorbed into Judah, while Judah was eventually to become the most important tribe. Any doubts we may have about Othniel's worth vanish when he later conquered Cushan-rishathaim, king of Mesopotamia, and delivered the Israelites (3.10). He conquered the enemy, without breaking any laws. Nothing bad is reported of him. We can conclude that, as in all fairy tales, the right hero has come along at the right time. Lucky Achsah.

But what if the wrong man had come along? The promise made by Caleb was a rash one, one not so different from the vow of the more unfortunate Jephthah. (Notice the "link"—the vow.) What if some very disreputable man had made the conquest? Poor Achsah.

Achsah vs. Jephthah's daughter. Caleb vs. Jephthah

Jephthah, too, was the father of a lively daughter, one who went to meet her father, not to ask for a present, but to celebrate "with timbrels and with dancing" (11.34). Unlucky daughter, to have danced out of the door at the wrong moment and to have a father whose vow, in contrast to Caleb's, brought her no husband. Like the son of Idomeneus in Greek myth, Jephthah's daughter deserved a better fate.[40]

Until we read the Jephthah story, however, we do not know the extent of Achsah's luck. Because of the difficulties in translation, it is not clear whether it was Achsah or Othniel who initiated the idea of asking Caleb for a present (1.14). What is clear is that Achsah went to her father fearlessly; and from him received the gift (or blessing) that she asked for—unlike what Jephthah's daughter got when she came to greet her father: she became a burnt offering, a gift to Yhwh (11.39).

Achsah had a husband; she did not have to wander on the mountains like Jephthah's daughter and bewail her virginity. Compared with other women in the book, she was not pushed out of the door to be raped by a gang of ruffians. Nor was she stolen from her town after everyone in town, except 400 virgins like herself, were slain and the virgins forced into a marriage with men of bad repute. Nor was she seized while she was dancing in the vineyard and abducted in a mass rape. Nor was she burnt, like the Timnite.

In the same way, the daughter of Jephthah goes to meet a triumphant hero, but is dealt a hideous blow. We notice her movements. First she dances out of the house (gaily) to meet Jephthah. (Dancing links her to the dancing daughters of Shiloh, whose fates were very different from that of Jephthah's daughter.) In contrast to Achsah, Jephthah's daughter, having come out of the house to meet her father, turns around and goes away from him. She moves away (sorrowfully) with her companions to lament her virginity; then she moves back (fearfully but courageously) to her execution, the sacrifice of herself to Yhwh. *She* is the gift.

Mieke Bal suggests that another "marriage" is involved here: "According to the tradition we see at work, for example in Judges 1, the victor is entitled to the chief's daughter as a bride. Just as Othniel . . . deserves Achsah, chief Caleb's daughter, Yhwh deserves [Jephthah's daughter]."[41] In my opinion, this would perhaps make Jephthah's daughter the first "bride of God (nun?)" in literature.

Table VII. Fathers and Daughters

Achsah (wife of Othniel) & her father	Jephthah's Daughter & her father	the Timnite (Samson's wife) & her father	the Levite's Concubine & her father
1. Girl (alive) on an ass	No ass mentioned	Dead ass (jawbone of an ass)	Girl (dead) on an ass
2. Dutiful daughter	Dutiful courageous daughter	Cowardly daughter when threatened by the Philistines; disloyal wife	Angry daughter who walked out on her husband; returned to her father
3. Good father	Erring father (consorted with worthless fellows)	Unwise father (misjudges wife's husband, Samson)	Convivial father, negligent of daughter's safety (father causes husband to delay departure)
4. Father & Daughter behave well	Father behaves badly, but daughter behaves well	Daughter speaks kindly to her husband but behaves badly	Husband speaks kindly to his wife, but later behaves badly
5. Father makes a (rash) promise and keeps it	Father makes rash vow; father keeps vow	Rash act: father gives away daughter; father tries to make amends; husband violates Nazirite vow	Israelites make rash vow (not to give daughters to Benjaminites)
6. Father breaks no law	Father breaks law (child-sacrifice)	Father breaks commandment in causing daughter to marry another (i.e. she commits adultery)	Wife played the harlot; husband forces wife to be raped (i.e., a kind of adultery)
7. One husband; good man (a hero)	No husband; Lack of husband bewailed	Two husbands Angry hot-tempered husband	Many "husbands" (gang rape). Negligent, cowardly, drunken(?), self-serving husband (saves himself, not wife)
8. Daughter happily married	Daughter (unhappily) unmarried; daughter given (or "married") to Yhwh	Daughter married to another man; husband divorced against his will	Daughter unhappily married

Achsah (wife of Othniel) & her father	Jephthah's Daughter & her father	the Timnite (Samson's wife) & her father	the Levite's Concubine & her father
9. Husband delivers Israel	Father delivers Israel	Husband kills enemy but causes trouble for Israel	Husband causes trouble for Israel, but kills no enemy
10. Girl going to her husband	Girl going out of house to father with joy; leaving father with sorrow; returning to him with fear	Husband storming angrily from wife; husband returning hopefully to wife, only to be disappointed	Wife leaving house angrily, away from husband, back to father. husband going to father retrieve his wife
11. Father gives daughter to husband	Father gives daughter to Yhwh	Father gives daughter to another man (two husbands)	Husband gives (pushes out) wife to many "husbands"
12. Father gives daughter present (basins of water)	Father gives a present (daughter) to Yhwh, but gives no present to daughter	Husband plans to give wife a present (a kid)	Wife given (a present) to base men
13. Daughter prospers	Daughter burnt	Father and daughter burnt	Daughter raped and murdered
14.Father, daughter, husband live	Father lives	Husband lives for a while, then dies in aftermath	Father and husband live
15. Lucky ending for father, daughter, Israel, saved	Unlucky ending for father and daughter; but Israel is saved	Unlucky ending for father, daughter & husband; but Israel begins to be saved	Unlucky ending for daughter; Israel split up by civil war; Israel reunited after civil war

Eventually when we understand Jephthah better, we may conclude that his rash vow was evidence not only of his cruel nature (cf. his treatment of the Ephraimites) but also of his folly in choosing the wrong solution to the dilemma in which he found himself, either to break a vow or to kill his child, both choices being taboo. Nobility lies not in Jephthah but in his obedient daughter who faces her unjust fate so courageously. The feminists believe, however, that this is evidence of a male text indoctrinating women to be servile to men. First, writes J. Cheryl Exum, "the androcentric message of the story of Jephthah's daughter is . . . submit to paternal authority." Second, when she comes out of the house and Jephthah realizes what this means, he "blames the victim."[42]

Table VII shows many more possibilities for comparison and contrast. We cannot cover them all here, but it should be noted that the book begins with Yhwh's anger at the Israelites' intermarriage with non-Israelites (3.16). Were the "marriages" at the end of the book, Israelites marrying Israelites, any better?

A mother (Sisera's) vs. a father (Jephthah)

Now to digress from the father-daughter stories to compare a mother in one story with a father in another—Sisera's mother with Jephthah. We will compare and contrast 1) the two parents; 2) the two children; 3) the two men; and 4) the two women.

1) Sisera's mother lost a son; Jephthah lost a daughter. The one waiting lost a hero (her son, Sisera). The hero (Jephthah) lost the one waiting (his daughter). A nice inversion.

2) Both children died. The death of Sisera was "justified" (he was an enemy); the death of Jephthah's daughter was "unjust" (she was an innocent victim). But *to the parents*, both deaths were tragic.

3) Sisera lost the war, but Jephthah won. Jephthah was an Israelite and thus a hero. Sisera was an enemy, the servant of a tyrant, and thus a villain. Sisera's loss meant grief for his mother and his country. Jephthah's victory meant joy for his country, but grief for him and his daughter. If we concede that Jephthah made a bad vow, then like Sisera, he got what he deserved, and his loss was just retribution. If Jephthah's vow was a good one, however, then his punishment was unfair, though if he had been a Canaanite, then the daughter's death might be dismissed as an abhorrent Canaanite practice. Both men can be seen as "bad" and thus deserving of their fate, while at the same time, to their own countries, both were heroes.

4) Both the mother in one story and the daughter in the other were awaiting the return of a hero. Both got a rude awakening, but with a difference: Sisera, the son, was dead, but his mother would live. Jephthah, the father, was alive, but his daughter would die. Sisera's mother would have been happy to have her son return, just as Jephthah's daughter was happy her father returned. Sisera's mother would not be happy when she learned that her son was dead. Jephthah's daughter would not be happy when she learned that *she* would die. How would Sisera's mother have felt if Sisera's safe return had also meant *her* death?

We sympathize with Jephthah's daughter because her death was not merited by anything she herself did. We do not sympathize with Sisera's mother because she was an "enemy" and relished the defeat of Israelites. She loved the idea of "captive women" as trophies for her men, but she no doubt did not love the idea of "captive men" for women. Comparison of the two stories, however, shows the neutral observer that Sisera's mother's fate was also "tragic."

(Jephthah is discussed in Chapter 2 as a comic character and in Chapter 4 under the categories of **vows** and retribution.)

Achsah vs. the Levite's Concubine

The keyword *ass* (חמור) at the beginning of the book is a signal pointing to another ass at the end of the book. (The reference to *ass* 5x in the Samson story indicates that this story, too, should be included among the parallels.)

So that we do not miss the signal, the word *ass* is mentioned 5x in the Concubine story—an excessive number of times. The asses are mentioned 4x before the abhorrent Benjaminites beset the old man's house in Gibeah, and the 5th time when the Concubine's body is being taken away home. Repetition is a form of emphasis.

Quite clearly, the second woman is not alighting happily from her ass of her own free will. The second woman is the Levite's Concubine, who has been placed, dead, on the ass by her husband and is about to be carved up by a knife and divided limb from limb into 12 pieces, a piece to be sent to each of the tribes.

The Levite's Concubine is, in fact, a meat offering to the tribes. There is another "offering" in the book—Jephthah's daughter, who was a burnt offering to Yhwh—and thus a flesh offering, like the meat which Gideon gave to the angel. Both the daughter and the Concubine are likened to slaughtered animals. In contrast to them, Achsah, we assume, lived happily ever after. (See *asses* under the category of Animals in Chapter 3.)

Wife/concubine. Happiness/anger. Beginning/end of marriage

Instead of a young girl going out to meet her bridegroom—lively and clear about what she desires—we have a contrasting situation in Ch. 19 in which a woman has become angry with her so-called husband (a Levite priest who on his return was "going to the house of Yhwh"), has run away from him, and has returned to her father's house. The Levite is called *her master* (אדני), also *her husband*. Though referred to as *woman* 2x (same word as *wife*), she is called his *concubine* 11x, *girl* (נערה) 6x, and *maid* (אמה, slave girl) 1x. She is not a full-fledged wife, like Achsah. We know that her status is inferior because of the way Jotham contemptuously refers to Abimelech's mother, Gideon's concubine (8.31), when he reminds the Shechemites that Abimelech is merely the "son of [a] maid-servant" (אמה, 9.18).

Whereas Achsah had gone to her husband joyfully (we may suppose), the Levite's Concubine when we last see her alive, is staggering (painfully) to her husband-master, horribly abused, perhaps even crawling, to the closed door that her husband has hidden behind. The climax of the story is swift and ruthless:

> So the man seized his concubine, and put her out to them. They wantonly raped her [knew her], and abused her all through the night until the morning. And as the dawn began to break, they let her go. As morning appeared, the woman came and fell down at the door of the man's house where her master was, until it was light. In the morning her master got up, opened the doors of the house, and when he went out to go on his way, there was his concubine lying at the door of the house, with her hands on the threshold. "Get up," he said to her, "we are going." But there was no answer. Then he put her upon the donkey, and the man set out for his home. When he had entered his house, he took a knife, and grasping his concubine he cut her into twelve pieces, limb by limb, and sent her throughout all the territory of Israel (19.25b-29).

Quite in contrast to how we imagine Othniel (Achsah's husband) awaiting Achsah's return from *her* father, the husband of the Levite's Concubine was *not* happily waiting for *his* wife in this scene. He was not even going to open the door. He had gone to bed. She dies before reaching him.

As in the Jephthah story, this daughter (the Levite's Concubine) dies *after* she leaves her father's house. And the Concubine's father, like Jephthah, is implicated in his daughter's death in having delayed the Levite's departure.

We see Achsah at the *beginning* of her married life (at the *beginning* of *Judges*), but the Concubine at the *end* of her married life (and also at the *end* of *Judges*).

Jephthah vs. The Concubine's Father vs. Caleb

The lengthy carousing scene in the story of the Levite's Concubine enables the author to stress the fact that the man drinking with the husband is not merely a *father-in-law* of the Levite (the relationship is mentioned 3x) but is also a *father.* Between verses 3b and 9 he is called *her father* 2x, *the girl's father* 6x, and *father-in-law* 3x (חתן), the word *father* being used a total of 11x in all.

What a different *father* he is compared with Jephthah, and yet we have the same consequence—the death of a daughter. This repetition invites us to consider the responsibilities of fatherhood and to compare this father with previous ones in the father-daughter stories in the book.

Although the Concubine's father is congenial, in contrast to Jephthah, he does not manifest any such high ideals as the keeping of a vow, no matter how rash, and because of his focus on "merriment" (i.e., drunkenness), he is low on the scale of values in comparison with Achsah's father, Caleb. These three men exemplify successive levels of degradation (in the Henry Adams sense of degradation through the course of history). (For further discussion, see the categories of Wine and Hospitality, in Chapter 3 and inebriation in Chapter 4.)

Husbands

As for the Levite, he too is a lesser husband than Othniel. Though indeed it was the Levite's intention, when he "went after the Concubine," to speak "kindly to her and bring her back" (19.3), he seems fonder of the father-in-law than of the girl. In the Carousing scene, the Concubine is conspicuous by her absence. Of course, this may be but an instance of the Middle East attitude toward women. But the Levite is in fact the opposite of heroic. First, he was negligent about getting his Concubine away early enough in the day so that they could reach home in good time, and second, when beset by the Benjaminites, instead of protecting her, he "seized" her and "put her out" to the rapists himself, who "knew her, and abused her all night until the morning." Apparently it was an *offense* for the Benjaminites to "know" *him*, but not an offense for them to "know" *her* (at least in the minds of the Levite and the old man). She is the scapegoat (Lev 16.8-27), just as Jephthah's daughter is a scapegoat.

Which is preferable: for a Levite priest to be subjected to this abuse, or a defenseless woman? Is this not one more coward to measure against Barak, Gideon, and Micah? Micah at least *made an attempt* to catch up with the Danites who were marching away with his images and his priest.

In marked contrast to his calling, can the Levite in the Concubine story be considered a "man of Yhwh"? The answer becomes clear when we compare his action with the corresponding episodes in the Lot and Gideon narratives.

Lot (Gen 19)

Both Lot and the Ephraimite host in Ch. 19 were willing to sacrifice their virgin daughter(s) for their guests. Can this be construed as hospitality par excellence? or does the author want us to question this interpretation? The situation in the Levite's Concubine story is quite different from that in the Lot story, however, for the host in Gibeah offers not only his own virgin daughter, but his *guest's* Concubine. This is presumptuous. The host does not fulfill his offer, because before he can act, the Levite pushes his Concubine out to the rapists. Why the Levite does not push out the Ephraimite's daughter as well is not made clear, but it might be construed as a sort of return for the hospitality he received. But two things are wrong with the scene: first of all, the Concubine is a wife, and wives must not commit adultery (can rape be called "adultery"?), and second, the Levite is sacrificing his Concubine *not* to save his *angelic* guests as Lot tried to do, but to save *himself*.

Had he *not* put her out, but had gone out himself, some angels might have "put forth their hands and brought [the Levite] back into the house" safely as they brought Lot back, in Gen 19.10 (so the author might have thought). But this Levite was taking no chances.[43] He is an abject coward.

Gideon's father

The father of Gideon was able to prevent a similar incident from developing into a massacre by using diplomacy, that is, persuasive logic (6.30-31)—reminding us, tellingly, of the contest of Elijah with the prophets of Baal (1 Kg18.24) and also reminding us of Gideon's later tact with the Ephraimites (8.1-2), as well as the diplomatic skill which Jephthah had but did *not* use with *his* Ephraimites (12.1-6). The Levite that night had no such trick up his sleeve.

The Concubine's Levite

When she managed to escape the rapists at dawn, the Concubine crawled to the closed (locked?) door. At the beginning of the episode, the Levite may have been cringing (we do not know), but he did not go out to look for her, not even after the commotion died down. Sooner or later, he went to bed. We assume this, for the author is careful to tell us that the next morning, "her master rose up."

That the husband might have slept through the attack astonishes us and adds to the horror. Perhaps he was suffering from a hangover after the 5 days of carousing and an additional evening with the old Ephraimite host "making their hearts merry" (KJV 19.22).

Where would Othniel have been if a group of men had tried to rape Achsah?

The Levite continues to show himself to be callous. When he first sees the fallen woman the next morning, he does not stop to commiserate nor inquire about her condition nor kneel down to make some loving "kindly" gesture. He simply issues an order, which she cannot obey, for she is dead. She is an Alcestis, who has died for an unworthy husband.

This interpretation may be questioned: are we not "adding something to the text"?—a strict no-no of the New Criticism. But in my opinion, the text is written in such a way as to invite us to "fill the gaps" ourselves, though *only* with likelihoods. We are judging the case. If we do not have all the data, we are obliged to ask, "What if?" and "What were the alternatives?"

Jephthah's daughter/the Concubine

Not to have a husband at all—was that indeed the worst thing that could happen to Jephthah's daughter? In the last story, had the Concubine been given a choice, she might have been glad to "go and wander on the mountains, and bewail [her] virginity" (11.37-38) rather than be raped by so many "husbands."

Lucky Achsah. Unlucky daughter of Jephthah. Unluckier Concubine. Unluckier still the virgins of Jabesh-Gilead and daughters of Shiloh. (Notice the "downward movement.")

Just as it would be nice to pick the right husband, so also would it be nice to pick the right father.

Samson's wife and her father

The fourth father is that of the unnamed woman of Timnah (hereafter called "the Timnite") who married Samson (15.1-2, 6). Here is a father who made the mistake of giving away someone else's property to another man—his daughter, who belonged at that point to Samson. He is a father who committed a rash act (a link with Caleb and with Jephthah) and like Jephthah, realized its consequences only too late. When Samson reappears, no doubt to sleep with the Timnite he had married, the woman's father seems to know only too well what kind of a violent man he is dealing with, for he speaks to Samson most obsequiously: "Her father said, 'I was sure that you had rejected [really hated] her; so I gave her to your companion.

Is not her younger sister prettier [better] than she? Why not take her instead?'" (15.2)—quite unlike how we might imagine Caleb to speak. Despite his effort, the Timnite's father is not able to propitiate the "hot anger" (14.19) of the dangerous ex-husband, whose rampage in reaction to the father's explanation ultimately causes the burning up of both the Timnite and her father.

The Timnite is another woman who, like the Levite's Concubine, would have been lucky not to have been blessed with *any* husband, much less two. One cannot say how much worse off she is than Jephthah's daughter, nor how much better off than the Levite's Concubine. The Timnite was only burned to death (like Jephthah's daughter), while the Concubine died from gang rape.

Notice also the pattern:

> no husband (Jephthah's daughter) (she dies),
>
> two husbands (the Timnite) (she dies),
>
> many "lovers" for one woman (the Concubine) (she dies),
>
> many husbands for many women (the daughters of Jabesh-Gilead and Shiloh) (they live—happily ever after?).

As is shown by **Table VII**, the woman's fate in each story goes from good to bad to worse to worst. Studied carefully, this chart shows a number of other points which the author of *Judges* invites the reader to compare and contrast.

Mother-son and father-son stories (See **Table VIII**.)

Parallel stories are inserted at definite intervals. The Jephthah story is approximately at the middle, while Achsah and Levite's Concubine are at opposite ends. Is there a story to balance the story of Sisera's mother (which lies between the beginning and the middle)? There is, and it is the story of another mother and her son Micah (which lies between the middle and the end). Both stories in turn are connected with other mother/son and father/son stories.

1. *Fathers and Daughters* (already discussed)
    1. Caleb father of Achsah
    2. Jephthah as father of a daughter
    3. Father of the Timnite
    4. Father of the Concubine
    5. Fathers of the daughters of Shiloh

2. *Mothers and Sons*
    (A) Sisera's mother near the beginning of *Judges* (5.28-30)
    (B) Abimelech's mother (a concubine) }
    (C) Jephthah's mother (a harlot) }
    B and C are not developed in the narrative.
    (D) Samson's mother in the middle of *Judges* (13.2-14.9)
    (E) Micah and his mother near the end (17.2-4)

3.   *Fathers and Sons*
    (a) the Gideon story about of ⅓ the way from the *beginning* of *Judges* (6.29-31)
        (i) at the beginning of the story, Gideon with his father, Joash; *Gideon* is
            cowardly and is hiding inside (6.30-31),
        (ii) at the end, Gideon with his son Jether; h*is son* is cowardly ("like father,
            like son") (8.20),
       (iia) Abimelech and (iib) Jotham in the next block are two more of Gideon's
            sons
    (b) Samson story about ⅔ of the way from the *end* of the book,
        (iii) Manoah, Samson's father, at the beginning of the story (13.6-14.10),
            and Samson's burial in his father's grave at the end his story (16.31)
        (iv) Micah's son [not developed in the story]

(The mother-son relationships are discussed fully elsewhere. Gideon's sons are discussed in the Gideon and Abimelech sections in other chapters.)

Table VIII. Parallel Stories at Intervals Within Blocks

Table VIII helps us to envision the kind of complexity and balance this author is aiming at as well as the way he uses parallel stories in order to engage his reader in thought. (Approximate locations of mothers and sons are shown by capital letters; locations of fathers and daughters by numbers; and fathers and sons by Roman numerals.)

VII. Folklore or History?

Of course, the stories have long been regarded as real "history." Look at any of the Introductions to the Hebrew Bible published in the 1960s, and see how a "history" of this period was constructed from *Judges*, its sole source.

On the other hand, how could anyone regard the book as history or even some sort of chronicle? If historical events lay behind these stories somewhere in the murky past, it is highly improbable that the author had any access to those events—oral-history traditions notwithstanding. As will continue to be demonstrated, *every detail* that the author used in the collection of stories fits too neatly into his design for it to represent the accidental, random, and formless nature of life—the *mess* that the artist has to find a *form* for—in Beckett's epigraph. To accomplish such symmetries, the author would have had to revise "reality," adding, subtracting, manipulating his materials endlessly to make the details satisfy his artistic purpose. Such *factual* information about real people as he needed for his symmetries would not be available at that time, or any time, for doing this.

Imagine writing a comparable series of symmetrical short tales about the outstanding presidents of our country since its founding, using historical documents and films and finding the right sort of parallel actions from president to president and comparable scenic backgrounds (buildings, artifacts, body parts—to mention only a few of the keyword categories listed and analyzed in Chapter 3) to fit into the design that *Judges* manifests. What a difficult—even impossible—chore that would be. Not all the biographies in all the libraries or all the films, documents, and recordings in the United States would yield material of that kind about our presidents, even if an author used the Internet and had several lifetimes to gather and analyze them. And if the author limited himself strictly to facts—the actual history—how different his book would be from *Judges*! The only way one could imitate the narrative scheme of the author of *Judges* would be to *imagine* and *invent*. Recently prominent scholars have placed this and other Deuteronomic compositions in the time of the late monarchy, the Exile or even the Hellenistic period, centuries after these alleged events, and some historians have recently cast doubt on whether the legends of the Hebrew Bible contain even a shred of "truth."[44]

More significant, to regard this book as a straightforward chronicle of history is do the author an injustice. In order to respect it as a literary masterpiece, we must free ourselves from the idea that it is history. My aim is not to disparage the search for Israelite history, for of course, that search must continue, and some insight into history *does* emerge from this book. My aim, however, is to show that some other, and possibly more important, purpose is being accomplished in *Judges* than that. The later redactors were surely not so unsophisticated that they could not perceive the difference between history and folktales. But if that is so, why did they retain folktales in the scriptures? Something about the stories must have met the standards of later, no doubt devout, editors.

Nevertheless, a kind of history can be perceived in *Judges*. Whatever else it does, this book presents us with views of a way of life, probably the life of those who originated the tales—evidently an early period of Canaanite or Israelite history, long before the development of such a civilization as is depicted in the reign of David and afterwards.

Judges focuses on the warfare that ensues when the tribes (not yet a "nation") are challenged by invaders. But the activity of the people in normal times is given in passing glances—how Samson's marriage was arranged by his parents and the marriage feast afterwards, for example, or in the Jephthah story, as Robert Alter points out, when we encounter such issues as

> the strife between brothers, the struggle over a patrimony, the opposition between the
> legitimate wife and the illegitimate mate, the bitterness of personal exile, the lines of
> political tension in the triangle of individual, community leaders and populace (*The
> World of Biblical Literature* 64-65).

The long inventory of varied relationships among people given in Chapter 3 shows that the author was deeply concerned with everyday life.

To judge from the number of words connected with agriculture and animals (again, see Chapter 3), these people are living the simplest kind of agricultural life. There is no technology of any kind—except for Sisera's iron chariots. Chariots were in use by the inhabitants of Ugarit, by the Hittites, by the army of *Keret*[15] and by the gods in the myths—even Yhwh. They were high-status weapons of the Trojan Wars. But the Israelites in the stories do not have them, nor do they have horses. They win the battle against Sisera only because of a downpour. The Midianites had camels, but the Israelites did not. They have no carts or wagons or wheels, only the donkey as a means of transportation. "Highways" are mentioned, and robbers are preying on travelers in three stories, but there is no reference to trade with other nations or peoples, though trade was extremely important in the city of Ugarit in the 12th C. BCE, even trade with distant lands.

The only money mentioned in *Judges* are the shekels that Delilah gets from the Philistine lords, shekels that Micah's mother has, and the annual salary of 10 shekels of silver that Micah paid his Levite. Gold and silver are mentioned, and ornaments are taken from the Midianite camels, but Israelite jewelry is not mentioned, and there are no craftsmen or artists, except for the person in the Micah story who smelted the silver (the word for *silversmith* is not used) and who, since he made idols, might also be considered a sculptor. In Ugarit and in its literature, precious stones, especially *lapis lazuli,* and gold and silver are mentioned often, and Ugarit had engravers, polishers, and borers, other professional people, and guilds (488). The arts are not completely unknown to the Israelites, however: they have music and dancing: the trumpet blasts by Ehud and Gideon, singing and piping in *The*

Song of Deborah, the timbrels and dancing of Jephthah's daughter, and the dancing of the daughters of Shiloh.

A few servants are mentioned in *Judges*, but no foreign slaves, as at Ugarit and ancient Greece. Essentially, there is no evidence of an elite class or wealthy aristocracy.[46]

This society is apparently without any kind of civic structure or leadership, except for an occasional military commander who might arise to lead the troops, if needed, and who afterwards, in certain cases, might do some kind of "judging."

No reference is made to administrative records as there were at Ugarit. There are allusions to legal language in the Gideon story (רִיב, *contend*, 6.31-32), in Jotham's fable, and in Jephthah's negotiation with the Ammonites, but no evidence of legal proceedings or law texts, and no mention of contracts or lawsuits, as in Ugarit. Only one example of literacy is mentioned, and that is the list of elders written down by the young boy in the Gideon story (8.14), although, to be sure, the name of the city of Kiriat Sepher means "Quarter of the Book."

The meaning of the word *judge* still confuses scholars, but it usually is taken to mean *a leader in warfare*, perhaps one seeming to have *charismatic* power. The only character we see in the act of judging is Deborah, but no specific information is given about what this comprises. In the Ugaritic stories like *Keret* and *Aqhat*, elders are making judgments about the everyday problems of ordinary people and helping the widows, orphans, and the importunate, which was looked upon as a high moral duty there,[47] but no mention is made of these issues in *Judges*. Poverty as such is not mentioned, nor are illness, bodily injury, nor oddly enough, even pain, referred to in any way, whereas these are of major importance in the Ugaritic story of *Keret*. By comparison with the Ugaritic society, which preceded the Israelite society, apparently by several centuries, Israel appears to be much less developed than Ugarit—at least so far as we can discern from this little book. The need for leadership, however, is one of the main thrusts of *Judges*.

We see some decision-making by "elders" in *Judges*. The elders of Succoth (and maybe also Penuel) made the decision not to give Gideon's troops food; those in the Jephthah story made the decision to make Jephthah their head; and those in the last story solved the dilemma of providing wives for the Benjaminites without, they tell themselves, violating their previously-made vow.

The most important judgment is made in the last story, and it is made by what seem to be all the people (with the possible exception of the tribe of Benjamin, which is on trial):

> Then all the Israelites came out, from Dan to Beer-sheba, including the land of Gilead, and the congregation [עֵדָה, assembly] assembled in one body [as one man] before the LORD [Yhwh] at Mizpah. The chiefs of all the people, of all the tribes of Israel, presented themselves in the assembly of the people of God [Elohim], four hundred thousand foot-soldiers bearing arms [swords] (20.1-2).

They assembled to hear the case against the Benjaminites as presented by the Levite, and after hearing it, made the judgment to attack the tribe of Benjamin. It was the "whole assembly" (כל־העדה, 21.13) which decided later how to get wives for the Benjaminites. (Incidentally, it is interesting that the Hebrew word for *swarm of bees* in the Samson story is the same word as *assembly*, עדה [14.8], a word that may have been chosen as a link between the stories.)

All "judgments" of disputes in the book concern warfare. Since it is a book about warfare, the lack of other kinds of disputes is understandable.

As for how religion was practiced in daily life, we are given the merest glimpse of religious practice. Bethel and Shiloh are alluded to as sanctuaries, but the only activity shown at a sanctuary is at Mizpah, where Jephthah spoke his words before Yhwh (11.11), when the tribes assembled in 20.1 (quoted above), and where the tribes swore the vow about not giving their wives to Benjaminites (21.1).

With respect to private life, the author shows us very little interaction between Yhwh and the people and no instruction about how to interact or what rituals to observe. After a heavenly messenger appears to Samson's mother, Manoah prays to Yhwh for the messenger-angel to return with information about Samson's future, and the divine messenger returns (13.8). Samson prays on two occasions—he calls (not *prays*) for water at Enhakkore and for divine help in the temple of Dagon (15.18, 16.28)—and Jephthah makes his vow to Yhwh (11.30), presumably in prayer. But if the people engage in prayer relating to their individual lives, as Hannah does in 1 Samuel, we are not given any examples. The chief attempt of the people to communicate with Yhwh occurs only when the Israelites build altars and present offerings, and when they are in distress and weep before Yhwh or *inquire* of him about "who should go up first." We are not, however, told how the act of inquiring was done. Very likely, it was done by lots (בגורל), mentioned only once in 20.9. Possibly lots (the *urim* and the *thummim*) are what are being referred to in the "inquiries" of Yhwh (1.1; 18.5; 20.18, 23, 27; 21.3, 8).

The people as a group appeal to Yhwh to relieve their sufferings, and the author shows that Yhwh feels compassion for them when they suffer from their own wrong-doings (usually apostasy) and when the suffering has lasted too long. Yhwh is a little like the Friend at Midnight in Jesus' parable (Luk 11.5-13), who responds (as to Samson) when sorely beseeched. Otherwise, the author sees Yhwh as having but two aims: to help the Israelites in battle when they are faithful to him, and to punish them for committing apostasy or for settling alongside non-Israelites. Religious ideas (always about apostasy) appear in the Deuteronomistic "formulae," of course, but these may be interpolations by a later redactor.

Prophecy is all but nonexistent. Deborah is called a prophet, and she speaks like one when she tells Barak that Yhwh has given the enemy into his hand. Another prophet, who is unidentified, appears at the beginning of the Gideon story to review the Exodus story and warn the Israelites against apostasy (6.8-10). But this passage is probably an interpolation, as Richard S. Hess has shown, for the copy of *Judges* found at Qumran does not contain this passage.[48] In addition to the messenger-angel visiting Samson's mother, there are two other messenger-angels: one cursing Meroz and its inhabitants in *The Song* and one commissioning Gideon. These messenger-angels are used to explain the otherwise inexplicable or the strange and wonderful.

The only priest who is shown in a religious role is Micah's Levite, and his role is no doubt negative, as he is using idols.[49] The Danites steal him and the idols, and the Danite priests continued this apostasy in the territory of Dan until the Assyrians removed the ten northern tribes, as the following passage, probably inserted by a later editor, testifies:

> Then the Danites set up the idol for themselves. Jonathan son of Gershom, son of Moses, and his sons were priests to the tribe of the Danites until the time the land went into captivity. So they maintained as their own Micah's idol that he had made, as long as the house of God was at Shiloh (18.30-31).

Apparently even the grandson of Moses can go astray. The other Levite, who is seeking lodging for himself in Gibeah, his Concubine, and servant, tells the old Ephraimite that the purpose of his journey is to return to the "House of Yhwh" in the hill country of Ephraim where he lives (19.18), and so we assume that he, too was a priest.

The ark of the covenant is said to have been at Bethel, but this information may have been inserted by a later editor, who is telling us of what happened "in those days" (20.27); otherwise the ark is not mentioned, and we do not know how it was used—though it may have played a part in the inquiries to Yhwh mentioned above.

This background to the stories, then, is "history," of sorts. How reliable it is, or for what early period of time, cannot be determined. But this, coupled with what we glean from keywords (see Chapter 3), is important information about how people lived *in illo tempore*.

The author of *Judges* focuses steadily on warfare. The incidents in the first two and a half chapters are allegedly about the "Conquest." The rest of the book is about *defensive* actions against the incursion of enemy tribes and the difficulty of living side by side with the enemy. *Offensive* action begins in Ch. 18, when the Danites pick up and migrate north to conquer the city of Laish, and further *offensive* action breaks out in Chs. 20-21, when the Israelites fight against one of their own tribes. This kind of warfare must have been typical all over the Middle East and elsewhere at this time; and although the stories themselves are fictitious, they were likely inspired by larger-than-life human beings who struck the fancy of the storytellers.

The stories were regarded as sacred probably because of the light they seem to cast on a distant historical period—the Conquest, Yhwh, and the superhuman strength with which Yhwh supposedly invested the heroes at moments of crisis. That the symmetrical arrangement of the stories was preserved suggests that the guardians of the text may have understood something about this collection of tales that modern critics did not guess. Otherwise, as already suggested, redaction would have ruined the symmetries. Interpolations were few and (as far as I can discern) consist mostly in the theological admonishments and the religious formulae inserted in places where the symmetries would not be ruined.

As already stated, the stories probably originated as simple folktales, then were put into the current design later, possibly during the time of David, and were handed down over the course of centuries, or generations, with only slight modifications after that. The tales could have been set down late, maybe even as late as the return from Exile, in the 5th Century BCE or afterwards.[50] If so, one would expect anachronisms. The fact that there are none except possibly the use of money in the Samson and Micah stories, may mean that the original stories remained intact, except for the possible introduction of bias in favor of Judah. (A theory of composition is discussed further in Chapter 6.)

Why would the guardians of the text be so careful to preserve the symmetries? Two answers are possible: first, the stories are like a resource book of "law cases" that enable readers to debate and argue endlessly about the ethics and morality in the stories, to render valid verdicts about human behavior, and consequently to learn how to become judges in real life situations. The arrangement, as will continue to be shown, gives many clues to help the reader do this. (Examples have been provided above. See also Chapter 4 about law and ethics).

Second, the book is about the gradual decline of the northern tribes. At the beginning of the book, we are told that Yhwh begins to raise up "judges," who are leaders in warfare. At the end, the judges are gone, and the country has fallen into anarchy. The angle of the downward slope does not waver; it is perfect. Any displacement of a part of the pattern would interrupt the decline. It is not interrupted, but steadily spirals downward.

The tribes of Dan, Benjamin, and Ephraim, powerful at the beginning of the book, cannot unite in action in the middle of the book, and are in disrepute by the end of the book. Dan has departed. Ephraim has proved itself contentious and indifferent to the welfare of Israel and been partly killed off by Gilead. The Levites have been shown to be violators of hospitality and/or to be pleasure-loving and negligent.[51] Benjamin has incurred the hostility of all the rest of the tribes and been nearly annihilated. And "all-Israel" has gotten involved in a civil war against Benjamin.

The meaning of the parable of the Levite's Concubine

The story of the *Levite's Concubine* is a parable, and as in the parables of Jesus, the message is concealed. The Bible does not give away its secrets easily. One has to dig for them.

The author of *Judges* planted an important clue for his readers, when he had Ehud say, "I have a message for you, O king" (3.16). The author himself had many secret messages for his audience. Later the Levite of the Concubine story says to the

Israelites: "Give your advice and counsel here" (20.7), echoing 19.30: "Think about it. Consider. Tell us what to do." Advice and counsel are what the author is asking from *us*. He is also answering the question that Gideon asks Yhwh when the Midianites invade his land and ruin his crops: "But sir, if the LORD is with us, why then has all this happened to us? And where are all his wonderful deeds that our ancestors recounted to us . . . ?" (6.13). The parable of the Concubine gives the answer.

In the parable, the Concubine is "Israel," ravished by the terrible tribe of Benjamin, and now being cut apart into 12 pieces (i.e., 12 separate dysfunctional tribes). The Concubine is the offspring of Judah (an indifferent father) married to a negligent husband (Levi/Ephraim), while the Ephraimite host in Gibeah represents a strong but trouble-making tribe. Israel is not even at this time a legal wife.

"Fallen, no more to rise, is maiden Israel" (Amos 5.2).

Those responsible for the rape of Israel (a daughter of Judah) are Ephraim, Levi, and Benjamin. The Levite (a priest from Ephraim) cuts Israel apart and provokes civil war. While the Levite and Ephraim carouse, Benjamin attacks Israel and at the end is all but annihilated. (The meaning of the allegory is discussed further in Chapter 6.)

Besides being an allegory of the history of the pre-monarchic period, *Judges* is also a commentary on, and counterpoint to, the history of the period that follows, from Samuel through to the death of David—for many of the incidents in *Judges*, if not most of them, have counterparts in *1* and *2 Samuel* as well as in *Genesis* (see Appendix 2 to this chapter). So many are the parallels that *Judges* might have been a series of cautionary tales for David or for subsequent monarchs (à la the Nathan tale of the "ewe lamb"). Thus the book could have been given its present design in the time of David or shortly after, though not written down until later.

Saul, a Benjaminite connected with Jabesh-Gilead (1 Sam 31.11-13), will indeed become king, but the tribe of Benjamin will lose preeminence. And David of the tribe of Judah will be called in to make peace among the warring factions. ("Who will go up first?" It is clearly Judah.) Ultimately the North (Ephraim and all the tribes except Judah) will separate from the South, and will disappear. Only Judah will remain, to "go up." This suggests a terminus post quem for the original composition of the book.

Here the matrilineal ties of the next generation of Benjaminites would be of great importance, for this is what makes the Benjaminites acceptable after their offense at Gibeah: their offspring will be hybrids—only one half Benjaminite, but the other half from two other tribes, Gileadite (the virgins of Jabesh-Gilead) and Ephraimite (the daughters of Shiloh). Significantly, not from Judah.

Judges is a dynamic book into which the author placed many varieties of human beings who as a whole may be regarded as a microcosm of the author's own society, with a heavy emphasis on women and on daughters and sons. (See "Relationships" in Chapter 3.) Since the women often turn out to be superior to the men, it is tempting to regard the author as something of a feminist. Alas, he probably was merely showing the depth of his contempt for the men of his times.

Every time one reads *Judges,* one discovers another of its many secrets. It is a polyphonic work. Viewed in this way, the book, despite its horrors, is a much more positive book than it is usually considered to be. It is a marvelous puzzle, a game with thousands of ingenious facets, a labyrinth or maze; one can either stay on this side of the looking-glass (or on the other side of it) or make one's escape from it as best one can. Or the book can be seen as an ingenious interweaving of contrasting comic and serious themes (as will be demonstrated in Chapter 2), or (as will become clear in Chapter 3) as a tapestry that would be worthy of the Gobelins and whose design would delight the Mozart who wrote *The Marriage of Figaro.*

It is a carefully contrived structure and design which may have helped teach Dante how to construct his *Divine Comedy* and Milton his *Paradise Lost* (not to mention *Samson Agonistes*) and may even have had some indirect influence on the literary structures of James Joyce.

These writers, however, needed immense canvases, whereas the author of *Judges* was a miniaturist who was able to pack almost an infinity of meaning into his tiny space. "Plots reduce the world," writes Don DeLillo, meaning that the world is always larger than anything that can be represented in a plot.[52] The author of *Judges* found a new way of "making meaning," however. Ideas keep flowing out from it in all directions, and they never seem to stop flowing. In this book, "the reduced world" is not so tiny after all.

Certainly, the design, intricacy, and cunning of this book would have been the envy of Gödel, Escher, or Bach. It is time that we accorded the anonymous author of the *Judges* a full measure of appreciation for his achievement.

Appendix 1. Chiasmus between Introductory Two Chapters and Last Three Chapters of *Judges*

Chiasmus would be one more example of artistry, and it also reinforces the importance of the inner relationships of the stories. Possibly the chiasmus is more intricate than the following table suggests and may include *all* the chapters in the book. It gives *Judges* an almost three-dimensional character. Homer's *Iliad* and *Odyssey* contain elaborate chiasmi. Readers are invited to develop these further on their own.

Chapters 1-2	Counterpart, Chapters 18-21
chaos at the beginning	chaos at the end
Israelites fighting outsiders	Israelites fighting each other
"the Israelites inquired of the LORD [Yhwh], 'Who shall go up first for us against the Canaanites, to fight against them?' The LORD said, 'Judah shall go up; I hereby give the land into his hand'" (1.1-2)	"The Israelites proceeded to go up to Bethel, where they inquired of God, 'Which of us shall go up first to battle against the Benjaminites?' And the LORD answered, 'Judah shall go up first'" (20.18) Drawing of lots (20.9)
defeat of Canaanites and Perizzites at Bezek (1.4)	defeat of the Benjaminites (20.46)
flight and pursuit of Adoni-Bezek	flight of Benjaminites to the Rock of Rimmon (20.47)
they "cut off his thumbs and his big toes" (1.6)	"grasping his concubine he cut her into twelve pieces, limb by limb" (19.29)
"the people of Judah fought against Jerusalem [enemy city] and took it. They put it to the sword [smote with the edge of the sword], and set the city on fire" (1.8)	"the Israelites turned back against the Benjaminites, and put them to the sword [smote with the edge of the sword]—the city, the people, the animals, and all that remained. Also the remaining towns they set on fire" (20.48)
"And Caleb said, 'Whoever attacks Kiriath-sepher and takes it, I will give him my daughter Achsah as wife'" (1.12)	"Now the Israelites had sworn at Mizpah, 'No one of us shall give his daughter in marriage to Benjamin'" (21.1)
"And Othniel son of Kenaz, Caleb's younger brother, took it; and he gave him his daughter Achsah as wife" (1.13)	"Benjamin returned at that time; and they gave them the women whom they had saved alive of the women of Jabesh-Gilead" (21.14) [Benjamin is the youngest son of Jacob]

"When she came to him . . . she dismounted from her ass" (1.14)	"Then he put her [the dead concubine] upon the ass" (19.28)
Achsah *goes to her father* and asks him for springs of water (1.14-15)	"But his concubine became angry with him, and she *went away* from him *to her father's house* at Bethlehem in Judah" (19.2)
Achsah asks her father for a present (blessing, ברכה) "So Caleb *gave* her the upper and lower springs" (1.15)	"No one of us shall *give* his daughter in marriage to Benjamin" (21.1) The Israelites say, "Cursed be he who *gives* a wife to Benjamin" (21.18) "Now the Israelites had sworn at Mizpah, "No one of us shall *give* his daughter in marriage to Benjamin" (21.22)
City of Palms (תמר) (1.16)	Baal tamar (תמר, palm tree) (20.33)
Achsah's marriage is properly arranged (1.13)	the fathers of the maidens refuse to give their daughters to the Benjaminites; the Benjaminites must steal wives for themselves (21.23)
the Kenites went up [north] and settled in the Negeb near Arad (1.16)	the Danites went north and settled there (18.29)
Judah and Simeon destroy four of the five Philistine cities (1.18)	the Israelites destroy the Benjaminite towns, animals and all (20.48)
"The house of Joseph sent out spies to Bethel (the name of the city was formerly Luz)" (1.23)	"They named the city Dan . . . but the name of the city was formerly Laish" (18.29)
"Judah went with his brother Simeon, and they defeated [smote, נכה] the Canaanites who inhabited Zephath, and *devoted it to destruction*. So the city was called Hormah" (חרמה) (1.17)	"Go, put the inhabitants of Jabesh-Gilead to the sword [smite (נכה) with the edge of the sword,] including the women and the little ones. This is what you shall do; every male and every woman that has lain with a male *you shall devote to destruction*" (חרם 21.10-11)

"When the spies saw a man coming out of the city, they said to him, '*Show us the way* into the city, and we will deal *kindly* with you'" (1.24)	"Put your hand over your mouth, and *come with us*, and be to us a father and a priest" (18.19) "Then her husband set out after her, to speak *tenderly* to her and bring her back." (19.3) "Be *generous* and allow us to have them . . ." (21.22)
after sending the spies, the man "showed them the way into the city; and they put the city to the sword [smote the city with the edge of the sword], but they let the man and all his family go" (1.25)	after sending out the spies, the Danites returned with the tribe to Laish and "put [the people] to the sword [smote them with the edge of the sword], and burned the city down with fire" (18.27).
"So the man went to the land of the Hitties and built a city, and named it Luz; that is its name to this day" (1.26)	"They rebuilt the city, and lived in it. They called the name of the city Dan . . ." (18.28-29)
Bethel (1.22-23)	Bethel (20.18, 26)
Rehab (רחוב) (1.31)	square (רחוב) (19.15, 17.20) the land is broad (רחב) (18.10) Beth-rehab (רחוב) (18.28)
"The Amorites pressed the Danites back into the hill country . . ." (1.34)	the Danites migrate north (Ch. 18)
"Now the angel of the LORD went up from Gilgal to Bochim" (בכים, weepers) (2.1) "When the angel of the LORD spoke these words to all the Israelites, the people lifted up their voices and wept (קולם ויבכו וישאו העם את־). (2.4)	"Then the Israelites, the whole army [people], went up to Bethel, and wept [בכה], sitting there before the LORD." (20.26) "And the people came to Bethel, and sat there until evening before God, and they lifted up their voices and wept with great weeping" (ישאו קולם ויבכו בכי גדול) (21.2) "The Israelites went up and wept [בכה] before the LORD until the evening" (20.23)
"I brought you up from Egypt and brought you into the land that I had promised to your ancestors." (2.1)	"the day that the people of Israel came up from the land of Egypt " (19.30)
death of Joshua. They buried him at Timnah (28-9)	death of Samson. They buried him between Zorah and Eshtaol (16.31) He had been married to a woman of Timnah (14,1, 2, 5)

Appendix 2. Selected Parallels (Intertextuality) between *Judges* and *Genesis, Joshua,* and *1 and 2 Samuel* and *1 and 2 Kings*

The correspondences between *Judges* and the other books of the Bible help us solve impasses in our judgments of the ethics involved in the various episodes.

Adoni-Bezek cutting off the thumbs and big toes of his enemies; likewise, the Israelites cutting off *his* (1.6-7)	David cutting off 200 foreskins of the Philistines (1 Sam 18.25-27)
Caleb's rash vow to give away his daughter to one who captures Debir (1.12); Jephthah's rash vow (11.31); rash vow made by the men of Israel (21.1)	Saul's rash vow to give away his daughter to the man who kills Goliath (1 Sam 17.25, 18.17-21); Saul's rash vow to put to death the person who violated the ban on food, even if it was his son Jonathan (1 Sam 14.39); Jacob's rash vow when Rachel was hiding the teraphim (Gen 31.21)
Achsah alighting from her ass before her father (1.14); Achsah is a Calebite (1.12)	Abigail alighting from her ass before David (1 Sam 25.3); Abigail is a Calebite (1 Sam 25.3)
man of Luz and spies (1.23-26); tribe of Dan sends spies to explore in the north for land (Ch. 18) They give a positive report, ending in Dan's victory and resettlement	Joshua sends two men to spy on Jericho (Josh 2.1-21; 6.1-27); Moses sends spies (Num 13.2 ff.) to explore Canaan; all but Joshua and Caleb give a negative report (when they go in, however, they are driven out by the Canaanites and Amalekites); he again sends spies (Deut 1.19-46), ending in the Amorites chasing Israel out
"Ehud made for himself a sword with two edges, a cubit in length; and *he fastened it on his right thigh under his clothes*" (3.16); "Ehud said, 'I have secret message for you, O king.' "Ehud said, 'I have a message from God for you.' So [Eglon] rose from his seat" (3.19-20) (his suspicion allayed)	"When they were at the large stone that is in Gibeon, Amasa came to meet them. Now Joab was wearing a soldier's garment and *over it was a belt with a sword in its sheath fastened at his waist;* as he went forward, it fell out. Joab said to Amasa, 'Is it well with you, my brother?' And Joab took Amasa by the beard with his right hand *to kiss him.* " (2 Sam 20.8)
When Ehud stabbed Eglon, "the fat closed over the blade, for he did not draw the sword out of his belly; and *the dirt came out*" לא שלף החרב מבתנו ויצא הפרשדנה (3.22)	"But Amasa did not notice the sword in Joab's hand; Joab struck him in the belly *so that his entrails poured out on the ground* (מעיו ארצה ישפך). And he died. [Joab] did not strike a second blow" (2 Sam 20.9-10) Abner stabbed Asahel in the stomach (fifth rib) and the spear had come out Asahel's back (2 Sam 2.23); "When Abner returned to Hebron, Joab took him aside in the gateway, to speak with him privately. And there he stabbed him in the stomach (KJV, fifth rib). So he died for shedding the blood of Asahel, Joab's brother" (2 Sam 3.27)

Jael kills Sisera (4.21) Gideon hews down (grh, implying ruthlessness) Zebah and Zalmunna (8.21)	Saul does not kill Agag (1 Sam 15.9); Samuel "hewed [Ps#] Agag in pieces" (1 Sam 15.33)
the Israelites are hiding from the Midianites in mountains, caves, and strongholds (Gideon story) (6.2); the Midianites are as numerous as sand on the seashore (7.12)	The Israelites are hiding in caves, thorn bushes, rock crags, tombs, and cisterns; the Philistine army is as vast as sand on the seashore (1 Sam13.5)
the theophany of Gideon (6.12) Jephthah's slaughter of 42,000 Ephraimites (12.6) visitation of the angel to Manoah and his wife saying that Manoah's wife will bear a son (13.3 ff.)	God's appearances to Abraham in Genesis; theophany of the angels to Abraham and Lot (18.2 ff.); theophany of Hagar (Gen 16.7-13)
Commissioning of Gideon (6.14) Gideon's modesty: "But sir, how can I deliver Israel? My clan is the weakest in Manasseh, and I am the least in my family." (6.15)	Saul's modesty (1 Sam 9.2); commissioning of Moses (Exod 3-4); Moses's modesty: "Who am I that I should go to Pharaoh, and bring the sons of Israel out of Egypt?" (3.11) "O Lord, I have never been eloquent, neither in the past nor since you have spoken to your servant. I am slow of speech and tongue." (4.10)
having seen Yhwh, Gideon fears he will die (6.22-23) Manoah thinks he will die after seeing the angel-messenger (13.22)	having seen Yhwh, Hagar is surprised that she did not die (Gen 16.13)
Gideon defeating Baal, Asherah (6.25-28) Samson defeating Dagon (16.30)	Elijah defeating the prophets of Baal (1 Kg 18.20-40); the Ark of the Covenant defeating Dagon (1 Sam 5.2-4)
Gideon's father being surrounded by the angry men of the town after he pulled down the altar of Baal (6.30); the Levite and his host surrounded by the base men of Gibeah (19.22)	Lot and the angels in Sodom being surrounded by the base men of Sodom (Gen 19)
Joash telling the Abiezerites to let Baal defend himself (6.31); Yhwh telling Israelites to let the God they have chosen (Baal) save them (10.14)	Elijah telling Israelites to follow Baal if he is God (1 Ki 18.21, 24)
The spirit of Yhwh clothes Gideon and he sends messengers out to recruit (Judg 6.34)	the spirit of Yhwh comes mightily on Saul; he sends out body parts of the oxen by messengers to recruit (1 Sam 11.6, 11)

Gideon asks Yhwh for a sign (6.36-40) Bargains with Yhwh	Abraham bargains with Yhwh about the destruction of Sodom (Gen 18.22-32); Moses asks God for his name (i.e. as a sign) (Exod 3.13-14)
Gideon's reducing the numbers so that he will not take credit for the victory (7.4)	King Amaziah is told to limit his force to Judahites in his army and to exclude Ephraimites of whom God does not approve (2 Chron 25.7-8); King Asa is informed by the prophet Hanani that his admission of weakness and reliance on God alone had allowed him victory over a massive force of Ethiopians and Libyans (2 Chron 16.8)
blowing of the shofars, with the empty pitchers, torches, and shouting, by Gideon's men (7.19-21)	priests with the ark blowing the shofars at Jericho (Jos 6.4)
Negative response of Succoth and Peneul to Gideon's request for food for his troops (8.6, 8) and its aftermath	Nabal's negative response to David's request for food for his troops (1 Sam 25.2-11 and its aftermath
Gideon overreaching his authority with the ephod (8.27)	Moses overreaching his authority in striking the rock (Num 20.11-12; 27.14)
Gideon's ephod (8.27)	Moses' serpent (Num 21.9)
Gideon's wives and one concubine (8.31) Samson's lust for women (14.2, 16.1, 4)	David's lust for Bathsheba (2 Sam 11); his many wives and concubines Amnon's lust for Tamar (2 Sam 13) Solomon's many wives and concubines
Abimelech surrounded by reckless and worthless men (Myzxpw Myqyr My#n)) (9.4); Jephthah as outlaw surrounded by reckless men (Myqyr My#n)) (11.3)	David as outlaw in band of outlaws with evil and worthless fellows (l(ylbw (r-#y)-lk) (1 Sam 30.22)
Abimelech's behavior is throughout that of a despot	Saul becomes a despot later in his reign
Abimelech cuts off his father's whole house, kills 70 brothers, one young brother–Jotham–alone escaping (9.5)	Saul destroys Nob, the city of priests, and only one person, the young Abiathar, escapes to David

Abimelech's murder of his 70 brothers (9.5)	David's murder of Uriah (2 Sam 3.11,15); Absalom's murder of Amnon; Solomon has his brother Adonijah killed (1 Kg 2.25); Jehu's slaughter of Joram (1 Kg 9.24) and the 70 sons of Ahab (2 Kg 10.6-7) (they were not Jehu's brothers, however)
Jotham's fable (9.7-20)	Nathan's fable of the one little ewe lamb (2 Sam 12.1-6); fable of the Woman of Tekoah (2 Sam 14.2ff.)
Jotham orates his fable from the top of a mountain (9.7)	David's rebuking of Saul from the top of a hill (1 Sam 26.13ff) (Garsiel, 98)
Abimelech's fall attributed to an "evil spirit" (רוח רעה), which Yhwh sends between him and the men of Shechem (9:23); The men of Shechem deal treacherously with him (9.23ff.)	Saul's degeneration is explained in terms of an "evil spirit" from Yhwh (same words, 1 Sam 16.14); Saul feels that everyone is betraying him (I Sam. 22:7ff); A "lying spirit" is sent to Ahab (1 Kgs 22.22)
Gaal mocks Abimelech and stirs the city against him (9.27-31 "If only this people were under my command! Then I would remove Abimelech; I would say to him, 'Increase your army, and come out.'"	Absalom stirs up the Judahites against his father David (2 Sam 15.1-6). "If only I were judge in the land! Then all who had a suit or cause might come to me, and I would give them justice."
Insurrection of Gaal under Abimelech (himself a usurper) (9.38)	Absalom's insurrection against David (2 Sam 15.10ff.) (David also perhaps a usurper)
Abimelech, Philistines, and Israelites lie in ambush many times in chs. 9, 16, 20	Joshua's ambushes at Ai (Jos 8.2-21)
Razing and salting of Shechem and killing of the people by Abimelech, as punishment for treachery towards the king (9.22 ff.)	Razing and killing all the people of Nob by Saul, done as a punishment for treachery towards the king (1 Sam 22.19)
"Then he called hastily to the young man his armor-bearer, and said to him, 'Draw your sword and kill me, lest men say of me, A woman killed him.' And his young man thrust him through, and he died." (9.54)	"Then Saul said to his armor-bearer, 'Draw your sword and thrust me through with it, so that these uncircumcised may not come and thrust me through, and make sport of me.' But his armor-bearer was unwilling; for he was terrified. So Saul took his own sword and fell upon it." (1 Sam 31.4)

the real sacrifice of Jephthah's only daughter, rash vow made in order to win victory in battle	the intended sacrifice of Isaa son (Gen 22.2); the threatened sacrifice of Jo (1 Sam 14.41) the King of Moab's sacrifice of his eldest son in order to turn the course of a siege (2 Kg 3:26-27)
the barrenness of Samson's mother	the barrenness of Sarah, Rachel, and Hannah
Samson is a Nazirite from birth until the day of his death (13.7)	Samuel is a Nazirite from birth until his death (1 Sam 1.11) (Samuel's birth was probably originally Saul's; Samson the vorspiel of Saul— Wellhausen)
Ch. 14-16 Samson's dalliance with women; Jael enticing Sisera into her tent; Delilah enticing Samson	warnings of Prov 1-9, e.g. 6.29, about enticements of women
Samson ordering his parents "get her for me," meaning the Timnite as wife (14.3)	Shechem's ordering his father to get "this girl" (Dinah) for his wife (Gen 34.4)
the feats of Samson: tore the lion in pieces barehanded (14.6); smote 30 Ashkelonites and stripped them of their clothing (14.19); burnt down the fields, orchards, and vineyards; slew many Philistines (15.5, 8); killed 1000 of them with the jawbone of an ass (15.15); broke all his bonds (15.14 etc.); blind and a slave, he broke down the temple of Dagon (16.30)	David's killing of Goliath (1 Sam 17.4); David's killing of 200 Philistines for their foreskins (1 Sam 18.25-27)
the giving away of Samson's wife (the Timnite) by her father (Samson enraged) (15.2, 3)	the giving away of Michal (David's wife) by her father Saul (David later wants her back) (1 Sam 27; 25.44; 2 Sam 3.14)
the importance of Samson's hair; connection of hair with death	the importance of Absalom's hair; the connection of hair with his death
the way Samson turned out, defeated but triumphant	the way Saul turned out, fearful and defeated
Samson blinded, grinding at the mill (16.21)	binding of Zedekiah and blinding of him (1 Kgs 15.7) Zedekiah blinded and grinding grain at the mill in the "house of the prisoners" (Jer 52.11)

temple of Dagon destroyed by Samson (16.30)	statue of Dagon toppled by the Ark (1 Sam 5.4)
Micah's idolatry (Ch. 17); idolatry of the tribe of Dan (Ch. 18)	Solomon's idolatry
600 fighting men of Dan (18.11, 16, 17)	600 contingents (Exod 12.37 and Num 11.21)
the sons of Belial (wicked Benjaminites in Gibeah) (19.22)	those in Gibeah despising Saul are called "the sons of Belial" (1 Sam 10.27) Others called "sons of Belial": Eli's sons (1 Sam 2.12); Nabal (1 Sam 25.17), some of the outlaws with David (1 Sam 30.22), and David's enemies, Shimei and Sheba (2 Sam 16.7; 20.1)
the rape of the Levite's Concubine (19.25) the abduction (rape) of the virgins of Jabesh-Gilead (21.10-12) and of the daughters of Shiloh (21.23-24)	the rape of Dinah by Shechem, son of Hamor (Gen 34); the rape of David's daughter Tamar by Amnon (2 Sam 13)
the position of the body of the Levite's Concubine with her hands on the threshold (19.27); her husband cuts her body into twelve parts	the similar position of the statue of Dagon with hands on threshold when it fell in the Philistine temple (1 Sam 5.4); the two palms of his hands have been cut off
the dividing of the Concubine's body into twelve parts by the Levite and sending parts to tribes to call to war (19.29)	the dividing of the oxen by Saul and sending parts to the tribes to call to war (1 Sam 11.7)
"Now the appointed signal between the men of Israel and the men in ambush was that when they made a great cloud of smoke rise up out of the city. . . . But when the signal began to rise out of the city in a column of smoke, the Benjaminites looked behind them; and behold, the whole of the city went up in smoke to heaven. . . . Therefore they turned their backs before the men of Israel in the direction of the wilderness; but the battle overtook them, and those who came out of the cities destroyed them in the midst of them." (20.38, 40, 42)	"So when the men of Ai looked back, the smoke of the city was rising to the sky. They had no power to flee this way or that, for the people who fled to the wilderness turned back against the pursuers." (Josh 8:20)
the wifeless Benjaminites (21.3)	Lot without grandchildren (Gen 19.36)
the complete disunity and chaos at the end of *Judges*; irreverence	the unity of the tribes with the covenant of Shechem at the end of Joshua; reverence (Josh 24.1 ff.)

This list of parallels in **Appendix 2** is by no means complete; it is intended only to give the reader an idea of the complexity of the biblical use of parallels. Some of these are discussed at length in Chapter 4 and elsewhere. Parallels like the insurrections fomented by Gaal and Absalom should induce the reader to make further analyses and judgments.

Chapter Two

THE COMEDY OF HORRORS

The whole of history is the sum total of human atrocity.

—Voltaire, *Essay on the Manners and Spirit of Nations*

Modern war is so expensive that we feel trade to be a better avenue to plunder; but modern man inherits all the innate pugnacity and all the love of glory of his ancestors. *Showing war's irrationality and horror is of no effect on him. The horrors make the fascination.* War is the strong life; it is life in extremis; war taxes are the only ones men never hesitate to pay, as the budgets of all nations show us.

—William James, *The Moral Equivalent of War* (1906) (my emphasis)

Our instincts salute the incommensurability of pain by preventing its entry into worldly discourse.   —Elaine Scarry, *The Body in Pain*

Man alone suffers so excruciatingly in the world that he was compelled to invent laughter.   —Nietzsche, *Will to Power*

Serious things cannot be understood without laughable things.   —Plato

I. The Horrors

If we read *Joshua, Judges, Ruth,* and *1* and *2 Samuel* in rapid succession, we find that *Judges* is radically different from the others in this series. *Judges* is a profoundly disturbing book. Why do we react to it as we do? *Joshua* is clean, orderly, almost grandiose. The promise apparently fulfilled, Joshua sweeps into the land of Canaan to conquer it with the help of his god, Yhwh.[1] The identity of the one dishonorable tribesman is discovered by the traditional casting of lots; and evidence for the crime is quickly uncovered in the man's tent. Everything happens in the light of reason and day, according to the law and the religious aims of the community. The book

72

ends with the renewal of the Covenant by all the tribes at Shechem. The book of *Joshua* is the *Iliad* of the Hebrew Bible. We might call it "classic" in style.

In *Ruth* (which follows *Judges* in many bibles, but not in the Hebrew Bible) we see the community at peace. Now the focus is no longer on the wars and leaders but on the life of the people for whom the wars were fought. All that Ruth and Naomi have to worry about are natural calamities, not man-made ones. *Ruth* is about the natural cycle of birth to old age and death and about the cycle of the seasons, especially the fruitful harvest and the reaping and threshing of grain. It is about the dependence of the common people on the bounty of nature, their sorrows, their hunger and misery, their love for each other, and their ways of solving problems. It is also about the sowing of seeds of plants and of children. The one scene that occurs at night is a romantic one: Boaz asleep on the threshing floor near a pile of grain with Ruth at his feet. At the end of the book, bad fortune has been followed by good. The birth of the baby and the continuity of the line are what this book and this religion are about. *Ruth* is a vision of the ideal way of life; it is Paradiso. It is no accident that the most Romantic of English poets, John Keats, used an image from *Ruth* for his most memorable lines in the "Ode to the Nightingale." We may call *Ruth* "romantic."

It can be argued that *1* and *2 Samuel* are history—one written by the victors. It is about the will to power, the succession, the rivalry of two kings, sibling rivalry, with all kinds of intrigues, deceptions, treacheries, insurrections, and usurpations, complete with ruthlessness, passions, intrigues, conspiracies, machinations, scandals, a rape, murders, mayhem. Heads roll. A wily old priest with two wayward sons. A prophet jealous of his powers who will not be upstaged by his protégé. A king who kills his great warrior in order to satisfy his lust for the warrior's wife and subsequently grieves over his dying baby and subsequently over a beloved, treacherous son. It's a psychological thriller, a whodunit. It's a cover-up, with the spin machines in full tilt, turning the monster into a sainted ancestor of future majesty. The winners seem to be those who are the most evil. In *1* and *2 Samuel*, we have a "realism" that is at times a "naturalism" almost contemporary in nature. Its plot surpasses any plot of Shakespeare's for viciousness, with no "knocking at the gate" for comic relief.

Then what is *Judges?*

The book's "naturalism" portrays a world of darkness and viciousness. It is a subterranean world, the world of neurosis, of the libido, of the id. It is the surrealistic land of our fears emerging from the subconscious as our worst nightmares. These people have been ejected from the Garden of Eden and have made their descent to the underworld. This is the Inferno of the Hebrew Bible. And like Dante's *Inferno*, *Judges* is reservoir of coarse humor. And also of judgments.

It is a dark book. Whereas almost everything in the story of Ruth happens in moonlight or in sun-drenched fields, many of the crucial events in *Judges* occur at night, under the cover of darkness. There are at least six main nighttime episodes. Gideon demolishes the altar of Baal and cuts down the Asherah at night "because he was too afraid of his family and the men of the town to do it by day." The two tests of the fleece and the dew take place at night. Gideon visits the Midianite camp in the middle of the night and hears the dream; it is the "middle watch" at night when he makes his surprise attack on the Midianites, and we see him using his strange weapons: the blaring trumpets, the blazing torches, and crashing jars.

Abimelech gets up at night and lies in ambush so as to catch his enemy Gaal off guard. When Samson visits the harlot of Gaza, the Gazites lie in wait for him all night, silently, but Samson tricks them by getting up at midnight and ripping out the gate and bars, and carrying them all the way to Hebron (16.2). The word for *spend the night* (לון) is used 11x between Ch. 19.4 and 20.4: the Levite spends four nights at his father-in-law's before he goes to spend the night in Gibeah. It is "all night until the morning" that the Levite's Concubine is abused (19.25), during which time her husband goes to bed, presumably to sleep. No doubt it is also by night that Samson goes to sleep on Delilah's knees; the sound of Delilah's name may remind us of the Hebrew word for *night,* לילה.

To be sure, some sun imagery is also to be found, especially in Chs. 14-15 in the Samson story. But much is happening at night. Night conceals things (see Chapter 3). Other hidden things (like Ehud's sword), fabric (covering), spies, and ambushes, are a few of the paramount themes of *Judges.*

It is above all a book about war. At the beginning of the book, we learn that the conquest of *Joshua* was not complete after all. The land is not at peace; it is in an uproar. The first few verses about some successful skirmishes are quickly followed by a series of failures in which we are told that eight of the tribes* could not drive out the inhabitants but had to settle down beside them:

> [Judah] could not drive out the inhabitants of the plain . . .
>
> the Benjaminites did not drive out the Jebusites . . .
>
> Manasseh did not drive out the inhabitants of Bethshean . . .
>
> Ephraim did not drive out the Canaanites . . .
>
> Zebulun did not drive out the inhabitants of Kitron . . .
>
> Asher did not drive out the inhabitants of Acco . . .
>
> Naphtali did not drive out the inhabitants of Beth-shemesh . . .
>
> The Amorites pressed the Danites back into the hill country . . .
>
> (1.19-34 passim)

—A list condemning all these tribes, specifically.

Gradually, when the camera focuses on the people in the book, *Judges* strikes us immediately as something hideous. Nothing preceding it prepares us for Ehud thrusting his sword into Eglon's belly or for Jael hammering a tent peg into Sisera's skull. All the time that we are reading about these horrors, however, we are assailed by the desire to laugh, and this tension creates an almost intolerable feeling of conflict and guilt. With no outlet for our laughter, we end up loathing the book that has

---

* It is important that the reader keep in mind what each tribe is doing.

caused us pain. But once we understand what type of literature we have under our microscope, this tension dissipates. The book, as it turns out, is a comedy of horrors.

Categories of Horrors

It is a Hobbesian world, a chaotic time when life was "solitary, poor, nasty, brutish, and short," with no dictator to come and put things in order. The horrors compose an impressive array.

War has to do with "uncreating," to use Elaine Scarry's term in *The Body in Pain: The Making and Unmaking of the World*. And the opposite of creating man in God's image, in her view, is the premature and wrongful mutilation, dismembering, and destroying of this creation.

War also has to do with numbers. The author of *Judges* concentrates on numbers. As Scarry tells us, this method is typically used by public relations experts: in references to an *army* or to a large numerical size of the army or to the number killed, we think in terms of an object moving, instead of individual human beings with bodies that can be hurt. Numbers are a disguise for crushed bodies, a method for concealing that injury is being done and pain is being felt.

One of the ways we use to tell who "wins" in a war is to compare the numbers of casualties of both sides, as Scarry writes. The side with the greatest number of enemy casualties "wins." The winner is the side which out-injures the other.[2] The author of *Judges* plays a numbers game throughout. The losses are phenomenal. They are given like scores in a sports contest. Our failure to give the score of the enemy dead today, is perhaps acknowledgment of our guilt and shame about the war and about our unfair advantage over those we have invaded.

The reader may study the lists below and reach an independent decision about who is the winner.

1. *Identifiable victims*

   The first list has 88 identifiable victims killed in a variety of ways:

   Adoni-Bezek, died after being mutilated—his thumbs and big toes cut off (1.6-7);

   Sheshak, Ahiman, and Talmai (the sons of Anak) smitten (נכה) in 1.10, but in 1.19 merely driven from Hebron;

   Cushan-rishathaim, king of Mesopotamia, killed by Othniel (3.10);

   Eglon, King of Moab, deceived by Ehud and assassinated by him with a sword thrust to the belly (3.25);

   Sisera, the general of Jabin's army, assassinated in his sleep by Jael with a tent peg driven into his temple (4.21)(5.27);

   Jabin, King of Canaan, destroyed (4.24);

   Oreb and Zeeb, two Midianite princes, killed and beheaded by the Ephraimites (7.25);

Zebah and Zalmunna, Midianite kings, executed by Gideon by sword (8.21);

70 half-brothers, probably including Jether, murdered on *one* stone by Abimelech and his reckless men (9.5);

Abimelech, killed by his armor-bearer after having his skull crushed by *one* millstone, dropped from a tower by a woman (9.54);

Jephthah's virgin daughter, sacrificed by her father as a burnt-offering (11.39);

the Timnite (Samson's wife) and her father, burnt with fire by the Philistines (15.6);

Samson, a suicide and martyr, killed when he pulled down the house of Dagon (16.30);

the Levite's Concubine, gang-raped and murdered by the men of Gibeah while her husband went to bed and had a good sleep (19.25).

Notice that in the first eight items on the list, the dead are all the enemy; but in the last six, the dead (except for the Timnite, and her father) are all Israelites. The Timnite, married to an Israelite, is not exactly an "enemy." This downward slope is apparent in all the lists.

2. *Slaughter for which numbers are given*

The second list of slaughtered people—both the enemy and Israelites—are of those for whom the number of casualties is given, if we translate the Hebrew word אֶלֶף as *a thousand* in the traditional way (instead of as "contingent," as suggested by Robert Boling).[3]

10,000	Canaanites and Perizzites killed by Judah and Simeon (1.4);
70	kings slain by Adoni-Bezek at an earlier time (1.7);
10,000	Moabites slain by Ehud and the Ephraimites (3.29);
600	Philistines killed by Shamgar (3.31);
120,000	Midianites killed by Gideon and his 300 men and by some Ephraimites (8.10);
15,000	Midianites under Zebah and Zalmunna apparently killed (8.10);
1,000	men and women in the Tower of Shechem burned by fire by Abimelech (9.49);
42,000	Ephraimites slain by Jephthah at the fords of the Jordan (12.6);
30	Philistines (in Ashkelon) slain in hot anger by Samson for their clothes (14.19);
1,000	Philistines killed by Samson with a jawbone of an ass (15.15);
3,000	Philistines on the roof of the House of Dagon killed, along with Samson himself, when Samson pushed the pillars of the building (16.30); an unknown number killed *in* the temple;
22,000	Israelites felled (שָׁחַת) by the Benjaminites at Gibeah (20.21);
18,000	Israelites felled the 2nd day (20.25);
60	Israelites killed by the Benjaminites (20.31, 39) [the second half of this number may be a duplicate of the first 30;[4] this would balance the 30 Ashkelonites killed by Samson];

25,100   Benjaminites killed that day (20.35) (600 fled to the rock of Rimmon);
1st repetition of the previous figure:

18,000   Benjaminites felled (20.44);

5,000   more Benjaminites killed in flight (20.44);

2,000   more killed (20.45);

2nd repetition:

25,000   Benjaminites killed (annihilation of all of the tribe of Benjamin, except
            600 men who fled) (20.46).[5]

Total: 267,860, more or less (not including the "repetitions" above).

Notice that, as before, in the first half of the list, those who are killed are the enemy; while, in the second half of the list—except for the Ammonites killed by Jephthah (in List #4, the "uncounted") and the Philistines killed by Samson—Israelites are killing Israelites.

3. *Cities and towers destroyed. Casualty figures not given* (cities and their relationship to
    the Israelites; list #4 is about the slaughter in various cities)

In the third list are the destroyed cities for which casualty figures are not given. Again, the cities are mentioned in a meaningful order. The first part of the list concerns *enemy* cities destroyed; the middle portion concerns *friendly* cities destroyed; and the last portion is about the *Israelite* cities destroyed by Israelites:

1) Enemy cities:
    Jerusalem set on fire (1.8);
    Hebron defeated (1.10);
    Debir/Kiriath-sepher attacked and taken (1.11-13);
    Zephath/Hormah devoted to destruction and "utterly destroyed" (1.17);
    Bethel/Luz smitten with the edge of the sword, except for one man and his
        family (1.25-26).

2) Friendly or allied or peaceful cities (the Ammonite cities being the single
    exception):
    The tower of Penuel destroyed by Gideon and all the men of the city slain
        (8.17);
    Shechem destroyed; all the people in it killed by Abimelech, and the land
        sown with salt (9.45);
    Tower of Shechem burned and destroyed by Abimelech (9.49);
    20 Ammonite towns;
    Laish smitten with the edge of the sword and burned with fire by the Danites
        (18.27).

3) Israelite cities (destroyed by Israelites):
    Gibeah, smitten and burned by the men of Israel (20.37, 41); all other
        Benjaminite towns (see List #4) (20.48);
    Jabesh-Gilead smitten with the edge of the sword (21.10-11).

There is no way of knowing the actual population of these cities. Archaeologists estimate that in Iron Age I, the land consisted of about 250 very small farming villages and hamlets with a population of a few hundred each, on the average.[6] The figures given in *Judges* are admittedly exaggerated. If the author thought that each of these cities had an average of 1,000 inhabitants, the destruction of 9 big towns (plus unnumbered smaller Benjaminite towns) would increase the number of casualties by 9,000. (This sum has not been included in the total in List #2).

4. *"Great slaughter." Casualty figures not given* (includes some overlapping with other lists)

Episodes of "great slaughter," in which the author does not estimate the number killed (not included in the total in List #2):

 people killed in Jerusalem (1.8), Hebron (1.10), Kiriat-Sepher (1.11-12), and Luz (1.25-26);

 Perizzites and Canaanites smitten (killed) by Judah (1.4, 5);

 all the army of Sisera, with 900 chariots, felled by the sword; "not a man was left" (4.16), an untold number swept away by the torrent Kishon (5.21);

 the Midianites killed when they set their swords against each other in their own camp (7.22);

 all the men in the Tower of Penuel killed (8.17) (apparently all the men of the city);

 Gideon's half brothers killed by Zebah and Zalmunna at Tabor (8.18, 19);

 Gaal's men, many of whom fell deadly wounded (חלל) when they reached the gate (9.40);

 the people in the fields smitten (slain) by Abimelech (9.44);

 all the people of the city of Shechem (not including the people in the tower) massacred (slain) by Abimelech (as well as Abimelech's men, some of whom we infer also fell in the battle) (9.45);

 tower of Shechem set on fire by Abimelech (9.49);

 Israelites shattered and crushed by the Ammonites (10.8);

 the "very great slaughter" of Ammonites by Jephthah (11.33);

 the Philistines, smitten (slain) "hip and thigh with great slaughter" by Samson after the Philistines burned the Timnite and her father with fire (15.8);

 great slaughter of Philistines by Samson in the house of Dagon, of many who "were more than he had slain in his life" (16.30), (not counting the 3,000 on the roof, who are included in List #2);

 all inhabitants of Laish killed (18.27);

 all inhabitants of Gibeah killed (20.37);

 the remaining Benjaminites (those not already numbered) with all animals, put to the sword (20.48);

 all the inhabitants of Jabesh-Gilead killed except 400 virgins (21.10-11).

Total: an inestimable number (not included in the total in List #2).
(Mutilation and dismemberment are discussed in section II.2. below.)

5. *Other kinds of fraud and violence* (those not included in other lists)

Finally, other instances of violence or wrongdoing, which did not involve people or did not result in the death of an individual. (I am following Dante in classifying the bribes and the graven images as horrors. The images would be classified as fraud in Dante, a sin of the intellect being a more heinous crime to him than violence.)

> the 77 elders of Succoth (a friendly city in Gilead), who were "chastened" or "threshed" with thorns and briers by Gideon (8.16);
> an ephod made by Gideon, which become a snare to him and his family (8.27);
> the bribe of 70 pieces of silver given out of the house of Baal-berith by the men of Shechem to Abimelech with which to hire assassins (9.4);
> a lion torn apart by Samson with his bare hands (14.6);
> 300 foxes caught by Samson, with their tails set on fire (15.4);
> the fields, orchards, and vineyards of the Philistines burnt up by Samson (15.4);
> the betrayal of Samson by Delilah for 1,100 pieces of silver (16.6);
> two eyes of Samson gouged out (16.21);
> 1,100 pieces of silver stolen by Micah from his mother, given back, and used in part to make a number of images (17.1, 4-5);
> the images as well as Micah's Levite priest, stolen by 600 Danites armed with weapons of war;
> the rape of the Levite's Concubine (19.25);
> the abduction and rape of the virgins of Jabesh-Gilead (21.12); and finally,
> the abduction and rape of the daughters of Shiloh (21.23).

This is a spectacular variety of horrors. One of the author's games in each episode is to try to top the preceding act. No two actions are alike. Until one compiles these lists, readers may be totally unaware of the extent of destruction and slaughter committed.

6. *Stages of fighting*

The fighting develops through at least twelve stages. What starts as normal or acceptable action gradually begins to degenerate until by the end, we have descended to the absolute bottom.

1. At the beginning of the book, Israelites skirmishing with the enemy cooperate with each other, trying to settle in the land (1st half of Ch. 1);
2. Israelites experience a series of failures against the enemy and have to settle down side by side with the Canaanites (1.27-36);
3. enemy tribes begin to make incursions from abroad, and Israelites defend themselves successfully (Ch. 3 through Ch. 14);

4. Israelites begin to fail to cooperate with each other in Deborah's war, though they are still successful against the enemy (Chs. 4, 5);

5. an Israelite (Gideon, of the tribe of Manasseh) fights first against the enemy Midianites; then he is threatened by furious Ephraimites (one of his own tribes) but avoids a military encounter with them (Chs. 7, 8);

6. an Israelite (Gideon) smites *friendly* cities; Gideon's brothers are killed by the enemy (Ch. 8);

7. Israelites now engage in fratricide, usurpation, and insurrection. Though in the hill country of Ephraim, if Shechem is not a foreign entity, it is at least an enemy to the house of Gideon. Gideon's sons are murdered by their own brother, Abimelech, who then makes himself king of Shechem; he himself is killed in the insurrection against him by an outsider who had moved into his city (Ch. 9);

8. an Israelite (Jephthah) fights an offensive war on foreign soil. Turning against the Ephraimites (an Israelite tribe), he spitefully slaughters 42,000 of them (Ch. 11).

9. Samson defies Yhwh and becomes entangled with Philistine women. He devastates the Philistines in a feud; his tribe is forced to leave the territory.

10. the Danites destroy Laish, an innocent undefended town which is not in their tribal allotment;[7]

11. an Israelite tribe (the Benjaminites) breaks all ties of decency toward an Israelite guest (a Levite priest) in their town and rapes the guest's wife (Ch. 19); and

12. all-Israel engages in civil war against Benjamin and comes close to annihilating their brother tribe as well as destroying many Israelite towns (including Jabesh-Gilead) (Chs. 20-21).

Structures like this abound in *Judges*, always with a progression of good to bad to worst, or, as Mikhail Bakhtin puts it, with a "downward motion."[8] Little by little, the chief troublemakers are the tribes. The worst of them are:

Ephraimites: they start out as "good" (Joshua and Ehud are Ephraimites), fighting beside Ehud and Deborah. In the Gideon story they are "fair," but inclined to be obstreperous. In the Jephthah story they are "bad" and definitely contentious—a steady decline;

Danites: Samson, a Danite, though endowed with the spirit of Yhwh, perhaps represents the trouble the Danites stir up with the Philistines; the tribe is "bad" in (a) stealing Micah's idols and priest, (b) attacking the friendly and defenseless town of Laish (Samson and Micah episodes), and finally, (c) continuing to worship idols;

Benjaminites: they start out as "good" (Ehud is a Benjaminite, and the Benjaminites help Deborah), but at the end they are "bad" in the story of the Levite's Concubine; while the following tribes—to judge by their representatives—come off none too well;

Manassahites (Gideon's tribe and location of the towns that refused Gideon's men succor);

Gileadites (slaughtering of the Ephraimites in the Jephthah episode); and
Levites (Micah episode and story of the Levite's Concubine).

Ultimately we must realize that the author of *Judges* apparently shares the hostility of
the south (Judah) toward the north (Israel) that resulted in the division of the
kingdom after Solomon and the eventual loss of Israel to Assyria. The south (Judah),
with its bias against the north, would be the original source of the stories. (See
Chapter 6 for further information about the tribes.)

Violence of the Language

Contributing to the aura of horror is the language. The English translations of
the most violent words in this book are in many cases benign. For example, the
phrase *be put to death* in English does not seem particularly vicious. Yet perceived
literally, it *is* vicious. *Falling* can refer to something *dropping;* but in these tales *falling*
is more often a euphemism for *dying* or *falling dead* in a pool of blood like Eglon:
"There was their lord fallen on the floor dead" (3.25). The word *fall* is also used of
the Concubine, and though it is not followed by the word *dead,* it probably would
have been followed by the word *wounded* or *injured* had she not been dead. Thus
Meir Sternberg and others are probably wrong when they speculate that the
Concubine might not have been dead when the Levite dismembered her. In Hebrew,
as in English, the *casualties* in warfare are called *the fallen,* but, whether in Hebrew or
English, the actuality of what occurred is *not being fully admitted* for what it is—blood
and guts. (The word *fall* is listed under expressions for destruction, below.)

For the expression *smite by the edge of the sword,* some translators prefer the gentler, but
less accurate, rendition, *put to the sword.* But the Hebrew phrase usually (perhaps always)
begins with the word נכה, which means *to smite* or *strike a powerful,* often *fatal, blow.*

The author uses many *different* Hebrew words to express destruction. In translations,
however, *one* English word can be used to represent several different Hebrew words;
for example, three or more different Hebrew words can be translated simply by the
word *kill* in English. And *one* word in Hebrew, on the other hand, can be rendered with
a variety of *different* English words. Thus an English translation (no matter how excellent
in other ways), prevents the reader from sensing how the author is using words. The
varied translations of the word *smite,* for example, do not matter so much when we are
merely trying to derive an accurate interpretation of the idea or sentence or story, but
variations blunt the impact that the repetition of the single violent Hebrew word נכה
conveys. Since the translator, as a rule, feels no compunction about translating a
specific word inconsistently, the reader of a translation cannot feel the same kind of
impact that a Hebrew reader would feel when one particular word has been used over
and over again, especially in a single passage.

A reader may not be completely alert to these words even in Hebrew. If one is
trying to focus on what happened to a nation, tribe, or character; or if one is
concentrating on a single story, separating it from the rest of the collection, without

keeping the whole book in mind; or if studying a certain theme (like position of women in the society) or trying to analyze the psychology of a character, one can easily overlook the way these words are used and not care about how often they appear or how many repetitions occur. In fact, for the modern reader, the repetitions of a word may be regarded as an inadequacy in the author. Further, sorting out a single thread of the narrative from the rest of the fabric may cause the reader to phase out deliberately everything else that distracts from the particular search at hand. Too much familiarity with the book, moreover, immunizes us to its horrors, and we cease to be affected by them.

There are all kinds of other reasons why we suppress the violence of these stories. Living in a culture which accentuates violence, we may be immune to it. We also may be unwilling to admit that the Bible can be as horrible as this book is—Oh, Samson just ripped a lion apart. Oh, he seized 300 foxes, tied their tails together, and set them on fire!—and the reason we do not think about these incidents realistically is that we have accepted it as a fictional world, perhaps unbeknownst to ourselves. Or we view them as we view cartoon violence: Tweety smashed Sylvester again. How the cat felt is of no importance, and that is because it is also comic.

Despite this, the reason for the bad reputation of this book is that most readers feel the force of these words on some level, are struck with the horror of the words, and have the uneasy feeling that the book is revolting—especially if they are reading it for the first time.

The author of *Judges* must have wanted us to understand the horror and be revolted by it. That is why he used at least 37 different words to express *destruction* for a total of at least 123x, and violent words like *seize* 98x and *smite* 29x, in addition to the great number of words for *fight, battles, warriors, weapons, mutilations*, etc., as well as the extensive instances of *horrors* listed above.

"Smite"

The word *smite* (נכה) appears 29x in the following places: 1.4, 5, 8, 10, 12, 17, 25; 3.13, 29, 31; 6.16; 7.13; 8.11; 9.43, 44; 11.21, 33; 12.4; 14.19; 15.8, 15, 16; 18.27; 20.31, 37, 39, 45, 48; 21.10. (Note: 7x in Ch. 1; 5x in Chs. 20-21, a possible chiasmus). The noun related to the word *slaughter* (מכה) appears in 11.33 and 15:8 (2x).

נכה (ידך, יכו, יכום) is a strong sharp onomatopoeic word, which in my opinion should always be translated the same way, and as *smite*. A strong heavy blow, it is translated in various ways: *slay, kill, strike down, defeat, attack.* When it is used in *with the edge of the sword*, KJV translates it as *smite* [the city or person] "*with the edge of the sword*," while NRS removes *smite* and uses *put to the edge of the sword*, or *defeat*, renderings too weak for the kind of destructiveness involved. *Smite* or *slay* is closer to the meaning than is expressed in more recent translations, which use the words *defeat* or *kill* or *put to rout*. BDB cites the following as *strike fatally*: 14.19; 15.16; 18.27; 20.31, 39, while the following instances are cited as *strike and destroy*: 1.5, 17, 25; 8.11; 20.37. (Some of these decisions are debatable.)

"Destroy," "humble" (The reader may want to look up these words on a CD-Rom such as BibleWorks.)

The following are 37 different words for the act of *destruction* in Hebrew, totaling about 125 occurrences. Some of the words are deadly:

massacre (murder, kill)	הרג	(15x)
fall in battle	נפל	(13x)
kill, murder, put to death (not included: *to die*)	מות	(11x)
tear down [an altar or a city], destroy, break down	נתץ	(8x)
cut down (not included: *cut a covenant*)	כרת	(8x)
destroy (cut down)	שחת	(7x)
overpower (afflict, subdue, humble, rape, BDB 776)	ענה	(5x)
strike (break down, defeat)	נגף	(5x)
cut down, abuse (rape)	עלל	(4x)
pierce through ([with a sword], slay, be deadly wounded)	חלל	(4x)
subdue (humble)	כנע	(4x)
fall upon (violently)	פגע	(3x)
take vengeance	נקם	(3x)
tear apart (tear off the bindings)	נתק	(3x)
cut up	נתח	(3x)
cut off	קצץ	(2x)
devote to destruction	חרם	(2x)
tear apart	שסע	(2x)
know (possible euphem. for rape), teach, thresh	ידע	(2x)
crush (crack)	רצץ	(2x)
discomfit (rout, drive away in terror)	חרד	(2x)
discomfit, rout	המם	(1x)
perish	אבד	(1x)
murder	רצח	(1x)
hew or hack down (related to name of Gideon)	גדע	(1x)
break open (split, cleave, as wood or rock)	בקע	(1x)
sweep away	גרף	(1x)
run someone through	דקר	(1x)
tear down	הרס	(1x)
wipe out (blot out, annihilate, eliminate)	מחה	(1x)
destroyer (חרב BDB 351)	מחריב	(1x)
gouge out, dig out [eyes]	נקר	(1x)
tear garments	קרע	(1x)
shatter	רעץ	(1x)
slaughter (as a beast for food, kill)	שחט	(1x)
violently destroy (ruin)	שדד	(1x)
lie ruined	שכב	(1x)

Comments made about the other two categories (*smite* and *seize*) also apply here. (For the words which fit into more than one list, the decision about which list to put them in is arbitrary.)

The translation for the word כ נ ע as *subdue* (or *humble*) has a softening effect in English. Because in Hebrew it means *conquer through warfare*, the translation should show the considerable force and brutality which this act requires. It is used in 3.30; 4.23; 8.28 (2x); 11.33 (5x). The other word for *subdue* (ע נ ה used 5x in all) also means *take by force* (16.5, 6, 19). In *subduing* or *humbling* Samson, it is not through warfare but by cutting his hair, gouging out his eyes, and casting him into prison; and the Concubine is *subdued* by rape (ע נ ה, 19.24, 20.5). In both cases, tremendous brutality is involved.

We also see this softening tendency in modern American English, especially in time of war. Some common euphemisms used currently are *take out* (for *assassinate* or *destroy*), *degrade* (for bomb to smithereens), *get their ordnance off* (for *drop bombs* from an aircraft on people and buildings), *cause collateral damage* (for killing the innocent noncombatant population by mistake), *friendly fire* (for killing one's own people by mistake), *make a humanitarian intervention* (for *bomb* and *destroy* buildings and people of an obstinate country), and more recently, *abuse* for *torture*, *soften up* for *applying torture* to get prisoners to talk, and *detainees* for *prisoners of war*. Another is the benign word *unacceptable*, when it is applied to some really heinous act. Such bland substitutions for violent acts signify guilt and shame about the action being taken, both in the past and present.

But, as Elaine Scarry writes in *The Body in Pain*, war is about injuring, and about injuring more bodies of the enemy than of one's own, and so we invent language to remove suffering from our consciousness,[9] to deceive ourselves that we are not committing "unacceptable" violence. We cover up. Oddly, though, even when we may feel the violence on an emotional or unconscious level, we may ignore it on an intellectual level. According to Scarry, in descriptions of war, "the movements and actions of armies are emptied of human content" and "the fact of injury is . . . so successfully enfolded within the language that we cannot even sense its presence beneath the surface of that language" (70, 69). Pain, misery, physical distress, suppurating wounds, blood (except in one instance, Abimelech's shedding of his brothers' blood [9.24]), injury, or cripples missing a limb trying to move around, etc. are completely absent in *Judges*, whereas the *Iliad* is filled with screams, cries, gory details, the exploration of all the different ways in which men can die. In *Judges*, we may not even notice the many violent verbs.[10] But they are there, and it is one of the things that makes this such a dynamic book. Possibly this ancient storyteller wanted the violence (as in an action movie), but he did not want to alienate the audience completely.

"Seize," "take possession"

The verb *seize*, one of the strongest and most frequent words used, should not be translated simply as *take*. The various words meaning *seize* total 90x:

bind	אסר (18x)	(all in Judg 15-16)
drive out (hifil)	הוריש (15x)	(companion to the following word:)
take possession of (qal)	ירש (11x)	
seize, grasp	לכד (14x)	
take, meaning "seize"	לקח (12x)	(excluding "to take" or "pick up")
seize	אחז (5x)	
drive away	גרש (5x)	
subdue, overpower, weaken, humble	ענה (5x)	
subdue (conquer)	בנע (5x)	
seize, lay hold on	חזק (3x)	
plunder (noun)	שלל (2x)	
seize, rob, tear away, abduct	גזל (2x)	
capture your captive	שבה שבי ך (1x)	
seize	חטף (1x)	
carry off	נשא (1x)	(excluding where it means simply *lift up*)

(הציל, meaning *rescue, snatch away, deliver* is not included here, as it is a benign word.)

When cities or the fords of the Jordan are *seized* or when a city is *seized*, a whole army is involved. In other situations, the word implies the use of the *hands* of one or more persons in order to *capture* someone or something through *prodigious* effort. What people or objects are seized? Cushan-rishathaim, plunder, the Ephraimites, the two princes Oreb and Zeeb, the two kings Zebah and Zalmunna, gates, Samson, the Concubine, and the daughters of Shiloh—all are *seized* in one way or another. When the Concubine is *seized* and *put out* to the rapists, the word for this act means *seized violently* (חזק 19.25, 29). Since this word is related to *strength*, the English translation should incorporate that meaning. The daughters of Shiloh are also seized (abducted) (גזל), that is, as in a *robbery*. According to Daniel I. Block, "Elsewhere the word is used of tearing off skin (Mic 3:2); seizing wells (Gen 21:25), fields (Mic 2:2), and houses (Job 20:19), and robbing property (Lev 19:13, etc.). The present usage of the forceful taking of women recalls Gen.31:31."[11] When Laban asked Jacob why he had stolen the teraphim, Jacob answered: "Because I was afraid, for I thought that you would take your daughters from me by force (גזל)."

Driving out (הוריש) the inhabitants and *taking possession* (ירש) of their land occur mainly in Chs. 1-2, which are about the entire process of conquest. Its qal form appears 11x (ירש, seize, take possession of): 1.19; 2.6; 3.13; 11.21, 22, 23, 24 (2x); 14.15; 18.7, 9. Its hifil form appears 18x (הוריש, drive out, dispossess): 1.19, 20, 21, 27, 28 (2x, a kind of double verb or infinitive absolute), 29, 30, 31, 32, 33; 2.21,

23;11.23 (uses both forms), 11.24 (4x; uses both forms 2x each—for great emphasis).
It can mean simultaneously both *expulsion* and *extermination*.[12] It also is used when
Jephthah is fighting with the Ammonites over possession of the land (Ch. 11) and
when the Danites take possession of Laish and its land (Ch. 18). Translators use a
wide variety of words to translate this one word: *possess, dispossess, drive out, take, take over,
evict, expel, expropriate, occupy, conquer, capture, inherit, rob,* and *give you to possess,* when each
time, in fact, it is only one Hebrew word and means simply *drive out* and *seize,* depending
on its form. Boling prefers the benign words *evict, dispossess,* and *expropriate.* Five different
words are used in one passage in one translation (NIV): *take over* (3x), *capture, drive out,
give* (2x), and *possess* (11:21-24). One would guess that translators find the strong
meanings of the words too distasteful, and try to soften the readers' impression of
what actually happened. In English there is a prejudice against mindless repetition
of a word, and translators seem bent on improving the author's style by varying the
translation. This lack of respect for the author, in my opinion, not only misleads the
reader, but also blankets the reader completely against the violence of the Conquest.

Yet here is a curious paradox for the reader. Most readers, though possibly
surprised by the amount of horror, do not question it. Why is all this fighting
occurring? For the Israelites, this is the "Promised Land," which the author and
perhaps the reader, too, believe that the Israelites have a "right" to conquer and
possess. The term *promised land* does not exist as such in biblical Hebrew;[13] in Hebrew
it is only "land about which Yhwh spoke to you [or to your forefathers] that he would
give you," every time clearly denoting Yhwh as the source of the gift. Of course it all
started in Genesis, where it is a gift already given, a covenant cut: "For all the land
which you see I give to you and your seed forever" (15.15). And the Israelites' god
Yhwh demands ruthlessness in gaining possession. *Psalms 2* reads:

> Ask of me, and I will give you the nations as your heritage [possession] and the ends of
> the earth your possession. You shall *break them with a rod of iron and shatter them in pieces*
> like a potter's vessel (8-9, italics mine).

Yhwh *swears* (שבע) an oath to give the land to the Israelites in Gen 50.24; Ex
13.5; 32.13; 33.1; Num 11.12; 14.23; 32.11. Other instances of this oath are in
Deuteronomy 1.35;10.11; 31.20, 21, 23; 34.4. In *Judges,* Yhwh says through his
messenger-angel, "I have brought you to the land which I *swore* to give to your
forefathers" (2.1, אל־הארץ אשר נשבעתי לאבתיכם, an oath). The land was
theirs, supposedly *given* to them by Yhwh.

In *Judges* the author clearly does not want the Israelites to believe erroneously
that it is *they* who are conquering the enemy, for he believes it is Yhwh who gives the
victory. At the very beginning of the book, when they inquire of Yhwh, the answer is:
"Judah shall go up [to fight]. I hereby give the land into his hand" (1:2). As Yhwh
says to Gideon: "The troops with you are too many for me to give the Midianites into
their hand. Israel would only take the credit away from me [lest Israel vaunt itself],
saying,'My own hand has delivered me'" (7.2). Thus when the Israelites try to *possess*
the land and to *drive out* the inhabitants, both they and most readers believe it is

done according to "the word of Yhwh." The readers, if they are among the faithful, naturally do not flinch at what Yhwh decides to do. Perhaps no reader really questions this command.

The two justifications for the Israelites' Conquest are, then, that Yhwh gave them the land and also that the indigenous inhabitants are pagans who for this reason deserve their fate to be driven out or exterminated.

Readers usually adopt the perspective of an author, whether it is the Bible or any other book. From the author's perspective, the Israelites' encounters with the enemy are defensive. The war is presented as a "just" war. Wars incur violence. Of course, these battles happened long ago, and it is easy to distance ourselves from them for that reason as well as all the others. So what's new? We accept the invasion by the Israelites without a qualm just as we accept Caesar's invasion of Gaul.

Yet it is odd that we readers fall so easily into the trap of thinking that it is the *Canaanites* who are wrongfully invading the *Israelites*, rather than the other way around. That we readers accept without question an invasion in the past that *in today's world* we would strongly condemn is a comment on literary perspective. Yet it is not totally inappropriate to suggest that the Israelites in about 1250 BCE were engaged in the same type of "ethnic cleansing" as the Germans annihilating the Jews in World War II and the Serbs driving out the Kosovars in 1999.

But we are postmodern critics (whether we like the term or not). And the postmodern critic, as David A. Clines says in *On the Way to the Postmodern* (1998), is interested not only in what texts say, but

> in what texts *do not* say. It is their silences, their repressions, their unexpressed interests, the social, religious, and political ambitions that they screen from us, that we are concerned with in the postmodern age. (italics mine)

The postmodern critic must ask, Clines continues:

> What does this text do to me if I read it? What ethical responsibility do I carry if I go on helping this text to stay alive?
>
> . . . [About texts, we must move] to the question of our complicity with their unlovelinesses as well as with their values, [and] the question of the ethics of biblical scholars like ourselves taking money from the state or the church for doing biblical scholarship.[14]

What does it do to us when we read the Bible? As he implies, it can injure us unless we read with the best part of our humanity.

Does the author of *Judges* use such language simply to express ferocity and strength, or to induce revulsion at so much horror? Is he gloating over the numbers of the fallen, or is he as horrified as we ought (but perhaps fail) to be? It is hard to decide. *Undecidability* is characteristic of the way we must interpret this text. This may not be accidental but part of the plan. The author forces *us* to decide. *Undecidability,* a postmodern term culled from recent scientific discoveries, is resisted by readers of the Bible, who do not want anything to be undecidable about it.

Is it nothing to us that Judah slew 10,000 Perizzites (1:4), in the next verse slew an untold number of Canaanites, in the next verse cut off Adoni-Bezek's big toes and thumbs, and two verses later set the city of Jerusalem on fire? That is a tremendous amount of carnage and destruction in the short space of five verses. On a gut level we may be shocked, but on the intellectual level, we do not blink. If we side with the Israelites, we may even smirk.

This is not a theological or historical or even ethical point, but a linguistic and literary one. It is an attempt to explain why interpreters usually ignore the viciousness of the book.

Another example of horror is the rape of the Levite's Concubine. Unlike the other horrors, this one happens in peacetime. It is the greatest crime committed in the book, at least according to the Israelites and perhaps the author as well. English translations, which tend to cool down the language, nevertheless grip most readers with pity and fear (Aristotle's terminology) as readers do not expect to find this kind of story in the Bible. Of course, even the Hebrew writer tones down the language in places, too.

The author achieves his effect through repetition. This is not to denigrate the great English translations, which tend to reduce repetitions of words by translating them in different ways. But the translator who holds appreciation of the author's style an important mission, must, in my opinion, always use the same translation for any particular word, though doing this may be at the sacrifice of some other benefit. I believe that the context of the word is sufficient for us to determine its meaning, just as it was for the original reader or listener.

Language used in the Concubine rape

In the story of the Levite's Concubine, translators shift inconsistently between the more violent expressions and the weaker ones. Euphemisms exist in Hebrew (especially words with sexual connotations, like *to know* meaning *to have intercourse* with), and they should be translated as such, though the reader should be informed about them. Some of these euphemisms were preserved in the Revised Standard Version but dropped in the New RSV. In the following list, the NRS translation is given first, and the older RSV second. The NRS attempts to put some of the violence back in:

19.22 *have intercourse*, instead of *know*,
19.25 *raped her* instead of *know her*,
20.3 *criminal act* instead of *wickedness*,
20.5 *raped* instead of *ravished* (but kept as *ravish* in 19.24),
20.6 *vile outrage* instead of *abomination*,
20.10 *disgrace* instead of *wanton crime* (a softer word but a more literal translation).

While the RSV tended to soften the keywords, the NRS is more explicit. (See **Appendix 1** to this chapter.)

In this story, the more violent expressions are closer to the author's intentions. The author is always aware of the extreme nature of the horror, and comes down hard on us in every chapter. This is not to say that the author is using these words to make us hate war and become pacifists. He could be using them in much the same way that violence is used in modern movies—accentuating the violence to increase entertainment. He may horrify us to stimulate, to excite, to make us participate in the action, to produce catharsis. But since he cannot do this through pictures, he must depict the various kinds of violence through words. To ignore the violence in our translations is to miss one of the author's most important aims: to show that the Israelites needed relief from these terrible times.

The repetition of certain words should also be preserved by translators, as repetitions are part of the code. (See discussion of repetitions of words in **Appendix 2**, Rules of the Game, in Chapter 3.)

The author's implicit aim is to convince us that in order to reduce this violence, Israel must become a monarchy. It would take the author of a subsequent book to realize that this alternative was not a solution to the problem, either, but the author of *Judges* did not have the advantage of hindsight that later editors had.

This is a book about horror. Horror should not be removed from the book.

Curious Weapons and Unique Ways to Kill

It has been enlightening recently to learn about the tribal warfare existing in Afghanistan to this day. Three millennia after the time of the Judges, and no progress toward unity in that region has been made. And men are still determined to exterminate those with different beliefs. It seems very biblical to me.

Modern readers may imagine the foot soldiers in *Judges* as organized disciplined troops moving in unison; but the recent war in Afghanistan (2001) gives a more likely picture: unkempt, bearded, disorderly, fierce men, terrifying in appearance, not wearing clean, recently-issued army fatigues, but scrambling over the rugged terrain in baggy pants, with a cloth wrapped around their heads like a turban. The author of these stories did not need to fill in any details about the warriors because his readers would have been familiar with their own kind of warfare. When modern readers imagine that all the military forays go along smoothly, we unwittingly remove violence and chaos which the listener of the times would have been able to supply.

We are told that "not a *shield* or *spear* was seen among forty thousand in Israel" (5.8). Likewise, in 1 Samuel, when Saul is fighting against the Philistines in an early battle, we learn that the Philistines have a monopoly on the production of weaponry, so that "on the day of the battle neither sword nor spear was to be found in the possession of any of the people with Saul and Jonathan; but Saul and his son Jonathan had them" (1 Sam 13.19-22). It seems a bit extreme. Not having been told what weapons the warriors fought with, we are forced to imagine them fighting with farm implements and probably the weapons of dead Philistines. *Arrows* are in use in *Joshua;* and *lances, javelins, barbs,* or *helmets* have been found at Ugarit and are mentioned in the myths.[15] But in *Judges*, no projectile weapons of any kind (such as the *lance*) are mentioned. An *armor-bearer* is mentioned in the Abimelech story (9.54), but what gear the man was carrying is not told. Sisera has *chariots* and horses, and the Midianites have *camels*, but the Israelites do not have any of these. All they have are *swords*.

The word *sword* (חֶרֶב) is used 23x, of which 15x are idiomatic (*edge of the sword* or *men that drew sword*). It is mentioned 3x in the Ehud tale; 5x in Gideon (once referring to the Midianites, the other times to Gideon, one of them implied); and 2x in Abimelech (one of them implied). The foot soldiers all apparently wield a *sword*, except for the 700 Benjaminites in the last story who are skilled with *slingshots* ("every one could sling a stone at a hair, and not miss" [20.16]), although we do not see them actually using them.

The main characters use the *sword* only 3x, and when they do, it is either with a difference (a double-edged sword on Ehud's right thigh) or with discredit— Gideon's execution of the courageous Zebah and Zalmunna, and Abimelech's death, when, mortally wounded, he is killed by his armor-bearer with a sword, "so that people will not say of me, 'A woman killed him'" (9.54).

Instead of traditional weapons, we have unconventional ones. The pretext for the use of these implements is found in the Deborah story, which gives us the information that the Israelites have no *shields* or *spears*. The implication is that Yhwh will provide.

Where there's a will, there's a way. The characters are what Lévi-Strauss calls *bricoleurs*, people who improvise their weapons on the spur of the moment. A few examples follow:

an enemy is killed by merely *cutting off his thumbs and big toes* (Adoni-Bezek) (1.6);

Ehud carries a two-edged (traditional?) sword, but in a *nontraditional* place (over his right thigh) (3.16);

Shamgar kills 600 Philistines with an *oxgoad* (3.31);

Deborah's enemies (all except Sisera) are killed *in a torrent* of the River Kishon, with the *stars* themselves *fighting* Sisera from heaven (representing the participation of the Divine Warrior, Yhwh) (5.20-21);

Jael, creeping stealthily up to Sisera with *a workman's hammer*, kills him by driving *a tent peg* through his temple (4.21-22; 5.26-27);

in the Gideon story, *a loaf of bread in a dream* strikes down a tent (7.13);

Gideon's first weapons against the Midianites are *trumpets, jars,* and *torches* (7.19-20);

Yhwh throws the Midianites into a *panic* (Yhwh's weapon), which causes them *to fall upon and kill each other* (7.22)—no weapons being needed when the enemy will *self-destruct*;

Gideon punishes the elders with *thorns* and *briers* (8.16);

a woman in the tower drops *a millstone* on Abimelech, crushing his skull, although his actual death is ultimately inflicted by his armor-bearer's *sword* (9.53-54);

Jephthah's *vow* might be considered his weapon against the enemy (11.30-31);

he makes *a burnt offering* of his daughter (*fire* is a weapon throughout) (11.39);

Samson kills a lion with *his bare hands* (14.6);

he *burns* the fields, orchards, and vineyards by *tying 300 foxes* by pairs together, by their tails, and *tying torches to them* (the weapons are *fire* and *torch-bearing foxes*) (15.5);

the Philistines slay the Timnite and her father *with fire* (15.6);

Samson slays 1,000 men with the *jawbone of an ass* (15.15);

bowstrings and *a weaving pin*, used as weapons, fail to vanquish Samson, but he is conquered when his *hair* (not his throat) *is cut* with a *razor* (ironically, nonviolently) (15.12-14; 16.7-9, 12, 19);

the *temple* of Dagon is a weapon: by leaning against the pillars and bending with all his might, Samson causes the temple to fall, killing 3,000 people who were on the roof and an untold number below (16.29-30); he has no *sword*;

threats are a weapon in the story of the Micah; though the Danites are heavily armed, the only weapon they use is *intimidation*. With their menacing presence (and *veiled* threats), they win over (coerce) the Levite (18.19), and with *real* threats cause Micah to flee (18.25);

the Abiezerites *threaten* Joash (6.30);

Gideon *threatens* the men of Succoth and Penuel and carries out his threat (8.16-17);

the Ephraimites *threaten* Gideon (8.3), but he propitiates them;

the Ephraimites *threaten* to burn down Jephthah's house but do not do so (12.1);

the Philistines *threaten* to burn the Timnite, her father (14.15) and her father's house, which induces her to entice the secret of Samson's riddle out of him; eventually, they carry out their threat (16.6);

finally, the Benjaminites surround the Ephraimite's house and *threaten* him and the Levite with a sexual crime (19.22); they accept a substitute victim, instead.

the Concubine is killed by *rape* (19.26-27), after which her husband, the Levite, dismembers her (violating her body) with a real weapon, a *knife* (19-29);

200 survivors of the tribe of Benjamin *seize* the daughters of Shiloh with their *bare hands* (like Samson with the lion), and carry them off, probably kicking and screaming and pounding the backs of their abductors (21.23);

finally, *taunts* and *mockery* are weapons in the Samson story (Samson *taunts* the Philistines with his riddle and jawbone, and he *mocks* Delilah three times) (14.14; 15.15; 16.15).

Curious weapons are the weapons of the underdog, the Trickster,[16] just as they are today. In the war in Iraq, the Insurgency and the terrorists use improvised electronic devices (IEDs). In literature, however, oddball improvised devices are characteristic of comedy, especially of folktales, grotesque comedy, and black comedy. The variety of these weapons in *Judges* is indeed a source of amusement, if only we can keep the horror at bay. It's a game of one-upmanship. Who wins the contest of ingenuity?

II. The Comedy

Judges is filled with comic situations. Because the book contains horror and humor in about equal parts, the genre may be classified as "comedy of the absurd," "black comedy," "noir," and/or "grotesque realism." Being out of touch with the manners of those days, modern readers undoubtedly miss some aspects of the humor of *Judges*, but much of it is obvious and pleasurable.

"Curious weapons," discussed above, are one of the connecting links between the horrors and the comedy. (See Item #8 below, Wrong Use of Common Objects.)

Only occasionally do critics factor into their interpretations the humor that pervades *Judges*.[17] As with the violence of the language, readers and interpreters who are focusing on their own topics of interest (history, women, theology, etc.) do not notice the prevalence of humor. With the Rorschach test, if you see the inkblot as a rabbit, you can no longer see it as a duck. Just so Comedy/Horror. How the reader perceives *Judges* reveals what kind of person he or she is, as will subsequently be shown.

In a recent psychological experiment, participants on two teams, one wearing black shirts and one wearing white shirts, were told to keep an eye on each other. At some point, a gorilla entered the room, walked to the center, thumped his chest, and then left. Half of the subjects did not see the gorilla. "The effect is inattentional blindness," writes Michael Shermer. "When attending to one task—say, talking on a cell phone while driving—many of us become blind to dynamic events, such as a gorilla in the crosswalk . . . . The perceptual system and the brain that analyses the data are far more complex. As a consequence, much of what passes before our eyes may be invisible to a brain that is focused on something else." One cause of many accidents is that we do *not* see what we do not *expect* to see.[18] Just so, the horror in these stories is phased out while we are perceiving the comic.

Or as in quantum physics, you cannot observe particles and waves simultaneously. Einstein regarded this as "spooky."[19] As with the Super Computer, the two themes in *Judges*—horror and comedy—are spinning simultaneously in opposite directions. It is what Yo Yo Ma calls "the 'edge effect' in music, when disparate elements converge to create unexpected contrasts."[20] Just such an "edge effect" is produced by the clashing of the horrible and the comic in *Judges*. When the reader tries to perceive both, he or she is caught in a cognitive dissonance and feels this edge effect throughout.

In the Anchor edition of *Judges*, Robert Boling calls these stories "historical romances" and suggests a festival occasion for telling them. He sees two types of romance—the ideal (with the exemplary figure) and the comic. I do not find any of the first type, except perhaps for Othniel and Achsah, and I have reservations about these. Boling provides five or six clues to the comedy, but he dismisses the comic in *Judges* as something that is "intended for more discriminating attention" (31-32).

Others mention comic situations from time to time, but do not remark about comedy as characteristic of the *whole* book. Failure to give this "discriminating attention" to the comic, as well to the other designs in the book, prevents one from discovering the underlying meanings of *Judges*.

Two sources of humor are the many intricate structures within the text and the complex use of keywords. (Structures have been discussed in Chapter 1. Keywords signifying *destruction* were analyzed above; other keywords will be discussed in Chapters 3 and 4.)

Definition of "Carnival-Grotesque"

Harry Levin's remark about a "resurgence of toughness during our more violent century," with its emphasis on "alienation," "absurdity," and "grotesquerie," perfectly describes the style of *Judges*:

> Comedy, with Bertolt Brecht or Samuel Beckett or Eugène Ionesco or Harold Pinter, has moved from sympathy to alienation. Absurdity is treated seriously, as indeed it must be when it breaks in on us from all directions and unsettles the presuppositions of daily living. Grotesquerie has come into its own. André Breton, two generations ago, rediscovered the roots of Surrealism in *humour noir* . . . . Swift was its "veritable initiator," in the testimonial of Breton . . . . [21]

The term "carnival-grotesque" encompasses all of these aspects of humor.

The word *grotesque* usually refers to monsters and monstrosities, like the grotesque figures on Gothic cathedrals. This also is its earliest meaning. One of its early definitions is to be found in an eighteenth-century French dictionary, where the grotesque is seen as that which is "odd, unnatural, bizarre, strange, funny, ridiculous, caricatural, etc."[22]

Also basic to its meaning is the concept of caricature, that is, "A representation . . . in which the subject's distinctive features or peculiarities are deliberately exaggerated to produce a comic or grotesque effect" (*American Heritage Dictionary*). Christoph Martin Wieland, the eighteenth-century German critic, distinguished three types of caricature: (1) "true caricature" with a natural distortion of the model found in reality, (2) "exaggerated caricature," in which the monstrosity of the model is enhanced but the model still can be identified, and (3) the "grotesque" or "purely fantastic caricatures," where the painter or author, "disregarding verisimilitude, gives rein to an unchecked fancy . . . with the sole intention of provoking laughter, disgust, and surprise about the daring of his monstrous creation by the unnatural and absurd products of his imagination" *(Underredungen mit dem Pfarrer von * * * (1775), ibid., 30).* In *Judges*, all the characters are caricatures. Micah is the "true caricature," in that he seems to behave in a rather normal fashion. Gideon is the "exaggerated caricature": the story is longer; he is truly absurd and truly comic. And Samson is the "purely fantastic caricature" or full-bodied "grotesque."

The grotesque is a means for describing hidden aspects of reality. Wolfgang Kayser, a twentieth-century critic, has identified the grotesque as "a form expressing the id" and stressing the theme of alienation (in the existential sense). Certain elements are essential to this form: suddenness, surprise, strangeness, and dynamic action. Grotesque literature makes the world seem to be unreliable, says Kayser, and inspires us with a fear of life. At the same time, the grotesque is an attempt to "subdue demonic aspects of the world" and thus, according to Bakhtin, has a kind of liberating effect (184-88 passim; Bakhtin 49). The grotesque is a way for the folk to try to control the elements of their environment which they fear.

It is Mikhail Bakhtin, a twentieth century Russian critic, who has given us a nearly complete analysis of the grotesque in his brilliant book *Rabelais and His World* (1965, 1968). Though *Judges* must be the most ancient example of this genre in extant literature, Bakhtin makes no mention of it in his study. Since all of the characteristics of the grotesque run rampant in the Samson cycle, it is strange that the name of Samson did not occur to him, the more so as Bakhtin was profoundly interested in the origins of the grotesque.

Bakhtin hypothesizes that the grotesque began with a "primitive grotesque," which had to do with the cycle of the seasons: "sowing, conception, growth, death." (These are also basic points of reference in *Judges*.) This primitive literature is followed by a more sophisticated grotesque, in which the "cyclic" topics are embedded and are thus connected with seasonal festivals.

He classifies two types of festivals, the official and the folk. Official festivals, exemplified by the church holy days, were humorless, characterized by respect for hierarchy, recognition of the inequality of human beings in the social order, and lack of change. Folk festivals, representing the binary opposite of the official religious festival, were humorous and were characterized by suspension of the hierarchy—the equality of all human beings lasting for the duration of the celebration—and acknowledgment of change. Folk festivals consisted of the carnival and other entertainments of the marketplace. Containing the laughter of all the people, the humor of the carnival is ambivalent: "it is gay, triumphant, and at the same time, mocking and deriding" (11). Bakhtin insists on the merry, positive aspect of the carnivalesque humor. (The occasion at which the daughters of Shiloh come out to dance may have been a joyous wine festival. See Chapter 3 for a discussion of festivals.)

The carnivalesque grotesque of Rabelais, Bakhtin believed, had a historical purpose. It marked the transition from a stern authoritarian period (the Medieval) to a period in which the individual was liberated from medieval superstition and fear (the Renaissance). The "monstrous" images of the grotesque literature have a "mighty awareness of history and of historic change . . . . The new historic sense that penetrates them gives these images a new meaning but keeps intact their traditional contents: copulation, pregnancy, birth, growth, old age, disintegration, dismemberment" (25)—again, all important to *Judges*.

Judges also clearly represents an historic process and marks a transition between the classic stories of the patriarchs and the more realistic literature of the reigns of

Saul, David, and Solomon. In the transitional period, the elements of the primitive grotesque are combined with hidden (or implied) messages about Israel.

The categories of the grotesque are not distinct items, but each overlaps some of the other characteristics. In what follows, I have sorted out the defining characteristics classified by Bakhtin that can be found in *Judges*. They will be discussed more at length in the analyses of stories which follow the list.

1. *Body parts*

"The site of comedy is the body," says Seth Lerer.[23] Bakhtin makes this clear in his study of grotesque mutilations, dismemberments, and references to what Bakhtin calls the "material bodily lower stratum"—the genitals, bowels, and other parts of the human body connected with food and sex (18-21 et passim).

Appearances to the contrary, Bakhtin finds the bodily element not negative, but "deeply positive." "It is presented not in a private, egotistic form, severed from the other spheres of life, but as something universal, representing all the people" (19).

Throughout *Judges*, all the limbs and even many internal organs or parts (*heart, brain, womb*, for example) are mentioned, some of them a number of times, and not only human parts, but animal parts as well (e.g., the camel's *necks, hooves* of horses, *jawbone* of an ass, *carcass* of a lion, foxes' *tails*). All the main parts of the body are represented in the Samson story, for the author means us to perceive Samson as a most physical being who loves physical contact of all kinds. Hands are important throughout. This is a book about bodies and the mutilation of bodies. (*Body* and *bodily parts* are discussed at length in Chapter 3.) The body is also the site of comedy in *Judges*.

2. *Dismemberment*

Grotesque literature shows us the body continually undergoing change, being taken apart, being reproduced. Nothing is fixed or eternal.

In *Judges*, mutilation and dismemberment occur in *every* story except the Achsah and Luz stories. It begins on a small scale (the thumbs and big toes of Adoni-Bezek) and ends on a large scale (the slicing up of the body of the Concubine into 12 parts). (What kind of a man is it, who would cut up the corpse of his wife?) It also includes disemboweling of Eglon, decapitating of Zebah and Zalmunna, and disfiguring of the body—as the gouging out Samson's eyes. (This is the only example of *torture* in the book, torture committed by the Philistines, not the Israelites.) Oddly enough, the usual dismemberments produced by warriors in battle are lacking.

In dismemberment, what is *inside* (hidden) is brought *outside*—the intestines and excrement of Eglon, the brains of Sisera, the skull of Abimelech. The slaughter that was described above, including the carnage of hundreds of thousands of people in battles and the destruction of cities throughout the book, is typical of the grotesque. Not only people, but also animals are victims, like the lion, the ass, and the foxes in the Samson story. Dead bodies are fertilizer.

Mutilations and dismemberment also abound in present-day black humor. In a recent *New Yorker* article, George Meyer (the chief writer for the TV series, *The Simpsons*), tells how, when he was growing up, he found the following parody of a Dennis the Menace cartoon in a *Mad* magazine to be uproariously funny:

> It was a cartoon that showed Dennis coming into the house holding a skull, and the caption was something like 'Hey, Mom, look what I found in Mr. Wilson's head.' That absolutely put me away. The next day my stomach muscles hurt from laughing. I felt like I'd been worked over by bullies.

Commenting on this cartoon, Meyer referred to what Michael O'Donoghue, the late writer for *National Lampoon* and "Saturday Night Live," used to say: "Humor has to be startling . . . . It has to re-frame reality in a way that is exciting. It's like seeing in two dimensions and then opening the other eye or looking through a View-Master and suddenly seeing in three."[24] He might be describing *Judges*.

Mike Scully, another writer for the *Simpsons*, tells about "the most intense laughter [he] ever heard in the rewrite room" of the show. The writers were discussing a scene where a criminal named Snake wants to get his car back, which Homer is driving. He stretches a wire across the road in hopes of decapitating Homer, but misses him. Homer's car is followed by another in which the driver is holding a sandwich up high, saying, "I told that idiot to slice my sandwich." It was obvious where the joke was going. But, as Scully relates, "George Meyer suddenly said, 'What if the wire cuts off his arm?' That made the people in the room laugh so hard that they were coughing—literally choking—because the joke was so unexpected. It was a shocked kind of laugh, and it started rolling, one of the laughs that build the more they reverberate through you" (66-67). All the jokes in this article about Meyer refer to mutilation or dismemberment. This is the type of black comedy we find in *Judges*. In the cinema, it would be *film noir*.[25]

Daniel Mendelsohn, reviewing Mel Brooks's *The Producers* in *The New York Review of Books*, writes about the prior film version of this musical comedy:

> Despite the mixed-to-terrible notices *The Producers* received when it opened in 1968 ("amateurishly crude," Pauline Kael wrote in *the New Yorker*; "a violently mixed bag," "shoddy and gross and cruel," Renata Adler wrote in the *Times*), Brooks' film soon established itself as a cult favorite. Today, it's not unusual to see it counted among the funniest movies ever made. This popularity surely owes a great deal to the same crudeness, grossness, cruelty, and amateurishness that the critics complained about . . . . To [Woody] Allen's intellectual *artiste*, Brooks has been more than happy to play the outrageous clown; like [his character] Bialystock, he gives his audiences access to their ids.
>
> . . . But then, *The Producers* was nothing if not a testament to the obstinacy of vulgarity, the tendency to bad taste; Brooks included that big neo-Nazi production number "right in the middle of the movie" because he knew that audiences occasionally *want* bad taste, have their faces rubbed in bona fide kitsch . . . . The impulse to force us to confront the grotesque is the germ of a certain kind of comedy—the kind that we're relieved to participate in because it frees us, temporarily, from everyday conventions and proprieties.[26]

—the last comment perhaps having been inspired by Bakhtin. One of the funniest episodes in film is in the Monty Python movie *Holy Grail*, where the two knights meet each other in single combat and begin hacking each other to pieces, until all that is left of them are two stumps.

The best-known exemplar of *black comedy* is no doubt Voltaire's *Candide*, in which the body is disfigured with syphilis, flogged, scourged, tortured, examined with surgical instruments and dissected, dismembered—legs, hands, buttocks, heads, testicles cut off—drawn and quartered, ripped to pieces, cannibalized, disemboweled, raped, hanged, burned, thrown upon a dunghill, and whatever—a series that ultimately ends in a bragging competition between Cunegonde and the old woman about which one has endured more suffering. Only the power of humor enables us to contemplate what the body endures in this story. Another exemplar is *Don Quixote*.[27]

Not all readers will find *Monty Python's Holy Grail, Candide, Don Quixote,* or *Judges* humorous, to be sure, as they are "black comedies." It's a matter of taste. And who is the audience? An *agelast* (unlaughing), to use Rabelais' term for a killjoy like Malvolio? Sir Toby, one of Malvolio's tormentors, asks Malvolio: "Dost thou think, because thou art virtuous, there shall be no more cakes and ale?" One can be *too* pious, as Shakespeare thought. Or would the audience be someone newly sprung from Comedy Central? *Judges* is in some respects the pulp fiction of the ancient world.[28]

3. *Food, wine, and banquets*

Bodily processes are connected with the intake and output of food, especially urination and defecation. The only reference in *Judges* to the bodily processes besides eating and drinking is defecation in the Ehud story, when the servants think that Eglon is "relieving himself" and when Ehud stabs Eglon through the belly, and the "dirt" comes out at his back. Other references may be hidden in other stories, but I have not found them.

References to wine, bread, and several varieties of grains are plentiful in *Judges*, especially in the Gideon and Samson stories and *wine* is notable in the carousing of Gaal and his partners in the vineyard and temple, probably at the wedding banquet of Samson and the Timnite, the carousing of the Concubine's Levite and his father-in-law, and the dancing of the daughters of Shiloh at the wine festival at the end of the book. (*Food/ drink* and *wine/ intemperance* are discussed in Chapter 3.)

4. *Degradation*

The motion of the action is always downwards. "The essential principle of grotesque realism," writes Bakhtin, "is degradation, that is, the lowering of all that is high, spiritual, ideal, abstract; it is a transfer to the material level, to the sphere of earth and body in their indissoluble unity" (19-20). This aspect in *Judges* may be what turns so many readers away in disgust.

In *Judges*, numerous characters are shown lying on the ground or in a prone position: Eglon, Sisera, Abimelech, Samson, and the Levite's Concubine. Notice especially the extended "falling" passage in the Jael scene (5.27, quoted below). The body of the Levite's Concubine, as I have already remarked, lies in a position exactly like that of Eglon, except that the Concubine lies *outside* a locked door, while Eglon lies *inside* a locked door. (This kind of symmetry, extremely important in *Judges*, and discussed in Chapter 1, is another aspect of its humor.)

Many other examples of this downward motion have already been given in the stages of fighting and some of the structures cited above.

5. *Positive aspect of this degradation*

Dismemberment, degradation, downward motion are not to be thought of as merely disgusting, for they lead to a rebirth (Bakhtin 20-21, 34). Only if something dies, can it spring up to new life. The comic element in *Judges* lends positiveness to an otherwise negative picture of the world.

6. *Weddings*

Comedies usually end with nuptials. Weddings, of course, ring in the new and lead to birth. They are normally connected with banquets (as in the Samson story). In Rabelais, they are sometimes connected with thrashings and warfare (Bakhtin 198-200, and passim). Samson follows this pattern, for the aftermath of his wedding is the slaughtering of the 30 Philistines for their festal garments.

Following the mass slaughter of the Benjaminites in the last story, the seizing of the women of Jabesh-Gilead and the daughters of Shiloh, during what seems to be a wine festival might be considered a "mock wedding." This signifies a somewhat bawdy *resurrection* of the tribe of Benjamin. After a mass rape of 600 virgins, a generation of babies will replenish the empty nests. (This item is closely connected with the next two.)

7. *Topsy-turvy world*

In the carnival-grotesque, the world is all upside-down, and the wrong people are often in charge. Two manifestations of this characteristic are usurpation and "uncrownings" (394). In *Judges, either* the "right" person is uncrowned (Eglon, though not the "right" king to the Israelites); *or* the "wrong" person is crowned and then rightly uncrowned (Abimelech); *or* the "wrong" person is uncrowned (Samson). As the author of *Judges* twice makes explicit, there was no order in Israel because there was no authority (18.1, 19.1) and everyone was doing what he thought right in his own eyes (17.6, 21.25). Chaos is the norm in carnival grotesque.

8. *Wrong use of common objects*

Odd uses of common objects, such as kitchen utensils being used as musical instruments, and household objects improvised as weapons, are also characteristic of the grotesque (411).

Examples of this in *Judges* are the curious weapons (discussed above), including a tent peg (Jael); a weaving pin (Delilah); horns, jars, and torches (Gideon); and the jawbone of an ass (Samson), etc. Of great interest is the upper millstone dropped on Abimelech by the woman in the tower of Thebez. Though stones are often traditionally used as weapons, this is a stone with a difference, and its user a woman with a deadly aim. Such weapons often involve trickery (deception). (This is discussed in Chapter 3 and elsewhere.)

9. *Suspension of normal rules of behavior*
The mood of the grotesque is like that of the Roman Saturnalia, "festive" and "joyous," symbolizing the suspension of ordinary rules of conduct (52, 92, et passim). From a realistic point of view, the ending of *Judges*, with the seizure of the dancing daughters, is a black one, but from another point of view it is one of madcap joy and success.

10. *Disguises and masks*
Disguises are not so prevalent in *Judges* as some of the other characteristics, but a few people do pretend that they are different from what they are: Ehud comes to Eglon as a right-handed man, Jael feigns friendship to Sisera, Abimelech masquerades as king—a usurper (himself usurped)—and the mighty Samson pretends that he can be made weak. All these are satirized.

11. *Exaggeration of numbers*
Numbers in grotesque fiction are "unstable," or may be over-precise and exaggerated to the point of monstrosity (463-465). They are important throughout *Judges*, as has been noted in the lists of horrors above. As is clear from the use of large numbers in all the battles, like Sun Tzu Wu in 500 BCE or General H. Norman Schwarzkopf, or General Colin Powell in the 20th and 21st Centuries, the Israelites understood the principle of "overwhelming force."

Though I have not taken time to analyze all the other dimensions of numbers in the book, I point them out from time to time, as for example, the doublets and triplets in the Gideon story (see item #17 below) and the frequent use of numbers involving "3" in Samson (for example, 3 kinds of animals: lion, fox, and ass, 3 agricultural crops that Samson destroys: vineyards, orchards, and grain fields, etc.) as shown by Robert Alter in "Samson without Folklore."[29] There are also the 3 mothers in the Deborah story, 3 trees in the fable of Jotham (olive, fig, and vine), while Gideon, Abimelech, and Jephthah are also a trio of sorts, etc.

The author is unusually exact in telling us the times of day or night when something happens—using the concrete, it would seem, to bolster the impression of factuality. Times of day and night are a category in themselves.

Sacred numbers are parodied in the carnivalesque-grotesque. Though I do not find this *in Judges*, it is possible that this kind of parody exists but that I have missed it.

12. *Heterogeneity*

Heterogeneous elements may be yoked (perhaps by violence) together. Bakhtin credits Möser and Schlegel with this idea (41), and we recognize it from techniques of the seventeenth century English metaphysical poets (e.g., our love is like "stiff twin compasses," from Donne's "Valediction Forbidding Mourning.")

In *Judges* this characteristic is embodied in the anomalies (discussed in Chapter 1). The strange weapons and mutilations are also examples, as are items #7, 8, and 9 above (topsy-turvy world, wrong use of common objects, and suspension of normal rules of behavior).

13. *Madness*

"Madness makes men look at the world with different eyes . . . . In folk grotesque, madness is a gay parody of official reason . . ." (39) as it is the opposite of wisdom (260). Samson is the most obvious example. A close cousin of madness is folly—like that of Abimelech, Gaal, and Jephthah.

14. *Parody, travesty, and burlesque*

These three related techniques are called "forms of the mask" by Bakhtin (39-40) or disguises—*travesty* being a grotesque or exaggerated *parody*, while *burlesque* means "making the subject seem ridiculous by treating it in an incongruous way." Bakhtin does not give much space to them, but they are plentiful in *Judges*. When the Levite thrusts the Concubine out of the house, this is a travesty of Lot offering his virgin daughters to the mob to save his angelic guests (Gen 19) (see Chapter 1); and the Gideon and Samson theophanies may be considered travesties of the Abraham/Sarah theophany in *Genesis*.

Akin to *parody* is the author's use of "parallel texts," or "inner intertextuality"—the use of correspondences and contrasts between stories (discussed fully in Chapter 1) and their connection with "keywords" and "hidden objects" (see Chapter 3).

Though the broader types of parody are open to all, as an art form they are mainly for discriminating readers, for they demand that the reader first, be able to spot a parallel text and second, be able to hold in mind not only the text itself but also the one it parodies or burlesques. This is what makes understanding the intertextuality of *Judges* so difficult. Lacking tremendous knowledge of two or more texts, the reader will not be sensitive to all the nuances of the differences between them. It is asking quite a lot of the human brain.

15. *Irony*

Unfortunately, Bakhtin does not elaborate on irony. His one comment, however, is helpful:

> In the world culture of the past there is much more irony, a form of *reduced laughter*, than our ear can catch. The literature, including rhetoric, of certain eras like Hellenism and the Middle Ages is flooded with various reduced forms of laughter, though we have ceased to be aware of some of them (135, my emphasis).

"Reduced laughter," a term which Bakhtin lifts from Jean Paul, describes the kind of laughter that *Judges* evokes. A most interesting and challenging game of intellect that the reader might play (either as solitaire or in groups) is to list and classify all the ironies in *Judges*. The longer the list, the more one continues to find. Because Lillian R. Klein presents such an excellent account of the ironies in *The Triumph of Irony in the Book of Judges*, I have not tried to duplicate her efforts here, but have merely added some here and there.[30] More ironies still remain to be spotted, however.

Kierkegaard, remarking on the relationship between comedy and religion, suggested that the ironic and comic are "border phenomena on stages in between the stages, irony preceding the ethical and humor the religious."[31] Here it would be accurate to say that humor is a servant to the religious, and irony is a means to the ethical. (See Chapter 4.)

16. *Satire*

Irony is a form of satire. According to Schneegans, a German critic of the late nineteenth century, the grotesque can be defined as "caricature that has reached fantastic dimensions, . . . exaggeration of the inappropriate to incredible and monstrous dimensions . . . . Therefore the grotesque is always satire" (Bakhtin 306).

What satire we perceive in *Judges* seems to be written with an ulterior motive, as Levin finds in the "primitive mind':

> For unqualified belief in the power of satire, we should have to turn back . . . to a primitive state of mind which believed as strongly in curses as in blessings. Seen within its own purview, malediction was a form of tribal magic, and Irish bards could exterminate rats by enunciating the appropriate rhymes. *Satirists are like witches who stick pins in the effigies of their enemies* (194, my italics).

To give but three examples from *Judges*, the story of Gideon satirizes the warrior, while the story of Samson satirizes machismo, and "women on the top" (Jael and Deborah) satirize male prowess.

In ancient times, satire had the function of trying to shame deviants into conformity, and it sometimes still does—whenever the public can agree on standards of behavior. "Satire addresses its appeal to a sense of shame, according to Evelyn Waugh among others" (ibid.). In my opinion, satire is "the last straw," a throwing up of hands in despair at the behavior of people or nations. (Curses and blessings are discussed in Chapter 4. I agree with Levin that they are reflective of a primitive state of mind.)

17. *Riddles, puzzles, and games*

The most obvious example of this category in *Judges* is Samson's riddle, which he propounds to the wedding guests. Another conundrum is the one the Israelites in the last story propound to themselves: how to give wives to the Benjaminites without violating their vow not to do this thing.

In this category of riddles, puzzles, and games may also be included not only the symmetrical designs (Chapter 1) and the category of keywords having to do with secrets (Chapter 4), but also the many diverse patterns that the author inscribes in each narrative. Upon first reading the book, for example, one is likely to regard the Gideon story as having a clumsy structure; the action and character at first seem blurred. But all comes into focus the moment one realizes that the writer has devised a structure of doublets. This strange case of presenting doubles of everything throughout is one of the author's many "games." But what meaning does it have? (See the analysis of comedy in the Gideon story below.)

Among the other games are the "law cases," which present the reader with many more riddles and puzzles to solve (discussed below and in Chapter 4).

18. *Women as destructive of men or as foils*

In grotesque literature, women are presented non-ideally, either as destructive of the male, or as a contrast to male behavior—the female as "the foil to his avarice, jealousy, stupidity, hypocrisy, bigotry, sterile senility, false heroism, and abstract idealism" (Bakhtin 240). Deborah is such a foil to Barak. And so is Jephthah's daughter to her father. Just as her father behaves stupidly, so she behaves nobly and tragically.

More numerous than one at first realizes, women in *Judges* are presented in all their various relationships to men: mother, daughter, sister, wife, concubine, and harlot among others. (See the list of Relationships in Chapter 3.)

Jael, Delilah, and the woman in the tower of Thebez in the Abimelech story are examples of women who destroy men. As if to more than even the score, in *Judges*, are men who destroy women—Jephthah's daughter, the Timnite, the Concubine, and the women of Jabesh-Gilead are killed by men.

19. *Focus on the common people*

The carnival-grotesque abounds with people—with the folk. "The comic stage, from its metropolitan standpoint, has habitually tended to ridicule the denizens of the small town," writes Harry Levin (157). Think Charlie Chaplin.

Most of the people in *Judges* have lowly origins. Aristocracy and luxury (except for the luxury items that Gideon captures in war) are mostly lacking. Though some critics claim Sisera's mother is a queen, there is no evidence for this (see Chapter 1, endnote 46). But she is elite, as is Eglon. The only two characters who have attendants are she and Eglon, and notably, neither is an Israelite. Abimelech has a steward. The only king among the Israelites, Abimelech, is an upstart. As for wealth, Delilah gets money; and Micah's mother has money. But the lifestyle of all the characters is simple. These are all small farmers, villagers, not urban dwellers. They don't live in elegant households with servants (עֶבֶד), though Eglon (King of Moab), Gideon, and the Ephraimite host in Gibeah have servants; and Sisera's mother has female attendants. There are no slaves.

The heroes are "folk" who do outstanding deeds. Interpreters of *Judges* usually focus on the heroes and fail to notice that many minor characters have significant and varied social roles, like the sons, brothers, lads such as Purah and Abimelech's armor-bearer, and the Levite's boy in the Concubine story. (For a complete list of the numerous folk, see Relationships in Chapter 3.)

20. *Accurate topography of the world*

Despite the invention and fantasy, "the topography of the grotesque world is described with remarkable precision" (444). Bakhtin does not explain why this should be, but perhaps it is to help suspend our disbelief willingly. The author of *Judges* gives the impression of being perfectly familiar with the lay of the land, though he suspects that the reader is not, for he gives directions on how to get to Shiloh (21.19). This seeming precision concerning cities, tribal areas, shrines, etc. is what tempts the reader to regard *Judges* as history. Geographical location is the anchor of concrete reality that holds the fantastic in place, lest it fly away like a hot-air balloon.

Place names in *Judges* seem to be actual names, and not invented for this book, but some places such as Akrabbim, meaning "Scorpion Pass" (1.36), may have been selected for their use as a gloss on the narrative. Scholars, moreover, have had difficulty connecting some of the locations with the known topography; this may be because the original stories were not Israelite but Canaanite.

21. *Nomenclature*

In comedy, nomenclature is a source of amusement. "Aristotle had indeed allowed that comedies might use invented names . . . . Comedy has habitually set great store by onomastics, the science of naming," writes Levin (73). "The zanies of the Commedia dell' Arte started as provincials from Bergamo; and communities along the Hudson River, with funny names like Hoboken or Yonkers, gain easy laughs for Broadway comedians" (157). Humor of this sort is found in *Judges*.

Gideon's name, for example, means *Hacker* or *Hewer*, a name appropriate to his occupation not only of chopping down the Asherah but also of chopping down the Midianites and especially the two kings, Zebah and Zalmunna, whom he hews as expeditiously as Samuel hews Agag to pieces. *Caleb* means *dog*; it is one more reference to animals, to add to the animal category of keywords listed in Chapter 3. The name *Micah* in its longer form (מיכיהו) means *Yhwh-the-Incomparable*, no doubt ironic for a man who is an idolater (Boling 258).

Not unusual in the Bible, this practice takes on added importance in *Judges* and was surely a source of enjoyment for the audience. Unfortunately, in translation, we miss these hidden meanings. (A partial list of names is given in **Appendix 1** of this chapter.)

The function of the Carnival-Grotesque

According to Bakhtin, the main aim of this genre is liberation:

> The function of the carnival-grotesque form is to *consecrate inventive freedom, . . . to liberate* from the prevailing point of view of the world, *from conventions* and established truths, from clichés, from all that is humdrum and universally accepted. This carnival

spirit offers the chance to have a new outlook on the world, to realize the relative nature of all that exists, and to enter a completely new order of things (34, my emphasis). Bakhtin was convinced that "folk culture was always based on the indestructible confidence in the might and final victory of man" (336n.).

Laughter was one route by which the folk overcame their fear of established authority and truth. Since this form seems to crop up during a transitional stage of history, as Bakhtin believed, it may well be that *Judges* was a means of trying to understand and control the transition from tribal independence and waywardness to "a less imperfect union," whatever that turned out to be.

The trickster

Oddly enough, Bakhtin does not distinguish the role of Trickster per se in his analysis. Yet obviously, this figure is one of the chief components of the grotesque, as it is in *Judges*.

The Trickster is anyone who achieves his ends by trickery, deceit, cunning, or design. In his ultimate contemporary avatar, he is the confidence man—like Thomas Mann's character in the novel of that name. The dictionary defines him as "a mischievous supernatural being found in the folklore of various primitive peoples, often functioning as a culture hero, and much given to capricious acts of sly deception" (*Webster's Third New International Dictionary* [1981]). According to the *Encyclopaedia Britannica*,

> He is a practical jokester who is depicted as clever, lascivious, gluttonous, vain, and deceptive, but is also a dupe. He is a culture hero, who brings knowledge of cultural skills, who steals fire, who releases impounded game, slays monsters, and ordains norms of social behaviour. He is a transformer, who, after creation, changes the often chaotic original world and primeval beings into the present world. In some traditions, he is the creator who establishes the earth.
>
> The characteristic trickster tale is in the form of a picaresque adventure: as the trickster was "going along," he encountered a situation to which he responded by knavery or stupidity, he met a violent or ludicrous end, and then the next incident is told.[32]

All these characteristics can be found in *Judges*. Samson in particular fits the job description perfectly. He and other characters of *Judges* have much in common with the great *picaros* like Don Quixote, all tricksters.

To Jung, the Trickster plot is a way of explaining to human beings that marvelous truth, that "anything can happen." (Who would have imagined the twin towers would be demolished not by bombs, but by airplanes improvised as missiles? Not Condoleezza Rice, for sure.) One of the best critics of the Trickster is Paul Radin, who says that this character explains tricks of fate or experiences in life when "everything goes wrong and nothing intelligent happens except by mistake at the last moment":[33]

> In American Indian myths, Trickster is at one and the same time creator and destroyer, giver and negator, he who dupes others and who is always duped himself. He wills nothing consciously. At all times he is constrained to behave as he does from impulses

over which he has no control. He knows neither good nor evil yet he is responsible for
both. He possesses no values, moral or social, is at the mercy of his passions and appetites,
yet through his actions all values come into being (xxiii).

The obvious character in *Judges* who is "at the mercy of his passions and appetites" is,
of course, Samson. Among the other Tricksters are Ehud, Jael, Gideon, the woman
in the Tower of Thebez, and Jephthah.

These Tricksters vary in the degree to which they use trickery to help Israel (and
Yhwh). As we progress through the book, the trickery becomes more self-oriented
and the Trickster more likely to be duped. Jephthah, Abimelech, and Samson are
"hoist in their own petard," as will be demonstrated below. Micah, who is perhaps
practicing trickery by relying on idols, is also duped when his icons arouse
covetousness and are stolen. In the last story, it is "all-Israel" (except the tribe of
Benjamin) who become the supreme tricksters in finding a way to supply wives for
the Benjaminites. They dupe themselves.

In *Judges*, we should take as much care to note when a Trickster is lacking as
when one is present. In the failure to save his daughter, Jephthah lacks the Trickster
element, though he certainly has a trick up his sleeve in capturing the Ephraimites.
Since trickery is so important to the characters who succeed, something must be
wrong with those who either have not got this knack, who lose it, or do not have it at
the right time.

In the most ancient literature, oddly enough, the Trickster has a divine nature.
Radin believes that this divine characteristic of the Trickster is always secondary and
was "largely a construction of the priest-thinker, of a remodeller." Priestly writers of
all literature, Radin says, equated the Trickster with Deity. "Thus he was a figure that
could not be forgotten, one that had to be recognized by all aboriginal theological
systemizers." Though martyrdom is not an essential part of the picture, the actions
of the hero bring about "ridicule and humiliation and result in pain and suffering"
(164). Again, think Samson.

In the American Indian myths Tricksters are not limited to the human species;
animals, supernatural beings, and monsters can be Tricksters. Neither animal or
monster Tricksters can be found in *Judges*, but there is one supernatural Trickster:
Yhwh and his role as messenger-angel. Though lacking all the characteristics listed
by Radin, Yhwh is the ultimate Trickster since it is only through him that anything
can be accomplished. Perhaps the reason why the human beings in the stories often
behave stupidly is that they serve as a foil to Yhwh, who though Trickster, is not
stupid. For Jung, too, "daemonic features exhibited by Yhwh in the Old Testament"
reminded him of

> the unpredictable behaviour of the trickster, . . . his senseless orgies of destruction
> and his self-imposed sufferings, together with the same gradual development into a
> saviour and his simultaneous humanization . . . . It is just this transformation of the
> meaningless into the meaningful that reveals the trickster's compensatory relation to
> the "saint."[34]

The characteristics fit Samson, although Jung does not mention him.

Edith Kern speaks of "the ambiguity of the trickster as both wounder and wounded of which Jung was so strongly aware."[35] They are "heroes both triumphant and suffering . . . . Tricksters therefore represent scapegoats of a special nature . . ." (117). One is reminded that Samson in his wounding and martyrdom is also seen by interpreters—beginning with Augustine's *Sermio de Samsone*[36]—as a "type" of Christ (that is, a representation of something yet to come).

To the Trickster figure Kern gives the epithet "the absolute comic" (116):

> Originating in that mythical stage of the human race and its subconscious, the trickster figure provides us, indeed, with insights that reach beyond life as we daily live it. By turning the world playfully upside down, by putting down the mighty from their seats and—though only in jest—exalting [those] of low degree, the trickster makes apparent the frailty of human existence and the proximity of laughter and tears. Quintessence of the absolute comic, he transports us into worlds where imagination and make-believe triumph (208).

The Trickster allows us to conquer over the mighty, at least in our imaginations. Trickery is the method of the underdog who has no other weapon.

The Trickster plot is closely connected with the grotesque: (1) it is comic, (2) it allows the author to play the wonderful game of "one-upmanship" ad infinitum (à la Rabelais), and (3) it is a way for the folk to vent their sheer frustration in trying to get some measure of control, or at least an understanding, of a world which has gone mad. (For further discussion, see #7 on *Samson*, below.)

III. Analyses of the Stories

The grotesque comedy and Trickster elements combine with the horrors and with other techniques of comedy in each story. One thing to keep in mind is that the text does not give us the whole story: the stories in the scrolls may have been only scenarios, which had to be fleshed out and embellished by the storyteller with traditional material handed down in the oral tradition, or with his own inventions. Depending on how he performed the story, it could be much more hilarious in performance than it is on the written page. The stories are but skeletons, with ample room for improvisation. (See further discussion in Chapter 6.) What is surprising is that there are so many comic elements in each story.

1. *Adoni-Bezek* (1.5-7)

Adoni-Bezek's punishment—having his thumbs and big toes amputated, the mutilation resulting in death—is innovative, bizarre, and grotesque. The story is told laconically with no hints from the author to increase or to decrease our horror at the mutilation. The reader may shudder, for Adoni-Bezek seems to be a real person. He has an identity; he speaks intelligently and with composed resignation to his fate. We do not as yet know how to react. To do anything but gasp in shock seems inhumane, but Adoni-Bezek himself calms us, testifying that the punishment was deserved.

Since Adoni-Bezek speaks after the punishment, we know that he survived for a time after the mutilation and must have felt it until he died under the table. How horrible. But how about the 200 Philistines whom David conquered and mutilated in order to hand over their foreskins to Saul and so win Michal? On the fate of these Philistines we cast a cold eye: they were killed by our hero, David; they were anonymous; and presumably they were not mutilated while still alive. Adoni-Bezek, however, is alive. He represents the good man whom Aristotle describes. On the other hand, he is an enemy, and readers do not, as a rule, sympathize with the enemy. Thus the reader is pulled in two different directions at once: sympathy and hostility. This very confusion is indeed a characteristic of the grotesque (one incidentally which Bakhtin did not note) and one of the bases of "black" or "savage" humor.

Henri Bergson, the great French philosopher whose ideas had an impact on literary critics of comedy, speaks of the "disturbing" effect of the comic. He remarks,

> It seems as though the comic *could not produce its disturbing effect unless it fell, so to say, on the surface of a soul that is thoroughly calm and unruffled.* Indifference is its natural environment, for laughter has no greater foe than emotion (emphasis mine).[37]

In *Judges* it is the author who feigns "indifference," and Adoni-Bezek who presents the "calm and unruffled surface."

One of the pleasing aspects of the story (and comic, since the punishment is just) is Adoni-Bezek's awareness of irony: "As I have done, so God has requited me." An eye for an eye; the punishment fits the crime. Thus the horrible mutilation is justified in the eyes of the very person who endures it. What is surprising is that he, an enemy, knows the Israelite law.

This mutilation, however, is contrasted by another that is by far more horrible, and in no way pleasing: the rape and mutilation of the Levite's Concubine near the opposite end of *Judges*. Such violence represents the Israelites' complete lack of *knowledge about the law of retribution* and *their lack of self-awareness.* When we contrast what happened to Adoni-Bezek with the Israelites' extremely severe punishment of the Benjaminites at the end, we begin to see him as tragic, a man of dignity and self-awareness, the only one of his kind in the entire book, ironically not an Israelite. Because of the long distance between the beginning of the book and the moment of insight at the end, however, these implications may escape all but the most discerning reader. But if we fail to see the real meaning, the joke is on us. The book is full of games of this kind.

The connection of his dismemberment with his gathering of scraps under a table of food—a banquet image—are earmarks of the carnival grotesque. Adoni-Bezek is also an example of the "uncrowning," and of things going topsy-turvy. Adonai-Bezek goes from the heights to the depths (in fact, under the table).

This story serves almost as a kind of "control," as does the Achsah story following so closely afterwards (discussed in Chapter I).

2. *Achsah* (1.12-15)

If the Adoni-Bezek story is about "the right kind of warfare," the Achsah story is about what seems at first glance to be "the right kind of marriage"—and Achsah, the commander's daughter, is the typical prize of story-book romance for the knight who conquers the dragon. Just as the stories in *Judges* show a progressive degeneration of morals and ethics, so also in the early stories, the humor is only faint (here it is simply "pleasure"), but grows more intense and more grotesque as we proceed. At the end, a new light is cast upon these early stories, and we may decide that Caleb is but another Jephthah (discussed below, and more fully in Chapters 1 and 3).

The Achsah story is not tragic; all ends well.

3. *Ehud* (3.12-30)

The first clue that the story is comic comes when we perceive the deceit by which Ehud gains admission to his enemy, Eglon, and his resourcefulness in drawing his sword from his right thigh. Ehud's swiftness and deftness in carrying out his mission are pleasurable.

Ehud is the first trickster or *eiron*. In Greek comedy, the *eiron* is a clever underdog who by his wit triumphs over the boastful character the *alazon* (*EB*, ibid.). Ehud exemplifies this in the way he gains admission—"I have a secret message for you, O king . . . a message from God (דבר־אלהים) for you." This message is something like Samson's riddle. Like Samson, Ehud was being deliberately deceptive, certain that the enemy would not guess what his statement meant. Ehud banked on a mystification.

Ehud's message is an example of *verbal irony*, "in which the real meaning is concealed or contradicted by the literal meanings of the words" (*EB*, Micro, V, 432). The second time we read the story, we experience *dramatic irony*—when the reader knows something that the character does not know. "The artistic achievement in dramatic irony," writes B. F. Skinner, "requires that the spectator respond to some extent as a member of both audiences"—that is, both the initiated and the uninitiated audience.[38] And so we do.

Eglon is fat, apparently lazy, slow to move, slow to catch on. He had been sitting in his cool roof chamber enjoying tribute from the Israelites for eighteen years, no doubt leading an idle, gluttonous life. As an oppressor, he knew that he risked being assassinated and should have been on guard. And his assassination ironically fits the crime, for Ehud actually removes the food (the luxury bought with the tribute money) from the fat oppressor's bowels:

> Then Ehud reached with his left hand, took the sword from his right thigh, and thrust
> it into Eglon's belly; the hilt also went in after the blade, and the fat closed over the
> blade, for he did not draw the sword out of his belly; and the dirt came out (NRS, 3.22).

"Humor," writes Skinner, "is preoccupied with tabooed subjects, in particular, sex, and with having aversive effects upon the listener or others" (287-288). Here the humor is scatological.

After Ehud has escaped, the servants, who should have set out in hot pursuit of the assassin had they but guessed, wait a long time, "till they were utterly at a loss." Note also the contrast: Ehud is swift, intelligent, and dynamic; Eglon and his servants are slow, stupid, and static. They are "dumb." They don't "get it."[39]

The servants conclude that their master is "only relieving himself in the cool chamber" (3.24). Why do they reach this conclusion? Possibly because they smell the "dirt" from Eglon's intestines. Ironically too, Eglon is not "relieving himself"; rather, his colon has "been relieved" for him.

Because of our lack of empathy with the enemy, these details are comic. Eglon, furthermore, as a disgusting (fat) oppressor could not possibly be tragic. Aristotle's definition of the tragic hero tells us why: the hero is "the character between these two extremes—that of a man who is not eminently good and just, yet whose misfortune is brought about not by vice or depravity, but by some error or frailty."[40] The story that depicts "the downfall of an utter villain" cannot be tragic since such an end satisfies the moral sense and therefore must be pleasing. It is comic also in that the murder of Eglon has released the Israelites from oppression (all ends well). Except possibly for Adoni-Bezek and Zebah and Zalmunna (8.21), who are rather noble, and possibly Jephthah's daughter, there is no candidate for the Aristotelian tragic hero in this book. Samson cannot be described as "eminently good and just," and his misfortune is certainly brought about by "depravity." Jephthah is a possibility, but as we shall see in our discussion of his famous vow, he may have been anything but noble. (See below and also Chapter 4.)

Perhaps this is as good a place to insert some of the "judgment" puzzles concerning ethics (discussed fully in Chapter 4)—Ehud's deception, to start with. Not only is the assassination a violation of hospitality and trust, but the message is a bald-faced lie. Was it unethical? Does the fact that the deception is practiced on the enemy, make any difference? Can this be called "self-defense" because it is a life-threatening situation? Does it make any difference that the name of Elohim was used? Can this be called using the name of God "in vain," that is, in an irreverent or disrespectful manner? Or does Ehud really believe that his "message" is from Yhwh? After all, he was the "deliverer" whom Yhwh had "raised up." Can Yhwh's chosen deliverer make a mistake?

Is Ehud better or worse than Jael, who feigns friendship for Sisera? Or Delilah who betrays her lover Samson? Ehud's plan was clearly premeditated: does this make his deception the more heinous? Later characters have to do quick thinking on the spot. On this account, in a court of ethics, their impulsiveness might be considered an extenuating factor in judging their guilt. Also they are "underdogs," whose violation of ethics interpreter after interpreter absolves as a necessary means to an end by people who were otherwise powerless.[41] *Judges* is shot through with such ethical conundrums for the reader to sort out. (See Chapter 4.)

The grotesque elements in the Ehud story include the "material bodily lower stratum" (bowels and bowel movement), food (the obesity of Eglon and the dirt in his intestines), and the uncrowning. The weapon is unusual in that it is the opposite of normal—or topsy-turvy—since the sword is drawn unexpectedly from the right thigh instead of the left. The hiding of the weapon is an aspect of the disguise or mask, and the secrecy of the message (דבר־אלהים) is akin to a *riddle*. Bakhtin makes a great deal of the "downward" movement in the grotesque: in the Ehud story, the servants find "their lord dead on the floor."

On another level, the story is also an exemplum to those in Israel who have rightful authority, not to be oppressive like Eglon. This is a legitimate aim of grotesque fiction.

The grotesque is a source of laughter. If you do not believe it, try reading the Ehud story aloud to a class of undergraduates. They always gasp, then laugh. Laughter such as this, says Bakhtin, has a therapeutic power to liberate and regenerate (56). Let us hope he is right.

As with all the other stories in the book, there are a number of unresolved mysteries in the Ehud story. Like Amit, Halpern worries about how Ehud accomplished his locked-door trick. Halpern's solution is pretty neat: what Ehud escapes through is the privy (מסדרון, a hapax legomenon, translated usually as *vestibule* or *porch*, 3.23). Halpern aptly compares this scene with Odysseus' killing of Polyphemos.[42]

As to whether this assassination bears any resemblance whatsoever to a historical event, there were thousands of other details in a real incident that the author could have focused upon. That the author selected these particular details to the exclusion of all others shows that his primary concern was to tell an amusing story.

4. *Jael* (Chs. 4, 5)

A source of pleasure in the Deborah/Jael story is the playful way it is constructed, with thirty or more different details paralleling and contrasting details in the Samson story (see Chapter 1).

The first of the comic touches is that of Barak who, like Lancelot of the Cart, hesitated for a fatal moment from lack of faith before going into battle. Deborah, called a mother in Israel, scolds Barak and takes away his candy. Jael is also a "mother"—tucking Sisera into bed and giving him his bottle. And then there is the *real* mother, the mother of Sisera waiting for her bad boy to come home with what he has gotten away with this time.[43] The three mothers are another nice pattern.

Finally, the irony of a possibly beautiful, gentle, motherly feminine woman, Jael, turning into woman-as-vicious-killer takes us aback. Woman, the symbol of powerlessness and dependency in a topsy-turvy world, overpowers the most powerful of males. She is the "unwomanly woman," to use George Bernard Shaw's term, or a "woman with a manly heart," to borrow a phrase about Clytemnestra from Aeschylus. Here men are foils to women—or is it the other way around?—a foil being a person "who underscores or enhances the distinctive characteristics of another" (*American Heritage Dictionary*). But the domination of women over men in this book does not necessarily signify women's *superiority* to men so much as the *degradation* of the male of the period.

By comparison with Ehud, Jael had little time to plan. She had had no clue that Sisera would drop by and had to think quickly. With no real weapon at hand, she is a *bricoleur*, or improviser, to use Lévi-Strauss' term again. The workmanlike way in which she wielded her hammer (her "weapon"), and her skill when she "drove the peg into his temple, until it went down into the ground" (4.21) are nothing less than amazing.[44] Despite the grisliness of the act, the situation gives the reader the pleasure of paradox, that a woman can wield a man's tool so deftly.[45]

A consequence of dismemberment in grotesque humor, according to Bakhtin, is that the *inside* of the dismembered thing can now be connected with the *outside*. Here, the brains of Sisera, like the intestines of Eglon, are no longer hidden from view. Abimelech's brains are shortly to come into view as well.

The death scene in *The Song of Deborah* gives us time to savor the grotesque or black humor fully; it also emphasizes the downward motion—here literal as well as metaphorical:

> He asked water, and she gave him
> > milk,
> > she brought him curds in a lordly
> > > bowl.
> She put her hand to the tent peg
> > and her right hand to the
> > > workmen's mallet;
> she struck Sisera a blow,
> > she crushed his head,
> > she shattered and pierced his
> > > temple.
> He sank, he fell,
> > he lay still at her feet;
> at her feet he sank, he fell;
> > where he sank, there he fell dead.
> > > (NRS, 5.25-27)

Milk, a soporific, is an image of the banquet or feasting so important in the grotesque. It symbolizes the mother's care for her child, and is also a symbol of Israel, like honey. Immediately after Jael has both given Sisera *more* than what he wanted—milk—she gives him what *he expressly did not want*, the blow in the temple—a contrast in gifts.

A few lines later, Sisera's mother is waiting expectantly for the return of her triumphant, spoil-laden son, who would have "a girl or two for every man," literally in Hebrew, "a womb, two wombs" (רחם רחמתים), bowdlerized in most translations. That she is waiting in vain affords the pleasure of dramatic irony, for the reader has information that the character lacks: her son is dead. The ending of the poem with the Israelite curse on "all thine enemies" brings us sharply back into reality. It is comic, nevertheless, in that all ends well for "our side."

Three women in *Judges* conquer men. Not so curiously, none of the women is pure Israelite. The topsy-turvy is involved in all three cases:

1. Jael, a Kenite, kills the noble enemy Sisera (the General Rommel of the day) and in so doing surpasses Barak (who if he had not misbehaved would presumably have had the honor of killing him);
2. the Shechemite woman in the tower mortally wounds a bad Israelite, Abimelech (the murderous Milošević of the day); and finally,
3. Delilah, a Philistine, subdues Samson (the Mike Tyson of the day).[46]

Whatever the situation, the woman-with-the-millstone had to act resourcefully and quickly—otherwise she would soon be burned up. In her trial for homicide or treason, she can plead self-defense, and the court must acquit her.

What is comic about these women is that women—symbol of powerlessness, femininity, seductiveness, and beauty—can kill so viciously. Whereas Judith has no imagination and does her killing in the traditional way, Jael takes us by surprise with her absurd weapon. Delilah pulls a fast one by committing a *non*violent act with a *violent* weapon used *nonviolently*. (She uses a razor, but not to cut Samson's throat.) The woman in the tower who kills Abimelech makes us gasp because her weapon is the last thing we might have thought to be found up there, and because she has such deadly aim.

A woman who *lacks* the Trickster quality is the Levite's Concubine, who cannot save herself. Her husband—the Levite—and the Ephraimite host ought to have had this skill, but lack it. Jephthah lacks it. Lack of this power may imply inferiority.

5A. *Gideon*

Gideon's behavior is comic throughout, yet few readers remark on this. Instead of being a "mighty man of valor," Gideon is an outright coward, as indeed are most of the Israelites and the Midianites in the story. His name means "Hacker," and this makes his cowardice all the funnier.

On least 13 occasions, Gideon shows fear at a time when he ought to have been brave:

1. When Gideon is about to be commissioned, the messenger-angel finds him hiding in a wine press (6.11).
2. When the messenger-angel calls him a "mighty man of valor" (6.12), instead of responding bravely, Gideon snivels that Yhwh has cast his people off.
3. When the messenger-angel speaks of Gideon's "might" and calls upon him to deliver Israel, he protests that he is from the weakest tribe and the least in his tribe (cf. Saul in 1 Sam 9.2). Though this might be construed as a polite way of accepting an honor (did not Moses also protest?), we must conclude from his other actions that he is being truthful. (Possibly, too, this passage shows the author's bias against Gideon's tribe, Manasseh.)
4. When Gideon is told that Yhwh would be with him in the battle, it is not enough. Gideon must have a sign (6.16, 17, 27, 29).

5. He runs off and brings an "ephah" of flour, a tremendous amount, as if to make certain to get the best help from Yhwh possible. A truly brave man would not need a bribe (cf. Jephthah).

6. The messenger-angel gives him a pyrotechnical display, but still Gideon lacks faith.

7. When he breaks (hacks) down the altar of Baal and the Asherah, he goes with a very large number of men (ten) to do so.

8. Fearful of his family and the men of the town, he does not do it by day, but by night in order to be invisible (6.27).

9. When the men of the town come to put Hacker (Gideon) to death, he is out of sight and does not utter a peep. It is his father (ironically, one of "his family" whom Gideon supposedly feared) who defends him.

10. When he finally gets his troops together, he asks for another sign from Yhwh that he will succeed. Yhwh supplies the sign of the dew on the fleece (6.38).

11. Such a sign would have satisfied an ordinary mortal, but not Gideon. He makes Yhwh perform a miracle, something contrary to normal: to find the dew on the ground and not on the fleece (6.40). The patient Yhwh, showing off his power, complies.

12. In the middle of the night Yhwh tells him to go down to the camp, but that if he fears to go down, he should go down to the camp with Purah his servant. Purah is a mere lad (נער). We might well ask how much more comfort Gideon would receive going down to this great multitude of the enemy with a child. Still, down he goes (i.e., he fears). A child is better than nothing—for a coward, that is.[47]

13. And ultimately, later in the story, Gideon is fearful of the Ephraimites.

It is not only Gideon who is terrified; his troops are, too:

1. Yhwh tells Gideon to thin them down by proclaiming, "Whoever is fearful and trembling, let him return home."[48] Instead of shouting, "We are not afraid," 22,000 of these valiant men from the tribes of Manasseh, Asher, Zebulun, and Napthtali return home (7.3, 6.35). (The author is again showing his bias against the north.)

2. At the test at the spring of Harod (the name meaning "trembling"), the 300 men who "lapped, putting their hands to their mouths" (7.6) are those who, it seemed, were too fearful to drink from a position that prevented them from keeping an eye out for the enemy. Or were they just wise?

Scholars have debated about why one method of drinking is "superior" to the other. The whole idea of thinning down the ranks of the Israelites to 300 men in this way, however, is to provide humor. Take a careful look at whom they are fighting against. More than once we are told that this army of Midianites was an army "that lay along the valley like locusts for multitude; and their camels were without number, as the sand which is upon the seashore for multitude" (7.12). Perhaps Gideon's fear was not cowardice but an intelligent appraisal of his chances of success with so few men. Who wouldn't tremble?

Wherever they went, Gideon never recalls to battle the men that he sent back to their tents. At the end of the story—though the Ephraimites have come out to fight on their own, and though Zebah and Zalmunna had 15,000 men left after 120,000 swordsmen had fallen [8.10]—Gideon is still fighting with his reduced force of 300 men [8.4]! The contrast in the size of the armies, especially when the tiny Israelite army of 300 men is being led by a quivering aspen leaf, has got to be funny. Perhaps the humor would be more apparent if Hacker were portrayed in a movie by Woody Allen.

When Gideon gets down to the Midianite camp with Purah, the information he receives is of no strategic value; instead, by luck (or by the planning of Yhwh?), he hears a Midianite relating a dream to another Midianite: "a cake of barley bread tumbled into the camp of Midian, and came to the tent, and struck it so that it fell, and turned it upside down, so that the tent lay flat" (7.13). It is a wild and amusing dream followed by a wild and amusing interpretation given by another Midianite: "This is no other than the sword of Gideon . . . ; into his hand God has given Midian and all the army" (7.14). How the Midianite reached this conclusion about the dream, who knows? What is amusing about this exchange is the utter confidence of the Midianite in his interpretation—on the basis of no evidence at all. This Midianite assuredly is no Joseph! (Or is he?) What we have demonstrated here is one of the chief sources of humor in comedy—lack of logic.

Equally amusing is that this interpretation, overheard by sheerest coincidence, is what inspires Gideon to take action. Though the ancient Israelites may have used dreams to predict future events like the outcome of battles (cf. Shakespeare's *Julius Caesar*), would such a dream galvanize this thinned-down army? Cowardly Gideon gains confidence *not* on the basis of *the promise that Yhwh himself made* to him—but rather on the basis of this unreliable and possibly unauthorized information from the enemy! The audience would have appreciated the joke better than we. It may be only the modern reader who takes this story seriously.

He was a trickster. Lucky Gideon wins this particular battle, not with real weapons but with a trick he apparently devised himself: the trumpets, jars, and torches. He instructed his men carefully:

> After he divided the three hundred men into three companies, and put trumpets into the hands of all of them, and empty jars, with torches inside the jars, he said to them, "Look at me, and do the same; when I come to the outskirts of the camp, do as I do. When I blow the trumpet, I and all who are with me, then you also blow the trumpets around the whole camp, and shout, 'For the LORD and for Gideon!'" (7.16-18)

This is paralleled later by his son, Abimelech, in instructing his men in gathering the branches to burn down the tower of Shechem:

> So he went up Mount Zalmon with all his soldiers, took his axe in his hand, and cut down some brushwood. This he lifted to his shoulder, then said to the men with him, "Hurry! Do just as you have seen me do" (9.48).

Yet it is Yhwh who allows Gideon's plan to work:

> So Gideon and the hundred who were with him came to the outskirts of the camp at the
> beginning of the middle watch, when [the Midianites] had just set the watch; and they
> blew the trumpets and smashed the jars that were in their hands. All three companies blew
> horns and broke their jars. They held the torches in their left hands, and in their right
> the horns they were blowing, and cried out, "A sword for Yhwh and Gideon!" Every man
> stood in his place all around the camp, and all the [Midianite] men in camp ran; they cried
> out and fled. When they blew the three hundred trumpets, Yhwh set every [Midianite]
> man's sword against his fellow and against all the army; and the army fled as far as Beth-
> shittah toward Zererah, as far as the border of Abel-meholah, by Tabbath (7.19-22).

(Note the exactness of the time.) The battle is a parody (it might even be called a
travesty, or burlesque) of the conquest of Jericho and the triumphant march of the
Israelites around the city related so straightforwardly in *Joshua.* The author is not ridiculing
the prototype of the parody, but the copy—Gideon's action. (A parody is a type of
parallel, and the reader must be alert to the ways in which the copy alters the original.)

Digression: preposterous acts

One of the most comic things about the book is that there are so many
preposterous acts, such as Gideon's, which make us wonder how they could possibly
have been committed.

They are most entertaining. There's a Rube Goldberg quality to the contrivances
of the characters. Absurdity is a staple of comedy. Only a few interpreters have given
these acts much thought, most commentators possibly being too concerned with
their own interests to question how these acts were accomplished. The interactive
nature of this book cannot be overemphasized. If specific details in each story had
been given by the author, the realism would be interesting, but less funny. What is
amusing is how the readers' imaginations work on these outrageous acts. The whole
book, as it turns out, is a riddle. Samson's is not the only one.

As to how Ehud escaped from the locked room without being detected, Halpern,
as has already been mentioned, suggests that Ehud escaped through the privy
(מסדרון). This possibility is consistent with the excremental nature of the story,
for "the dirt came out" of his intestines when Ehud struck him, and also the
attendants believe that the reason Eglon did not unlock his door is that he was
"covering his feet"—that is, relieving himself (3.22-4) (Halpern 58). This adds to
the scatological humor of the story. Ehud must have been pretty smelly when he
emerged. If Halpern is correct, the privy would also be one of the many "hidden
places" in the book. In *Johnny English*, a recent parody of James Bond movies, the way
that Johnny—a Peter Sellers clone—infiltrates the castle to try to prevent the villain
from becoming King of England, is by climbing up inside the sewage pipe to the
toilet room at the busiest time of day. The toilets above get flushed and he emerges
covered with bad-smelling "poop," the difference being that Johnny goes in, while
Ehud comes out. It is apparently a very very old joke.

Then, could one man really kill 600 Philistines armed only with an oxgoad as Shamgar ben Anat does? Or does this happen only in action films?

The picture of Gideon's 300 men doing their juggling act with jars, torches, and trumpets is amusing to imagine (7.19-20). Shock and awe of an ancient cast. But consider: in order to effect the surprise, the torches could not be lighted until the 300 men were all in position. How was the lighting of the torches done? Were they started from a single flame and lighted one by one along the line of battle? Too slow. The sleeping Midianites might wake up before they all got lighted. Yet how could each man possibly carry his own flame without being detected by the enemy on watch, and wouldn't the flames blow out as the men ran to take position? How big were the torches? Wouldn't they need to be huge in order to throw a huge army into panic? How big were the jars? They would also have to be huge, as small jars would not raise much of a clatter when broken. The author does not explain these things, but takes pains to tell us exactly the order in which the acts were performed and exactly which hand held which object: "They blew the trumpets, and smashed the jars that were in their hands. So the three companies blew the trumpets and broke the jars, holding in their left hands the torches and in their right hands the trumpets to blow; and they cried, 'A sword for Yhwh and for Gideon!'" (NRS 7.19-20). What each man needed was a third hand! But how scared would the Midianites be of a mere 300 men with torches, when the numbers of the Midianites with their camels were massive: as countless as locusts and the sands of the seashore (6.5, 7.12)? And where did Gideon get so many trumpets and jars?[49]

This juggling trick might be compared with Delilah's weaving Samson's hair into the loom. Daniel I. Block imagines that Delilah had Samson lie on the floor while she did it,[50] but in my opinion it would have been easier if he lay on a bed at the same height as the loom. (What mental exercises this book puts us through!) "He awoke from his sleep and pulled up the pin and the loom, with the fabric." Not only is Samson's body strong, but his hair is strong, too (16.15)! And how did she manage to get his locks into the loom without waking him up?

Just how did Gideon identify and round up the elders of Succoth whom he was going to thrash with thorns and briers (8.16), those who had been listed for him by the literate youth (8.14)? Did he call roll?

Another deed that must have taken some skill to manage is the killing of Abimelech's 70 half brothers on "one stone" (9.5, 18). Possibly an armed posse swooped down, and killed the whole group, forthwith, but that would entail having an occasion to bring all the brothers together in once place, as Absalom did when he murdered Amnon (2 Sam 13.28). It might be hard to arrange: since Abimelech went to his father's house at Ophrah and murdered them there, he would not have invited them to a party. The murder is more like an execution than an assassination, because of the fact that the brothers were killed "on one stone." Were they all rounded up, put in shackles, lined up to take their turn, and executed "serially" on a single day, as Block speculates (312)? Or were they brought in one by one over a period of time? And what does "one stone" mean (עַל־אֶבֶן אֶחָת ... יַהֲרֹג) (9.5, 18)? Was it a big broad platform on which all 70 could be struck down at one time (with swords), or was it a small slaughtering stone, such as was used for animals, to which each of the captive brothers was led and beheaded one at a time? Was the execution done single-handedly by Abimelech himself, as 9.5 seems to imply, or by *all* the men of Shechem, or by only the "reckless adventurers" or "worthless and reckless men" whom Abimelech hired (9.4, 18)? On the other hand, "one stone" may merely be a literary device, an inclusio, for at the end of the story, Abimelech is himself mortally wounded with "one stone." Finally, was the assassination of his brothers done out of view, or as a public spectacle, for 9.6 implies an immediate assent by the citizens: "Then all the citizens of Shechem and Beth Millo gathered beside the great tree at the pillar in Shechem to crown Abimelech king"(NIV)? It's a brain-teaser, the kind of problem typical of much humor, even though realistically, a mass murder is very black indeed.

Another problem is how Jephthah, the Gileadite, distinguishes the Ephraimites from the non-Ephraimites by getting them to pronounce the word "Shibboleth" (12.5-6). This involved 42,000 men! It certainly one-ups Abimelech's slaying of a mere 70 brothers. Like the brothers, one can imagine 42,000 Ephraimites lined up in a long queue patiently waiting, while someone at the head of the line questioned each individual and lopped off the head of whoever mispronounced the word. Here's the *real* stumbling block, however: how would a Gileadite ask an Ephraimite to say "shibboleth" without pronouncing it himself? In a way, the word *shibboleth* is another curious weapon.

Like most other readers, Block does not wonder how this was done, but he is stymied by how Samson pulled off the fox trick (441), trapping 300 of them, tying their tails together by pairs, attaching torches, and sending them through the Philistines' fields in order to destroy the fields, orchards, and vineyards (15.5). We have to ask: where and how did he capture so many foxes? How did he bring them to the fields? How did he keep them from running away before he used them? Did he have a great number of cages? If so, how did he get them there? How could he control these wiggly biting creatures long enough to tie their tails together and put lighted torches on them? How did he accumulate and light enough torches? How could the foxes be forced to keep on the right destructive path? Why in "pairs"? Block speculates at considerable length, that it is because "the animals' attempts to separate would force them to zig-zag up and down the fields, and to stop periodically, long enough for the torches actually to light the crops, rather than hurrying off in straight lines and snuffing out the torches." How far could foxes go with torches blazing on their tails? And how straight? Would not the foxes attack each other in an effort to get free? While he was doing all this, how come the Philistines let him do it? Surely once they observed one blazing pair, they would have put a stop to this insanity. How long did the job take? The story gives the impression that this was done in a single act, not over a period of days, or weeks, or months. In any case, was this a rational way to burn fields? The rational way would be to have his henchmen do it. But Samson was a loner. And no one has ever accused him of being rational, to this day. We do not ask questions such as these when watching cartoons. Nevertheless, underlying comedy are just such unanswerable questions.

Another puzzle is how the virgins in Jabesh-Gilead in the last story were distinguished from the non-virgins in order to supply wives for the Benjaminites (21.11-12). All kinds of possibilities might occur to us. Block in all seriousness offers a suggestion: "a rabbinic midrash tells us that each female child was asked the question. If she had slept with a man, her face would pale; if she had not, she would blush" ("as rendered by Milgrom") (575, n.382). A clue as to how it *realistically* could have been done, is found in *2 Samuel*, where we are told that Tamar, who was raped by Amnon, "was wearing a long robe with sleeves; for this is how the virgin daughters of the king were clothed in earlier times" (2 Sam 13.18). But in truth, the author provides no clue as to how this or any other preposterous feat was done. What we are supposed do is to wonder, and brainstorm, and laugh—with a taste of chagrin.

The text is interactive, and in forcing us to imagine how such acts could be perpetrated, the author of *Judges* is providing us with another kind of comic picture or icon. As the many drawings, paintings, films, and scholarly interpretations of these stories demonstrate, we all picture the details differently. Perhaps we might appreciate the comedy more if these stunts were being performed by Charlie Chaplin or Jim Carrey.

Incidentally, this is an example of the kind of "gap" I have mentioned elsewhere. The text puts the reader to the task of supplying the details. The author of *Judges* is forcing us to picture how such feats could be accomplished, and that is part of the humor.

5B. Gideon (continued)

To return to the Gideon story and his "weaponless weapon" (the trumpets, torches, and jars), the real joke is that it is not Gideon who is doing the winning, but (in the author's view) Yhwh. Against the numberless Midianites, Gideon and his 300 men could not have made it alone. But like many another comic hero, Gideon takes the credit. According to the story, Yhwh's very reason for thinning down the ranks is "lest Israel vaunt themselves against me, saying, 'My own hand has delivered me'" (7.2). One hint that Gideon may have "vaunted himself," is given when he rushes to battle and has his men shout: "'For Yhwh and for Gideon'" (7.18) instead of "For Yhwh" alone. Another is the use of his plunder.

Amusingly enough, the trumpets, torches, smashing of jars, and shouting throw the Midianites into a panic, and in their camp, Yhwh (not Gideon) "set every man's sword against his fellow and against all the army" (7.22), suggesting that the Midianites were as cowardly as those "fearful and trembling" Israelites who had taken the easy way out and gone home earlier in the chapter. Many of the Midianites, in fact, are not so much conquered by Gideon in this episode but rather that in their panic they kill each other. That the hoped-for result is ironically brought about by the weakness of the enemy and the cleverness of Yhwh rather than by the hero's strength and power, and that the coward wrongly attributes the success to himself is another source of humor. The main character lacks self-knowledge.

Another amusing incident, and perhaps a fourteenth instance of cowardice, occurs when the contentious Ephraimites challenge Gideon and "upbraid him violently." Appearing to keep his cool, Gideon replies obsequiously: "What have I done now in comparison with you? Is not the gleaning of the grapes of Ephraim better than the vintage of Abiezer?" (8.2). (Compare the obsequious reply of the Timnite's father to the angry Samson [15:2] and Micah's speedy retreat from the angry Danites [18.25-26].) Diplomacy is often disguised cowardice. This is a typical Trickster technique and comic device.

Gideon vaunts himself again (again forgetting Yhwh's warning) when he gets revenge on friendly Manassehite cities. When the towns refuse to grant his demand for bread, he destroys the first town, and in the other town, he "chastises" or "teaches" the offending elders with "thorns of the wilderness and briers" (8.16)—once again, "weaponless weapons." An ingenious Trickster.

Finally, he again vaunts himself with the ephod. Gideon's misuse of plunder, by making the hated ephod, is testimony that Yhwh's fear was well-founded. Could it be that Gideon began to think he was above the Law? The seriousness of this violation of PC religious behavior should correct our vision of Gideon if we have imagined him to be a unalloyed hero.

The last grotesquely "amusing" episode occurs when Gideon orders Jether, his first-born son, to slay the two Midianite kings, Zebah and Zalmunna. We are told that "the youth did not draw his sword; for he was afraid, because he was still a youth" (8.20). The child's fear, as the author explains, is understandable. But is not the son a "chip off the old block"—that is, a coward like his father? Gideon may be vaunting himself once more when he draws his sword, kills the enemy kings, and robs them of their crescents. Though it establishes the genuineness of his nickname, "Hacker," once and for all, the incident cannot be construed as evidence of his bravery, for he was only slaying defenseless captives. Anyone, except perhaps a child, could do that. It took no courage. The humor lies in the irony that it is the enemy kings who show courage, for they say: "Rise yourself, and fall upon us; for as the man is, so is his strength" (8.21). Like Adoni-Bezek, they have noble stature. These—not Gideon— are "the mighty men of valor" (גבור החיל 6.12, 11.1).

The Gideon story illustrates for us the comedy of the character who has one overriding personal trait or habit. In Jacobean drama, comedy of this type is called "the comedy of humors." According to Bergson, comedy seeks to expose human weakness for the purpose of correction. Since the correction must reach as great a number of the audience as possible, it does not focus on *unusual* faults, but rather on *common* human failings (170). Gideon is a coward. But who in his right mind would *not* be scared of those numberless Midianites? Gideon is all the more amusing because we can identify with him, as we do with Charlie Chaplin. As an ordinary man playing hero, Gideon is an antihero.

Finally, a bit of amusement is in store for readers when they discover that the entire Gideon episode is constructed as a series of doublets. Everything happens by twos:

2 named enemies: Amalekites
                 Midianites
2 names for the hero: Gideon
                      Jerubbaal
2 pagan deities: Asherah (Astarte)
                 Baal
2 altars: Yhwh (El)
          Baal
2 altars for Yhwh built by Gideon: on the rock
                                   on the stronghold
2 meat sacrifices: a kid (6.19)
                   the second bull (N.B. not the 1st or 3rd bull) (6.25)
2 threatening mobs: clansmen (angry about altar) (6.30)
                    Ephraimites (angry at being left out) (8.1-3)
2 fleece tests: dew on the fleece, dry on the ground (6.37)
                dry on the fleece, dew on the ground (6.39)
2 ways to reduce size of troops: send the fearful home (7.3)
                                 sift by their way of drinking (7.4)
2 ways of drinking water: putting their hands to their mouths
                          kneeling down to drink
2 terrified armies: Israelites (7:3)
                    Midianites (7:21)
2 people to go down to Midianite camp: Gideon (7.11)
                                       Purah
2 lads with names: Purah, the boy going to the enemy camp
                   Jether, Gideon's eldest son (8.20)
                   (+ one unnamed lad, who wrote down the 77 names)
2 items in dream: bread (7.13)
                  tent
2 actions: blowing trumpets (7.19)
           smashing jars
2 main tribes: Manasseh (Gideon's)
               Ephraim
2 towns needing chastisement: Succoth (8.4, 16)
                              Penuel (8.8, 17)
2 punishments of the towns: chastising with thorns & briers (8.16)
                            breaking down tower, slaying men (8.17)
2 princes of Midian with names of 2 animals: Oreb (wolf) (8.25-6)
                                             Zeeb (raven)

2 kings of Midian: Zebah (8.10)

Zalmunna

2 kinds of plunder: ornaments (8.26)

garments

2 kinds of women: wives (8.30) (presumably Israelite)

a concubine (8.31) (a Shechemite, probably not an Israelite)

There are a few triplets as well:

clefts, caves, strongholds (6.3)

sheep, cattle, donkey (6.4)

jars, trumpets, torches (7.20)

the three lads mentioned above.

The game of doublets in Gideon demonstrates the skill and ingenuity of the author to follow his unvarying rule that all the events must occur twice, without the doubleness being noticeable or irritating to the reader.

There are a number of possible reasons why the author chose to construct the Gideon story in this way:

1. The doublets link the Gideon story with the preceding story of Deborah, which is also twice told—first in prose, then in poetry—and which has its own bizarre correspondences with its "fraternal twin story," Samson. Gideon, too, has parallels with Samson.

2. In Samson, the author plays a game with the number 3; in Gideon, the main number is 2 (the double), though Gideon's 300 men remind us of Samson's 300 foxes. Another link.

3. The doublets are an artificial device, like those in grotesque literature and twentieth century by "black humorists" and postmodernists, who often experiment "with the printed page—incorporating charts and prints, using different type faces and alignments, introducing random factors," etc., in order to "distance us by calling attention to their artifice."[51] It is an "alienation technique."

4. Doubling is a favorite device in comedy: mistaken identities, impersonations, twins, siblings, etc. This kind of comedy existed almost from the beginning, going back at least as far as Plautus and picked up by Shakespeare and other English playwrights and used until the present. In the plays of Oscar Wilde and Noel Coward, for example, according to Seth Lerer, "doubling is the essence of what we would now call the 'camp' sensibility: the recognition that there is always another, seemingly similar version of the same thing or person out there—one live, one dead; one city, one country; one straight, one not; one sincere, one ironic,"[52] and in this case, one coward/one brave, one pious/one idolatrous.

5. The doublets may be a key to the secret code of this story: the author may want us to discover a "duplicity" in Gideon: the coward masquerading as the hero. Or are the doublets simply the artist's exhibitionism?

Gideon *is*, in fact, a bifurcated psyche: after 8.35 and in the story of his son Abimelech, Gideon is always referred to as *Jerubbaal*, never as Gideon. It is conceivable that stories about two different men have been amalgamated and that Abimelech was originally the son not of Gideon but of another man, whose name was Jerubbaal. If so, the amalgamation was seamlessly done. Or more likely, this second name testifies to how seriously Gideon went astray with the ephod in his old age (8.27); it is possible that he reverted to Baalism, since his second name incorporates the theophoric element of the despised Canaanite god, Baal, and also since the temple in the city of Shechem (the city of Gideon's son Abimelech) is the temple of Baal Berith. We must ponder the reason why the author never once uses the name *Gideon* in the story of Abimelech.

Although we have noted three boys in the list of doublets, actually there is a fourth one, but he appears in the Abimelech story. It is Jotham, Gideon's youngest son, in contrast to Jether, who was his oldest. Jether, we have seen, was cowardly, while Jotham is brave enough to shout his fable to the Shechemites. But is he brave? At the end, he "fled, going to Beer, where he remained for *fear* of his brother Abimelech" (9.21) (i.e., fearful like his father and his brother Jether). Thus we have 4 young men (two pairs): two cowardly (Jether and Jotham) and two possibly brave (Purah and the young man of Succoth).

Other grotesque characteristics in the Gideon story: food and drink (there are many references to wine, animal sacrifice, and bread or grain, from beginning to end); strange weapons; disguise or mask (as the use of the trumpets, pots, and torches); and the exaggerated numbers of people killed. The proportions are also exaggerated. Cowardly Gideon and his 300 men are pitted against more than 135,000 Midianites. This is a link with the Micah story where one weak weaponless Ephraimite, Micah, is pitted against 600 Danites "armed with weapons of war" (mentioned 3x). In this latter story, Micah is no Trickster, and a coward; and the story is also significantly not Israelite-against-enemy but Israelite-against-Israelite.

6. *Abimelech* (Ch. 9)

Though it is fairly grim throughout, the tale of Abimelech nevertheless affords some comic relief. The comedy consists mostly of ironies. We also have the following grotesque characteristics: the eating and drinking and cursing in the wine orgy "in the house of their gods" promoted by Gaal ben Ebed, with stolen grapes; the banquet/festival/violation of a religious sanctuary; the challenging of the "son of a king" (Abimelech) by a "son of a servant" (Gaal ben Ebed) (attempted usurpation); and finally the crowning and uncrowning of Abimelech and his comic-grotesque death at the hands of a woman. That he is killed both by a woman (the theme of women as destructive of men) and by a Trickster with her unusual weapon (the millstone) also fits into Bakhtin's scheme. (The woman-with-the-millstone and Abimelech have been discussed in Preposterous Acts and in the section about Jael above.) Some readers, because of their abhorrence of treachery, are likely to be enticed into siding with Abimelech, against this woman and against the intruder, the treacherous Gaal, forgetting that Abimelech is also an intruder and equally treacherous himself, if not more so. Finally, it is comic that the punishment of Abimelech so appropriately fits the crimes he committed. He who killed his 70 brothers *on one stone* is himself killed *by one stone*.

7. *Jephthah* (Chs. 10, 11, 12)

(Jephthah is discussed in Chapters 1 and 4. Here the focus is solely on comedy, but some overlapping and repetition are inevitable.)

Jephthah is one of the main characters who might be considered *tragic* rather than *comic*—perhaps the only one, though to Milton, Samson was profoundly tragic. The story is *comic* in that Jephthah is a typical folk hero who rises from lowly birth (the son of a prostitute), was unappreciated and rejected by his family and brothers, became an outcast of society, sowed his wild oats (with outlaws), but turned out to be the very man the community needed in a crisis. He is brought back, rehabilitated, fights heroically, and becomes the ruler. Horatio Alger, from rags to riches.

But if the main plot shows a man who, through *a tragic flaw* (an error in judgment), inadvertently makes a vow that brings about the death of his only child, Jephthah could be classified as *tragic*, according to Aristotle's definition. On the other hand, he also may be considered *comic* in that he is a man who has only the *appearance* of the heroic, while underneath, he is some (or all) of the following: cowardly, corrupt (making bribes), stupid, absent-minded, and excessively zealous, perhaps even evil. If he is behaving reprehensibly and what we see is the "downfall of a villain," then Jephthah gets his just deserts, and the story is a *comedy*.

Since these two possibilities are in collision, as it were, we must consider both sides of the argument. The following considerations list the ways that he was not tragic, but comic. The story is not an downright knee-slapper, however. It is a black comedy.

The case for Jephthah as parody

The story can be seen as a parody of the Abraham/Isaac story. In a contest about piety, Jephthah comes out the loser. Something was wrong with him, as is proved by the fact that the vowed object was not somehow saved.

The case for Jephthah as boastful, hypocritical, and sanctimonious

Under this heading, Jephthah has one all-consuming desire: to become head. He is willing to offer Yhwh whatever.

It is comic because Jephthah is also sanctimonious—excessive in his zeal, proud of his piety and obedience to Yhwh. Like the Pharisee in the New Testament praying hypocritically in public, Jephthah made the vow perhaps as much to impress others as to get help from Yhwh. He also has materialistic aims. A storyteller might perform him as a Malvolio or a Tartuffe—in that he is a materialist who expects his piety to be of profit. As Francis Landy puts it, "the content of humour [in the Bible] is frequently terrible, centred around man's obsessive preoccupations, sexual failure and fear of death—gallows-humour, smut and the like."[53] Yet Jephthah's obsession with getting it "right" can also be seen as tragic.

It is *comic* in that Jephthah *got what he bargained for*. It is funny because he was so sure of his piety—until it hurt. He regrets it because he does not like the results. The vow was *about* the results; thus he could not change his mind. He goes through with the pretense because he is the arch-hypocrite. He cannot back down. He cannot admit to anyone: I love Yhwh, but not *that* much. This story may be a lesson about not going overboard to demonstrate one's piety.

Grotesque literature is a way of *mocking those in authority*, especially *those who are sanctimonious or legal-minded*. Jephthah, like Malvolio, got his comeuppance.

The case for stupidity and lack of foresight and the case for irony

Because of Jephthah's diplomatic ability with the Ammonites, we infer that he is highly intelligent. He also uses intelligence in finding a way of distinguishing the Ephraimites from the non-Ephraimites. And he was apparently wise enough to judge Israel for six years.

Yet his vow seems stupid. Why did he offer an *unidentified* person or animal instead of a *specific* one? Perhaps he had something else in mind than his daughter, some lesser object—as if that lesser object did not matter. Was Jephthah so obtuse that he did not dream that his daughter might emerge?

Whatever the answer, the vow is comic in that it is ironic. In folktales, when a man is given the opportunity to wish for any three things in the world he desires (Jephthah desires victory and power), if he is stupid, he wishes for the wrong things and ends up with a sausage on his nose. Jephthah is just such a fool.[54] Here Jephthah's stupidity is a link with the stupidity of the character who follows, Samson.

Jephthah as absent-minded

Or perhaps Jephthah is absent-minded, the type of comic character who makes a mistake because he has his mind too fixed on his goal, a person who, in Auden's words, is "ignoring the present for the sake of the future."[55] He has slipped on a banana peel.

One of the functions of *comedy*, according to Bergson, is to teach us to be farsighted about what might result from our impulsive actions. Through humor, writes Bergson, the character is brought back into conformity with his society, whose logic and conventions he abandons when "he slackens in the attention that is due to life" (*EB*, Macro 4, 958). The author of *Judges* is giving the rules of vow-making. Don't be rash.

The case for simple human error and for making excuses

Perhaps Jephthah meant well, but was the victim of the law of unintended consequences.

In a very human way, Jephthah puts the blame for the disaster on the daughter. When she emerges from the house, he exclaims: "*You* have brought me very low!" This is surely comic, as *she* did not choose to make her father miserable.

The case for cowardice

We know that this is a book about a series of "tests" Yhwh devised for the Israelites (2.22) and that they did not pass these tests. Since cowardice is one of the themes of the two preceding stories (Gideon and Abimelech), as well as of the last two stories (Micah and the Levite's Concubine), the Jephthah story may be one more example of this failing. The reason he makes the vow is *to take the stigma off himself if he does not win against the Ammonites*. That is, it will be *Yhwh's* fault—or plan.

On two other counts Jephthah may be considered a coward: first, he was not brave enough to go into battle without making a bargain with Yhwh; and second, he offered to sacrifice *someone else, not himself.* He is like Admetus in Euripides' comedy *Alcestis,* who persuades his wife to die in his place.

We might have more respect for Jephthah's piety if he had offered to immolate himself, instead of an innocent, defenseless child. The Levite in the last story also sacrifices someone else (also a woman, his Concubine), rather than himself. This is cowardice. Take anyone else, but not me, Yhwh!

The case for being on the horns of a dilemma and being too legalistic

One very important source of the comic is the clash between two codes of conduct. In the Jephthah story we are in the characteristic predicament of an audience in comedy—hanging between "two self-consistent but incompatible frames of reference at the same time" (*EB*, Macro, IX, 5).

Jephthah is hanging fire between keeping his vow, or disobeying the injunction against murder. Although it is not really comic that he keeps his vow, it is amusing that even he, who is so legal-minded with the Ammonites, does not know or think about the injunction not to murder, which could have saved his daughter's skin.

His failure as a trickster

A smarter man (or a Trickster) would have found some way to avoid fulfilling a vow which would cause him to make a burnt offering of his only child. Isaac, having given the blessing to the wrong son, managed to call up something so that Esau would not be utterly bereft (i.e., eventually Esau would break the yoke of Jacob's dominion over him) (Gen 27.40). And at the end of *Judges*, the Israelites find a way to give Israelite wives to the Benjaminites, without (or so they think) breaking their vow to Yhwh.

So why does the author not show Jephthah a crumb of mercy and devise a way out of the trap he had built for himself? Folk sayings give us the answer: He had made his own bed. Let him lie in it. Hoist with his own petard.

Other examples of humor in the Jephthah story

Another comic-grotesque element in this story is that the daughter is the burnt offering. She is the "edible" element in the feast. Her destruction is also a kind of dismemberment. Likewise, she may be connected with the origin of a puberty festival such as the Greek festival at Bauron.[56]

Rash vows, parody or travesty, irony, satire, an "uncrowning" (in that the people are led by a man of dubious breeding, one of the "folk"), the wedding (or rather, lack of wedding), the use of the word "shibboleth" as a kind of weapon (i.e., mispronouncing it causes your death), the trickery involved in sorting out the enemy, the testing of both Jephthah and of the reader, and women as a foil to men (i.e., Jephthah's daughter is the pious one, not Jephthah), and the festival for the sacrificed daughter—these are some of the carnival-grotesque elements.

8. *Samson* (Chs. 13-16)

(See Retribution in Chapter 4.)

Though the Samson story is widely regarded as comic, certain intricacies of this humor need to be unpacked.

The theophany at the beginning of the story (Ch. 13) is a parody (or travesty) of the Gideon theophany, which in turn is a parody of its serious prototype, the Abraham and Sarah theophany. In what ways is the one in the Samson story amusing? First, it takes Manoah (but not his wife) an inordinately long time before he trusts the messenger-angel of Yhwh. Samson's parents are depicted as "folk," or peasants—otherwise, why do we find Manoah's wife (Samson's mother-to-be) sitting "in the field" (13.9)? They are simple people, obtuse, and the message must be repeated more than once to Manoah (that his wife will bear a child and that the child must be a Nazirite) before it finally sinks in. After that, they have to confirm that the messenger-angel is indeed authentic. And at the end of the chapter, even after they have seen the miracle of the messenger-angel ascending in the flame of the altar (13.20), Manoah still fears that this visit will be fatal for them. In their peasant ignorance, the couple speculate about whether or not they will now die, having just seen Elohim. The woman's reasoning is charming: would Yhwh have made such an announcement if he intended to kill them (13.23)? The humor rises not because their logic is bad (it is in fact sensible), but that it is so childlike. What would be obvious to any other character in the Bible has to be "figured out" and explained to her husband: the notion that the prophecy could not be fulfilled if they were to die. The stupidity of Samson seems thus to have been inherited from his parents. Ironically, after the divine intervention at the beginning of the story, Samson turns out to be anything but the ideal son. He is no Isaac.

In the next episode (after Samson has violated the Nazirite vow in touching the carcass), the picture of Samson, his mother, and father all eating sticky honey out of their hands as they walk along the road is comic in the grotesque sense. Samson, as we shall soon see, is a monomaniac. Honey symbolizes his mania for sweetness, sweetness especially in women. He becomes obsessed with three women, enemy women at that. Only Philistine women seem to turn him on. Each of them betrays him; but comically, he cannot seem to learn from experience. Women in this story are of the first type mentioned by Bakhtin and like the notorious scarlet women of Proverbs: those who are destructive of men. Like a madman, Samson goes unwittingly and recklessly from one to the other and keeps repeating his mistakes. Monomania and repetition of one's foolishness are the trademarks of comedy. Writes Auden: "A miser is satirizable because his desire for money overrides all other desires, such as a desire for physical comfort or love for his family. The commonest object of satire is a monomaniac" (68). The definition also applies to Jephthah.

In the episode with Samson's Timnite wife, the amusing nature of the riddle, with its sexual innuendos, needs no discussion. Obvious also is his wife's way of wheedling and enticing her husband—the traditional way the male writer thinks women get what they want. We chuckle at the universality of this experience, at the power of sexuality, and more so at Samson's inability to withstand his wife's argument. His anger at being cheated in the riddle contest (especially since he had only himself to blame) and his resourceful way of getting the thirty festal garments and the thirty linen garments to pay off the debt are amusing (though not to the men of Ashkelon), as is the obsequiousness of the father-in-law in dealing with this unrequited and extremely frustrated lover.

The way in which the lunatic Samson vents his rage at not being allowed to "go in to my wife in the chamber" needs careful examination. His logic is that of a madman. When told that she has been given to another man, he immediately remarks: "This time I shall be blameless in regard to the Philistines, when I do them mischief" (15.3). But how blameless is he when, instead of punishing the father-in-law, who if anyone, was the guilty party, he turns around and burns up the fields of the Philistines, who had nothing whatever to do with his sexual frustration?

And what a spectacular way he has of burning them up! Another person might have used flint and a little tow here and there around the fields. But Samson caught 300 foxes and "turned them tail to tail, and put a torch between each pair of tails" (15.4). Quite possibly a Canaanite fertility myth lies behind this scene in *Judges*. According to Soggin, at the annual Roman feast of the goddess Ceres, foxes with torches tied to their tails were apparently released "in the circus or in the fields." At another Roman festival in the same month, reddish puppies were sacrificed so that rust would not infect the fields and to promote fertility.[57] Gaster also mentions this, but misses the point when he remarks that this was "a customary way" to remove mildew from the fields and that the Arabs did this thus to promote fertility.[58] (I have complete skepticism that Arabs ever did this as I have no faith that a fox with a burning tail would remove much mildew. Wouldn't a man with a torch be more reliable?) In any case I would imagine that such a ritual was never so sensational as Samson's performance.

When we see it in the context of this book, however, it is one of those preposterous situations commented on above. Here is a story which requires so much "willing suspension of disbelief" on the part of the reader that we know we have entered the realm of fantasy, a fantasy symbolic of Samson's extreme sexual frustration. This is the third type of caricature mentioned by Wieland, "purely fantastic caricatures or grotesques" in which the writer "disregarding verisimilitude, gives rein to an unchecked fancy . . . with the sole intention of provoking laughter, disgust, and surprise about the daring of his monstrous creation by the unnatural and absurd products of his imagination" (Kayser 30). And it exemplifies Schneegans' definition of the grotesque as "caricature that has reached fantastic dimensions, . . . exaggeration of the inappropriate to incredible and monstrous dimensions" (Bakhtin 306).

The logic of the Philistines in this scene is equally askew. It is comic that the Philistines take revenge not on Samson, but on the Timnite and her father, when it was Samson who burned their fields! Were they so afraid of dealing with Samson that they had to vent their rage on some other object which would not endanger their own lives? But maybe there's an iota of justice here, for it was her father's rash decision to give her away to someone else which had first enraged Samson. (This is also a link both with Jephthah's rash vow and with Caleb's rash act in disposing of his daughter to whomever.) In other words, the punishment finally falls on the offender—though, amusingly, in a roundabout way. But it is comic that Samson, who was mad at the Timnite and her father, now uses the Philistines' revenge on the ex-wife and her father as a pretext for killing more Philistines. The Quixotic logic of the way these characters think, once we have perceived their mental processes, is equal to anything in Rabelais or Cervantes or Lewis Carroll's *Alice in Wonderland*.

Samson is the Trickster par excellence. In addition to his ingenuity with the foxes is his resourcefulness in killing a lion with his bare hands and in using the fresh jawbone of an ass to slay a thousand men. And his prowess when he "took hold of the doors of the gate of the city" of Gaza "and the two posts, and pulled them up, bar and all, and put them on his shoulders and carried them" forty miles away "to the top of the hill that is before Hebron"[59] must make us smile, especially as it is after a night of love-making (16.3). Samson on steroids. In the scene with the foxes, we have the hyperbole of his sexual frustration; while in the scene when he carries the city gates all the way to Hebron, we have the hyperbole for his sexual stamina and hubris.

Also amusing is the variety of women in Samson's life. Again, we see a deliberate downward progression of events:

1. The Timnite was a wife. She betrayed him innocently; no money was involved in her transaction with the Philistines, and she could be said to have acted in own self-defense.

2. The harlot of Gaza was only doing her job; she no doubt got paid. But

3. Delilah, of the valley of Sorek (the wine region of the Philistines) was treacherous; she sold him for 1,100 pieces of silver. It is one thing to play informer to help your own people; it is another to betray a lover for money. She is a Judas.

Samson should have learned from the first experience. Each predicament is worse than the one that preceded it. But by the third woman, he has an exaggerated sense of his own power and his ability to escape with impunity. Delilah tricks him not once but four times. Like his father, he is obtuse. He finally catches on—but only when he is seized. Any man in his right mind would have gotten up and gone home after Delilah deceived him the first time. Samson is a case of all brawn and no brain.

Delilah tries to trick him, but is not a *true* Trickster—first, because she is in no danger herself, and second, it is not with her own wits that she succeeds. She simply follows Samson's suggestions in all that she does. She succeeds by her admirable persistence, as well as greed. "The triple pillar of the world transformed into a strumpet's fool" (*Anthony and Cleopatra*, I.i.13).

No doubt the Samson story rises nearly to a tragic level in the last episode. But if we cannot weep for the Samson of the Bible as we might for the protagonist of *Samson Agonistes*, we should not feel too guilty about it. As Aristotle explains in the passage already cited, the truly tragic figure is a person "who is not eminently good and just, yet whose misfortune is brought about not by vice or depravity, but by some error or frailty" (33). Error or frailty Samson surely had plenty of. But he also had vice and depravity.

And he did not keep his vows. Here is another link with Jephthah: Jephthah kept a vow he should *not* have kept; Samson did *not* keep vows he should have kept. But, we might ask, did *he* make the Nazirite vow himself? Or did his mother? If it was she who made the vow, does *her* vow bind *him*? The answer makes a difference. Hannah also made a vow about her son Samuel, a vow which was kept. Anyway, Samson who had always done what was "right in his own eyes" (the formula for self-indulgence, ever a target for comedy) receives an appropriate punishment in having his two eyes gouged out.

Unexpected appropriateness of an unexpected punishment (an instance of irony) is a source of pleasure, if not of comedy. Very interesting is Bakhtin's comment on the connection of grotesque literature with the Saturnalia, when the uncrowned king becomes a slave. Ancient slaves were sent to the mill for punishment, where they were beaten and made to tread the millstone (198)—like Samson. Samson is the perfect example of the man of prowess who has lost his laurel wreath. It is the uncrowning of the hero.

But even the great final event of martyrdom is not itself without comedy. Though Samson is down and out, blind, being made sport of by his enemies in the house of their god, so helpless that he must be guided by a boy (but not fearful, as Gideon was with Purah—a contrasting parallel), at the end he is still the Trickster. He is as ingenious as ever, and in the house where the Philistines were marking sport of him, he found his greatest, as well as his most unusual, weapon—pillars (16.25). We feel pleasure in this triumph and in the paradox that at his most powerless, he was ironically his most powerful. "So the dead whom he slew at his death were more than those whom he had slain during his life" (16.30). Maybe where women were not concerned, a little brainpower was there, after all. Or maybe the extremity of his predicament enabled him (as Samuel Johnson put it of the man condemned to be executed in the morning) "to concentrate his mind powerfully."

Samson as Trickster

The Samson story is an archetype of Trickster fiction. In the Native American myths, the Trickster is a displaced deity, and (like Samson) is connected with rock and sun. In a Native American myth, the Trickster is represented as being punished by the supreme deity for having brought shame and ridicule upon the gods and is condemned to go to the world and remain there not merely to be without friends but to be hated by all mankind (Radin 165). A loner, Samson (a Danite, we must remember) seems to be feared, and possibly hated, even by the men of Judah, who bind him and turn him over to the enemy. "The Trickster has two types of adventures: the first deals with his self-education, his progress from insecurity to security; the second, with his endeavours to make the earth habitable for man, and with the establishment of man's customs" (166). Samson plays the first role, if not the second, though the Israelites, at the end, might have thought he played the second.

Trickster's primary traits are "his voracious appetite, his wandering and his unbridled sexuality" (167). All these are characteristics of Samson. Trickster is a picaresque hero:

> In a world that has no beginning and no end, an ageless and Priapus-like protagonist is pictured strutting across the scene, wandering restlessly from place to place, attempting, successfully and unsuccessfully, to gratify his voracious hunger and his uninhibited sexuality. Though he seems to us, and not only to us but to aboriginal peoples as well, to have no purpose, at the end of his activities a new figure is revealed to us and a new psychical reorientation and environment have come into being (167-168).

This is exactly like Samson, especially when it comes to his need "to gratify his voracious hunger and his uninhibited sexuality."

Karl Kerényi's comment about the Trickster, when applied to Samson, helps us understand what Samson is doing in the Bible:

> Nothing demonstrates the meaning of the all-controlling social order more impressively than the religious recognition of that which evades this order, in a figure who is the exponent and *personification of the life of the body.*[60] *never wholly subdued, ruled by lust and hunger, forever running into pain and injury, cunning and stupid inaction.* Disorder belongs to the totality of life, and the spirit of this disorder is the trickster. *His function* in an archaic society . . . *is to add disorder to order and so make a whole* . . . (Radin 185, emphasis mine).

(Incidentally, as all the above shows, the Samson story is a macho, not a feminist, narrative, as all grotesque fiction seems to be.)

What figure is more "disorderly" in the Bible than Samson? The trickster story, says Kerényi, shows us "within the fixed bounds of what is permitted, an experience of what is not permitted" (Radin 185). The Trickster has an important role in making the bad world good. Jung, in analyzing the Native American legends, goes even further and attributes a divine aspect to the Trickster:

> *He is a forerunner of the saviour*, and, like him, God, man, and animal at once. He is both subhuman and superhuman, a bestial and divine being, whose chief and most alarming characteristic is his unconsciousness. Because of it he is deserted by his (evidently human) companions, which seems to indicate that he has fallen below their level of consciousness . . . . [Ultimately this falls] away from him; instead of acting in a brutal, savage, stupid and senseless fashion, *the trickster's behavior towards the end of the cycle becomes quite useful and sensible* (Radin 203, 206, emphasis mine).

Here we have an explanation for the typology which sees Samson as a forerunner of Christ. The darker aspects of Trickster have not really disappeared, Jung says, but have withdrawn into the unconscious (206). It has become a "shadow," awaiting an opportune moment to reappear. So too with Samson when he pulls down the temple.

The story of Samson, then, may be seen as a priestly way of keeping control of this "other side" of man's nature. According to Jung, the Trickster myth has a therapeutic effect: "It holds the earlier low intellectual and moral level before the eyes of the more highly developed individual, *so that he shall not forget how things looked yesterday*" (207, my italics). None of these writers—Radin, Jung, Kerényi—was thinking specifically of Samson, yet how well their remarks fit him.

Besides the Trickster, we can list many other examples in the Samson story of Bakhtin's category of grotesque literature, such as the burlesque of the pious person (the Nazirite), sexuality in abundance, the woman as destructive of the male, festivity, wedding and feast, a wedding followed by thrashing and killing, an uncrowning, an ordinary and stupid man as superhero, strange weapons, a large number of killings, numerous bodily references (there are more body parts mentioned in the Samson chapters than in any other story), the dismemberment of both animals and people (lion, ass, Samson), the carnivalesque spectacle at the temple of Dagon (with those on high falling to the bottom), the topsy-turvy (in that the helpless is really the powerful), the use of the number three,[61] etc.

The Samson story is the carnival-grotesque played with all the stops out.

9. *Micah* (Chs. 17, 18)

The last two stories of the book, grisly though they are, are not without humor. The Samson story and the story of Micah (an Ephraimite) with his graven images are carefully linked. Each character behaves stupidly and breaks one or more important laws (i.e., the so-called "natural laws" which are fundamental and elemental to most societies). Samson breaks the Nazirite vow (an apodictic law); Micah and his mother break commandments (also absolute). They do so without self-awareness.

The main characters are strongly contrasted. Samson is brave; but Micah is craven and fearful. Samson is a single Danite who confronts and defeats thousands of

Philistines (the enemy); while in the Micah story, one single Ephraimite (Micah, i.e., not an enemy) confronts, but is defeated by, 600 armed Danites (another inverted parallelism) who ultimately go on to "utterly annihilate" a defenseless town, which the author clearly regards as not dangerous but even friendly. Samson broke his religious vows. Micah violated the prohibition against idols; he was excessive, in that he had four kinds of idols. And the Danites violate one of the rules of holy warfare, not to mention the 2nd and 8th commandments—against graven images and theft.

The main grotesque feature of this story is its burlesque of pious behavior, thus linking it with the Jephthah story. A burlesque is a "literary or dramatic representation that ridicules something, usually the serious and dignified . . . but sometimes the trivial and commonplace . . . by means of grotesque exaggeration or comic imitation" (*Webster's Third New International Dictionary*). What does Micah want the idols for? They are his insurance for prosperity (17.13). The story proves how *in*effective idols can be. The very things that were supposed to protect him against loss of prosperity (against theft) are stolen. Wonderful irony.

No character in this story plays the role of Trickster. This is an important lack. Had Micah been a Trickster, or had he the backing of that Ultimate Trickster, Yhwh, he could have outwitted the Danites in one way or another and kept his priest, if not his images. That he fails no doubt is meant to show Yhwh's disapproval both of the four types of images he acquired (which are mentioned numerous times) and consequently of Micah.

The tale begins with a funny about-face. Money has been stolen from Micah's mother, and she has cursed the unidentified thief, ironically unaware that she is bringing disaster to the one she loves. Micah confesses to his mother: "The eleven hundred pieces of silver which were taken from you, about which you uttered a curse, and even spoke it in my ears, behold, the silver is with me: I took it" (17.2). Immediately upon hearing this, without *aye, yes,* or *no,* the mother replies: "Blessed be my son by Yhwh."

What is going on here? The curse which the mother had spoken was a rash vow. Like Jephthah, her "attention had slackened"—to quote Bergson again. Had she guessed that the thief was her son, she would hardly have uttered a curse. Quickly— as fast as Laurel to Hardy, or Hope to Crosby, or Tinker to Evers to Chance—she now tries to undo the effect of the curse and change it to a blessing. Under the belief-system of this society, however, a curse could not be retracted, any more than Isaac could take his blessing away from Jacob and give it to the rightful heir or than Jephthah could retract his vow. (And this would be important knowledge for the audience to learn.) Possibly one might alter the outcome, but one could not remove it. In this story, the mother did not remove the effect of the curse, for all ended badly after all. One moral of the story might be: be careful whom you curse.

Micah's mother is close to being a Trickster, but she is inept. Superstitiously, Micah's mother tries to bribe Yhwh: "I solemnly consecrate the silver to Yhwh from my hand for my son to make an idol of cast metal" (17.3). But the end of her sentence instantly (ironically) nullifies the effect of her good intention, for "to make a graven image and a molten image" is something that certainly cannot please the Yhwh who gave the Ten Commandments to Moses.

Micah had already broken two of the commandments when he failed to honor his mother and when he stole from her. Now we see a third commandment being broken—graven images. To make matters worse, after boasting what she will do with the silver, it turns out that she gives only 200 of it to Yhwh. She withholds 900 pieces. The humor includes that the errors come in quick succession and that though she is trying to please Yhwh, what she is doing is ironically contrary to what Yhwh might desire. This is rudimentary humor, when the characters build up an elaborate protection system only to see it collapse in an unforeseen way.

Likewise, when Micah installs the Levite as a priest in his house, he says: "Now I know that Yhwh will prosper me, because I have a Levite as priest" (17.13). Bribery again. Could installing a priest nullify the effect of breaking the commandments? This seems unlikely since the commandments are "absolutes." (The usual question arises: were the characters aware of the Deuteronomic law? Even if not, surely the reader or listener was.)

The entire story illustrates another characteristic of comedy observed by Auden: "The comic butt of satire is a person who, though in possession of moral faculties, transgresses moral law beyond the normal call of temptation" (67).

Micah is also a perfect example of the persona in the poem by John Betjeman whom Auden quotes:

> Although, dear Lord, I am a sinner,
> I have done no major crime;
> Now I'll come to Evening Service
> Whenever I have time.
> So, Lord, reserve for me a crown,
> And do not let my shares go down (69).

The picture of the Levite priest in the Micah story standing idly by, as the Danites decide to steal the images that they covet (another commandment being broken, bringing the total up to four—or five, if the mother's curse is a violation of the commandment not to misuse the name of Yhwh) is especially amusing when one considers how helpless the priest would have been against the Danite force in preventing it:

> While the six hundred men of the Danites, armed with their weapons of war, stood by the entrance of the gate, the five men who had gone to spy out the land proceeded to enter, and take the idol of cast metal, the ephod, and the teraphim [and the molten image], while the priest and six hundred men armed with weapons of war stood at the entrance to the gate (NRS, 18.16-17).

No wonder the Levite aids and abets the crime and goes along with the Danites. So that we will not fail to notice the vulnerable position of the priest, the author gives us a neat inclusio and tells us twice—once before the objects are stolen and once afterwards—that there were 600 Danites standing there armed with weapons of war.

600 armed Samsons, we might remind the reader. What could a little Levite priest do? Was this not intimidation?

When the Danites persuade him that he should come along on their migrating expedition, they seduce him with visions of sugar plums dancing in air: "Is it better for you to be priest to the house of one man, or to be priest to a tribe and family in Israel?" (18.20). (Is the correct answer to this question "yes" or "no"?) This makes "the heart of the priest glad." He has had a delusion of grandeur—a favorite target of folk humor. But is this any justification for stealing, i.e., breaking one of the commandments—especially by a priest? Amusing, too, are Micah and his neighbors, chasing so boldly after these Danites at first, then promptly returning home with their tails between their legs:

> When they were some distance from the home of Micah, the men who were in the houses near Micah's house were called out, and they overtook the Danites. They shouted to the Danites, who turned around and said to Micah, "What is the matter with you that you come with such a company?" He replied, "You take my gods which I made, and the priest, and go away, and what have I left? How then can you ask me, 'What is the matter?'" And the Danites said to him, "You had better not let your voice be heard among us, or else hot-tempered fellows will attack you, and you will lose your life with the lives of your household." Then the Danites went their way. When Micah saw that they were too strong for him, he turned and went back to his home (NRS, 18.22-26).

Micah is no Samson.

There is not much humor in the rest of the story; it can hardly be considered amusing that the Danites continue on in their bullying way and wipe out an undefended and powerless people. But a serious message emerges from the comedy. If Micah can be said to stand for the tribe of Ephraim, this tribe has again been shown to be reprehensible: it is materialistic, immoral, physically weak, and cowardly. And the Danites are thieves, bullies, and idolaters.

10. *The Levite's Concubine; the Punishment of Benjamin* (Chs. 19-21)

In the last story, the prevailing mood seems at first to be tragic. But this is because the comedy is "black." As for grotesque characteristics, this story has them all: brutality, sexuality, feasting, carousing, wine, dismemberment, degradation, license, thrashings, beatings, killings, travesties, etc.

As is true of the story of Adoni-Bezek and really of all the stories in the book, however, the comedy cannot be fully perceived until the story is viewed in all its complexities and seen against the entire book of *Judges* as well as of the Law ("natural" or otherwise) (see Chapter 4).

The Carousing Scene between the Concubine's father and the Concubine's husband (the second Levite) (19.4-9) begins amusingly because of the way the good-natured father-in-law, in bonding with his son-in-law, prevails upon the Levite to "spend the night and let your heart be merry" night after night after night until eventually, on the fifth day (the author carefully counts the days for us), the Levite delays so long that it is too late in the day for any person in his right mind to depart. (Again, notice the explicit reference to the time of day, as is common in this book.)

The cowardly behavior of the Levite in Gibeah when the base men surround the house is comic because it is a parody, or even a travesty (i.e., a debasement), of the Lot story with significant differences. (See Chapter 1.) Part of the joke is on the reader who does not see what is really going on, that the Levite is not out to save two messenger-angels, as in the Lot story, *but to save himself.*

Also comic is the irony that in the feud and civil war that develop, "all-Israel" is as much to blame as the tribe of Benjamin. True, the Law states: "You shall extirpate evil from your midst." But the Israelites make three mistakes. First, their revenge is excessive. The Law clearly states "an eye for an eye," as the author has carefully pointed out in the first story of the book—the punishment of Adoni-Bezek. Second, the Israelites make a rash vow and, like Micah's mother, seek to repudiate it directly. Third, they ironically permit the Benjaminites to commit the same lawless act at the end of the story that they were punishing them for at the beginning!

That the Israelites (like the Danites of the preceding story) have inquired of Yhwh (20.18) does not alter this interpretation. Boling (who is looking at this as history, not fiction) thinks that the Israelites made the mistake of using "archaic institutions" (277)—i.e., using the *ban* against *Israelite* towns. Other commentators have questioned the authenticity of the inquiry. But what happens afterwards is so clearly wrong that we must question whether the author himself thought Yhwh backed the war. One possibility is that the inquiry is improper. Another is that a later redactor inserted the inquiry in order to make the operation seem *kosher.*

In the first inquiry, the Israelites simply asked, "Who shall go up first?" They got their answer: "Judah." But maybe they asked the wrong question. Had they asked, "Shall we fight against Benjamin?" the answer might have been "No." Then they would have tried to find another way of taming the Benjaminites. (Perhaps Jephthah should have inquired of Yhwh, "Do you want me to sacrifice my daughter?")

In the second inquiry of Yhwh (20.28), they *do* ask whether they should continue to fight against their brothers, the Benjaminites, or whether they should desist. The answer is that they should continue, for Yhwh has given the Benjaminites into their hands. It was now too late for the Israelites to withdraw.

The comedy of the last chapter consists of the Israelites' rash vow (discussed in Chapter 4). The Israelites had sworn in one moment: "No one of us shall give his daughter in marriage to Benjamin" (21.1, meaning the tribe of Benjamin). But in the very next sentence, when they realize that this means that the Benjaminites will not have good Israelite wives, they sit down and weep pitifully, asking, "O Yhwh, the God of Israel, why has this come to pass in Israel, that there should be today one tribe lacking in Israel?" (21.2-3). They seem utterly unaware who was to blame. Like Jephthah, and like children, they do not seem to be able to connect cause with effect. It is another case of faulty logic and of characters "ignoring the future for the sake of the present" (Auden 60) or of slackening "in the attention that is due to life" (*EB* Macro 4, 958).

It reminds one of a play by Aristophanes or Molière, in which the characters have a "happy idea" in the first scene, but in the very next scene, the law of unintended consequences sets in. In Aristophanes, the "typical hero is a dyspeptic old man who gets fired up by an idea and in pursuing it, turns the world topsy-turvy."[62] The "happy idea" of the women in *Lysistrata* is that in order to stop the war, the women, who have no power at all in that society, except the power of sex, will issue an ultimatum to their husbands: either make peace with Sparta, or the women will stage a sex strike. The ultimate result of the happy idea is that *everyone* is miserable. The misery ends only when all reconcile and exit to a feast of revelry.

The happy idea to solve the Israelites' dilemma in Ch. 21 comes not from Yhwh, but from themselves. The Israelites play the Trickster role: they find a way out of their self-contrived trap, to do something that they have vowed not to do—give good Israelite wives to the Benjaminites—without violating their rash vow. Here, too, is a link with the Micah story. Like Micah's mother, they are trying to undo the effect of a curse, for violation of a vow brings on a curse.

What is funny is that the Israelites in their zeal are oblivious to the fact that not only have they invented a fairly preposterous way of supplying wives (it is like the "wrong logic" from Aristophanes' *The Clouds*), but also their method of doing so *contradicts* their moral case against Benjamin. Though on a literal, realistic level, it is no more amusing that Jabesh-Gilead is utterly destroyed than that the city of Laish was annihilated (18.27), the Israelites have a reason— which they construe as valid—for declaring a ban on Jabesh-Gilead: it did not respond to the muster.

While Jabesh-Gilead may have been wrong, the punishment of the city was a worse wrong: first, it was surely excessive, and second, the *ban* (or *herem*, i.e., the complete destruction of a town according to the rules of Holy War) was not intended to be applied to Israelite towns, but to Canaanite towns. What the author wants to show us is the extreme to which these people will go. It is the comedy of exaggeration and of paradox. One smiles despite oneself.

The last ruse is sheer comedy (though perhaps not for the daughters of Shiloh):

> And they said, "There must be heirs for the survivors of Benjamin, in order that a tribe be not blotted out from Israel. Yet we cannot give any of our daughters to them as wives." For the Israelites had sworn, "Cursed be anyone who gives a wife to Benjamin." So they said, "Look, the yearly feast of [Yhwh] is taking place at Shiloh . . . ." And they instructed the Benjaminites, saying, "Go and lie in wait in the vineyards, and watch; when the young women [daughters] of Shiloh come out to dance in the dances, then come out of the vineyards and each of you carry off [seize] a wife for himself from the young women [daughters] of Shiloh, and go to the land of Benjamin" (21.17-21).

From the point of view of males in the audience of *Judges*, this might be considered a merry carnivalesque scene, especially if we imagine all the participants to have first partaken of a goodly amount of new wine at the festival, and even more amusing if we imagine each of these crude left-handed Benjaminites to be an Ehud with a difference. Another source of amusement is to imagine that Saul's mother was a young woman from Shiloh or Jabesh-Gilead and that Saul was the offspring of one of these wild Benjaminites. Surely the connection was clear, though perhaps not so amusing, to the ancient audience. But it certainly supplies an explanation for Saul's failure as a king.

The final touch is the Israelites' charming way of reasoning (the equivalent of that of Manoah and his wife in the Samson story) when they say:

> "Then if their fathers or their brothers come to complain to us [contend with us], we will say to them, 'Be generous and allow us to have them; because we did not capture in battle a wife for each man. But neither did you incur guilt by giving your daughters to them." (NRS, 21.22).

That is, if the fathers or the brothers of these girls get angry at the way their daughters and sisters have been seized, the Israelites will say to them: "It could be worse. After all, we *could* have *seized* your women in *battle*. Or you might have had to *give* your daughters to these Benjaminites, breaking your vows in the process. Come on now, be polite."

On a realistic level the rape is repulsive to us and must have been repulsive to the ancient Israelites *who reacted so violently, after all, to the rape of the Concubine.* Yet the ending is presented as a merry one.

The humor consists not of the actual rape, but of the *paradox* of the cause of the civil war: that the Benjaminites raped *one* woman (who was not a virgin), while at the end, the very people who are punishing them are now ironically aiding and abetting them in abducting and raping *600 virgins*—400 from Jabesh-Gilead and 200 from Shiloh.[63] Not only did these Benjaminites learn nothing from the lesson taught by the Israelites; it was the Israelites themselves who reprogrammed them, and were now condoning the behavior that they had first punished them for. The joke is on the reader. The author makes us loathe the multiple rape of the one girl, but tricks us into countenancing the seizing of the 600 screaming and kicking innocent virgins—all of these women, it might be remarked, *representative of the innocent victim, Jephthah's daughter.* Thus we wonder if, after all, it was such a bad thing that Jephthah's daughter died without knowing a man or that the Timnite was burned to death. Some fates are perhaps worse than to be a burnt offering. It is marvelous sleight-of-hand trick by the author.

There is perhaps another irony here. This festival at Shiloh should remind us of the one instituted to commemorate the death of the daughter of Jephthah, who had not "known a man." At the end of this book, 600 virgins are about to be forced to "know a man."

The reader's common misreading of this scene says something important about our social attitudes toward rape. The author is testing our knowledge of the Law. If you are among those who guffaw and slap your thighs in laughter, you will earn his eternal scorn. But laugh with a tug of blackness in your heart, and he will recognize you as his fellow. If we have any doubts about this interpretation, contrast the raucous ending of this book with the dignified ending of *Joshua* and its celebration at the assembling of the tribes to hear the covenant. The ending of *Judges* should not be funny, yet it is.

After all the preceding slaughter, the book concludes with a "merry" drunken sexual orgy at the wine festival at Shiloh. Like most comedies, this one ends with marriage—many marriages. This story culminates in an energetic *gamos*, though it is hardly a *hieros gamos*. It is a huge fertility rite. "The world must be peopled!" cries Benedick at the end of *Much Ado About Nothing*. The tribe will be replenished with a generation of baby boomers. "In a fundamental sense every comedy is a thinly disguised re-enactment of the rebirth of the world," writes Erich Segal (13). Tragedy moves toward death, comedy toward the continuing of life. Comedy reintegrates everyone back into society. That is why comedies end in marriages.

Dionysus, who was the titular god of Greek drama as well as of wine, also rules here. The final scene of *Judges* should bring to mind the Dionysian orgies, the religious origins of Greek drama and the Satyr plays, and the comedies of Aristophanes (with their licentious sexuality), given at just such wine festivals as this. It is also, of course, the Rape of the Sabine women in Roman legend, as well as the Roman Saturnalia, with all the carnivalesque license which, according to Bakhtin, lies behind grotesque comedy. Of one of the wedding episodes in *Gargantua and Pantagruel*, Bakhtin. in a marvelous passage, writes:

> This is the "Vineyard of Dionysus," the vendenge, the feast of the grape harvest . . . . Beyond *the blood-saturated mass of torn bodies* . . . [is given] a glimpse of the vats of that purée septembrale (September-pulp) so often mentioned by Rabelais. *Blood is changed into wine* . . . . *Bloodshed, dismemberment, burning, death, beatings, blows, curses, and abuses— all these elements are steeped in "merry time."* . . . The figure of propitious time symbolizes in folklore the end of evil days and advent of general peace. For this reason Rabelais develops a popular utopian theme: the *triumph of peaceful labor* [the vineyard] *and abundance over war and destruction* (211, 227-8, my emphasis).

Battles are followed by weddings. This incredible description applies perfectly to the seizing of the daughters of Shiloh. The story of the Levite's Concubine is "black humor" or "savage comedy," which uses humor to attack evil. "Rapacity is one hallmark of savage comedy," writes Kenneth Steel White in *Savage Comedy Since King Ubu: A Tangent to 'Absurd.'*[64] Like scenes in another famous black comedy, Joseph Heller's *Catch-22*, the humorous scenes of *Judges* are always profoundly ambivalent and deeply disturbing.

Judges as a whole is Dionysian. Disorder rules, but throughout there is a longing for order, the rule of Apollo. Can we find Apollo here? (See Chapter 4.)

When we read this book as simple history about great heroes, we are offended by its horrors and find the book abhorrent. When we discover that many episodes are comic, we no longer feel that we are being force-fed with hateful medicine. We can relax and enjoy it. *Judges* has been redeemed.

But there are deeper mysteries yet to be explored.

Appendix 1. Translations of Keywords in the Story of the Concubine

In the following paraphrase of the story of the Levite's Concubine, I give literal translations of the Hebrew words. A comparison of significant words (in italics) in four translations follows the Notes below. Readers may judge the translations for themselves.

The scene: the Ephraimite is plying his new guest, the Levite, with food and drink in his house at night (unless otherwise noted, translations are mine, using present tense).

Paraphrase of Lines

19.22 While they are enjoying themselves, *evil men* (בני־בליעל, sons of Belial) surround the house, *pound* on the door, and tell the old man [the Ephraimite] to bring out his guest so that they can *know* (ונדענו) him [have intercourse with the Levite].

19.23 The Ephraimite goes out to them and says, "Do not be *evil* (אל־תרעו), . . . do not do this *outrage* (הנבלה)."

19.24 The Ephraimite offers to *bring out* his own *virgin* daughter and the Concubine. "You can *abuse* (ענו, rape) them, do to them *whatever seems good in your own eyes*, but don't do this *outrage* (הנבלה)."

19.25 The base men do not want to listen to [the old man]. Then [the Levite] *seizes violently* (יחזק) his Concubine and *takes (puts) her outside to them* (ויצא אליהם החוץ). The men *know* her (ידעו) and *cut her down* (יתעללו; see also 20.45 NRS trans.) *all night* until *morning* and let her go at *dawn* (שחר).

19.26 At *the break of morning* she goes back to the door and *falls down* and *lies* there until [*day*] *light*.

19.27 When her master gets up in the *morning* . . . there *lies* his Concubine *fallen* at the door of the house, with her hands on the threshold.

19.29 When the Levite reaches home with his dead Concubine, he *cuts her up* into 12 *cut-pieces* and sends *her* to all the areas of Israel. When the Israelites see this, everyone says:

19.30 "Such a thing has *never been seen or done*, not since the Israelites came up out of Egypt" (NIV trans.)

20.3 When the Israelites assemble, they say to the Levite: "Tell us how this *evil* happened." [This pretext allows the author to repeat the story, with a number of charged words.]

20.4-5 The Levite—now called "the husband of *the murdered woman*"—tells that the men of Gibeah intended to *kill him*, but they *raped* (ענו) her, and *she died*. (KJV has "the woman who was *slain*)

20.6 He tells how he *cut her up* and sent her out to all the territories because [the Gibeahites] had committed this *act of unchastity* (זמה) and *outrage* (נבלה).

20.8 All the listening Israelites rise *as one man* and vow not to go home until the Gibeahites are dealt with.

20.10 They want the army to do to [requite] Gibeah of Benjamin [as they deserve] for all the *outrage* (נבלה) they did in Israel.

20.12 They go to Gibeah and ask the people: "What is this *evil* (הרעה) that was done among you?"

20.13 They demand that the city turn over [i.e., let the Israelites extradite] the *worthless men* (בני־בליעל) so that the Israelites may *put them to death* (נמיתם) and *burn out the evil* (רעה) from Israel. But the Benjaminites refuse. This is the cause of the war against the Benjaminites that follows.

Notes

19.22 "Enjoying themselves" (המה מיטיבים את־לבם) is a euphemism for "getting drunk." This euphemism is repeated six times between 19.3-22 to make sure we do not overlook what is happening. Biblical writers, says Carey Ellen Walsh, do not distinguish between *drinking* and *intoxication*.[65] (See Chapter 3, Subcategory: Wine and Intemperance.) *Men of Belial* (בני־בליעל) probably means *Sodomites*. The context tells us these are disgusting, obscene, threatening, worthless, base, wicked, perverse, evil men. The word is echoed by the 4 uses of *outrage* (נבלה) and may be intended to connect them with the followers of Baal.

19.22, 25. *To know* means *to have sex*. These are the only places in *Judges* where this euphemism is to be found.

19.25. KJV and NRS have "The men of Gibeah *abused* her." A more violent word than *abuse* is required here. The Hebrew is יתעללו, a metaphor referring to *evil practices* (2.19, ממעלליהם); literally, עלל means "gleaning" of the vineyards (8.2, BDB 760); it is translated as the "cutting down" of the Benjaminites in battle (NRS 20.4-5).

19.24. ענה, *abuse, afflict*, means *rape*.

19.23, 24; 20.6, 10 *outrage* (נבלה). The *outrage* is not against the Concubine, as we modern readers would surmise, but against the Levite. The old man and the Levite thrust her out in order to *avoid outrage* against themselves. They seem to consider the rape of the Concubine a lesser crime than sodomy. NEB may be confirming this when it describes the Levite as "the man to whom the murdered woman belonged" (20.4) (i.e., his property) instead of "the husband of the woman who was slain (or murdered)" (האיש הלוי איש האשה הנרצחה). Or perhaps NEB was reluctant to call the Concubine's master her *husband*. Though she is usually called the *Concubine*, she is also referred to as *wife* (or *woman*?) in this story.

19.25. The men do not want to listen to the old man's request. In 20.13 the Benjaminites again, this time as a whole, will not listen when the Israelites ask them to turn the criminals over to them. We need to catch on to this *deafness*. Had the Benjaminites been at all "reasonable," the war might have been avoided.

19.25, 26, 27. Through 6 mentions of *morning* (given in various ways) and one mention of the *abuse* having lasted *all night long* (19.25), the length of time is being hammered in. The word *fall*, as has already been pointed out, can also mean *fall dead*, the meaning it usually has in battle scenes. It is particularly poignant that the Concubine falls with her hands on the threshold—close enough, one would think, to have aroused someone within to come to her aid. Her position suggests that she made one last pitiful plea, with no response.

19.30.   Presumably a long time (since the Israelites had come up out of Egypt); thus the remark shows how unusual and terrible the crime was.

20.5.   The Levite seems to be establishing that the Concubine was already dead when he dismembered her. Some scholars think that the Levite himself killed her, perhaps reasoning that after the rape, she would presumably be useless to him as a wife. *And she died* is not in 19.26, as it is in 20.5. It is not explicit that the men of Gibeah actually killed her or caused her to die. The reader assumes that she is dead, however, and that it was her corpse that the Levite laid across the back of the donkey.

　　　　Some interpreters think she was placed alive on the donkey. If the Levite killed her after he got her home, however, I believe the author would have told us, though this cannot be proved. That would be murder, and the author would have had to bring up this charge against him. Even if she *was* dead, did the Levite have a right to desecrate her body by cutting it up into pieces? This is the question we must try to answer.

20.6.   The word for *unchaste act* (זמה) is mentioned 3x in Leviticus and concerns the sexual abuse of women.

Variations in Translations

	author's language	NIV	NRS	NEB
19.22	making their hearts merry*	enjoying themselves	enjoying themselves	enjoying themselves
	men of Belial	wicked men	base fellows	scoundrels
	pounded on door	pounded on the door	beat on door	hurled themselves against the door
	said	shouted	said	shouted
	know	have sex	have intercourse	have intercourse
19.23	not be evil	not be vile	not act wickedly	do nothing wicked
	outrage	disgraceful thing	vile thing	outrage
19.24	rape (עוה) them	use them	ravish them	rape them
	do the good in your eyes	do whatever you wish	do whatever you want	do whatever you please
	outrage	disgraceful thing	such a vile thing	outrage
19.25	seized, violently	took hold of	seized	took hold of
	brought her out**	sent her out	put her out	thrust her outside
	knew her	raped her	raped her	abused her
	cut her down	abused her	abused her	assaulted her
20.3	the evil	awful thing	criminal act	wicked thing
20.5	raped (עוה)	raped	raped	raped
20.6	unchaste act and outrage	lewd and disgraceful act	vile outrage	filthy outrage***
20.10	outrage	vileness	disgrace	outrage

*as stated above, *making hearts merry* probably means *getting drunk*

**In Hebrew, the implication is that she resisted strongly.

***NEB uses *filthy outrage*, combining *unchaste act* and *outrage* into one expression.

By comparing the keywords of several translations with the literal words that the author used, we can begin to see how the philosophy of the translator affects the meaning. The translators try to convey the horror but do it in different ways.

144   Intricacy, Design, & Cunning in the Book of Judges

Appendix 2. Meanings of Names[66]

Abdon	servile[67] service
Abinoam	"my father is delight" or "Darling of my father (epithet in Ugarit)
Abiezer	father of help (God of my father will help)[68]
Achsah	anklet; bangles[69]
Adoni-Bezek	lord of Bezek [zedek=righteousness]
Aijalon	deer
Akrabbim Pass (1.36)	scorpion
Anak	long-necked, necklace [the ancient giant people are also called long-necks]
Asher	happy one; of Asherah
Barak	lightning
Benjamin	son of the right hand
Caleb	dog
Cushan-rishathaim	Superblack double villain[70]
Dan	judge, a function of the sun god in antiquity[71]
Deborah	honey bees
Delilah	of the night;[72] diminishing;[73] related to Arabic word "to flirt,"[74] falling curl" or "be humble"[75]
Ebed	servant (in the name of Gaal ben Ebed)
Eglon	calf-like; young bull, fat calf (Boling 85)
Ehud	Where's the splendor? God of praise (Block 160)
Elon	oak; terebinth
Ephraim	fruitfulness
Etam	place of birds of prey[76]
Gaal	contempt, loathing[77]
Gershom	exiled
Gilgal	circle
Gibeah	hill
Gideon	hacker
Hakkore	caller (Spring of the Caller, formerly Partridge Spring)
Harod	trembling
Heber	association; comrade (Radday, 67); friend
Ibzan	swift (Block 388)
Jabesh	dry
Jabin	he understands; yoke
Jael	mountain goat [Athtart is also called "wild goat"][78] or "she who goes up"[79]

Jair	may [God] enlighten
Jephthah	set free; Yhwh opens[80]
Jerubbaal	let Baal contend (strive)
Jether[81]	one who is superior (Radday 67); abundance
Joash	given by God
Jonathan	given by God (Block 511)
Joshua	salvation
Jotham	Yhwh is perfect (honest, blameless)
Laish	lion
Lehi	jawbone
Luz	deception
Machir	sold
Manoah	rest, freely giving[82]
Micah	who is like Yhwh
Oreb	raven
Othniel	my strength is God
Phinehas	negro
Purah	bud, sprout
Rephaim	giant
Samson	man of the sun,[83] sunny.
Shaalbim	foxes
Shamgar	sword
Shechem	shoulder
Sheshai	princely
Sisera	leader
Talmai	make furrows
Tola	worm
Zalmunna	shadow, protection refused[84]
Zebah	sacrifice, sacrificial victim (idem)
Zebul	high, exalted; habitation;[85] big shot (Boling 175), prince
Zeeb	winepress

Chapter Three

HIDDEN OBJECTS: WRESTLING WITH ANOMALIES, SOLVING THE ENIGMA

The trick is not to arrange a festival. The trick is to find people who can enjoy it.

—Nietzsche

Man plays only when he is in the full sense of the word a man, and he is only wholly Man when he is playing.   —Schiller

It is the glory of God to conceal things, but the glory of kings to search things out.

—Proverbs 25.2

Patience, and shuffle the cards.   —Cervantes, *Don Quixote*

I. The Categories

Though a minimalist, the author of *Judges* was not a mere primitivist, using his folk legends carelessly and clumsily; he was a conscious craftsman with an ambitious aim. He was thinking like a lawyer. He seems to have believed that no single action stands alone; that it is always connected with other actions, and that we cannot understand any single situation in isolation from others, but must constantly make comparisons and contrasts between situations in order to make judgments about them.

The author created a design that would enable him to take ten different stories, including two of the "short shorts" in the Introduction, and judge them (like law cases) with all their ramifications, thoroughly and completely in the smallest possible space, but without forcing his own judgments upon the readers. The book seems designed to make readers reach their own conclusions. Every part of every story has a relationship with every part of every other story, offering new perspectives and, consequently, different insights with each story. Possibly even the author himself was not fully aware of the extent to which these comparisons could be made.

146

An art game

In a sense, the author of *Judges* is playing a game of designs—a game of horror and humor, a game of hidden things, and a game of law or ethics. The book is full of puzzles and riddles for us to solve. Solving puzzles and riddles is play. As Johan Huizinga wrote in *Homo Ludens* (1938), a long scholarly study of play, games are the basis of culture, and play-activity is a voluntary activity which absorbs the player but which exists outside of everyday life. "The play-concept is of a higher order than is seriousness. For seriousness seeks to exclude play, whereas play can very well include seriousness." We could view all culture *sub specie ludi.*[1] In fact, we all play games, whether we are conscious of it or not. This is true of biblical scholars, who are trying to unlock the secrets hidden in the Bible.

The pieces used in the game

Here is the game plan of *Judges:* elaborate relationships among hundreds of objects, with all kinds of parallelisms and symmetries, but *with stories so compelling that the general reader is not aware of the author's contrivances.* Undoubtedly these objects affect us subliminally, but once discovered and analyzed, they provide us with important data about the characters, the society, and the nation.

The game was for small groups of admirers or students, who played the game continually, endlessly discussing the right and wrong in each action and situation of each part of the story. The group would be a kind of jury, debating, and their leader would be the judge, though if anyone then or now could make definitive judgments in any of the cases, is difficult to imagine. We are left, at the end, with as many questions as answers—as in scientific inquiry. In a book review in the *New York Times* about the Super Computer, the question is asked: "But when the computation is over, how do you read the results? Since you started with a great big mixture of questions, you're left with a great big mixture of answers. And quantum theory says you can't see each of them individually."[2] That is what we have in this study: a great big mix of both questions and answers and the inability to see completely what is going on. In *Judges* we are impelled to continue until the answers finally become clear to us. (See Chapter 4 for law and ethics.)

Whether the ancient author of *Judges* ever achieved any kind of recognition for his intricate design, we cannot know. But I believe the Deuteronomic editors knew that the book *had a secret message that could be deciphered by this method*: Look for and study the hidden objects.

How do we play the keyword game? The author has hidden many objects in the dense texture of his material and is asking us to find them. This is like being in a scavenger hunt. After one has found an object, one must *collect* all the other objects in its category and *analyze* the list in order to determine how the relationships of every object with all the others produce new information to be used in interpreting each story individually. An important difference between this scholarly game and typical biblical scholarship is that we are looking not only at each story in a linear fashion from beginning to end, but also at the book *as a whole, interpreting all the actions as if they were happening simultaneously.* (See **Appendix 2** of this chapter for "The Rules of the Game.")

The categories in Ugaritic myths and in Judges *compared*

The Ugaritic myths contain a large number of objects, which can be fitted into general categories. The chief Ugaritic categories are: Kinship Relationships, Animals, Nature, Food, Drink, Body Parts, Buildings, and Places.[3] In the myths, however, the words have no literary function; they don't relate to each other; but seem merely to testify to the author's pleasure in the use of specific language. In *Judges*, however, they are crucial to our understanding of the meaning of the stories.

A number of these same categories are found in *Judges*. One of the most substantial categories in *Judges* is *Kinship Relationships*, represented with an unbelievable number of different items. The category of *Animals* consists chiefly of agricultural animals, especially the ass, but it also includes a bird, a few insects (locusts, a scorpion, and by implication, a spider [Delilah with her web]), but no fish, or snakes—which are found in the myths—and a number of wild animals, which are not found in the myths. Many more *Body Parts* (including *Hands*) than in the myths are strewn throughout *Judges* from place to place, with almost all the body parts being mentioned in the Samson story. Whereas in the myths most of the food is the meat and wine consumed by the gods in their banquets, in *Judges* the *Food and Drink* category concentrates on food of ordinary people: grain, produce from orchards, meat, water, and bread and wine, with mentions of milk and honey.

In contrast to the Ugaritic tales, Nature receives little attention in *Judges*—except for the mention of trees, springs, rivers, caves, mountains, and one storm, and then never as an object of beauty, as in the myths, but as utilitarian signposts in the plot. Geography is important in both. Many of the geographical references in the myths are mythical, but a few references to actual places are given from time to time. In the Israelite stories, the author gives the impression that he is speaking of real sites when in fact these are sometimes hard to locate. And though he seems to be talking about *all* the tribes of Israel, the action is mainly limited to the tribes and territory of Manasseh, Ephraim, Dan, Benjamin, and Gilead, with Judah receiving very slight, though significant, attention.

In addition, *Judges* contains the following categories: Agriculture, Tools, Instruments, Vehicles, Fabric, Building Parts (like Doors and Rooms, Entrances and Gates, Open/Shut, Inside/Outside), Containers, Water, and Invitations and Hospitality, among others. These will be discussed in the present chapter. The significant categories of Warfare and Strange Weapons; Mutilations; and Destruction (seizing, smiting, tearing apart, demolishing, etc.) were discussed in Chapter 2. The categories having to do with Evil and Good, as well as Anger, Concealment (including Hidden Things, Secrets), Vows, and Retribution, among other related topics, will be discussed in Chapter 4 under the rubric of ethics and law.

Unlike the Ugaritic texts, the objects in *Judges* are fundamental to meaning and are intimately related to each other. For example, the Food and Drink theme is connected to Invitations, Requests, and Hospitality; and both are connected to Containers. Containers are connected to Hiding Places, for the author regards hiding places as containers of sorts: a prison, for example, contains a prisoner, a den contains an outlaw, a winepress contains an Abiezrite who is threshing grain, etc. Hiding Places are connected to Ambushes, Spies, Secrets, and Riddles and also to Buildings, and so on. To get an idea of what is going on here, examine the scene in which Jael (in a tent) throws a covering or rug over Sisera. The outcome of the story of Sisera and Jael depends in no way upon this detail. Perhaps the rug is meant to allay Sisera's suspicions. As critics have pointed out, Jael is also ironically behaving like a nurturing mother, while nurturing murderous intentions in her heart. What they fail to notice is the Concealment theme. Just as the fabric conceals Sisera, so Jael is concealing her true intentions. As such, the rug is only one of the many threads of an intricate tapestry.

Binary opposites

Binary opposites are one of the fundamental ways that languages establish meaning. In *Judges*, polarities are a seminal aspect of the categories (both material objects and concepts). The polarities may exist within one character or between characters; within a story and between stories; and in some cases throughout the book. Some stories contain many or most of the binaries. The following list is not complete, either of the binaries nor of the examples but will serve to indicate the complexity of the ideas the author is playing with:

angry, dismayed/happy (Yhwh, Samson, Philistines);

blessings/curses (Jotham, Micah);

complete body, living body/dismembered body, carcass (throughout; Adoni-Bezek, Samson, lion cub, Levite's Concubine);

bravery/fear, cowardice (Gideon, Jether, Jephthah's daughter, Micah, Benjaminites);

comedy/tragedy (throughout);

compassion/ruthlessness (Yhwh, Abimelech, Jephthah);

construction, build/destruction, tear down, destroy (throughout; Gideon's altars, Abimelech, civil war at end, where Benjaminite cities are destroyed and rebuilt);

cooperation/dissension (tribes in Deborah, tribes in Jephthah story and at the end; Ephraimites in Ehud, Gideon, Jephthah);

cover/uncover (Jael, Samson);

dancing/not dancing (Jephthah's daughter, daughters of Shiloh);

eat, drink/not eat, be thirsty, be famished (Sisera, Gideon's men, "empty" men (ריקים) in the Abimelech and Jephthah stories, Samson, Levite in Levite's Concubine story);

exhaustion/rest (Sisera, Gideon's men, Samson);

give, lose/take, seize (throughout; Yhwh gives the enemy into Israelite hands, Jael gives Sisera a drink, Succoth and Penuel refuse to give bread to Gideon's men; many people, land, objects are seized; Caleb gives Achsah to Othniel, the Israelite fathers refuse to give their daughters to the Benjaminites, but the Benjaminites seize the daughters of Shiloh);

good/evil (throughout);

hero, courage/villain, enemy, cowardice (throughout);

hidden/exposed (Sisera, Gideon, Abimelech, the Philistines in the Samson/ Delilah episode);

honor/shame (Barak);

hunger/thirst, abundance of food; drink/lack of food or drink (Sisera, Gideon, Samson);

in/out (Ehud, Jephthah's daughter, Levite's Concubine);

know/not know (Samson);

love/hate (Samson, the Timnite, Delilah);

loyalty/disloyalty (man of Luz, Abimelech, Zebul/Gaal);

night/day (Gideon, Abimelech, Samson, Levite and his Concubine);

noise, loud/silence, quiet (Gideon, Samson, Micah);

open, unlocked/shut, closed, locked (locked door in Ehud, the door in the Levite's Concubine story);

planting crops/destroying crops (Gideon, Samson);

pursue, run after/flee, stay (Barak/Sisera, Abimelech/Gaal, Micah/the Danites);

rise/fall (Eglon, Sisera);

safety/danger (Gideon, Samson);

see/not see (Abimelech, Gaal, Samson—seeing the Timnite and later being blinded);

sleep/wakefulness (Sisera, Midianites, Philistines before the harlot's house in Gaza, Samson);

strength/weakness, exhaustion (Gideon's clan, Gideon, Samson);

tears, weeping, sadness/laughing, joy (Israelites from time to time, Abimelech, the Timnite, Jephthah's daughter and her companions, Samson/the Philistines, Levite and his father-in-law);

up, high/down, low (towers in Gideon and Abimelech stories [high], hiding places [low]; Jotham orating from top of Mt. Gezerim, people on roof in Temple of Dagon in Samson story);

wet/dry (Gideon's fleeces, Samson's bindings);

virgins/non virgins (Jephthah's daughter, Civil War at end);

war/peace (throughout).

In the Samson story, for example, as James A. Freeman points out, the wet/dry opposition includes honey as opposed to a carcass, a fresh jawbone to a brittle one, the "Spring of the Caller" to the arid land, and 7 pieces of undried gut to 7 dessicated thongs.[4] Samson's strength is magnified by comparison with the weakness of other men or with his own weakness when his vow is violated. The fruitful land Gideon is trying to save is more flourishing when contrasted with the land after the Midianites raid or with the crops that Samson destroys. The success of the tribes in cooperation with each other when battling the enemy is in stark contrast to the failure of the tribes in conflict with each other, etc.

The author achieves emphasis for concepts about his society and attributes of characters that might otherwise escape our notice through this dynamic *system of communication.* It may also be a necessary device in a language where the vocabulary is small and does not offer discriminating choices. Perhaps the binary opposites may also be a mnemonic device set up for storytelling purposes, as well as a simple means to elicit our delight, for these objects are like gems sewn into the fabric of the design. The use of them is a most wonderful juggling skill of the artist. The author looks at life through a Yin/Yang lens. (See also Chapter 6, Conclusion.)

The purpose of the method; lack of tropes

The categories with their binary opposites also show that the author was working with a method similar to what T. S. Eliot called *objective correlatives:*

> "The only way of expressing emotion," wrote Eliot, " . . . is by finding an 'objective correlative'; in other words, a set of objects, a situation, a chain of events which shall be the formula of that *particular* emotion," and which will evoke the same emotion from the reader.[5]

Instead of establishing a set of objects to evoke emotions, however, the author of *Judges* used them to trigger and reinforce ideas and themes.

As Carolyn Spurgeon pointed out decades ago in *Shakespeare's Imagery* (1935), Shakespeare used this technique consistently to pound certain ideas into the reader's unconscious (like associations of the color red with blood and violence in *Macbeth* and images having to do with rot, decay, and poison in *Hamlet*) in order to affect the reader subliminally, without the reader being able to put up his defenses or reducing the effect of the narrative line. It is something like how a musical score works in contemporary cinema.

The author of *Judges* is not using tropes to achieve such effects. Tropes, of course, exist in even the most primal of languages. In *Judges*, for example, fire is said to *devour* the offering; when one is angry, *the nose blazes*; and Yhwh "gives" the enemy "into the hands" of the Israelites or "sells" the Israelites "into the hands" of their enemy because they were "whoring" after other gods. These metaphors are idiomatic and conventional. (Wordplay, like the play on the word *knees* in the Jephthah story, is also abundant throughout.)

The basic tropes with which all languages are constructed[6] are lacking in *Judges*, those used creatively by an author for a variety of reasons: to articulate the inexpressible, to evoke strong emotions, to manifest ambiguity or demonstrate the many facets of an idea, to make a thought memorable or beautiful, to avoid directness, to evoke a picture, etc. We find a few in the books of Samuel, such as when Hushai, speaking to David, says, "You know that your father and his men are warriors, and that they are enraged, like a bear robbed of her cubs in the field" (2 Sam 17.8). Shakespeare could seldom utter a sentence that did not contain a trope: "He jests at scars that never felt a wound" (embedded metaphor referring to a painful experience in love), "the milk of human kindness" (embedded), or "Pity, like a naked new-born babe, Striding the blast" (explicit) and so on.

Creative tropes like this, though common in the Ugaritic myths, are rare in *Judges*, except perhaps for the line from *The Song*, "The stars fought from their courses in the skies" (5.20) or the line in which the leaders are called *cornerstones* in Hebrew (פנות) (20.2). When Gideon threatens to *thresh* the elders who refuse to give him bread, *thresh* may not be a common metaphor of the language, but one that the author creates as part of his agriculture theme. We first see Gideon beating out wheat (חבט חטים, 6.11) in the wine press, but later *threshing* (דוש, 8.7)—that is, beating—the townsmen who inhospitably rebuffed him when he needed food for his troops. The word is used to depict the deterioration of Gideon. He went from engaging in a suitable occupation, to becoming angry and vindictive. Like other keywords, references to wheat, incidentally, are to be found throughout the entire book.

Such references are ligatures between stories. They are the building blocks of his main creative technique—abundant use of comparisons and contrast, which he points out by his careful planting of strong, elemental keywords, their synonyms, and the repetition of them or of related ideas (not always the identical word) whenever a connection is needed. An example of the kind of keyword that might easily be overlooked: that Ehud "allowed *not* a man *to pass over*" (עבר) the Jordan is a deliberate parallel and contrast with Jephthah who *allowed only* certain ones "*to pass over*."[7] Another is the word *ass*, which shows the parallel between the Achsah and the Concubine stories, while the word *stake* or *pin* (יתד) points out the parallel between Jael and Delilah (discussed at length in Chapter 1).

Since these keywords, objects, and ideas are crucial to the author's narrative system, we cannot finally appraise his style or appreciate the vastness and complexity of his achievement, until we unearth as many of them as possible, create lists of all of them, analyze them, and notice how skillfully he has strewn his objects one by one evenly throughout the book, with larger clusters appearing where he wants greater emphasis.[8]

Such lists provide us with statistics, a way of measuring the extent of the task. The reader cannot truly grasp what the author is doing with Kinship Relations, for example, by merely remarking that there are many of them. We have to see the concrete evidence in the astonishing array of relationships that are to be found in the landscape. To know the real value of a mine, we cannot guess how much ore it contains; we must enter the mine, descend, blast out the ore, bring it up to light, have it appraised, and then sell it on the open market. Finding these hidden objects is in effect like working in an archaeological dig.

The lists are useful in many ways. First, they sharpen our ability to interpret the stories accurately. Without the parallels, we run the risk of misinterpreting the meaning of the stories. Proust and Joyce tell us everything that is to be known; we simply sit and read their work and absorb their interpretations. We are never in doubt about how to construe their stories. But the author of *Judges* makes *us* work. He leaves all kinds of gaps, trusting that we will labor to fill them in correctly. He *never* draws conclusions for us, *never* interprets. But he has supplied all the clues and more, through this use of keywords, that enable *us* to work out our own conclusions. The text is intentionally interactive.

Second, the keywords reveal the author's appreciation of the complexity of ordinary life. We live among buildings, we depend upon certain agricultural products, animals appear in our everyday experience, we wear or touch certain fabrics, we put on our ornaments—scarcely aware that these things exist. Like the living person, the characters and the reader of *Judges* are focused on the plot, the suspense of how events are going to turn out. The author appreciates the items of daily experience, however, and wants us to appreciate them, too. They are not there merely to provide a connection with the phenomenal world, however. They do much more than that. As we shall eventually see, they serve an artistic purpose as well.

Third, his method enabled him to compress his ideas into the smallest possible space. Perhaps by temperament he was a miniaturist who simply liked little things. Several millennia before the invention of electron microscopes, this author was carefully examining certain tiny aspects of society through one. He is a *nano*-engineer.

Fourth, in order to do this, he had to understand how "meaning" is produced in texts. His text exemplifies this better than any other writer's, except the great writers of literature—like Chaucer, Cervantes, Ibsen, and Joyce. They too worked with intertextuality as a device to expand meaning (though not particularly with keywords), and they also incorporated deliberate parallelisms within or among their stories or poetry. But their writings are long and complex, whereas the author of *Judges* worked within a very *small* compass.

Fifth, in his understanding of language, the author of *Judges* is a forerunner of Derrida. Indeed, *Judges* may be the best text in world literature that can demonstrate the kind of understanding and use of language that modern literary theorists have been trying to explain to us since the late 1960s. (More about this in Chapter 6, Conclusion.)

The language he used (except in *The Song of Deborah*) was basic, elemental, simple. The words by themselves are largely denotative—especially for modern readers three millennia later, for whom the ancient contexts are lacking. Since it is only through differences in contexts that words acquire connotations, *Judges* gives us many opportunities to compare and contrast the contexts of the words in one story with all the other words and contexts in this book. It is this continual cross-referencing that causes meanings to multiply almost infinitely—like the legendary jar of meal in the Elijah cycle (1 Kgs 17.6).

Difficulty of classifying and analyzing the hidden objects

The reader of this chapter will find his brain cells continually sapped trying to follow the logic and complexity of meaning given by this author. The multiplicity of meanings can become so great, as one weaves back and forth between stories, that once one begins working in earnest with the method, one is thrown into confusion. For discovering them is to let all chaos loose: meanings begin to undermine meanings, and the result could be complete "deconstruction," if not the disappearance of the text. One ceases to see the forest for the trees and the trees for the forest.

The task is too daunting, for there are too many details to contend with. If, for example, we have 100 details, all related to each other in every possible way (and this writer is dealing with far more than 100 items), the number of "transactions" between them would be too large for any of our computers to handle. Everything is related to everything else; and one must make an almost infinite number of calculations in order to grasp what is going on. That is the kind of puzzle that the author has set up for us to solve in this book.

Assailed by so many meanings, we may find it difficult to reach conclusions and, if not careful, will cease to notice the curious objects swarming around us as we proceed. When we begin to be discouraged and to suspect that making the effort is a waste of time, we will be tempted to revert to the traditional method of following the simple plot lines to discern the causes and effects of each incident, and let the "hidden objects" slip back into obscurity.

It takes a tough mentality, patience, and expertise even to perceive these objects, let alone understand what they are doing. And it takes a great deal of time before one can become proficient playing the "game." Like the chess player, the reader needs perhaps years of study before one becomes a Master.[*]

Both the collecting and the analyzing of these objects are extremely time-consuming.

Once the words and concepts are collected in separate categories, we want to see how a single word (with its synonyms) is used in each story, and then we want to compare and contrast how they are used in all of the stories. We can set up an imaginary chart of columns representing each keyword, and rows representing each story and then read up and down and across the grid.

In the sections about *body parts* below, for example, I used both methods: I listed *body parts* (section 1) and *hands* (section 3) of all the stories *except Samson*. And in Section 2, I listed *all* the *body parts*, including *hands*, in the Samson story by itself. After we have found and listed all the references to *noise* and *silence*, for example (see **Table** in the **Appendix 1** to this chapter), we have to analyze the data to

---

[*] Unless the reader is thoroughly familiar with all the stories in *Judges,* the following analyses may be confusing.

determine what they mean, like what Kepler did when he analyzed Tycho Brahe's data and derived from them the three planetary laws of motion.

Because of the constant interweaving of words and themes, a certain amount of repetition of ideas is inevitable in my account, but it is hoped that each repetition will produce significant variations from ideas expressed elsewhere. Besides, there is something kaleidoscopic about each repetition: the objects seem to shift position and produce different patterns each time we come back to a story with a change in our perspective.

Up until now, critics in general have found *Judges* disorderly and incoherent. Discussing the Micah story, Soggin, for example, remarks: "However, the effectiveness of the account is lessened by the *confusion* in the text, which is full of *redundancies and repetitions*" (emphasis mine).[9] As we study each category carefully, certain orderly patterns emerge. What seemed like confusion is really "method in the madness." The redundancies and repetitions are there for a purpose. One point in analyzing these categories is to derive the author's artistic principles.

The topic of the development of ideas of ethics, law, and justice cannot be avoided here, as human error is what the book of *Judges* is about, and the author seems to be testing the ability of the audience to evaluate each incident. The main discussion of this topic, however, is in Chapter 4.

People and Relationships

Given the vast number of the deaths (approx. 267,860, not including enormous numbers of uncounted deaths) and the many acts of violence committed, the author persuades us of the density of the Israelite population, as well as that of the enemy. In this period, Iron Age 1 (1250-1020 BC)—if indeed the period can be pinpointed—there were actually only 50,000 inhabitants, or fewer,[10] in the whole region. Villages were also very small, 43% under 2.5 acres by the end of that period, and 52% between 2.5 and 12.5 acres. The activities in the book seem more appropriate to a sparsely settled landscape than the numbers in the text imply.

If we want to extrapolate some kind of history from this book, we should apply what Baruch Halpern calls the "Tiglath-Pileser" principle of "minimal interpretation"; that is, one asks,

> What is the minimum the king might have done to lay claim to the achievements he publishes? Looting a town? He shoplifted a toothbrush from the local drug store. Ravaging the countryside? Perhaps he trampled crops near a farmstead. Receiving submission from distant kings in lands one hadn't invaded? A delegation arrived to inaugurate diplomatic relations. Each small mark of prestige becomes the evidence for a grand triumph.[11]

The author's figures were no doubt hyperbole. (See Chapter 2.)

Judges is teeming with life, not only of people inside the country, but also of outsiders who make incursions and maraud. People are all over the place, mainly farmers and farmers-turned-warriors. Yet for such a short book, it is amazing how many other kinds of people, with their occupations and relationships, are included. What we have is more than a mere cast of characters. The author seems to have made an attempt to give us a complete cross-section of kin relationships. When we first read the book and concentrate on the main characters (the so-called "heroes"), we may fail to notice how many other people surround each of them—people of all ages and of all levels of society from the slave (Samson) up to Sisera's mother, who has been called *queenly* because of her "wisest ladies" in attendance, and to the nobles and princes mentioned in *The Song*, the kings and princes in the Gideon story, and "lords of Shechem" (i.e., "rulers") in the Abimelech story. A most wonderful microcosm, a miniature world carved into a walnut shell.

The following lists are of relationships which function in the plot. Notice the tremendous variety of roles.

Subcategory: Men (outstanding men in their relationships)

fathers of sons (the word *father* is strongly emphasized in Chs. 7-9, 11, 14-15, and 19.): (1) Anak, father of Sheshei, Ahiman, and Talmai; (2) the sons of the Israelites who marry foreigners and the foreign sons who marry Israelite women (3.6); (3) Joash, father of Gideon (Gideon is the youngest son); (4) Gideon, father of Jether (oldest son), Jotham (youngest son), Abimelech, and up to 70 or more other sons; (5) Abimelech, who is not depicted as a father, but has the word "father" in his name; (6) the father of Abimelech's mother ("house of the father," meaning Abimelech's maternal grandfather) (9.1); (7) the minor judges Jair (30 sons), Ibzan (30 sons, who married foreign daughters), and Abdon (40 sons); (8) Gilead, the father of Jephthah; (9) Manoah, father of Samson; (10) Micah, a father to an unnamed son and "like a father" to his Levite; (11) the same Levite, whom the Danites want to be "as a father" to them; (12) the genealogy from Moses (great-grandfather) to Gershom (son of Moses), to Jonathan (son of Gershom), then to Jonathan's sons (18.30). (Most of the patronymics and national or tribal designations have not been included— e.g., Othniel, son of Kenaz, nor "Sons of Israel" for "Israelites," etc.)

fathers of daughters: (1) Caleb, father of Achsah; (2) Jephthah, father of an unnamed daughter; (3) Ibzan (30 daughters who married foreign men); (4) unnamed father of the unnamed Timnite and her sister (including the "daughters of the Philistines" in 14.2); (5) unnamed father of the Concubine in Bethlehem; (6) the old Ephraimite in Gibeah who offers his daughter to the rapists; and (7) the fathers of the young women of Shiloh whom the elders allowed the Benjaminites to seize (21.22).

grandfathers and great-grandfathers: the clan of the father of Abimelech's mother (see also the genealogy of Jonathan, above [18.30]).

grandsons: Gideon's future grandson whom the Israelites want to be their ruler after Gideon and his son (8.22); (see also the genealogy of Jonathan [18.30]); Eleazar's son, Phinehas, who is Aaron's grandson (20.28).

fathers-in-law: Caleb, Othniel's father-in-law (or possibly his uncle); the Timnite's father, briefly Samson's father-in-law; the unnamed father-in-law (word used 4x) of the Levite (the Concubine's father); Hobab, the Kenite (Moses' father-in-law) (4.11).

brothers: (1) three brothers: Sheshai, Ahiman, Talmai; (2) Othniel's father Kenaz, who is Caleb's younger brother [or nephew]; (3) Simeon, Judah's brother; (4) Gideon's brothers (the sons of his mother) who are slain by Zebah and Zalmunna; (5) the *brothers* (*kin*) of Abimelech's mother (Abimelech's maternal uncles); (6) Abimelech, brother to Jether, Jotham, and the 70 brothers whom he killed (these presumably include Jether but not Jotham) (the word *brother* is used 13x in the Abimelech story, emphasizing the importance of this relationship); Abimelech is also *brother* (*kin*) to the men of Shechem; (7) the *brothers* (kin) of Gaal; (8) the half-brothers (unnamed) of Jephthah who drive him out; and (9) Samson's brothers (unnamed). (Excluded are others for whom *brother* means *kinsman*.)

husbands: (1) Othniel, husband of Achsah; (2) Lappidoth, husband of Deborah; (3) Heber, husband of Jael; (4) Gideon, husband of many wives and at least one concubine; (5) Manoah, husband of Samson's unnamed mother; (6) Samson, temporary husband of the Timnite (marriage likely not consummated); (7) the Benjaminites after they marry the women of Jabesh-Gilead and the daughters of Shiloh.

uncles: Caleb to Othniel;[12] Abimelech's uncles (his mother's "brothers") (9.1, 3).

nephews: Othniel to Caleb.

cousins: Othniel and Achsah.

lovers (the Heb. word for *lover* is not used): Samson (of the prostitute and of Delilah).

sons (see the list of "fathers of sons" above).

sons of mothers (specifically mentioned): (1) Sisera; (2) the sons of Gideon's mother who were killed by Zebah and Zalmunna (odd that Gideon says "sons of my mother," not "sons of Joash"; this probably means that Joash had more than one wife); (3) Abimelech (son of Gideon and a Shechemite concubine); (4) Jephthah (son of Gilead and a harlot); (5) sons of Gilead's wife (Jephthah's half-brothers 11.2); (6) Samson, the son of an unnamed mother (and Manoah); (7) Micah, the son of an unnamed woman.

sons-in-law: see fathers-in-law above.

illegitimate sons: Abimelech (?); Jephthah.

outlaws: Jephthah's band. Abimelech's group may also have been "outlaws."

young men (נער, lads, servants): (1) Purah (Gideon's lad); (2) the scribe at Succoth who wrote down the names of the elders for Gideon; (3) Gideon's son Jether; (4) the lad who kills Abimelech; (5) Samson, called a *lad* 5x; (6) the lad who helps the blind Samson in the temple; (7) the Levite priest in the Micah story, called a *lad*; and (8) the lad who accompanies the Levite in the story of the Levite's Concubine. נער is also a term for elite warriors and a term of affection.[13]

bachelors (בחורים), those accustomed to give wedding feasts (14.10).

bridegroom (Hebrew word not given): Othniel, Samson.

elders (old men): the elders who outlived Joshua (2.7); the officials and elders at Succoth in the Gideon story (betrayed by a young man) (8.14) and threshed by Gideon (8.16); the elders of Gilead in the Jephthah story (used 6x), who go to Jephthah the way the Greeks go to Achilles, to implore him to lead them to battle (11.5-11); the old man, an Ephraimite, at Gibeah who is host to the Levite;

and the elders who make the decisions about finding wives for the Benjaminites (21.16). (Elders are mentioned 6x in 11.5-11; 4x in Ch. 19.)

master: the Levite in the story of the Levite's Concubine (called *master* [אדון] 4x); the old man in Gibeah (the host) (called *master* (בעל) *of the house*). (Cf. with *lord* below.)

lords (בעלי שכם): men of Shechem in the Abimelech story (mentioned 16x, meaning "rulers," but called בעלי perhaps to associate them with Baal).

wicked men: the base friends (called ריקים, *empty*) of Abimelech and Jephthah; the men of Gibeah (*men of Beliat*, בני־בליעל) who surround the Ephraimite's house.

friends (רע): *friends* (*companions* or *others*) mentioned 4x in the Gideon story (6.29; 7.13, 14, 22); thirty *companions* at Samson's wedding feast including the one to whom Samson's wife is given; the commanders of the Gileadites who speak to one another (10.18); Gaal's *brothers* (or *kin*) (no doubt base) in Shechem; Abimelech and Jephthah's "base friends" (listed above under "wicked men"). (Friendships, such as that of Enkidu and Gilgamesh or Achilles and Patroclus, are not to be found in this book. Some of the main characters, like Ehud and Samson, are loners, as far as the story is concerned, though in his youth, Samson is seen with his mother and father.)

child (טף) 2x. The Danites have their families, including children, in the vanguard as they migrate (18.21). In 21.10 the text pointedly tells us that the Israelites are going to kill all the married women and *children* of Jabesh-Gilead as well as the men.

families: We do not see *families* in the usual sense. Some of the characters have other members of their family or tribe in the vicinity. Samson has a mother, father, and brothers. His *whole family* (כל־בית) is mentioned (16.31). The word *family* (משפחה, *clan* or *tribe*) occurs only twice: the family of the man of Luz (Bethel) (1.25); and Abimelech's mother's family (9.1). *House* (בית) may represent a household, as the house of the Timnite's father or Jephthah's household, for example, but Jerubbaal's *family* (8.27, 35) for whom the *ephod* is a snare is probably the extended clan. Gideon had 72 sons (including Abimelech and Jotham), the number 70 meaning a "large number." The book abounds in the use of the words *sons of* or *children of* and *inhabitants*. Biblical authors are especially interested in blood relationships. But of the "*nuclear family*"—nothing.

Subcategory: Women

mothers (they are listed under "sons of mothers" in the subcategory of "men" above): Deborah is called "mother of Israel."

mothers-in-law: none.

grandmothers: none.

sister: the Timnite's (sole).

daughters (listed under "fathers of daughters" above; there are no mothers of daughters): the Israelite *daughters* who marry foreign men and the foreign *daughters* who marry Israelite men (3.6); the 30 daughters and 30 daughters-in-law of the minor judge Ibzan (12.9), 3 references to daughters of the Philistines and of the Israelites (14.1-3), 2 references to Achsah as the daughter of Caleb; 1 reference to the host's daughter in the story of the Concubine. The references to *daughter* in the Jephthah story (5x in Ch. 11) and in the story of the *daughters* of Shiloh (5x in Ch. 21) call for a comparison and contrast of these stories. Perhaps the *daughters* of Shiloh are also to be considered "offerings." The five-fold repetition is significant.

girls: the Levite's Concubine is called a *girl* (נערה) 8x emphasizing her youth. Incidentally, the Concubine, though a major character, does not speak, but the young man (נער), a minor character in the same story, does. Significantly, the only other reference to *girls* are the virgin girls of Jabesh-Gilead (נערה בתולה) (21.12).

orphans: maidens of Jabesh-Gilead, though not called such.

virgins of marriageable age (בתולה): (1) Jephthah's daughter, who bewails her virginity; (2) the old Ephraimite's daughter in the story of the Levite's Concubine; (3) the 400 virgin *girls who have never known a man* of Jabesh-Gilead (women who are *not* virgins are killed) (4) the daughters of Shiloh (called *daughters* [*women* 1x], not *virgins*). (Whether the *companions* [בחורים *bachelors*] at Samson's wedding feast are virgins is not clear [14.10].)

wives: (see list of husbands above).

brides: Achsah; the Timnite.

concubines: Gideon's; Abimelech's mother; the Levite's Concubine (the word is used 11x in 19.1, 2, 9, 10, 24, 25, 27, 29 and 20.4, 5, 6. We are not allowed to forget what this woman's relationship is to the Levite).

maidservant: Abimelech's mother (אמה, 9:18, also translated as *slave*); the *servant* in 19.19 (referring to the Concubine).

lover: Delilah (harlot?).

prostitutes (זנה noun and verb): The Israelites play the *harlot* (2.17). Gideon's people *prostituted themselves* to the ephod (8.27, 33). Jephthah's mother is a prostitute (11.1); Samson has a prostitute in Gaza (16.1); and the Concubine prostituted herself (19.2).

captive women (רחם רחמתים Heb. *wombs*): what Sisera's mother expected Sisera to return with (5.30). The women of Jabesh-Gilead and daughters of Shiloh are *captives*, though they are not called such.

destructive women: Jael; the woman who drops a millstone on Abimelech; the Timnite; Delilah.

friends (רעה, female companions): the friends of Jephthah's daughter who help her celebrate her virginity, mentioned 2x (counterparts of Samson's 30 *companions* at the wedding feast).

wise women (חכמות שרותיה, sole) of Sisera's mother; they might also be considered *ladies-in-waiting*.

foreign women: passim.

Comment about the women in the book

Not surprisingly, women are seen mainly in their relationships to men, either as wife, mother (of Israelites), mother of an enemy, daughter, concubine, prostitute, or slayer. They are not depicted as friends to any other men, though in two cases women have female companions (Sisera's mother and Jephthah's daughter).

The word for *woman* or *wife* (אִשָּׁה) is not used nearly so often as the word for *men*. Nevertheless, it appears about 69x. The primary emphasis on women is in two stories: Samson (31x) and the Levite's Concubine (18x). By comparison, the total of all other uses of אִשָּׁה is only 19x: 2x in the Achsah story, 8x in the story and poem about Deborah, 1x in the Gideon story, 4x in the Abimelech story, and 4x in the Jephthah story (concerning the wife of his father, Gilead).

What is surprising is that women are in all of the stories and like the men, play a variety of significant roles. (The following list overlaps with "Women" and "Occupations" so as to point out the variety of women's roles.)

A young woman given as wife (trophy) to a conqueror (Achsah).

The Canaanite women whom the Israelites marry; the Israelite women who marry Canaanite men (3.6, 12.9).

A female judge and prophet as well as military leader (Deborah).

A nomad woman in a tent alone with a visitor she is about to kill (Jael).

A noblewoman awaiting the return of her conqueror-son (Sisera's mother, mother of a commander).

Wise women or ladies-in-waiting with Sisera's mother.

The many wives of Gideon.

A concubine who is a mother (Gideon's concubine, the mother of Abimelech, also called a *maidservant* or *slave*).

Ordinary women in a tower, one of whom drops a millstone on a tyrant's head (Abimelech story).

Gilead's wife, who had many children (beginning of Jephthah story).

A daughter awaiting the return of her conquering father (Jephthah's daughter).

A virgin daughter who had no husband (Jephthah's daughter).

A prostitute whose son is first an outcast, then a chief (Gilead's prostitute, who is Jephthah's mother).[14]

A barren wife, visited by a messenger-angel of Yhwh (Samson's mother, apparently a peasant).

A Philistine bride whose father takes her from her husband and gives her away to the best man at her wedding (the Timnite in the Samson story).

The younger sister of a bride (the Timnite), who is offered to the groom (Samson) to replace his wife.

A prostitute who sleeps with the hero (Samson's prostitute at Gaza).

A woman (Delilah, possibly a prostitute) who is alone with Samson in her chamber and about to do him in.

The Philistine women in the house of Dagon and on the roof (16.27).

A rich mother whose son steals her money but later returns it (Micah's mother).

A Concubine who plays the prostitute, and then becomes a runaway, is raped, and brutally murdered (Ch. 19).

All the women of Jabesh-Gilead who had "known a man" (not virgins) and were killed by the Israelites (21.12).

400 virgin girls (who had *not* "known a man") whose entire town of Jabesh-Gilead has been annihilated in order that they might be given as wives to the Benjaminites (21.12).

200 dancing *daughters* of Shiloh (*virgins* by implication), who are seized by lustful men to be their wives (last chapter).

Subcategory: Occupations

In general, other types of workmen—such as carpenters and masons—are lacking, except for the silversmith (specific word not given) in the Micah story. Though villages are depicted (Timnah, Shechem), the author depicts life outside the towns, especially the life of the farmer. Most of the action occurs outdoors, with a few exceptions, like the killing of Eglon in a house and Sisera in a tent, the marriage feast of Samson (which possibly could have been outside), Delilah's tempting of Samson; and the two drinking scenes of the Levite in the last story. The main occupations are as follows:

judge: Yhwh is the main judge (11.27). Others said to have "judged": Othniel (3.10); Deborah; 5 minor judges, Tola, Jair, Ibzan, Elon, and Abdon (Chs. 10, 12); Jephthah; and Samson. The meaning of the name of the tribe *Dan* is *judge*. Deborah is the only one who is shown "judging." Jephthah negotiates with the Ammonites.

deliverer (מוֹשִׁיעַ): Yhwh; Othniel; Shamgar; Ehud; Gideon; Tola (a minor judge); Samson. The word is not used specifically of Jephthah, though he does "deliver." Jael is a deliverer of sorts; the woman with the millstone is a deliverer of the Shechemites in the Abimelech story, though the word is not used for either of these women.

messenger-angels of Yhwh: (2.1, 4; 5.23); in Gideon (7x in Ch. 6) and in Samson (12x in Ch. 13).

messengers (men): sent by Gideon (6.35, 7.24), by Zebul to Abimelech (under cover) (9.31), by Jephthah to the Ammonites and by the Ammonites in return (11.12-19).

warriors (the predominant, though no doubt temporary, occupation throughout). Gideon and Jephthah are *mighty warriors* (גִּבּוֹר הֶחָיִל).

chief or head (רֹאשׁ): the heads of Sisera's army (5.30); Abimelech as head (10.18); Jephthah as head (11.8, 9, 11).

commander (leader, prince, or ruler) (שַׂר): Sisera (4.2, 7); the princes of Issachar (5.15); the princes of the Midianites—Oreb and Zeeb (7.25,

8.3); the officials of Succoth (8.6, 14); Zebul, ruler of Shechem (Abimelech's deputy) (9.30); the commanders of the Gileadites (10.18).

commanders (מחקקים) in *The Song* (5.14).

commander (קצין): Jephthah's title, given by the elders (11.6, 11).

overlords: the Philistine rulers (סרן, 3.3; and 7x in Ch. 16).

mercenary (no Hebrew word for this in *Judges*): *worthless and reckless men* by Abimelech are probably *mercenaries* (they are said to be *hired*, שכר).

foot soldier: both Israelite and enemy (mentioned throughout).

spies (שמרים): the Israelite spies informed by the man from Luz (1.24); the young man who writes down the elders' names for Gideon; the five Danite spies in Ch. 18.

ruler (משל, verb only): Gideon refused "to rule" over the Israelites (but Abimelech did).

king: Cushan-rishathaim, Jabin, Eglon (3.17, 19), and Abimelech are kings; there are "kings of Canaan" in *The Song* ; Zebah and Zalmunna, kings of Midian in Gideon; king of the Ammonites (in the Jephthah story); kings of Edom and Moab (11.17); Sihon (earlier king of the Ammonites); and Balak (king of Moab). Jotham's fable has to do with anointing a king. The chaos in Israel is attributed to the fact that they have no king (17.6; 18.1; 19.1; 21.25).

prince: see *commanders* above (1st mention)

nobles: *Song of Deborah* (פרע [5.2], אדירים [5.13]).

officer of a city (deputy, פקיד): Zebul.

prophet: Deborah (4.4); a prophet, beginning of the Gideon story (6.8).

farmers: Gideon (especially as a thresher); the old Ephraimite coming from the fields in the Levite's Concubine; Samson's parents (Samson's mother is sitting *in a field*).

shepherds: *Song of Deborah.*

servants (עבד, can also mean *slave,* see also categories of "men" and "lads"): Eglon's servants (3.24); they are also called *attendants,* that is "those standing around" (העמדים, 3.19); Gideon takes 10 of his servants (אנשים מעבדיו) to tear down the altar of Baal; 2 "lads" act as servants: the lad who leads the blind Samson in the temple; and the lad accompanying the Levite and the Concubine; two armor bearers (listed below). Joshua is "servant of Yhwh" (2.8), and Samson, praying to Yhwh, describes himself as "your servant" (15.18).

Gaal ben Ebed ("son of a servant") rebels against *serving* Abimelech; Jerubbaal and Zebul are said to have "served Hamor." Gaal asks: "Why should we *serve* [Abimelech]?" (9.28). (*Serve* is used 4x in this one verse, including Gaal's patronymic. Gaal's patronymic may be contemptuous, identifying him as of a low class in contrast to Abimelech, who is the "son of a king.")

Yhwh reminds the Israelites that he has saved them from *the house of slavery* (same word) (6.8).

forced laborers (מַס): Canaanites are used as forced laborers (1.28, 30, 33, 35), but word not mentioned thereafter. Other references: the "house of slavery" of the Israelites in Egypt (6.8); Samson, considered a *slave* in the mill (16.21, but specific word not used).

armor-bearer (הַנַּעַר נֹשֵׂא כֵלָיו, *the lad bearing his gear*): Gideon's lad, Purah; and the lad who obliges Abimelech (9.54).

villagers: (פְּרָזוֹן rural people) (5.7, 11).

Subcategory: Others

assassins: the men hired by Abimelech to kill his brothers (see *worthless men* below).

bribers: Jephthah, who can be said to have tried to bribe Yhwh; the Philistines who bribe Delilah; Micah's mother, who tries to bribe Yhwh in order to counteract her curse.

captives: (שֶׁבִי) for Deborah's army to take (5.12) (see female captives above).

priests (כֹּהֵן): Micah's son and the Levite in the Micah story (word used 15x in Ch. 17-18); Jonathan and his sons (18.30); Phinehas who inquires of the Lord at Bethel (20.28).

prisoner: Samson.

robbers: robbers apparently terrorizing wayfarers at the beginning of *The Song*; Midianites, who are robbing the Israelites at the beginning of the Gideon story; probably Jephthah's outlaw band of "worthless" men; men of Shechem who lie in wait on the hilltops and rob all who pass by (9.25); Micah, who steals money from his mother; the Danites who steal the priest and icons from Micah; and the Benjaminites who steal the daughters of Shiloh when they come out to dance.

silversmith (word implied, not used, in the story of Micah) (the only craftsman).

travelers: *Song of Deborah* (5.6), Abimelech story (9.25) (i.e., those who pass by or walk on the path or road).

traitors: the man of Luz who helped the Israelites against his own people; Jael helping the enemy of her allies; the young man of Succoth who gives Gideon the list of names of officials and elders of his town; Abimelech in betraying his father, Gideon; Gaal in betraying Abimelech; Delilah betraying Samson; the Levite who abandons Micah and colludes in the Danites' theft of Micah's idols.

unknown occupation: Samson's father asks the messenger-angel of Yhwh: what will (Samson) do in his life?

worthless men: the empty (רֵיקִים), reckless (פֹּחֲזִים) men hired by Abimelech (9.4); the followers of Jephthah (empty men). Gaal in the Abimelech story is *worthless* (but the word is not used), and the Benjaminites of Gibeah who surround the host's house (בְּנֵי־בְלִיַּעַל, the sons of Belial, 19.22, 20.13).

Some men are dangerous: simple warriors like Sisera and Gideon as well as the more savage type like Samson; the Abiezerites who threaten Gideon (6.30); the Ephraimites in the Gideon and Jephthah stories; the Danites to Micah and city of

Laish (Chs. 17-18); and the Benjaminites of Gibeah (Ch. 19-21). And others are cowards: Barak, Gideon, the tribe of Judah (in turning Samson over to the Philistines), Micah, and the Levite (husband of the Concubine) (see **Cowardice** under **Good and Evil** in Chapter 4 and in the discussion of Gideon in Chapter 2.)

Subcategory: Remnants, Escapees, Survivors, Fugitives, Renegades

There are two types of "left-over" people:

1. remnants; those who remain (שריד, יתר, survivor) after some kind of action, like remnants of (to) the nobles (שריד לאדירים) (5.13); those who remain (שאר) after Gideon sends the fearful home (7.3); the rest (יתר), who kneeled to drink water (7.6); Midianite survivors (ונתרים) of the battle with Gideon, including Zebah and Zalmunna (8.10); Jotham, who survived (was left over, יתר) after his brothers were killed (9.5) (curiously, his older brother is named Jether [יתר 8.20]); and finally, the Benjaminites left over (נותרים, *survivors*; later called פליט, *fugitives*) after the civil war, and for whom wives and an "inheritance" had to be provided (21.7, 16).

2. fugitives (פליט)—either the Ephraimites (who are *fugitives* from the Gileadites), or the Gileadites (as perhaps originally being *fugitives* from Ephraim) (12.4, 5); and the Benjaminite *survivors* of the civil war (21.17).

Boling translates פליט (12.4, 5) as *fugitives* "For the *fugitives* of Ephraim said: 'Oh Gilead, you are in the midst of Ephraim and Manasseh!'" and notes that "the meaning of the taunt is obscure . . . the disabling of 42 contingents [42,000] of Ephraimites is one of the most puzzling in the book."[15] Notice that Boling calls the 42,000 Ephraimites *disabled*, when they were actually slaughtered. Perhaps he thinks that they were easily slaughtered because they had been disabled.)

NRS has: "You are *fugitives* of Ephraim, you Gileadites—in the heart of Ephraim and Manasseh" and also calls the Ephraimites *fugitives* as they attempt to flee. Soggin translates the word as *survivors*: "for [the Ephraimites] had said, 'You are mere *survivors* of Ephraim, you Gileadites, half-way between Ephraim and Manasseh!'" Soggin thinks the Ephraimites are accusing the Gileadites of being outcasts from Ephraim and Manasseh (200).

NIV translates the word as *renegades* and has it that the Gileadites struck down the Ephraimites because the Ephraimites had called them "*renegades* from Ephraim and Manasseh." In other words, the Gileadites accused the Ephraimites of having deserted them or rebelled against them.

There is no consensus as to the meaning.[16] Perhaps the Ephraimites are taunting the Gileadites because they are not a bona fide tribe in and of themselves but were a composite of other tribes. To the Ephraimites, the Gileadites lack credibility. The episode may be a foreshadowing of the Benjaminites, who certainly become outlaws, fugitives, and *remnants* (21.17).

Another reference to *survivors* (שריד, survivor, BDB 975) is found in *The Song*: "Then down marched the *remnant* of the noble; the people of the LORD marched down for him against the mighty" (5.13). The meaning of שׂרִיד is unclear here: perhaps it refers to those who had survived a battle with the oppressor and remained to fight.

Juan-Pablo Vita's discussion of the problem of *fugitives* from the city of Ugarit in *Handbook of Ugaritic Studies* may be helpful:

> As is known, the pursuit and extradition of fugitives was an important matter in the international relations of the ancient Near East. Ugarit, like the other states in the period, confronted this situation by means of bilateral treaties and internal legal mechanisms . . . . Since the *nayyalu* or runaway could not fulfil the economic obligations towards the administration . . . , he was pursued and lost his lands in favor of third parties . . . . It was another possible way of becoming a servant.[17]

Possibly the Ephraimites in 12.4 were addressing Jephthah's band of outlaws, who had been fugitives in the sense of the *nayyalu* of Ugarit. Possibly Gilead had harbored many men who in some way had fled their responsibilities or, like the early settlers of Australia, been banished for misdeeds.

What is the reason for this vast variety, this panoply, of people? Despite the limitations caused by the small size of the book, the author finds a way to show us that a thriving civilization exists in the background—a civilization, we might deduce, that is very important to him, for it consists of families, with their various interconnections with each other. Whether the author realized it or not, these lists counteract the depersonalized language of warfare discussed by Elaine Scarry. They bring home to us how the action of the "heroes" affects the lives of all kinds of people and make clear just what is being wiped out when the Danites annihilate the defenseless city of Laish, and the Israelites all but annihilate the Benjaminites and the people of Jabesh-Gilead.

Body

Keywords relating to the *body* give life to these people and indirectly make a statement about what is lost when the body is destroyed through mutilation or death in battle. These words are distributed rather evenly throughout all the stories, but are most plentiful in the Samson story. Some body parts have already been discussed in Chapter 2 as traditional sites of humor for comedy. What follows is a different way of analyzing the material. Some of the references to the body are made in common idioms, but even those may affect the reader's mind subliminally.

In my analysis below, I will discuss the body parts one by one. Of course it must be remembered that in the various stories, we have different clusters of body parts. For example, in the Ehud story, four body parts stand out: *hand* (3x), *thigh* (יָרֵך, 3.16, 21), *belly* (בֶּטֶן, 3.21, 22), and *back* (פַּרְשְׁדֹנָה, perhaps meaning *entrails* or *bowels with excrement*, 3.22, [BDB 832]). If פַּרְשְׁדֹנָה means *excrement*, as is likely, this is an implied reference to *intestines*. KJV and NRS translate the last part of the verse as "The dirt came out." Eglon's *body*, of course, lies on the floor.

The Samson story contains more body parts than any other story, and more or less covers the entire body. In the first and third sections below, I take the body parts one by one in each given story *except the Samson story*. In the 2nd section, I analyze the body parts in the Samson story only.

1. Body parts (Excluding Samson's) (Excluding Hands)

Whole body. Bodies are found in certain positions, and these give the book its character. *Dead bodies* abound, as discussed in Chapters 1 and 2.

A possible reference to the *torso* is in the statement that the Canaanite gods will be "as (thorns) in your *sides*" (2.3).

As already shown in the section about Iconicity in Chapter 1, a number of *bodies* are described as *lying on the ground*: Eglon (sword through his abdomen), Sisera (tent peg through his temple), Zebah and Zalmunna (sliced by Gideon), the lion (torn apart by Samson, first seen with fresh flesh, later as a decomposing carcass), the ass (a skeleton or a piece [jawbone] of a skeleton), Abimelech (head crushed in, sword through his body), Samson (under the rubble of the temple, amid a tangle of corpses), and the Concubine (fallen down dead outside a closed door). Because the decapitation of Oreb and Zeeb occurs off-stage, we do not see the bodies, but we do see their *heads*, which were brought to Gideon (like the head of Hadji Murad to the Russian soldiers in Tolstoy's novel of that title). Neither do we see the bodies of Abimelech's 70 brothers but, as in a Greek tragedy, hear about them being "killed on one stone," offstage. These are Gideon's sons, who, we learn, came from his *body* (or *loins*) (8.30, יְרֵךְ).

Hundreds of thousands of warriors are killed in battle, but we see no actual dismemberments, decapitations, or entrail-ripping of the warriors themselves, like that of Eglon, though bodies must have littered the field after each battle. The author did not distance himself completely from this carnage, however, because his use and repetition of many different verbs and nouns indicating mass destruction, such as *smite*, *destroy*, and *death*, force upon us the stark reality of the horrible extent of the devastation, despite the omission of groans and shrieks (discussed fully in Chapter 2).

It is interesting that Eglon's body lies on the floor (אַרְצָה) *inside* the house *behind a locked door* (3.22), while the Concubine lies fallen on the threshold *outside* the house *in front of a door* that was no doubt locked (19.27), an intentional iconic pattern.

The Levite cuts up (נתח) the Concubine's *body* (19.29 and 20.6, word for *body*, however, is not given) by *limbs* (עֲצָם, *bones* [cf. 9.2, *flesh* and *bone*]). He cuts her body into 12 cut portions (נתחים, same word as *cut*) and sends the cut portions to all the territory of Israel. (It does not say "to all the tribes of Israel." One wonders to whom the 12th portion was given—to Benjamin?) What are the 12 parts? Possibly (though not necessarily), 1 head, 2 arms, 2 legs, 2 hands, 2 feet, 1 neck, 2 halves of the torso. (If the body had been that of a man, would there have been 13 parts?) This final mutilation is a summing up of the Dismemberment Theme (see Chapters 1 and 2). Presumably, the *whole* body is referred to, whereas in other tales (with the exception of Samson), only a selection of body parts appears in each story.

If we remember that the Concubine "played the harlot," this horrible incident might be viewed as a cautionary tale for women. Was it a kind of retribution (the prostitute raped, the body given to many in a kind of hideous communion)? That is the question that the author poses and the kind of question that will be discussed in depth in Chapter 4. (This interpretation is grimly reflected in the attitudes of serial murderers of prostitutes in the last hundred years, beginning with Jack the Ripper: prostitutes "deserve" to be killed.)

Soul, spirit, or *life* (נפש). Although the *soul* is not strictly speaking a body part, it is the animating principle, and fits into no other category. To translate the word as *soul* is misleading, for it is not the same as the modern meaning of *soul,* which derives from Plato and the Greeks. The Hebrew *soul* is not akin to the *soul* that Faust sells to Mephistopheles; rather it is what the Sibyl at Cumae in Petronius is forced to keep when she asked for eternal life but neglected to ask for eternal youth. It refers to *life* and sometimes to *temperament* or *spirit* (but is not the same thing as רוח, as in the *spirit* of Yhwh). It does not seem to represent the "I" in all its uniqueness (as some definitions maintain)—at least, not in *Judges.* Rather, it is what one loses when one dies. We must try to elicit suggestions as to its meanings from the contexts. (Cf. Gen 2, where Yhwh breathes life [נפש] into man's nostrils and Exod 21.23 where the *lex talionis* [law of retaliation] requires life for life: נתתה נפש תחת נפש.)

נפש is the word used in the following passages: Yhwh's *spirit* was grieved because of the Israelites' suffering (10.16), and Samson's *spirit* was vexed by Delilah (16.16), as it had been by the Timnite (14.17). The tribe of Naphtali risked their *lives* (נפשו) to fight against Sisera (5.18). And it is what the poet of *The Song* addresses in 5.21 ("March on, my soul, in strength"—תדרכי נפשי עז). Jotham reproaches Abimelech for not appreciating Gideon's risk of *life* for them against Midian (9.17), while Jephthah scolds the Ephraimites for not appreciating his having put *his life in his palms* for them (12.3). Samson prays that his *life* be allowed to die with the Philistines (16.30). In the story of Micah, the word is used 3x in one sentence when the Danites threaten that men of bitter temperament (*life*) (אנשים מרי נפש) will remove (אסף) Micah's *life* and the *life* of his house (נפשך ונפש ביתך) (18.25). The importance of נפש or *life* is signified by its being used 10x in the book.

The other word for *spirit* is רוח, as in Gen 1.2. In *Judges,* the *spirit* of Yhwh (יהוה רוח) represents incoming of power as when the adrenalin surges into the body. It is used 3x when the spirit rushes in to rescue the heroes—Othniel (3.10), Gideon (6.34), and Jephthah (11.29). It is used 6x in Samson (see **Body Parts in the Samson Story** below). It is also used to depict the angry *mood* of the Ephraimites confronting Gideon (8.3), and it is an *evil spirit* (רוח רעה) sent by Elohim to stir up insurrection between Abimelech and the Shechemites (9.23). It is what Saul gets when he "prophesies" (1 Sam 19.23) and when an *evil spirit* comes on him (רוח־אלוהים רעה, 2 Sam 16.14).

Blood. For such an otherwise bloody book, it is surprising that *blood* is used only once—in reference to Abimelech for having slain his seventy brothers: "their blood be laid on Abimelech . . ." (9.24).

Bones are mentioned twice, not counting the *jawbone* in Samson. The word *bone* is used when the Concubine is dismembered "by the *limbs*" or "*bone* by *bone*" (19:29). The second time is when Abimelech woos the Shechemites by reminding them that he is"their *bone* and their *flesh*" (9.2).

As for *flesh* (בשר, *meat*), Gideon threatens the princes of Succoth to tear (flail) their *flesh* and then does so (in 8.7, 15). (The word has not been included here when it refers to food.)

The word for *head* (ראש) is used frequently to mean the "top" of something like a mountain or stronghold, or for "leader" or in certain metaphors, such as when Yhwh returns evil deeds on the *heads* of the Shechemites (9.57). It is hard to determine how much force such metaphors have to evoke the real *head* of a real *body*.

However, real *heads* are referred to 4 or 5x, as when Jael crushes Sisera's *head* (5.26) and pierces and shatters his *temple* (רקתו, another body part) (4.21, 22; 5.26); when the decapitated *heads* of Oreb and Zeeb are brought to Gideon (7.25); and when Abimelech's *skull* (גלגלת) is crushed by a millstone (9.53).

Hair and *head* are most important, of course, in the Samson story (see Section 2 below). Later in the book, we learn that the Benjaminite slingshooters can "shoot a stone at a *hair* (שערה) and not miss" (20.16).

On top of heads are *necks* (צואר). Sisera's mother is waiting for embroidered work for her *neck* (5.30). Gideon takes collars and *neck*laces off the *necks* of the camels (8.21, 26).

The *mouth* (פה) is mentioned at least 7x (not including figurative uses). "The edge of the sword" in Hebrew is figuratively "the *mouth* of the sword." Ehud's sword is "two *mouthed*, meaning *double-edged*." Some of Gideon's men lap water by putting their hands to their *mouths* (7.6). Zebul taunts Gaal by asking, "Where is your *mouth* now?" while the Jephthah story emphasizes the *mouth* by repeating 4x that Jephthah has opened his *mouth* ill-advisedly (11.35, 36 [3x]). In Micah, the Danites silence the priest by telling him, "Keep quiet! Put your hand over your *mouth* and come with us" (18.19).

In the *mouth* is the *tongue* (לשון). Some of Gideon's men lap water with their *tongues*, while others lap with their hands to their *mouths* (7.5, 6, 7).

People speak with *voices* (קול, which come out of their mouths, as does Jephthah's. The word for *voice* is common, idiomatic, and scarcely noticeable. But at times it is emphasized. In *The Song of Deborah*, a voice is singing, reciting (5.11). Jotham raises his *voice* as he shouts his fable from the top of the mountain (9.7). The Danites recognize the *voice* (the dialect—as Jephthah recognized the dialect of the Ephraimites?) of the young Levite living with Micah, and this is what draws them into Micah's house (18.3). Eventually, they warn Micah not to raise his *voice* lest angry men attack him (18.25).

Ears (אזן) appear 6x, used idiomatically to mean *to hear*: to say something in another's *ears*, as when Yhwh tells Gideon to *"proclaim in the ears* of the people" (7.3) or when Micah's mother "spoke the curse *in my ears*" (17.2). *Ear*rings (נזם), are made into the ephod that becomes a snare to Gideon. Though the word also serves as a reference to the Israelites' exodus from Egypt (Exod 32.2, 3), the author may want to make still another reference to this bodily part (8.24, 25, 26).

Eyes (עׁיׁן) and the verbs *to see* and *appear* are included in this category only when they advance the narrative, though they are used idiomatically as many as 10x or more, as in the expression good or evil "in the *eyes* of someone" (2.11, 3.7, 19.24, for example), or "departed from his *eyes*" (6.21), or "the old man lifted up his *eyes*" (19.17).

Used as keywords, verbs *to see* are strewn evenly throughout the book, as when Gaal *saw* the people rising against him (9.36) and when the Benjaminites *saw* that disaster was upon them (20.41). *Seeing* and the *eyes* are fundamental in the Samson story: "she was *right in his eyes*" (14.6). This expression is also used of David's arranged marriage to Michal: "David told Saul that the thing was *right in his eyes*" (1 Sam 18.20). The implication may be that the desires of Samson and David are wrong. (The only thing that is *right* is what is *right in Yhwh's eyes*.)

Toward the end of the book, *eyes* are emphasized when the clause "the people did what was right in their own *eyes*" is repeated twice (17.6; 21.25). The implication is clear. Like the secret message of Ehud to Eglon, this is one of the most significant sentences of the book. (See Chapter 4 under the heading **Good, Right, Happiness, Distress**).

The *nose* (אַף) appears only in the idiom "*nose burned*" meaning "became angry," but it is significant in that it appears at least 7x (2.14, 20; 3.8; 6.39; 9.30; 10.7; 14.19) (see **Anger** in Chapter 4).

The *face* is mentioned often, but only idiomatically—*face* of the sword, seeing Yhwh *face to face*, turning their *faces* (meaning *turning around*), etc. The only non-idiomatic use is perhaps when Manoah and his wife fall with their *faces* to the ground (13.20). *Teeth* are not mentioned.

The word *heart* (לֵב) is usually used idiomatically to express such inner feelings as sincerity, inclinations, and states of contentment as in the following: "My *heart* goes out to the commanders" (5.9) and there were "great searchings of *heart*" (5.15, 16), "their *hearts* inclined to follow Abimelech" (9.3), and "the priest's *heart* was glad" (18.20). (The repeated use of this word in Ch. 16 is discussed below, under **Body Parts in the Samson Story**.)

Such idiomatic expressions may indicate that the author wants us to be conscious of it as a body part.

The many repetitions of the word *heart* in the Concubine story are significant. The Levite goes to the Concubine to "speak to her *heart*," that is, to speak "kindly" to her (19.3), an ironic reference, since what he was ultimately going to *do* was not kind. In this story, the word *heart* (לֵב) is also used 5x in rapid succession (19.5, 6, 8 [לֵבָב], 9 [לֵבָב], 22) as a code to evaluate that what the men are doing—getting intoxicated—is wrong. All these uses are similar: the father-in-law is urging the Levite to remain and carouse with him: "Strengthen your *heart*" and "Let your *heart* be merry," are the two expressions he uses (alternately, it might be added). The last time is a bit different, for then the Levite is a guest in the house of the old Ephraimite in the town of Gibeah. They too are carousing: "As they were making their *hearts* merry, behold, the men of the city, certain sons of Belial, beset the house round about, beating on the door . . ." (19.22). This could be a simple case of binary contrast: *inside*, the people are innocent and happy, while *outside*, the men are evil, and a terrible plot is being fomented. The word *heart* is being used ironically here. But its use should remind us of how gleeful (כטוב לבם) the Philistines were in capturing and humiliating Samson (16.25).

The word is repeated 5x to signify bodily refreshment and pleasure to the point of drunkenness (19.5, 6, 8, 9, 22). The many repetitions force us to acknowledge the pleasure-loving aspect of the Levite and both his hosts; and it underlines the Levite's negligence toward his duties. (For Drunkenness and important references to the heart, see below under **Food and Drink**.)

Arms (זרע) are found in the Samson story (see below), but not elsewhere. The only *shoulder* (besides Samson's in 16.3) is Abimelech's when he puts a bough on his *shoulder* (שכמו) with which to burn the stronghold (9.48).

Hands are so numerous that they have been put in a separate category. However the *thumbs* and *big toes* of Adoni-Bezek can be inserted here. Since they are cut off (4 parts), they introduce the Mutilation Theme and parallel the dismemberment of the Concubine into 12 parts at the end (discussed above and in Chapters 1 and 2).

Knees (ברך) are alluded to when Sisera sinks to his *knees* (כרע, repeated 3x in this passage) between Jael's feet (5.27). Gideon's men *kneel* on their *knees* (ברכיו־כרע אל, repeated 2x) (7.5, 6). Jephthah puns several times on this word. When he sees his daughter (כראותו), he tears (יקרע) his clothes, and says, "Alas, my daughter, you have brought me to my *knees*" (הכרע הכרעתני), and continues with a similar sound, "You have become a great trouble to me" (בעכרי) (11.35).

Feet (רגל) occur often idiomatically, as in the expression *to go on foot*, meaning *walk* or *follow*. Deborah *follows* Barak, at his *feet*, while Issachar also sets out behind him at his *feet*. Gideon has his troops at his *feet*, and the spies in the story of Micah (18.2, 14, 17) and the troops in the last story "go on their *feet*" (i.e., are *foot* soldiers, 20.2). Adoni-Bezek's *big toes* are described as the "big *toes* of his *feet*" (1.6, 7). Eglon is thought to be *covering his feet* (a euphemism for *relieving himself*). On two occasions *feet* are not strictly idiomatic: when Sisera falls at Jael's *feet* (word used 2x) and when the travelers wash their *feet* in the Ephraimite's house (19.21). The washing of the feet in this story is really a superfluous detail, completely incidental to the plot. While it highlights the *hospitality* theme, it is an example of how the author takes the opportunity to insert another body part. Achsah's name means "anklet." Possibly the horses' *hooves* (עקבי־סוס) in *The Song* should also be placed in the category of *feet* (5.22).

Wombs. Eglon's *belly* (בטן, 3.21, 22) links with Samson's mother's *belly* (same word, *womb*), and it is the term Sisera's mother uses twice for *captive maidens—wombs* (though a different Hebrew word, רחם) (5.30). *Captive maidens* are a pointer to the last chapter, the captive virgins of Jabesh-Gilead and the daughters of Shiloh, who are soon to have their wombs filled. When one analyzes the significance of the keywords, this decoding is by no means outrageous. It is backed up by a great deal of evidence in this and the following chapter.

Thus we find references to body parts in every story. This cannot be accidental. They have a relationship with the dismemberment theme discussed in Chapter 2.

2. Body Parts in the Samson Story (Including Hands)

Nearly *all* the parts of the *body* are included in the Samson story, with the interesting variation that not all of them are *human* parts and not all are *living* parts. Two of these have to do with *carcasses*. When Samson returns to look at the lion cub which he has torn apart, he finds its *carcass* (מפלת); in its *body* (גוית) is the honey, which he takes (14.8). The second *carcass* is the (implied) *skeleton* of an ass, from which he takes the *jawbone* (לחי־חמור,15.15). That he takes something from each *carcass* is not accidental. He is violating one of the Nazirite rules, not to touch a dead body. The foxes, whose *tails* (זנב, mentioned 3x) he ties together by pairs and sets on fire, are soon to be charred *carcasses* (15.4-5). All these destroyed bodies are part of the Mutilation/Dismemberment Theme.

Samson certainly tears the lion's whole *body* apart, but the word is not used.

As has already been mentioned, Samson's *life* (נפש) was vexed to death by Delilah. And in the temple of Dagon when he prays to Yhwh, he asks that his *life* die (16.30, תמות נפשי).

Outstanding is that the *spirit of Yhwh* (רוח יהוה) comes upon him 4x (13.25, 14.6, 14.19, 15.14). It probably came a 5th time when he calls upon Yhwh to quench his thirst and when his spirit (רוח) revives after he drinks from the spring (15:18, 19); and a 6th time when he calls upon Yhwh and topples the temple (16.30). Whether or not the 5th and 6th instances imply the coming of the *spirit of Yhwh* (רוח יהוה), the *spirit* comes to Samson more times than to all the other main characters combined. This presents a dilemma in judging Samson's ethics: would the author believe that the *spirit* of Yhwh comes to a rank sinner? Or does the fact that the *spirit* of Yhwh comes to him mean that all his peccadillos were forgiven, or even that they were not peccadillos at all? Or that because he was divinely endowed, his peccadillos were worse than they would be to an "ordinary man"? Or that the coming of the *spirit* has nothing whatsoever to do with the ethics of the receiver? (See Chapter 4, where ethics are discussed.)

What would the Samson story be without *hair* (or *locks*) on his head (ראש)? Actually, his *head* is mentioned 5x: in the command that "no razor shall come to his *head*" (13.5, repeated to Delilah in 16.17) and in the phrases "locks of my *head*" (16.13, 19) and "hair of his *head*" (16.22).

Initially, his *hair* is referred to 3x as the "seven *locks* of my *head*" (מחלפות ראשי, plaits or braids) (16.13, 14,19). The sole appearance of the words of *hair of his head* (שער־רושו) comes when his hair begins to grow in prison (16.22); no doubt the

hair is too short then to be plaited and could no longer be called locks (מַחְלְפוֹת).
Samson's glorious hair might remind us of, and may be a reference to, the hair of
Absalom (2 Sam 14.26), whose head got caught (probably by his luxurious *hair*) in
the branches of an oak tree (18.9). *Hair* was a danger to them both.

The *mouth* is represented by the *jawbone* of the ass (15.15) and is alluded to when
Elohim hears the *voice* of Manoah (13.9).

The word *face* is used when Manoah and his wife "fell on their *faces* (עַל־פְּנֵיהֶם)
to the ground" (13.20), signifying prostration in adoration or submission. *Ears* are not
referred to in Samson.

Eyes (5x) and *vision* are crucial to the story. The first sentence of the story sets the
mood: "The Israelites did evil in the *eyes* of Yhwh." Samson's mother tells Manoah of
the visit of the stranger, whose "*appearance* was like the *appearance* of a messenger-
angel" (מַרְאֵהוּ כְּמַרְאֵה מַלְאָךְ, from the word *to see*) (13.6). The source of Samson's
error is his *eyesight*: in finding the Timnite to be "right in his *eyes*" (i.e., pleasing)
(14.3, 7). He no doubt felt the same way about Delilah. When his *eyes* are *gouged out*,
his punishment "fits the crime" of seeing and desiring foreign women. When he
prays for vengeance, he asks for "one vengeance for his two *eyes*" (16.25). *Eyes* are
clearly his problem, reminding us of A. E. Housman's line in Poem xlv,

> If it chance your eye offend you,
>
> > Pluck it out, lad, and be sound,
>
> 'Twill hurt, but there are salves to friend you,
>
> > And many a balsam grows on ground.

But the poem continues:

> And if your hand or foot offend you,
>
> > Cut it off lad, and be whole,
>
> But play the man, stand up and end you
>
> > When the sickness is your soul.

As already mentioned, the Israelites are supposed to do what is right in *Yhwh's eyes*,
not what is right in *their own eyes*. *Judges* lacks a Helen of Troy, but it does not lack the
theme of duty vs. desire.

The *heart* is mentioned 5x. Delilah tries to arouse Samson's guilt when she accuses
him, "How can you say 'I love you' when your *heart* is not with me?" (16.15). Twice we
learn that he has told her all his *heart*, and she repeats this to the Philistines (16.17, 18
[2x]), meaning that Samson has at last revealed what was hitherto hidden or secret
(another keyword). And it is when the *hearts* of the Philistines are merry (כְּטוֹב לִבָּם,
meaning *intoxicated*) that they call Samson to the temple so that he can entertain them
(יִצְחָק לִפְנֵיהֶם) (such as doing feats of strength before them) (16.25).

The *heart* is also mentioned 5x in the Concubine story, when the father-in-law is
urging the Levite to remain and carouse with him: "Strengthen your *heart*" and "Let
your *heart* be merry." The pleasure-loving Samson is to be compared with the pleasure-
loving Levite. Samson did not succeed in his marriage or love affairs. Neither did
the Levite. Samson, who ought to be the observer of (Nazirite) laws is parallel to the

Levite, who ought to be the giver of laws. This comparison denigrates the Levite. Samson at least killed some Philistines. The Levite did nothing to protect Israel against its enemies. He was the cause (not the Benjaminites?) of the civil war that almost destroyed Israel.

Samson is a muscle man. After visiting the harlot of Gaza all night, his strength is not sapped, for he puts the city gate and posts on his *shoulders* (כתפיו) and carries them up the hill to Hebron (16.3). Several times when he has bindings on his *arms* (זרע—mentioned in 15.14, 16.12), he either snaps them off easily, or they become as flax burned with fire and melt off his *hands* (15.14). When he tears the young lion apart, he has "nothing in his *hand*" (14.6). *Hands* as *tools* and *weapons* (two other categories) are implied. (Cf. Léon Bonnat's wonderful painting of the muscular nude Samson prying open the jaws of a fierce lion with his bare hands.) When Samson ties the 300 foxes together in pairs by the *tails* and burns them, we visualize him doing this with his bare *hands*. When he takes up the *jawbone* with murderous intent, the author tells us—unnecessarily it would seem—that "he *reached* his *hand* and seized it" (15.15) and then *sent* (*threw*) the jawbone from his *hand* (15.15, 17). This feat was accomplished solely by *hand*. (*Reached* and *sent* are also keywords.)

At the beginning of the Samson story, Yhwh is said to have taken the two offerings "at our *hands*" (מידינו—i.e., the hands of Manoah and his wife) (13.23). Samson scoops out the honey with his *palm* (כף) and goes along eating from it. (Pretty gooey.)[18] Samson gives some of the honey to his parents, who also, we assume, eat from their *palms* (14.9). The word *hand* is used twice in 15.18 when Samson asks Yhwh, "After you gave this great victory to the *hand* of your servant, shall I now die of thirst and fall into the *hand* of the uncircumcised?" (15.18). When he drinks from the spring, no doubt he either uses his cupped *hands*, or *laps* like a dog with his *tongue* (à la Gideon's men), though we are not told which way. When Samson rips up the gate and its bars at Gaza, we visualize him doing this with his *hands* (16.3). In the Delilah scene, the Philistines bring Delilah the money in their *hands* (16.18). (The word *hand* is not necessary to convey meaning; again the author was able to insert this body part one more time.) Near the end, the lad leading the blind Samson into the temple is holding his *hand* (16.26). Here the *hand* serves both a real and a literary purpose, reminding us that the reason he needs help in order to get into the temple and to get his hands into the position is that he is blind. "Let me *feel* (הימשני) the pillar on which the house stands, so that I may lean on them" (16.26)—another implied reference to *blindness* and to *hands*. And finally in the temple, Samson leans his weight against the pillars, "his *right* [hand] on one and his *left* [hand] on the other" (16.29); in this verse, the actual word for *hand* is only implicit.

All together, the word *hand* is used at least 7x in Ch.15 (15.13, 14, 15, 17, 18[2x]) and 4x in Ch. 16 (16.18, 23, 24, and 26). Amazingly, although these references are provided in an unnoticeable manner, the author is surely focusing on this particular bodily part throughout the Samson story. Samson never wields a sword.

The 300 foxes have *tails* (זנב, repeated twice). Samson smites his enemies *hip* (שוק, leg) and *thigh* (ירך) (15.8). Delilah has Samson sleeping on her *knees* (ברכיה) (16.19).

Though the sexual organs are mentioned explicitly in the Ugaritic myths, they are not mentioned in *Judges*. That the Philistines are *uncircumcised* is an allusion to the penis (הערלים, *having foreskins*) (14.3, 15.18). (Two hundred *foreskins* are collected by David [1 Sam 18.27], a Samsonesque feat, to say the least. The word *foreskins* does not appear in *Judges*.)

Finally there are 2 allusions to the *womb* (when we are told that Samson's mother was barren (עקרה ולא ילדה) (13.2, 3), 3 references to *conception* (הרה, 13.3, 5, 7), and 3 direct mentions of the *womb* (בטן) (13.5, 7; 16.17). Samson is a bodily man who emerged from that bodily *womb*. And again, this is a link with two events, the captive maidens (*wombs*) Sisera's mother is expecting and the abduction of the maidens of Jabesh-Gilead and the daughters of Shiloh at the end of the book.

3. Hands (Excluding Samson's)

The word *hand* is used at least 92x in the book; the *palm* (כף, *fist*) of the *hand* is used 6x.

Many references to *hand* appear in the expression of how someone (including Yhwh or a god) will give (or sell) an enemy into someone else's *hand*. Though idiomatic, these instances play at least a subliminal role in the category. The following is a sampling: Yhwh gave the Israelites into the *hands* of plunderers (שסים) who plundered them, and he sold them (ימכרם) into the *hands* of their enemies (2.14); Yhwh sold them into the *hand* of Cushan-rishathaim (3.8); Yhwh sold them into the *hand* of Jabin (4.2); Deborah says Yhwh will give Sisera into the *hand* of Barak (4.7); that Yhwh will sell Sisera into the *hand* of a woman (4.9); yet Deborah tells Barak that Yhwh has given Sisera into *his hand* (4.14); Yhwh sold them into the *hands* of the Philistines (10.7); Yhwh gave them into my *palm* (12.3); our Elohim has given Samson into our *palm* (16.23); our Elohim has given our enemy into our *palm* (16.25); the land is rich on both *hands* (meaning, from one side to the other) (18.10); and finally, Yhwh said: "Tomorrow I will give him into your *hand*" (20.28). (For usage in the Gideon story, see below.)

In this list we see how often Yhwh, who had once freed the Israelites from slavery in Egypt, threatens to return them to that condition. When they lapse and worship false gods, Yhwh *sells them* into their enemies' *hands*. Paradoxically, the Israelites are also enslaving, or trying to enslave, the inhabitants of the land of Canaan (1.28, 30, 33, 35).

Beyond these idioms, the word *hand* is often used deliberately and significantly, and we are often told which hand, *right* or *left*, was involved. In the Ehud story, we learn that Ehud's *right hand* is impaired (אטר, bound, 3.15), but he triumphs over the enemy despite this handicap (3.19). *Left-handedness* existed among the

Benjaminites, and it is ironic that the name "Benjamin" means "son of the *right hand*." The book thus begins with one *left-handed* Benjaminite with a sword who is an Israelite *hero*, and ends with 700 *left-handed* Benjaminites with slingshots (20.16), who now are Israelite *enemies*—"every one of them able to sling a stone at a hair and not miss." A nice parallel inversion.

As already mentioned, the word *reach* (שלח) is a marker for intentional parallelisms. "Ehud *reached* with his *left hand*, *took* his sword from his *right thigh*" (belly) (3.21). Jael *reaches* her hand (*left*, implied) to the tent peg and her *right hand* (explicit) to the workman's hammer (5.26) (implying that she reached for the two objects simultaneously); presumably she left the peg in Sisera's temple and no doubt *dropped* the hammer. Samson *reaches* for the jawbone, but *throws* it away. Gideon's men and Samson, like Jael, are also wonderfully ambidextrous: Gideon's men go to battle with torches in their *left* hands and trumpets in their *right* hands:

> So the three companies blew the trumpets and broke the jars, holding in their left hands the torches, and in their right hands the trumpets to blow; and they cried, "A sword for the Yhwh and for Gideon!" (NRS, 7.20).

Since the torches were in the pitchers (7.16), the pitchers must have also been in their *left hands*. It is hard to imagine how the men could blow the trumpets while holding the pitchers and torches as well: this great juggling act is comparable to Samson's feat with the 300 foxes (notice parallelism with Gideon's 300 men). Samson must have used both hands with the foxes, and, as already noted, it is explicit that Samson uses *right* and *left* [*hands* implied] on the columns in the temple (16.29).

In the Gideon story, the oppressiveness of the *hand* of the Midianites is emphasized: Yhwh delivers the Israelites into the hand of the Midianites, and the Midianites prevail (6.1, 2); Gideon accuses Yhwh of having given the Israelites into the *palm* of Midian (6.13); but Yhwh tells Gideon that he will save (הושעת) Israel from the *palm* of Midian (6.14); Yhwh promises to give the Midianites into Gideon's *hand* (7.7); Yhwh says that he has given the army into Gideon's *hand* (7.9); Elohim has given Midian into Gideon's *hand* (7.14); Elohim has given the princes of Midian into Gideon's *hand* (8.3); and the people of two cities ask Gideon: "Is the *palm* [of the hand] of Zebah and Zalmunna in your *hand*?" (8.6, 7, 15); finally, the men of Israel say that Gideon has delivered them from the *hand* of Midian (8.22). Why so much stress on the word *hand*? I do not know the answer.

Yairah Amit finds that in certain passages, the word *hand* is linked with the word *deliver* or *save*: the *hand* of Gideon (6.36, 37; 7.9, 14; 8.6, 7, 15); the *hand* of Israel (7.2 [2x], 7, 15); the *hand* of Ephraim (8.3).[19] That *hands* are used mainly on objects (instead of on swords) underlines Yhwh's fear "that Israel will attribute the victory to the might of its own *hands*." And, Amit continues, the word *to save* (ישע) is linked with the word *hand* (in 6:14 [2x],15, 31, 36, 37; 7:2, 7; 8:22) and believes that the outstretched hand is not a human *hand*, but "the divine hand" (ibid.).

Some of the other references to *hands* in this story include: the messenger of Yhwh *reaching* (שׁלח, that keyword again) with a staff in his *hand* (6.21); Gideon squeezing the fleece and wringing the dew out of the fleece (6.38), no doubt with his *hands*—how else? (the counterpart to Samson with the honey); and his men lapping (water) with *hands* to their *mouths* (7.6).

In the Abimelech story, Zebul tells Abimelech to do to Gaal as his *hand* finds (to do) (9.33). Abimelech takes an axe in his *hand* (9.48). Jephthah defends himself against the protesting Ephraimites: "I tōok my life in my *palm*" by fighting the Ammonites (12.3).

Micah's mother consecrates the silver to Yhwh from her *hand* (17.3). Micah installs a son as priest (literally, ימלא את־יד, filled the *hand)* (17.5) and later installs a Levite as priest (17.12). The Danites warn (threaten) the priest when they are stealing him from Micah: "Keep quiet (החרישׁ); put your *hand* upon your *mouth*" (18.19).

In the story of the Levite's Concubine, the placement of her *hands* seems at once both pitiful and sinister: after she is raped all night and crawls back to the house, she is found the next morning by her husband: "fallen down at the door of the house, and *her hands were upon the threshold*' (סף) (19.27).

This scene is strangely parallel to 1 Samuel 5.4, where "Dagon had fallen on his face to the ground before the ark of Yhwh, and *both his hands were lying cut off upon the threshold*' (a different word for *threshold* is used, however, מפתן). Dagon was apparently headed *outside*, while the Concubine was headed *inside*. What the *threshold* signifies in the ark episode, I do not know (*thresholds* are discussed under the heading **Buildings** below), but the dismembered body indicates that Dagon had been defeated. The Concubine, however, was stretching out for help. The position of the *hands* emphasizes how near to safety she got, and yet how far from it she was. Because she was that close, we are meant to ask: why did no one inside the house come to her rescue? The Knights in Shining Armor inside the house were snoring.

In the last scene, where the 200 Benjaminites "seize" the 200 daughters, we have to supply the details and imagine the men grasping the women with their *hands* and throwing them up on their *shoulders*, with the daughters' *arms* and *legs* flailing about furiously and *fists* pounding against the *backs* of their abductors (as in Poussin's two paintings of the *Rape of the Sabine Women*), knowing that they are soon to be raped (a bodily experience, to say the least). It is a "merry scene" from one point of view, but from another, it is a bodily horror.

Hands are also important in the Ugaritic myths, and we told at times which hand was used. For example:

'Anatu took [his hand],
  'Athtartu took his left hand . . . . (KTU III.1.40)

She took her spindle in her hand,
  (And) the spindle fell from her right hand . . . . (KTU IV.1.3-4)

> Take your nose in your hand,
>> your windpipe in (your) right hand . . . .
>
> Then the hero Ilaha'u
> took his nostrils in his hand,
>> his throat in his right hand. (*Keret* III.i.42-43, 46-48)

> "Let her take the cup from my hand,
>> the goblet from my right hand!"
>
> They brought Pughatu in and she gave him drink.
> She took the cup from his hand,
>> the goblet from his right hand. (*Aqhat* III.iv.53-57de Moor' . . . passim)[20]

The messengers who come to Anat in the Baal Cycle tell her that Baal has gone hunting (indeed, a strange thing for a god to do):

> His bow he took in *his (left) hand,*
> and his arrows in *his right hand* . . . . (1.10.ii.6-7, Wyatt, *Religious Texts,* 156)

And

> Baal spoke:
> the axe his (left) hand indeed brandished,
> the cedar (was) in his right hand. (1.4.vii.40-2, ibid., 110-111)

Nicolas Wyatt mentions "the complex symbolism of left and right in ancient thought."[21] Other body parts are also mentioned often in the myths—notably, the head, skull, heart, and (quite vividly) sexual organs, as well as those in the quotations above. But these parts do not seem to play a part in the *design* of the myths, as the patterns and codes do in *Judges.*

As the analysis of these body parts indicates, the author of *Judges* tried unremittingly to compel us to be aware of how the characters were affected by everything—not only mentally and emotionally, but also *in the material body.* Body parts have been tucked in everywhere, though paradoxically, they are scarcely noticed by the reader. This is not merely a story about violence, the horrors of war, justice, retribution, vows, apostasy, mother-son and father-daughter relationships, etc. It is not even merely about warfare and chaos in Israel and the need for the rule of law. But it is a story about the *connection of all these things* to the *body.* The author of *Judges* has "covered up," concealed, and hidden the pain and the suffering involved when these body parts become disabled, mutilated, or destroyed when the battles are done, but the many parts should alert us to the fact that he had not forgotten the site of all the action, and all the wounding: the human body. And as in modern media, the actual damage is covered up. Elaine Scarry should have used *Judges* in her book *The Body in Pain.*[22]

(The reader should remember that if sections 1 and 3 above had included the body parts from the Samson story, each keyword group would have been much larger.)

Tools, Weapons, Instruments, and Vehicles

All these *objets trouvés* provide insight into the author's creativity.

The category of *Tools* provides an interesting connection between war and peace. Most of the military *tools* (*weapons*) have already been discussed in Chapter 2. In addition, a *commander's staff* (שבט ספר) (5.14) and the *tip* of the (messenger's) *staff* (קצה המשענת) (6.21) are also mentioned in the book. Most of the other tools, however, are everyday items, the ordinary implements of the household and a person's occupation, though they may be used in violent actions. Domestic life is not slighted in this book.

An unspecified tool is used to cut off Adoni-Bezek's toes and thumbs (1.6, 7), probably a *sword*, though a *knife* might have done the job more efficiently and prevented the amputation of the other fingers and toes.

Ehud locked (נעל) the doors after he made his exit following the murder of Eglon (3.23). We are not told what tool he used; perhaps he took the *key* from the inside of the doors, locked them, and left with the key. Eglon's attendants got a *key* (מפתח) to unlock the door (3.25). According to Philip J. King and Lawrence E. Stager, Eglon had a tumbler lock that could be locked from the outside by putting one's hand through a hole beside the bar and sliding it shut. The key was a bent stick with teeth at the end that matched the pins in the lock. When it was inserted from the outside, it fitted into the pins and allowed the bolt to be drawn.[23] What was previously a how-was-it-done mystery turns out to have a simple explanation.

Shamgar uses an *ox-goad* (מלמד־הבקר) to smite 600 Philistines (3.31).

Jael wields a *hammer* (מקבת) and a *tent peg* (יתד 4.21 [2x], 22; 5.26) to kill Sisera. A different word is used for *hammer* (הלמות) in *The Song*, (5.25) the same word supplying the verb for Jael's action of hammering (הלמה) Sisera with the peg (5.26). The word is used again in for the *hammering* of the horses' hooves.

Two musical *instruments* are mentioned: the *tambourine* or *timbrel*, used by Jephthah's daughter when she comes dancing out to meet her father, and *the shofar*, used by Ehud (3.27) to summon his troops and later by Gideon and his men. *Shofars* are strongly emphasized in the Gideon story, where they are referred to 9x (6.34; 7.8, 16, 18 [2x], 19, 20 [2x], 22), seven of them with the verb *to blow* (יתקע בשופר). The *shofar* is also *blown* in 3.27 to muster the troops.

Incidentally, *Judges* is not so noisy as the *Iliad*, but it does contain many sounds, especially in Ch. 7, Gideon's attack on the Midianites. (See **Appendix 1**, this chapter, for a table of references to *sound/noise*.)

Abimelech uses *axes* (הקרדמות) to cut the branches with which to burn the tower of Shechem (9.48, 49), and he is fatally injured with an *upper millstone* (רכב פלח) (9.53). Many scholars have wondered how the woman in the Abimelech story got her millstone up to the top of the tower (9.53). If we are imagining the kind of millstones common in the 19th Century CE, we may visualize her as something of an Amazon, as many interpreters like Block have done (333). But it is a פלח רכב, an upper millstone, which, as King and Stager describe it, fits into the miller's hand (95) and thus was probably not very heavy. This information, however, does not diminish our admiration for the woman's quick thinking (her bricoleur quality) in taking the millstone with her when she mounted to the top of the tower, or for the excellence of her aim.

Samson uses the *jawbone* of an ass to kill 1,000 Philistines (15.15).

Delilah uses a *weaving pin* (16.13, 14 [2x]) to weave Samson's hair into the fabric on her *loom* (הארג) (16.14), but of course he breaks loose. Note once more that the Hebrew word for *weaving pin* (יתד) is the same as that of the *tent peg* used by Jael (4.21[2x], 22; 5.26). Ehud *plunges* (תקע) the sword into Eglon just as Delilah *plunges* (same word) the weaving pin against Samson's hair into the fabric on the loom. (In Gideon and in Ehud, however, תקע means *blow* on the trumpets.)

Though Samson was not supposed to allow a *razor* (מורה) (13.5, 16.17) on his head, he foolishly lets his hair be shaved (גלח, 16.17, 19, 22). Finally, he is bound by bronze *shackles* (נחשתים), which unlike the cords, seem to hold him (16.21).

Micah's mother takes her money to be smelted into idols by a man whom we assume works with *tools* (17.4). In the last story, the two asses have something (probably *saddles*) bound (חבושים) on them (19.10). Finally, the Levite cuts up the Concubine's body with a *knife* (מאכלת) (19.29), recollecting for us the cutting off of Adoni-Bezek's thumbs and big toes at the beginning of the book.

The only vehicles in the book are *chariots* mentioned in the first chapter, prominent in the Deborah story (4.7, 13[2x], 15, 16; 5.28[2x]) and said to be made of *iron* 3x (רכב ברזל) (1.19; 4.3, 13). The enemy alone has them. The people of Ugarit had chariots, but the iron part of the chariot is apparently an anachronism. One might expect to see a cart, but none is shown. The *lack of vehicles* is important, for it gives us a possible early date for the origin of the oral tales.

This is about the extent of the technology used, except for the weapons, which are discussed in Chapter 2. The society represented is pre-technological, and perhaps not quite so advanced as the Canaanites (with their chariots) and the Midianites (with their camels). Not the whole of the society is depicted, of course, only what serves the purpose of the narrative. In the following categories, however—fabric, agriculture, and buildings—we see a society of industrious, thriving, and knowledgeable people.

Fabric

A domestic item already mentioned above, *fabric* is extremely important. Since *fabric* in this book is also a *covering*, it is connected with the Hiding/Secrecy theme (discussed in Chapter 4) and as such is one of the most important objects in the book.

Ehud *covers* the sword on his right thigh with his *clothing* (girds it under his clothing, מתחת למדיו). Jael *covers* (כסה) Sisera with a *rug* (שמיכה) when he lies down in her tent (the verb *cover* is repeated for emphasis) (4.18, 19). Derived from the verb "cover" (סכה) is the *fabric* (המסכת) being woven on Delilah's loom (16.13). When Eglon is thought to be relieving himself, the idiom for that is "covering his feet" (מסיך הוא את־רגליו) (3.24).

Clothing or fabric is a prize in the spoils of war. Sisera's mother expects beautiful *clothing* from the victory:

Are they not finding and dividing the spoil?—	הלא ימצאו יחלקו שלל
A girl or two for every man;	רחם רחמתים לראש גבר
spoil of dyed stuffs for Sisera,	שלל צבעים לסיסרע
spoil of dyed stuffs embroidered,	שלל צבעים רקמה צבע
two pieces of dyed works embroidered	רקמתים לצוארי שלל
for my neck as spoil? (5.30)	

The four-fold repetition of *spoil* (שלל) is for emphasis—the taking of plunder for selfish reasons being under question in Israelite law. The word *dyed stuff* (צבע, colorful) is repeated 3x, and *embroidered* (רקמה) is repeated 2x. This word (רקמה), incidentally, is a wordplay with the two repeated words for captive women earlier in the same verse (רחם רחמתים, wombs). His mother wants *two* pieces of cloth for her neck. Each man is expected to get *two* wombs.

Gideon spreads an outer *garment* (שמלה) to collect from each of his men an earring from their *spoil*. Besides the earrings, Gideon got ornaments, pendants, other gold things, *collars* from the camels' necks, and *purple garments* of the kings of Midian (בגדי הארגמן שעל מלכי מדין) (8.26)—no doubt like what Sisera's mother was expecting. Since there were "camels without number" [6.5], the plunder must have been great. (*Theft/Plunder* is discussed in Chapter 4.)

The *fleece* (גזה) (also connected with the Animal category) that Gideon uses to test Yhwh is a *fiber*. The word is repeated 7x to signify its importance: 6.37(2x), 38(2x), 39(2x), 40. That the *fleece* is specifically a fleece of *wool* (הצמר) is mentioned once. In *The Song*, a saddle *blanket* (or garment or carpet) is mentioned (מד) (5.10), while the spirit of Yhwh *clothes* Gideon (רוח יהוה לבשה) (6.34) (a verb used only two other times in the Bible in this way, in 1 and 2 Chr). Jephthah tears his *clothes* when his daughter dances out of the house (11:35). Samson promises, and then gives, *clothing* as a reward for the Philistines for solving the riddle (14.12, 13, 19): thirty *linen garments* (סדינים, wrappers) and thirty sets of ordinary *clothes* (בגדים חליפת) (14.12) torn off the corpses of the 30 Ashkelonites he had killed. Part of Micah's annual payment to the Levite is a set of *clothes* (17.10).

Fabric, yarn, cords, ropes, and the *weaving of fabric* are stressed in the Samson story. First of all, the Judahites bind him with two *new ropes* (עבתים חדשים, *weavings*), which of course he breaks easily. The *ropes* become like *flax* (פשת) (a fiber), when melted with fire (15.13, 14). To weaken him, Delilah binds him with *seven fresh cords* (bowstrings, יתרים לחים) (S&M?). Again, he breaks them easily: they become like a *thread* (פתיל) *of fiber* (הנערת) when it nears the flame (16.7, 8, 9). When, like the Judahites, she binds him with *new ropes* (בעבתים חדשים) that have never been used, Samson also easily snaps them (16.11, 12 [2x]) as if they were *threads* (חוט).

Delilah's third attempt to bind Samson is an intricate allusion to the *weaving* process. He tells her: "If you *weave* (ארג) the seven *plaits* of my head" (מחלפות, i.e., braided like *weavings*, BDB 322) "into the *web*" (מסכה, fabric) ("on the *loom*" is implied), "I will become weak as any man" (16.13). So she takes the seven *locks of his head* and does this, plunging the *weaving* pin (תתקע ביתד) against the locks so as to imprison him securely. But he pulls the pin loose from the *loom* (ארג) and the *web* (מסכה) (16.14). (Strong hair!) (The spider and the web.) The seven braids (or *weavings*) are mentioned again when Delilah has them shaved off his head (16.19).

The numerous references to *fabric, web,* and *weaving* are surely meant to be noticed. They give us a glimpse of the domestic life of the times. They also emphasize cover (hiding) and secrecy. Finally, the emphasis on both *weaving* (the *web*) and the *threads* in the fabric is an allusion to, or metaphor of, the *intricacy* of the author's style. The book is a woven object of many threads and designs.

Animals and Agriculture

Agricultural references remind us of what most of the Israelite wars were about: protection of the land and the sustenance of the people.

Animals not related to agriculture include *camels, horses, deer,* and *fawn. Horses* are completely lacking except in the phrase "the sound of the *horses*' hooves" that Sisera's mother in *The Song* is expecting to hear (5.22). No doubt Sisera's chariots were pulled by *horses,* but the Israelites themselves have no horses.[24] Since the Israelites had only *asses,* Sisera's 900 *horse*-drawn chariots of iron and the Midianite camels were guaranteed to inspire terror. Asses are not mentioned as being used in warfare, but as a means of transportation in domestic life as well as in agriculture.

Camels were introduced at the end of the Late Bronze Age (Boling, 129). Because of their speed, endurance, and ability to survive without food and water for long periods of time,[25] camels were a formidable presence. The absence of camels among the Israelites probably attests that the "history" depicted in these stories is quite early.

The only people in the book who have *camels* (6.5; 7.12; 8.21, 26) are the Midianites, who, along with their livestock and camels, were as numerous as swarms of *locusts* (6.5) and whose camels as innumerable as the sand on the seashore (7.12). Thus the Midianites were very powerful. It was from the camels' necks that Gideon took his spoil—certainly a vast number of ornaments! Oddly enough, there is no mention of his having kept and used the camels.

Ass is a crucial keyword. The *ass* signals the parallel between the Achsah story (where a *live* woman is riding an *ass*) and the Concubine story (where a *dead* woman is slung across the back of an *ass*). The jawbone of an *ass* figures as a weapon that Samson uses against his enemies. *Ass* is mentioned 5 times in the Samson story and 5 times in the Concubine story in which the asses are used for transporting the

Levite, his supplies, the lad, and the corpse of the Concubine. Since there were two *asses* in this episode, it may be presumed that the Concubine rode on one of them while she was alive, as she did when she was dead. The lad probably walked. *Asses* aplenty are also used by some of the minor judges.

Agricultural animals include 1) benign animals like *goats, kids of she-goats* (the author is at least minimally interested in relationships and ages among animals), *sheep, goats, kids, flocks, dogs, asses, calves, beasts (cattle, bull, heifer)*, and *honey bees*, and 2) creatures harmful to the farmer such as *locusts* and *scorpions* (in a place name), *foxes, cub of a lion, raven* (name of Oreb), and *wolf* (name of Zeeb). *Serpents* are not shown in this particular Eden. The *spider* and its web are alluded to when Delilah weaves a web on her loom to catch Samson.

References to *agriculture* are fundamental. The author is advocating the *growing* of *crops* and *rearing* of *animals*, and opposing wanton destruction of them. (Since most agricultural items appear in the analysis of the **Food and Drink** category below, only those connected with the actual act of farming will be discussed here.)

In the Deborah story, Deborah's name contains the allusion to *honey bee*, while the milk Jael gives Sisera provides an allusion to *sheep* and *goats*; *cows* are not specifically mentioned, though a *bull* and *oxen* are. *Bees* are producing honey in the Samson story. *Locusts*, alluded to when the Midianites invade, are a metaphor for the Midianites' destructiveness. Birds are not mentioned except for the reference to a *raven* in Oreb's name. There are no fish.

At the beginning of the Gideon story we have the *planting of seed* by the Israelites and the *destruction* of *produce* and *farm animals* (*sheep, ox, ass*) by the Midianites. Parallel to this is the destruction of Philistine crops (*vineyards, orchards*, and *grain fields*) by Samson. (This important contrast has been largely unnoticed.) Samson destroys some dangerous beasts: one *lion cub* and 300 *foxes*, but he is primarily a wanton destroyer of *crops* and people.

While Gideon *threshes grain* at the beginning of the story, he is *threshing people* at the end (8.7). Instead of weeding out *thorns* and *briers* from his own crops to a good purpose, he is inflicting these scratchy things on people (his own) to a bad purpose. Was he justified? the author may be asking. In any case, as mentioned above, we see a deterioration of Gideon's purpose in life. The *fleece* he uses in the wet/dry test is a reminder of the importance of *sheep* and *goats* as well as of fabric.

Besides the three kinds of trees (*olive, fig*, and *vine*) in Jotham's fable, we have again *brambles* (which are a nuisance to farmers). The *vine* in the fable connects with the *vineyards* which Gaal and his men cut down and trod on to make wine (9.27)—an act of devastation, as the *grapes* had not been planted by *them*. Wine also connects with the Philistine *vineyards* destroyed by Samson, with the *vineyards* where the Benjaminites hide in order to seize the daughters of Shiloh, and with the various *drinking episodes* (Samson, Gaal, and the Levite of the Concubine story, all discussed below). Abimelech's *sowing of salt* over the destroyed city of Shechem is not only a *violation* of a good farmer's practice (sowing seeds) but a destruction of mother earth herself. No one can grow anything there after that.

In the Samson story, Samson's mother at the outset is found sitting "in a *field*." Why in this particular location? The author may merely want to make clear that she is alone, not with her husband. But why a *field*? Possibly in the Middle East, then as now, women— not men—worked the fields. In any case, she is associated with agriculture.

(Yair Zakovitch, following Lord Raglan's analysis of heroes in myth, shows that Samson has many of the characteristics of semi-divine heroes. In the original myth, from which the Samson story was supposedly derived, the god would have seduced the hero's mother in a field. In the Israelite version, Samson's father becomes a mortal. Some recent interpretations include the possibility that Samson's mother was impregnated by the messenger-angel, not by Manoah. The scene in the field and the heavenly messenger in *Judges* 13, according to Zakovitch, are all that remain of the original mythological birth story.[26] We are also meant to recognize the mother's lowly status, like Mary in the New Testament. Samson has long been seen as a prototype of Christ.)

A *kid of a she-goat* is mentioned both in the scene when Gideon feeds his messenger-angel and also where Manoah (Samson's father) serves a *kid of a she-goat* (3x) to the messenger-angel. Samson takes a *kid of the flock* when he goes to visit the Timnite woman he assumed was still his wife.

Significantly, this is at the time of the *wheat harvest*. Instead of *harvesting* crops, Samson *destroys* the *shocks of grain*, the *vineyards*, and *olive groves*, all of which ominously echo Jotham's warning (9.7-20). Samson like Abimelech may also be a something of a *bramble*. Just as the Midianites had been to Gideon and the Israelites, so was Samson to the Philistines "the destroyer of our land" (16.24). Ironically, whereas in this scene he is destroying Philistine crops (depriving the Philistines of nourishment), at the end when he is blinded, he is *grinding grain* at the mill, presumably for *flour*, which will be used to *nourish* the Philistines.

In the Micah story, the Danites covet the *fertile (good) land* of the people of Laish, where "there is no lack of anything." As they migrate northward, they drive their *cattle* before them (18.21) just as the Midianites once did in the Gideon story (6.5). It is surely for the purpose of this contrast that the author gives us these parallel details. The Danites now have become like the Midianites.

In the last story, the old Ephraimite returns to Gibeah after a day's *work* in the *field*. Though the Levite has *straw* and *fodder* for the asses, and food and wine for himself, Concubine, and lad, the Ephraimite instead provides fodder for the asses and probably the food and drink for his guests.

In the civil war at the end, the tribes are pursuing vigorously (רדף, 20.43) their brother tribe, the Benjaminites, and in an act of Holy War, destroying everything under *the ban* (חרם)—i.e., destruction of males and beasts and everything else, and burning of the Benjaminite cities (20.48). They, too, are doing what their enemy, the Midianites, had been doing to the Israelites in the Gideon story. Significantly, it is also a parallel to the destruction of the city of Luz (under the ban, ויחרימו אותה) (1.17) at the beginning of the book. The Israelites have become their own enemy.

The analysis of *agriculture* reveals what was hidden to former interpreters of this book, that the Israelites themselves are going from bad to worse, eventually wantonly destroying their own sustenance and that of innocent people. The author is perhaps the first ecologist in literature.

Buildings

The inclusion in the book of so many buildings and building parts may be more than an evocation of realism; perhaps the author delighted in the variety of stage sets he provided for his characters. They also remind us where these particular episodes are happening—in villages and towns.

As with all the lists, there are two different ways of analyzing this one: 1) citing (analyzing) the different buildings throughout each consecutive story; and 2) classifying the buildings by types and parts and showing how each appears in consecutive stories. Both methods are equally important, and we learn something different from each of them, but under constraint of time, I apply only the second method here.

The binary opposites are *building/destroying*. Frequently the *destruction* and *construction* occur one after the other. An important pattern emerges: at the *beginning* of the book, the Israelites *destroy* the city of Luz, and the Canaanite man from Luz goes elsewhere and *builds* himself a new city (1.26); near the *end* of the book, the Israelites (Danites) have *destroyed* the city of Laish, exterminated the inhabitants, and *rebuilt* it for themselves (18.28); while at the *end* of the book, the Benjaminite cities are *destroyed* by their *fellow Israelites* and afterwards the *Benjaminites* are *rebuilding* them (21.23).[27]

Gideon's act of *destroying* the *altar* to Baal is mentioned 5x (6.25, 28, 30, 31, 32), his *cutting down the Asherah* 3x (6.26, 28, 30), and his *building an altar* to Yhwh 3x (6.24, 26, 28). This destruction has Yhwh's approval. There is destruction for good reasons vs. destruction for bad reasons, another binary opposite. We have to distinguish between them.

Corresponding to Gideon's altar, an altar is also *built* at the end of the book (21.4) when the Israelites want Yhwh to identify those who had failed to respond to the summons to come out against the Benjaminites.

The literal *houses* spoken of are those of Jephthah; the Timnite's father (both houses are threatened with fire); Micah; the father of the Concubine; and the old man in Gibeah who takes in the Levite and the Concubine for the night. (Idiomatic uses of "house of," as in the expression "house of Joseph" to refer to the two tribes of Ephraim and Manasseh, have not been included.) The four-room Israelite houses of Iron Age I (1200-1000 BC) that have been dug up by archaeologists generally consist of a courtyard surrounded by rooms on three sides.[28] It is this type of four-room house that we may picture Jephthah's daughter as dancing out of.

While it is sometimes conjectured that Sisera's mother is waiting in a *palace* for her son to return, that word is not used in the book.[29] All we know about her building is that it has a *window* with a *lattice*. Buildings described as "palaces" have been found by archaeologists, but many of these are simply larger houses than the normal four-room courtyard house (64). A monumental palace has been found in Samaria from Iron Age II (139), but if the author had had this kind of structure in mind, he would have been specific. Eglon probably had one of the larger houses; at any rate, his house seems to have a cool room on an upper level (מקרה, 2x; עליה, 4x) (3.20-25), which is also translated a "cool roof chamber," while NIV and NEB place it in a "summer palace"—a fanciful addition, in my opinion. Though Eglon is a "king," this translation for his dwelling gives a more grandiose impression of Eglon's building than the Hebrew does. The upper room has an area that has been translated as a "porch" or "vestibule" (מסדרונה, 3.23) as well as some kind of toilet facility. Boling has the servants remark that their master must be relieving himself "in the palace *rest*room," instead of simply a *cool* r*oom* (חדר המקרה) (3.24). And has Eglon, awaiting Ehud, sitting on a *throne*, another grandiose word, instead of the simple Hebrew word, *seat* (כסא) (3.20).

These are primitive times, and the book gives no evidence of luxury such as a Cecil B. De Mille liked to depict. The earrings and necklaces (signs of luxury) that Gideon took as plunder (1,700 shekels) were probably in reality small change; the silver of the five Philistine lords in the Samson story (5,500 shekels) and of Micah's mother (1,100 shekels) are also no doubt exaggerations like those reported of casualties in the battles and the number of Midianite camels.

Many of the inhabitants live in *tents*. The *tent* of Jael is prominent (4.11, 17, 18, 20, 21), and she is called "most blessed of *tent-dwelling* women" (5.24). Most of the other references to *tents* are in the Gideon story. The marauding Midianites come, as we might expect, with their *tents*, destruction of Israelites in mind (6.5). One of the Midianites dreams of a *tent* (mentioned twice) which is knocked down by a round loaf of barley bread (7.13). And Gideon, on one of his treks, passes through an area where people live in *tents* (8.11). Gideon's men who were rejected in the water-drinking scene are allowed to return to their *tents* (7.8). Whether they went back to their tents in the *camp* or to their *homes* is not clear, but they never return to battle.

The following are some of the instances where the word *floor* or *ground* (ארץ) is used: Eglon is on the *ground* (3.25), Jael smites the peg into Sisera's temple and nails him to the *ground* (4.21); Gideon places the wool fleece on the threshing *floor* (בגרן 6.37), the first time, to test if the *ground* (ארץ) is dry; and the second time, to test if the *ground* is wet (6.39, 40). Manoah and his wife "fall on their faces to the *ground*" (13.20); and the Concubine is on the *ground* (though the word is not specifically used), with her hands on the *threshold* (סף 19.27). Of course fighting men are "falling" all over the place, and of necessity, to *the ground*.

There are also a number of *temples*: in Shechem, the *house of Baal Berith* (9.4), the *house of their gods* (9.27), and the *house of El Berith* (9.46), which has a *stronghold* attached to it (all in the Abimelech story and likely one and the same temple). Remains of a remarkable broad-roomed temple, dating from the Middle Bronze Age, has been excavated at Shechem.[30] Other *temples* in *Judges* are the *house of Elohim* in the Micah story (17.5); the *house of Elohim* in Shiloh (18.31); and the *house of Yhwh* to which the Levite says he is returning in the story of the Concubine (19.18). The only *temple* which is described is the *house of Dagon*, with its unusual architectural feature, the pillars.

The meaning of *pillar* (or palisade מצב) at the oak where Abimelech was crowned king (9.6) is obscure, though it may well be an asherah. The *pillar* of smoke in the civil war (עמוד 20.40) may be meant to echo the *pillars* (עמודים) in the house of Dagon in the Samson story.

Pillars are integral to the Samson story (16.25, 26, 29).[31] According to Boling, just such a Philistine temple has been excavated with *two pillars* supporting the roof of the building (252). A small temple like this would not have had a roof large enough to hold the 3,000 men and women (not counting those on the floor below), who were able to watch Samson while he entertained them. But we are accustomed to hyperbole throughout *Judges.*

Part of the humor of the story consists of the fact that readers—even those who regard the story as pulp fiction—are compelled to figure out how such an episode could happen. Possibly the temple was like a peristyle or circular *arcade*, with an unroofed center over an *atrium*-like space as in a cloister. In trying to imagine this, readers must *construct* a temple in their imagination. This is an example of that "fourth or fifth dimension" in writing that Hemingway speaks about, the dimension in which the gaps of the narrative must be filled in by the reader. The text is an interactive one.

In our mind's eye, when the roof collapses, we can visualize the mass of bodies falling on top of "the lords and all the people below," tumbling like those bodies plunging into Hell in Michelangelo's *Last Judgment* in the Sistine Chapel, or in *The Last Judgment* of Hans Memling.

There is only one other *roof* in *Judges* and that is on the *tower* of Thebez, which Abimelech was attempting to destroy. The *cool room* (עליה המקרה) (3.20) in the Ehud story is thought by some to have been on the *roof*, but the word *roof* is not mentioned.

Towers predominate. The name Mizpah (in the Jephthah and Concubine stories) means *watchtower, high place* (BDB 859). This city name appears 10x in chs. 10-11, 20-21. Gideon, in his anger at the people of Penuel for not supplying his troops with food, swears he will tear down their *tower* (מגדל), and does so (8.9, 17). Abimelech destroys the *tower* of Shechem and "the thousand men and women" in it. Immediately he moves to destroy the *tower* of Thebez where the many people congregated on the *roof* barely miss sharing the fate of the people on the *roof* in the Temple of Dagon in the Samson story—and this because of the marksmanship of the woman who drops the millstone on Abimelech's skull before he can do his intended damage (9:49-52).

In the Gideon story, instead of living in *houses* or *tents*, the Midianites have forced the Israelites into *dens* (מנהרות), *caves* (מערות, hiding places), and *strongholds* (מצדות, masadas) (6.2). Gideon builds his altar on *top* of a *stronghold* (מעוז, high place) (6.26). After Abimelech strews the city with salt, the Shechemites retreat to their *strongholds* (צריח) (9.46, 49). Samson hides in the *cleft* (סעיף) of the *Rock* of

Etam (15.8, 11). Even the *prison* where Samson is held might be considered a lower place, although of course it was not necessarily underground. In contrast to such lower places, Eglon's *upper room*, the *roofs* and *the towers* would represent the *High* in the *High/Low* binary pair.

Besides Eglon's cool *roof chamber* in the story of Ehud (עליה המקרה) and a possible porch (מסדרונה, or colonnade), other architectural features or structures consist of sheep*folds* (a contested translation) in *The Song;* a *latticed window* (האשנב) through which Sisera's mother is gazing (5.28); a *prison* (בית האסרים a place of bindings) in the Samson story; and *rooms* (חדר) in two places in the Samson story (the Timnite's *room* and the *room* where the five Philistine lords hide while Delilah tries to wrest Samson's secret from him). The leaders of the people are called *cornerstones* (פנות, in 20.2), one of the rare metaphors.

Architectural features serve the purpose of lending authenticity to the stories. The author delights in them. He has a keen interest in how things are constructed—again, a possible interest mirrored in the structure of his book.

Subcategory: Doors (Entrances, Gates) (Open/Shut, Inside/Outside)

A minor theme is played with *doors,* which can be *opened, shut,* or *locked or unlocked.* Most, if not all, of the *doors, entrances,* and *openings* are dangerous *thresholds. Doors* and *entrances* separate the *inside* from the *outside.* People *enter* and *depart* through them. The *Inside/Outside* theme is announced where we see the Israelites intermarrying with the Canaanites and worshiping their gods (3.6) (the words *inside* and *outside* are not used, but are used in other like passages): Ibzan sent 30 daughters from *inside* to the *outside* (שלח החוצה) to be married, and brought 30 women from the *outside* (מן החוץ) to the *inside* for his sons (12.9). The "outside" is a euphemism for intermarriage with foreigners. Gaal, we might note, is an *outsider* who moves into Shechem, Abimelech's town. The reason that the Levite is besieged in Gibeah is that he is an *outsider* there, though the word itself is not used in these two cases. The word is used elsewhere only in 19.25, where the Concubine is pushed *outside.*

The author is playing with the *In/Out* theme in Ehud's attack on Eglon. Eglon's attendants *go out* (יצא) of the room and leave him alone with Ehud. Ehud strikes: "the hilt *went after* (אחר meaning *into* the flesh) the blade, the fat closed *upon* (בעד ... יסגר) the blade, he did not *draw* the sword *out* from his belly (שלף ... מבטנו לא), [and] the dirt *came out*" (יצא) (3.22). After assassinating Eglon, Ehud *comes out* (יצא) of the room, *closes* (יסגר) the doors after him (just as the fat *"closes"* over the blade), and *locks* (נעל) them. The lifeless Eglon has been *closed in.* When Ehud *goes* (יצא), the servants stand *outside* the room, find that the doors are *locked* (נעל), and realize that they cannot get *inside.* Finally, when Eglon still does not *open the doors* (איננו פתח דלתות), they get a key, *open* (יפתחו) the doors, and find their master dead on the floor *inside.* (3.19-25) (*Doors* are emphasized through 3 repetitions.) The *opening* and *closing* of *doors*, the locked *door*, the verb *come*, and that "the hilt went in after the blade" have sexual overtones, according to Alter and Brettler, among others.[32]

Jael lures Sisera into her tent: "Turn in, turn in, do not be afraid," repeated 2x (4.18). Sisera *turns in*, that is, comes from the *outside* to the *inside* of the tent. In the last scene, Sisera's mother is *inside*, looking *outside* (בעד, repeated a second time) through a *window*. The people in the Abimelech story enter *into* the *stronghold* of El Berith (9.46), where afterwards they are burned up by Abimelech. Likewise the people of Thebez *shut* themselves up (סגר, same word as when the fat *closed* over the blade in 3.22, 23) *inside* the *tower* (9.51).

Jephthah swears to make an offering of whatever *comes out* (יצא) of the *door* of his *house* when he returns; it is his daughter who *comes out* (יצאת). She tells him, "Do to me according to what has *come out* (יצא) of your mouth." (*Come out* is emphasized equally with the word *open* in the Jephthah story.)

In the solution to Samson's riddle, the word *come out* (יצא) is used twice: "*Out* of the eater *came* (יצא) something to eat, *Out* of the strong *came* (יצא) something sweet. Samson's riddle is foreshadowed by Jotham's riddle: "if not, let fire *come out* (יצא) from the thornbush . . ." (9.15). Samson wants to *go in* to his wife's room (אבאה אל־אשתי החדרה), but he is kept *out* (15.1).

The Levite *enters* Micah's house (17.10); the Danites *turn into* Micah's house when they hear the Levite's voice; and the Levite *goes out* (יבא) with them (18.20).

While the Ephraimite and the Levite are making themselves merry *inside*, the evil men of Gibeah are gathering *outside* with thoughts about *another* kind of "merriment." They pound on the *door* of the *house* and demand that the old man *bring out* (הוציא) the Levite (19.22), a parallel to the occurrence in the Gideon story, "*Bring out* your son" (הוציא) (6.30). The old Ephraimite says he will *bring out* his daughter and the Concubine (19.24); and finally, the Concubine is *brought out* (19.25). In the morning, the Levite *opens* the *door* of the house, *goes out*, and finds the Concubine's body (19.27). At the end of the book, when the daughters of Shiloh *come out* (יצא) to dance, the Benjaminites *come out* (יצא) *from* the vineyards and each man seizes a wife for himself (21.21).

The verb יצא, incidentally, is used when Yhwh brings (יצא, delivers) the Israelites up out of Egypt, "*out* of the house of slavery" (2.1, 6.8. and 7x or 8x elsewhere).

The other *goings in* and *comings out*, as the people *going into* the caves and towers, etc., are too many for these to be accidental.

Entrance (פתח) and its related words, *to open* and *gates*, are *openings* into cities and towns that must be kept secure; they *open* into *towers*, and *strongholds*, *hiding places*, and private *homes* where one expects to be safe. It is through an *entrance* that an enemy or some kind of disaster comes: consequently, *entrances* are of more importance to these stories than they might be in other fiction or history and should be given attention by the reader.

The man of Luz, who is a traitor to his own people, shows the Israelites the secret *entrance into* his town so that they can devastate the city (1.25). Thus the man of Luz story is an announcement of the *In/Out* theme. In *The Song*, we hear that "war was in the *gates*" (5.8). When Sisera comes to the *tent*, Jael has *come out* (יצא) and apparently is standing at the *entrance*, luring Sisera in, though the word *entrance* is not used until Sisera later commands her to stand at the *entrance* (פתח) and warn away anyone who comes searching for him (4.20). Gaal is standing at the *entrance* of the city when Abimelech and his men rise up from ambush (9.35).

When the rest of the Shechemites flee to the *stronghold* of the *tower* of Thebez, Abimelech approaches the *entrance* to the *tower* in order to burn it (9.52), but of course he is outwitted. Samson seizes the *doors* of the *gate* of Gaza and two *posts* (מזוזות) and the *bar* to the gate (הבריח) and carries the *gate* all the way up to Hebron (16.3), incidentally getting rid of the *entrance*. This is a clear echo of, and contrast to, the Luz story. In the Micah story, 600 Danites stand by the *entrance* of Micah's *gate* menacing him (18.16, 17). Finally, the author is careful to note that the Concubine's body lies at the *entrance* of the house (mentioned 2x) and her hands are on the *threshold* (הסף) (19.26, 27). She did not make it back into the place of safety (*inside*).

Obviously, *doors, entrances,* and *thresholds* are liminal. They are the line between friend and enemy, between safety and danger, between secrecy and awareness. The stories are all about being let in, or discovering a way to be let in, or forcing oneself in—or it is about being shut out. From the narrative point of view, the opening door leads to an event. We find out what happens, and our suspense ends.

Particular building parts—sometimes implied, when not actually stated—fascinated the author. The words furnished him the means to increase the amount of information in the narrative about his society.

Containers

The category of Containers is in some respects a subcategory of both Concealment (see Chapter 4) and Food and Drink. Some of them are simple everyday *household* or *agricultural utensils,* which contain the expected commodity, while others are surprises. The connection between Containers and Concealment is obvious in the following items: *dens, prisons, traps, ambushes,* and other *hiding places,* which contain people, and also *buildings,* like the *towers* in the Gideon and Abimelech stories, and the *prison* and the *temple* of Dagon in Samson.

Common containers include: two *basins* (גלת or *springs*) of water (Achsah story), a *skin* of milk (נאוד, 4.19), a lordly *bowl* (ספל אדירים, 5.25), a *basket* (סל) of meat and *a pot* (פרור, 6.19) of broth (to feed the messenger-angel in the Gideon story), a bowl (ספל) to catch the water from the fleece, 300 *empty pitchers* (or *jars*, כדים), which Gideon's men break, *cupped hands* which hold water (Gideon story) and *cupped palms* which hold honey (Samson story), a *well* (at Beer, to which Jotham flees), and another *spring* from which Samson drinks, undoubtedly from his hands.

Containers which are strange—for the way they are used or the fact that they are mentioned at all—include: the *wine press* holding Gideon, a *fleece* holding dew (when wrung out, it contained enough water to fill a *bowl*),[33] *the empty pitchers* holding torches, *hollow places* on the rock holding the food offerings (odd at least in that the hollow places are even mentioned) (both in Gideon and Samson), and the lion's *carcass* containing honey. Some of them perhaps do not hold their contents very well (*the hands* of Gideon's men and of Samson holding honey from the lion or the water from En Hakkore).

Even though small in number, the variety of *containers* indicates their importance to the tales: the whole book is a container of infinite meanings. These objects are not thrown in at random but are deliberately placed and emphasized.

Food and Drink

Closely connected with Containers is the Food and Drink category, which in turn is linked with Invitations, Requests, and Hospitality and with Animals and Agriculture. The theme is introduced early with the *scraps* under the table in the Adoni-Bezek story and with the *field* (for food) and the *water* (for *drink* and *irrigation*) in the Achsah story. These belong rightly in the category of Agriculture, but also announce the theme of food and drink.

Subcategory: Food

Food is present by implication in the Ehud story: Eglon, the tyrant, is *fat*; no doubt from *food*, perhaps from the very tribute exacted from Ehud's people. *Milk* (*curds*) is in the Jael episode (4.19; 5:25), and an allusion to *honey* is in Deborah's name, which means *honey bee*. This is matched by *honey* in the Samson story, a real parallel, which will cause the reader to reflect: So *this* is the land of milk and honey.

But it is not until we reach the Gideon story that food and drink play a major role. The subtitle of the Gideon story could be *Bread and Wine*, or *The Trials and Tribulations of an Israelite Farmer*. We may ask some questions:

Why are the Midianites compared with *locusts* so many times?
　　Ans. Because a plague of locusts is one of the most terrifying things that can *devastate crops*.
Why does Gideon use a *wine press* as a place to beat out his *grain* when he might have found other places to hide?
　　Ans. Because the image is symbolic: *bread and wine*.
Why does Gideon run to get a huge *ephah* of flour with which to *feed* the messenger-angel? And why does he mention the *unleavened cakes* (matzot) 4x, the *meat* (*flesh*) 4x, and the *broth* 2x?
　　Ans. To emphasize strongly the theme of *grain* and other *food*, the *unleavened bread* linking him to the Exodus, which he questions the messenger-angel about (6.13 and also 6.8, 9).

Why is the *bullock* (6.25, 28) mentioned as a sacrifice 3x? Note that this is the *2nd bullock*.

Ans. That Gideon's father has (or had) a *team* means that not only is he a farmer, but a prosperous *farmer* with two bulls.

Why does the test of Yhwh involve *dew* on *fleece*?

Ans. Because *dew* is a precious source of moisture in arid lands, and *fleece* represents the sheep and goats, which are the source of milk, meat, clothing, rugs. That the fleece is lying on the *threshing floor* is an allusion to Gideon's peacetime occupation.

Why does the test of the men involve *drinking*—some of them lapping *like dogs*?

Ans. To emphasize *water*. The *dog*, then as now, was the *farmer's* helper.

What is that preposterous *loaf of barley bread* (or moldy barley bread [Boling 146]) doing in the Midianite's dream?

Ans. It may be called a Freudian dream of *wish fulfillment*. The Midianite craves *food*. That's what the incursion is all about. But the dream also represents Freudian *fears*: that the *bread* may be bad and that the incursion will result in the Midianites' defeat.

Why is Oreb (Heb. for *raven*, the only reference to birds in the book) killed at a *rock* (צור threshing floor or rock for slaughtering animals) and Zeeb (Heb. for *wolf*) at a *wine press*? (Cf. Abimelech killing his brothers on one stone [אבן, 9.5, 18].)

Ans. Because these are the leitmotifs of *bread (or food) and wine*, and *meat*, while *ravens* and *wolves* are enemies of the *farmer*.

What is the significance of the aphorism that Gideon thinks up about the *gleaning and vintage* to propitiate the Ephraimites?

Ans. It's another allusion to the theme: *bread and wine*.

Why does Gideon *thresh* the elders of the city of Succoth with *thorns and briers*?

Ans. *Threshing* (as well as *hacking* [meaning of Gideon's name]) is what he is good at. The *thorns and briers* are weeds, which infest the fields and plague the farmer.

Why did he punish the elders of Succoth and Penuel?

Ans. They refused to give his *hung*ry men *bread* (8.6, 8).

The reference to *threshing* at the *beginning* of the story where Gideon is beating out (חבט) *wheat* in the *wine press* (6.11) is balanced by the allusion to *threshing* (דוש) the elders near the *end* (8.7), while *fleece* on the *threshing* floor (גרן) (6.37) is in the *middle*. It's a neat little pattern, a triangle.

When he sends some of the troops *back to their tents*, he keeps their *provisions*, undoubtedly *bread* or *flour*. (This detail, superfluous to the plot, shores up the food imagery while perhaps it is also an explanation for the *empty jars* he later used in the night attack.) The name of his lad, Purah, is connected with the Hebrew word for *fruit*.

The story is packed with allusions to *flour and wine*: it begins with the planting of *seed* by the Israelites and the laying waste of the *fields* by the Midianites ("Whenever the Israelites put in seed, the Midianites . . . would . . . destroy the produce of the land . . . and leave no sustenance in Israel, neither *sheep* nor *ox* nor *ass*" [6.3, 4]), and it ends with the *loaves* that Gideon begs from Succoth and Penuel for the men faint with *hunger* (famished) pursuing Zebah and Zalmunna. Their *hunger* in the middle of the book, incidentally, is to be compared with Sisera's thirst ⅓ of the way from the beginning of the book and Samson's *thirst* ⅓ of the way from the end. Another triangle.

Although Animal and Insect imagery is a category by itself (already given above), it is a subcategory of Food in the Gideon story, particularly of the production of Food. The animals valuable to the farmer are: *ass, kid, bullock, dog, sheep* or *goats* (alluded to in the episode of the fleece), and the destructive ones: *locusts, Midianite camels,* a *raven,* and a *wolf.* (The *ass*—an animal important to the whole book—is mentioned only once, as a clear connection to agriculture, in 6.4.) These references validate Gideon's reasons for attacking the Midianites: the Midianites threaten the abundance of his food supply.

Parallel to the *stone* in the Gideon story, where Oreb is killed, is the *one stone* on which Abimelech kills his 70 brothers and the *one stone* dropped on him from above, mortally wounding him. Both the first two stones are probably allusions to *slaughtering stones* for *animals.* While this allusion is "acceptable" (from the Israelite point of view) in Oreb's case because he is an enemy, it is hideous when an Israelite slaughters his brothers like animals in Abimelech's case. These references to *slaughter* are subtle allusions to the category of *Food.*

In Jotham's fable (part of the Abimelech story) we are shown some of the *trees* and *plants* that are most useful to the Israelite farmer:

> o*live* (fatness),
>
> *fig* (sweetness), and
>
> v*ine* (refreshment),

while the *bramble* is a hazard. Like the phrase *land of milk and honey,* the three terms, *fatness, sweetness,* and r*efreshment,* are symbolic of Israel. In this fable, fire will *devour* (eat) (9.15). Fire also *devours* the offerings of Gideon and of Samson's parents.

The word for *wine* is not used in the Gaal episode (Abimelech story), but after Gaal and his companions are shown treading out the *grapes* and *drinking,* we know that what they are drinking is new *wine:*

> They went out into the field and gathered the grapes from their vineyards, trod them, and celebrated. Then they went into the temple of their god, ate and drank, and ridiculed Abimelech (9.27).

That he and his companions are drinking in the temple (of Baal Berith) is a link with raucous scene in the House of Dagon where Samson was later brought to be taunted. Why does the author give this information in both stories? It is to discredit Gaal and the Philistines. *Wine* in the temple may have been considered sacrilegious by the Israelites.

The author may also be linking the untrustworthy and disloyal newcomer, Gaal, with the careless Levite in the carousing scene of the last story. Gaal has to be emboldened by alcohol before he can utter his (drunken) treacherous, bellicose words in the next verse: "Who is Abimelech and who is Shechem that we should serve him?" Finally, the scene allows the author to squeeze in another reference to the word *vineyards,* which figures so importantly elsewhere in the book. The *wine* from the vineyards in the Gaal orgy connects with the *wine*press in Gideon, with the *vineyards* that Samson destroys, with the *carousing* of the Levite and his father-in-law (19.4-9), and with the orgy of the *vineyards* where the Benjaminites hide before seizing the daughters of Shiloh (21.21). (See the separate categories of *Wine and Hospitality* below.)

That Abimelech *sows* the destroyed city with *salt* instead of *grain* highlights the fact that Abimelech is anything but a nurturer. Our ecologist author is no doubt outraged by that.

An allusion to *grain* is made when the *millstone* is dropped on Abimelech's head. Why a *millstone*? Why not simply a *big stone*? The *millstone* here, instead of being used in the *nurturing* process, serves a function for which it was not intended: *destruction.* It is also a link with the Samson story, where we see Samson *grinding* at the *mill* in the prison, or as Milton puts it, "eyeless in Gaza, at the mill with slaves."

In our categories, we must also pay special attention when something is lacking. The single reference to food in the Jephthah story is the *ear of corn* found in the word *shibboleth.* The lack of other references to food there, especially in such stark contrast with the abundance of food in the Gideon story, may be a clue first, that Jephthah's reason for fighting against the Ammonites is *not* so valid as that of Gideon against the Midianites, and second, that he is *not* a nurturer. The Midianites are depleting the land, and Gideon is forced to *protect* his very *sustenance.* Gideon's war, at least at first, is defensive.

Though the Ammonites have already camped in Gilead, Jephthah's war may be more imperialistic. This possibility is supported by the author's technique of *disproportion*: Jephthah *"passed through* Gilead and Manasseh, and *passed over* to Mizpah of Gilead, and from Mizpah of Gilead he *passed over* to the Ammonites " (11:29; *passed over* is repeated 3x). Any information which occupies a disproportionate space in this book is a demand for special interpretation: Jephthah, we suspect, may have gone too far; he may really be fighting for his own selfish power, rather than for the defense of Israel. He is the only champion who bargained to become chief *before* he achieved victory; the others became leaders as a *result* of their achievement. And in the end, his slaughter of 42,000 Ephraimites was ruinous to Israel.

A different interpretation for the length of his march, however, might be that it shows his energy and resolve. Nevertheless, a suspicion about him has been raised. Our suspicion may be confirmed by his character: like his resolve in going after the Ammonites, he is also pious to an extreme, even straight-laced, unrelenting in his treatment of his daughter and the Ephraimites. Slaughter seems to have gone to his head.

In the Samson story, references to *food* are manifold, though most of them are what *belong to the Philistines.*

At the beginning of the story, Samson's parents try to feed the messenger-angel with a *kid* and a *grain* offering (13.15-16). Samson (or at least his mother) of course is forbidden to drink *intoxicating drink* (שכר, 13.4, 7, 11, perhaps date wine or grain alcohol), a word that is not used elsewhere in *Judges.*

Samson *eats the honey* which he finds in the lion's carcass on the way to the wedding (14.9). Much *eating and drinking* no doubt were done at the wedding feast, since many guests (30 companions and an unknown number of other guests) stayed at least 7 days.

The meaning of מִשְׁתֶּה, the Hebrew word for *feast*, which is mentioned twice, is a *drinking bout*. We can imagine that here Samson broke his Nazirite vow and became intoxicated, and that his rage, when the Philistines learned the solution to the riddle, was one of drunken fury. For Samson, the Philistine food was also no doubt *unclean*. Though we cannot say whether this author knew of the dietary laws, the later audiences did.

Eating (*refreshment*) and the *taste of food* (*sweetness*) are fundamental in Samson's riddle. Throughout the entire Samson story are mentions of *wine, strong drink* (refreshment), *cereal offering, food, honey* (sweetness), and *wheat;* the *grain fields, vineyards* (wine), and the *olive orchard* (fatness) which Samson destroyed by fire; the *water* at Lehi; and the *grain* which he grinds at the mill as a slave. These echo Jotham's three symbolic references to Israel in a wonderful way: *fatness, sweetness* (*honey* replacing the *fig* in the fable), and *refreshment*. As suggested earlier, Samson, like Abimelech, is also a *bramble*, for *fire* literally *comes out* of Samson in the scene with the foxes (15.5) (cf. Jotham's fable [9.15, 20]), just as fire comes out of Abimelech when he sets fire to the stronghold (9.49). A bodily person, Samson may be something of a *glutton*— linking him with both the fat Eglon and the olive trees in the Jotham fable. Perhaps his tribe, Dan, is, too, lusting after the fertile fields of Laish.

At En Hakkore Samson is *ravenously thirsty* (repeated 2x), cries bitterly to Yhwh, and receives *water* that restores his spirit.

In contrast to the Samson story, food and drink images are *lacking* in the Micah story. Micah is far more interested in other things than food: *money, silver images, priests,* and *worship*. His chief interest in his religion may not be righteousness but covetousness, a desire for material prosperity, first indicated by the theft of his mother's money and second by his comment when he hires the Levite: "Now I know that Yhwh will prosper me, because I have a Levite priest" (17.13).

This lack of food imagery links Micah with Jephthah. When objects in any category are "missing," their lack is likely to point up contrasts: here, between (1) the bodily *food-producing* Gideon and the bodily *food-consuming* Samson and on the other hand, (2) the ruthless, ambitious, "lean and hungry" Jephthah, the materialistic (ascetic) Micah, and imperialistic (gluttonous?) Danites (going out to seize a land rich in food).

Here, then, is another of the author's numerous patterns:

food-producing Gideon (Midianites destroy food)

vs.

pious (legalistic?) nonfood-producing, nonconsuming and
ambitious (imperialistic?) Jephthah

and

food-consuming gluttonous Samson (Samson destroys sources of food)

vs.

pious (materialistic) nonfood-producing, nonconsuming Micah
and the imperialistic food-lacking Danites.

The Danites are another comparison to Jephthah in that like Jephthah, they may have gone too far out of their assigned territory.

We may have four other allusions to *food* in the book: (1) the slaughter of Eglon, whose name means *calf* (this is a contrast to the "tribute offering" which Ehud brought to Eglon) and who is depicted as obese—thus the "fatted calf" ready for slaughter as an offering;[34] (2) Abimelech's 70 brothers who were killed on one (slaughtering) stone; (3) the sacrifice of the daughter of Jephthah, who is a *flesh offering*; and (4) the dividing of the Concubine's body *limb by limb* with a knife, where her body is being carved *like a slaughtered animal*. She is an animal offering. Since flesh offerings were normally eaten, a horrible cannibalism may be implied. Compare this with Saul's carving up of the ox and distributing it to the tribes. Add these to the 3 *offerings* made by Gideon, Samson's parents, and the Israelites in 20.26, and you have 7 food offerings in the book.

Subcategory: Water

The verb *to eat* is used at least 17x in the book (8x in Samson, 4x in Abimelech). In the scene with Sisera, although the words *to eat* and *to drink* are lacking, they are implied through the words *water, thirsty,* and *milk (curds)*. The verb *to drink* is used at least 10x in the four stories: Gideon, Abimelech, Samson, and the Levite's Concubine. Great *thirst* is a keyword which links Sisera, Gideon's men, and Samson.

Water is the liquid most frequently drunk. Sisera pleaded with Jael, "Give me a little *water to drink*, for I am thirsty," but she gave him *milk* (4.19); in the poem, "he asked for *water*, she brought him *curds* (חמאה) in a lordly bowl" (5.25). Yhwh tells Gideon to take his men down to the *water* (7.4) and separate those who *lap water* with their tongues, as a *dog laps*, from those who kneel down *to drink*, with their hands to their mouths (7.5). 300 men *lap*, all the rest kneel down *to drink water* (7.6); Yhwh tells him to use the 300 men who *lapped* (7.7) and let the rest return to their tents. Repetitions demonstrate how much emphasis is given to these words: *lap* [water] 3x; *water* 4x, *kneel to drink* 2x.

When Samson was very *thirsty*, he asked Yhwh: "Am I to die of *thirst*?" Yhwh scooped out a hollow place at Lehi, the *Spring* of Hakkore burst forth (15.18), and Samson *drank*—whether lapping like a dog, or kneeling down to drink (no doubt out of his hands—a parallel with Gideon's men).

The numerous *bodies of water* include: the *springs* (or *basins*) of *water*—the upper and lower springs that Achsah requested (1.15); *watering places* (5.11); the *waters of Megiddo* (probably the Kishon) (5.19); the *River Kishon* (4.17, 13; 5.21 [2x]); the *spring of Harod* (7.1); the *Spring of Hakkore*, from which came water for Samson (15.19); *the Jordan* (11x in 3.28; 5.17; 7.24, 25; 8.4; 10.8, 9; 11.13, 22; 12.5, 6); and *fords over the Jordan*: Ehud prevented the *Moabites* from crossing the Jordan at a ford (מעבר, 3.28)—this is good—while Jephthah prevented the *Ephraimites* from crossing (12.5, 6)—this is bad. Finally, *the waters of Beth Barah* (*Beth Barah* meaning *house of the ford*) and *Jordan* are mentioned in the Gideon story (7.24).

Rain is referred to only once, and not by the word נשם but in the clause "the clouds dropped water" in *The Song*. (5.4). *Dew* and *dryness* figure in the Gideon story and *dryness* in the Samson story. The *wet/dry* theme in Gideon—the tests of the fleece (6.37, 39, 40)—should be compared with the fresh/dried bowstrings in the Samson story (16.7, 8). The last reference to *water* is rather different, for the travelers visiting the Ephraimite in Gibeah are not drinking, but *washing* their feet (19.21).

The author has kept the reader continually aware of the importance of water to this otherwise arid land.

Subcategory: Wine and Intemperance

Allusions to *milk* in the reference to *milk*-producing animals have already been mentioned. And *milk* is significant of course in Jael's seduction of Sisera.

But in many passages, *to drink* implies use of strong drink, although specific words are not always used. *Wine* (יין) appears in the book 5x (13.4, 7, 14[2x] and 19.19) and *strong fermented drink* (שכר) 3x and only in the messenger-angel's mandate to Manoah and his wife (13.4, 7, 14). Other references to intoxicating drink, however, abound: *vine* (9.13), *vintage* (8.2), *winepress* (6.11 and 7.25—different words), and *vineyards* (5x: 9.27; 14.5; 15.5; 21.20, 21). When the author uses the words *to drink* in these scenes, he is *not* referring to water (Samson) or milk (Sisera).

As mentioned earlier, Carey Ellen Walsh finds that biblical authors do not always distinguish between drinking and intoxication.[35] Drinking at Samson's wedding feast (משתה, meaning *a drinking*) was likely heavy and probably lasted all the time that the Philistines were trying to guess the riddle. Since a regular part of banqueting was "play," Samson's riddle would have been part of the "play" (22). Walsh writes, "When Samson forgets the play nature of riddles, his wedding משתה becomes a fiasco of frustration, enmity and annulment. Samson's belligerence is self-defeating and perhaps due to or accentuated by *intoxication* (although the word *intoxication* is not used)" (27, my italics). He was berserk, no doubt from drink, when he rushed down to Ashkelon to commit mayhem in order to get the prize garments.

One of the code terms for being drunk is that "their *hearts are merry*" (כטוב לבם) (16.25), and this is a clue that the gathering in the Temple of Dagon to make fun of the vanquished Samson was probably also a "drinking" (משתה) and that the Philistines are drunk. They had called for Samson so that he might entertain them (צחק, 16:25)—another "play." We do not know what that "play" was—perhaps Samson was to perform feats of strength for them, or perhaps they simply wanted to mock him. Likewise, we catch on to the drunkenness of Gaal and his men, who after they trod the grapes, "*made merry* [יעשו הלולים—celebrated; literally, held a festival] and went into the house of their god where they did *eat* and *drink* and cursed Abimelech" (KJV, 9.27). It is also a clue to the drunkenness of the Levite and his two hosts in Ch. 19.

Feats of drinking are celebrated a number of times in the Ugaritic tales. Danel in *Aqhat* has no son; he needs a son for many reasons, among them,

> To grasp my arm when I'm drunk,
>
> To support me when sated with wine,[36]

a refrain he repeats 5x. And there is more than one poem in which the gods get drunk. Here are Baal and a minor deity preparing for a banquet for the gods:

> He [the minor deity] did stand up, he spread a banquet and gave him drink;
>> he gave a cup into his hand(s),
>> a large jar, huge to see,
>> a cask of mighty men,
>> a holy cup which no woman could regard,
>> a flagon which no goddess could look upon;
>> he took a thousand pitchers of wine,
>> ten thousand he mixed in his mixture. [Gibson "The Palace of Baal 3 A, 8-17, 47.][37]

Another poem focuses on El's drunkenness:

> El summoned his drinking-companions:
>> El took his seat in his feasting house.
> He drank wine to satiety,
>> new wine until intoxication.
> El went off to his house;
>> he stumbled off toward his dwelling;
>> Thukamun and Shanim supported him.
> A creeping monster approached him.
>> with horns and tail!
> He floundered in his (own) feces and urine:
> El fell down as though dead;
>> El was like those who go down into the underworld.
> Anat and Athtart went hunting . . .
> Athtart and Anat [returned]
>> And they brought back meat [ ]
> When they had cured him, he awoke. [KTU 1.114, 18-35 Wyatt, *Religious Texts.* 70-71.][38]

De Moor claims that we cannot infer the importance of alcohol to Ugaritic society from their poems (*The Rise of Yahwism* 83), but the references in *Aqhat* prove otherwise.

In *Judges*, Jotham's fable contains an odd reference to *wine*, where he says that it is *wine* that "*cheers* gods and men" (i.e., with which they are *honored*, כבד) (9.13). What "gods" is he referring to? This plural indicates the Canaanite origin of the fable or refers to a time when the Israelites were still polytheistic (see Ps 82).

The (bad) connotations given to drinking in *Judges* may thus be an attack on another one of the "abominations" of the Canaanites and Philistines. For readers of the Hebrew Bible, a warning against drunkenness is given in the story of Noah's drunkenness (Gen 9.21-24), a story which the author of *Judges* may or may not have known.

Drinking is prominent in the story of the Levite's Concubine, which begins with two Carousing scenes: (1) the *drink* and *bread* served by the father of the Levite's Concubine, and (2) the allusion to the *food* and *drink* served by the old Ephraimite host at Gibeah. The author repeats *heart* 5x in Ch. 19, either "refresh (or fortify) your heart" or "make your heart merry (good)":

³He was glad to meet him (ישמח לקראתו) (1ˢᵗ day)

⁴His father-in-law, the girl's father, made him stay, and he remained with him three days; so they ate and drank, and he stayed there. (2ⁿᵈ and 3ʳᵈ days)

⁵Fortify (comfort, refresh) your heart (סעד לבך) (4ᵗʰ day)

⁶Spend the night and make your heart good (be merry, enjoy yourself) (ויטב לבבך לין)

⁸Fortify (comfort, refresh) your heart (סעד־נא לבבך) (5ᵗʰ day)

⁹Spend the night here and make your heart good (be merry, enjoy yourself (לבבך לין פה וייטב)

¹⁰But the man would not spend the night; he got up and departed . . . .

²²While they were making their hearts good (enjoying themselves) (המה מיטיבים את־לבם) [adaptation of various translations]

"We'll teach you to drink deep, ere you depart," says Hamlet cynically to Horatio (I.ii.175), as the father-in-law might have said to the Levite.

Notice also the 5-day scheme. At Ugarit and elsewhere, 7-day schemes were a traditional stylistic device.[39] (This scene is also discussed under **Body Parts** [the heart], above, and **Hospitality**, below.)

In the first episode, the Levite and his father-in-law continue eating and drinking until the evening of the 5th day, when the Levite finally pulls himself away—no doubt drunk, as he has been drinking all that day (19.9), not to mention the four days before.

In the second episode, when the Levite finally finds a place to stay the night in Gibeah, he tells his host he has "*bread and wine*" with him, but the host is too polite to accept that arrangement (19.19). Then they "*ate and drank,*" apparently out of the host's store (19.21), "making their hearts merry" (19.22), and were doing so when the house was surrounded by the evil Benjaminites, who were perhaps equally drunk.

From this, we are meant to understand that the Levite may have been in a state of drunkenness when he thrust his Concubine out to the rapists.

Finally, the story ends with an allusion to the possible *drunkenness* of the Benjaminites lying in the vineyards waiting to seize the daughters of Shiloh as they came out to dance. We suspect that the Benjaminites too are drunk, for we know from 1 Sam 1.14 that *wine* was being drunk at the festival at Shiloh which Hannah attended (probably the same festival some years later), because Eli assumed that the distressed Hannah was drunk, though she was actually only praying (1 Sam 1.13). Incidentally, by the time of the final composition of *Judges*, Shiloh had disappeared, for the author of *Judges* finds it necessary to give careful directions on how to reach Shiloh (21.19).

The seizing of the daughters of Shiloh by the Benjaminites, no doubt drunken roisterers, at the end of the tale forms an Inclusio of sorts with the two carousing scenes at the beginning of the tale.

The story also tells us in other ways that the author has no high regard for people who carouse: Gaal, the Levite, the Concubine's father, and the Ephraimite host in Gibeah. We find this same negativity toward excess in *1* and *2 Samuel*, beginning with Eli's suspicions about Hannah's condition during the Shiloh festival. The rude inhospitable Nabal, Abigail's husband, we learn, "was holding a feast (מִשְׁתֶּה, a drinking bout) in his house, like the feast of a king. Nabal's heart was merry within him, for he was very drunk [שִׁכֹּר עַד־מְאֹד]." He dies from apoplexy "after the wine had gone out of him" (1 Sam 25.36), to David's good fortune. In the Bathsheba story, David gets Uriah drunk so that he will forget his religious duties and go to sleep with his wife (2 Sam 11.13). The way Absalom kills Amnon is that he bids his men watch when Amnon "is merry [or befuddled] with wine," and then strike him (2 Sam 13.28). Wine is a gift of a drink to be offered to exhausted men in a gesture of hospitality (1 Sam 1.24, 10.3, 16.20, 25.18, and 2 Sam 16.1), but in the Bible, it has its negative side as well and can be used for nefarious ends.

The end of *Judges*, as a scene of drunken abandon, is a strong condemnation of Israelites as a whole and is a calculated contrast to the ending of *Joshua*, where the Israelites are *not carousing* and seizing women but paying reverence to Yhwh.

And thus the book is as much about the misuse of Food and Drink, "Yhwh's plenty," as it is about flawed heroes and warfare.

Subcategory: Festivals

The stories in their original form may have had to do with seasonal festivals: Achsah with some kind of *rain* or water festival, Deborah with a festival honoring the *storm* god (Baal), Gideon with the *autumn grain* harvest, Abimelech and the rape of the daughters of Shiloh in the last story with a *grape* or *fertility* festival, Samson with a midsummer celebration or a festival honoring the *Sun* God, who is necessary for growing crops, and Jephthah with a *fertility* festival lamenting the loss of a *goddess* (a death and resurrection rite) or celebrating the transition of the girl to womanhood (a puberty rite). Such festivals tie in with the Agriculture and Food and Drink categories. They need further study. (See information about festivals in Chapter 2.)

Subcategory: Invitations, Requests, and Hospitality

The Food and Drink category is closely connected with the category of Invitations and Hospitality. Hospitality is one of the important themes in the book; and its rules are violated in many of the stories.[40]

The reason that the rules of hospitality are so important in the ancient world is that they help to define an individual. As Alasdair MacIntyre explains in his chapter on Heroic Societies in *After Virtue: A Study in Moral Theory* (1981):

> the given rules which assign men their place in the social order . . . also prescribe what they owe and what is owed to them and how they are to be treated and regarded if they fail and how they are to treat and regard others if those others fail.

The rules help establish one's identity, both for himself and for others:

> It is precisely because of this that the heroic societies commonly have a well-defined status to which any stranger who arrives in the society from outside can be assigned. In

Greek the word for 'alien' and the word for 'guest' are the same word. A stranger has to be received with hospitality, limited but well-defined. When Odysseus encounters the Cyclopes, the question as to whether they possess *themis* (the Homeric concept of *themis* is the concept of customary law shared by all civilized peoples) is to be answered by discovering how they treat strangers. In fact they eat them—that is, for them, strangers have no recognised human identity.[41]

The Benjaminites of Gibeah are Cyclopes: they rape strangers.

In *Judges* there are at least eight main types of *invitations* and *requests* (including *violations*): 1) to fight, seize, destroy, rule, become someone's priest, 2) to eat or drink, 3) to use or give something, 4) to marry, 5) to enter a place, 6) to visit, 7) to solve a riddle and get a prize, and 8) to have sex.[42] Not all invitations are accepted. Some invitations are rejected outright. Some invitations are issued too late. Some people invite themselves. Some people refuse to invite others. Fine distinctions exist between the words

1) *inviting* and *commanding*,

2) *inviting*, *requesting*, and *enticing*;

3) *inviting oneself* and *begging* something *from* another; and

4) *good* invitations and *bad* ones.

(These are all exemplified in the analyses following.)

In the tale of Ehud, Eglon *invites* Ehud to reenter for a private conference because Ehud has promised Eglon a secret message from Elohim; instead Ehud stabs Eglon. Joke. But one must also ask: is this a proper use of "the Word of Elohim" (דבר אלהים)?

In *The Song of Deborah*, all the tribes are *invited* to fight against Sisera, but some *do not accept*. Sisera asks for water; Jael *invites* him to enter and *invites him* to drink milk; then she *invites* Barak to enter to see what she has done. Are she and Ehud Cyclopes, too?

David Chalcraft looks at behaviors such as violations of hospitality from an anthropological point of view, in which "deviance" would be the label of actions that one's own social group would disapprove of if committed toward one's own society. Though Ehud misuses the divine name, though his method of murdering Eglon is disgusting, and though he also violates the hospitality code, his act is *not* deviant, according to Chalcraft, because the enemy is depicted as "subhuman" and as "deserving" of maltreatment.[43]

Jael is a temptress who *entices* Sisera into her tent ("Turn in, my lord! Turn in. Fear not," she coos [4.18]), then lulls him to sleep with milk, and treacherously slays him. For this, Israel calls her *blessed*. But is she indeed any better than the sinister Delilah, the "hostess," who lulls Samson to sleep on her lap and then sells him to the Philistines? Do Israelites or friends of Israelites have a right to violate hospitality when it is in their own (Israelite) interest, while enemies of Israelites do not, when it is in *their* (Philistine) interest? Here is an example of the intentional enigmatic aspect of the tales—of the uncertainty principle—as well as an example of how the reader's perspective can shape his or her interpretation. Compare Jael's "hospitality" (really "inhospitality") with the inhospitality of the men of Gibeah who do not invite the Levite in and the hospitality of the Ephraimite host, who does (see below).

In Chalcraft's opinion, Jael's action is potentially deviant for many reasons: "she breaks the code of the host; indeed she uses the trust of her guest to betray him and to carry out the murder." She also breaks the obligation she has to her husband and his obligation to Sisera. But her "crime" is against Israel's out-group. In her actions, she "chooses for Israel." And this exonerates her in Israel's eyes, "because it is performed within the out-group against the out-group" (182-183). Chalcraft is not recommending this behavior; he is only trying to explain how her inhospitality might be interpreted by the Israelites. (Chalcraft's theory of deviance is discussed further in Chapter 4.)

In the Gideon story, (1) Yhwh invites Gideon to rescue Israel, but Gideon finds excuses *not to accept the invitation*. (2) Gideon is *hospitable* to the messenger-angel when he *invites* him to a meal, but the fire, not the messenger-angel, consumes the meat and cakes. (3) He *requested* bread for his hungry men from Succoth and Penuel, but they refused him. (4) He *invites* 4 tribes (Manasseh, Asher, Zebulun, and Naphtali) to participate against the Midianites, then sends all but 300 of the men away (dis-invites). (5) He *invites* the Ephraimites to come to battle (7.24) but nevertheless is accused by the Ephraimites of *not having invited* them (8.1). (6) He *requests* (*begs*) two towns to feed him and his hungry men, but *they refuse* outright (are *inhospitable*). (7) He is *invited* to become king, and his son and his grandson after him (8.20), but he refuses.

In contrast to Gideon, his son Abimelech *invites himself* to be king and is *accepted* by the Shechemites. In Jotham's fable, the trees *invite* the olive, the fig, the vine, and finally the bramble (one after another) to become king. The genuine plants *refuse*, only the bramble *accepts*. The fire is also *invited* ("Let fire come out") to devour the cedars of Lebanon and to destroy Abimelech and the citizens of Shechem and Beth-Millo. Gaal *indirectly invites* his cronies at the wine-drinking to remove Abimelech (9.28, 29). The Gileadites *invite* Jephthah to be their leader. The Ephraimites again claim that they were not *invited* to fight, but Jephthah claims they were (12.2).

Manoah and his wife show *hospitality* when they *invite* the messenger-angel to a meal, but the messenger-angel *declines* and tells them to *invite* Yhwh instead. Samson's mother at her annunciation is *invited* (*ordered*) to avoid drinking or eating anything unclean because her son is to be a Nazirite. Samson *invites* his parents to eat the honey, which he removed from the lion's carcass (though he does not tell them where he got it). Thirty companions and other guests are *invited* to Samson's wedding feast. Samson *invites* the wedding guests to solve the riddle. After going off mad, he later *invites* himself to visit his wife, but the *invitation is denied* by her father. The Philistines *invite* (or *command*) Samson to come to the temple to make sport of him.

Micah *invites* a Levite to become his priest, and the Levite accepts. 600 armed Danites *invite* (through intimidation) the same Levite to become their priest, and he accepts.

But did not the Danites *violate* Micah's *hospitality*? And did not the Levite in the same tale also *violate the hospitality* of his benefactor, the man who had given him a home and a salaried position? Are they not Cyclopes?

How does the behavior of Micah's Levite compare with that of Gaal's in the Abimelech story? Like the Levite, Gaal is an outsider (another bramble) "who moved into Shechem with his kinsmen." Like the Levite, instead of being loyal to his new master, Gaal stirred up the city against Abimelech. Abimelech was reprehensible, and Gaal was an instrument of retribution. But does this excuse Gaal's violation of hospitality? (This dilemma is discussed along with other ethical issues in Chapter 4.)

Hospitality in the Story of the Levite's Concubine (Ch. 19-20.7).

(See discussion of this story under the subheading **"Food and Drink"** above.)

In the story of the Levite's Concubine, the father-in-law has no rancor for the Levite (as he might have had if he thought the Levite had treated *his daughter* badly), but is overjoyed to see him (perhaps because he thought his daughter had treated the *Levite* badly), so overjoyed that he *invites* the Levite in to eat, drink, and be merry, and day after day to continue to stay. Even on the 5th day, he is trying to prevent the Levite from leaving. The Levite succumbs to the *hospitality* and finally overstays his visit. He eventually goes on to Gibeah, where other acts of hospitality and inhospitality are done to him.

The story is told in one chapter (19):

Intro. to the Story	1-3	(19.1-4 are the 1st 3 days)
First Carousing	4-9	(19.5 begins the 4th day)
	8	(19.8 begins the 5th day)
Departure	10	(departs evening of 5th day)
Search for Hospitality	10-21	
Second Carousing	22a	
Rape	22b-26	
Aftermath (Mutilation)	27-30.	

This neat little structure is a "bell-shaped curve": 3 verses, 6 verses (to v. 9), 12 verses (to v. 21), 5 verses (to v. 26), 3 verses. Six verses devoted to the First Carousing (approximately 1/5 of the story) is an excessive amount of space to devote to the father's chummy affection for the Levite—at least in comparison with other parts of the story. As already shown, all along the author has been playing the game of "What is wrong with this picture?" In this case, the excessive amount of space given to this carousing should alert us to the fact that these men are intoxicated (discussed under **"Wine and Intemperance"** above).

From one point of view, the two men in the First Carousing are only having comradeship and pleasure (like male friends having beer and chips while watching the Super Bowl). From another point of view, however, the excessive amount of time spent drinking is the cause of the Levite's impaired judgment about departing in good time. He keeps on delaying his departure until he finally leaves his host's house so late in the day that he cannot possibly get home that same night but must seek refuge from strangers.

He rejects going to the town of Jebus, because the inhabitants are *not* Israelites and will *not be hospitable* (i.e., would-be Cyclopes). He goes instead to Gibeah, a Benjaminite town that he thinks will be *hospitable* to him. In Gibeah, however, he is ironically confronted by extreme *lack of hospitality*. Not one of the inhabitants *invites* him in.[44] It is instead an old Ephraimite (an "outsider" in the town), coming from his work in the fields, who proffers the *invitation*.

The Levite had brought his own *straw* and *provender* for the *animals* and *bread* and *wine* for himself and his host's household. One reason for giving this information is to show the *lack of hospitality* (selfishness) of the inhabitants of Gibeah, for the Levite was not asking for charity—he only wanted a place to sleep. Another reason is to show the *hospitality* (*generosity*) of the old man, who will not hear of the Levite using his own provisions but insists on supplying these things himself. Here, we think, is a very "good" Ephraimite, unlike the other Ephraimites in the book. But is this evaluation accurate? Wait and see.

The Levite ate, drank, and was "merry" for five whole days in Bethlehem and for one evening in Gibeah before the Benjaminites (no doubt drunk) beset the house and *invited* themselves to *know* the Levite (have sex). The host begged them not to insult his guest in this way, and *offered* them instead his virgin daughter and the Levite's Concubine. The Levite thrust out his Concubine, and the Benjaminites *accepted her* in lieu of the Levite.

The fact that the Ephraimite offered the base men his virgin daughter and the Levite's Concubine if only they would leave the Levite unscathed may be considered an act of *hospitality*, albeit a weird one.[45]

But is this *hospitality*, or an *act of a drunk*? And what right did the Ephraimite have to offer the *Levite's* Concubine? In the parallel episode in *Genesis* 19, where Lot offers his virgin daughters to the base men, there is a feast (מִשְׁתֶּה), but *no* mention of *drink*, only an emphasis on *bread*. Lot's offer was made soberly. He made the offer in honor of *angels*, not of a drunken Levite. Whereas the Ephraimite offers the Concubine belonging to the Levite, Lot does not offer anything belonging to the *messenger-angels* to the base men.

After the Levite pushes his Concubine out, and while she is being raped, he goes to bed and sleeps. Either he is extremely callous, or extremely besotted. Or both.

The merriment of the father-in-law, the Levite, and the Ephraimite host immediately before the multiple rape intensifies the horror of the woman's fate which follows. More important, the juxtaposition of the drinking with the rape expresses a cause/effect relationship. What the men did was to drink to excess. What they did led to the death of the young woman. The judgment of the men was impaired, no doubt by their drinking—especially the judgment of the Levite, who by that time had been drinking for six days. Too much hospitality in one case (the girl's father), and abuse of hospitality (the Ephraimite) in the other.

Clues to the author's attitude toward carousing are to be found in parallel stories in the book: the Gaal drinking episode in the Abimelech story (9.27) and Samson's wedding feast of 7 days (מִשְׁתֶּה, 14.10). Though Samson as a Nazirite may have abstained from intoxicating drinks, his rash way of acquiring the garments for the prize from Ashkelon is the style of a drunk (14.19).

This author does not state outright that he has contempt for Gaal, Samson, the Levite, and the father-in-law. Rather, he leaves judgment to his readers. We are supposed to notice that evil, only evil, results from each of these scenes, and we are supposed to figure out why.

These are not the last *invitations* in the book. After the outrage, the Levite *invites* all the tribes to come to fight against Benjamin. It turns out that one town, Jabesh-Gilead, rejects the *invitation* and is punished. Although the Israelites refuse to *invite* the Benjaminites to *marry* their daughters, they *invite* the Benjaminites to *seize* (חטף) them.

It is through a careful examination of instances of hospitality and lack of it in the book, that we can make character evaluations that will later help us assign verdicts in our cases of ethics and law (see Chapter 4).

II. Conclusion

Though *Judges* is a serious work of art, the author is playing games, amusing himself and us in performing many sleight-of-hand tricks with all kinds of objects: People and Relationships; Body and Body Parts; Tools, Instruments, Vehicles; Fabric; Agriculture and Animals; Buildings, Doors, Entrances, Gates (which represent the Open/Shut, Inside/Outside of experience); Containers; Food and Drink, Water; and Invitations and Hospitality. These objects we may call "hidden" because previous interpreters have scarcely noticed them, and when they do, see only a precious few and, as far as I know, do not list and analyze them in the way that I have. As *objets trouvés*, they serve an artistic purpose. The author presents these keywords in such a way that the reader or listener is not even aware of them, and in doing so is telling us something about how life is organized. Seth Lerer, lecturing on comedy, compares the "stone" passage in Samuel Beckett's *Malloy* with Rabelais' *Gargantua and Pantagruel*, the passage in which Malloy is passing sixteen stones from pocket to pocket and sucking on them:

> Rabelais is similarly interested in finding comic ways of organizing experience, of organizing the things of this world. Now Rabelais does this by in effect *creating catalogues, great lists* that . . . are comic parodies of the encyclopediac tradition—that is the way you organize experience by making *great lists* . . . (emphasis mine).

To what purpose are Rabelais' lists?

> The central question is, How do we organize the things that experience or nature has provided for us? But secondly, how do we organize them in such a way that we are not given to monotony or boredom . . . . The rut of the job can be varied . . . by in effect making sure that you don't suck the same stone twice in a row, . . . that you don't have the same experience over and over again, that you have some variety in life and also that you have what you think is a rational way of giving you that variety.[46]

Beckett's Malloy comes to the conclusion that variety is an "illusion," and he does not "give a fiddler's curse about it." The author of *Judges*, has lists, too, but the items in his lists are scattered and distributed throughout. He delights in them.

All these categories of objects give us glimpses of the peace and quiet that exist in this otherwise violent, vicious world with its deadly combats, warfare, slaughter, and rapes. Such details are comparable to the way that Homer brings in the domestic lives of ordinary people through his profusion of epic similes—little islands of peace amidst the raging battles of the *Iliad*.

In a recent review of the translations of Anton Chekhov's stories, Philip Hensher remarks on Chekhov's "evocations of the world" through the listing of objects and "the astonishing, unelaborated concreteness" that they give to this world:

> These details very rarely attain the status of descriptions . . . . More characteristically they are simply lists of objects. Each object appears unnecessary and even surprising in so *frugal a writer*; cumulatively, though, they create not just *a world of unprecedented solidity* but the sensation of human lives lived in the world. And every so often we do get a glimpse of what Chekhov surely felt—a sort of *ecstasy induced by the simplest objects and self-effacingly* ascribed to his characters . . . .
>
> The appearance of life was an illusion, but perhaps it would be a truer to say that Chekhov's manner reflects a conviction that there is nothing for the writer to talk about but *the physical world and people's lives within it*; the means by which the conviction is conveyed are not naive ones, and are clearly identifiable by analysis. But the effectiveness and subtlety of Chekhov's conventions do not mean that his supreme artifice is, in any sense, a conjuring trick, or meretricious.[47] (Emphasis mine).

So too the author of *Judges* gives "solidity" to his world though conjuring up his many themes and hiding so many objects. He too is a "frugal" writer and a "supreme artificer," but although a playful gamester, he too is never "meretricious."

His objects all convey richness of meaning about plot, character, ethics, and history, but a different kind of history than is usually meant by the term, not a history about men and women who actually lived, though they may have had prototypes in the distant past, but about how we have to make judgments about human behavior, how difficult it is to do this, yet how important to history.

What I have tried to establish in this chapter can be called a Special Theory of Relativity. We have discovered a boiling cauldron of objects bubbling around and colliding with each other at a furious rate and have tried to comprehend—to a certain extent—how these collisions affect meaning. By forcing us continually to compare and contrast various aspects of each story, the author makes us realize that everything is relative, that with all their various ramifications, no case is clear-cut, black-and-white, that values are not, and cannot be, absolute, with one exception: in this book, it is always wrong to worship any other god but Yhwh.

Most modern critics of the stories want, and expect, to deliver one definitive interpretation for each story. That is where they go wrong. The author leaves us with questions, not answers. If we want answers, we have to think, and think, and think again, as we shall learn in Chapter 4 on Law and Ethics.

Did the author expect his readers or listeners to perceive this complexity?

Presumably the author had not studied higher mathematics and may not have comprehended, in the chaos he created—in which every single atom is related to every single other atom—what a nearly infinite sum of relationships would be involved. It is a vast network of relationships like the neural network of the human brain, a wiring problem with millions, maybe trillions, of connections. There ceases to be any such thing as merely *one point in time*; everything flows seamlessly into everything else. This complexity did not get into the book fortuitously. It is too consistently present to be an accident. The author no doubt was aware of the complexity, though perhaps not the extent of it. What program was he running on his computer? Possibly his software was beyond the grasp of his hardware. Or vice versa.

But would he not have been amused to hear some of the scholarly debates on his book during the past half century, those who noticed the forest, but not the trees in it, and who failed to grasp the larger overall picture of his world that these details supply?

Appendix 1. A. First Method. Noise/Silence

Not only do the stories have pictures (the icons mentioned in Chapter 1), but they also have a sound track. In order to analyze sounds and silence, the first method is to list the sounds heard within each story. The second method (which follows) is to classify the sounds and list them in their respective categories (for example, to *weep* and *groan*). The first method follows:

INTRODUCTION

the Israelites *lift up their voices* and *weep* (וישאו העם את־קולם ויבכו) (2.4) (repeated almost word-for-word in 21.2)

the Israelites *groan* (נאקה BDB 611) (2.18)

EHUD

the Israelites *cry out* (זעק) to Yhwh (3.9) (This occurs also in 3.15; 6.6, 7; 10.10, 14, not to mention the times the Israelites weep—probably loudly)

the land is said to be *quiet* (שקט, undisturbed) (3.11, 30; 5.31; 8.28)

the King commands his attendants to "Keep silence" (הס binary opposite of *noise*) (3.19) (Cf. the *silence* of the Gazites in 16.2 and the Danites in 18.19)

the servants *knock* (word not used) on Eglon's door (3.24, 25)

Ehud *blows* on a shofar (3.27) (the shofar is a call to arms)

DEBORAH

Barak calls out (פעם, summons) Zebulun and Naphtali (זעק is also used when they *cry out* to Yhwh) (4.10, 13)

Deborah and Barak *sing* (שיר) (5.1)

singing, music mentioned (5.4); *song, voice, singers, reciting* mentioned (5.11) (Cf. the friends of Jephthah's daughter, who *recite* or *commemorate* her death [11.40])

utter (speak) a *song* (דברי־שיר) (5.12)

pipings to the flock are heard (5.16)

the horses' hooves *hammer* (הלמו, 2x) (5.22) (See *hammer* in category of Tools)

Sisera's mother is waiting to hear the *beats* (פעמי, implying *hoof beats*) of his chariot (5.28) (The same word used in Samson, when the spirit of Yhwh *pounds* Samson [13.25])

Sisera's mother *cries out shrilly* (תיבב) (5.28)

GIDEON

Gideon *blows* on a shofar (ויתקע בשופר) (6.34) (Cf. Ehud's blowing the shofar [3.27]) (*Shofar* is used 10x in Chs. 6 and 7.)

Gideon calls out Abiezer and four other tribes (זעק, 6.34, 35)

Chapter 7 is a very noisy chapter. First, Gideon throws the Midianites, Amalakites, and other Eastern people into a *panic* (7.21)—the whole camp was "running and *shouting* (רוע) and fleeing." The *shofars* are brought out in 7.8, 16, 20, 22 the men are told to *blow* the *shofars* (7.18 [2x]); they actually *blow* them in 7.19, 20 [2x], 22

they are told to *shout,* "For Yhwh and for Gideon!" (7.18); actually they *shout* (with an addition), "A sword for Yhwh and for Gideon!" (7.20)

they are not told beforehand to break the jars, but this is understood; and the jars are *smashed* (נפוץ) (no doubt for their *noise* effect) (7.19)

a cacophony occurs when the three companies (i.e., 300 men) *blow* the trumpets, *break* (שבר) the jars, and *cry:* "A sword for Yhwh and for Gideon" (7.20)

the Midianites *cry out* ((רוע) (7.21) (cf. 15.16)

ABIMELECH

Jotham, from top of Mt. Gerizim, *lifted up his voice* and *cried out* (ישא קולו ו יקרא) (9.7)

JEPHTHAH

Jephthah's daughter dances out of the door shaking her *tambourines* (11.34)

Jephthah's daughter asks permission to *bewail* (בכה, no doubt loudly) her virginity (11.37, 38)

her friends *commemorate* (תנה) (probably by *singing* or *reciting*) (11.40) (same word used in *The Song,* 5.11)

Jephthah called the Ephraimites, but they did not come (12.2)

SAMSON

the spirit of Yhwh begins to *pound* in Samson (13.25 same word as the *pounding* of the hooves above)

the young lion of lions *roars* (שאג) coming to meet Samson (14.5)

the Timnite *weeps* (בכה) before Samson (probably loudly) (14.16, 17)

Philistines come toward him *shouting* (רוע BDB 929) (15.14) (same word used of the Midianites (7.21)

Samson *calls* to Yhwh (קרא) and thereafter the place is named Spring of the *Caller* (En Hakkore) (15.19)

the Gazites are *silent* (חרש) all night (16.2) (Cf. other situations of *silence:* Gideon's men before they made their clamor; the Philistines in Delilah's room; Micah; the various people in ambushes)

MICAH

voice of the Levite is *heard* and recognized (18.3)

the spies on their return tell the Danites that the land they have spied out is *quiet* (שקט) (18.7)

silence is invoked: the Levite is told to *be quiet!* (החריש, sole) and to *put your hand over your mouth* (18.19) (Cf. the Gazites waiting for Samson [16.2])

Micah's men are *called out* (זעק, summoned [noise implied] (18.22)

they *shout* (קרא) to the Danites, and the Danites ask them why they *called out* (זעק, 18.23)

silence is again invoked: Micah is warned by the Danites: *Don't let your voice be heard* (קולך אל-תשמע) among us (18.25)

LEVITE'S CONCUBINE

worthless fellows *pound* on the door (דפק, beat violently BDB 200) (19.22) (Cf. Eglon's servants who probably *pounded* on the door in 3.24)

the Israelites *weep* (20.23, 26)

the Israelites *raised their voices* and *wept* with *great weeping* (ישאו קולם ויבכי גדול) (21.2)

B. Second Method. Noise/Silence

The following is the same information organized by the different kinds of noise and silence:

WEEPING

2.4 the Israelites *lift up their voices* and *weep* (ישאו העם את־קולם ויבכו) (2.4) (repeated almost word-for-word in 21.2)

2.18 the Israelites *groan* (נאקה BDB 611))

11.37, 38 Jephthah's daughter asks permission to *bewail* (בכה, no doubt loudly) her virginity

14.16, 17 the Timnite *weeps* (בכה) before Samson (probably loudly)

20.23, 26 the Israelites *weep*

21.2 the Israelites *raised their voices* and *wept* with *great weeping* (ישאו קולם ויבכי גדול)

SILENCE

3.11, 30; 5.31; 8.28, 18.7, 27 the land is said to be *quiet* (שקט, have rest, be undisturbed)

3.19 the King commands his attendants to "Keep silence" (הס binary opposite of *noise*) (Cf. the *silence* of the Gazites in 16.2 and the Danites in 18.19)

16.2 the Gazites are *silent* (חרש) all night (16.2) (Cf. the various people in ambushes)

18.7 the spies on their return tell the Danites that the land they have spied out is *quiet* (שקט)

18.19 silence is invoked: the Levite is told to *be quiet!* (חרש, sole) and to *put your hand over your mouth*

18.25 Micah is warned by the Danites: *Don't let your voice be heard* (אל־תשמע קולך) among us

CRY OUT (CALL, SUMMON

3.9 the Israelites *cry out* (זעק) to Yhwh (This occurs also in 3.15; 6.6, 7; 10.10, 14)

4.10, 13 Barak calls out (זעק, summons) Zebulun and Naphtali (זעק is also used when they *cry out* to Yhwh)

5.28 Sisera's mother *cries out shrilly* (יבב)

6.34, 35 Gideon calls out Abiezer and four other tribes (זעק)

7.20 the Israelites *cry* (קרא): "A sword for Yhwh and for Gideon"

7.21 the Midianites *cry out* ((רוע, raise a shout)

12.2 Jephthah called the Ephraimites, but they did not come (זעק)

15.14 Philistines come toward him *shouting* (רוע BDB 929)

15.19 Samson *calls* to Yhwh (קרא) and thereafter the place is named Spring of the *Caller* (En Hakkore)

18.22 Micah's men were *called out* (זעק, summoned [noise implied])

18.23 Micah and his men *shout* (קרא) to the Danites, and the Danites ask them why they *called out* (זעק)

NOISE

3.24, 25 the servant may make some noise or *knock* (no specific word used) on Eglon's door

3.27 Ehud *blows* on a shofar (the shofar is a call to arms)

5.22 the horses' hooves *hammer* (הלמו, 2x)

5.28 Sisera's mother is waiting to hear the *beats* (פעם, implying *hoof beats*) of his chariot (The same word used in Samson, when the spirit of Yhwh *pounds* Samson [13.25])

7.8, 16, 20, 22 the *shofars* are brought out

7.19, 20 [2x], 22 the men are told to *blow* the *shofars* (7.18 [2x] and they do (Chapter 7 is a very noisy chapter.)

7.19 they are not told beforehand to break the jars, but this is understood; and the jars are *smashed* (נפוץ) (no doubt for their *noise* effect)

7.20 the cacophony occurs when the three companies (i.e., 300 men) *blow* the trumpets, *break* (שבר) the jars, and *shout*

13.25 the spirit of Yhwh begins to *pound* in Samson (same word as the *pounding* of the hooves above)

14.5 the young lion of lions *roars* (שאג) coming to meet Samson

18.23 Micah and his men *shout* (קרא) to the Danites, and the Danites ask them why they *called out* (זעק)

19.22 worthless fellows *pound* on the door (דפק, beat violently BDB 200) (Cf. Eglon's servants who probably *pounded* on the door in 3.24)

MUSIC, SINGING

5.1 Deborah and Barak *sing* (שיר)

5.11 *singing, music* mentioned (5.4); *song, voice, singers, reciting* mentioned

5.12 she is told to *utter* a song (דברי־שיר)

5.16 *pipings* to the flock are heard

6.34 Gideon *blows* on a shofar (יתקע בשופר) are mentioned 10x in Chs. 6 and 7)

7.6 to 7.19 shofars are brought out and blown (see above under "Noise")

11.34 Jephthah's daughter dances out of the door shaking her *tambourines*

11.40 The friends of Jephthah's daughter *commemorate* (תנה) (probably by *singing* or *reciting*) (same word used in *The Song*, 5.11)

SPEAKING AND SHOUTING (direct discourse not included)

7.20 Gideon's men are told to *shout*, "For Yhwh and for Gideon!" (7.18 but; actually do so with an addition), "A sword for Yhwh and for Gideon!"

7.21 Gideon throws the Midianites, Amalakites, and other Eastern people into a *panic*—the whole camp was "running and *shouting* (רוע) and fleeing."

9.7 Jotham, from top of Mt. Gerizim, *lifted up his voice* and *cried out* (ישא קולו ויקרא)

18.3 *voice* of the Levite is *heard* and recognized

18.9 the spies on their return, urge the Danites to *speak*

15.14 Philistines come toward Samson *shouting* (רוע BDB 929) (same word used of the Midianites [7.21])

Appendix 2. The Rules of the Game Explained

A great deal has been written about games since the publication of *Homo Ludens: a Study of the Play Element in Culture* by Johan Huizinga in 1938 (trans. 1955).

What follows are some of the rules followed by the author. A few examples will be supplied to help the reader remember other examples given in the first three chapters of this book. (I have omitted wordplay and the rules about comedy and horror.) Some of the rules are gleaned from subsequent chapters of this book. The reader is invited to add other rules, as they are discovered.

Rule 1A. *The author has used about 100 or more keywords (nouns and verbs) and synonyms of these keywords. In any category, significant keywords and motifs will appear in every story. Keywords and motifs are generally distributed fairly evenly throughout the book and serve to give information and to unify the book. Every word in the book is there for a purpose.*

They are "hidden objects" because readers scarcely notice them. Though their function seems to be that of verisimilitude, every keyword is a thread of the tapestry.

Example 1. The father-daughter/mother-son stories (as well as several father-son stories).

Example 2. Hiding and secrecy.

Example 3. Body parts. This includes mutilation of bodies, starting with small mutilations and ending with the dividing of the Concubine's body into 12 parts. Nearly all the main parts of the body are mentioned in the Samson story. The story of Jephthah is an exception in that body parts are lacking.

Rule 1B. *The author provides meaning through the use of binary opposites.*

Some of these are Love/Hate, Night/Day, Inside/Outside, Cowardice/Bravery, Food production/Food consumption (destruction). (Longer lists of these are given above in this chapter and elsewhere.)

Rule 1C. *Missing items can be as important as well as other objects, hidden or not. The author often uses keywords through implication only*

Example. Use of hands: the Samson story has at least four incidents in which both hands are used but not always mentioned: the tearing apart of the lion (but "there was nothing in his hand"), the scraping out the honey from the carcass with *his palms*, but the tying up of the foxes and the tearing off of the gate of the city of Gaza and the two posts (hands not mentioned).[48]

We can imagine the oral storyteller acting out such scenes using his hands.

Rule 2. *Many patterns are established, little structures which are used to unify the book. As each part of the structure appears, the object or situation goes from good (or fair) in the beginning to bad in the middle of the book to worse at the end. The structures differ from each other each time: no rule can cover all the variations.*

Example 1. See the author's "table of contents" (discussed in Chapter 1) or Stages of Fighting (discussed in Chapter 2.)

Example 2. *Idols* are specifically mentioned in three stories.

> Ehud (*idols* are part of the landscape, ⅓ distance from the beginning of the book);
>
> Gideon (an ephod used by him and his community) (middle);
>
> Micah/Dan stories (4 kinds of idols, stolen to become the founding religion of a tribe ⅓ distance from the end of the book).

Note the increasing degree of the abuse. (Discussed in Chapter 4.)

Example 3. *Threatening men* appear 4x:

> early in the book: men (not *base*, however) surround the house of Gideon's father, threatening Gideon;
>
> middle of book: Abimelech uses *empty* (ריקים) and *reckless* (פחזים) men to assassinate his brothers;
>
> middle of book: Jephthah consorts with *empty* (ריקים) men;
>
> end of book: sons of Belial (בני־בליעל, *base fellows*) surround the house of the old Ephraimite in Ch. 19, threatening the Levite.

As we go down the list, the evilness of the men increases.

Example 4. Three *riddles* are also distributed:

> Ehud's secret message (⅓ distance from the beginning of the book);
>
> Jotham's fable (middle of the book);
>
> Samson's riddle (⅓ distance from the end of book);

The conundrum posed by the Israelites at the end of the book—how to give wives to the Benjaminites without violating their vow not to give them wives—is a riddle. In fact, the whole book is a riddle. (See Chapter 4.)

Example 5. A *numbers game* is being played throughout the book: in the Samson story, we have 3 women, 3 animals, 30 wedding guests, 300 foxes, 3000 Philistines on the roof of the temple—just one of many such patterns.)[49]

Example 5A. Also in the Samson story are *animals*:

> one lion (mentioned 3x) first alive, then dead;
>
> one ass (mentioned 5x in the jawbone-of-an-ass incident) also dead; and
>
> 300 foxes (mentioned 1x, their tails mentioned 3x) first alive, then assuredly dead.

Such designs are part of the author's style (other examples are given under rules about other devices).

Rule 3A. *Stories are meant to correspond or contrast with each other. Each story may have a special relationship with one other story. Stories are "hinged" together like a polytych, sometimes with keywords, other times with structures and themes, signifying comparisons and contrasts. Closely-related, or "companion stories" have a preponderance of items that are parallel or relate to each other. A story may have more than one counterpart.*

Rule 3B. *Stories linked together in this way are sometimes adjacent, sometimes not.*

Example 1. For example, the right-handed Jael is hinged to the left-handed Ehud in the preceding story.

Example 2. But Jael also contrasts with Delilah in a much later story; they are linked through the word *pin.*

Example 3. Gideon's outstanding characteristic is *cowardice.* Samson's is *bravery.*

Example 4. Defeat of Luz (beginning of book) is compared with annihilation of Laish (end of book).

Rule 4. *Keywords and stories are placed in a specific order, the sequence being from up to down or from smaller to greater or from good to worse.*

The most common sequence is in a downward direction; that is, something which may be fairly good at the beginning of the book starts to deteriorate toward the middle of the book, and finally becomes the worst that it could be at the end. (See examples under Rule 2.)

Rule 5. *The book abounds in "curious details." Though this information may seem to be gratuitous, curious details are an especially important means of linking two stories together.* (See discussion of anomalies in Chapter 1.)

Examples:

the curious weapons used throughout;

the loaf of bread which knocks down the tent in the Midianite's dream.

Rule 6. *Characters, actions, and attitudes are characterized by a cluster of keywords especially if used more than once. The narrator contrived unique ways to do this.*

Example 1. As is appropriate to Samson, the most physical of characters in the book, almost every important part of the body is mentioned except the sexual organs; the genitals are implicit in his encounters with women, as well as the fact that the Philistines are described as *uncircumcised.* The three bodily parts that most represent Samson are *hands, heart,* and *hair.* The ancient writer probably had the same connotations in his mind as we do:

hands have to do with his natural prowess;

heart has to do with his weakness for women and perhaps his strength;

hair represents his vow (all of which he breaks) and the mystery of his strength.

Example 2. The author slips in references to the body parts with the animals—carcass (lion), jawbone (ass), and tail (fox). We are being shown iconically what animals he likens Samson to: Lion = strength; Ass = stubbornness and stupidity; Fox = cunning.

Rule 7A. *A cluster of repeated uses of a word may be a signal or code. 5 repetitions of a word in rapid succession always have a special meaning. (3 repetitions are perhaps a different code, as yet undeciphered).*

Rule 7B. *Disproportion or "overdetermination" of any kind is a signal for the reader to look for a special message.*

Example 1. The word *ass* that is repeated 5x in the Samson story. This signals us to look for other asses in the book. The first ass that is the one that Achsah alights from (1:14). The other woman on an ass is the dead Concubine (19:18). In this last story, the word *ass* is also used 5x.

That the Levite puts the body of the Concubine on the ass is an arrow that points us back to Achsah where we see a romantic (ideal) story that ended happily, in contrast to the Concubine's miserable marriage and her horrible end.

Example 2. The word *hands* is repeated 3x in the following passage.

and they blew the trumpets and smashed the jars that were in their hands. So the three companies blew the trumpets and broke the jars, holding in their left hands the torches, and in their right hands the trumpets to blow (7.19-20).

Like Jael and Samson, Gideon's men use both hands when they are trying to harm the enemy. An excess of details is a signal of the importance of this information.

Rule 8. *The book is iconic. Each story contains one or more graphic pictures with which we can identify the whole story.* (See Chapter 1.)

The author had no camera, but he was thinking iconigraphically.

Example: As mentioned above, about ⅓ of the way from the begnning of the book, we see Eglon, who has fallen (נפל) dead on the floor *inside* a room behind a locked door; while about ⅓ the way from the end of the book, we we see the Concubine outside a house, fallen in front of a locked door. (See Chapter 1 for a list of other iconic tableaux.)

Rule 9. *Not only are there parallels (comparisons and contrasts) within the book, but there are many parallels with other books of the Bible.*

This is the art of intertextuality and allusion.[50] Parallels aid the reader to interpret the meaning of the stories in *Judges*. More often than not, the models elsewhere in the Bible are good, and the parallel in *Judges* bad. (See Appendix 2 in Chapter 1 for a partial list of parallels. See also Chapter 6.)

Example 1. Judges 19 (the base men in Gibeah) is parallel to Genesis 19 (the base men in Sodom). One story ends happily; the other story ends tragically.

Example 2. The carving up of the Concubine and sending the parts to the tribes as a summons to war is parallel to Saul's carving up the oxen for the same purpose (1 Sam 7.11). The acceptable method by Saul increases the horror of the unacceptable carving up of the Concubine.

Example 3. The *near* sacrifice of Isaac is parallel with the *actual* sacrifice of Jephthah's daughter (one good, the other bad).

Rule 10. *Many of the details are arranged in chiastic order. Smaller chiastic patterns may exist within the larger one.* (See Appendix 1 in Chapter 1.)

Examples already given: 1) Achsah on an ass (beginning of book) and the Levite's Concubine on an ass (end of book). 2) the dead Eglon on the floor and the dead Concubine on the ground. (3) graven image in the Ehud story, ephod in the Gideon story, four kinds of images (including the ephod) in the Micah story.

Possibly all the details fit into one huge chiasmus, while smaller chiastic patterns within the whole, which are independent of the larger one, were created. The chiasmus is not simply an illustration of the ingenuity of the craftsman, but serves the purpose of spotlighting comparisons and contrasts.

Rule 11. *When a speech between two people is reported to another, the differences between the original and the report may be meaningful.*

When it is not clear whether the report has been erroneously or deliberately altered, an addition or omission may mean that the truth is being manipulated by the reporter.[51] Or perhaps we are to assume that the story was told accurately but that the author did not find it necessary to repeat all the details.

Example 1. When Samson's mother reports to her husband that Samson will be a Nazirite, she adds that he will be a Nazirite to the day of his death. This has been taken to be the actual *cause* of Samson's death, as it was his mother who linked the violation of his Nazirite vow with his death.[52]

Example 2. When reporting the rape of the Concubine, the Levite stresses that the Gibeahites intended to kill *him* but omits the fact that he thrust her out to them in order to save himself.

Rule 12. *The stories should be laid out side by side and read both diachronically and synchronically and thereby gain increased meanings.*

12A. down from beginning to end (diachronically)

12B. across the matrix (synchronically) (i.e., comparing and contrasting parallel stories) (see Chapter 1).

Rule 13. *Summary: the fundamental way that meaning is derived is through the similarities and differences between and among the stories. To fail to examine these similarities and differences is to fail to understand the meaning of the book.*

Conclusion to the Rules.

This list of rules by no means exhausts the possibilities concerning the author's artistry nor of the examples available. Not only are these rules functional, but they also add to the pleasure of the game played by the author. It is a strange narrative art.

We do not know whether or not this technique was used by other writers as a design for a whole body of writing. So far as I know, there is no other literature like it, although the chiastic pattern of the *Iliad*, observed by Cedric Whitman, has affinities with this. A theory of composition is offered below, in Chapter 6.

Chapter Four

HIDDEN OBJECTS: CASE LAW

It is the glory of God to conceal things, but the glory of kings to search things out.
—Proverbs 25.2

It is the merit of the common law that it decides the case first and determines the principle afterwards. —Oliver Wendell Holmes, Jr., Chief Justice of the Supreme Court

"Tut, tut, child," said the Duchess. "Everything's got a moral if only you can find it."
—Lewis Carroll *Alice's Adventures in Wonderland*

I. Introduction to Case Law

As shown in previous chapters, *Judges* is a group of stories containing numerous parallel elements: actions, situations, and words. Once we have investigated the parallels and binary opposites closely, we realize that their dialectical purpose is to compel us not only to compare, but also to contrast, the different situations in order to arrive at the best possible judgment of human behavior by logical arguments concerning the variations in similar situations.

To make valid judgments about the stories, we must keep the *entire* scope of activities in the book within our purview, for as in present-day common law, no case can be really understood in isolation from the others, but must be evaluated in *comparison* with other cases. In the process, we will notice what a difference perspective makes and try to understand how much we are swayed by our subjective points of view.

The only *absolute* that we discover in this book is, as we might expect, that it is always wrong to worship any other god than Yhwh.[*]

Most interpreters concentrate on one story, one episode, one character, perhaps one aspect of the character. Like lawyers, they usually defend a single point of view. Perhaps not even realizing what they are doing, they are engaging in an act of

---

[*] Yhwh is the author's explanation for why things happen as they do.

judgment and are trying to prove and *win* their case. They want definite answers. The author of *Judges*, I believe, puts everything in question.

These stories may have been used in the way that Homeric epics and the Icelandic sagas were used. In Book IX of the *Iliad*, for example, when the Greek embassy approaches Achilles to beg him to return to battle, the strategy of Phoinix was to tell Achilles the story of Meleagros, which was roughly parallel to Achilles' own experience of losing Briseus. Phoinix says: "Look at how heroes behaved in the old days. Let me tell you a story . . . . Let me tell you how heroes are supposed to behave." And he tells this tale, hoping that Achilles will see where he went wrong. This is what the people in ancient civilization got from the *Iliad*. Elizabeth Vandiver writes:

> How should we behave in a certain situation? Let's look to Homer and see how Achilles, Agamemnon, Odysseus behaved. Just as we have Achilles performing epic inside the epic, here we have Phoinix citing epic or citing the authority of antiquity inside the epic, which itself is the authority of antiquity, a nice kind of double vision of how epic works.[1]

The stories in *Judges* also provide "authority" and give positive and negative examples.

The Icelandic sagas go further; they are repositories of legal information. In *Hrafnkel's Saga*, for example, the narrative embodies problems concerning customs, kinship relations, property rights, and rules of warfare, and makes legal judgments concerning these issues. Homer and the authors of *Judges* and the sagas sensed that only with vivid examples of actions set in a narrative can we understand what happens when human beings go wrong, and find clues about how to deal with problems of power. The more exciting the narrative the more memorable and useful these examples.

Judges, like the sagas, is "existential," in that the author seems aware that no philosophy or system of ethics can be understood or evaluated or built *apart from human experience*. Abstractions do not grab us as experience does. And as Kant believed, pure unembodied abstract speculation is too difficult for us to engage in for long. We need to be driven by some urgent need. Ethics is like common law in that no law of behavior can exist abstractly, apart from its cases.

All human beings, says Daniel N. Robinson, must grapple with three serious questions: "What kind of knowledge do we need to have about our world? what is 'right' conduct? and how should we be governed?" Questions about the first of these areas are answered in epistemology and metaphysics; the second in ethics and moral philosophy; and the last in political science and jurisprudence (to paraphrase Robinson).[2] All three domains receive close attention in *Judges*. *Judges* is philosophical in this sense.

Some of the particular questions it asks are: How do we understand our world and what do we do in the face of the danger and uncertainty of our lives? How do we solve our problems? How do we keep ourselves safe? How much help can we expect to get from Yhwh? To what degree can we expect our own tribe to protect our interests? How trustworthy are our brother tribes? How do we avoid danger from "outsiders"? Are human beings "victims" or "agents" in the game of life? What is "honor" and how is it manifested? Is there a difference in our treatment of a guest who is "one of us" and a guest who is an "outsider"? How do individual flaws like pride or *hubris* (Jephthah) and wrath (Samson) affect our future? What is wrong with gross cowardice (Gideon) and blind fury (Samson)? What is loyalty and to whom should we be loyal? What is the right way to conduct warfare? Is it right to take plunder for oneself from a defeated enemy? Who is our best ruler? And so on.

Some of the conclusions that the Israelites might have reached after studying and judging the cases in *Judges* are: that they should not worship foreign gods, not use idols, not make graven images, not deceive, not violate the rules of hospitality, not treat "sojourners" (visitors to one's city) disrespectfully, not take plunder in holy warfare and/or use it unwisely, not slaughter members of fellow tribes, not destroy friendly cities, not make rash vows, not violate marriage vows, not be disloyal, not be lazy or cowardly, not be overly pious, not be overly ambitious, not be ruthless, not love wine and good fellowship too much, not marry "foreigners," not fall prey to the blandishments of women, not underestimate the power of a woman, not choose a leader frivolously, etc.

The negative particle throughout is meant to show how one's judgments might emerge as commandments, like the Ten Commandments, which begin with the Hebrew word *not* (לא). Positive rules might be deduced as well, such as *dulce et decorum est pro patria mori*.

One can imagine these stories being read or told to a group of ancient Israelites studying law, perhaps sitting cross-legged on the floor in a circle around their leader, who is explaining that they must carefully scrutinize all the clues before judging a person's behavior and study all the similar cases, prior and subsequent, before reaching a decision. A long discussion of each case will ensue, as among members of a jury, in an attempt to arrive at a consensus. As with the Upanishads and philosophical and religious literature, we have not only students, but also the master, who will answer their questions.

This is the beginning of wisdom literature. However, we are *not* given the wisdom, *only the building blocks* with which to arrive at wisdom, for the author does not supply us with an answer-key at the end of the book. Maybe the real truth was only for the initiated, for those who passed the test of the Law, who proved their ability to judge cases, got their law degree, and went on to be judges.

Dante clearly gives us the sentences and punishments of the criminals; all we have to do is figure out the *why*, and Virgil is there to supply that information when Dante does not know. Virgil intervenes and prevents Dante from misjudging the miscreants in Inferno or feeling undeserved sympathy for them. Readers of *Judges* have only themselves, or their discussion leader, to guide them to reasonable conclusions. Perhaps the verdicts and sentences could have been transmitted orally by such leaders though generations, and were a predecessor to the Jewish law in the Pentateuch.

Actually, there is one key in *Judges* and that is the order in which the author places the stories. As already discussed (see Chapter 1) and as will be discussed below, the characters are presented in descending order, from fairly good, to poor, to worse, to worst. The judicial sentences or punishments may have been implied there, too, but they are more cryptic than in Dante. To give but one example: Was Jephthah guilty of a grievous error in killing his only child, and if so, what should his punishment be? Our clue can be found in the list of minor judges before and after him. They form a pattern: first, a judge with no children, then a judge with 30 children, then Jephthah (a judge) with none, then a judge with 60 children, then a judge with none, then a judge with 40 children (See **Table III** in Chapter 1). Jephthah, the third judge in the pattern, does not disarrange it. Because he ended up by having no children—almost the worst thing that could happen to an Israelite— we may conclude that he was guilty of wrongdoing. The punishment is that he will have no progeny. Basically the key to unlock the door is *retribution.*

Like all great literature, *Judges* gives present-day readers an opportunity to fine-tune their own powers of judgment. Readers might judge the cases against their own laws, ethics, and morals, and not dismiss ancient behavior as being of no concern today. It muddies our own thinking to allow a different standard from our own to prevail. Moreover, comparison with modern judgments may clarify our thinking. We would like to arrive at "moral clarity" in each case.[3] Law itself is not fixed. As Derrida says, the judge "has to reinvent law each time" he makes a judgment. Justice is "always incalculable," and Derrida quotes Levinas, who says that "justice is the relation to the other . . . . Once you relate to the other as the other, then something incalculable comes on the scene, something which cannot be reduced to the law or to the history of legal structures."[4] Though in the larger respect, law is supposed to remain the same from case to case, the law is ever changing in subtle ways.

Is there a body of Israelite laws against which we should measure our decisions about these stories? We cannot know. We may assume them to be something like those found in the Pentateuch. But since we cannot be sure when the laws were codified, and thus do not know if they were set down before or after the composition of *Judges,* we must infer the "laws" from the stories themselves. We should not go to this book with preconceived ideas about what it means. Let the book speak for itself.

Judgment demands impartiality; but we are always at the mercy of our own personal perspectives. This may be the author's reason for offering us several perspectives on a single behavior, as we shall subsequently see. Not that the author was completely objective himself. No doubt, he, too, had his own perspectives and expected that his immediate audience would eventually agree on what Yhwh desired of them as judges. But the author *never* interferes in our process of judging; he lets us work on these cases on our own.

The first time we read it, we come to *Judges* completely unprepared to make these judgments. But because of the vast distance between that ancient world and ours, we are automatically behind a "veil of ignorance," as the late philosopher John Rawls puts it.[5] Though Rawls was referring to distributive justice, the "veil of ignorance" is a good term to describe the contemporary reader's viewpoint of the events of the book, as we are really ignorant of this society, and despite our own theological doctrines, should have no personal stakes in it when we judge. The law requires that we be "disinterested." Yet we must judge.

An important consideration is whether or not we in the modern age can presume to judge ancient behavior. Can we ever attain moral clarity? Most interpreters hunt for the author's (or Yhwh's) morality and try not to intrude with their own opinions. On the other hand, if we try to rationalize behavior that we otherwise would condemn, or excuse it because we fear how a frank opinion might be seen as a criticism of religious institutions, we are doing no service to modern beliefs. Ancient behavior and our opinion about it do affect how we think and act today and vice versa.

As shown in Chapter 1 and elsewhere, the characters make mistakes from beginning to end, with the mistakes at the end more egregious than at the beginning.

David Chalcraft believes the author of *Judges* is studying "deviance" and in the process seeking "to create and maintain the boundaries" of behavior in his own social group.[6] From the stories, Chalcraft lists certain actions that *are not* legitimate if practiced against one's *own* group, but when practiced against the *out-group* in order to maintain one's own social group "in the face of external threat," they *are* legitimate:

1. Use of Violence
2. Use of Trickery/Treachery
3. Breakage of Kinship Obligations
4. Non-deference
5. Disregard of Social Obligations
6. Pursuance of Societal Ends [i.e., achieving societal ends by doing deviant acts]
7. Non-normal Interactions with Out-Group
8. Choosing for Israel (184)

On the other hand—according to the ancient ways of thinking—*not* doing these things with the out-group, that is, having *normal* relationships with the out-group— is wrong but with the in-group is correct behavior (185, 196). Chalcraft's list works well today in describing how we (or some of us) judge the present attacks on our nation by the Other, and our conflicts with those who threaten our society.

The acts of Jael and Ehud are "potentially deviant" but legitimate because their behavior is against the out-group. Samson is an example of the reasons for a policy of nonfraternization: why one should not cooperate with the out-group or be too friendly or intermarry with them (182, 186). The Danites in Ch. 18 are wrong because their actions are against Micah, who belongs to the in-group. Chalcraft does not make a judgment on the Danites' annihilation of Laish, but if we believe Laish to be an out-group, then all is fair in this war against Laish. (Or is it?) And was it right for the Danites to steal the idols and the priest from one of their in-group?

In Ch. 19, the men of Gibeah break the code of hospitality and commit rape and murder. This behavior is deviant because it is committed against their own people, but if committed against the enemy, would not be. In the case of the rape of the Concubine, "the narrator indicates how punishment should be regulated," according to Chalcraft (181). Is the narrator right, or can we question the Israelite judgment against Benjamin?

Others claim that as "underdogs," the Israelites have no alternative than to act subversively. Using this excuse along with Chalcraft's tables of permissible and impermissible actions, all of the Israelite characters may escape censure.

But do we today accept this theory of "underdog" ethic—that ethics toward one's own group is rightfully different from ethics toward another group?

We are often warned against applying 21st century ethics to the past. But first of all, are we really able to switch to a different ethics every time we plunge into the past? Second, how can we view the past except through our own lens—much less judge and evaluate the behaviors, the more so since our ethics are derived largely from the Hebrew Scriptures and from the New Testament?

The ideology of the terrorism of September 11, 2001, and its Al-Qaeda perpetrator—which, incidentally, may be said to have has its origin in the events of the Hebrew Scripture—has been called "evil" by the President of the United States. The terrorists are underdogs. The only weapon they, like the Palestinians, have against their powerful enemy is terrorism. Only if they are not classified as "evil," can the Israelite underdogs in *Judges* be regarded as "heroes." But if we allow the underdogs in *Judges* their deviant behavior, how can we refuse to allow the Al-Qaeda terrorists the same?

The underdog still acts subversively—has to. Human nature has not changed. What has changed is the "side" that the terrorists are on. Today it is not the Israelites who are the underdogs, but it is the enemies of the Israelites who are the underdogs. What we do not like is being the target.

Whatever ethics we apply to the present events, should we not apply them to the forerunners of these events? Finally, if our modern western ethics *are* different, there's a value in both being critical of the underdog and yet understanding him.

What may confuse readers ethically (whether they are religious or not) is that they tend to think that in the past, the land truly belonged to the Israelites and that Yhwh gave it to them and was on their side.

From a nonreligious perspective, however, we may acknowledge that this land was always up for grabs by any people stronger than those residing in it. Then the ancient and the modern pictures must be viewed differently. To absolve the Israelites from error because in the narrator's perspective they seem to be on "our side" is wrong. The fact that they are underdogs, however, is an extenuating reality, in that it is unjust that the weaker be crushed by the powerful simply because they are weak. If they don't resort to terrorism, then injustice prevails. Where we have to draw the line, then, is the consideration of whether the victims of terrorism are innocent bystanders or justifiable targets: a contrast exists between Ehud's justifiable target and Samson's innocent victims.

What also confuses us ethically is that as readers of literature, we naturally fall in line with the author's perspective, and in this case, we tend not to question what the book tells us. But once we think of the characters in *Judges not as* models of behavior for us to emulate, but as negative examples for us to judge, and once we accept that in the author's mind Yhwh was *testing* these people (as the story says), we are relieved

of that confusion. The ancient author himself provided two different perspectives
of similar cases, such as the case of Jael and the case of Delilah—doubtlessly to test
the readers' objectivity, or at the very least, to provide them with an ethical puzzle.

These problems are wrenching to us today. And they were wrenching to the
author of *Judges* back then.

Emile Durkheim believed that if we were left to our own devices for too long a
time, our moral beliefs and convictions would weaken in strength. We need
institutions like religion and government to require reinforcement.[7]

Judges ends the way it does because the characters had no rules to follow. The
society went from bad to worse and ended with that "worst of evils,"according to
Alasdair MacIntyre, civil war.[8] The main thrust of these cases is to show how behaviors
deteriorate when people have no external controlling authority and no body of law.

II. Evil and Good

One reason some readers may feel disgust upon reading *Judges* is that there is so
much evil in this book and very little "high moral ground" and because most of us
are unprepared to find that in the Bible.

If we are reading with active minds, we must apply some standard by which to
judge the characters' actions. One obvious approach is to be guided by the Ten
Commandments and the Deuteronomic laws. Another approach would be to locate
instances of the seven deadly sins: pride, envy, covetousness, anger, sloth, lust,
gluttony. Ehud, Barak, Deborah, and Jael seem to have none of these sins. Sisera's
mother is guilty of pride and covetousness. Gideon is angry at the towns who refuse
to help him. Jephthah is angry at the Ephraimites. Samson commits all of the deadly
sins except perhaps envy. The Danites are covetous both of Micah's idols, the Levite
priest, and the prosperity of Laish. The Levite in the last story is guilty of sloth and
gluttony. The men of Gibeah are guilty of lust. The book is full of angry people,
including Yhwh (see the category Anger below).

Let us keep these approaches in mind as we continue our analysis. It must also
be remembered that the author is always thinking in terms of the binary opposites of
the values and actions being observed.

Subcategory: "Evil," Sin, Disobedience

When we analyze the keywords for *evil* and its synonyms, we find that it is much
more prevalent in the text than we had realized upon first reading.

Disobedience (*disloyalty*) to Yhwh is naturally condemned. Beginning with 2.2,
Yhwh rebukes the Israelites for disobedience in 22 instances and says that they have
transgressed (עבר, lit., gone over) his covenant (2.20). "We have *sinned* (חטא, missed)
because we have abandoned (עזב) our Elohim and served (עבד) the Baalim," cry
the Israelites (10.10). The word *sin* is used when Jephthah protests to the
Ammonites, "I have not *sinned* (חטא) against you; you do me wrong (רע, evil) by

making war on me" (11.27). (חטא means *miss* when the Benjaminites are said to be able to shoot at a hair and not *miss*. [20.16])

The Israelites do *evil* I (רע) in the eyes of Yhwh very often (2.11; 3.7, 12; 4.1; 6.1; 10.6; 13.1). Usually the crime is forsaking Yhwh (עזב, a word which is used 5x in *Judges*: in the sense of *forsake*, 2.12, 13; 10.6, 10, 13). Abimelech did *evil* (רע) to his father in murdering his father's 70 sons (9.56). It is an *evil spirit* (רוח רעה) that Elohim sent between the Shechemites and Abimelech (9.23). We are told that "the *evil* of the men of Shechem fell on their heads, and on them came the curse (קללה) of Jotham" (9.57). Samson declares himself to be *innocent* (נקה) if he does *evil* to the Philistines (15.3). But is he justified at all, in harming them to the extent that he did? In the battle with the Israelites, the Benjaminites did not realize, but later saw, that *evil* (רעה, *defeat*) was touching them (20.34, 41). The rape of the Concubine is also called *evil* (20.3, 12, 13).

Disloyalty/Loyalty/Treachery

To turn away from Yhwh and worship other gods is the supreme act of disloyalty. But many personal disloyalties can also be uncovered: for example, the failure to do one's *duty* may be *disloyalty*. Who are the *disloyal* ones? The author may not relate these incidents as evil, but the reader reaches these conclusions from the information in each story.

The man from Luz is an informer; he shows the Israelites the secret way into his own city (1.25). Though to his own people, he is a traitor, this is not shown in the story, and he is not recognized as such by the author. It is something we must realize by our own critical thinking.

The youth in the Gideon story who writes down the names of the elders in Succoth to help Gideon is another informer, disloyal to his people (8.14), though not recognized as such by the author. But the author reproves Gideon's people, who did not show kindness, loyalty (חסד) in return for *the good* Gideon had done (8.35). This reproof is also given by Jotham (9.16-20).

Abimelech is disloyal to his "house" when he kills his brothers and becomes the king of Shechem (whether he is also king of the Israelites is not clear). Jotham gives the Shechemites a sermon on loyalty:

> for my father fought for you, and risked his life, and rescued you from the hand of
> Midian; but you have risen up against my father's house this day, and have killed his
> sons, seventy men on one stone, and have made Abimelech, the son of his slave woman,
> king over the lords of Shechem, because he is your kinsman (9.17-18).

Perhaps we are meant to hear the author's own voice in this.

Gaal and the men of Shechem deal treacherously (בגד) with Abimelech (9.23), but Zebul shows loyalty to his king when he sends a message to Abimelech that the Shechemites are stirring up the city (צרים את־העיר) against him (9.31). Zebul, in fact, is an anomaly in the book that is brimming over with treachery. His loyalty to his master Abimelech marks him as a relatively decent servant, although from another point of view he may only be acting in self-interest.

Samson is not doing his *duty* to Yhwh and thus is disloyal by wasting his promise dallying with women. The Timnite is intimidated by the Philistines into *betraying* Samson. Judah may be considered *disloyal* in turning Samson over to the Philistines (15.13). And Delilah is, of course, *disloyal* to her lover Samson, though loyal to her own people. The clan of Meroz seems to have been *disloyal* to Deborah (5.23), as were the cities of Succoth and Penuel to Gideon (8.6, 8) and the city of Jabesh-Gilead to the Israelites (21.8). The offense of Meroz and Jabesh-Gilead was failure to answer the muster. Succoth and Penuel failed to supply Gideon's troops with food. Or were there extenuating reasons for these cities to act as they did?

Loyalty and its binary opposite are never far from the author's mind.

Idolatry

The outward manifestation of disloyalty to Yhwh is idolatry. Yhwh complains against the Israelites' idolatry throughout the book.

In the Hebrew Bible, those making and worshiping idols are anathema (Exod 20.4, 5). "Do not turn to idols or make cast idols" (Lev 19.4) and "Curst be the man who makes carved images and cast idols, an abomination to Yhwh . . ." (Deut 27.15), though of course, the author and his society may not have known these laws.[9] Immediately after five references to the images in the Micah story, however, the author remarks: "Each man did what was right in his own eyes" (17.6) and repeats it following the description of Micah's establishing of the sanctuary (18.1). Image-making was clearly wrong.

Images (פֶּסֶל) are mentioned twice in the Ehud story. The *carved images* at Gilgal (פְּסִילִים) (3.19, 26), where Ehud turns back, are very likely idolatrous. We do not know what they represent or who has put them up or worshiped them or if Ehud had any connection with them. They are a mysterious artifact in the landscape. Whatever the case, they are in the story for a reason. They are literary signpost to what is to come.

Gideon tears down an altar to Baal and Asherah at the start of his career (6.27-32). But at the end he ironically sets up an *ephod* (אֵפוֹד) in Ophrah, which became "a snare to him and his family" (8.27). This must mean that it was evil and therefore is evil in the Micah story, too. Jacobus Marais, in fact, thinks that when Micah set up the ephod, he was serving Baal.[10] The concentration of images in Chs. 17 and 18 emphasizes the extreme to which Micah had gone:

carved image (פֶּסֶל, *pesel*, 17.3, 4; 18.14, 17, 18, 20, 30, 31).

cast idol (מַסֵּכָה, *masekah*, 17.3, 4; 18.14, 17, 18)

ephod (אֵפוֹד 17.5; 18.14, 17, 18, 20).

images (תְּרָפִים, *teraphim*, 17.5; 18.14, 17, 18, 20) (cf. Rachel in Gen 31.19).[11]

A total of 23x. The author will not allow us to lose sight of these objects.

Some Israelites were no doubt idolaters in the ancient pre-Deuteronomic world before the rise of Yhwism (see Chapter 5). Rachel had her father's teraphim, and Michal had an idol with which to deceive Saul about David's whereabouts. Such idols were perhaps not regarded as totally abhorrent until the time that these stories in *Judges* were committed to writing.[12] In focusing intently on the idols, the author is asking us to think about them over and over again.

When the Danites arrive at Micah's door, Micah has all four of the forbidden items of worship. The Danites steal the *carved images* and set them up in their new territory (18.30, 31). This must be a condemnation of Dan.

Cowardice/Courage

Judges is about bravery, with the heroes running the gamut from derring-do and bravado to intrepidity, fearlessness, and resolute courageousness. The different characters represent different attitudes of *bravery* or its opposite, *timidity* and *cowardice*.

Barak will not go to battle without Deborah (4.7). This seems cowardly, but later he fights well in battle: "Barak pursued the chariots and the army to Harosheth-ha-goiim. All the army of Sisera fell by the sword; no one was left" (NRS 4.16). Perhaps he was not so much cowardly as superstitious or cautious. Jael tells the mighty Canaanite commander *not to fear* to come into her tent (4.18). Sisera *lacks caution*. He makes his fatal mistake and enters. Gideon is *fearful* that he will die when he sees a messenger-angel, but Yhwh tells him not to *fear* (6.23). *Fearing* his father's house, Gideon tears down the altar of Baal by night rather than by day (6.27). Joash, his father, however, is *courageous* when he confronts the mob surrounding him (6.30)—while Gideon is no doubt *shrinking* behind his father's skirts. (His cowardly acts are listed in Chapter 2.)

Compare him with the Levite and the old Ephraimite in the story of the Rape of the Concubine, where the Ephraimite, like Joash, shows considerable *bravery* in confronting the crowd of rapists (19.23) but immediately *loses courage* when the Benjaminites do not heed him.

On the eve of battle, and in accord with Deut 20.8, Gideon allows the *fearful and trembling* among his men to return home (7.3), and 22,000 take him up on the offer. A vast number of men are fearful and trembling. And Gideon himself continues to show *fear*, for rather than go down to the enemy camp alone in the middle of the night, he follows Yhwh's advice: "But if you fear to go down, go down to the camp with your lad, Purah" (7.10). Purah must be seen as *braver* than Gideon. But then Gideon becomes brave. When Gideon smites the Midianite army, it is *they* who flee *terrified* (8.12). (Now the shoe is on the other foot.) Next, however, Gideon's son Jether is *afraid* to slay Zebah and Zalmunna (8.20), but they (the enemy) are *brave* and challenge Gideon to play the man[13] and do the job himself. He does so.—But, of course, it is at no personal risk.

Another son of Gideon—Jotham—is *brave* in shouting out his fable to Abimelech and the Shechemites, although he climbs up a mountain, out of reach, to do this, and afterwards *flees* to Beer (9.21).

And Jephthah's daughter was *courageous* to face her destiny so resolutely. No doubt about it.

The Alpha Male of the book is certainly Samson. Extremely powerful, he *inspires fear* in everyone, but *never shows* a single moment of *fear* himself. Although his crouching in the peculiar remote hideout on the rock of Etam may imply *fear*, it is more likely a case of sulks. (He is fed up with everyone.) The Judahites in the Samson story are *cowardly* when they confront him, for they are 3,000 to 1. And they are *cowardly* in handing him over to the Philistines in order to save themselves (15.13). Samson's meekness in allowing this is to be wondered at, but he had a trick up his sleeve that they did not know about. Micah is an Epsilon Male, the binary opposite of Samson. The *craven* but wise Micah turns tail and runs when threatened by the Danites, 600 of them armed with weapons of war (18.26).

The Levite and the Ephraimite host are the most *cowardly* of all: first, when the Ephraimite offers the base men his virgin daughter and the Concubine and tells the men, "Abuse them, do whatever you want with them" (19.24). Next, it is cowardly when the Levite pushes his Concubine out to the rapists while he and the old man cower *inside* the house, letting the gang do its pleasure *outside* with the defenseless woman (19.25).

Many other people *flee for their lives* (נוס) in battle: Adoni-Bezek *flees* (1.6), but is captured; Sisera *flees* (4.15, 17), but meets his death anyway; the Midianites *flee* in panic from the torches and the racket Gideon is making (7.21, 22); Zebah and Zalmunna *flee*, allowing Gideon to throw their army into *panic* (8.12), but afterwards the two kings stand their ground *bravely* when all has been lost; Jotham *flees* after delivering his fable (9.21). Gaal, after boasting what he will do to Abimelech, *flees* for his life when attacked (9.40). The Shechemites *flee* to the tower (9.51) Finally, the Benjaminites *flee* from the Israelites and *hide* in the wilderness at the Rock of Rimmon (20.45, 47). (Ironically, or not so ironically, these are the remnants of the mob in Gibeah that did not fear to attack a lone, defenseless woman.) (Notice the dynamism of this list.)

Hiding is also *fleeing* (נוס). When Gideon hides as he threshes wheat in the winepress, the verb used is *flee* (6.11). The word *flee* is used 13x in *Judges,* usually characteristic of enemy behavior, but here of Gideon and in Ch. 20 of the Benjaminites.

But of bravery: Deborah (staunch), Ehud (intrepid and resolute), Gideon (fearful, then brave, then ruthless), Jephthah (resolute, brave, then ruthless, straight-laced, grim), and Samson (arrogant, reckless, brutish, feral, bloodthirsty, but ultimately resolved and courageous)—all are *brave*. Gideon, Jephthah, and Samson, however, are also *bullies*. Assign your own adjectives. Make your own judgments.

Rape (already discussed in Chapters 1 and 2.)

Theft/Plunder

Not much thievery is reported in *Judges,* and when it occurs, it is committed either by the enemy or by corrupt characters—up until the Micah story. Yhwh allowed the tribes to be plundered by enemies and then raised up judges to save them from being *plundered* (2.14, 16). Sisera's mother is waiting for *plunder* (שלל). *Plunder* of course is one of the rewards to the troops and their incentive to go to battle. But in *Judges*, *plunder* seems to be a bad word, for *plunder* is supposed to belong to Yhwh, not to the people (Josh 6.21). We know what happened to Achan (Josh 7.25). *The Song of Deborah* expressly states that "they took no silver money as spoil" (בצע כסף לא לקחו, 5.19; בצע signifies "unjust gain"). This amounts to a boast and is in stark contrast to Gideon, who did take spoil. Gideon may have thought he was devoting his *plunder* to Yhwh, but the ephod he made of it debauched his people (8.27). Deborah's lack of avarice (in taking no plunder) is also in contrast to Delilah's cupidity in betraying Samson for money.

As for *theft*, the lack of safety on the highways from enemy incursions or simple banditry is stressed in the Deborah story (5.6). The Midianites in Gideon invade to destroy the produce of the Israelites and also to *pillage* (6.3-4). The Shechemites, out of hostility to Abimelech, begin *robbing* everyone passing by on the highways (9.25), probably robbing other Shechemites as well as outsiders; they—not the enemy—are robbing their own people. Samson's wedding companions complain to the Timnite, "Have you invited us here to *rob* us (ירש dispossess)?" (14.15). In Ch. 17, a *robbery* is also done by an Israelite—significantly, an Ephraimite, Micah—who *steals* money from his mother (17.2). Later in the story, the Danites, with the help of the Levite, *steal* Micah's idols and then *steal* the Levite from Micah (18.20). Three bad tribes.

The importance of *theft* to the author will elude us unless we stop to analyze each instance of *theft*.

Impatience

Impatience as a human defect occurs only with Yhwh and with Samson. After the Israelites complain so heartily about the incursion of the Ammonites, Yhwh relents: "Yhwh's soul (life) was *worn out* (קצר, *impatient*) because of Israel's misery" (10.16). With Yhwh, it is a sign that he is going soft. Thus, קצר is included under **Compassion** below.

With the Timnite's nagging, Samson's soul (life) was *tired to death* (נפשו למות תקצר) (16.16), and he gives in to her. Though the same word is used in both sentences, in the first one Yhwh is feeling *compassion* because he sorry for Israel's suffering, while in the second, Samson is giving in because he is *vexed, worn out*. Samson's behavior after the wedding guests crack his riddle is *anything but patient*. When his sexual expectations have later been cruelly dashed by the Timnite's father, he goes completely berserk, although amusingly enough, he calls himself "blameless" (15.3) for the damage he is about to wreak. In justifying his action to others, however, he is also showing some self-awareness, though he is not wreaking vengeance on the guilty party, his father-in-law, but on the Philistines in general.

While Gideon is *patient with* the Ephraimites (8.2), Jephthah is *impatient* with them (12.1-2). (More about this under **Cooperation** below.)

Mockery, Taunts

Only a few instances of *mockery* are given in *Judges*, but when it occurs, it is regarded as wrongdoing. To utter a *curse* or *mock* anyone in authority was apparently a serious offense, judging at least from a story in a later period of history when the boys who *mocked* (קלס) Elisha were immediately gobbled up by she-bears (2 Kg 2.23).

Gideon accuses the elders of Succoth of having *mocked* him (חרף, 8.15) and punishes them severely. Gaal and his men mock (ridicule, curse) Abimelech (קלל 9.27). Zebul taunts Gaal: "Where is your mouth now?" (9.38). The Ephraimites *taunt* the Gileadites. When the Ephraimites say, "You Gileadites are renegades from Ephraim and Manasseh" (12.4), Jephthah's Gileadites strike them down. (See Chapter 3, Subcategory on **Renegades**).

Delilah accuses Samson of having *mocked her* (תלל, התל, 16.10, 13, 15). If her accusation is just, but nevertheless we do not find her worthy of respect, perhaps Samson is *not* blameworthy. In the cases of Gideon and Gaal, mockery was a sign of *disrespect*, if nothing else.

Curses

Curses are more serious. Curses can be given in two ways: first, an outright or simple curse, especially to punish a wrong that cannot be punished in any other way—if, for example, the identity of the perpetrator of a wrong is unknown. The curse (קללה) that Jotham put on Abimelech and the Shechemites for the *evil* they committed (9.57) may not be an offense, first, because the wickedness of those he cursed is unquestioned and second, because he had no way of bringing about their punishment. As we are told at the end of the story of Abimelech, his curse brought about retribution. Second, nonfulfillment of an oath incurs a curse as punishment. Possibly all unfulfilled oaths were believed to be under a curse of some sort.

In the Ugaritic myth of *Keret*, Keret makes a vow to Athirat (Asherah) of how much he will pay her when he has found a wife. He neglects to fulfill his vow. His punishments are his illness and also the treachery of his son Ysssib.[14] As a result of Yassib's treachery, Keret curses him:

> But Kirtu, the nobleman, answered:
> "O son, Horonu break
>   Horonu break your head,
>   (and) 'Athartu, consort of Ba'lu, your skull!
> May you fall down at the height of your years,
>   in the prime of your strength, and yet be humbled!"
> (*Keret* III.iv, de Moor 54-59.)

Here the text breaks off, as the subsequent tablet is missing. De Moor writes:

> It has to be assumed that the death-curse on Yassubu became effective and that Kirtu eventually lost all his other children but one [the youngest girl].[15]

Though the whole story, including the curse, may be tragicomic, as Baruch Margalit finds it to be,[16] we get a clear example of how an unfulfilled vow was followed by a curse in this ancient literature (ca. 1450 BCE). Danel in the Ugaritic story *Aqhat* issues a number of curses concerning his son's death, but we are given no evidence as to how these turn out. Their purpose may be to establish the extent of Danel's grief.

Micah's mother made an outright *curse* (אלה) on the thief who stole her 1,100 shekels, not knowing the thief was her son Micah (17.2). Even though she tried to nullify the curse, we can infer that it had its intended effect, because things turned out badly for Micah. Like Jephthah's vow, the mother's *curse* was certainly rash and had unintended consequences. It is one thing when you know who or what you are cursing, and are cursing something truly *evil*, but another thing when you do not know.

Victor H. Matthews writes:

> The Israelites were admonished in Exod 2:.7 not to make "wrongful use" of the name of God. Therefore a curse or a vow, such as Jephthah's in Judg 11:30-31, is very serious business and subject to divine wrath if taken frivolously or without a clear thought for what is at stake. For example, in the case of the blasphemous son in Lev 24:10-12, the episode hinges on his using God's name in a curse in the heat of a fight with another man. Micah's concern over his mother's curse is therefore quite understandable, if somewhat ironic, in the face of his violation of the statute against theft (Exod 20:15) and their subsequent violation of the statute against idolatry (Exod 20:4-6).[17]

The young man in *Leviticus* was to be stoned. Of course, we do not know whether Micah and his mother even knew these stories and commandments. No doubt, however, Micah feared the effect of the curse, which as we learn from very ancient literature like the Ugaritic myths, was thought to be dire.

In the case of Meroz, the city was *cursed* bitterly because it did not answer the muster (ארו ארור ... מרוז אורו—3x) in the Deborah story (5.23). Possibly the muster included an oath that violators of the call-to-arms "be put to death." Annihilation of a city may have been standard practice for such an offender. Look what happened in *Judges* to Jabesh-Gilead, which also failed to join the battle: it was wiped out (21.5, 8, 11).

When the fathers in the last story swore not to give their daughters to the Benjaminites, the implication is that whoever does this will be *cursed*. That is why they invented a ruse to escape the severe punishment awaiting those who violate their oath.

A clear example of a simple curse is when Gaal and his cronies *curse* (קלל ridicule, dishonor) Abimelech (9.27). It brought on a war, and Gaal and his kin were driven out of the city. This is but another example of the ill-advised behavior of people who are drunk.

One might infer from these contexts that *cursing* in the time of *Judges*, if done at all, must be done with care and directed at a deserving target.

Bribery

There are three possible instances of *bribery*: bribery of Yhwh by Jephthah (11.30, 31, discussed elsewhere); bribery of Delilah by the five Philistine lords; and bribery of Yhwh by Micah's mother (17.3). Jephthah and Micah's mother suffer as a result. It is left to the reader to decide whether their subsequent suffering was punishment for this offense. The author may want us to reflect on this.

Lies (See Concealment, Subcategory: Deception)

Subcategory: Good
"Good," Gratitude, Right, Happiness/Distress

No indication is given that human beings ought to be holy. The word *holy* (קדש) is used but once, in the term *consecrate* when Micah's mother dedicates the money to Yhwh (17.3). The main word used for *goodness* is simply *good* (טוב) and, like the word for *bad*, appears so many times that it is almost unnoticeable, yet makes a strong subliminal impact by continual repetition throughout.

The following is a list of how the word *good* (טוב) is used. All the italicized words are translations of this simple word.

"Is not the gleaning [of grapes] of Ephraim *better (more good) than* the vintage of Abiezer?" (8.2). "Which is *better* for you? (That all seventy rule or . . .)" (9.2). In the fable, the fig tree speaks of its *good fruit* (9.11). Jotham asks if the Shechemites "did *well* with Jerubbaal" (i.e., Gideon) (9.16). "Jephthah fled to the land of *Tob*," ("the land of the *good*" [11.3]). Jephthah asks the Ammonite king, "Are you *better* (אתה הטוב טוב) than Balak?" (11.25). The father-in-law told Samson that the younger sister is "*more good*" (טובה ממנה, attractive) than Samson's wife (15.2). The Philistines call for Samson "when their hearts were *merry*" (*good*, 16.25). "Yhwh will be *good* to me since the Levite is my priest" (17.13), says Micah. The Danites find the land of the people of Laish very *good* (18.9). They ask Micah, "Is it *better* to be priest to one man or to a tribe and clan of Israel?" (18.19). (But *is* it?) The Benjaminites have "700 *good* men" (20.15, that is, good with slingshots). Finally, as has just been pointed out, Samson declares himself to be *innocent* (נקה, blameless) for the *bad* (*evil*) he is about to do to the Philistines (15.3).

Happiness and *merriment* are also expressed with the word טוב: "Yhwh will do me *good*" (כי־ייטיב יהוה לי, make me glad) (17.13); "the priest's heart was *glad*" (18.20); "let your heart be *glad*" (19.6, 9); and "they were being *glad*" (19.22). Another word used to express *happiness*, שמח, is translated as *rejoice*: "my wine which causes gods and men to *rejoice*" (9.13); "then *rejoice* in Abimelech and let him *rejoice* in you" (שמח) (9.19); and the Levite's father-in-law "came with joy (שמח) to meet him" (19.3).

In Samson's wedding feast, where everyone should be *happy*, we see that Samson is first probably *happy*, and the 30 companions *are not*; then the 30 companions are *happy*, and Samson *is not* (their happiness or unhappiness stated only by implication, however). At the end of his story, the Philistines are happy (טוב). They have called for Samson to "entertain" them (שחק, make them laugh) in their temple, and he does so (16.25, 27). But of course their downfall is imminent.

Wine festivals usually make people *happy*, but at Gaal's festival, the text implies that Gaal has become *restless, discontented*, and we know that he is loosed-mouthed. In the two Carousing scenes of Ch. 19, the father and the Levite-husband make *merry* (3x) and are *refreshed* (1x), but these two words also connote carelessness, neglect, and intoxication and certainly bring about their opposites, *suffering* and *discontent*, rather than joy, for the Concubine and in fact for all-Israel. (See the binary opposites in the subcategories **Anger** and **Threats** below.)

Related to the word *good* is the word *right* (יֹשֶׁר). One of the most significant statements in *Judges* is that "there was no king in Israel, and each man did what was *right in his own eyes*" (אִישׁ הַיָּשָׁר בְּעֵינָיו יַעֲשֶׂה) (17.6), repeated word for word in 21.25. Compare this with the weeping Israelites obsequiously pleading to Yhwh when they know they have done wrong: "Do to us whatever is *good* (הַטּוֹב) *in your eyes*," they plead (10.15).

This phrase is repeated in Samson's statement to his parents about getting the Timnite: "She is *right* (יֹשֶׁר) *in my eyes*" (14.3, 7). And it is what the old Ephraimite says to the vicious men of Gibeah: "Do to them whatever is *good* in your own eyes" (הַטּוֹב בְּעֵינֵיכֶם, 19.24). Since 10.15 is addressed to Yhwh, the implication is that *right* will be done. But Samson's judgment about the Timnite (14.2, 7) was *wrong*, and the intentions of the men of Gibeah in 19.24 were certainly *evil*. Deut 6.18 says: "Do what is *right in the eyes of Yhwh*"; it does *not* say, "Do what is right in your own eyes." Most crucial is Deut 12.8: "You shall not all do as we are doing today—every man doing what is *right in his own eyes*." As David A. Clines reminds us, "doing as they pleased," is a sign of "godless license," as in Dan 8.4.[18] Yhwh knows what is *right*, but men do not. Throughout, the author is stressing *good* and *evil* and *right* and *wrong* and wants us to judge between them.

Compassion/Lack of Compassion (Pity, Kindness, Generosity)

Compassion is used only twice, and oddly so, since this is such an important word in the Hebrew Scriptures. First, the Israelites promise *kindness* (*mercy*) (חֶסֶד) to the man of Luz, an enemy-informer (1.24), and second, the cities of Succoth and Penuel are miserly toward Gideon and unwilling to give him bread (8.16, 17), and after his death, the people do *not* show *kindness* (חֶסֶד) to his family (house) for the *good* that Gideon had done for them (8.35). חֶסֶד means "covenant love," that is, something that is due, like the necessary return or payment in a contract.[19] In other stories, the omission of this word may also signify a general lack of concern for others.

In five other instance of, or references to, *compassion* or *lack* of it, the specific word חֶסֶד is *not* used. First, there is the *compassion* of the old Ephraimite on the Levite's traveling group when he offers them hospitality (19.21). Second, when the Israelites have all but destroyed the Benjaminites, the Israelites finally have compassion (נָחַם, *grieve for*) for Benjamin for being cut off from Israel (21.6) and again have *compassion* (נָחַם) for Benjamin because Yhwh had made a gap (פֶּרֶץ) in the tribes of Israel (21.15). Notice, however, that the deplorable gap is blamed not on themselves, but on Yhwh. (But if Yhwh had ordered the massacre, did the Israelites then have the right to nullify what Yhwh caused?)

Third, the Danites have no compassion on the city of Laish (again, this is strongly implied but not stated).

Fourth, the Israelites had *no compassion* (the word, however, not used) whatsoever for Jabesh-Gilead (21.10-11), which they ruthlessly destroyed except for the virgins, whom they set aside for the Benjaminites, nor for Shiloh, whose daughters they allowed the Benjaminites to seize (21.23). When the Israelites try to calm the indignant fathers of the girls, they call on *the fathers'* compassion: "Be *generous* to us (חָנֻּ, sole instance of this word) and allow us to have [your daughters]" (21:22).

Fifth and most important, when they were oppressed, Yhwh has *compassion* (נִחַם) for the people because of "their groans" (2.18). At another time, once the Israelites cast out the foreign gods, "His soul (נֶפֶשׁ) could not *bear* (קָצַר, *was impatient* with) the misery of Israel" (10.16).

When Yhwh is *angry* with them, however, he does *not* show *compassion* and allows the enemy to prevail. *Compassion* is otherwise usually lacking or scarcely exists in these stories.

Cooperation/Dissension

The book begins with *cooperation* of the tribes against the enemy, such as between Judah and Simeon in the first chapter. Then little by little, *cooperation* dwindles until at the end the tribes are *fighting against* each other. (There is no specific Hebrew word for *cooperation* in this book, however.) In Ch. 2 of *Judges* we learn that a number of tribes apparently did *not* do their part in driving out the Canaanites, but settled down and lived with them. The house of Joseph (Ephraim and Manasseh) appears to be doing its part (1.22) and succeeded against the Amorites, but they and the others are faulted for not actually driving out *all* the Canaanites (1.27, 29). Zebulun, Naphtali, Asher, Dan, and Benjamin are also singled out for this failure (1.21, 30-34). Even though it also failed in this way, Judah has the excuse that the enemy had formidable chariots (1.19). The main explanation for the tribes' troubles is that Yhwh was punishing the Israelites because they had not broken down Canaanite altars (2.3).

In Ch. 3, the tribes are *cooperating*: Ehud, the Benjaminite, blows on his *shofar* in the hill country of Ephraim and calls out the Israelites (most of them probably Ephraimites) against the Moabites (3.27), and they come. Later, the Ephraimites quarrel with both Gideon (8.1) and Jephthah (12.1) for not having called them out (discussed under **Deception** below). We see that Benjamin and Ephraim start out as "good" in this respect (Ch. 1) but end up "bad" (Chs. 19-21).

In the Deborah story, "the people *offer* themselves" (הִתְנַדֵּב, i.e., volunteer for war) (5.2): Ephraim (Deborah's tribe), Naphtali (Barak's tribe), Zebulun, Machir (western Manasseh), Benjamin, and Issachar *cooperate* (in Ch. 4, Zubulun and Naphtali are the most important). Reuben, Gilead, Dan, and Asher, however, *fail to respond* to the call. Judah and Simeon are not on the roll call (Ch. 5).

In the Gideon story, the two Israelite cities of Succoth and Penuel of the Transjordan flatly *refuse to help* Gideon when he and his troops are famished. Next, the Ephraimites are hostile to Gideon because they allege that he spurned them and did *not let them cooperate* with him (8.1). However, they came out anyway and in fact killed Oreb and Zeeb, the princes of Midian. Gideon assuages their hostility by flattering them, claiming that they were more successful than he. Actually, Gideon *had* called them out (7.24), though perhaps he had not called them early enough. They are spoiling for a fight with him.

In the Jephthah story, the Ephraimites repeat the charge (12.1-2). Jephthah claimed he did, but the upshot is that Jephthah *fights* and *kills* 42,000 of them outright. At the very least, they are malcontents and troublemakers—an *uncooperative*, carping tribe. But Jephthah is impatient, angry, and severe. Ironically, it is Gideon who negotiates with them, while Jephthah, noted for his diplomatic skills with the Ammonites, does not.

In the Samson story, Judah *cooperates with the Philistines* and not with Samson (this cannot be good). In the last story, all the tribes (except Benjamin and the town of Jabesh-Gilead) are *cooperating* (this is good), but they are fighting viciously against Benjamin, *one of their own tribes* (this is bad). (See Chapter 6, Conclusion, for a final analysis of the tribes.)

Favor, Glory, Honor, Truth, Integrity, Faith, Righteousness

A code of *honor* is implied in these stories but is directly stated only in Jotham's fable. Jotham sarcastically warns the Shechemites that they are not behaving *honorably*:

> And the bramble said to the trees, "If in *truth* [באמת, good faith] ye anoint me king over you . . ." (9.15).

> "Now therefore, if you acted in *truth* and *honor* [באמת ובתמים] when you made Abimelech king, and if you have done *well* (אם־טובה עשיתם) to Jerubbaal and his house, and have done to him as his actions deserved (כגמול ידיו עשיתם, the *deserving* of his hands) (9.16).

> "If . . . you have acted in good *faith* and *honor* [באמת ובתמים] with Jerubbaal and with his house this day, then rejoice in Abimelech, and let him also rejoice in you" (9.19).

The words *good faith* (truth), *honor*, doing *well* (טוב), and *deserving* are strongly stressed in these passages. They cast a light on the other actions in the book and imply that we should be looking at all these actions the way Jotham does. This is the single passage in the book that defines ethical and moral behavior.

When Barak demands that Deborah go to battle with him, Deborah agrees but warns him that the outcome of the battle will not be to his *honor* (תפארה, glory), that because of his demand, Yhwh will let Sisera fall into the hands of a woman, instead of Barak (4.9). In the Gideon story, Yhwh is anxious that Israel not claim *honor* for itself (יתפאר vaunt itself), thus avoiding the deadly sin of Pride (7.2).

Gideon hopes he has found *favor* (חן, 1x only) with his messenger-angel (6.17). Jotham says that it is with olive oil and wine that gods and men are *honored* (כבד) (9.9, 13). Manoah begs the messenger-angel to give his name "that we may *honor* you" (כבד) (13.17).

Righteousness, oddly enough, is mentioned only once—in *The Song*: "They shall rehearse the *righteousness* of Yhwh" (צדקה, 2x) (5.11).

Slight though these references are, they are evidence of the existence of a code of ethics of some kind. *Violations* of this code are what the book is about.

Honor (*timê*) in battle and *glory* (*kudos*), which are so important to the warriors in the *Iliad*, are not referred to in any way about the warriors in *Judges*. But *Judges* does represent *fame* or *renown*—if not necessarily with *honor*. And though not what warriors were aiming for, their fame has nevertheless lasted millennia.

Deliver, Save

Deliver (ישע, *save*, and מושיע, *savior*) is used 21x in *Judges*, including, Othniel (3.9 [2x]); Ehud (3.15); Shamgar (3.31); Gideon (8.22); and Tola (10.1), who *deliver* their own people; and Samson at least *begins* to *deliver* Israel from the Philistines (13.5). Jephthah accuses the Ephraimites of not having *delivered* him from the enemy (12.3).

Yhwh raised up judges to *deliver* the Israelites from oppressors (2:16, 18). Yhwh *delivers* them in 10.12. He refuses to *deliver* them in 10:13, 14. Yhwh tries to persuade Gideon to *deliver* his people, but Gideon is reluctant: 6.14, 15, 36, 37; 7.2, 7. When townsmen surround him and threaten to punish his son for destroying the altar of Baal, Joash, Gideon's father, asks sarcastically if they are trying to *deliver* Baal and challenges them: "If he is a god, let him contend for himself, because his altar has been pulled down" (6.31).

The other word for *deliver*, נצל, is used 6x: Jotham reminds the Shechemites that Jerubbaal (called "Gideon" in ch. 6-8) *delivered* them (9.17); Jephthah asks the King of the Ammonites: if they had the right that they claim, why had the disputed land not been *delivered* long ago (11.26). And we are told that when the Danites attacked and destroyed it, no one *delivered* Laish (18.28).

This is the word used when Yhwh reminds the Israelites that he *delivered* (נצל) Israel from the Egyptians (6.9; 8.34). When the Ammonites are oppressing Israel, and Yhwh rebukes the Israelites for disobedience, the Israelites plead, "We have sinned; do to us whatever seems good in your eyes, but *deliver* us *this day*" (same word, 10.15).

This passage is echoed when the old Ephraimite tells the Gibeahites surrounding the house to "do to [his daughter and the Concubine] whatever is good in your eyes" (19.25). He does not add the phrase "but *deliver* us *this day*," though that is what he no doubt was hoping for.

These two words for *delivering* (*rescuing, saving*) have been studied carefully by scholars and need not be rehearsed further here. At the end of the book, we see that Yhwh has not really *delivered* Israel.

Trust, Security, Prosperity

Another word that shows understanding of ethics is the word for *trust* (בטח), which is used 6x in the book: "the lords *trusted* [Gaal]" (9.26); the Israelites "*trusted* the ambush" (20.36), and "Sihon did not *trust* (אמן)" Israel (11.20).

(It has a slightly different meaning when a people or a military group believes itself to *be secure* or unassailable or not likely to be attacked: "The camp [of Zebah and Zalmunna] was *secure* [had trust]," but Gideon attacked it [8.11].)

When the Danites are looking for a land to migrate to, their spies find an innocent and vulnerable people in the city of Laish. The prosperity and the vulnerability of Laish is repeated 4x.[20] Not only do the Danites steal Micah's idols and priest, but they annihilate a perfectly *peaceful, prosperous, serene, trusting, defenseless* town instead of a vicious enemy. It is a town where *nothing is lacking* (מחסור כל־דבר אשר בארץ אין שם, 18.10). (The passage 18.7, 9-10, 27-28 is quoted at length in the discussion of the Danites near the end of this chapter.)

Two others for whom *"nothing at all on the earth is lacking"* are the Levite (כל־דבר אין מחסור, same words as in 18.10) (19.19), who is asking for lodging for the night and is not imposing on anyone, and the old Ephraimite, who says that he will supply whatever the visitors need (again, same word, כל מחסורך עלי, 19.20). But now we are into a related topic—hospitality—which of course involves trust. (See **Invitations, Requests, and Hospitality** below.).

III. Fire, Anger

The author does not represent emotions as a rule, except for anger and happiness. *Anger* and *fire* are interconnected.

Subcategory: Fire

Fire pervades *Judges* and is one of the most important keywords. The theme of *fire* (שלח באש) is announced when Jerusalem is set on fire at the *beginning* of the book (1.8). To balance this, the author has placed the burning of the innocent city of Laish by the Danites near the *end* of the book (20.45). In between are many other burnings. The word for *fire* (אש) is used at least 14x in the book. Also used are the following words for *burning*:

to *burn* (שרף באש) [5x] 9.52, 12.1, 14.15, 15.6, 18.27);
to *set on fire* (שלח באש) [3x] 1.8, 18.27, 20.48);
or to *set* (the stronghold) *on fire* (יציתו באש) [1x] 9.49) (a different verb);
or to *set fire* to (יבער־אש, *light* something [4x] 15.5, 6, 14) (different verb).

Fire can be referred to indirectly. Barak's name, for example, means *Lightning* or *Torches*, as does Deborah's husband's name, Lappidoth (לפידות, torches, 4.4). This word, *torches,* appears in three stories: Deborah's husband's name (1x), Gideon (the torches in the pitchers 2x) and Samson (the torches on the foxes, 3x)—a neat little triangle, devised by the writer.

Burnt offerings are mentioned 5x in the book. (1) Gideon presented an *offering* to a messenger-angel, who *burned* it (6.21, 26, 28). (2) Samson's parents also presented an *offering* to a messenger-angel, who *did wonderously* with it, after which it *burned.* In

the episode with Samson's parents, the messenger-angel himself goes up (יַעַל)
with the *flames* (לַהַב, 13.16, 20, 23). (3) Jephthah's daughter is also a *burnt offering*
(עוֹלָה, 11.31). (4) The Israelites make a burnt offering to Yhwh when they beseech
him for help against the Benjaminites (3x, 20.26) and again (5) when they have to
figure out how to provide wives for the Benjaminites (2x, 21.4).

Doubtless the emphasis on these *offerings* highlights the contrast between the
persons making them and the occasions for which they are made. Gideon and
Samson's parents are doing it properly, in thanksgiving and appreciation. Jephthah's
act is questionable, though the text implies that it is done in sorrow and grim
determination. (Here we have to fill in the gaps.) The Israelites at the end are
acting, as we are told, in complete humility: they are weeping, fasting, praying for
help, and making burnt offerings (21.4), putting themselves at the mercy of Yhwh.

Fire imagery is especially prominent in both the Abimelech and Samson stories.
Jotham's fable in the Abimelech story prophesies that the bramble will *burn* the
cedar, that *fire* will come out of Abimelech and *devour* the citizens of Shechem and
Beth-millo, and that *fire* will come out of Shechem and *devour* Abimelech (9.15, 20).
(Notice that *fire devours*, a metaphor in Hebrew, as well as in English.) Abimelech
gathers wood and *sets* the stronghold of Shechem *on fire* (9.49), killing the people in
the tower. He intends to give the same treatment to the tower of Thebez, but is killed
before he can do so.

The Ephraimites threaten to *burn* Jephthah *with fire* (12.1), but do not do it. In
the Samson story, Samson does his Houdini-like trick of tying the tails of 300 foxes
together by pairs, attaching *torches* to them, and *burning* the fields, orchards, and
vineyards of the Philistines (15.4, 5). In retaliation, the Philistines threaten to *burn*
the Timnite and her father, and do it (15.6). Samson also twice breaks his bonds as
easily as if they had been flax or a strand of fiber that had caught *fire* (15.14, 16.9).

Abimelech and Samson are prone to *anger*. *Fire* is indeed a linking word for the
two stories. Abimelech premeditates and plans; he is slower and more methodical;
while Samson is more volatile, quick to *burn*, quick to subside. They are both arsonists
and incendiaries.

In the case of the original Samson of the folktales, he may have been the Sun God
(שֶׁמֶשׁ), for whom fire would have been most apt. (See Chapter 5 on the Ugaritic myths.)

Subcategory: Anger

Closely identified with *fire*, the anger of people *is kindled* or *blazes* frequently in this
book. The idiomatic expression for *getting angry* is that the individual's *nose burned in
anger* (יִחַר אַפּוֹ at least 7x). Yhwh gets *angry* often, and *his nose burns* (in 2.14, 20; 3.8,
6.39 [where Gideon asks Elohim not to get angry], and 10.7). In Yhwh's case, it cannot
be a deadly sin. Only two human beings have *anger* that *blazes*: one is Zebul, Abimelech's
loyal steward, who becomes *angry* at Gaal, the insurrectionist (9.30). The other, as
might be expected, is Samson, who after smiting the 30 Ashkelonites to get their
clothing, rushes away from the wedding feast in *anger* (14.19).

There are obviously many angry people, for whom the word *anger* is not specifically used. Among them are Yhwh's messenger-angel in *The Song* who curses Meroz (5.23); the men of Gideon's clan who *threaten* him for cutting down the Asherah and destroying the altar of Baal (6.30); and the Ephraimites, who are *angry* with both Gideon ("they chided him strongly," 8.1) and Jephthah (they threaten to burn his house, 12.1). Gideon is *angry* at Succoth and Penuel for their lack of generosity (8.16, 17); Jotham is *angry* at Abimelech and curses him (9.20); Gaal's *anger* at Abimelech is expressed in his curse (9.27, 28); Abimelech behaves like an *enraged* man at Gaal and Shechem (9.40, 49, 52); the Ephraimites are *angry* at Jephthah; and in return, Jephthah is *enraged* at them (12.4, 6). Samson's *anger* is kindled against the Timnite and the Philistines (14.19); he *burns* up the fields in *anger* because the Philistines *burnt* up his wife and her father (15.9); and later he is "*vexed* to death" (קצר) by Delilah (16.16).

Gideon, Abimelech, Jephthah, and Samson in fact go berserk in their *rage*. They inflict excessive harm, certainly not the even-handed justice of life-for-life (*lex talionis*). Their behavior is not "righteous indignation." Rather, it is *blind fury*. Compare their *anger* with the *wrath* of Achilles in Homer.

Micah's mother is angry and utters a curse against the unknown thief (17.1); Micah is angry at the Danites for stealing his images and priest (18.24); and the Danites threaten, in turn, that angry fellows (אנשים מרי) from among them will fall on Micah if he does not get lost (18:25). The Concubine's reason for running away from her Levite-husband is that she *quarreled* with him (and presumably was *angry*). The Levite apparently recovered from *his* anger, though it took him four months before going after her to kiss and make up. The author has been specific about the lapse of time (four months!), and we must figure out *why*. Whether he is merely neglectful—i.e., not strongly-enough motivated to fetch her, and is hoping she will return without his making an effort—or is careless and lazy, is not clear, but when the Levite approaches his Concubine, he intends to speak *kindly* to her. If she really "played the harlot," as we are told in 19.2, perhaps the Levite's forgiving attitude in that culture is wrong, and anger would have been appropriate. In any case, his attitude is a binary opposite of *anger*.

Angry and *base* men surround the house of the Ephraimite (19.22). And finally all-Israel is *angry* at the tribe of Benjamin (20.8), and *curses* anyone who gives a daughter as wife to one of them (21.18). In Christian morality, anger is one of the Seven Deadly Sins, but in the world of the *Judges*, it may not be so serious.

Distress is akin to *anger* in that it is a feeling of unhappiness. "They were in *distress*" (צרר, in a narrow, tight place) (2.15) we are told of the Israelites when Yhwh was angry at them. "Israel was greatly distressed" (10.9) when the Ammonites came out against them. "Let them [the false gods] deliver you in your time of *distress*" (10.14), says Yhwh, rebuking the Israelites for their apostasy. "Why do you come to me now when you are in *distress*" (11.7), Jephthah says—echoing Yhwh—to the elders of Gilead when they bury their pride and invite him to be their head. And then there are the Ephraimites, whose mood of resentment (רוח, i.e. bad spirit) subsided when Gideon appeased them (8.3).

The opposites of *anger* and *distress* are *contentment* and *enjoyment*. (See **Good, Right, Happiness, Distress** above.)

Fires spring up and burn and flare all over the land of Israel, signifying the anger, destructiveness, fear, and cruelty of the Israelites. Consider the burning up of the house of the Timnite and her father (arson), and the burning up of Jephthah's daughter (unnatural), and the burning of the Philistine fields and orchards by Samson (wanton) done for different reasons, but equally cruel and terrible. "Is there any cause in nature that makes these hard hearts?" Lear wonders in *King Lear* (III.vi.81), as well might the author of *Judges*.

In Greek philosophy, the four fundamental constituents of the universe are water, fire, earth, and air. *Earth* in *Judges* is represented by many keywords connected with *floor, ground, land* and those connected with *agriculture* and *animals*. *Fire* and *Water* have their own categories. The only one not clearly exemplified in this book is *Air*. Israelite substitutions for Air might be *Life* or *Temper* (נפש) and certainly *Spirit* (רוח), benign or malevolent.

Subcategory: Threats

Threats is another important category in the author's scheme, as the following list shows.

There are at least six threats: The Abiezerites *threaten* Gideon, (6.3), but Joash (Gideon's father) saves Gideon with a diplomatic rejoinder. Ephraimites *threaten* Gideon (8.3), but he propitiates them with an aphorism. The Ephraimites *threaten* to *burn* Jephthah's house down over his head (12.1), but he gets them first. The Philistine wedding guests *threaten* to burn the Timnite and her father's household if she does not reveal the secret of Samson's riddle (14.15), but doing this does not save her, for eventually they burn her anyway (15.6). The 600 armed Danites with their bitter spirits (hot tempers, מרי נפש) (18.25) *threaten* Micah, and he flees. The Benjaminites *threaten* "to know" the Levite (19.22), but he gives them the Concubine to rape instead. Later in recounting the "outrage" to the Israelites, he added that the Benjaminites intended to kill him (20.5) (thus doubling the threat). Threats are a form of intimidation and inspire fear.

In some states in our society, threats are liable to prosecution and punishment. A *threat* is a *promise* with a pejorative meaning, based on a condition (See **Subcategory: Promises** below). The binary opposite of *threat* is *reward* and perhaps *bribe*. I will deal further with *threats* and *rewards* while discussing other topics that follow.

IV. Concealment

Concealment and everything associated with it—*Fear, Deception, Spying, Traps, Secrets, Riddles*—are found in every chapter of *Judges* and are perhaps its most important theme. Human beings in these stories *conceal* an object or themselves either because they are afraid or because they are intent on harming another.

Cunning, a form of *deception*, at times has a negative connotation, but it is one of the virtues in heroic societies, according to Alasdair MacIntyre (116), as it often is in *Judges*, especially when used to conquer the enemy. *Cunning* is a strategy of the underdog (already discussed above) and is used especially to devise ways of surprising an enemy. It was a strategy that Sun Tzu Wu advocated in *The Art of War* in about 500 BCE:

> *All warfare is based on deception.* Hence, when able to attack, we must *seem unable;* when using our forces, we must *seem inactive;* when we are near, we *must make the enemy believe we are far away;* when far away, we *must make him believe* we are near. Hold out baits *to entice* the enemy. *Feign disorder,* and crush him. If he is secure at all points, be prepared for him. If he is in superior strength, evade him. If your opponent is of choleric temper, seek to irritate him. *Pretend to be weak,* that he may grow arrogant. If he is taking his ease, give him no rest. If his forces are united, separate them. Attack him where he is unprepared, *appear where you are not expected.* These military devices, leading to victory, must not be divulged beforehand. The general who loses a battle makes but few calculations beforehand. Thus do many calculations lead to victory, and few calculations to defeat: how much more no calculation at all! It is by attention to this point that I can foresee who is likely to win or lose.[21] (Italics mine.)

Above all, *calculate.* Sun Tzu Wu might have been writing about the battles in *Judges*, and had the author of *Judges* analyzed those battles. he might have given similar counsel. *Concealment* is found throughout and is linked to *deception, secrecy,* and *surprise.* Surprise with its companion, suspense, are elements in most successful narratives, and it is in this one.

(The overlapping of this section with the other sections on law and judgment is to an extent unavoidable.)

Subcategory: Deception, Deviousness, Mendacity
(See also **Evil/Good, Disloyalty/Loyalty** above)

The book begins with the story about Adoni-Bezek, which is perfectly aboveboard—*no deviousness, concealment,* or *secrecy* here.

In the story of Achsah, the next pericope, the situation is fairly ideal. Someone in the background, seems to have persuaded Achsah to ask for a special gift (1.14) ("he nagged her [פות, incite] to ask tilled land from her father"[22] may be a better translation than "she urged him" as in the NRS). Perhaps Achsah desires simply to make an otherwise arid land productive with basins of water; or perhaps her motive is to improve her material wealth. Although Achsah may be maneuvering (or being manipulated) to get special privilege, *nothing* indicates that she is *practicing deception* on her father. She is not like Lot, who chose the best land and let Abraham be contented with the worst.

The next story announces the theme of *Deception*, for that is the meaning of the name "Luz" (1.23; Boling 52). The man of Luz betrays his own people by showing the Israelites the way into the city. After that, deceptions of various kinds occur in almost every episode.

Ehud, the crafty one, is *devious* when he *conceals* a sword under his clothes on his right thigh. He *deceives* Eglon into thinking that he has a "secret message" (דבר־סתר) for him from Elohim (3.19, 20). It is amusing, from one point of view, what the "secret message" turns out to be. Still, that it is deception cannot be gainsaid. And it is a violation of the hospitality code.

Jael *pretends* to help Sisera, perhaps even seduces him—whether literally or not—but she *treacherously* slays him instead.

The Ephraimites claim that Gideon had failed to call them out to fight against the Midianites (a *deception*). But Gideon had (7.24). They also claim that Jephthah did not call them out (12.1-2). Jephthah denies this. Because they had already *lied* to Gideon, we suspect that they are *lying* again, though it is not clear why they would do so. Yet we have no reason to suspect Jephthah of lying. Probably the Ephraimites became angry because they feared losing their share of the spoil (see 5.30 and 8.24-26), and their accusation is meant to intimidate. It did not work. (This was discussed under **Cooperation** above.)

Samson does not tell his mother and father about the lion or the honey (a deliberate *deception*, as is discussed under **Promises** below). Delilah accuses Samson of *lying* (תלל) to her in not divulging the secret of his strength (16.10, 13, 15), and perhaps he did. But when trying to wheedle Samson's secret out of him, Delilah *deceives* him by feigning innocence when her intention is to turn him over to the Philistines, who are hiding in a nearby room (a kind of ambush). Micah *deceives* his mother when he steals her money, though he later confesses and returns the money. (We might ask: does the confession and return of the money totally wipe out his guilt?)

The Levite perhaps *lies* to the Israelites when reporting the rape of his Concubine; at least his story is different from what we had read (20.5). He exaggerates the threat of the Benjaminites—saying that they were trying to kill him. Actually, they only expressed their intent to have sex with him. But who knows? Since they killed the Concubine, it is likely they would have killed the Levite, too, had he come out to them. Maybe his fear was justified, though not his method of escaping from them. And the Israelites in the last story practice *casuistry* in order to avoid violating their vow not to let Benjaminites marry their daughters.

The author, too, is d*evious*, in that he is concealing so many hidden objects in each chapter of his book, as well as his many *secrets* concerning the meaning of his work.

Subcategory: Hiders, Spies, Ambushers

Connected with Deception and somewhat overlapping it are the Hiders, Spies, Watchers, and Ambushers (Heb. *Liers-in-Wait*). *Ambushes* occur frequently in *Judges* and should be linked with two other occasions: when men surround Joash's house and threaten Gideon and when base men surround the Ephraimite's house and threaten the Levite in the story of the Concubine, though these are not ambushes, strictly speaking.

The ambush depends upon the element of surprise, when those lying-in-wait (an oft-used expression) spring out against their enemy. On the other hand, a threatening mob surrounding a house is in full view, its success depending not on surprise, but on how menacing, violent, and determined the mob appears to be.

The theme of *Spying* is included here because it is a form of *hiding*; it is *secret*, and similar to the *ambush* except that the spies do not spring out to attack others. This theme is announced, along with the theme of deception, when the tribe of Joseph *sends spies* (תור) to Luz (1.23, sole use in *Judges* of the specific verb to *spy*). Thereafter, we find spies cropping up in a number of stories.

Eglon, murdered, is *hidden* in a locked room. In *The Song*, travelers take to the *hidden byways* (if 5.6 has been translated correctly) because they fear the main highways. Jael *hides* Sisera under a covering or rug, pretending to nurture and *conceal* him.

At the beginning of the story of Gideon, the Israelites are *hiding* in dens, caves, and strongholds so as not to be seen by their enemy (6.2). Gideon beats out wheat in a winepress to *hide* (נוס) from the Midianites (6.11). He breaks down the altar under *cover of darkness;* he is *hiding* when the Abiezerites surround his house—threatening him; on the battlefield, because he is afraid to go alone, he goes with the youth Purah to *spy* and *eavesdrop* on the Midianites by night; and finally he engages the services of a young *spy* at the city of Succoth to write down the names of the (up-til-now-hidden-from-him) elders there (8.11), that Gideon might punish them on his return.

In the Abimelech story, we learn that his brother Jotham had escaped being murdered by *hiding* (חבא, 9.5). Abimelech's steward Zebul, a *spy* of sorts who remains in the city while Abimelech is away, sends messengers to Abimelech *under cover* (בתרמה, also translated "to Arumah," 9.31) so as to prevent Gaal from anticipating Abimelech's return, and he *lies* when he tells Gaal that only shadows are coming down from the mountains, though he knows the "shadows" are Abimelech's men (9.36) *hiding* under the branches that they have cut down.

Samson *hides* out at the cleft of the Rock of Etam (15.8, 11). His blindness is another *kind of hiding*, for now the *world is concealed or hidden* from *him*. Locked away in prison, he in turn is *hidden* from the world. Freeman mentions the importance of enclosed places in the story: lion's body, wedding chamber, Delilah's room, prison, and Philistine temple, and he remarks that enclosed places harbor not only sensory pleasures but also dangers.[23]

In the story of Micah, the Danites send five men to *spy* out the land and the unsuspecting city of Laish. (Actually, the word *spy* is not used; the men simply *explore*, but since of necessity they do so *secretly*, it is usually translated as *spying*.) In the last story, it is implied that the Levite *hides behind the door* while the Benjaminites rape and kill his Concubine.

Ambushes (called *lying-in-wait* [ארב]) occur 5x in the Abimelech story, with the Shechemites laying traps for travelers on the highways (9.25), and Abimelech's men twice trying to ambush Gaal (9.32, 34, 35, 43). In the Samson story, the Philistines *lie in wait* to capture Samson outside the prostitute's house (16.2) and they again *lie in wait* to capture him in Delilah's house (16.9, 12).

Finally, *ambushes* occur 6x in the civil war in the last story when the Israelites try to ambush the Benjaminites (20.29, 33, 36, 37 [2x], 38) and once when the Benjaminites lie in wait in the vineyards to seize the daughters of Shiloh (21.20). When we list these occurrences, we are surprised by the large number of them. Obviously, Deception is an important theme of the book.

Subcategory: Traps (See also Doors in Chapter 3)

The many ambushes listed above are *traps*. But there are other *traps* as well, though this word is used only twice. This topic of traps is announced when the messenger-angel of Yhwh warns the Israelites that the Canaanites "shall be in your sides, and their gods shall be a *trap* to you" (מוקש 2.3). The Baalim *snare* the Israelites over and over again. But the Israelites also *trap* others, and others *trap* them.

Eglon is caught in Ehud's *trap*, and Eglon's attendants are *locked out* of Eglon's room. Sisera is caught in Jael's *trap*. Gideon beats down the tower of Penuel and kills the people who had *trapped* themselves in it (8.17, word *trapped* not used). Then Gideon and his people get caught in the *snare* (מוקש) of the ephod (8.27). The people in the Tower of Shechem are *trapped* (implied) and burned by Abimelech, while the people in the city of Thebez narrowly escape a similar *trap* he set for them. Jephthah is *trapped* in his *own vow*. And he *traps* the Ephraimites at the Jordan with the way they pronounce the word "Shibboleth." Women are obviously a *snare* for Samson. Samson is *trapped* in prison, but he in turn can be said to set a *trap* for the Philistines in the Temple of Dagon. Money is a *snare* for Delilah and, at first, for Micah.

Of course, the Big *Spy* (or *Trapper*) is Yhwh, who, as explicitly stated, is *testing* Israel and watching the Israelites throughout (2.22; 3.1, 2).

Subcategory: Secrets and Riddles

Another aspect of Concealment and Cunning connected with the *trap* is the *Secret* or the *Riddle*.

The *dream* of the Midianite in the Gideon story is a *riddle* until it has been interpreted. "Gideon heard the tale of the dream (את־מספר החלום) and its interpretation (שבר)" (7.15). שבר means *breaking open of the sealed dream*, a *solution* to its *mystery*; it is connected with the *breaking* (same word) of the jars (7.20) and obviously with the *solving* (breaking the code) of Samson's riddle. The name of the messenger-angel in the theophany of the Samson story is *wonderful* (פלא, secret, incomprehensible) (13:18), and he keeps his name secret. In the next verse, the messenger-angel does *wonderful* deeds (using the same word, מפלא לעשות, deeds difficult to do, beyond ordinary powers).

Jotham's fable is a *riddle*, albeit one that Jotham interprets when he finishes telling it: *out of* the bramble (Abimelech) *will come* fire (insurrection), which will destroy the "cedars of Lebanon"(9.15). Who the "cedars" are is uncertain, but may be the "rightful" rulers, whoever they may be.

Jotham's fable is an exact parallel to Samson's riddle: *out of* the eater *came* something to eat, *out of* the strong *came* something sweet: lion (the strong, Samson), honey (his amorousness, his wife). Whereas Jotham *wants the meaning* of his *riddle to be known*, Samson *wants his to be kept secret*, but his wife wheedles the *secret* out of him.

Samson's riddle emphasizes the enigmatic aspect of his character. The *source of his strength* is also a *riddle*, a *secret*. The word *riddle* (חידה), strongly emphasized in this story, is used 12x or more; the verb *solve* or *find out* (מצא) is used 3x while the verb *tell* (נגד), which is used only 4x elsewhere in the book, is used at least 23x here. Thus we have a strong emphasis on the solving of Samson's riddle.

In the last story, the Israelites set themselves a *conundrum* (or puzzle) to solve: how to keep their vow *not to give* maidens to the Benjaminites while *still giving* the maidens to the Benjaminites. To the reader, the whole book of *Judges* is a riddle. And riddles, we must remember, are play.

What is the significance of this large category of words connected with words like *deception, traps, ambushes, spies, secrets,* and *riddles*? One function is perhaps to condemn the northern tribes, for in the tales, these are the tribes which resort to such practices. For them, the number of concepts represented by the *binary opposites* of these terms—such as *trust, loyalty, openness, heroic combat, spies used properly, clear-cut truths,* and *wisdom*—though not altogether lacking, are in short supply. *Deception* has become a way of life, and it leads to anarchy and chaos. The exception to this seems to be the southern tribe of Judah, although in handing Samson over to the Philistines, Judah is not 100% pure, either. Another aspect of this fabric of deception is to remind us of the author's own deviousness and secrecy. Playfully, perhaps, he uses the very characteristic he condemns, and in his own text has hidden from plain sight all kinds of objects and messages for us to ferret out. Some of the objects, indeed, ambush us.

Always remember Ehud's words to Eglon: "I have a *secret* message to you O King" (דבר־סתר, 3.19); "I have a message from Elohim for you", (דבר־אלוהים, 3.20). It is as if the author himself also had said, "I have a secret message for you, O reader."

V. Vows, Oaths, and Promises

Judges is permeated with ideas about contingency, the notion that events are not predetermined, that any event may or may not occur. The author does not manifest a belief that things can happen by sheer chance, however, but no evidence of a belief in fate *per se* can be found, such as we find in classical Greek literature. There always is a cause, and it is usually a human cause, deliberate or inadvertent.

In the author's view, Yhwh is making the decisions about the outcome of battles and in *some* cases working out divine retribution, but his decisions are contingent on human behavior. If Yhwh gives the Israelites into the hands of the enemy, it is because the human beings have done something wrong. Good behavior (remaining faithful to Yhwh) brings victory. Bad behavior (unfaithfulness) brings defeat. The author (or the Deuteronomic interloper) attributes long intervals of Israelite distress to Yhwh's withholding of favor. But why is Yhwh withholding favor? Because the Israelites turned to other gods. The author is then something of a believer in free will, though had we asked him his opinion, he might have answered that Yhwh was in charge of everything and agreed with the philosophical system of "double causation" as espoused by van Rad, and explained by Robert Alter:

> . . . everything in the story is determined by its human actors, according to the stringent dictates of political realism; yet, simultaneously, everything is determined by God, according to a divine plan in history. David, informed that his own shrewd political advisor Ahitophel is part of Absalom's conspiracy, urgently and breathlessly invokes God, "Thwart, pray, the counsel of Ahitophel, O Lord." Then he reaches a holy site . . . and here he sees Hushai . . . coming toward him. Theologically, Hushai is the immediate answer to David's prayer. Politically, David seizes upon Hushai as the perfect instrument to thwart Ahitophel's counsel, so from a certain point of view David is really answering his own prayer through human initiative. Yet the encounter with Hushai at a place of worship leaves the lingering intimation that Hushai has been sent by God to David.[24]

Concerning serendipitous experiences like this, believers attribute them to God, while nonbelievers call them lucky chance. If Hushai succeeds in his mission, then it *is* due to double causation. However if it *does not* work out, then what is it?

The author of *Judges* would subscribe to the double causation theory up to a certain point. What he focuses on in his stories is good and bad behavior. When Samson insists upon marrying the Timnite (a Philistine) against his parents' objections, the author tells us: "This was from Yhwh, who was seeking an occasion to act against the Philistines" (14.4). If this is so, then how could Samson be blamed for consorting with foreign women?

On the other hand, the author clearly faults Samson for breaking the Nazirite vow against shaving his hair—it is the precipitating cause of his loss of power and his subsequent imprisonment. *Not* breaking the vow would have let him remain free, we conjecture, since once his hair grew back, he regained his power. Thus he succeeds in pulling down the temple, an act against the Philistines.

The author, however, did not think that all the evil that happens in the book was merely a pretext on the part of Yhwh to accomplish his aims. If Yhwh was the cause of everything, Yhwh would have no need to issue the warning against intermarriage. If everything was determined by Yhwh or even by preceding events, a system of morality would be meaningless. Clearly, the book is about the need for leadership. People continue to do "what is right in their eyes," however, instead of what is right in God's eyes.

On the human level, the characters also seem to believe that they can change the course of events. One way to do this is by obedience, vows, promises, or by conditions, threats, and revenge. The stories show that it is usually the characters' free choice of disobedience, or bad behavior, that brings them trouble. Thus the author is not a "hard determinist," but more of a "middle-of-the-roader" philosophically.

When we view the stories as law or ethics cases to be judged, we see why so many complex relationships exist between stories. In human relationships, the devil is in the details. We need the details in order to work out a system of morality or ethics.

Subcategory: Promises

Related to *vows*, but not exactly the same, are *promises*, a number of which are made in *Judges*. A binary opposite is *threat* (see **Subcategory: Threats** above). A threat, if fulfilled, brings harm, while a promise, if fulfilled, brings benefit.

Though the word *promise* does not occur in *Judges* (according to Tony Cartledge the word does not exist in biblical Hebrew),[25] promises are implied, and as such, amount to *oaths* that must be fulfilled, even though the words for *oath* and *swear* are also lacking in these incidents. *Violations of promises* and agreements do not occur in *Judges* except when the Timnite's father gives his daughter away to another man. The *keeping of promises* seems to have been as important then as now.

The first *promise* in *Judges* is Caleb's statement that he will give Achsah, his daughter, to the man who seized Kiriat-Sepher (1.12). Although the word for *vow* or *swear* or *promise* is not used, it is a *promise*, and Caleb honors it. (The way Caleb expresses the promise suggests that there were other candidates besides Othniel.) Othniel seizes the city, and receives Achsah as his reward. This fulfillment of the promise is unquestioned by the reader because it is fairy tale situation. It does not occur to us that an unsuitable person (someone like Abimelech or Samson or Micah, who each would have been totally inappropriate for Achsah) might have seized the city and won the bride. That Caleb's offer is really a *rash vow* does not enter the reader's mind, either. But after we see what happens to Jephthah, we might return to judge Caleb's offer differently.

There are at least three rash promises in the Pentateuch (without the verb *to swear*). The first is the situation when Laban has pursued Jacob and complains that his household gods have been stolen. Jacob swears to Laban, "'Anyone with whom you find your gods shall not live.' . . . Now Jacob did not know that Rachel had stolen the gods" (Gen 31.32). Fortunately for Jacob, Laban did not find the *teraphim*, and Rachel (through her cleverness) was saved. The second rash promise is a curse: Saul curses any of his men who touches food before the battle. Unfortunately, Jonathan dips his spear in honey (1 Sam 14.24). When Saul inquires of Yhwh and Yhwh does not answer him, Saul believes that it is because some sin has been committed and swears of the person who sinned, "For as Yhwh lives who saves Israel, even if it is in my son Jonathan, he shall surely die!" (1 Sam 14.39). Had the people not redeemed Jonathan, Saul would have been forced to keep his promise. (With this information in mind, we have to ask: why was Jephthah's daughter not also redeemed?)

The third rash promise or vow is like Caleb's. Saul apparently promises that whoever goes against Goliath and wins will have Saul's daughter as bride, with an added benefit: "The king will give great wealth to the man who kills him. He will also give him his daughter in marriage and will exempt his father's family from taxes in Israel" (1 Sam 17.25). Though Saul tries to wiggle out of his promise, eventually he gives Michal to David (not the promised Merab, however)—but for a price of 100 (or perhaps 200) Philistine foreskins (1 Sam 18:17-21).[26] This was another rash promise that was regretted by the one who swore it. The obvious moral is: if you do not want to keep your promise, do not make the promise in the first place.

Parallel to Caleb's disposal of his daughter and Jephthah's "giving" his daughter to Yhwh is the disposal of Samson's Timnite wife by her father. "Vows" may not been exchanged in Samson's marriage ceremony, but even so, Samson had been terribly wronged when his father-in-law gave away Samson's wife to another man. The father-in-law soon found out how rash his act was (15.2), for it was followed by the episode with the foxes and ultimately the burning of the father's entire household. Perhaps we are to question which of the three daughter-gifts is the worst: Caleb's, Jephthah's, or that of the Timnite's father.

Another *promise* is made by Gideon when he threatens to punish the inhabitants of Succoth and Penuel because they refuse to provide food for his men when he demands it (do they defy the law of hospitality?) (8.7, 9). Unlike Jephthah, Gideon is specific about what he will do, to whom he will do it, and why. He makes good his *threat* (i.e., it is a promise that bodes no good).

Still another *promise* is made by the Gileadites to Jephthah. Like Caleb, the elders first issue a promise with no definite person in mind: "Whoever launches the attack . . . will be head . . ." (10.18). How rash this promise was would have been apparent if someone like Abimelech had volunteered. Apparently no one took up their challenge until Jephthah did. Jephthah bargains with them and becomes head.

Subcategory: Vows

A number of *oaths, promises,* and *two vows,* are made in *Judges,* the most significant being the *vow* made by Jephthah. They are closely related. Jephthah makes a bargain with Yhwh; it is what is called a *do et des* exchange: I will *give . . .* if you *grant . . . .*

According to Tony Cartledge,

> In the Hebrew Bible, one may swear to another person, but may vow only to God. Thus, vows must always be understood as taking place within the context of prayer, in an address to God. In biblical usage, vows *are always conditional promises to God, to be fulfilled only when and if God answers the petitioner's request.* (12)

Either this society had the Deuteronomic laws, or, if it did *not* have them, was moving toward them. These laws give us a basis for making judgments about each case.

The Deuteronomic laws make it clear that one shall not swear falsely and that once one makes a vow, the *vow* must be kept. "If a man *vow a vow* unto Yhwh or swears an oath . . . he shall not break his word; he shall do all that proceeds from his mouth" (Num 30.2, repeated in Deut 23.23). "Or when any of you utter aloud a rash *oath* for a bad or a good purpose, whatever people utter in an *oath* and are unaware of it, when you come to know of it, you shall in any of these be guilty" Lev 5.4). As this translation implies, if you utter an oath unthinkingly, once you become aware that you made this vow, you are responsible if the vow is not kept.

Deut 23.21 specifically warns against postponing the fulfillment of a *vow.* Unfulfilled vows, according to Mal 1.14, bring on a curse. As already noted above under **Curses**, this was the case in the Ugaritic story of Keret, who because he failed to fulfill his vow to Athirat (Asherah) was punished with illness; and because of the curse, his son Yassib, instead of being the strong supporter that his father had hoped for, turned out to be treacherous. According to Simon B. Parker, "the vow is a species of contract." If the vow-maker does not keep his part of the bargain," says Parker, "Deut 23.22 . . . warns that Yahweh himself will then seek what is owed him . . . . Presumably, the penalty for the non-fulfillment would be even more costly than the fulfillment of the vow."[27]

A *sacrifice* must be offered when one *fulfills a vow* and as substitute for the object or service offered in the vow. "When anyone offers a sacrifice . . . in fulfillment of a vow, . . . to be acceptable it must be perfect" (Lev 22:18-23). *Leviticus* and *Numbers* both specify that animals from the flock may be substituted, but in Lev 27.1-8, persons are involved. Cartledge finds "the implications of this . . . unclear," that is, whether human sacrifice is what is referred to (13). *Leviticus* speaks of equivalents in money for *a person* who had been offered to Yhwh; the equivalent for a male age twenty to sixty is 50 shekels of silver, or for a female, 30 shekels, or for a female between the ages of five and twenty, 10 shekels (27.3-5), etc. *Leviticus* must be referring to human sacrifice, for the equivalents for animals are given in the next part of the chapter. This sounds like a contradiction to Deut 18.10, 12, which *forbids burnt offerings of children,* saying that this is abhorrent to Yhwh. Of course the people "offered" in the Leviticus text need not have been put to death, but may have been offered in some kind of service, as Hannah offered Samuel. This may be a later modification, however, meant to attenuate the cruel nature of human sacrifice.

The vow maker, according to Parker, was released from the contract if the deity did not respond to the vow; nevertheless, he gained something: "the alleviation of (personal) anxiety and of (social) shame, by putting into the deity's sphere some of the responsibility for changing the situation" (86). This may have been in Jephthah's mind. The vow relieved him of responsibility. If he lost the battle, the blame for the sacrifice could be put on Yhwh, not on Jephthah.

We have no idea what laws the author of *Judges* was familiar with. He does not refer directly to any laws, such as those in *Leviticus, Numbers,* and *Deuteronomy.* If the laws did not exist at the time in which the stories were set, they, or similar traditions about behavior, may well have existed when the author put the stories into their present form. And if the actual laws did not exist, *Judges* may show us something of the evolution of their development.[28]

This is why it is so important to determine whether the author approved or disapproved of Jephthah keeping his vow. If the author *approved*, then perhaps a law against child sacrifice did not then exist. If the author *disapproved*, it may be because he had some understanding of the Deuteronomic laws.

Of the many vows and swearing of oaths in the Hebrew Bible, the most memorable are the following (the specific word that describes each deal is given):

Abraham and Abimelech *swear* not to deal falsely with each other (Gen 21.23, 24, 31). Yhwh *swears* to Abraham that he will multiply Abraham's descendants (Gen 22:16-18) and that he will give the land of Canaan to Abraham and his descendants (in Gen 24.7 and many other passages). Jacob made Esau *swear* to give him the birthright before he gave Esau the pottage (Gen 25.33). Jacob *vowed a vow* that if Yhwh protects and feeds him, then when Jacob returns to his father's house, Yhwh would be his Elohim (Gen 28.20-21). In a deal with his father-in-law, Jacob kept his *agreement* with Laban about the flocks, though he connived to increase their number. His increasing of the flock may be regarded as fair, if we think he was entitled to some compensation for Laban's deceit in giving him Leah as wife instead of Rachel (Gen 29.18). Since there were no judges and no laws at the time, people had to work out their own system of justice.

The Israelites *vowed* to utterly destroy Arad (the *ban*) if Yhwh gave it into their hands (Num 21.2). They conquered it, and they utterly destroyed it as they had *vowed*. The Israelites kept the *oath* they *swore* to Rahab the harlot in Jericho in return for their safety (Josh 2.17, 20). They also kept their *agreement* when they *swore* to the Gibeonites that they would not attack them (Josh 9.19). Hannah *vowed a vow* to give her son to Yhwh as a Nazirite if she should conceive (1 Sam 1.11). She of course offered Samuel to Eli (1 Sam 1.21, 25), and she and Elkhanah sacrificed a bull when they fulfilled the vow. David promised (*made a covenant with*) Jonathan not to cut off Jonathan's house (20.15, 42); but a way to do away with Saul's descendants was found, by letting someone else kill them. Solomon found reasons to violate his father's vow and kill the rest of Saul's family.

Compare also the *promise* made by Ahasuerus in Esther 3.12. Once Ahasuerus had told Haman to "do with [the Jews] as seems good to you" (3.11) (like what the old Ephraimite said to the Benjaminites in *Judges* 19.24), permitting a pogrom of the Jews, and had put it in writing under his seal, he could not rescind it. But wanting soon afterwards to help the Jews, he invented a way out of the dilemma: he allowed the Jews to defend themselves. In retaliation against those who would harm them, the Jews then did "as they pleased to those who hated them" (9.5). This is similar to the way the Israelites solve their dilemma in the last chapter of *Judges*. They had *sworn* never to give wives to the Benjaminites, yet they found a way to procure wives for them without breaking their vow not to give them wives.

In the New Testament, when Salome danced before Herod, he rashly vowed (ωμοσεν) to give her anything she wanted (Mark 6.17-29). She asked for the head of John the Baptist, and got it. This, of course, removed the onus from Herod: it was not his fault that John the Baptist's head was what she wanted. Perhaps Jephthah's vow also was the author's attempt to remove the onus from his having killed his daughter. The story in its origin may have been a *do et des* or *quid pro quo*, and its cruelty for us softened by turning the sacrifice into something either accidental, or Yhwh's choice.

In *Judges*, the word for *vow* (נדר) appears twice—but only in the Jephthah story. The word *swear* (שבע) appears 6x: 2x in Ch. 2 (of Yhwh), 1x in Samson (15.12), and 3x in the last chapter. The word is used often in Deuteronomy, but only of Yhwh's *swearing* to give the land of Canaan to the Israelites. In *Judges*, Yhwh *swears* to give the Israelites the land and says he will never break that covenant (2.1). However, when the Israelites do not obey him, Yhwh changes his mind and *swears* not to help them in their battles with the enemy (2.15). (Would this be considered a broken promise? Not if obedience of the Israelites was part of the deal.)

Evaluating Jephthah's Vow

(See Chapter 2, as well as below under **Retribution**.)

Whether or not we are looking at this story from the perspective of 1) Yhwh, 2) the author, 3) Jephthah and the Israelites of that time, or 4) us today—all this makes a big difference in our evaluation of Jephthah's act. Evaluation is a most difficult problem.

Negotiation with the elders

When the Ammonites attacked, the Gileadites approach Jephthah and beg him to be their commander (11.5-6). He sarcastically reminds them of their having once rejected him and driven him out of his father's house (11.7). Doubting the elders' sincerity and distrusting their word, Jephthah makes them repeat the offer—"You may fight with the Ammonites and become head over us" (11.8)—and then responds, "*If Yhwh gives them to me*, I will be your head" (11.9), a slightly different, and better version (better for the elders) than what the elders had proposed. The elders again promise: "Yhwh will witness (hear) between us; we will do as you say" (11.10). This amounted to a solemn *oath* when "Jephthah spoke all his words before Yhwh at Mizpah" (11.11). When the elders of Gilead agreed to make Jephthah their "head," was not this also a "rash vow"? It is a foreshadowing, in fact, of Jephthah's mistake.

Why this very elaborate 6-part negotiation? Why does the author repeat this contract 4x and then tell us 2x that it was repeated a 5th x before Yhwh? Is it to show us how careful a negotiator Jephthah is? Or to make us doubt the elders' trustworthiness? Or to emphasize how badly Jephthah wants to be the "head"? Or to call our attention to the fact that Jephthah is very particular about making *others* keep *their* promises and consequently would have been a sheer hypocrite if he had not kept his *own vow*, which he afterwards famously made?

The intense focus on the negotiations seems to hint that his main aim was to become "head." If so, this makes a big difference in our judgment of him. ("Caesar was ambitious.")

The vow

Jephthah made his vow just after he had been endowed with the Spirit. Maybe having the Spirit meant that a man was swept up in a manic state and mistakenly felt he could do *anything*. Thus maybe the story has to do with being on guard against mania.

Despite being imbued with the Spirit, he nevertheless, to be doubly sure, makes his vow. What does the author mean by Jephthah's reaction to the Spirit?

that Jephthah did not know he had the Spirit? Or

that he doubted the Spirit (if indeed heroes were aware when the Spirit descended on them)? Or

that having the Spirit did not necessarily mean one was going to win? Or

that Jephthah wanted to win so badly that he would sacrifice *anything* to Yhwh? Or

that he is desperate to be "head"?

He *vowed a vow* (וַיִּדַּר יִפְתָּח נֶדֶר) that if Yhwh gave the Ammonites into his hands, then he would sacrifice whoever (whatever) first came out of the door of his house when he returned home (11.30-1). The first thing out of his door proved to be his daughter—his only child. She it is who honors the bargain Jephthah made with Yhwh. "If [or since] you have opened your mouth [vowed] to Yhwh, [then] do to me according to what has gone out of your mouth" (11.36), she declares, and Jephthah does with her as he had vowed. She becomes the scapegoat, like Iphigenia in Aeschylus.[29] If you sacrifice a child, you will win a war. (The reader assumes that Jephthah's daughter was precious to him—because of his shock when it is she who comes out of the door. But perhaps she was not so precious to *him* as the reader thinks. The vow he makes shows him to be as hard-hearted as Agamemnon.)

Cartledge asks: Why did Jephthah not vow to perform the ban on the Ammonites—that is, dedicate everything that he won to Yhwh? His answer is that Jephthah's hands were probably tied. In order to reimburse his troops, he could not devote the spoils to Yhwh because he had to distribute them among his men. Jephthah possibly thought that while seeming to promise the most precious thing he had, something else would actually come out of the house first. His words thus "are a cunning attempt to promise one thing while hoping for a lesser outcome, and effectively forcing Yhwh to make the choice!" (179). Bribery.

From the Israelite determinist point of view, Yhwh *is* in control of everything. As with the *urim* and the *thummim* (the roll of the dice), the decision about who or what will come out of the house would be made by Yhwh, and his decision would be the *right* one.

From the point of view of free will, however, the consequences are the result of a person's behavior or of chance.

If the author, and possibly the Israelite reader, believed that Yhwh was in charge of everything, Jephthah would be satisfied (though sorry) with Yhwh's choice. This rules out the element of chance, and puts the blame squarely on Yhwh—not on the human being—for the result. It is hard to believe that this is what the story means.

Jephthah is often credited with great piety (as in Handel's oratorio), greater piety than Abraham in fact, since he *proved* that he could kill a daughter in order to fulfill a vow to Yhwh, while Abraham was allowed *to avoid this ultimate proof.* (So who *is* the more pious?)

Comparison with the intended sacrifice of Isaac

Perhaps Jephthah (in the author's mind) knew of Abraham's attempted sacrifice of his son Isaac and expected the same praise and help from Yhwh. And would not the Israelite audience expect the same reaction from Yhwh?—This may be the point: Yhwh's reactions to the two cases differed.

The first difference is that it was *Yhwh* who asked Abraham to sacrifice his son, whereas it was *Jephthah* who originated the idea. Abraham made no vow. Jephthah did. The vow was an act of his own will.

The second difference is that Abraham had nothing to gain from the sacrifice and everything to lose. Jephthah hoped to win the battle and become the ruler of Gilead. Abraham is more like Jael (gaining no apparent reward), Jephthah more like Delilah (acting for a reward).

Third, Yhwh saves Isaac, but he does not save Jephthah's daughter. Had Jephthah been right to offer his daughter, had the intended vow been done in absolute faith, had Jephthah really *trusted* Yhwh to provide the offering (Gen 22.8), would not the messenger-angel of Yhwh have said to Jephthah, as he did to Abraham, "Do not lay your hand on [the child] or do anything to [her]; for now I know that you fear God, seeing you have not withheld your [daughter], your only [daughter] from me" (Gen 22.12)? That no messenger-angel saved the daughter may be author's clue that something was wrong either with the vow or with Jephthah's faith.

The fourth difference is that Abraham was a man of faith and courage while Jephthah lacked both these qualities in that he lacked confidence and had to bribe Yhwh. Of course he shows courage with the Ammonites, while with the Ephraimites he shows brutality.

The parallel between the two stories helps us assess Jephthah's sacrifice as wrong.

The Bible and human sacrifice

Although the Hebrew Bible inveighs against child sacrifice and considers it a Canaanite abomination, there is no doubt that child sacrifice continued to be practiced by the Israelites, although how extensively is not known. John Day writes that.

> we have independent evidence that child sacrifice was practiced in the Canaanite (Carthaginian and Phoenician) world from many classical sources.
>
> There is overwhelming evidence that the Old Testament itself implies that children were offered up in fiery human sacrifice to Molech. The next question . . . is whether . . .

[we should] follow certain modern scholarly sceptics who claim that the Old Testament allusions are simply unreliable polemic. However, no concrete evidence has been cited to support this supposition.[30]

Deut 18.10 forbids child sacrifice, saying that anyone who does such a thing is abhorrent to Yhwh: "There shall not be found among you any one who burns his son or his daughter as an offering . . . ." The punishment for this crime was, theoretically, death.

> Any of the people of Israel, or of the aliens who reside in Israel, who give any of their offspring to Molech shall be put to death; the people of the land shall stone them to death (Lev 20.2).

We have to assume that Jephthah was ignorant of this law, for since he is pious—or pretending to be—he would not deliberately transgress. Leviticus offers an escape route: monetary redemption. Even had Jephthah known such a possibility, he might have regarded this option as the easy way out, and not chosen to put his piety in doubt this way. Saul did choose this route and redeemed Jonathan, but it was not ultimately to his advantage, and it could be argued that he did wrong. (Incidentally, the Jephthah story is most apropos *during a time when the Israelites were committing child sacrifice*—the time of the later kings, when it is believed child-sacrifice was practiced.)

Was redemption not possible in Jephthah's time, but possible in Saul's? To give your first-born (animal or human) to Yhwh was an ancient Israelite custom. That the prophets debated the issue of human sacrifice means that the issue had not been resolved by their time. Jeremiah did not believe that Yhwh ever ordered such a thing. Ezekiel testified, however, that Yhwh did order it, but only to test ethics, that the good man would not do it (Ezek 20.25-26).

Had Jephthah been a Canaanite, modern interpreters would consider the sacrifice of Jephthah's daughter as just another Canaanite abomination, and they would not need to ponder its meaning. Compare the Moabite king sacrificing his first-born son in order to force the Israelites to turn back in their siege against him (2 Kgs 3.27). The Israelites turned back. It might thus seem to the reader that *the Moabites'* god approved of the sacrifice.[31] One's perspective makes a difference.

Naomi Steinberg argues that Jephthah expected women to come out of his house (his בית, or *household*) to greet him, implying that the vow was about one of them, not his daughter.[32] But to my mind, this makes the vow even more heinous. What right would he have to sacrifice *someone else*? Another woman would have cost *him* nothing. Jephthah is like Agamemnon: going to war and victory were so important he was willing to sacrifice anything—a daughter, if need be.[33]

Those who want to reconcile the hideousness of human sacrifice with their own theology assign "higher meanings" to it. Hubert and Mauss, for example, saw that the sacrifice is a way of bridging the two realms of the profane and sacred, of combining immanence and transcendence.[34] First, we do not know if ancient Israelites ever saw sacrifice in this way. The most we can say is that they thought Yhwh wanted sacrifice. Second, Hubert and Mauss's thinking transforms the heinous deed into something spiritual and right. I find this explanation casuistic.

At a conference on biblical literature in a respected university on the East coast, a noted scholar from a prominent theological seminary made the statement, that if put to the test, she too would obey God, even if it meant sacrificing her only child, that she put her love of God higher than her love for anything on earth. It seemed to me an appalling statement; she had struck within me a chord of one of the most critical taboos for our humanity: thou shalt not kill thy child. The meaning of life on earth is that it must be perpetuated. This is a fundamental principle. At a recent SBL annual conference, Jacques Derrida declared more than once that Abraham was a criminal[35] even though Abraham only *intended* to kill his son, while (as we know) Jephthah actually did kill his daughter.

Yet this vow was Kierkegaard's yardstick for determining Abraham to be the "truly religious person," superior to the "ethical man." Does it console us to know that Kierkegaard reached this conclusion only after "much torment of soul"?

Jephthah offered a gift to Yhwh. Did Yhwh accept it? If so, was Yhwh delighted with the offering? (Was he delighted with Samuel's barbarous treatment of Agag in 1 Sam 15.33?) The author does not say.

But as in the Iphigenia legend, that a person could kill his child is profoundly disturbing—particularly in Jephthah's case, his *only* child. The emphasis on "only" is meant to make the sacrifice, and thus his piety, all the greater, meaning that if he had had several children, the killing of one child would not be such a great loss. This kind of thinking is equally unacceptable, in my mind. Then why was the word "only" inserted in both *Genesis* and *Judges*? In *Genesis* the entire race of Israelites was hanging in the balance. In *Judges*, only Jephthah's progeny was involved. That difference, to my way of thinking, does not however alter whatever verdict that we must give in either case. As Lucretius put it, "Tantum religio potuit suadere malorum." "So much evil can religion bring about."

The dilemma

Jephthah is caught in a dilemma. Presumably he had something like the Deuteronomic Law on the one hand, and the problem of keeping his vow on the other. He zealously obeys one law (keeping his ill-conceived vow) while breaking another (committing murder). Should we commend him for breaking the one he chose to break? Which is the lesser of the two evils?

1) Why did Jephthah not invent a clever way out of his dilemma? Ans. Jephthah *was* pious (or was he pig-headed?) and thus could not alter his vow.

2) Why did Yhwh not provide an escape route? Ans. Yhwh (in the author's mind) thought Jephthah did wrong. (He deserves his punishment.) Or Yhwh thought he did right. (Jephthah sacrificed himself.) Which of these alternatives is the correct one? The author is silent on the subject. Some might suggest that offering your most precious object might be acceptable *only* on the condition that you do not violate any higher ethic, like the commandment not to kill. When two ethics conflict and a choice must be made, the choice must be

made on the side of the "higher" one, as Antigone chose to do. Because it is one of the 10 apodictic commandments, the violation of the commandment not to kill probably is the higher principle. This is the dilemma that caused Kierkegaard such anguish.

Kierkegaard called Abraham's decision "the teleological suspension of the ethical," which he made in *the faith that God would not let ethics be violated*, meaning, I assume, that God would not let the son die. Perhaps that is what Jephthah hoped.

Kierkegaard could reach this conclusion, for the story shows God supplying the sacrifice. But by Kierkegaard's standard, in Jephthah's case, either God *did* let ethics be violated, or if the choice was unethical, Jephthah should have broken his vow.

If you break your vow, how do you prove that you broke it for a higher reason? Would not the public assume you are a vow-violator, a boaster? Is it important to consider what the public thinks? Jephthah *is* a model. But of what? Goodness or evil? Let us not forget an important fact: the vow was a bargain. Yhwh supposedly kept his part of the bargain, letting Jephthah win the battle. Should Jephthah then get off free? Do we neglect to pay the mortgage and still get to keep the house?

Why did Yhwh not intervene?

Yhwh (the author might have supposed) could have saved Jephthah from the consequence of his vow, but this would have been a bad message for the Israelites: do not worry, if you make a bad vow, Yhwh will get you out of the scrape you have got yourself into. That said, the right interpretation must be that Yhwh wants you to take your vows seriously. Yet a correlation to this is: if you promise Yhwh something *less* than the most precious thing you have, why should Yhwh find it worthwhile to help you? Would not the "truly pious man" vow the most precious object he possesses? Then is Jephthah a saint? Or a careless man? What kind of sacrifice did the author think acceptable to Yhwh? But would Yhwh visit such a loss on an *innocent* Jephthah? Did the author believe Yhwh would do this?

Since the daughter is innocent, one wonders why the author has Yhwh *punish her* instead of *him*. We know that she is not overjoyed by her sacrifice: she laments the loss of her virginity (of her life?) for two months before she is killed. We sympathize with her because she did nothing evil herself to cause her own death and was noble (or was she craven?) in support of her father. (Feminists say that we can tell that this is a *male* text, because it commends the female's abject submission as ideal filial piety—to a male society, of course. A *real* daughter might have protested—like Antigone.)

If Jephthah did wrong, does the punishment of Jephthah "fit the crime"? Is it not unjust that the innocent daughter received a worse punishment than her father? Or was Jephthah's punishment at least as bad, in that he was denied descendants? Of course, she was denied descendants, too.

Why is the daughter's "virginity" stressed? Perhaps it was to assure us that she qualified as a "perfect" specimen for the offering, as the law demands in Lev 22.21;

perhaps to stress that she had no offspring and this was Jephthah's punishment; or perhaps to increase our sympathy for her.

The story may be an etiology explaining the origin of a festival that emerged from the incident.[36] The festival is an important consideration, for it is a hinge to the festival at Shiloh in the last chapter of the book, underlining the fact that the daughters of Shiloh—dancing *just as Jephthah's daughter danced* out of the house— are also *virgins about to be "sacrificed"* to the Benjaminite brutes.

Let us go to court with the case. Jephthah stands accused of having made a rash vow. After the above evidence has been offered, the case continues:

Defense Attorney's Peroration: *The Case For Jephthah*

Jephthah was glad to receive the Spirit, but had no assurance that it alone would guarantee victory.

Yhwh was pleased that a man could love him to this degree.

Yhwh had the power to determine Jephthah's fate.

Yhwh did not provide an appropriate animal (as he did for Abraham) because this would diminish the value of the vow and would also deny Jephthah the opportunity to prove his piety.

Yhwh was testing him to see just how pious Jephthah would turn out to be. Jephthah could prove his piety only if he actually sacrificed the valued object. You do not prove your piety if you are prevented in mid-act from fulfilling the vow. What kind of lesson would the Israelite learn if these models of behavior got away with unfulfilled vows?

Jephthah had no qualms about the vow: He was so "sure" of Yhwh that he was willing to take whatever chance and abide by it. He was willing to offer his most precious object. Though sorry it turned out to be his daughter, this only gave him a better opportunity to prove his love for Yhwh. He also was man of honor. Nothing could prevent him from fulfilling his vow.

Jephthah's vow was not a bribe, but an offering or sacrifice made in *advance* in return for victory. We all have to show our gratitude. Victory was a great gift. We have to reciprocate greatly. We can only do so if we forfeit something which hurts us deeply to lose. The vow was the best way to prove his gratitude. *He left the choice in Yhwh's hands.*

Prosecutor's Peroration: *The Case Against Jephthah*

Jephthah was not pious; he was vainglorious, ambitious, and evil.

From the beginning, he was a bad seed, the son of a prostitute. He was also an outlaw, consorting with "reckless men." What were these outlaws doing? As we know from other stories in *Judges* and from the story of David, they were robbing people. This does not attest to his piety. (The defense attorney would protest that having been rejected by his community, he had no other option than this. Objection would be denied.)

Endowed with the Spirit of Yhwh, he should have been fearless. It was not *his* strength; it was *Yhwh's*. He cannot claim ignorance of the Spirit, because strength by its very definition is a sign of the Spirit. The vow signifies that he was afraid to rely on Yhwh.

Would the "truly great man"[37] (as some have acclaimed him) have bargained nigglingly with the elders for payment, as he did (11.7, 9)? Would he not have volunteered and fought against the enemy gratuitously?

Jephthah's vow is not an offering or sacrifice made in *advance* in return for victory. It is an attempt *to bribe* Yhwh (cf. Gideon and Micah).

In the case of the vow, he was so indifferent to *all* human life that he did not mind sacrificing *any* person who came out.

His love for his daughter was a shallow one. He would not have made such a vow if his only child were a son. As feminist critics point out, the gender of the child is an important distinction between the Abraham and Jephthah stories.

If Jephthah really acted out of piety, Jephthah is a martyr and, in the Israelite system, as a martyr, he would receive some *reward* eventually besides becoming "head"—like David, with a second child, or like Job, with a second family. The fact that Jephthah does not get this reward means that the sacrifice of his daughter, and thus his vow, were evil.

And can you prove your love for Yhwh *by killing another human being*? Only an evil person would think this.

Afterwards, Jephthah slaughtered 42,000 Ephraimites willy-nilly. That the Ephraimites were contentious is no reason for his violent treatment of a fellow tribe. Since he was so good at diplomacy, he could have used a little of his skill here, chastised the Ephraimites, and avoided bloodshed. Like the example provided by Gideon, he could have put them off with an apothegm. About the Ephraimites, we know we are not to sympathize with these irritable fellows, since after Deborah, nothing good is said of them. But why did he slaughter so many? This certainly shows a cruel nature and a lack of regard for life.

Jephthah fits Auden's definition of "the devilish," that is, the type of person who "causes serious suffering to the innocent."[38]

The ultimate way to show his love for his daughter might be either to sacrifice his standing with Yhwh, or to commit suicide ("Greater love has no man . . ."). Jephthah made a bad decision in the wording of the vow. Unless Jephthah is punished, the rest of us might all hallucinate that we are Abrahams. Jephthah was not really pious; otherwise he would not have been punished, but rewarded. Being made "head" of Gilead for a mere six years, was scarcely a reward for such a great loss.

The Outcome

We must now confront the persistent rumor raised by a small number of interpreters who believe that Jephthah did not actually put a knife to his daughter and make her a burnt offering, but consigned his daughter to an isolated life as a virgin. Solomon Landers, for example, prefers this ending. The word חנה, he believes, should be translated to show the women *consoling* her four days each year, not *lamenting* her (11:40).[39]

I cannot agree. First, if she lives, the story does not make sense. She is obviously meant to be compared with the Timnite, who was burned to death and with the Levite's Concubine, to whom the Levite also took the knife. Second, the author delighted in telling how the tricksters win out against ill fortune by quick thinking, so that *not* to tell us how she escaped death would be to fall down in his storytelling art. The author would have to explain how Jephthah could do this yet not violate his vow. Third, if child sacrifice could be *avoided*, it would be important for his audience to learn how it was done. This valuable information is not given. Fourth, there are just too many parallels and contrasts with other stories, including the Abraham/ Isaac story, that would completely lose their significance if this alternate ending is allowed to survive. Finally, children in Israel were sacrificed, as Eissfeldt argued, not to Molech, but to Yhwh.[40] Thus we will proceed with the understanding that the author meant what he said when Jephthah "did to her as he had vowed" (11.39).

To Naomi Steinberg, he is a hero, for "Jephthah, a man without a lineage, saves his people who *do* have a lineage, paradoxically *by giving up* his own chance for *a lineage* through his daughter" (126, my italics). Possibly this is what the *author* thought and maybe what the character *Jephthah* thought, but to me, it is ethically dangerous for *us* to exonerate or ennoble Jephthah in this way. How did giving up his lineage help the Israelites? There were plenty of other lineages for them to count on. And is this not what some Palestinians think today, when they send *their* beloved sons and daughters out as suicide bombers? Jephthah may have saved his people through his military leadership, but do we think that the vow was essential to his victory? If it was essential, why do none of the subsequent leaders use this same means?

Conclusion to the Case

The author actually does not answer any of our questions, but forces us to consider *all* the possibilities and to make the judgment ourselves. Maybe it is safer for the reader *not* to judge, for judgment shows not so much what kind of person Jephthah was, but what kind of person the *reader* is. The author's purpose is to test our understanding of the morals and ethics involved, and he plays many tricks on us to make us think. Are the consequences a *just retribution* for an evil that Jephthah committed? Maybe the Yhwh of this book stood back and let events take their course. One thing we should learn is that human behavior has consequences. (See further discussion of Jephthah under **Retribution** below.)

Not counting the Nazirite agreement made by Samson's mother, Jephthah's is the main *vow* made in *Judges*, and it tells ancient readers in no uncertain terms that it is dangerous to make vows—unless they know what they are doing. Be careful what you wish for; you may get your wish. Jephthah expected the Gileadites to keep their oath to make him head; and he had to keep his own oath. Another moral is Shakespearean: "'Tis a sport to have the engineer hoist with his own petard" (*Hamlet* III.iv.206).

Possibly the main lesson of Jephthah's vow was that the people needed a standard by which to make and judge vows.

One might also question Jephthah's ambition. He is like Agamemnon. MacIntyre points out that Agamemnon had not learned the truth about *honor*. He is

> the prototype of the Homeric hero who has never learnt the truth that the *Iliad* was written to teach: he wants only to win and to have the fruits of victory for himself. *Everyone else is to be used or overcome*: Iphigenia, Briseis, Achilles. So the sophist . . . makes success the only goal of action and makes the acquisition of power to do and to get whatever one wants the entire content of success. (130) (My emphasis.)

It is a damning comparison. Or, as Kant put it in his corollary to the *categorical imperative*, "So act as to treat humanity whether in your own person or that of any other, in every case as an end, never as a means only." For Jephthah, his daughter was a means.

There is danger in thinking that nothing succeeds like success.

But there is one more way of viewing Jephthah and, in fact, of viewing all the main characters—as types of men auditioning for the role of leader of all-Israel.

So what kind of leader would Jephthah be? He would be a diplomat and negotiator, he would not be a usurper but make sure of his legal right to rule by getting the governors (elders) of the land to vote for him, and he would be an excellent and victorious military commander who could take swift successful action to defend his people, as well as a man devoted to Yhwh, to such an extent that he would scrupulously observe all official rituals piously and in doing so demonstrate to all that he was obeying Yhwh's precepts. Further, like Creon in *Antigone*, he would be incorruptible, and would not allow his personal comfort, needs, or family to obstruct his devotion to duty, and he would also reprimand and punish those who violated even in the slightest way what was right. He would be harsh, stern, and ruthless in enforcing obedience and righteousness—righteousness as he saw it—proving this by sacrificing his daughter and 42,000 Ephraimites.

But isn't he also a model of what Yhwh represented to some, both giving life and taking it away, setting standards, and demanding obedience? And isn't the daughter the model of the obedient servant? We find the same conflict between Antigone and Creon. Antigone and Creon did not know how to negotiate; thus both came to bad ends. Jephthah's daughter, unlike Antigone, bows to her master and in doing so, in effect, admits: "I know that you can do all things, and that no purpose of yours can be thwarted . . . . I despise myself, and repent in dust and ashes" (Job 42.2, 6).

And Jephthah is like a father, whipping a child: "This hurts me more than it hurts you." This is construed by some as compassion.

The Vow in the Samson Story

Another important discussion, or debate, about vows and promises is found in the Samson story, where a messenger-angel orders Samson's mother to follow the

Nazirite *rules* herself and specifically orders *an* additional rule for her son, the taboo against shaving his hair. Although neither the word *vow* or *promise* is mentioned, the implication is that she *agreed*—i.e., made a contract. Samson did *not keep* his mother's *agreement* (a wrong action, presumably) and a dire thing happened to *him*. Jephthah *kept* his *vow* (a right action, possibly); nevertheless a dire thing happened to his *daughter*. In this comparison, it would seem that "right" actions do not necessarily pay off. Who says life is fair?

Is a son obligated to keep a vow made by a parent? If so, in not keeping the vow, Samson may be said to violate the 5th Commandment about honoring his mother. The story implies obligation. In realistic fiction, we might assume that Samson also agreed to the vows at some point in his life.

But this is not realistic fiction. Everything in the story counts. We must not disregard important details. We have to fill in the gaps, but must not do so too liberally. Readers do not always observe these rules.

Before Samson is put to the test of vows, he makes a rash *promise* to give a prize to the Philistine wedding guests if they guess the riddle; they guess it, and he fulfills his *promise*, though surprisingly, not the way anyone expected. When the Philistines burn up his wife and her father, Samson *promises* to continue to wreak havoc until he has taken his proper revenge (15.7), and he does this. When the Judahites come to take him prisoner, he makes them *swear* first (שׁבע) that they will not attack him (15.12). They fulfill their *sworn statement*: they merely bind him, but they turn him over to the Philistines. These are three subsidiary *promises*, which are kept, in addition to the *chief promise* (the Nazirite *vow*), which Samson did not keep and which did him in. Remember that nonfulfillment of a vow incurs a curse. Perhaps what the author is showing here is that Samson was a man who generally kept his promises, but had one fatal lapse, to his great misfortune. (Further discussion of these "promises" will be found below, under **Revenge**.)

Or was this merely the last of four lapses, his having already violated the other three parts of his Nazirite commitment? He violated the Nazirite rules when he touched the lion's carcass and when he picked up the fresh jawbone of a dead donkey (the stricture against touching anything dead, though this has been challenged by some scholars).[41] He no doubt ate unclean food at the feast in the Philistine's house and may have drunk fermented drinks there. We cannot be sure about the food or drink, but circumstantial evidence is against him. We also note that Samson did not tell his parents where he got the honey. Was this merely a necessary plot device to assure us that his parents' ignorance about the lion meant also ignorance about the secret to the riddle? Or was it so that Samson (being guilty, we suspect, of the deadly sin of Gluttony) deceived them about the honey, because he knew that his parents would not have eaten it and would not have allowed him to eat it, had they known that it was taken from a carcass, and was therefore unclean (Lev 5.2)? The shaving of his head was then the fourth and last of the broken rules. This is usually judged the most critical part of the commitment, although possibly he had to violate *all* the rules before he would lose his strength, and this was just the last one. (We should keep in mind that we do not know what beliefs about the Nazirite law were held at this time.)

Why did he not keep this rule? Although it is possible that he did not really know that the shaving of his head would deprive him of strength (nothing else had, so far), one answer to this question is: carelessness, inattention (the deadly sin of Sloth), or overweening self-confidence in his strength (Pride, or hubris), or sexual desire for Delilah (Lust). We saw that Yhwh is certainly concerned with Pride when Yhwh made Gideon cut down his forces lest his troops "vaunt themselves" and take the entire credit for having defeated the enemies (7.2). Of course (as we have already noted), when Samson wanted to marry the Timnite, the author had told us, "This was from Yhwh, who was seeking an occasion to act against the Philistines" (14.4). But if (in the author's opinion) Yhwh was behind the scenes directing Samson's behavior, would it be unfair to call any of Samson's choices in life "bad"? You might even call his behavior "right" (though possibly the comment about Yhwh in 14.4 is some editor's or copyist's interpolation, as a way of whitewashing Samson.)

In a system of retribution, if dire punishment is the consequence of bad behavior, then what the author teaches in this story is that one must not violate a vow, whether made by a parent or by oneself.

But perhaps what caused him to lose strength was the dallying with Delilah, not the loss of hair. The hair was merely the *symbol* of his errancy. Yhwh may have arranged for Samson to marry the Timnite, so that Samson could begin the elimination of Philistines. But Yhwh disapproved of the Delilah episode because Samson had by then forgotten his mission—or so the author thought—just as Henry IV rebuked Prince Hal, for consorting with lowlifes: "Thou hast lost thy princely privilege with vile participation" (*Henry IV, Part I*, III.ii. 86-87). Samson lost his power through his relationship with Delilah. In other words, "the gods are just, and of our pleasant vices make instruments to scourge us" (*Lear*, V,iii,172). The growing back of the hair signified his having returned to the right path again, having discarded his lust and returned to treating the Philistines as enemies.

Or maybe it was just Samson's superstition and subsequent dread about having violated his vow that caused him to lose strength, as the modern reader might think. The story can be read in many different ways, but Samson cannot be completely exonerated of wrongdoing.

Micah and His Mother's Vow

(See also Chapter 2 on humor in Micah.)

In the story of Micah and the Danites, when Micah returns the stolen money to his mother, his mother *dedicates* (הקדש הקדשתי) the money for an image and an idol to Yhwh (17.3). Because of the religious language, this amounts to a *vow*, though the word *vow* is not used. The inference is that she will dedicate the total amount (1,100 shekels); however, she dedicates only 200 of them. This is often interpreted as a *breaking* of an *oath* and makes her seem hypocritical. She was perhaps guilty of the deadly sin of Avarice. (All the deadly sins, we remember, are punished in Dante's *Purgatorio.*) Since the silver had been stolen, moreover, it may also be contaminated and unworthy of being sanctified.

Disaster follows for Micah, but the reason is not clear. We may suspect that his mother's rash curse, following immediately after the story of Jephthah's *vow*, may be the root cause. Like Jephthah, she did not think through the ramifications of the curse. Though she immediately blessed her son as soon as he returned the money and as soon as she identified the thief, perhaps it was impossible to neutralize a curse in this way. Or was she guilty of breaking the 3rd commandment against taking Yhwh's name in vain?

Was Micah alone responsible for his disaster: because he stole his mother's money (breaking the 8th Commandment) and worshiped idols (breaking the 2nd Commandment)?[42] The consequence of acquiring the idols was that the Danites coveted and stole them; thus the Danites broke the 10th and 8th commandments.

Because the idols are mentioned so many times, the emphasis implies that we must pronounce judgment on them. Deuteronomic Israelite audiences of a later period would certainly have regarded idols as evil. (See discussion of **Idolatry** above in this chapter.)

In the free will/determinism debate, one cannot construe the story of Micah and the Danites as simply Yhwh's way of getting the Danites some idols and a priest for their new territory in the north (like Yhwh's way of getting Samson to exterminate some Philistines). But it does provide the author with an explanation of why Yhwh allowed the idolatrous Danites to be carried off by the neo-Assyrians in 722 BCE, a fact which is mentioned in the next-to-last verse of the story, and which therefore is of profound importance. The story is thus an *exemplum*[43] of the bad consequences of possessing idols. Micah, his mother (both Ephraimites), and the Danites did wrong.

All these possibilities must be sorted out by the reader.

The Vow and the Curse in the Story of the Levite's Concubine

(See Chapter 2 for the humor of the story.)

In the last story in the book—the Israelites' revenge on the Benjaminites of Gibeah—the Israelites *promise* each other not to return to their tents or houses— that is, not to stop fighting until the Benjaminites are punished (20.8, 10). This amounts to a *vow*, although again the specific word for *vow* or *oath* is not used. Next, however, the Israelites take an *oath* (שׁבעה) that whoever did not come to Yhwh at Mizpah to fight on their side should be put to death (21.5). At Mizpah, they also *swear* (שׁבע) (21.1) not to give their daughters as wives to the 600 remnants of the Benjaminites (all Benjaminite women having been killed in the destroyed towns). To the oath they added an unfortunate *curse*: "*Cursed* (ארור) be anyone giving a wife to Benjamin" (21.18). A customary part of a *swearing an oath*, the *curse* brings severe punishment if the oath is not fulfilled (Cartledge, 15). (See discussion of **Curses** above.)

Like Ahasuarus in the story of Esther, the Israelites in the last story of *Judges* consequently have to devise a means of *avoiding the oath and the curse they unwittingly put on themselves* (a parallel to Micah's mother's curse), yet not literally violating it, which would incur the curse. When the Israelites discover that Jabesh-Gilead had not come to fight with the rest of them (21.10), they impose the *ban* on it—their "happy idea" to solve their dilemma of providing the Benjaminites with wives. They utterly destroy the town except for 400 virgins, whom they turn over to the Benjaminites. This, they reason, is not a violation of any *vow* because the fathers of the daughters of Jabesh-Gilead, not having come to Mizpah, had thus not sworn the oath about daughters, and anyway, they killed all the fathers, and thus eliminated *that* problem.

The 200 daughters of Shiloh are a different matter. *Their* fathers had sworn the oath at Mizpah not to *give* their daughters to the Benjaminites. But the Israelites rationalize that if the Benjaminites *seized* the daughters, the fathers would *not* actually *be giving* the women to them. Through this sophistry, the fathers are persuaded not to feel guilty (אשם) of having violated their oath (21.22).

It is up to the reader to decide if this ruse protected the fathers against the *curse*. The ominous statement at the beginning and end of this story, "All the people did what was right in their own eyes," implies that the people were lawless and that their sophistry did not fool the author. And it should not fool us.

Again, we must not forget that daughters are being *given away* throughout the book. This was the last such occasion.

Subcategory: Conditions and Cause/Effect

The book seems to be a fabric of various kinds of *promises* and their good or bad results, expressed not only through stories, but also in sentence structure. Many of the *conditional sentences* in *Judges* are really *promises* and as such are akin to *vows* and *sworn* statements. Conditionals also disclose the author's philosophy of *contingency*, of what *consequences* of the actions are *possible* or *likely*. They often show hesitation about the rightness or wrongness of an action. Human beings are given the opportunity to make choices. They are each responsible for their own destiny through their judgments. This is not the philosophy of a pure fatalist. The author is asking us to judge these characters and learn from what they do. (An analysis of conditional sentences can be found in **Appendix 1** of this chapter. There are too many to be listed here.)

VI. Punishment/Reward: Retribution, Requital, Revenge

Punishment of one sort or another usually follows from the bad or evil behavior of characters in this book. Most of the punishment is deserved. Some of it supposedly comes from Yhwh (success or defeat in battle). But much of the time, the characters themselves impose punishment on others through *revenge*. The author of *Judges* gives us a number of examples of how the system of revenge worked in his society.

First, we must define terms[44] so that the reader may refer back to the definitions, as needed.

Retribution: something justly deserved, recompense, something given or demanded in repayment or punishment, especially for an evil done. In theology, it may be punishment (or reward) distributed by the divinity in the *afterlife* and is based on performance in this life. As far as the people of the time are concerned, however, there is no *afterlife*. In their thinking; retribution occurs in *the here-and-now*, not after death. The author of *Judges* tells us when he thinks the retribution is *divine*.

On the whole, the author believes that people get their just deserts. Innocent victims, like Jephthah's daughter and the virgins of Jabesh-Gilead and daughters of Shiloh, however, suffer as a consequence of *others'* bad decisions or evil deeds and are not redeemed, at least in this text.

About the justice or injustice of the destruction of Jabesh-Gilead (21.8), we may infer that to the Israelites, such cities had an obligation to cooperate, and their punishment was *just retribution* for their not cooperating with the Israelites in their attack on the Benjaminites. (No evidence or rule for such an obligation, however, is shown.)

But maybe Jabesh-Gilead's commitment was *only* to the tribe of Benjamin, and this ruse by the Israelites was an injustice. We see the close connection between this city and the Benjaminites during the time of Saul (1 Sam 11.1-9; 2 Sam 2.4-5; 21.12). Of course, a reason for the later close relationship between Jabesh-Gilead and Saul may have simply been the intermarriage of the 400 virgins of that town and Saul's tribe, the Benjaminites, Saul presumably being the offspring of such a union.

These stories are part of the debate about tribal obligations and about the proper punishment for failure to honor them. Loyalty to "all-Israel" had still to be created and would not come into being until the time of David, if then. This story may illustrate one of the ways the idea of unity was begun, developed, encouraged—and enforced. But since we have before our eyes the existence of very powerful tribal rivalries in Afghanistan and Iraq and other Middle Eastern countries today, perhaps the unity of "all-Israel" was, as for these modern countries, always only a dream.

Such destruction as that of Jabesh-Gilead was another example of the excesses committed by the Israelites because they lacked a strong leader. "There was no king in Israel, and each man did what was *right in his own eyes*" (איש הישר בעיניו יעשה) (17.6; 21.25). This is a *cause-and-effect* statement, implying that chaos, lawlessness, and anarchy are the *retribution* visited on people who do not have a king. Yhwh, so far as the author informs us, had not commanded that they get a king so it cannot be said that they disobeyed him. The sentence implies, rather, that it is *their responsibility* to do something about the deteriorating situation themselves. That this idea seems to be promonarchical may be a clue (barring interpolations) to the time period in which the stories of *Judges* were being told orally, before being written down—and before the monarchy had proved to be a failure.

Retaliation: return like for like, especially evil for evil. To pay back an injury in kind. Note the etymology of this word from the *lex talionis*, the principle of justice based on the Mosaic law in Exod 21:23-24. (Block—mistakenly, I think—calls the lex talionis a "Canaanite ethic.")[45] The ancient law recommends an equivalent payment for a crime—something equal to, but not greater than, the crime. The *eye-for-an-eye* motif is not largess, generosity of soul; it is justice, but grim justice.

Tit-for-Tat and *Reciprocity* are related to this principle. *Tit-for-tat* is specifically a blow given in return for a like blow; an equivalent injury given for an injury, but also (in modern Game Theory) a good for a good. *Reciprocity* refers to mutual action (usually beneficent) between two parties.

Proportionality means that the punishment or revenge shall not be excessive. According to Susan Jacoby, "Proportional punishment serves a dual function: it must be severe enough to reflect society's estimation of the seriousness of a crime, but not so harsh or excessive as to exceed the harm done by the offense."[46] (Tit-for-tat, or retaliation.)

Reprisal, requital, and *revenge* are other methods of punishing behavior regarded as negative or evil. *Reprisal*: retaliation for an injury with the intent to prevent further loss and to inflict at least as much injury in return. It might include the seizing of property or persons belonging to someone else by way of recompense. It is usually an action taken by the injured party.

Requital: like *retribution*, repayment or return for something as a service or injury. It differs from most of the other terms in that it can be a deliberate agreed-upon repayment for either kindness or evil. Not exemplified in this book is *requital* in its special sense of a fine or a voluntary payment made by the perpetrator to offset the crime. In cases of murder, Jewish law forbade absolution "through payment or through substituting another man's life for the life of the murderer" (Jacoby 125). But *redemption* (such as an offering or fine) was provided in the Deuteronomic laws, exemplified by the redemption of Jonathan (1 Sam 14.39-45). The line drawn between *absolution* and *redemption* is a fine one.

Revenge: infliction of a hurt on the injurer in order to get satisfaction of one kind or another for injuries. *Revenge* should not be confused with *retribution*. *Retribution* is supposed to be proportional as well as deserved. *Revenge* may be a method of incurring *retribution*, but it may have no regard for equity.

Modern society tends to disdain revenge systems, but revenge is a system of retaliation devised as deterrence against violence in the time before the development of law enforcement. Revenge systems still exist today and have some justification. Richard A. Posner writes:

> Revenge is . . . a system of social control, like law itself, rather than a sign of the absence of all social control . . . . A potential victim who seeks to deter aggression against himself . . . must *convince potential aggressors that he will retaliate* even if the expected benefit of retaliation, calculated *after* the aggression has occurred, are smaller than the expected costs at that time . . . . Cultures in which revenge plays a significant role in the

regulation of social interactions place great emphasis on honor . . . . Out of the interplay of honor, shame, and revenge grow notions of exchange, balance, reciprocity, "keeping score"—notions later taken up by law, initially under the rubric of "corrective justice."[47]

And, in fact, "in the long prehistory of the human race," writes Posner,

people who were endowed with *an instinct to retaliate* would have tended *to be more successful in the struggle for survival* than others. The desire to take revenge for real or imagined injuries, *without calculating the net benefits of revenge* at the time when it is taken, may therefore have become a part of the human genetic makeup (51). (Emphasis mine.)

(This idea takes Samson off the hook.) Modern systems of justice replace, to some degree, the individual need to exact revenge.

Corrective justice—the idea that *the task of the legal system* is to restore a preexisting balance between persons—reflects the revenge-inciting feeling of indignation caused by the infringement of one's rights. (58)

Systems of revenge exist today in tribal societies and in urban gangs. As Posner says, the instinctive desire for retaliation and revenge is part of our genetic heritage, surfacing as our anger at violent acts that have affected us personally. Even among law-abiding people, the instinct for revenge manifests itself when it encourages them to cooperate with law enforcement in order to obtain justice for the victim instead of taking the law into their own hands. In other words, representatives of law enforcement take revenge for us.[48]

Reward: money (or a valued object) given in payment for some service. A reward is given freely as positive reinforcement for an approved act or behavior, not an obligatory debt such as is implied in *requital*. Jephthah is presumably *rewarded* for fighting against the Ammonites by being made "head."

Justice: the upholding of fair treatment and due reward in accordance with honor, standards, or law.

The author of *Judges* is asking us to distinguish between the following binary opposites:

divine/accidental *retribution*,

appropriate/excessive *retaliation* or *revenge*,

just/unjust *punishment*, and even

r*eward*/*punishment* (as with the Jephthah/daughter conundrum).

Analysis of Retribution, Revenge, etc. in the Stories

The *retribution* theme is announced in Ch. 1, the introduction to Judges, when after having his thumbs and big toes cut off by the Israelites, Adoni-Bezek, their enemy, says: "Seventy kings with their thumbs and big toes cut off used to pick up scraps under my table. As I have done, so Elohim has *paid me back* for what I did to them" (1.7).

The first *reward* given is the one promised by Caleb: "To the one who conquers Kiriat-Sepher I shall give Achsah my daughter as wife" (1.12). Othniel receives the *reward*. Interpreters uniformly judge this as appropriate. No questions asked. As we shall see, questions about this should be asked.

All of Ch. 2 of *Judges* has to do with the *punishment* or *divine retribution* inflicted by Yhwh for the Israelites' apostasy. The author believes Yhwh regards the worship of "other gods" as evil, and certainly it was wrong by the standards of the time. At least the time when the stories were committed to writing.

Ch. 3 seems to have no instances of *retribution*. Of course, Eglon deserves to be assassinated—from the Israelite point of view—and his death may be considered retribution for his evil, though such is not stated. Readers generally agree that he got what he deserved.

In Ch. 4, Barak receives *retribution* for his cowardice in refusing to go to battle without Deborah. As she prophesies, he does not win the honor of defeating Sisera but is humiliated by having that honor go to a woman. This, however, is relatively mild punishment compared with what follows.

Gideon

The Gideon story recounts one possible incident of *retribution* and two instances of *revenge*.

Gideon's decision *not* to rule over the people—"Yhwh will rule over you" (8.23)—is usually regarded as the right decision, but it could be considered wrong, for look at the consequences: Abimelech's murder of his brothers and usurpation of power, his ultimate assassination, and the destruction of Shechem. Had Gideon become King, Abimelech's cause would have been weakened, and Gideon's rightful successor might have had the power to prevent Abimelech's murders.

Gideon may have refused the title of king, but he nevertheless had the trappings of kingship—the plunder from the Midianites and the ephod—and some interpreters think he wielded power like a despot. His refusal of the title did not prevent debacle for his descendants, and the weakness of his house resulting from the lack of authority in the land may even have caused the problem. Interpreters' opinions are divided on this issue. After we have read the two statements about the chaos in Israel because there was no king (17.6; 21.25), we have to rethink the decision made by Gideon. *Retribution* fell on his sons through the instrument of Abimelech, and on Abimelech through the *evil spirit* thought to have been sent by Yhwh.

In the first instance of *revenge*, Succoth and Penuel refuse bread to Gideon and his troops. When he returns after his victory, he *punishes* them: he chastises the elders of Succoth with thorns and briers, breaks down the tower of Penuel, and kills all the people (8.5-9, 16-17). That these are Gileadite cities and perhaps not authentic Israelite cities may be important, as we infer from the way the Ephraimites taunted Jephthah: "You Gileadites are renegades [fugitives] from Ephraim and Manasseh" (12.4, discussed in Chapter 3 under **Relationships**.)

But is he not merciless in trampling the men of one of these cities and in breaking down the tower and killing the men of the other? The soldiers, the reader might notice, *did* manage to survive their exhaustion without the donations of food Gideon demanded. It might help to compare Gideon's action with what David and his outlaw band intended to do to Nabal (1 Sam 25:8-13ff.). Nabal had refused David provisions on the reasonable grounds that Nabal had not asked for protection. David's "protection," was possibly a "racket," which Nabal could rightly be annoyed at. But perhaps Nabal, and the people of Succoth and Penuel, should have been grateful for the service provided by these warriors. These towns very likely benefitted from the peace that Gideon and David secured for them from marauders, invaders, and other enemies. At least the stories suggest that we had better be grateful for services rendered even if we had not requested them. At best, try to be tactful. David was furious with Nabal and was bent on destroying him. Gideon was furious at the two Gileadite cities.

Were Gideon and David protectors of the defenseless, or were they bullies preying on vulnerable people? Nabal's people and his wife witnessed for David against Nabal (or so the author would have us believe). Predatory raids were the usual way for the army to forage for food and provisions. Armies on the march must be fed, and those who do not feed them must be penalized as a warning to other cities (so the thinking might have been). Thus Gideon's punishment of the cities might be considered appropriate punishment. Cooperation is a good. Was the punishment, however, excessive?

Gideon also gets *revenge* on Zebah and Zalmunna. He would not have killed them, he claims, had they not killed his brothers (8.19). We might also call this *retribution* for Zebah's and Zalmunna's lack of mercy. But one wonders if Gideon's claim to them was sincere: marauding kings with armies fighting against Israelites would never forbear killing the enemy merely because they were the brothers of an enemy leader, nor would those being invaded forgive *their* enemy and send them back to their homeland unscathed for such kindness. This speech is rhetoric justifying his anger. But it also serves an important purpose: it underlines the parallel between Gideon and his son Abimelech. Gideon's love for his brothers is contrasted with Abimelech's lack of love for his.

After Gideon's death, the Israelites (possibly including all of Gideon's sons) do not honor (לֹא עָשׂוּ חֶסֶד, i.e., do not do *hesed* to) the house of Jerubbaal/Gideon nor remember the good (הַטּוֹבָה) Jerubbaal had done for them (8.35). This black mark against the sons should be remembered when judging Abimelech for his crime of assassinating them. In a curious way, their deaths might be considered a form of retribution for their disloyalty to Yhwh.

After 8.35, Gideon is always referred to as *Jerubbaal*, never as Gideon. Possibly stories about two different men have been amalgamated; Abimelech may originally have been the son not of Gideon but of another man, whose name was Jerubbaal. Or maybe this second name, which incorporates the theophoric element Baal, implies that going astray with the ephod in his old age signified that Gideon, like his sons, reverted to Baalism. The change of his name to Jerubbaal tempts us to think so. Certainly "the Israelites . . . made Baal-berith their god" (8.33)—a much overlooked statement. Shechem, the home of Gideon's concubine, Abimelech's mother, was the site of the temple of Baal Berith.

Abimelech and his Brothers

Though the murder of Jerubbaal's sons by their brother Abimelech may be seen as *divine retribution* on Jerubbaal for having led his house astray with the ephod, Abimelech's cold-blooded murder of his brothers was in no way justified, as Abimelech himself was *not* seeking *revenge* for his brothers' disloyalty to their father or to Yhwh (a cause that might be considered good) but was committing fratricide just to gain power. *Retribution* is subsequently meted out to Abimelech when the author tells us Yhwh sent an "evil spirit" to him in order to avenge the killing of his brothers (9.23, 24).

Compare Gideon with his son, Jotham (Abimelech's brother), a survivor of the mass fratricide by Abimelech. Jotham did *not* seek *revenge* on *his* brothers' murderer. Perhaps this makes him a lesser man than Gideon, who did avenge his brothers. But since the murderer of his brothers is his own (and only surviving) brother, Jotham's killing of Abimelech would be fratricide, as clearly as the fratricide that Abimelech committed. The question might be: was it proper in that society to commit fratricide in order to get revenge?

Here the author clearly wants us to understand the relationships that he has so carefully set down. Gideon's brothers were *full* brothers, the sons of his own mother (8.19), and his indignation over their murder is righteous. But Gideon "had many wives" (8.30), as the author so carefully tells us. So *his* sons, including Jotham, were *not* full brothers of Abimelech. Abimelech's mother was a Shechemite concubine (very likely not an Israelite), a "lesser wife" of Gideon/Jerubbaal (cf. the Concubine in Ch. 19). This possibly made Abimelech "a lesser brother" of those he killed. The question the author may be raising is: does it make any difference whether the brother you are murdering is a *half* brother or a *full* brother? Or if your mother is not the social equal of the father's other wives? In a society where *revenge* is the substitute for the rule of law, the answer to this question might matter. Comparing these relationships may modify our judgment in subtle ways. We do not know how revenge was viewed by the author or by the society of his time. We have to infer from evidence.

In his fable, Jotham, speaking to the citizens of Shechem, calls for just *retribution*:

> If you have acted in truth and integrity [בתמים] with Jerubbaal and his house, then rejoice in Abimelech and let him rejoice in you . . . . If not, let fire come from Abimelech and consume the citizens; let fire come from the lords of Shechem and Beth Millo and consume Abimelech (9.16, 19, 20).

At the end of these *if . . . then* statements is his curse. Jotham may have desired, and deserved, to get revenge, but he cannot be faulted for not getting it, as he was completely powerless, except for the power to curse. Though Jotham gets no *revenge*, he does perhaps get a kind of satisfaction in having predicted the consequences of the collusion of Abimelech and the Shechemites.

In *revenge* for Gaal's treachery, Abimelech attacks the city of Shechem, kills all the people therein, razes it, and sows it with salt. *Carthago delenda est*. Abimelech here is irrationally destroying his *own* city, cutting off his nose to spite his face. Next he burns down the tower of Shechem with the people in it and goes on to attack the tower of Thebez, but at this point he himself is killed (9.45). Were these people so disloyal that it was right for Abimelech, evil though he was, to retaliate in this way? Or is this excessive *revenge* on his part? To be sure, he had been disloyal to his own brothers, and now gets paid back in the same coin—with the disloyalty of Gaal and the Shechemites to him. One of the corollaries of this story might be: A worthless man who gathers "worthless and reckless men" around himself (9.4) should not expect his followers to treat him honorably. It is also another case of being hoist with his own petard.

The parallel to Gideon's treatment of Succoth and Penuel is significant. Like father, like son. It is also parallel to the Israelites' destruction of the cities of their own tribes, the cities of Benjamin and Gilead (Chs. 20-21).

Whereas Gideon refused to rule over the Israelites because he considered it offensive to Yhwh, Abimelech seems to care nothing for Yhwh; he covets power. Like Macbeth and Caesar, he was too ambitious.

We are to make no mistake about Baal Berith, the god to whom he apparently holds allegiance, for as we have seen, "As soon as Gideon died, the Israelites relapsed and prostituted themselves with the Baals, making Baal-berith their god" (8.33). The 70 shekels Abimelech used to hire reckless fellows as assassins came from the temple of Baal Berith. And on the occasion when Gaal and his friends are gathering grapes from the vineyards (probably stealing them), they remove to the temple of their god for a "festival," at which they eat, drink, and curse Abimelech. Perhaps the author wants us to understand that this is no temple of Yhwh, or (should it happen that the Israelites were also using *their* temples for like festivals) that this kind of behavior was an abuse of the god.

That Abimelech and the Shechemites receive *divine retribution* is carefully spelled out 2x, the first in 9.24 and the second time at the end of the chapter (echoing earlier statements by Adoni-Bezek and Samson):

> Thus Elohim returned the evil that Abimelech did to his father in murdering his
> seventy brothers. All the wickedness the bad men of Shechem did, Elohim returned
> [יָשֵׁב] on their heads, and on them came the curse of Jotham (9.56-57).

Instead of getting *revenge* himself, Jotham fled, having made his statement: that only evil will come from evil.

Jephthah

Another person who flees from evil brothers is Jephthah (9:21); but while Jotham flees from a brother who committed *mass* fratricide, Jephthah flees from brothers whose crime was merely injustice, not mass fratricide. The story of Jephthah begins with the elders' *promise* of a *reward*: "Who is the man who will fight against the Ammonites? He will become head over all the inhabitants of Gilead" (10.18). The elders choose Jephthah.

Like the evil Abimelech, Jephthah surrounded himself with "worthless" fellows (אֲנָשִׁים רֵיקִים). Abimelech's mother was a concubine; Jephthah's mother was a harlot—details used by the author in judging the characters of the men. Jephthah's heritage is even a bit lower than Abimelech's. His father is only "Gilead" (a place name) while Abimelech is the son of the renowned hero, Gideon. And do not forget the Ephraimites' taunt about the people of Gilead being *fugitives* or *renegades* (12.4). (Also see the discussion of Jephthah's vow above.)

Jephthah's brothers had driven him out and refused him a share in the inheritance (11.2). Nevertheless, Jephthah is not spiteful; he did *not* seek *revenge* on his oppressors but returned to help them. Though in *repaying* unkindness with kindness, he may seem rather noble, he really is not. First, the reason Jephthah did not seek *revenge* might be that he was not so strong as Abimelech, who had money to pay his henchmen. Second, he did not offer his services to his town free of charge; he demanded *recompense* for helping instead of selflessly rushing out against the enemy from the goodness of his heart. (If we think this, then Othniel was not a pure savior either. Was he not also "bribed" with the promise of a wife if he won a victory? When does *reward* shade over into *bribery*?) Jephthah returned to his city not out of generosity, but to gain power.

In a deliberately-constructed parallel situation, Gideon can be *persuaded* (by Yhwh) to fight against the Midianites, but Jephthah has to be *bought* to fight against the Ammonites.

In another parallel, Abimelech left his father's town of his own free will and killed his seventy brothers without provocation—for his own aggrandizement. Though Jephthah had provocation for *revenge* (he was disinherited), he exercised restraint and demonstrated to the Gileadites their mistake in driving him out. The Jephthah story shows that Abimelech could have found another way to obtain power. Of course, Jephthah does get revenge on his townspeople when they have to come crawling to the man they had abused and ostracized, an observation that I think the author wants us to make.

Jephthah's promise to the elders needs further scrutiny. While the Gileadites have not made his becoming head of Gilead contingent on victory, he says he will become "head" (רֹאשׁ) *only* if Yhwh gives the enemy to him. Since he *did* conquer the Ammonites, his part of the bargain was kept. Theirs was, too, for he judged Israel for six years.

In order to obtain victory, he made his horrible vow. Yhwh *rewarded* Jephthah with a victory, but Jephthah paid heavily for it. The death of his daughter may be interpreted as *retribution* for something—no other than the vow he should not have made.

Jephthah then slaughtered 42,000 Ephraimites as they crossed the Jordan (12.6). Though the Ephraimites threatened to burn Jephthah's house with him in it, was Jephthah justified in taking such a *brutal* and *excessive revenge* on them? Parallel to this, Ehud prevented the Moabites from crossing the Jordan, and slew them. But they were the enemy; while the Ephraimites were Israelites (3.28-29). In another parallel situation, Gideon deflected the Ephraimites through diplomacy. Though Jephthah had diplomatic skills and could have negotiated with the Ephraimites, he chose to do otherwise.

Admittedly, the Ephraimites were one of the thorns in Israel's side (2.3). Since that tribe was the chief rival of Judah in later Israelite history, the author is building up the case for why the Ephraimites were carried off with Dan and the other northern tribes by the Assyrians in 722 BCE, for their "removal" (translated as *captivity*) is mentioned in the last words of the story (18.30, עַד־יוֹם גְּלוֹת הָאָרֶץ). The parallel battle of the Israelites against the Benjaminites and near annihilation of them in the last chapter, helps us to judge with certainty that Jephthah's treatment of the Ephraimites was wrong as well.

Finally, Jephthah got to be head, but only for 6 years instead of 20 or 40. Was ever such a small duration of power bought at such dear cost?

Samson

Now let us consider the multiple revenges and retaliations perpetrated on the Philistines by Samson, in his feud with them.

As the consequence of Samson's Pride (a deadly sin) in believing that his famous riddle cannot be solved, a series of crimes and *retaliations* is launched. The binary opposite of *pride* (hubris) is *fall* (nemesis) in this case.

1) When the Philistines cheat and learn the solution of the riddle unfairly through intimidating Samson's wife, the Timnite, and through her subsequent treachery (14.18), Samson runs amok and kills 30 Ashkelonites in *revenge* (14.18-19). He commits mayhem.[49]

Incidentally, here is another conundrum: how wrong is Samson's wife in betraying him? Can she not plead self-defense? The wedding guests have threatened to burn her and her father's house if she does not worm the secret out of Samson. *Her life* and *her father's life* are at stake, while what is at stake for Samson are merely 60 garments. Intimidation and threats against one's life or property are forms of harassment. Most readers feel sympathy for Samson, however. They think that she is just another nagging wife. But we can imagine her fear: how could her one lone husband, an Israelite, possibly save her and her family from 30 angry, brawny Philistine men? Besides, what difference would it make if she told them the secret? It was only a game. Is the Timnite really another Xantippe? A Dame Van Winkle? Does she not have the right to defend herself in the only way that was possible at that time? She was an underdog.

If we are in doubt that the Philistines meant business, see what happened after Samson pulled his trick with the foxes: "So the Philistines came up, and burned her and her father" (15.6). She was right to be afraid. Let us rehabilitate her and restore her reputation.

On the other hand, just how wrong were the Philistines in cheating in order to solve an unsolvable riddle? There have been a number of attempts to prove that the riddle was fair, but the author does not present it as fair. Yet was cheating not a reasonable kind of tit-for-tat on the part of the wedding guests? But the bargain was also unfair for Samson: if *he* won, the 30 Philistines had to give him *only 2 garments each* (a total of 60 garments in all), whereas if *they* won, he *alone* had to get *60 garments* for them. But not to worry! He was certain to win! (Or so he thought.)

Still another conundrum: how wrong is Samson in promising this extravagant prize? The only way to get the prize was to *kill*, as the Ashkelonites certainly were not going to *give* him the shirts off their backs willingly. This might be a place for the teacher of ethics to pause and give a lecture on the law of unintended consequences. Everyone gets angry. Everyone has felt a desire for vengeance. And can we really fault Samson for *not* having a sufficiently developed prefrontal cortex to plan a workable strategy in advance? He was impetuous and uncontrolled from the beginning. Samson never had any inhibitory capacity. This story may serve to exemplify the dangers of lack of self-control and thus show society the need to develop institutions for moderating such intransigence. Of course, the Philistines were the enemy, and his success surely delighted the audience.

2)　When his wife is taken away and given to another man (14.20) (cf. Michal being taken away from David [1 Sam 25.44]), Samson takes *revenge* by using the foxes to burn the shocks, the standing grain, the orchards, and the vineyards of the Philistines (15.4). We might agree with Samson that such an insult and loss deserved a huge settlement in compensation. But against *any* Philistines, not against the *actual offenders*? Though the damage done by Samson was excessive, so was his frustration, and the amount of damage is testimony to the amount of anger he felt.

3)　When the Philistines r*etaliate* and burn his ex-wife and her father (15.6), Samson's counter *retaliation* is to "smite them hip and thigh with great slaughter" (15.8). Nothing proportional about this.

4)　Again in *retaliation*, when the Philistines invade Judah (15.9), the Judahites bind Samson and turn him over to the Philistines. Was it wrong for the Judahites to give Samson over to the enemy? This question can be answered in two different ways:

No, it was not. First, because of all the trouble with the Philistines that Samson has caused, which is ricocheting back on the Judahites (15.13), provoking the Philistines in turn to invade them. Second, because it was the only way to put an end to this crazy *series of retaliations*. In revenge societies, as Richard A. Posner tells us, "People have an incentive to *police their kin*, lest a *kinsman's misbehavior* lead to retaliation against them rather than against him" (52). If someone did not stop him, the Judahites may have reasoned, he would only continue *ad infinitum.*

Yes, it was wrong. First, Samson was an Israelite. It was cowardly of the Judahites not to fight on *behalf* of Samson. One of the functions of kin in this kind of society is to act as a deterrent to violence against the family (51). They may have thought they were doing this. But by handing Samson over, the Judahites were not only *aiding the enemy* but also *showing themselves to be weak*—pushovers for attack. Second, in the Israelite scheme of things, it is good to get rid of the Philistines; it is bad to sacrifice your own hero.

A question here is: by whose standards are we going to make *our* judgments today?

Again, *no*, the Judahites were not wrong. First, because although Samson killed the enemy, he did not wage war against the enemy as he should have and as the other heroes of the book did. He fought out of spite and for personal satisfaction—though the Israelites of the time may not have objected to that, thinking that the only good Philistine was a dead Philistine. Second, the Judahites may have reasoned that Samson was not worth saving: he had been fraternizing with the enemy and had participated in a "mixed marriage," something expressly forbidden by Yhwh. Finally, though a member of a brother tribe, Samson was not a Judahite but a *Danite*. The Danites, according to Israelite history in the Bible, were despised because they became idolaters (18.30, 31). The audience of this book, especially during the later monarchy and exile, may have justified Judah's behavior on that ground. Moreover, the Judahites at this time were really quite independent of all the northern tribes—as we can see from their lack of activity in this book and the fact that there is no story in the book centered on Judah. Judah's role in the Samson story is another breakdown in the hoped-for tribal unity.

5) Samson, however, breaks loose and again runs amok, retaliating once more by killing 1,000 Philistines with the jawbone of an ass (15.15). With each step in the series, the price the Philistines must pay grows steeper.

6) Finally, through Delilah's treachery, the Philistines, seeking to incapacitate him, imprison Samson and gouge out his eyes (16.21). But Samson refuses to be subservient. He had one more weapon under his sleeve: his biceps. Again Samson *retaliates*—not, however, on his betrayer, Delilah (unless she happened to be in the temple when it was destroyed), but on a vast number of people, "more than he had killed in his lifetime" before.

When he is about to pull his final trick, Samson prays: "let me get *one revenge* for my *two* eyes" (ואנקמה נקם־אחת משתי עיני, 16.28). Why did the author give us these numbers? Because it is not "two eyes for two eyes," but two eyes for perhaps 4,000 people or more—the 3,000 men and women on the roof of the temple of Dagon, and also all those uncounted who were underneath (16.27, 30). Unlike Adoni-Bezek's justice, Samson's *revenge* is *excessive* to an extreme. Maybe he is being ironic in calling this *one revenge*. And is killing himself in the process a "true" instance of *retaliation*? For in punishing the enemy, is he not also helping them rid themselves of their favorite enemy?

In this series of retaliations, the Philistines never seem to get the message, that it is dangerous to mess with Samson. Only through his death can the feud be ended and the danger stopped. The Philistines pay an enormous price—but they do get rid of Samson. Samson, however, has destroyed the temple of Yhwh's rival, Dagon. And of course, we know that the greater the damage that Samson caused, the greater the ancient audience of *Judges* cheered. From their point of view, Samson is a martyr. He is an archetype, Samson agonistes. Samson may be the first "suicide bomber" in literature. Suicide bombers are to this very day also considered heroes. By their own side.

The fact is that shortly afterwards, the Danites had to move from their territory. The place got too hot for them. That was perhaps one of the unintended consequences of Samson's behavior.

(For a comparison of Delilah's ethics with Jael's, see Chapter 1.)

Samson and Game Theory: The Alpha Male

Samson's quarrel with the Philistines is a feud, or a Tit-for-Tat series, which Game Theory[50] teaches us is not the worst strategy against an opponent, but neither is it the best.[51] A variety of strategies is best. But Samson was playing a zero-sum game (that is, "a situation in which a gain for one side entails a corresponding loss for the other side" [Webster's *New Collegiate Dictionary*])—as were the Israelites and other warriors in the book. The Holy War is a zero-sum game: the enemy must be *completely* annihilated. Samson wanted a huge profit, and zero for the enemy. "Most of life is a zero-sum game. Generally both sides can do well, or both can do poorly," writes Axelrod (110). But this idea did not enter Samson's head.

The Philistines had told the Judahites that they only wanted the *justice* of *lex talionis*: "to do to [Samson] as he did to us" (15.10), whereupon Samson gave an identical explanation for going berserk, "As they did to me, so I have done to them" (15.11). If they had stuck to this plan and let things go once the punishments were equal, things would have turned out differently. However, Samson never had a thought about *even-handedness* and *proportionality*.

Once started, the Tit-for-Tat system is poor strategy, as both parties feel they have justification on their side for whatever havoc they wreak. The stakes keep escalating. The Samson story is a perfect example of the continuing classic feud, in which there is no way out except the extermination of one or both of the feuders. To prevent this, one side must "cooperate" (that is, be "forgiving," and not insist on punishment of the other) at least once, preferably early in the game. This gives the opponent a chance to reduce the penalty as well.

The value of Game Theory has been brought to our attention by two recent Nobel Prize awards. In 1994, John Nash won the Nobel Prize in Economics for his contribution to Game Theory (Nash's Equilibrium), while in 2005, game theorists Robert J. Aumann and Thomas C. Schelling won the same prize for their addition to this theory—namely, that *each side must be a little bit forgiving. You may lose in the short term, but can win in the long term.* Advice that came a little too late for Samson. Of course, the danger of this advice is that the enemy will think your are "soft" and take advantage of you.

The reader might pause here to reflect on a modern day feud, Palestinians vs. Israelis in Israel. At this writing, whenever it looks as if this feud could draw to a close, some Samson rises and strikes again. Shibley Talhami, Anwar Sadat Professor of Peace and Development at the University of Maryland, recently spoke in just these terms: "The Palestinians and Israelites have played the tit-for-tat game for the last 20 years and each time end up worse than they were before. They have to cooperate, but won't unless someone on the outside intervenes."[52] The author of *Judges* understood the danger of feuding.[53]

The series of retaliations begin with the riddle at Samson's wedding feast. Since the Philistines cheated, Samson could have said, "No fair" and stomped off without paying. Samson, however, kept his word and gave his wedding companions their promised prizes. But his way of obtaining the prizes was intended to infuriate the Philistines in turn, and it did.

What is wrong is that Samson believes his opponent is out to get him, and he assumes that the opponent will always make the move he fears most—i.e., increase the stakes. This leads him never to "cooperate," but always to "defect"—that is, never to be forgiving but always to engage in behavior which is harmful to the opponent. This brings about unending punishment, says Axelrod.[54] Samson's tit-for-tat strategy is a perverse version of the gift-giving of the Kwakiutl, in which each gift had to be repaid with interest.[55] Repaying every blow given by the Philistines, he always increases the stakes with exorbitant "interest." His vendetta is a kind of negative potlatch, in which everything ultimately is destroyed.

In a computer simulation of game strategies, Axelrod found that "the player that scored the best was the one that was least forgiving—i.e., the one that employs permanent retaliation." (36). However,

> *if everyone else is using a strategy of always defecting, then a single individual can do no better than to use this same strategy* (116). Permanent retaliation may seem clever because it provides the maximum incentive to avoid defection [by the opponent]. *But it is too harsh for its own good* (122, italics mine).

The going got too rough. In the feud between Samson and the Philistines, neither side cooperated. "Once mutual recrimination sets in, it can be difficult to extract oneself" (34). And Samson did not want to extract himself. Neither side would let bygones be bygones, which would have brought an end to the feud. Both sides were totally unforgiving. In such a situation, neither dares to soften, for the danger of forgiving an opponent is that "you risk appearing to be exploitable" (117).

The hope of those who use the strategy of retaliation is that the opponent will either be completely destroyed or will give up and leave the territory. It might have worked had Samson's whole tribe been strong enough to engage in it successfully. But for a loner, the strategy is foolish: it can only lead to mutual harm. It should be remembered that the Israelites were forbidden by Yhwh to live alongside of the Philistines, and Samson was ignoring that charge. In the author's mind, compromise was not approved by Yhwh, and Samson, and anyway his tribe were presumably absolutists, as we learn from the Danites' behavior in the next story. What could have prevented the stalemate in Samson's case was negotiation and compromise, but Samson (like, or unlike, Jephthah) did not think of this. He was a man of action, not of words or reflection. His weapons were his hands.

One of the recommendations given by Axelrod to prevent such a series of retaliations is "to enlarge the shadow of the future" (126). This might be a good rationalization for the Judahites' behavior in handing Samson over to the Philistines—the shadow of the future has loomed over *them* because of his behavior.

At first, Samson gets what he wants: he is feared by the Philistines, and "the shadow of the future" also looms over *them*. His brawn brings Samson—the alpha male—status and women. He was taking away Philistine women. This would give the Philistines another reason to loathe him. According to anthropologists, there is intense antagonism between groups when men stay in their native bands while women migrate. "Where . . . a group of closely related men live together as a social unit . . . , feuding and raiding between groups is chronic," writes Matt Ridley.[56] It might also be argued that when the men of Gibeah in Ch. 19 form a coalition and steal the Concubine, they are behaving just like the bottlenose dolphins and the chimps that Ridley uses as examples: the males form alliances in order to kidnap the desired female (161-162). Seen as an archetypal pattern, the outrage of the Israelites in Chs. 20-21 that follows the rape of the Concubine is understandable, though pathetic.

Presumably, as an alpha male, Samson's selfish genes were at work,[57] but as far as we know, he had no offspring. The book would have told us had he had offspring, for it makes so much of offspring, and lack (or loss) of offspring elsewhere—of Gideon, Jephthah, and the minor judges. Nevertheless, if he is not helping his own genes, Samson is trying to help his tribe to satisfy *their* selfish genes. But in tribal situations, "to neutralize the power of an alpha male requires a large coalition," Ridley admits (160). Neither the Philistines nor Danites can manage it. Samson seems to be someone whom no brute force can conquer.

His remarkable successes up until his capture no doubt make him overconfident, and he begins to court greater and greater dangers. It would take the power of a woman to do him in. But he keeps up his high-stakes game until the very last, and his opponents never succeed in crushing him, though his game requires that he sacrifice himself in the process.

With this ancient model in mind, one wonders how the Palestinian/Israeli conflict will turn out in the present day. We incline toward pessimism. The upshot of the Samson's feud with the Philistines is that Samson's tribe left the territory.

The Danites in the Micah Story

(This was partially discussed in Chapter 2.)

Eventually, the tribe of Dan had to migrate to the north (Ch. 18). One infers that the Philistines were too much for them and that the Danites eventually lost the game that Samson had forced them to play. And so instead of being on the defensive, the Danites now became the invaders and marauders.

How do we judge the Israelites of that day? Are they entitled to a different ethics from that of the modern reader? Was extermination of the enemy a necessity? It might have been the only way to guarantee one's own safety.

It was a matter of survival. The Israelites believed that the land they were to possess had been promised them by Yhwh. The battles in *Judges*, beginning with Ehud's were defensive—battles against invaders—until we come to the Danites' migration in the next story. The modern reader studying ethics is stuck with a problem of immense importance. We understand the tribes' need for *lebensraum*, but do we have to view it as a theological "right"? Especially today, when we can see where this "promise" has led? And in this particular story, the author himself did not approve of the Danites' brutality. So should we?

In conquering the town of Laish, the Danites are bullies. (See short discussion of this under **Trust, Security, Prosperity** above.) We know this because the author gains our sympathy for Laish *3 different times* within a very short passage by telling us that it is a "quiet and unsuspecting [trusting] city far from help."

> [They] came to Laish, and saw the people who were there, how *they dwelt in safety,* like the Sidonians, *unsuspecting and secure,* lacking nothing on earth, and possessing wealth. Furthermore, they were far from the Sidonians and had no dealings with Aram [any one] (18.7).

> [The spies report back:] "Come, let us go up against them; for we have seen the land, and it is very good. Will you do nothing? Do not be slow to go, but enter in and possess the land. When you go, you will come to *an unsuspecting people.* The land is broad— [Elohim] has given it into your hands—a place where there is no lack of anything on earth" (NRS, 18.9-10).

The peacefulness and vulnerability of Laish is contrasted with the brutality of the heavily-armed Danites:

> the Danites . . . came to Laish, to a people *quiet and unsuspecting,* put them to the sword, and burned down the city [with fire]. And there was no deliverer because it was far from Sidon, and they had no dealings with Aram [any one] (NRS, 18.27-28).

That the Danites are after the wealth of the land may be viewed as a violation of Holy War, the rules of which were intended to remove greed, lust, and rapaciousness from the Israelites' conquest of Canaan. Cities devoted to the *ban* were not supposed to be occupied afterwards by the Israelites, yet the Danites not only rebuild Laish and live there, but it becomes one of the two great shrines of the north (Israel) where idolatrous golden calves were subsequently worshiped (1 Kg 12.29).

Whether or not the Danites ought to have practiced *herem* (the ban) on this occasion is under question because Holy War was only for the tribal territory allocated by Joshua, and Laish was apparently not what was allotted. Maybe the author thought they should have stayed where they belonged and driven out the Philistines rather than let the Philistines remain and continue to be a threat to Israel. As the Danites had learned, however, they could not live side by side with them. But if they had to go north, could they not have settled elsewhere in that "broad land" (ארץ רחבת ידים) (18.10)? Why pick out Laish? Like Lot, they wanted the best.

Readers are bothered that in this story and the next ones, the actions seem unworthy of a "holy people." Yet the actors "inquired" of Yhwh and got the go-ahead sign: the oracle of the Levite priest indicated that Yhwh has given his blessing, and the returning Danite spies state that "Yhwh has given [Laish] into [our] hands" (18.10). We are tempted to assume that the author thought Yhwh was behind them.

The Levite's oracle, however, when he is asked to inquire of Elohim, is like the oracle at Delphi, abstruse and noncommittal: "The journey which you go on is before (under) the eye of Yhwh" (18.6). This might be said of any act, good or bad. It might also be interpreted to mean: "Beware! Yhwh is watching you." We have to be careful about reading more into this than the oracle actually says. That the Danites entice the Levite priest to become their accomplice in their theft of the images discredits both them and the Levite. Because of the idols, the author may be suspicious of the Levite's power to know Yhwh's will.

But the two oracles are nevertheless disturbing. How do we know if Yhwh approves or disapproves of these actions? We are forced to weigh the evidence ourselves. This is a text book.

Parallels to this event are to be found in the story of the spies of Moses spying out the land (Deut 1.22 ff.; Num 13-14), in the conquest of Jericho (Josh 2 and 6), and in the story of Bethel-Luz at the beginning of *Judges* (1.22-26). Jericho and Luz seem to be cities rightfully designated in the Conquest of Israel. In both cases, leniency toward the families of the informers in both cities shows that the Israelites knew something about compassion (חסד) or at least about gratitude. In contrast, the Danite parallel shows the Danites as unfair and lacking in compassion in their conquest of Laish. It would seem that they were violating both law and ethics.

Earlier in the story, when Micah's priest and idols are stolen by the Danites, Micah does not get *revenge*. The theft of the idols was likely punishment for his sins: 1) He stole his mother's money. 2) He was under his mother's curse; and her immediate blessing of him did not avert the curse. 3) He worshiped the hateful idols. And 4) his idols did not save him.

Abimelech and Micah are the only two protagonists in these stories who are defeated. (Samson is defeated but ultimately conquers.) Abimelech broke civil laws; Micah broke commandments; Dan broke the Deuteronomic law of warfare. This may explain why the Micah story is placed close to the end of the book rather than directly after Abimelech, for Micah's crimes—though he was no fratricidal murderer—are crimes against the Israelite religion, and may thus be considered worse than Abimelech's.

For Micah, the outcome of the story is appropriate. What was stolen at the beginning of the story is stolen at the end. This just retribution forms a triangle with the just *retributions* of Adoni-Bezek in 1.7 and Abimelech in 9.66.

The Levite's Concubine

(See Chapters 1 and 2 and brief discussion above under **Vows**.)

The story of the Levite's Concubine and the civil war that follows is about the *vengeance* Israel takes against the tribe of Benjamin for the rape of the Concubine: "that they may do to Gibeah for all the outrage (הנבלה) that they did to Israel"

(20.10)—a deliberate echo of the words of just retribution quoted above of the Philistines and Samson (15.10-11). However, is this not also *excessive* punishment?—to destroy *all* the members of *1* tribe (except a mere 600, spared in a last-minute decision) in *retaliation* for the rape and murder (however horrible that is) of *1* Concubine? There is nothing "proportional" about that.

In a way, this is "trial by battle," the method resorted to when aggressors cannot be brought to justice in any other way, when the personal revenge system has broken down. Like the duel, Posner tells us, it is one of the intermediate stages in the evolution from revenge to public enforcement (57). (Posner, of course, makes no reference to *Judges*.) The danger of the revenge system is that a *miscalculation* of the enemy's strength may lead to civil war, and this one does. (Compare the problem of insurgency and the threat of civil war in the U.S. invasion of Iraq. A *miscalculation?*)

The rape of the Concubine is something like the rape and abduction of Helen in Greek legend. The war that ensues in each case is meant to teach a lesson for all time: a wife or concubine is the property of her husband or master. No man can violate this relationship without bringing on himself the wrath of the entire society. Steven Pinker in his discussion of war in *How the Mind Works*, writes:

> But one motive that is surprising to Westerners appears over and over. In foraging societies, *men go to war to get or keep women*—not necessarily as a conscious goal of the warriors (though often it is that), but as the ultimate payoff that allowed a willingness to fight to evolve . . . . *The desire for women not only helps to fuel blood feuds; it also helps to spark them in the first place.* Usually the first killing was over a woman: a man seduces or abducts someone's wife, or reneges on a deal to trade a daughter. (Emphasis mine.)[57]

Examples from the Bible of men going to war for women that he cites are: Num 31.7, 15, 17-19, Deut 20.10, 12-14, and Deut 21.10-14. Women are essential to male reproductive success, and in those days men simply went out and seized them.

This is the explanation of the Rape of the Sabine women. According to Roman legend, the problem arose that there were no women for the Romans to marry. When Romulus sent out envoys asking for *ius conubii* (right to intermarry), all envoys were refused. Then Romulus invited all the local peoples, including the Sabines, to the Consualia, a festival of games. While the games were in progress, Roman youth dashed out and seized the Sabine maidens. Romulus' explanation was that the rape came about "owing to the pride of their parents in denying right of intermarriage to their neighbors."[58] Is this not what the fathers in *Judges* had done? And then changed their minds about, and permitted—instead of abhorring—the rape and also at a festival?

Laws had to be devised to prevent this from happening again. Were the virgins of Jabesh-Gilead and the daughters of Shiloh "willing," as so many interpreters seem to think?

A classical example of unwilling brides is *The Suppliant Maidens* by Aeschylus (463 BCE). In the first play of the trilogy, the 50 maidens fled to Argos rather than marry the sons of Egypt. The city of Argos sheltered them. In the remaining plays of the trilogy, which are lost, they are forced to marry against their will. They vow to kill their husbands and do. But one of the daughters spares her husband and is brought to trial. Aphrodite acquits her, testifying to the sacredness of love and marriage. What is interesting about this is the sympathy for the maidens and the extremity to which they will go to avoid being married against their will. We must not imagine that the 600 Israelite maidens were ecstatically happy about their arranged marriages.

Although I discussed the comedy side of this scene in Chapter Two, the series of stories about fathers and daughters shown in **Table VII** of Chapter One tells another story. The series of disposals of the daughter by their father has the same pattern as all the other parallels: a downward motion. Achsah, we may assume, was a happy bride, despite the fact that her father's offering of her on the auction block can also be seen as discreditable (a rash vow). Jephthah's daughter is offered to Yhwh as a burnt offering. She was murdered. Samson's wife, first given to Samson and then given to one of the wedding guests, has two husbands, the first of which she possibly chose herself, but the second of which was her father's decision, and it led to her death by fire. In the story of the Levite's Concubine, we have a "lesser" kind of marriage, in which the negligence of both the husband and the father put her in danger, and whose husband throws her out to the dogs, who gang-rape her and kill her. Finally, the women of Jabesh-Gilead and Shiloh aren't even offered by their fathers. The women's families and a whole town are utterly destroyed, and the daughters of Shiloh are not "taken" (לקח) but "seized" 21.21 (חטף). Whereas the Concubine had "known a man"—i.e., she was married—these women are only girls. Because of the pattern set up by the author, of the downward progression of all the stories, this story represents the nadir. The terrible wound between the tribes has been patched up, but as subsequent stories in 1 and 2 Samuel and beyond prove, the wound never fully healed.

The Rape of the Sabine Women has been painted numerous times, notably by Poussin, Rubens, and Picasso. Picasso's portrays real horror, the kind that he depicts in *Guernica*. Poussin's gains pathos by depicting aged parents trying desperately to wrestle their terrified daughters from the rapists. These scenes may be said to depict as well the abduction of the daughters of Shiloh. It is not a pretty picture.

VII. Conclusion

Literary criticism has always involved criticism of moral and ethical issues. Artists are different from philosophers or ethicists in that they conjure up human situations in which philosophy and ethics can be embodied. The greatest literature is often that which is also able to handle the greatest complexity.

When we begin to realize that we are investigating "cases," somewhat like law cases, we cannot but conclude that the author of *Judges* sees everything as relative, that behavior is good or bad only by comparison with the good or bad behavior of others.

Yhwh's priority is seen to hold the tribes together. The tenor of the book is that anything that destroyed unity would be wrong. Would the tribes have tried to annihilate each other if they had been acting in good faith? Clearly the Benjaminites had done wrong, they were recalcitrant, they would not deliver up the offenders, and so there was no option but to punish the whole tribe. But was civil war the answer? According to MacIntrye, "Both Plato and Aristotle treat conflict as an evil and Aristotle treats it as an eliminable evil . . . . Civil war is the worst of evils" (147).

Possibly the most important themes of the book are the need for self-defense and the horror of war. And this will continue to be the case in the future. Little by little, things go from bad to worse. The people could not rule themselves, and all ended in a full-scale civil war. For, in Bacon's phrase (which Jacoby uses for the title of her book), "Revenge is a kind of wild justice, which the more man's nature runs to, the more ought law to weed out."

Judges demonstrates how urgently these people needed a rule of law to take vengeance out of their own hands and vest it in the hands of some recognized authority who could act for all the tribes together. How this stage was reached in Greece is shown by Aeschylus in his *Eumenides*, when the Greeks turn to Athena to render judgment on Orestes, thus ending the system of feuds.

The idea of avenging a wrong done to oneself or one's people is an accepted part of the system that the author is showing. Yet human beings are shown as often going overboard in getting *revenge* and even Yhwh does not always mete out proportional *retribution*. Yet by the system of parallel stories and their successive outcomes, the author shows the need for proportionality in dealing out punishments. In this, the author is perhaps ahead of his times, as the idea of proportional retribution did not enter modern thinking fully, until after the Enlightenment (Jacoby 132), and in some cases, not until the latter half of the twentieth century. One of the lessons Robert McNamara learned from his years as Secretary of Defense during the Vietnam War was "Proportionality should be a guideline for war."[59] It is not clear whether this lesson will ever be heeded.

At this point, the best system of government for the Israelites seemed to be a monarchy. The stories show why the experiment in monarchy came about. As the author predicted when he showed the weaknesses (deadly sins) of his heroes and the tribes, this too would fail.

In addition to being an allegory about Israel (see Chapters 1 and 6), the stories are negative examples, cautionary tales, from which the future kings and leaders of the nation could learn lessons about law, ethics, and human behavior.

One is tempted to believe that the book might have been written to educate a king, perhaps David himself.

What kind of ruler did Israel need?

Appendix. Conditional and Cause/Effect Sentences

Closely related to *vows, oaths,* and *promises* are *conditional statements* (if . . .). The *conditional* statement is a *promise* with a *condition* attached, but without the use of the word *vow, oath, swear, or promise.* In *conditional statements,* according to Greenbaum's *Oxford English Grammar,* "the host clause is dependent upon the fulfillment of the condition in the conditional clause."[60] In other words, in a conditional statement, if the *condition* is *not* fulfilled, then the *promise* is null and void. Some conditional statements, it should be added, are threats.

Jacob *vowed a vow* (already quoted above): "If Yhwh will be with me, and will keep me . . . and give me bread . . . and clothing . . . and bring me home . . . then Yhwh will be my Elohim" (Gen.28.20-21). This is clearly conditional. In our thinking today, vows are not necessarily conditional, but according to Cartledge, biblical vows are (12).

Cause-and-effect and *if . . . then* statements are closely related to conditional statements when they express consequences of actions. It is sometimes hard to distinguish between conditionals and cause-and-effect. (In some grammars, all *if* [adverbial] clauses are classified as conditional.)

The *if . . . then* statement may give a future sequence of events: B is not *caused* by A, but follows A. An example of this would be: "If there is dew on the wool, then I shall know . . . ." The dew does not *cause* anything; it is simply a sign. These are incidentally indications neither of free will nor determinism.

At least two "*if*" statements in *Judges* also are *contrary-to-fact.*

These sentences are important to the subject of judgments, though the sentences are difficult to analyze from this point of view.

Deborah

1. "if you will go with me, I will go, if not, then I will not (4.8)." (*Conditional.*) Barak was wrong to impose this condition on Deborah, since the command to go to battle was from Yhwh. He must have thought he could not win without her.

2. "if anyone . . . asks you . . . , say no" (4.20). (*If . . . then.*) Sisera is imposing a condition, but Jael did not promise, and she did not obey. She cannot be said to have "disobeyed," either—as she was under no obligation to obey a guest in her house. Sisera was not her master. He mistakenly thought she was a willing accomplice. Or was he used to commanding—troops and women—and not used to being defied? Or did the relationship between Heber and Jabin imply not only loyalty but obedience? Perhaps women were supposed to obey men, no matter who the men were. This we do not know.

Gideon

All the following "if" clauses are *if . . . then,* except the last one, which is *contrary-to-fact.* Most of them show uncertainty or cowardice.

1. "if I have found favor with you, then show me a sign" (6.17). This is something of an inverted *conditional,* in which the speaker tries to elicit the following promise from Yhwh:"I will give you a sign to show that you have found favor with me (Yhwh)."

2. "if he is a god, [then] let him contend (רֹיב) for himself"—i.e., let him conduct his own law case (6.31). This is Joash's method of determining a theological question.

3. "if you will save Israel by my hand, then [give me a sign]" (6.36). This suggests hesitation in Gideon's making a choice.

4. "if there is dew on the wool, . . . then I shall know . . . (6.37), and if it is dry on the wool, etc." (6.39).

5. "if you lap like a dog, you will be chosen to fight" (7.5). This is "descriptive": i.e., those who lap like a dog will be chosen.

6. "if you fear, then go down to the camp with Purah" (7.10). Since Gideon did go down with Purah, we can assume he was afraid.

7. "if you had saved them alive, I would not kill you" (8.19). This *contrary-to-fact* sentence can be seen as "past" *conditional*. Since they had not saved them (Gideon's brothers), Zebah and Zalmunna were killed.

Jotham's fable in the Abimelech story

Jotham's four "*if . . . then*" statements are predictions about what will follow *from the choices made*. In each of his statements, the individual has free will, whether to anoint someone as king or not, and take the consequence of his choice:

1. "if you are anointing me king, [then] take refuge in my shade . . ." (9.15).

2. "if not . . . [then] . . ." (9.15).

3. "If you have acted in truth and integrity [תֹמִים] with Jerubbaal and his house, then rejoice in Abimelech and let him rejoice in you" (9.19).

4. "if not, [then] let fire come from Abimelech and consume the citizens; and let fire come from the citizens and consume Abimelech" (9.20). This is the curse; it takes effect immediately, for Yhwh sends an "evil spirit" to breed discord between Abimelech and the lords of Shechem. This in turn leads to Abimelech's downfall and the destruction of the city. Yhwh does not cause this. As Jotham points out, the faulty choice of the Shechemites causes it.

Jephthah

1. "if Yhwh gives the Ammonites to me, I shall be your head." Jephthah is asking the elders for confirmation. In some translations, the "host" clause (see Greenbaum, above) is a question (11.9): "Will I be your head?" *Conditional.*

2. "if we do not . . . , Yhwh witness among us." (11.10). *Conditional* or *cause-and-effect*

3. "if [since] you have given your word, [then] do to me according to your words . . ." (11.36). *Cause-and-effect.* Jephthah's daughter acknowledges that her father must take responsibility for his freely-given vow.

Samson

#1-2 of the following are *conditional*; the rest are *if . . . then (cause-and-effect)*; #11 is *contrary-to-fact*:

1. The messenger-angel puts demands on Samson: that "he will be a Nazirite until the day

of his death" (implying the following taboos for himself, including the taboo against touching a dead body), that his mother shall not eat wine or strong drink or eat unclean food, and that no razor shall touch his head, (13.5, 7). No condition, promise, reward, or consequence is attached. Actually, as it turns out, there is a condition, meaning that *if* he does not keep these commands, something dire may happen. We cannot, however, tell if his weakness is purely psychological, if it was caused by the shaving of his head, or if it was punishment for philandering with the enemy.

2. "coax your husband to explain the riddle to you, or we will burn down you and your father's house" (14.15). This is a *condition* (threat): "If you do not do this, we will burn down . . . ."

3. "if you can declare [the riddle], [then] I will give you . . ." (14.12). This is a *promise*.

4. but if you cannot . . . , [then] you shall give me . . ." (14.13). A *demand*.

5. "if they bind me, [then] I shall become weak" (16.7). *Cause-and-effect.*

6. "if they bind me with new ropes, [then] I shall become weak" (16.11). *Cause-and-effect.*

7. "if you weave the locks of my head . . . , [then] I shall become weak . . ." (16.13). *Cause-and-effect.*

8. "if I am shaved, [then] my strength will leave me" (16.17). *Cause-and-effect.*

9. "if you detain me, [then] I will not eat your food, but if you want to prepare an offering, [then] offer it to Yhwh" (13.16). *Cause-and-effect.*

10. "if Yhwh meant to kill us, [then] he would not have accepted [the offering] . . ." (13.23). *Cause-and-effect* and *contrary-to-fact.*

11. "if you had not plowed with my heifer, [then] you would not have found out my riddle" (14.18). (*Contrary-to-fact* but expressed positively, *cause-and-effect.*)

Micah

This story has two *cause-and-effect* statements; the first is a *promise*, the second is a *threat*:

1. "[if] you dwell with me, [then] I shall give you ten pieces of silver" (17.10).

2. "[if] you raise your voice, [then] angry men will attack you" (18.25).

Levite's Concubine (*If . . . then*)

1. "if their fathers or brothers complain, [then] we will say . . ." (21.22). Here's a clear-cut example of the host clause being inoperative if the condition is not met.

Cause-and-effect and *if . . . then* statements are included in this study of the development of law and the category of Promises because some do show consequences, and others show some kind of manipulation of one person (or god) by another and thus are evidence that the author is thinking in terms of "free" will. In some conditional statements, A *will* bring about B. An example of this is "if you will go with me, I will go." This seems to be a promise. The distinguishing feature is whether or not a promise is being made.

There may be more to these conditional statements than I have been able to determine. I relegate them to the unsolved parts of the puzzle of the book.

Chapter Five

SUBMERGED UGARITIC MYTHS IN *JUDGES*

Myth is what we call other people's religion.   —Joseph Campbell

I. Introduction

One of the most amazing archeological finds of the 20th Century was the discovery of thousands of "Canaanite"[1] clay tablets from the ancient city of Ugarit at Ras Shamra, Syria, in 1928. The tablets had been inscribed in a then-unknown cuneiform script concerning all kinds of government, business, and social information with eight languages represented.[2] They continue to be found, even recently. Most of the Ugaritic tablets derive from the last fifty years of the existence of the city before it was destroyed by the "Sea People" between 1200 and 1175 BCE.[3] At that time, a dispersion of refugees doubtless occurred, with some refugees possibly going as far away as Israelite territory and taking their myths with them.

In 1931 a collection of these myths was uncovered. The tablets containing the myths, when deciphered, were found to be written in the Northwest Semitic, a close kin of Biblical Hebrew. Most of them date from about 1350 BCE.

The stories in *Judges*, though probably not written down until the period of the late monarchy or after, are believed to be laid in the premonarchical period of approximately 1250-1020 BCE, and as folktales, they originated then and were perhaps being transmitted orally by storytellers as early as 1000 BCE. This is approximately the time when the city of Ugarit was destroyed.

Many traces of the myths have been detected in the Bible and are evidence that Israel and Ugarit have a common linguistic lineage and—at least in some respects— a shared literary heritage. As Jonas Greenfield believes, many Israelite literary traditions and rituals were shared by a number of sites, including Ugarit, Tyre, Ashkelon, Shechem, and Jerusalem.[4] Greenfield writes:

> . . . there can be no doubt that similar myths, epics and tales, as well as hymns and prayers circulated in both oral and written form throughout Canaan proper not only in the Late Bronze Age, but also in the Iron Age, that is, from 1400-600 B.C.E., a period of

a thousand years. We may also assume that the various cities also had variant versions, using different words and phrases and on occasion crediting different gods with the same deeds.[5]

As Smith comments in *Origins*,

> . . . ancient Ugaritic and early Israelite literatures were not completely different, especially in the general parameters of language, social structure, religious terminology, and religious practices (prayer, sacrifice, and religious experience), and even conceptualizations of divinity. [Israel's] monotheism emerged only midway through Israel's history. It was heir and reaction to a long tradition of Israelite polytheism (17).

And Baruch Margalit writes,

> Ugaritic literature is indeed 'Canaanite literature' . . . the origins of the mythological and Ugaritic literary traditions we call 'Ugaritic' lie in northern Canaan and Transjordania (Bashan/Golan) and not in northern Syria . . . [and] the language we call '(literary) Ugaritic' was that spoken in Ashtaroth and Edrei around 1500 BCE.[6]

Because of the references to the region of the Galilee in the Ugaritic story of *Aqhat*, Margalit believes that it was composed by an author living in the Transjordan: it is *Aqhat* "which reveals the closest affinity with the literary corpus of the O.T., [and it is] nearly certain . . . that it alone was known in one form or another to the Israelites of the Iron Age" (489-90). Upon closer examination, we can uncover many other traces of this pre-Israelite mythic material in the Hebrew Scriptures.

For these reasons alone—the date, the language and style, the manifest connections between their religions, the possibility of communication between the two peoples, and the shared material in the Bible—Ugaritic literature continues to be closely examined by scholars to determine what influence it had upon the Israelite religion and literature.

Because the dating of the Ugaritic texts is separated from the *composition* of the Bible by perhaps even as much as a millennium, it should be kept in mind that the beliefs of the "Canaanites" in Ugarit or the Transjordan may have differed somewhat from those of the Canaanites living in Israel when the stories of *Judges* were orally composed and at a much later time when they were put into writing. The reason the Ugaritic myths are so important is that except for *Enuma Elish* and *Gilgamesh*, they are the only extant evidence of a pre-Israelite religion that is extensive.

Whatever we find when we compare and contrast both sets of narratives may improve our knowledge about the meaning of the stories in *Judges*.

Date and authorship of the Ugaritic poems

Before the discovery of the Ugaritic texts, the little that was known about Canaanite myth and religion came from the writings of Sanchuniathon, the author of *Phoenician History*. Although this work is no longer extant, fragments of it are found in Eusebius' *Preparation for the Gospel* (315 CE). According to Porphyry of Syria (133-204 CE), whom Eusebius quotes, Sanchuniathon lived in the time of Semiramis (who reigned from 810-805 BCE) and collected his stories from ancient history because of his "love of truth." With the discovery of the Ugaritic texts, it became evident that Sanchuniathon's work was more reliable than had earlier been thought.[7]

Curiously enough, whereas most of the biblical books are anonymous, a number of the Ugaritic texts were signed by the name Ilimilku (Elimelek). Ilimilku was not merely a scribe or compiler, but a creative author with a style of his own.[8] The other poems are anonymous.

II. The Canaanite Gods and the Ugaritic Myths

First, we must identify the gods and goddesses and summarize the content of the Ugaritic tales. Further details will be supplied along with the arguments for the influence of this literature on *Judges*.

The gods

El is called "the Bull," "the kindly one," "Latipan" (or "Benevolent," "Compassionate"), "King," "the Creator and Lord of the Gods," He is the father of the gods and of all created things, the "Father of Years," and "Ancient of Days"—all epithets of the Hebrew Yhwh Elohim. He is depicted in some of the poems as old (with a beard) and wise, impotent (but not sexually impotent) and remote, yet deferred to by the other gods. He lives at the source of the two rivers. Baruch Margalit identifies his abode as Mt. Hermon (430, 473).

Baal, or Hadad, called Aliyn Baal ("Almighty Lord"), "our King and Judge," is the storm god and "Rider on the Clouds," wielder of lightning, bringer and withholder of rain. Baal is also called "Savior," "Healer,"[9] and "Judge." He represents the realm of earth. Although he is the son of Dagon and is an outsider to the pantheon, in some texts he also seems to be the son of El.[10] He and his sister Anat are the beloved of each other. Baal is killed more than once but rises again. He dwells on Mt. Zephon (Saphon, Sapon), which can be identified as Mt. Casius, the highest mountain in Syria.[11] He is the patron of the city of Ugarit.

Yam (the Hebrew word for *sea*), a son of El and Athirat, is called "Prince Sea," but he is also "Judge Nahar" (River). At the beginning of the cycle, El has granted him his own palace—in the sea. When in conflict with Baal, he is a dragon or seven-headed sea monster. At first Baal is his slave and is defeated by him. Eventually Yam is killed once by Baal and once by Anat. He is equated with Poseidon and Neptune.

Mot (the Hebrew word for *death*) lives in the miry underworld in filth. He represents the realm of death. He swallows Baal with his large gaping maw, but "never in the Ugaritic texts is divine death a permanent condition . . ." (Smith, *Origins*, 98). Eventually Mot is slain by Baal and confined to the underworld.

Dagon, apparently the god of grain, is the father of Baal, but he is not a character in any of the myths, though Ugarit had a temple of Dagon.[12]

Athirat (Asherah) is the consort of El. She is called "She who Treads on the Sea," "the Creatress of the Gods," and "the Queen of Heaven," and is identified with

Tanith (the Serpent Lady) in other cultures. She is also identified as Havah (Eve). She and El have 70 or more sons (including Yam and Mot, but not Baal), who are eventually killed by Baal. In the Hebrew Bible she is (mistakenly) regarded as the consort of Baal. In a 10th-8th century BCE Israelite inscription, she seems to be the consort of Yhwh. She does not live with El, but by the sea.

Anat, the virgin (or "Adolescent"),[13] represents warfare and fertility. She is called "the Mistress of the Gods," "Wanton Widow" (de Moor 8), "in-law of the nations,"[14] or "sister-in-law of peoples." (In one poem on a rampage of slaughter, she wears a necklace of human heads and a belt of human hands. "She revels in destruction for its own sake."[15] A sister of Baal, she may have been his consort, though this idea has been challenged.[16] She will fight fiercely for her brother Baal and ultimately will slay Yam and Mot. She lives on a mountain called Ughar and Inbar (an unknown place).

Athtart (Ashtart, Astarte, Ashtoreth), "Name of Baal," a goddess of love, fertility, and warfare, is sister of Anat and also a warrior. She is often identified with both Aphrodite and Ishtar. She too was sometimes thought to have been the consort of Baal (Gibson 4, n. 6), but not in these myths. In the Bible she is called Ashtoreth and is conjectured to be the "Queen of Heaven" in Jeremiah (Day 148). She is only a minor figure in the myths.

Athtar, El's son, is given the throne of El for a time, but being found unfit for the position, is removed and Yam installed instead.

The content of the major poems

Baal and Yam[17] concerns the battle between these two gods. With the help of his marvelous clubs, Baal defeats Yam and becomes king.

The Palace of Baal. Baal wants his own palace so that he no longer has to live with El. Athirat (Asherah), the foe of Baal, is persuaded to get permission from El for Baal to build a palace. (Gibson says this is "a foundation myth of Baal's temple at Ugarit" [14].) When it is built by the craftsman Kothar-and-Khasis, it has a window of singular import. Anat is shown in her bloodthirsty career of slaughter. Baal recklessly invites Mot to visit his new palace.

Baal and Mot concerns the rivalry between these two gods. Shapash (the moon goddess), knowing that Mot is out to enslave Baal, encourages Baal to procure a substitute and to hide in the underworld among the dead. Before he departs, Baal conceives an offspring, a boy, from a heifer in the fields, whom he offers to Mot. Anat scours the earth and then finds her brother's substitute, dead. Anat, El, and all the gods mourn. For a time Athtar (son of El and Athirat) rules but is ineffectual and is deposed. Eventually Anat cleaves Mot with a sword, burns him, and scatters ("winnows") him. El dreams that Baal is still alive. Eventually Baal is restored, and Mot and Baal meet in single combat. Mot loses the battle. Baal kills the 70 sons of Athirat.

Aqhat is about a mortal named Danel who, through the help of El, was enabled to have a son, Aqhat. Anat covets Aqhat's miraculous bow, but Aqhat refuses to give it up. At the behest of Anat, her henchman Yatpan kills Aqhat. Pughat, Aqhat's sister, disguises herself and visits Yatpan for revenge. Here the poem breaks off, but it is likely that Pughat kills Yatpan. Both Danel and Keret are called "men of Rephaim." Who the Rephaim are is not known; they may be "dead and deified kings," or "legendary heroes" of semi-divine origin, perhaps connected with the "sons of God" in Gen 6.1-4 (del Olmo Lete 326) or "living members of the aristocracy," etc.[18] Margalit believes that the story shows the author's contempt for Anat and those devoted to her warlike ways (487).

Keret is about a mortal king, called a "son of El," who is childless. Through the help of El, he procures a son, Yassib, and other offspring. He becomes ill, his authority is challenged by Yassib, and the poem ends with Keret cursing his son. Del Olmo Lete calls it "a 'sacred history' or ancestral history, intended to preserve the memory of the origins of the royal dynasty" (330). Margalit thinks that this story is a parody of the notion of divine kingship.[19] De Moor calls it "a protest against the current concepts of divine rule" (*The Rise of Yahwism 95*). Wyatt thinks it possible that the text is "discrediting one king in order to legitimize his successor" (Wyatt, *Religious Texts*, 243, n. 298).

Shachar and Shalim and the Gracious Gods and *Nikkal and the Kotharat* are marriage poems. The main theme of the myths is the conflict among the gods to determine who shall be the king of them all. It is the family of El vs. the assembly of Baal.

III. The Hebrew Bible and the Canaanite Religion

According to the stories in the Bible, the Israelites left Canaan and lived for more than four hundred years as slaves in Egypt, having taken with them the god of Abraham, Isaac, and Jacob, a god known as El Shaddai (El the Almighty), El Olam (El, the Eternal One), and El Berit (El of the Covenant). By the time they returned to Canaan, they had become monotheists, and began to call Elohim by the name traditionally given by him to Moses, *Yhwh*. All the above epithets of Yhwh Elohim are also epithets of the Canaanite El, and very likely derived from him.

Considerable doubt has been raised about the historicity of this version, as well as of the Exodus story and the Conquest.[20] It now seems likely that the people called Israelites never left Canaan at all. Perhaps consisting in part of *habiru*—the "uprooted elements" or "social outcasts"[21] mentioned in the *Amarna Letters* and referred to in some of the Ugaritic texts—the Israelites in fact were in all likelihood indigenous, sharing with others the Canaanite religion, a belief system similar to that found in the Ugaritic myths, in which El was the king or head of the pantheon, and Baal Hadad, a younger rival and contender for the throne.

In any case, El was the god of the Patriarchs, as is indicated by the name *Israel*, which contains the divine name El, not Yhwh. Smith and other scholars conjecture "that El may have been the original god connected with the Exodus from Egypt and that the event was secondarily associated with Yahweh when the two gods coalesced" (Smith *Origins* 141, 142, 146).

Introduction of Yhwh to the Canaanites; his likeness to El and Baal

At some point, a new god, Yhwh was introduced by a group of people coming from the south, as a passage from *The Song of Deborah* attests:

> "Yhwh, when you went out from Seir, when *you marched* from the region of Edom, *the earth trembled, and the heavens poured, the clouds indeed poured water. The mountains quaked before Yhwh*, the One of Sinai, before the Yhwh Elohim of Israel" (5.4-5, itals. mine).

The italicized phrases show the similarity of Yhwh to Baal. One theory of the origin of the Israelite religion is that the people coming from Edom and Sinai with their god Yhwh had had a liberation experience resembling that of the Israelites' liberation from Persia after the Exile.[22] After the Return from the Exile, these two experiences were combined in the somewhat fictitious story of the Exodus as a "charter myth,"[23] created to inspire and unify what was left of the tribal confederation after the return from Babylon. The Exodus story, believes Allan Rosengren Petersen, was created "to give identity to a group of exiled 'Canaanites', or Israelites, and to justify their territorial demands in Palestine."[24] And Thomas L. Thompson believes that the redactors of the Persian period created the story from "fragments of memory: written and oral, chains of narrative, complex literary works, administrative records, etc." The Babylonian exile is "the governing principle . . . . 'Radical trauma of exile is used as a literary paradigm in terms of which both newly-formed tradition and its collectors acquired identity as Israel.'"[25] Monotheism itself, believes Mark S. Smith, was not developed until the Exile, or slightly earlier.[26] Polytheism continued for a long time.

De Moor has discovered a scenario of a possible Exodus-like experience of a small group from Egypt, which occurred at the end of the 13th century under a "chancellor" Beya, an Israelite who served Queen Tausret. He identifies Beya as Moses and Queen Tausret as perhaps Miriam. The gods of that time were Seth (equated with Baal) and Amon-Re (with attributes similar to those of Yhwh/El). After a change of dynasties, Beya and Tausret fled, eventually arrived in the Transjordan, and joined Beya's kinsmen in Bashan. This would be the origin of the Exodus story. Though not even Moses was a monotheist at that time, "the other gods had a reduced status" for him. De Moor conjectures that these proto-Israelites became strict Yahwists only after the Israelites were dislodged by the Sea-Peoples (*The Rise of Yahwism* 214-244 et passim; also 372-373). (Discussions of De Moor's speculations can be found on Internet.)

It seems clear now that Yhwh as a god was fashioned, at least in part, out of the Canaanite gods El and Baal. In his ground-breaking book *Canaanite Myth and Hebrew Epic* (1973), Frank Moore Cross wrote:

> Yahwism also owes a debt to the myths of Baal. In the earliest poetic sources the language depicting Yhwh as divine warrior manifest is borrowed almost directly from Canaanite descriptions of the theophany of Baal Hadad as storm god.[27]

And Patrick D. Miller writes:

> Yahweh came into existence as a worshiped deity out of the world of the gods with discernable antecedents, so we may speak of Yahweh as coming out of the gods and the

divine world of Canaan . . . . [But] we may also recognize that the gods are present in Yahweh . . . [and that there is a] *conflictual relation between Yahweh and the gods* . . . .

The characteristics of Yhwh, like those of the Canaanite El, include

El's compassion and wisdom, being divine judge and head of the divine council as well as creator and father, El's kingship, his tent and cherubim throne, to name some of the major shared elements. So also were fundamental dimensions of the god Baal basic to Yahweh. The patterns and motifs of Baal as storm god who rides the clouds and whose theophany has such powerful effects on the natural world were present in [Yahweh]. The imagery of Yahweh as the divine warrior reflected the character of El and other gods and goddesses, but most particularly Baal . . . .[28]

Marjo Korpel estimates that "fifty percent of all terms describing the gods and their world in the Ugaritic literature is also used to describe Yhwh and his entourage in the Old Testament" (cited by de Moor, *Rise of Yahwism* 111-112). In *Judges* 5.4-5 (quoted above), Yhwh is like Baal, a warrior marching, causing a downpour.

Psalm 68, the first part of which is one of the oldest writings of the Hebrew Bible,[29] contains a number of descriptions of Yhwh Elohim that are identical to those of El and Baal of the Canaanite religion. In it,

Elohim is called El-Shaddai (El the Almighty, or El of the mountain) (Ps 68.14)

his home is on a high mountain (like El and Baal) (Ps 68.15, 16, 18)

he is the Divine Warrior, lord of vast (רב) "hosts" (צבא), Yhwh Sabaoth (usually translated "God Almighty" but means "God of Armies" Ps 68.7, 11, 12)

he marches with his tens of thousands of chariots (Baal also has chariotry) (Ps 68.17)

he brings back captives from the depths of the sea (as Baal conquers Yam) and spoil (Ps 68.12, 18)

he rides upon the clouds (Baal is called "Rider of the Clouds" at least 12 times in the myths) (Ps 68.4, 33);

he thunders and casts lightning (Ps 68.8, 9, 33)

rain and snow fall when Yhwh (like Baal) comes (Ps 68.8, 9, 14)

he shatters heads and spills blood (like Baal and Anat) (Ps 68.21, 23)

In the lines of Ps 68 below, similarities with the Ugaritic gods are in italics:

[4]Sing to Elohim, sing praises to his name; lift up a song to him *who rides upon the clouds*—his name is Yhwh—be exultant before him.

[7]O Elohim, when you went out before your people, when *you marched* through the wilderness, Selah . . . .

[8]*the earth quaked, the heavens poured down rain* at the presence of Elohim, the One of Sinai, at the presence of Elohim, Elohim of Israel.

[9] *Rain in abundance, O Elohim, you showered abroad;* you restored your heritage when it languished . . . .

[11]Yhwh gives the command; *great is the host* of those who bore the tidings;

[12]"The kings of the armies, they flee, they flee!" The women at home *divide the spoil* . . . .

[14]When *Shaddai scattered kings* there, *snow fell on Zalmon.*

[15]O *mighty mountain*, mountain of Bashan; O many-peaked mountain, mountain of Bashan!

[16]Why do you look with envy, O many-peaked mountain, at *the mount that Elohim desired for his abode*, where *Yhwh will reside forever?*

[17]With *mighty chariotry, twice ten thousand, thousands upon thousands*, Adonai [another name for Yhwh] came from Sinai into the holy place.

[18]You ascended the *high mount, leading captives* in your train and receiving gifts from people, even from those who rebel against Yhwh Elohim's abiding there.

[21]But Elohim will *shatter the heads of his enemies*, the hairy crown of those who walk in their guilty ways.

[22]Adonai said, "I will bring them back from Bashan, I will *bring them back from the depths of the sea,*

[23]so that you may *bathe your feet in blood*, so that the tongues of your dogs may have their share from the foe."

[33]O *rider in the heavens*, the ancient heavens; listen, *he sends out his voice, his mighty voice.*

(See also Ps18.8-16; 77.17-20; and 97.1-5.) As de Moor puts it, Yhwh-El had "usurped" the attributes of Baal in the Transjordan and elsewhere, just as Baal had assumed El's attributes farther north (*The Rise of Yahwism* 208).

Bashan—roughly the Golan Heights, in the northern Transjordan east of the Kinnereth (the Sea of Galilee) and occupied by the half-tribe of Manasseh—seems a strange place for Yhwh's residence (for Yhwh is a southern god associated with Edom and Sinai), but not strange if the psalm originally was about Baal, a northern god.

Zalmon, its location unknown but possibly near Mt. Hermon (Margalit, *The Ugaritic Poem of Aqht* 473), was like Zaphon (a Hebrew word meaning *north*), the dwelling place of Baal. This was taken over by Yhwh-El (de Moor, ibid. 169).

The first part of *Psalm* 68 has been thought by some to be a Canaanite hymn transformed into an Israelite one. Others who do not accept the Ugaritic origin of Yhwh's characteristics regard *Psalm* 68 as an Israelite *imitation* of a Canaanite hymn intended as polemic against Baal, one that tells who the *real* rider of the clouds is. This interpretation, however, does not alter the fact that the attributes of Yhwh-Elohim are the same as those of El and Baal. It seems apologetic.

Other similarities

Other likenesses between the Israelite depictions of their god and the Canaanite gods include:

1)   Both Baal and Yhwh are enthroned. In the following Ugaritic hymn Baal is described flashing out lightning, thundering, and pouring out snow and water:

Baal sits like the base of a mountain;
Hadd se[ttles] as the ocean,

in the midst of his divine mountain, Saphon,
in [the midst of] the mountain of victory.

Seven lightning-flashes [   ],
eight bundles of thunder,

a tree-of-lightning [in his] right hand,

His head is magnificent,
His brow is dew-drenched.
His feet are eloquent in (his) wrath.

[His] horn is [exalted].
His head is in the snows in heaven,
[with the god there is abounding water.]
His mouth is like two clouds [   ],
[his lips] like wine from jars,
his heart [   ] (KTU 1.101, Wyatt *Religious Texts*, 388-389).

Notice the striking similarity to Baal in Ps 18.8-16, and also in Ps 29, one of the enthronement psalms, where Yhwh is depicted as king after a victory over the waters, flashing out lightning and shaking the landscape:

[3]The voice of Yhwh is over the waters; the God of glory thunders, the Yhwh, over mighty waters.

[4]The voice of Yhwh is powerful; the voice of Yhwh is full of majesty.

[5]The voice of Yhwh breaks the cedars; Yhwh breaks the cedars of Lebanon . . . .

[7]The voice of Yhwh flashes forth flames of fire.

[8]The voice of Yhwh shakes the wilderness; Yhwh shakes the wilderness of Kadesh.

[9]The voice of Yhwh causes the oaks to whirl, and strips the forest bare; and in his temple all say, "Glory!"

[10]Yhwh sits enthroned over the flood; Yhwh sits enthroned as king forever.

In the following passage about El's sons, we see Baal sitting on his throne after seizing it from El.

   2) El has seventy sons. These are the ones whom Baal later kills:

   Baal seized the sons of Athirat
   he smote the great ones with the broad-sword,
   he smote the 'pounders' of the sea with the mace,
   he dragged the yellow ones of Mot to the ground.
   (Then) did Baal [sit] upon the throne of his kingdom,
   [on the cushion] on the seat of his dominions.

(*Baal and Mot*, KTU VI.v.1-6, Gibson 79; de Moor uses the future tense in this passage, 94 n. 452; see his translation below.)

Yhwh Elohim also has "many" sons (mentioned in Job 1.6; 2.1; 38.7, and elsewhere). In *Genesis* 6.4, the "sons of God" came down to earth and "went into the daughters of humans, who bore children to them." Possibly this mysterious passage is meant to account for the disappearance of these lesser gods from Yhwh's heaven. Deut 32.8 is a special case, for in the Septuagint and the Dead Sea scrolls, Yhwh is not the father of "the sons of God" but one of them, as in *Ps* 82. But instead of "divine sons," the MT has "sons of Israel" (Smith, *Origins*, 48-59), thus changing the meaning entirely.

3) Yhwh/Elohim has a large council. In Ps 82, Elohim is standing amid the "assembly of El" where all the other gods are condemned to death for not having administered justice. In verse 8, Elohim is called to judge the world, and told that he has inherited all the nations.[30] In the Hebrew, it is not "God's council" but El's (בעדת־אל), a term in the myths referring to the assembly of El, and the condemned gods are not "the sons of the Most High" (i.e., God's) but "sons of Elyon" (עלו ן־ בנ י), among them, Yhwh. The standard interpretation of this psalm, however, is *not* that it is an attack on all the other gods *by El*, but an Israelite polemic *of Yhwh* versus the pagan gods (the "elohim").

Compare "the assembly of the sons of the gods" (KTU 4.iii.14, Gibson 58) or "the convocation of the Council" (1.2.i.13)[31] in Ugaritic myths with the divine council described in Daniel:

> As I watched, thrones were set in place, and an Ancient One took his throne, his clothing was white as snow, and the hair of his head like pure wool; his throne was fiery flames and its wheels were burning fire.
>
> A stream of fire issued and flowed out from his presence. A thousand thousands served him, and ten thousand times ten thousand stood attending him. The court sat in judgment, and the books were opened (1.9-10NRSV).

These numbers should be compared with Yhwh's "ten thousand, thousands upon thousands" in Ps 68.17.

The councils of El in KTU 1.1 and 1.2 can also be compared with Yhwh when he is sitting in judgment or consulting with his hosts on warfare (1 Kg 22.19; Zech 3; Dan 7.9ff.; Job 1-2ff.) (Miller 27 et passim).

4) The gods have messengers who do their errands. Baal has Gipanu and Ugaro, for example, who go to Anat and ask her to bring peace to the earth (KTU I.iii.33, de Moor 10). Likewise, Yhwh has messenger-angels.

5) Both the gods in Ugaritic myths and Yhwh live in tents. The Ugaritian gods are seen going to their tents in *Keret*:

> Having pronounced blessings, the gods went,
>> the gods went to their tents,
>>> The family of Ilu to their dwellings.
>
> (KTU 1.5 iii 17-19, de Moor 207).

Yhwh has the tent of meeting, and also has a cosmic tent, as Nicolas Wyatt points out. In *Isaiah, Psalms,* and *Job,* Yhwh is stretching out the heavens like a tent:

> It is he who sits above the circle of the earth, and its inhabitants are like grasshoppers; who stretches out the heavens like a curtain, and spreads them like a tent to live in (Isa 40.22);
>
> You stretch out the heavens like a tent (Ps 104.2-3);
>
> [Yhwh] who alone stretched out the heavens and trampled the waves of the Sea (Job 9.8)

The cosmic tent in the myths, says Wyatt, was made from the skin of Yam (*Space and Time,* 177, 173).

6) El in the Ugaritic texts is called "Bull" and is represented by the golden calf. Yhwh too was connected with the bull. Aaron built the Golden Calf, and Jeroboam made two calves, one in Bethel and the other in Dan (van der Toorn 321) for the worship of Yhwh.

7) El had astral associations, and so does Yhwh (323). In *The Song of Deborah,* Yhwh commands both the rain and the stars in their courses:

> The stars fought from heaven, from their courses they fought against Sisera. The torrent Kishon swept them away, the onrushing torrent, the torrent Kishon. (5.20-21)

Note the solar items destroyed by Josiah in 2 Kg. 23, connected to Baal (quoted below). Also attesting to solar worship in Israel, possibly by Israelites, is the town of Beth Shemesh, which translated, means the House or Temple of the Sun.

8) Yhwh's conquest of the dragon and the sea in the Bible have their antecedent in the myth of Baal and Yam.

9) The "revolt-in-heaven myth" may also have been derived from the Baal cycle. These last two similarities need further discussion.

Conquest of the dragon

Comparing the victory of Baal over Yam with Yhwh over Leviathan and the final form of the dragon-conqueror in literature, Wyatt writes:

> The fight of the storm-god with Yam appears in adapted form throughout the pages of the Hebrew Bible, spills over into the intertestamental literature, turns up in the New Testament, and flourishes in slightly disguised form, by way of a hybrid which also takes on Perseus and Andromeda . . . in the stories of George and the dragon.[32]

This is the battle as found in the Baal epic:

> Although you defeated Lotanu, the fleeing serpent,
>> destroyed the coiling serpent,
>>> the Tyrant with the seven heads,
>> you were uncovered, the heaven came loose
>>> like the girdle of your cloak! (KTU 1.5, 1-5a, de Moor 69-70)

This same Lotanu, called Leviathan in the Bible, is described in *Isaiah* and *Psalms,* where Yhwh is the slayer of the dragon of the sea (yam), behaving much as Baal with his lightning:

On that day Yhwh with his cruel and great and strong sword will punish *the fleeing serpent, Leviathan the twisting serpent,* and he will kill *the dragon that is in the sea.* (Isa 27.1)[33]

Awake, awake, put on strength, O arm of Yhwh! Awake, as in days of old, the generations of long ago! Was it not *you who cut Rahab in pieces, who pierced the dragon?*

Was it not you who *dried up the sea, the waters of the great deep; who made the depths of the sea a way for the redeemed to cross over?*

So *the ransomed of Yhwh shall return,* and come to Zion with singing; everlasting joy shall be upon their heads; they shall obtain joy and gladness, and sorrow and sighing shall flee away. (Isa 51.9-11; italics mark parallels with the myths)

Only substitute "Baal" for "Yhwh" and "Zephon" for "Zion." The "ransomed" are the dragon's liberated captives. The dragon is Yam. The conqueror is Baal.

You divided the sea by your might; you *broke the heads of the dragons* in the waters;

You crushed the heads of Leviathan; you gave him as food for the creatures of the wilderness. (Ps 74.13-14)

And *he sent out his arrows, and scattered them; he flashed forth lightnings, and routed them.*

Then the channels of the sea were seen, and the foundations of the world were laid bare at your rebuke, O Yhwh, at the blast of the breath of your nostrils. (Ps 18.14-15)

See also Ps 89.10-11:

Thou dost *rule the raging of the sea;* when its waves rise, thou stillest them.

Thou didst *crush Rahab like a carcass,* thou didst *scatter thy enemies* with thy mighty arm.

Ps 29 (quoted earlier above) has such a striking similarity to Canaanite beliefs about Baal that some have "supposed [it] to be a translation or adaptation of an old 'Canaanite' hymn" (Wyatt, *Space and Time,* 102). Others, who do not accept the Canaanite origin of Yhwh's characteristics, however, claim that Ps 29 is another polemic against Baal, showing that anything Baal can do, Yhwh can do better. This does not alter the fact that Yhwh's actions imitate Baal's.

In the myths, Baal thunders out of his window in his newly-built palace, as does Yhwh:

"Let a window be opened in the mansion,

a lattice in the middle of the palace!"

Ba'lu opened a rift in the clouds,

Ba'lu gave forth his holy voice,

Ba'lu repeated the ut[terance] of his [li]ps.

His holy voice made the earth [qu]ake,

[the utterance of] his [lips] the mountains . . .

(IV.vii, 26-32, de Moor 63)

In Ps 29 "the 'voice of Yahweh' (*qôl yhwh*), mentioned seven times in the text, . . . appears to echo the 'seven lightning-flashes, eight bundles of thunder' of Ugaritian Baal" (Wyatt, idem):

Ba'lu was seated, as immoveable as a mountain,

Haddu r[ested] like the ocean

on his mountain, the divine Sapanu,

    [on] the mountain of victory.

Seven lightnings [he had].

Eight storehouses of thunder,

          the *shafts of lightning* he [   ]. (I.i.3-4, de Moor 1-2)

We clearly see Yhwh as the Storm-God Baal in Ps 29.

Frank Moore Cross thought it likely that the Exodus and Crossing of the Reed Sea (a conquering of the sea) had their origin in the story of the defeat of Yam (Sea) by Baal, while the miracles of the crossing of the Jordan represent a defeat of the river (Nahar) aspect of Yam (147).

The revolt myth

(The revolt myth is referred to in Gen 6.1-4; Isa 14; Eze 28.1-9, 11-19; Ps 82.1-8; Job 38; Dan 11.21, 31-39, 45 and Dan 12.1-3; and Enoch 6-11, as well as in the New Testament.)[34]

Hugh Rowland Page and others believe that the revolt of Lucifer and his attendants in heaven and their subsequent fall into the underworld have their origin in the Canaanite myth of Athtar. When the god Athtar briefly occupies the throne of Baal, he is found to be unsuitable and so descends "and became king on all the divine earth" (KTU VI.ii.65, de Moor 86). The myth does not tell us what happened to Athtar after that, but Page conjectures that the nonextant part of the myth was known to the ancient world.

In the extant myths, Athtar *comes down to earth.* In the Jewish and Christian lore, however, the displaced god goes down into "the pit" like Baal to "die a violent death in the heart of the seas" (Eze 28.8). The author of *Ezekiel* used this myth in order to condemn a bad king (151). According to Page, Athtar had been demonized by Jewish, Christian, and Islamic lore (204). In the myth, the gods do question his qualifications, however, and find Athtar unsuitable (KTU VI.i.49-53; 60-61). Perhaps Athtar was demonized in some other Canaanite myth, no longer known. It seems likely.

Not only can Canaanite myths help us unravel some of the mysteries of the Hebrew Bible, but—and this is very important—the Hebrew Bible can help us reconstruct the Canaanite myths which have been lost or are preserved only in fragments. As Page writes, "Canaanite mythological allusions are ubiquitous in Hebrew literature and can be used productively in reconstructing certain elements of older Canaanite tradition" (204). A lot of sleuthing nevertheless remains to be done.

Absorption of Canaanite myths by the Israelites

Gradually, El came to be "reinterpreted at the end of the tenth century BCE as an allomorph of Yahweh" (van der Toorn 327). Other gods continued to be worshiped, but the god called Yhwh began to dominate them. Eventually the other gods disappeared or dissolved into the "hosts (armies) of heaven" in the Hebrew Bible or became the "messengers" (מלאכים, angels) of Yhwh, whose functions were similar to those of the messengers of the Canaanite pantheon. This transformation is perhaps alluded to in the Commandment, "Thou shall have no other gods before me" (i.e., other gods are not to be more important than I am). In Ps 82, all the other gods are condemned to death "for their failure to maintain justice on earth and [Yhwh] takes over the total rule of the divine world" (Miller 27).

According to de Moor, the use of the term *Elohim* (the plural of El) in the Bible signifies that Yhwh Elohim contained all the gods of the pantheon (*The Rise of Yahwism*, 334):

> The religion of the early settlements, writes van der Toorn, was predominately a matter of the family or clan . . . . The clan god was commonly a god of the Canaanite pantheon, El and Baal being the most widely worshiped (254-55) . . . . The situation of religious parity [between Yhwh and El or Baal] was condemned by some groups among the Yahwistic clergy, but never abolished in the course of the existence of Israel as an independent state (376).

Even after Yahwist worship became predominant, some Canaanite families continued to prefer Baal worship. The Gideon story—of the destroying of the Baal and Asherah altars—may reflect the conflict about the gods during a transitional period (329).

The temple of El Berith in Shechem (El of the Covenant in 9.46—Baal Berith in 9.4) was a center for Baal worship, while the temple at Bethel, with its images of bulls, was a center for El worship (2 Kg 24.4). Smith writes:

> In addition, as a function of the identification of Yahweh-El at cultic sites of El, such as Shiloh, Shechem, and Jerusalem, the old religious lore of El was inherited by the priesthood in Israel. At a variety of sites, Yahweh was incorporated into the older figure of El, who belonged to Israel's original West Semitic religious heritage (*Origins* 140).

Idols were popular. The teraphim (mentioned in the Gideon and Micah stories) were "household gods," not necessarily Baal and Asherah, but somewhat like the *penates* of the Romans and were used in family worship and perhaps consulted as oracles, though it is not known how answers to questions were given (219, 223-224). Many female figurines have been found throughout the area, possibly representing Asherah or some other fertility goddess. D. V. Edelman, in her study of deities on coins from the Persian to the Hasmonean period, believes that Micah's image was of Yhwh.[35]

Baal worship continued side by side with Yhwh worship for a long time, as is affirmed by the high percentage of names with the theophoric element of Baal in the Samaria ostraca: 7 for Baal to 11 for Yhwh. A study of the names in the tribes of Manasseh, Ephraim, and Benjamin in the period of the Judges through Samuel's judgship shows that 16 have the name of El, 10 the name of Baal and various other gods, while only 7 refer to Yhwh (van der Toorn 238). Van der Toorn comments,

> The complete absence of the name of Yahweh from early Iron Age toponyms . . . must be taken as a reflection of the relative unimportance of the worship of Yahweh among the early Israelites (241).

The Israelites may have always practiced the worship of Baal to some extent. Otherwise, Arvid Kapelrud asks, how was it possible that Saul and David, who themselves were Yahweh worshippers, should give their sons names compounded with the name of the god Baal? There is, in fact, only one possible explanation. In their time Yhwh must have been identified with Baal. Yhwh had absorbed the mightiest and most important of the gods of Canaan.[36]

Another explanation is that both gods were worshiped. Ozwald Loretz believes that except for intermittent tension and warfare, the Israelites co-existed peacefully with the Canaanites until David's time, with a common government, and with similar rights and duties. Only after David's time did communication and intermarriage with the "Canaanites" begin to be forbidden as in the many references in *Judges*.[37]

El and Baal were not the only Canaanite gods represented in the Israelite religion. There was also Asherah (Athirat), thought to be the consort of Yhwh. Two inscriptions dating from 950-850 BCE found at Kuntillet 'Ajrud and another found at Khirbet el-Qom in Israel mention "Yahweh and his Asherah." An ongoing debate is whether "the Asherah" refers to a female being, Yhwh's consort, on the one hand, or to a sacred pole, on the other. Some Biblical scholars reason that Yhwh's consort would never be referred to as "*his* asherah"; it would just be "Asherah"—for Yhwh, they reason, did not have a consort.

But since the asherah is a "sacred pole," which is the goddess' iconic form and since Asherah is El's consort in the myths, and "El" was the original name of Yhwh,[38] the inscriptions apparently corroborate this marriage relationship in the Israelite religion. Smith agrees (*Origins* 47).

But in the Bible Asherah is the consort of Baal, not Yhwh. According to Saul M. Olyan, however, "the asherah [pole] was a legitimate symbol in Yahweh's cult," for in the Canaanite religion, Asherah was never associated intimately with Baal (73). Her association with Baal (instead of with El) was made by the Deuteronomic writers, Olyan continues, in order to detract from the cult of Asherah, which was popular at the time and which the Yahwists wiped out. Originally, references were not to "Baal and Asherah" but to "El and Asherah." When El became Yhwh, Asherah came along with him into the Israelite religion. Olyan writes:

> If Asherah were the consort of Baal [i.e., not of Yhwh] in the Iron Age, as so many scholars assume, surely her cult would have been opposed by conservative and even radical Yahwists like Elijah, Jehu, Amos or Hosea [*but they did not oppose her*] . . . . In the light of the intense rivalry between Yahweh and Baal and their respective votaries during the period of the divided monarchy, it is difficult to imagine that they could share the same consort.[39]

Van der Toorn likewise thinks that because she was the consort of El in the Ugaritic myths, she must also have been the consort of Yhwh among Yahwists (321). Today in scholarship, Asherah is "increasingly recognized as having been the consort of Yahweh in the Solomonic temple, and the mythical mother of the king," as Wyatt writes (*Space and Time* 168). John Day agrees that the substitution of "Baal and

Asherah" for "Yhwh and Asherah" in the Bible was "probably a polemical move to discredit her . . . whereas in fact other evidence suggests she was regarded as Yahweh's consort by many Israelites, and this was probably an appropriation from El" (34, 48).[40]

The whole population had begun as "Canaanites" (or non-Yahwists) but when opposition to Baalism arose, the term "Canaanite" came to be applied as a pejorative to the non-Yahwists. According to the Deuteronomists, the worship of Baal persisted until Jehu, King of Israel (9th C.), destroyed the Baal cult in Samaria with its temple and worshipers (2 Kg 10.18-27). The reason that Asherah remained, however, was that she was still considered to be Yhwh's consort.[41]

It was not in the northern tribes alone that Asherah was worshiped.[42] Josiah, King of Judah, two hundred years later cleansed the temple in Jerusalem and also removed—from Bethel, Samaria, and other "high places"—all signs of the worship of Baal and Asherah still remaining:

> [4]The king [Josiah] commanded the high priest Hilkiah, the priests of the second order, and the guardians of the threshold, to bring out of the temple of Yhwh *all the vessels made for Baal, for Asherah*, and for all the host of heaven; he burned them outside Jerusalem in the fields of the Kidron, and carried their ashes to Bethel. [5]He deposed the idolatrous priests whom the kings of Judah had ordained to make offerings in the high places at the cities of Judah and around Jerusalem; those also who made offerings to Baal, to the sun, the moon, the constellations, and all the host of the heavens. [6]He brought out the *image of Asherah* from the house of Yhwh, outside Jerusalem, to the Wadi Kidron, burned it at the Wadi Kidron, beat it to dust and threw the dust of it upon the graves of the common people. [7]He broke down the houses of the male temple prostitutes that were in the house of Yhwh, where the women did weaving for Asherah . . . .
>
> [10]He defiled Topheth, which is in the valley of Ben-hinnom, *so that no one would make a son or a daughter pass through fire as an offering to Molech.* [11]He removed from the entrance to the temple of Yhwh *the horses* that the kings of Judah *had dedicated to the sun* . . . . Then he burned the *chariots of the sun with fire.* [12]The altars on the roof of the upper chamber of Ahaz, which the kings of Judah had made, and the altars that Manasseh had made in the two courts of the house of Yhwh, he pulled down from there and broke in pieces, and threw the rubble into the Wadi Kidron. [13]The king also desecrated the high places that were east of Jerusalem on the south of the Hill of Corruption—the ones Solomon king of Israel had built for Ashtoreth the vile goddess of the Sidonians, for Chemosh the vile god of Moab, and for Molech the detestable god of the people of Ammon. [14]He broke the pillars in pieces, *cut down the sacred poles,* and covered the sites with human bones . . . . [19]Moreover, Josiah removed all the shrines of the high places that were in the towns of Samaria, which kings of Israel had made, provoking Yhwh to anger; he did to them just as he had done at Bethel. [20]He slaughtered on the altars all the priests of the high places who were there, and burned human bones on them . . . . Then he

returned to Jerusalem. [24]Moreover Josiah *put away the mediums, wizards, teraphim,*
idols, and all the abominations that were seen in the land of Judah and in Jerusalem . . . .
(NRSV 2 Kg 23 passim, italics mine)

As this long excerpt shows, the religion of El, Baal, and Asherah was pervasive and
was removed only with considerable effort and cruelty. Baal was removed because he
was one of the gods condemned in Ps 82. Asherah removed because it was by
then concluded that Yhwh had no consort.

Idolatry in Judges

Judges seeks to discredit the northern kingdom of Israel and such northern
shrines as Bethel, Shechem, Shiloh, and Dan. The stories of *Judges* contain many
references to idolatry, including the altar of Baal in the town of Ophrah, which
Gideon destroyed, and Gideon's ephod. Probably Abimelech and the city of Shechem
were idolaters, and Micah and the Danites had idols. Except for the altar of Baal in
the Gideon story and Micah's installation of idols, these stories are not principally
about worship of idolatry, yet Yhwh in the religious "formulae" of these stories is
perpetually inveighing against it. The admonitions against idolatry were likely
inserted at a later time by the Deuteronomists in order to explain why things went
from bad to worse in Israel in the period of the judges, and why Israel's powerful
god allowed the Israelites to be conquered by the Assyrians and the Babylonians.
Ziony Zevit thinks that the Yhwh-alone movement gained momentum only after the
Assyrian destruction of Jerusalem in 722 BCE and that it did not become
"widespread" until the Exile and the Persian period.[43"]

"[To] ground monotheism, or even monolatry, historically before the seventh
century is difficult . . . . [A] group of scholars, including T. J. Meek, date the
emergence of monotheism around the time of the 'Exile' (587-538 BCE)," writes
Mark S. Smith, who reminds us that monotheism is clearly attested in the sixth
century prophets like Second Isaiah (*Origins* 150, 153-154).

The most important lesson to be taught, in the minds of the priests returning
from Babylonian Captivity, was that Yhwh alone was to be worshiped, not the Canaanite
gods. Even at that late date, however, the Canaanite gods must not have been totally
eliminated; otherwise these repeated warnings would not have been necessary.
And what is not clear is how extensive either religion was, nor how many followers it
had when it emerged—whether a whole people, or just a priestly group, those who
wrote the text.

IV. Ugaritic Myths Compared and Contrasted with Judges

(See chart of differences and similarities of the Ugaritic poems and of *Judges* at
the end of this chapter.)

The stories of *Judges* are not a simple revision of the extant Ugaritic myths; they
differ from the myths in many ways. But the numerous similarities between them

suggest that the Canaanite myths may be an ancestor of the stories in *Judges*, though at least one remove. According to Mark S. Smith,

> pre-monarchic Israel (ca. 1200-800) may share as much, if not more, with the religious outlook expressed in the texts from Ugarit (ca. 1350-1150) than with later Israel (ca. 800-200) and the monotheistic faith it eventually produced (*Origins,* 10).

One problem in comparing the myths with *Judges* is that the only Canaanite texts we have are the Ugaritic ones, and there are relatively few of them. Other Canaanite literature in all likelihood existed, which was either never written down or was irretrievably lost. Thus the Israelites may have been familiar with variants, rather than the extant ones. This makes the task of collating *Judges* with the Ugaritic poems more difficult than if the gods and goddesses in the ancient Middle East had been presented with a stable array of actions. Further are the gaps in the clay tablets and the problems created by the differences in translations.

The extant Ugaritic literature is not a primitive production. The poems show the use of certain conventions such as word pairs, syntactical and other kinds of parallelisms between lines, multiple repetitions of lines and passages, alliteration, word-play, stock epithets, and mixture of dialogue and narrative.[44] Scholarly conclusions of the linguistic and stylistic studies of Ugaritic poetry are too complex to be discussed here, but they demonstrate a sophistication of narrative in the Ugaritic myths of the kind that in my opinion can only be the result of a centuries-long evolution of language and narration, as long an evolution as the Gilgamesh epic and perhaps with even as widespread an audience.

The Ugaritic poems are short, brisk, beautiful tales, with a charmingly comic tone. Even the bloodthirsty description of Anat is not without its light touches. The poems are pictorial, the descriptions rich in details. The marriage poems, *Shachar and Shalim and the Gracious Gods* and *Nikkal and the Kotharat,* for example, are sensuous and lyrical, like *The Song of Solomon.* The society depicted is not primitive. Signs of luxury in the stories are frequent: cups of silver and gold, jewels, and precious stones like lapis lazuli. The action may be dynamic from time to time, but on the whole the narratives are presented in a leisurely fashion. Dialogues are common and more extended than those in *Judges.*

Actual locations like Byblos, Memphis, and Crete are referred to, but in general the action takes place in mythical settings—in brightly-lighted landscapes, on plateaus on the tops of mountains, in "the recesses of Zaphon" (Mt. Sapon), where Baal abides, on the seashore, or in mythic sites like the city of Mot (Death), called "Miry," "where a pit is the throne on which (he) sits, filth the land of his heritage" (*Baal and Mot,* 5.ii.15-16, Gibson 70). The place where the gods reside is somewhat unearthly, but it is not the heaven of later imagination.

We often see the gods feasting like mortals, eating meat and drinking wine—even carousing in drunkenness—in their palaces. "Clearly one of the main activities of the general assembly [of gods] is feasting," writes Smith (*Origins* 45). We even see Athirat's attendant fishing in order to give the visiting gods fish to eat. (Gibson

"Palace of Baal," 4 ii 30-47, 57). Their palaces are built of earthly materials—cedar-wood, bricks, and precious metals—and they have the same kind of furniture as mortals. But the gods also live in tents.[45] In moving about, they are able to fly, as Anat explicitly does in one of the love poems (II.ii.10-11, de Moor 113) and as Yam's messengers do (2.i.12, Wyatt, *Space and Time*, 57). They can take subterranean routes as well (de Moor 13); but they also (to our amusement) ride on asses; and like patriarchs of *Genesis* and ordinary people of *Judges*, they walk.

The picture in *Judges* is different. Except for *The Song of Deborah*, *Judges* is in prose. Though also comic in the actions depicted, *Judges* is a black comedy of the grotesque. Despite the many objects and people in this book, descriptions as such are in short supply. Money is mentioned on several occasions to connote treachery, but except for the spoil expected by Sisera's mother (and never delivered), the spoil taken by Gideon, and the silver idols of Micah, luxury items are lacking. Instead, what we have are predominantly common tools and household utensils. The Israelites have no vehicles and very few asses. They and their warriors go on foot.

In contrast to the leisurely pace of the myths, the action of *Judges* is dynamic. Single figures, and hundreds, even thousands, of people lurch around a terrain that is usually dark. The settings are on earth. The map of Israel is always in the storyteller's mind. He keeps reminding us where people are and what time of day it is and how many days have passed. Dialogues are kept to a minimum and are crisp and brief, with only one or two exceptions (like Jephthah's messengers' long speech to the Ammonites). Bizarre episodes and curious objects and details abound. The people are very different from the noble patriarchs of *Genesis* or the myths. They are simple rural people, who do not live in palaces, but dwell in tents (sometimes in tent communities), or in small houses in small villages.

Though the Ugaritic myths—those signed by Ilimilku—are related to each other, we do not know if they were presented in any set order. We cannot speak of them, except loosely, as a "book," nor can we determine whether the corpus ever had a structure.

As I have shown elsewhere, *Judges* is a "well-wrought urn." The stories are all closely interconnected, including the last two stories, which scholars have long (mistakenly, I believe) regarded as "appendices." What gives *Judges* structure and design is the common theme of warfare and the many parallel situations in the stories, whereas parallel structure is not a design element in the myths. In *Aqhat*, the murder of Aqhat by Anat and Yatpan is paralleled by Pughat's avenging of her brother and killing of Yatpan.[46] This parallel is *within* a story. In the Baal cycle, Anat's saving of Baal is parallel to Pughat's avenging of Aqhat. This parallel is *between* two stories. There might be others. The method of parallelism was, at least, known and used. But parallels are not a regular device in the myths.

The term "judge"

An important link between the two corpora is the term *judge* used in both of them. In the Ugaritic myths Prince Yam (or Sea) is called Judge Nahar (River) many times.[47] Baal is called both King and Judge at least once (KTU I.v.33-34, de Moor 17). El is known as El Dan, which means "El the judge." Incidentally, El Dan might possibly have been the patron of the Israelite tribe of Dan, as Asherah might have been of Asher, which implies a polytheistic origin. The location of these tribes in the far north—toward Ugaritic, rather than Israelite, territory—may give us one more reason to suppose a polytheistic origin of these tribes, and consequently of their narratives, rather than a Yahwist one.[48]

In the myths we see El in the act of *judging* when he has to decide whether or not Yam or Baal will prevail and whether or not they will be allowed to build palaces for themselves. When he agrees to Anat's request for Baal to build a palace, Anat replies to him:

> "Your *judgment*, Ilu, is wise.
>> May your wisdom last forever!
>>> Long live the sharpness of your judgment!"
> (I.v.30-32, de Moor 17)

El also judges whether or not he will allow Anat to wreak revenge on Aqhat, and he decides whether or not to give Keret and Danel children. He is the only god who can bless people with children (de Moor, *Rise of Yahwism* 72) (compare Yhwh's intervention with Sarah and with Samson's mother). No doubt, El made other judgments as well.

When Canaanite gods become the "sons of god" (sons of Yhwh) or dissolve into the "hosts" of heaven in the Bible, they continue to engage in judging (see Dan 7). In the mysterious passage Gen 6.1-4, the "Bene Elohim" who have just come down to earth, are, Graves and Patai believe, "sons of judges."[49]

In contrast to *Judges*, in which no mortal actually engages in explicit judging, mortals in the Ugaritic myths do. In *Aqhat*, Danel is sitting on the threshing floor (with dignitaries) judging a case of a widow and orphan when Pughat approaches him with dire information about Aqhat's death (III.i.20-25, de Moor 249; also 17.v.7-8, Gibson 107). The Daniel mentioned in Eze 14.14 and 28.3; the brilliant young judge Daniel in the apocryphal story of Susannah; and Daniel in *Daniel*—all three are likely derived from this tradition.[50] Daniel in the book of *Daniel* is known for his righteousness and wisdom.

When Keret, a "just king" in the Ugaritic myth of that title, becomes ill, he is accused by his son Yassib of having fallen down in his duties.

> You have let your hand fall down in slackness;
> You do not judge the case of the widow,
>> You do not try the case of the impatiently waiting,
>>> You do not drive the robbers away for the poor,
> Before your (eyes) you do not let the orphan eat,
> (nor) behind your back the widow . . . .
> Abdicate the kingship, let me be king!
> (*Keret*, III.vi.45-50, 53, de Moor 222)

Parker compares this with Ps 82 (discussed above), in which El movingly condemns the other gods of failing to do justice:[51]

> "How long will you judge unjustly and show partiality to the wicked?
>
> Give justice to the weak and the orphan; maintain the right of the lowly and the destitute.
>
> Rescue the weak and the needy; deliver them from the hand of the wicked."
>
> They have neither knowledge nor understanding, they walk around in darkness; all the foundations of the earth are shaken.
>
> I say, You are gods, children of the Most High, all of you;
>
> nevertheless, you shall die like men, and fall like any prince."
>
> Rise up, O Elohim, judge the earth; for all the nations belong to you! (*Ps* 82.2-8)

Because of this, the other gods will die, and Yhwh shall rise up. This is the kind of failure that Absalom accuses David of in 2 Sam 15.2-6.

But except for the brief mention of the Israelites coming to Deborah for judgment (4.5), we do not see any actual judging in *Judges*. Because of this lack, many scholars claim that the term *judge* means simply *leader*. As with most stories in a culture, however, the contemporary audience likely understood more about these characters than was written down. Possibly in nonextant parts of the stories, the characters made judgments. Just because we do not see them judging does not mean that they did not engage in this activity.

When the stories were adapted as Israelite stories, the title "judge" as an honorific was transferred to the human characters derived from the Canaanite divinities. The title *judge* is one small but important bit of evidence of the Ugaritic connection.

Warfare

An important difference between the two corpora is that the myths are about internecine conflicts among the gods, while warfare in *Judges* is directed against outsiders up until the last story, when civil war breaks out.

In *Keret*, the king musters an army and marches through the countryside (much like Jephthah)—not to despoil and seize cities, but to lay siege to one city in order to force its king to give his daughter in marriage to Keret (*Keret* I.iv to II.i, de Moor 198-204).

The gods have large armies, but prefer (like Samson) single combat. Actual warfare between armies is described only once—when Baal goes out on a spree after giving a great feast for all the gods to celebrate his new mansion:

> The god [Haddu] removed himself from the mountain
>
>> while the gods were [eating] on Sapanu.
>
> He marched from town to town, turned from city to city,
>
>> Sixty-six towns he seized, seventy-seven cities,
>
> Ba'lu st[ruck] eighty,
>
>> Ba'lu expelled ninety.

(Then) he came [back] in the house,

      Baʻlu (back) inside the house. (IV.vii.5-14, de Moor 61-62)

He is no doubt attacking human cities, as the gods do not have towns.

Except for this, the gods of the myths do not attack an enemy outside of their realm, but vie with each other over control of the forces of life—rain, sea, death. In some respects, they are like tribal leaders competing for power. Despite these differences, both groups of stories are alike in that warfare and conflict are important themes.

Transference of myth to Hebrew legend

As to how the Ugaritic myths came into the Hebrew tradition, we may hypothesize that Canaanite folktales, not identical to the extant Ugaritic myths, but using some of the same characters and situations, were being shared with the Yahwists. When the Yhwh religion deposed the other gods (Ps 82), the tales involving the Canaanite gods were given a human provenance and Israelite associations. The Israelite authors in effect "demythologized" them, as Susan Ackerman puts it (66). This transition occurred long before the stories were written down.

V. Possible Influence of Canaanite Myths on Judges:
The Song of Deborah

The strongest influence of the Ugaritic myths is to be found in the stories of Deborah, Abimelech, and Samson, with traces of the myths in the other stories.

The Song of Deborah resembles the myth of Baal against the forces of El and Yam in so many ways that it can be argued to be a translation of sorts. The Song may have been a favorite poem of the Canaanites. Not wanting to lose the great victory hymn altogether when the Israelites had become monotheistic, the Yahwists would have modified it to make it fit into the new religion, presumably at a time when the two religions were not so far apart as they later became. After Israel began to condemn Baalism, the poem would be modified even further in order to express the new developments. Such transformations are the kind of syncretism that results when two cultures blend together. An example of this is Beowulf, which combines both the older Anglo-Saxon pagan culture with the newer Christian one. Susan Ackerman believes that the people "in Israelite culture responsible for the text of Judges 5 adopted older Canaanite mythological traditions concerning Baal and Anat and adapted them in describing the Holy War Israel waged against Sisera" (36).[52]

Ps 68 (quoted in part above) likewise illustrates the overlap of two theologies. De Moor notes the similarities between the two both in language and theme and finds that the psalm "fits a time close to the texts of Ugarit . . . ." He believes that Ps 68 is older than The Song, but does not venture to guess how much older.[53] The similarities are found especially in vv. 4, 7-9, 12, 17-18 with references to Yhwh's march from Seir, the great hosts, the captives, and the women dividing the spoil. In Ps 68 the armies and the chariotry are cosmic ones. Likewise, the armies in The Song originally could also have been cosmic.

The style and vocabulary of *The Song* (Ch. 5) are very different from anything else in *Judges*, and the Hebrew contains many language puzzles, with about 25% of the poem untranslatable.[54] This suggests that *The Song* represents some kind of transition or an intermediate language between its original Semitic dialect and biblical Hebrew.

The prose version (Ch. 4) may have been created to elucidate the meaning of the poem, though it is equally possible that it is an Israelite variant of the same story, with the older Canaanite version being retained at a time when both dialects were understood by the audience.

Identification of Deborah with Anat, and Barak with Yatpan

P. C. Craigie and Glen Taylor, two early Ugaritic scholars, saw a close connection between characters from the Ugaritic poems and the characters of *The Song*. Craigie identified Deborah with Anat, and Barak with Yatpan (Anat's assistant). Taylor identified Jael with Athtart, the sister or double of Anat.

The main thrust of Craigie's argument had to do with the cosmic aspect of both battles, especially a comparison of the host of stars at the command of the warlike Anat, with the stars in *The Song* (now the heavenly host of Yhwh) fighting for Israel. In Ugaritic myth, the stars served as the "army of the sun." Craigie found an allusion to this in the last line of *The Song* when the victors are compared with "the sun as he rises in his might" (5.30). "'Sun'(*Sps*) and her army of stars in the Ugaritic material have been translated into Yhwh (//*Sps*, 5.31) and his army (//'stars' 5.30)"[55]

In another article, Craigie associated Barak with Anat's assistant, Yatpan, who carries out Anat's commands in the poem *Aqhat*.[56] In my opinion, however, this is not a convincing comparison, for Yatpan is a cruel and merciless assassin, whereas Barak is not, and nothing in the Ugaritic poem suggests, moreover, that Yatpan would behave in the cowardly way that Barak does at first. Rather, Yatpan, Anat's henchman, carries out his task of murdering Aqhat—too well.

That Anat is a patroness of warriors, Craigie observed, can be seen in the strange epithet of Shamgar ben Anat (Shamgar, son of Anat) (3.31), meaning that Shamgar was a mercenary soldier and protégé of the warrior goddess of Ugaritic myth.[57]

Craigie saw Deborah as like Anat, in that she inspires warriors to volunteer for war. He called Anat a "mistress of dominion" (*drkt*), a word he linked with Deborah's battle cry, "March on, my soul, with might," which he translated as "you shall dominate (*tdrky*), O my soul, mightily."

Although Anat is a virgin, while Deborah is a wife, Craigie nevertheless found the theme of virginity in the thoughts of Sisera's mother and her ladies-in-waiting who imagine that Sisera is collecting female booty, "a maiden or two for every man," though ironically, unbeknownst to the mother and her ladies, Sisera has just been *defeated* by two women—Deborah and Jael.

Craigie concluded that the Israelite poet was alluding to the Canaanite myth, and that this imagery "not only dramatizes Deborah's role in the war, but points ultimately to that power . . . which resided in Yhwh and in his 'friends' [as being] greater than any divine Canaanite power" (*ZAW* 381). In other words, the Israelite poet was using Ugaritic materials to demonstrate that the Israelite Yhwh was superior to the Canaanite El. (Compare this opinion with the interpretations of *Pss* 29 and 68 given above.) The story does not, however, reveal this to me.

Glen Taylor found Jael to be like the Ugaritic goddess Athtart (Astarte), Anat's sister. If Deborah is Anat, then Jael, he reasoned, must be Anat's sister. Taylor notes that Athtart's warlike character in the Ugaritic myths is supported by other sources. In Egyptian myth, she appears on horseback and bears a shield and spear; in Mesopotamian literature she is related to the warlike Ishtar; and in the Bible, when Saul is killed, the temple that the Philistines hang his armor in is the temple of the goddess of warfare, Ashtoreth (Athtart) (1 Sam 31.10). In an ancient curse, found two times in the Ugaritic myths, moreover, Athtart is shown to be as violent as Anat; and she is also the smasher of heads (KTU III.i.8-9, de Moor 30). (This curse is quoted below).[58] In *Keret*, when Yassib challenges his father's (Keret's) right to rule, Keret responds with the same curse directed to Athtart. This curse, said Taylor, is uttered in response to a "challenge of dominion."[59]

Taylor observed that the lines in *The Song*, "In the days of Shamgar ben Anat, in the days of Jael," imply that Shamgar and Jael are *oppressors* (*not saviors*, as they are otherwise depicted), for the passage is describing the *bad* state of affairs before Deborah arose. Why would Jael be linked with Shamgar, since in *Judges* she does not exist until *after* the time of Shamgar? If the original meaning of the lines, however, was a reference to the "days of Anat and Athtart" (Shamgar being the son or retainer of Anat and Jael being Athtart), then the storyteller is telling us something that happened in the time of these goddesses.

Another link between Jael and Athtart is that Athtart in the myths is associated with hunting and is called "the huntress," while Jael's name means "wild goat." According to Judith M. Hadley, Athtart's name also means "wild goat."[60] Taylor saw an irony here in that the huntress has become the "hunted one." These parallels, he thought, are "subtle allusions" to the Canaanite goddesses by the author of *The Song of Deborah* (100).

A hypothetical scenario of the myth transformed into The Song by the Israelite storyteller

In my opinion, however, the more likely comparisons are that Jael is Anat, and Deborah is Athtart. Deborah goes to battle, but we do not see her engaging in warfare. We do, however, see Jael in an act of vicious killing, like that ascribed to Anat. Then Barak would be Baal, Sisera would be Yam, and Jabin would be El.

The story is about the rivalry between Baal and Yam. In the *extant myth*, Baal has declared: "I alone am the one who can be king over the gods, who can fatten gods and men, who can satisfy the multitudes of the earth" (KTU 1.4.vii.49-52 de Moor's trans. in *The Rise of Yahwism* 80). For that reason, El orders Yam to kill Baal, Yam's powerful rival, so that Yam can become king.

In a *hypothetical scenario*, Yam, under El's command, challenges Baal to meet him in battle. Baal refuses to fight unless Athtart is by his side. Athtart accuses Baal of cowardice and shames him, but consents to accompany him. They go together. The armies fight. Yam is defeated and flees. He seeks haven with Anat. He imagines he will be safe with her, for all the gods are considered to belong to the "family of El." Nevertheless, she hates Yam because he has enslaved her brother (1.2.i.37, Wyatt, *Space and Time*, 61), and her loyalty is solely to Baal. She lures Yam into her home with feigned hospitality and sexual favors, and then treacherously kills him while he is asleep. She cannot really be called treacherous, however, because it was never a secret that Yam is her enemy and also because she has never had more than an uneasy truce with the family of El. (End of hypothetical scenario.)

Just as El and Yam had oppressed Baal and exacted tribute from him (KTU III.i.37, de Moor 33), so in *Judges*, Jabin and his commander Sisera have oppressed Barak and Deborah (Baal and Athtart) and perhaps even exacted tribute from them. Just as El has commanded Yam to drive out his rival Baal, so Jabin has commanded Sisera to drive out Barak and Deborah.

All of the hypothetical scenario is taken from the extant myths, except for the seduction of Yam by Anat, but her use of her sexuality in this way is consistent with other details of the myths. Thus the scenario could be a variant of one of them, which the original Israelite storyteller modified slightly for his own purposes—for like myths of other cultures, the Ugaritic myths come in more than one version. In one of the myths, Yam is killed by Anat, but in a variant, he is killed by Baal. In another story, Mot is also killed by Anat, but in a variant by Baal. Baal too is killed. But, as Smith writes, "Baal does not remain permanently dead, for never in the Ugaritic texts is divine death a permanent condition . . ." (*Origins* 98). This need not be considered inconsistent. The deaths of Yam [Prince Sea], Mot [Prince Death], and Baal are related to the annual passing of the seasons. After a short death, the gods rise again. And then the cycle begins anew.

What the myth adds to our knowledge of the story in *Judges* is more background information and the motivations for the actions, which are lacking in the Israelite scenario.

Identification of Jael with Anat

In the myths, El's people are not Anat's people. This helps explain why in the Deborah story, Jabin's people (Canaanites) are not Jael's people (Kenites).

In the Deborah story, no reason is given for Jael's killing Sisera (Anat's killing Yam). But as an Ugaritic myth converted into an Israelite tale, we understand that Anat's primary loyalty is to her brother, Baal (Barak), and not to his enemies. Peace between the factions had been declared, but when Yam (Sisera) went to war against Baal (Barak), that peace was violated, and she then had a right to kill him.

Barak of course is not Jael's brother in the Israelite story. But we are talking about an adaptation of the myth. The storyteller had to drop the sibling/wife relationship of Anat and Baal and create a new relationship in its place.

The transformed Anat became a Kenite, a clan long associated with Judah. The Kenites are supposedly descendants of Cain, *and Cain was the murderer of a brother*. Being considered a "*daughter*" of El (Yam's father), Anat can also be said to have murdered a "*brother*" when she killed El's son Yam—but not her *real* brother. The clan of Kenites were substituted by the author for the "brother" connection.

It might be asked why the storyteller did not invent an Israelite connection for Jael. The answer may be that it was offensive to the Israelite author for the killer to be an Israelite *woman*. It is a little less offensive if the killer is a Kenite. The woman in the tower who killed Abimelech was a Shechemite (a suspect city, with its temple of Baal-Berith [9.4]); and Delilah was a Philistine. In the Hebrew Bible, *Israelite women do not kill*. (Judith is in the Apocrypha, not in the Hebrew canon.)

There are four reasons for identifying Anat as Jael. First, Anat is a warrior goddess. She is like the Amazons of Greek myth, and she rides through the sky like the Valkyrie of Valhalla. Her destructiveness is made clear in a famous scene from the Baal cycle:

> And look! 'Anatu fought in the plain,
>> she slaughtered between the two cities.
> She smote the people of the sea-shore,
>> silenced the men of the east.
> Heads were under her (feet) like clods of earth,
>> on her were hands like locusts,
>>> like scales of a plane-tree the hands of the warriors.
> She attached the heads to her chest,
>> tied up the hands with her girdle.
> She plunged her knees in the blood of the guards,
>> her buttocks in the gore of the warriors.
> With a staff she chased the old men,
>> with the stave of her bow the veterans
>>> (KTU I.ii.6-17, de Moor 5-6).[61]

Still not satisfied, she continues battling; finally when she surveys the scene of carnage:

> Her liver shook with laughter,
>> her heart was filled with joy . . . (Ibid. 25-27, de Moor 6).

Even so, she continues battling the warriors until, finally sated, she washes their blood from her hands and fingers and rearranges the furniture of her house.

> She scooped up water and washed herself
>> with dew of heaven
>>> oil of earth,
>> with the drizzle of the Rider on the Clouds [i.e., Baal],

> dew that heaven poured out for her,
>
> drizzle that the stars poured out for her.
>
> (Ibid. 38-40, de Moor 7)

After that interlude, she takes her lyre and sings of her love for her brother Baal. (In Wyatt's translation, it is an attendant who plays the lyre and sings [*Religious Texts* 76].)

Second, Anat is desperately invested in the power struggle between Baal and the sons of El. Yam and Mot are the two most important sons of El and Athirat, and both are called "beloved of El" many times. This is significantly *not* Baal's epithet. Baal is the son of Dagon, not of El, and Anat is his beloved sister.

The reason that El's family fears Baal is that Baal is determined to rule over all the gods (KTU I.4.vii.49-52, de Moor *The Rise of Yahwism* 80). El has granted Yam the right to have his own palace and Mot already has his—in the underworld—but El will not at first grant an equivalent right to Baal. The likely reason for his reluctance is that Baal is competing with El's sons and will eventually kill all of them. Baal is Yam's enemy. Thus Yam is Anat's enemy, too. Twice in the myths she has killed Yam. She does this because Yam has enslaved her brother.

On one occasion, when Baal sends messengers for her, she jumps to the conclusion that some foe is threatening her beloved brother. Filled with rage, she exults over the killings that she has already committed for Baal, especially the killing of Yam. In her fierce outcry, the words *river, serpent,* and *dragon* (Tunnanu) all refer to Yam:

> She raised her voice and cried: . . .
>
> "What enemy has risen against Ba'lu
>
> What foe against the Rider on the Clouds?
>
> Did I not slay Yammu, Beloved of Ilu?
>
> > Did I not destroy River, the god of the Big Ones?
>
> Did I not muzzle Tunnanu?
>
> > Did I not stop his mouth?
>
> I did slay the coiling serpent,
>
> > the tyrant with the seven heads! (I.iii.35-42, de Moor 10-11; see
>
> also (KTU 1.5, 1-5a, de Moor 69-70, quoted above.)

Notice that it is Anat, and not El, who slays the serpent in this passage. Anat boasts about other children of El (Ilu) that she also slew:

> I did slay Arishu, Beloved of Ilu [El]!
>
> > I silenced 'Atiku, the bull-calf of Ilu!
>
> I did destroy Ishatu, the bitch of Ilu!
>
> > I did destroy Dhubabu, the daughter of Ilu!
>
> I shall battle for the silver,
>
> > (and) gain possession of the gold
>
> of anyone who tries to expel Ba'lu from the heights of Sapanu,
>
> > who tries to make (him) fly up like a bird from his aerie,
>
> who tries to chase him from the chair of his kingship,
>
> > from the seat of the throne of his dominion!

> What enemy has risen against Ba'lu
>> What foe against the Rider on the Clouds?"
> (I.iii.43-48, I.iv.1-4, de Moor 11-12)

Margalit finds Anat to be "a sadistic goddess who revels . . . in the massacre and mutilation of young warriors" (482). Though she represents warfare in general, here she especially directs violence against anyone who threatens Baal.

Third, both Baal and Anat, though not offspring of El and Athirat, are members of El's court; they visit him and have feasts with him. But they are also independent of him. Baal wants his own palace—as an expression either of his equality with the other gods or his desire to be superior to them. Anat has to fly to El and beseech him to get his consent, and when he hesitates, threatens to cast him to the ground, make his gray hairs run with blood, and even seize his children with her right hand if he does not agree. This threat is repeated two times, first as she thinks about approaching El and then when she actually does so (KTU I.v.20-25, de Moor 17). El wisely acknowledges her power:

> "I know you, my daughter, (I know) that you are like a man,
> (and) that among goddesses your scorn is unequaled!" (Idem, line 27)

(This threat and response are repeated in *Aqhat* when Anat wrings permission from El to kill Aqhat [1.18.8-18, de Moor 241-242].) Despite this, El does not relent about the palace for Baal until El's wife Athirat, after being both intimidated and bribed by Baal and Anat, also beseeches him.

Fourth, throughout the tales, Anat is passionately, fiercely devoted to Baal and *to no one else*. After her ferocious battle, when she washes the blood off herself, and sits down to sing of her love for Baal (KTU I.ii.6-7, quoted above; I.iii.4-9, de Moor 5-6, 8), Baal sends for her and returns her affection by preparing a meal for her (I.iv.41-42, de Moor 14). This mutual devotion is one of the most prominent themes of the myths. Anat and Baal are "inextricably intertwined," writes Ackerman, so that "Anat's triumphs in battle are also Baal's" (55).

The Ugaritic tale provides us with the reason why Jael is alone when Sisera comes to her tent, for her motive for slaying Sisera, and for why killing Sisera would not be considered treachery toward Jabin (with whom she and her family had "peace").

The marriage status of Anat and Jael

Anat, though called a virgin, is also considered the consort of Baal. Her counterpart, Jael, is usually regarded as married, but the Hebrew text is uncertain, since the word for *wife* in Hebrew is the same as the word for *woman*. Although the English translations make her to be the wife of Heber, J. Alberto Soggin argues that she was not a *wife*, but a *woman* of the *clan* of the Kenite tribe called Heber (67).

Anat's killing of Mot in the poem *Baal and Mot* is similar to the way Jael dispatches Sisera:

> She grasped mighty Mot!
> She split him with a sword,

　　　winnowed him with a sieve,
burnt him with a fire,
　　　and ground him with millstones;
she scattered him in a field
　　　for birds to eat his flesh
　　　and sparrows to chew his limbs.
Flesh cried out for flesh![62] (also VI.ii.31-39, de Moor 88-90),

but she is more ferocious than Jael, as Anat personifies war and is not a tent-dwelling woman like Jael. Jael's killing of Sisera in the Israelite tale, however, is also cold-blooded and ruthless:

She put her hand to the tent peg
　　　and her right hand to the
　　　　　workmen's mallet;
she struck Sisera a blow,
　　　she crushed his head,
　　　she shattered and pierced his
　　　　　temple.
He sank, he fell,
　　　he lay still at her feet;
at her feet he sank, he fell;
　　　where he sank, there he fell dead (NRSV, 5.26-27).

Jael, too, might have cried, like Anat: "Did I not make an end of Nahar [Yam]? I did destroy the tyrant . . ." (I.iii.35-42, de Moor 10-11, quoted earlier). Deborah could not have made this claim, for she was not the one who killed Sisera. Deborah is more like Athtart, who fought with and for Baal (Barak), but did not defeat Baal's enemy Yam (Sisera).

Milk and mothers

　　Why is there such strong emphasis in *Judges* on the milk that Jael gave Sisera? As already remarked, food and drink are a category of objects found both in the Ugaritic myths and *Judges*. (See Chapter 3.) In one Ugaritic poem, when Baal is seated on his throne: "His mouth is [craving] for bowls of milk" (KTU 1. Frag. 8-9, de Moor 2). In another, milk is served to guests by El

'El sits in [his banqueting hall] . . .
He did give (them) curdled milk . . .
to drink, he gave [the cup into (their) hand(s)],
the flagon into both (their) hands [　　　] . . .'
(*Baal and Yam*, KTU I.iv.4, 8-10, Gibson 39. Mark Smith also has *curdled milk*)[63]

Although the passage is somewhat unintelligible due to the damage on one side of the column, enough of it remains for us to see the similarity with the passage in *Judges* when Jael fetches milk for Sisera: "He asked water and she gave him milk, she brought him *curds* in a lordly bowl" (5.26). As in the myth, the milk was *curdled*.

Milk is associated with the word *mother*. As Freema Gottlieb proposed, *The Song* is about three mothers: Deborah (a mother of Israel), Sisera's mother, and Jael, who "mothered" Sisera by serving him milk and then covering him with a blanket.[64]

Milk also symbolizes Jael, a tent dweller whose occupation would be the raising of flocks, and the production of milk. The meaning of Jael's name is "wild goat" or "mountain goat." And this connects her with Anat, who lives on a mountain and who is described in the myth as a cow who mates with Baal and conceives a bull by him (*Loves*, II.iii.1-24, de Moor 114-115; *Myth and Ritual* IV.1-2, 30-35, de Moor, 138, 139).[65] When the Israelite poet adapted the Ugaritic myth, "cow" got changed into "wild goat." The drink that Pughat gave Yatpan in *Aqhat* is wine—to make her victim drunk. Likewise in the Jael story, the drink might have been wine but was changed to milk to give it an Israelite connection.

Seductiveness of Anat/Jael

Anat and Athtart are beautiful, as we learn in the story of Keret. "When Lady *Hry* [Huray], *Krt*'s [Keret's] noble bride, is described, her loveliness is like 'Anat's loveliness,/her beauty is like 'Attrt's [Athtart's] beauty" (Oldenburg 42). In the myth called *Loves*, Anat is shown in a rather torrid sexual scene with Baal (idem). As some interpreters think, Anat may have attempted to seduce Aqhat when she tried to wheedle his bow from him (*Aqhat*, I.vi.15-34, de Moor, 237-239).[66]

Although Jael is not described as beautiful, it is likely that she seduced Sisera or was raped by him. We see her outside the tent, enticing him three times to "turn in," like the harlot in *Proverbs*. The sexuality of the Samson/Delilah episode suggests the probability of sexuality in its companion piece, the parallel story of Jael and Sisera. "At [or between] her feet he fell" is the clue that makes Jael both a seductress and a fertility figure.

Rabbinic commentaries are divided as to whether or not Jael slept with Sisera before she murdered him. Freema Gottlieb argued that she did (199), and so does Ackerman (61). Victor H. Matthews and Don C. Benjamin think that Sisera was "planning to rape her and take over the household of Heber" when he went to her tent.[67] This idea, which seems far-fetched is not so far-fetched when viewed as possibly derived from the Ugaritic tale. Anat is the prototype for the danger of seductive women. Men are supposed to fear, not trust, them. So it is with Jael.

One of the points of Anat's killings in the Baal cycle and in *Aqhat* is to show how women (like Pughat in *Aqhat*), as well as men, learn violence from this goddess, the woman warrior. Margalit calls the story *Aqhat* a polemic against the worshipers of this violent goddess, Anat:

> A universe ruled by Anat is indeed evil and capricious; the rejection of Anat in favour of Baal and El will bring in its wake a more just world and redress the balance in terms of just reward and punishment.[68]

(See the discussion of Pughat, a character in *Aqhat*, and Jael below.)

Identification of Deborah with Athtart

Athtart is the shadowy double as well as sister of Anat and possibly another consort of Baal. And equally bellicose. She is a goddess both of love and of war.

According to Sanchuniathon, the Phoenicians identified Athtart with Aphrodite (Oldenburg 43). She may also be identified with Ishtar, who marches before the militant Assyrians. On monuments, Ishtar is depicted with her animal—the lion—and in literature she is described as a furious lion (Oldenburg 40, de Moor 150 n. 13). She is also recognized as Astarte.

"'Athtart, name-of-Baal' is a title designed to describe her as a manifestation of Baal, whose consort she in fact is," notes Gibson (4 n. 6). Philo of Byblos reported that Astarte and Baal ruled the land together, with the consent of El, though not in Ugarit.[69] That "the name itself has some kind of radiance or glory, attests to her martial character and special relationship to the warrior god Baal," writes Smith (*Origins* 74-75). She is represented by the curse mentioned above:

> "May [Horon] smash, [O Yam]
> [may Horon smash] your head,
> Athtart-the-na[me-of-Baal your skull]!"
> (KTU1.2.i.7-9, Wyatt *Religious Texts*, 56; or III.i.7-9, de Moor 30).

An almost identical curse is given by Keret on his son Yassib (*Keret* 1.16.vi.55-57, Wyatt, ibid. 241; also III.vi.55-57, de Moor 222-223). Thus, like Anat, Athtart is known as the smasher of heads. Though not so prominent in the myths as her sister Anat, neither is Deborah when compared with Jael.

Deborah, like Athtart, is also a warrior. She has no lion, but she marches with Barak. In one of the myths, Athtart rebukes and shames Baal for being slow to take advantage of his enemy, just as Deborah rebukes Barak for his unwillingness to go up to battle without her. Baal is sometimes afraid. In the Bible, where Athtart appears under the mistaken name of Ashtoreth, she is a fertility figure.[70] Deborah, whose name means "Honey Bee," represents both sweetness (honey) and fertility (the bee's pollinating function), like Athtart.

Finally, some goddesses in the myths are warriors and fight battles. Israelite women do not. Another reason Jael and Deborah are exceptions may be that they originated as Canaanite goddesses.

Identification of Barak with Baal

Baal and Barak have many similarities.

First, Baal is the god of lightning. As Baal tells Anat, his secret is that "I understand lightning, which the heavens do not know" (3 C, 23, Gibson 49; KTU I.iii.26, de Moor 10). In *Judges*, the meaning of Barak's name is *Lightning*.[71] And the name of Deborah's husband seems to be Lappidoth, meaning *Torches* or *Flasher*—i.e., *Lightning*. In other words, it is a name with the same meaning as *Barak's*. Translations of the Bible make us think Lappidoth and Barak are two different men, but *Lappidoth* may be only an epithet, not a name. Thus it is plausible that Barak (or Lightning) is Deborah's husband (Torches). For two synonymous epithets to refer to a single man would not puzzle an Israelite audience.[72]

Athtart, we have seen, is thought to be one of the consorts of Baal. Though this is not represented in the extant myths, it may be a relationship known in Ugarit. Thus Athtart, wife of Baal (god of lightning) in the Israelite story becomes Deborah, wife of Barak (*lightning*). Jael is disqualified for this role because she is better identified as Anat.

Near the beginning of *The Song*, in a passage already quoted above, Yhwh, the Divine Warrior, like Baal, creates thunder and rain as he marches:

> Yhwh, when you went out from Seir, when you marched from the region of Edom, *the*
> *earth shook, the heavens dropped, the clouds dropped water. The mountains quaked* before the
> Yhwh, this one of Sinai, Elohim of Israel (5.4-5, itals. mine).

And the stars come out to fight against Sisera. In the original Canaanite poem, this might have been a description of Baal. Baal's domain was the weather and the astral bodies that control it; the heavenly bodies and the elements would fight for him, the god of thunder and lightning, against Yam. "Haddu," Baal's epithet, moreover, means "thunderer." Cognate Arabic words denote "demolishing with violence, with a vehement noise," "sound of rain falling from the sky," and "thunder." Another epithet of Baal is "Ilumer," signifying "wind, rainstorm" (Oldenburg 59-60). In an Egyptian stele, the Storm god is depicted "with horns on his head and dressed in a short kilt with his right hand raised to wield a bludgeon and holding the lightning bolt in his left hand." Figurines of the Storm-god found at Ugarit are similar (79).

In *The Song*, the stars and the torrent Kishon are now under Yhwh's command, but they still fight for Barak (Baal) and disperse Sisera's (Yam's) army (5.20-21). Sisera has an equipage equal to Yhwh's, but Barak, a human being with a human army, has no chariots and must rely on the army of Yhwh (Lord of hosts), which no doubt had chariots on the march in 5.4-5 and certainly did in *Ps* 68.

Second, Barak, like Ehud to Eglon, in all likelihood had to pay tribute to Sisera/ Jabin, just as Baal, as Yam's captive, had to pay tribute to *Yam* (KTU 1.ii.37-38, Gibson 42, quoted below). Israel had been oppressed by Jabin for 20 years, and Deborah exhorts him: "Take captive those who have made you captive" (5.12).

Third, in the myths, when Baal is about to kill his captive, instead of merely taking him prisoner, he is scolded roundly by Athtart:

> 'Athtartu rebuked the Name [Baal]:
> "Be *ashamed*, o Ba'lu Almighty!
> Be ashamed, o Rider on the Clouds!
> For his Highness Yammu is our captive,
> [for] Judge Naharu is our captive!"
> (itals. mine. KTU III.iv.29-30, de Moor 41)

In a parallel scene, when Baal takes a "slaughtering axe" in his hand in a fit of rage and is about to murder Yam's messenger, Anat and Athtart hold him back and again shame him (III.i.39-44, de Moor 33-34, quoted below). This is like the scene in which Barak too is scolded and shamed by Deborah when he refuses to go to battle without her. Why would Barak (Baal in the original myth) be afraid to go without Deborah (Anat or Athtart)? Given the warlike nature and fierceness of both these goddesses in the myths, Baal's reluctance to go without his sister would not be surprising. It would be like an Israelite going to war without invoking Yhwh. In the Israelite tale, Barak gives no reason for wanting Deborah to accompany him, and he appears to be a coward. But in the myths, warrior goddesses were expected to engage in violence and win, and sometimes Baal lets them. On one amusing occasion, when he accompanied Anat to induce El's wife, Athirat (Asherah), to persuade El to give Baal a palace, Athirat got on her ass to go to El, but Baal faded away and let his sister Anat accompany Athirat on the mission: "Baal did depart to the height(s) of Zephon," his home (*Palace of Baal*, KTU 4.iv.19, Gibson 59).

Finally, just as Baal fights Yam, but lets Anat kill Yam, so Barak (Baal/Lightning) fights against Sisera (Yam/Sea) and scatters Sisera's hosts, but Sisera flees—for Jael to kill, just as Anat killed Yam.

Identification of Jabin with El

Scholars have great difficulty with Jabin, for they do not believe that Canaan had a king, and since he does not participate in any action himself, they cannot figure out what he is doing in the Deborah story, as Soggin writes of Jabin in Ch. 4 of *Judges*:

> here he appears as an immediate superior of Sisera, and is clearly distinguished from him because *he does absolutely nothing*. Mention of him therefore seems *useless for narrative purposes*; at most it adds one extra fact, that there was *another superior authority above the commander* of the coalition; however, this is an authority who is conspicuous by his absence . . . . He is completely absent from ch. 5 (70) (itals. mine).

In the myth, the king is El. Canaanite storytellers familiar with El's remoteness and passivity in the Ugaritic myths would understand Jabin's remoteness when the story became an Israelite one. They would not question why Jabin (El) himself does not do battle with Barak (Baal), but orders Sisera (his son Yam) to do it. And they would see why Jael (Anat) was loyal to Barak (Baal), rather than to Jabin (El).

Jabin, Sisera's king, lived in Hazor, and we might expect Sisera's city, Harosheth-ha-goyim (of the Gentiles), to be nearby. Though the precise location of Harosheth is not known, it was apparently not close to Jabin. All we know is that it is not Israelite. But the gods in the myths do not live near each other either. And a storyteller adapting a myth probably did not have a map at hand.

Identification of Sisera with Yam

Sisera would be derived from Yam/Nahar, the god of the sea and river. While Ugarit was a thriving maritime port, Israel was in the hills, far from the sea. The story of Deborah is incongruously connected with the sea, but this discrepancy can be explained if the story had originated in a thriving seaport like Ugarit.

Sisera as Yam, the sea god, helps explain some of the disputed meanings in *The Song*. Dan abiding with the ships and Asher sitting still at the coast of the sea (5.17) are troublesome passages since the Bible locates those Israelite tribes not by the sea, but in the north, the area of Kedesh, Hazor (supposedly Jabin's city), and Naphtali, the locations of the Deborah story in Ch. 4. The names *Dan* and *Asher* are Canaanite gods in their origin, as C. F. Burney reminds us (197, 392, et passim). *Dan* means *judge* and refers to El, while *Asher* is the masculine form of *Asherah*. That Dan and Asher remain by the ships or at the coast would signify loyalty to Yam (son of El and Asherah) rather than to Baal (son of Dagon). As gods in "El's family," they would naturally not fight *against* Yam, who is their brother, nor would they fight *for* Baal, who is not their brother. At the time of the transformation of the tale into an Israelite story, they remain in their original location, though the storyteller has now identified them as Israelites. Israel does not seem to have had any seaports until at least the time of Solomon, and precious few after that.

The name of Sisera has always mystified interpreters, who do not recognize it as Semitic and connect his name with the Sea People (Boling, 94; Soggin 63, 68). Yam, the god of the Sea, has been identified with the Greek god of the sea, Poseidon. Poseidon is also known as "Hippios," i.e., *of horses*. Sisera's name (סיסרא) contains two samechs as does the Hebrew word for *horse* (סוס) and may be intended to echo that word. Poseidon, like Yam, has chariots drawn by horses, and Sisera has 900 horse-drawn chariots of iron. Keret and Danel in the myths have chariots, the "shades" of the underworld have chariots, as did the people of Ugarit, but the Israelites in *Judges* do not, for they lived in the hill country, where chariots were not practical, and the society was not yet prosperous enough to make them obtainable. (They probably had no chariots until the time of David.) The reason that the storyteller allowed Sisera, when transformed into a human being, to keep his equipment, while Barak had none, is to emphasize the disparity between the forces, making Barak's and Jael's victory all the more unlikely and thus more astounding.

Other reasons for identifying Sisera with Yam will be given in the next section.

Identification of Sisera's mother with Athirat

In the myth, the mother of Yam is Athirat, and she hates Baal for good reason. Both Athirat and Sisera's mother lose a son. Athirat is called "she who treads the sea"—an important link with the sea god Yam—and when Anat and Baal come to her to ask her to intercede with El for them, they find her at the seashore, doing the laundry.[73] As Baal and Anat approach her, she cries:

> 'How (is it that) mightiest Baal has arrived?
> 'How (is it that) the virgin Anat has arrived?
> 'Are my enemies come to smite my sons
> 'or [make an end of] the company of my kinsfolk?'
> (*Palace of Baal*, 4.ii.21-26, Gibson 57)

As the mother of both Yam and Mot, both of whom would be defeated by Baal, Athirat naturally fears Baal. Eventually he would also kill her 77-88 children, an event alluded to in the above passage and predicted in the following:

> "Ba'lu will seize the sons of Athiratu.
> The big ones he will slay with an axe-blade,
>> those who are like Yammu he will slay with an axe,
>>> the small ones he will pull to the ground.
> Ba'lu [will sit down] on the chair of his kingship,
>> on the seat of the throne of his dominion."
> (*KTU* VI.v.1-6, de Moor 94; Gibson's translation, uses the past tense [quoted with the enthronement psalms above].)

In the Hittite myth of Elkunirsa (meaning "El creator of the earth"), "the storm-god boasted of having killed the many sons of Asheratu or Athirat" (Gibson 11, n. 1).

Gibson believes this myth was based on a Canaanite original in which Baal did kill the sons of Athirat and El. So Athirat's fear of Baal was well-grounded.

Athirat, called Asherah in the Hebrew Bible, is regarded as Baal's consort in the Bible (as in the Gideon story, for example), though in Israelite inscriptions, she is the consort of Yhwh and is the goddess for whom women are weaving "hangings" in 2 Kg 23.7. The later redactors believed that by the time Jezebel brought Baal worship to Jerusalem, Baal had taken Athirat as his consort when El was old, and such was reported by Philo. She was never Baal's consort in the Ugaritic myths, however.

The pairing of Asherah and Baal in the Bible may be a polemic against her in order to tarnish her reputation and thus remove her from her position as *Yhwh's* consort, as she may have been at the time of the Kuntillet 'Ajrud inscription. In the Baal cycle, Athirat (or Asherah) is El's consort and a foe to Baal.

Four more details in addition to the death of her son Yam may link Sisera's mother with Athirat of the Ugaritic myths: the window and the lattice out of which she is looking, the "wise women" with her, the captive maidens, and the dyed materials.

The window

In the myths, after he defeats Yam, Baal asks El for a palace, and the Ugaritic poet goes to great length to express the importance of there being a window in it. In the myth of Baal, the word *lattice* is paired with *window* just as it is in *The Song* (5.28). Baal at first does not want the window, but at last reluctantly agrees to it and ultimately seems to be delighted with the effect he can create by roaring out his window far and wide. Perhaps his reason for at first not wanting it is that a window could allow the dangerous waters of Yam to re-enter the firmament (Gibson 14). The significance of this window to either the Ugaritic or Israelite poet, however, is none too clear, nor is it clear why a window is mentioned in *The Song*, unless it is just another building-part of an important keyword category.

But why was Sisera's mother at a *window* instead of a *door*? For Susan Ackerman and others, it calls to mind the "woman at the window" plaques of Asherah and other Canaanite goddesses (159).[74] But of course, it is also a natural place for a mother to wait for the return of her son from battle, wondering what is keeping her loved one so long. The question of whether or not this window relates to the Ugaritic myths remains to be answered.

The interesting thing is that it is the mother, not a wife, who is waiting for the returning hero. Yam, Athirat's son, is apparently not married and is still young. In the myths, his mother is the character most concerned about him.

The captives and the spoil

Why does Sisera's mother imagine Sisera as bringing not gold and silver spoil, but rather "dyed stuff" and captive women (רחמתים), specifically *two* for each man? Could these items be a link with Canaanite religious practices mentioned above when Josiah "broke down the houses of the male cult prostitutes which were in the house of Yhwh, where the women wove hangings for the Asherah" (2 Kg

23.7)? Sacred prostitution was one of the Yahwist charges against Canaanite religion, as mentioned in 2 Kgs. Whether this was a valid charge is not known.

The captive women in *The Song* were viewed by Craigie as an important irony, in that Sisera himself had already been taken captive—by *two* women. Women have always been part of the spoils of war. Yhwh (created from the Canaanite El) marched and took captives and spoil, as we saw in Ps 68:

> "The kings of the armies, they flee, they flee!" The women at home divide the spoil . . . .
>
> You ascended the high mount, leading captives in your train and receiving gifts from people . . . (Ps 68.12, 18).

The spoil in the Ugaritic story would have been received by a god or a goddess like Athirat, now Sisera's mother.

The wise women

The "wise" women waiting with Sisera's mother (5.29) who give answer to her question are possibly the Kotharat,[75] whose name means *skillful* (Gibson n. 4, 24). In the Ugaritic pantheon, they are guardians of weddings and protectors of the marriage bed. They are also the midwives of the gods. As the *Danel* and *Keret* myths show, they are:

> swallow-like daughters of the crescent moon,
>
> those [artful] in pleasure(s) of the bed of conception,
>
> delight(s) of the bed of childbirth.
>
> (*Aqhat*, 17.ii.40-41, Gibson 106)

But why would Sisera's mother have midwives in attendance? The answer is found in the Hebrew word for "captive maidens," which is *wombs* (רחם 5.30) (see also Burney 155). The wise women therefore may be present to assure the "delights" referred to in the quotation above, "the pleasures of the bed of conception" when Sisera (Yam) returns home. Had Sisera been victorious, the two captive wombs might have been those of Deborah and Jael. Thus how much greater the impact of that penultimate line in *The Song of Deborah*, "So perish all thine enemies, O Lord!" (5.31a).

The window, the "wisest ladies," and the cloths are hard to explain as elements of the Israelite story, but have significance as traces of an Ugaritic one.[76]

The geographical problem

A further question for biblical scholars to ponder is why all the main characters and events of the story of Deborah (Ch. 4) are in locations so remote from each other, why the tent of Heber is near Kedesh-Naphtali, but the battle is fought far away along the river Kishon, and why Sisera musters troops from Harosheth instead of Hazor where Jabin resides—details not fitting in well with the known Israelite geography. It is also odd that Hazor never seems to have had a king, that the city had supposedly been destroyed by Joshua (before Deborah's battle took place), and that Deborah in Ephraim recruits Barak, who lives so far distant from her in Naphtali—Barak, north of the Sea of Galilee and Deborah, who lives south of Galilee between Ramah and Bethel. What power she would have over Barak, so far away from her, is hard to fathom. Compare the Israelite locations with the Ugaritic ones:

Table I. Geographical Locations Compared

El lives in a remote abode on high mountains (Margalit says it is at Mt. Hermon) "where the rivers and oceans emerge from the earth" (Gibson 10).	Jabin (El) lives to the far north in Hazor, near the upper Jordan and Lake Huleh, not far from Mt. Hermon.
Baal lives on Mt. Zaphon (the north).	Barak (Baal) lives in Kedesh-Naphtali (in the north in the territory of Naphtali).[1] He significantly descends from a mountain (Tabor) for the battle.
Anat lives on Ughra and Inbubu (an unknown mountain some distance from Baal).	Jael (Anat) lives in Kedesh near Elonbezaannim (in the north), 30 miles from Tabor, where the battle begins, a considerable distance from Barak.
Athtart's location is not given in the myths.[2]	Deborah (Athtart) lives in Israel, between Bethel and Ramah under a palm on "Mt. Ephraim." It is perhaps significant that she is associated with a mountain.
Athirat lives by the sea, not with El.	Sisera's mother lives with or near Sisera, as she expects to see him return.
Yam lives in his palace in the sea.	Sisera (Yam) is from "the place of the pagans."[3]

---

1   Two significantly-named towns in Naphtali are mentioned in *Judges* 1.33: "Naphtali did not drive out the inhabitants of Beth Shemesh or Beth Anath . . . but those living in Beth Shemesh and Beth Anath became forced laborers for them." Perhaps the author of *Judges* assumed that these Canaanite towns became the source of forced labor after Barak's conquering of Sisera.

2   Since she and Anat are doubles and since both of them are called the consort of Baal, perhaps she lives on the same mountain as Anat. Although Athtart and Anat are sometimes seen as identical, sometimes they are not. Neither is Deborah identical to Jael.

3   Various locations are given for Harosheth-ha-goiim: near the foot of Mt. Carmel (Soggin, 63) (i.e., not far from the sea) or in the forests of Galilee (Y. Aharoni, cited by Soggin 63), or on the plain of Sharon (Boling 94), but not up north, near Hazor. Jabin lives in Hazor, which is near the Sea of Galilee. Thus Harosheth may be nearby.

Everything in *The Song of Deborah*, writes Nadav Na'aman, is a geographical problem:

> ... The conclusion is inevitable: either the author of the story or a late redactor was not acquainted with the geography of northern Israel and mixed up the narrative elements in a way that excludes any geographical sense from the description.

Na'aman notes the differences between the geography of the prose story and that of *The Song*. "The author further replaces certain geographical names by others, which presumably were better known to his readers."[77] All of these locations with respect to each other make bad sense if we are dealing with real Israelites in a tribal battle circa 1125 BCE, but good sense if we are dealing with Canaanite gods in the dim past.

In theory, the Canaanite gods, though in some vaguely cosmic realm, are thought of as belonging to the region of Ugarit. Yet Margalit shows that the location of *Aqhat*, a story about human beings, is in the region of Lake Kinneret (Sea of Galilee), in the same region as some of the locations in the Deborah story.

In the Galilee region, says Margalit, "plastered skulls," such as *Aqhat* describes, have been found. Danel throws the body of Aqhat into Lake Kinneret (Galilee), in fact.[78] And Bashan, associated with Mot and the Rephaim (which may be the spirits of the dead), is actually nearby in the Transjordan (251, 309).[79]

Margalit also connects Aqhat's father Danel with both the tribe of Dan and the Daniel mentioned in several places in the Hebrew Bible, and he notes that the tribe of Dan was located near Mt. Hermon, the source of the Jordan River and Lake Kinneret. "Even as late as Hellenistic times (ca. 200 BCE), it is not unlikely that El is still 'the god who is in Dan,' a situation conceivably anticipated already in the name of the Ugaritic hero 'Dan'el'" (430). From these reasons, we can deduce that the Canaanite myths were not confined to the area of Ugarit, but were also available in Israel, the land to the south.

The Song may represent an intermediate stage in the transformation from Ugaritic myth to Israelite story. The main outline of the Ugaritic myth remained, even though the names were translated into Israelite forms. The transition audience would have no difficulty with the changes made, just as we have none when *Romeo and Juliet* appeared as *West Side Story*.

VI. Samson and the Myths

Identification of Samson with Baal

The complete interdependence of the Deborah and Samson stories (with their numerous parallels, as listed in Chapter 1) suggests that they were a connected pair from their origin, or at least from the time they were placed in the Hebrew text of *Judges*. Since *The Song* apparently contains a submerged Ugaritic myth, it is quite likely that its companion piece, the Samson story, does as well.

No Ugaritic myth corresponds as well to the Samson story as the *Baal and Yam* myth does with *The Song*. But a hypothetical myth constructed out of Ugaritic materials can help reconstruct the archetype we are searching for. As Hugh Rowland Page reminded us, Canaanite allusions in Biblical literature "can be used productively in reconstructing certain elements of older Canaanite tradition" (204).

Let us consider the possibility that Samson is Baal.

1.   Like Samson, Baal is none too intelligent. Whereas El is known for wisdom, cunning, and craftiness (Oldenburg 21, 24), Baal is sometimes obtuse.

2.   Like Samson, Baal is a man of few words. "Great are the deeds of Baal," writes Oldenburg, "but rather few his words. Greater is his strength than his wisdom" (70, 74).

3.   In contrast to El who in the Ugaritic myths is normally portrayed as "physically weak, indecisive, senile, procrastinating, and submissive" (23), Baal is young and active. The reader will remember many examples of Samson's hyperactivity: tearing apart a lion, killing a thousand Philistines with the jawbone of an ass, tying the tails of 300 foxes together and setting fire to them, carrying the gate from the city of Gaza forty miles away up the hill before Hebron, continually pursuing women (exhibiting his sexual prowess), and tearing down a temple with his biceps. No bonds can hold him. Nothing can keep him from doing mischief until Delilah comes along to tame him (as the temple priestess/prostitute does to Enkidu in *Gilgamesh*).

Smith speaks repeatedly of Baal as being weak.

> The presentation of Baal as a relatively weaker figure needing extensive divine assistance is consistent with his presentation throughout the cycle. Indeed, Baal is no super conquering god like Marduk in Enuma Elish or Yahweh in so much Israelite poetry (*Origins* 129).

In my opinion, though he may be weak in character, he is not weak in body as we see in his battle with Mot:

> They eyed each other like burning coals;
>
> Mot was strong, Baal was strong.
>
> They gored like wild oxen;
>
> Mot was strong, Baal was strong.
>
> They bit like serpents;
>
> Mot was strong, Baal was strong.
>
> They tugged like greyhounds;
>
> Mot fell down, Baal fell down on top of him.
>
> (*Baal and Mot*, 6.vi.16-22, Gibson 80.)

4.   In Ugaritic myth Baal is often angry. Like Samson (and, as we have seen, like Anat and Athtart), Baal is connected with breaking skulls. "El always blesses," writes Oldenburg, but "Baal mostly curses . . . . Dn'il cries, 'May Baal break the wings of the eagles,/may Baal break their pinions that they may fall at my feet.' This Baal does . . ." (71). Samson too is a troublemaker, and directs his anger against everyone, even the lion cub and the innocent foxes, just as Baal does against the eagles.

5.   Baal (like Samson) is a loner. As Oldenburg writes, "the whole battle with Yamm is described as a single combat, like his other battles" (70).

> Baal is constantly seen in battle. In his earlier battles with Yamm and with his other enemies he uses long range weapons: the two swooping clubs given by *Ktr w Hss*, which

fly from the hands of Baal like eagles down into the deep where Yamm is sitting [UM 68:11-25] or, according to another text, the cedar wood which speeds from his right hand [UM 51:VII:35-41]. Later in time, he fights with Mot and the sons of Asherah in hand-to-hand fighting . . . (74). (See *Baal and Yam*, 2.iv, 23-25, Gibson 44.)

Baal and Mot met in single combat, not with armies.

Although Baal uses clubs in conquering Yam, he uses no weapons against Mot. Samson uses his bare hands to tear the lion cub apart and has no weapons against the Philistines except the jawbone of the ass, which he finds on the ground.

6.   Like Samson, Baal is impetuous, full of unruly passions, and he lunges into battle without preparation, rhyme, or reason. Of the scene where Baal is prevented from killing the messengers, Oldenburg writes:

> Baal is a very emotional young hero. His youth is mentioned in the early texts of the Baal-Anat cycle; he is called "the lad," and all his emotions are as those of an adolescent. When the messengers of Yamm have delivered their message, and El has surrendered Baal as Yamm's slave, "then Prince Baal is a man of the field of Mot" [i.e., he runs amuck] [UM 137: 38, 3]); seizing a knife, he rushes against the messengers. Only two goddesses can keep him back and bring him to reason. That it is not strong gods, but only goddesses alone who can hold him, shows his state of adolescence . . . . Women are his best servants, whom he dispatches on most important errands . . . (70). (See KTU III.i.39-44 and III.iv.29-35, de Moor 33-35 and 41.)

In Oldenburg's description, Baal is remarkably like Samson. Samson, too, is called "the lad." Oldenburg cites the poem in which Baal has a fit of rage in the assembly of the gods.

> He arises and spits in the midst of the assembly, rebuking the gods because of some displeasing act [UM 51: III: 1-22]. Raging because of the hypocrisy of El and other gods, he calls them, "Impious, profane persons" [UM 133 rev.: 8]. Without taking into consideration who will be on his side and who against him, nor preparing much for the battle, Baal goes in person against Yamm. Dire curses he utters against Yamm [UM 137:6-9] . . . (70). (See KTU IV.iii.12-14; III.i, 6-9, de Moor 49, 30; or 2.i.38-44, Gibson 42.)

Baal is the equal of the headstrong angry Samson in this respect.

7.   Like Samson, Baal prefers the company of women to men. We never see Baal with the male gods. In fact, "the young Baal is sexually highly potent. This is seen from the love scenes so vividly describing his sexual intercourse with Anat in the meadow of *Smk* and with a heifer in the field of failings" (Oldenburg 71). In one of the Ugaritic poems, Baal mates with a cow, and he has a steer by Anat. In his rage when the wedding guests solve his riddle, Samson accuses them of having "plowed with his heifer" (14.18). This is not merely a crude metaphor, but is perhaps a reference to the mating described in this Ugaritic myth. It is significant that Baal himself had once "plowed" with a heifer. Unlike Baal, however, Samson is unlucky with women.

8.   Like Baal, Samson collapses from the heat (15.18). His tremendous thirst at En Hakkore (15.18-19) has its counterpart when Baal is enticed to leave his land and go to the fringes of the desert to attack the Devourers and Rippers—El's "voracious offspring" (Schloen 355)—where he too is stricken by the heat.

> Ba'lu was walking around and scouring (the area),
>> rushing along the fringes of the desert . . . .
>
> (But) Ba'lu fell into the marsh
>> [Haddu] felt heat in his nose,
>
> [Motu] sent fever into his loins,
>> [he consumed] his horns like branches,
>
>> he himself, as when he scorches [the olives] . . . .
>
> The growth on the fields turned brown
>
> Seven years the god completed,
>> eight cycles of time . . . .
>
> Then had Ba'lu fallen like a bull . . . .
>> down into the middle of the marsh.
>
> (*Myth and Ritual*, KTU 12.II.i.34-35; ii.36-40, 44-45, 54-55 de Moor 133-134.)

He kills the offspring (Schloen idem) and is himself killed (Oldenburg 76). The death of Baal brings about seven years of drought. It was the lack of rain that made the fields turn brown. Baal was apparently powerless to change this, until he revived. Samson, however, in his thirst, called upon Yhwh and received water to drink.

9.   As with Baal, Samson's enemies are "out to get him" and make many attempts. Samson becomes a slave to the Philistines (Dagon's people) just as Baal becomes a slave to Yam.

10. Both Samson and Baal are resurrected. Though defeated, blinded, and enslaved, nevertheless Samson still rises. He is "like the sun as he rises in his might" (5.31)—both when he rises from the slave mill and when he crushes his enemies as he dies.

Thus we have at least ten ways in which Samson resembles Baal. Though perhaps Baal is more charming and Samson more grotesque, the two are counterparts of each other. The main obstacle to identifying Samson as Baal, however, is that while Baal's chief opponents are Yam and Mot (sons of El), Samson's—in addition to the Philistines—is Dagon, who is considered the father of Baal.

The Ugaritic myths do not include a story about Dagon, but since Baal is a son of Dagon and since a temple to Dagon existed at Ugarit, myths about Dagon may have circulated there at one time.[80] But unless this is another Freudian (Oedipus) situation, we have no reason to think that Baal would engage in a series of battles against his own father or the "family of Dagon." And such a hypothesis is not borne out by the extant Ugaritic texts, though they do contain other Oedipus figures, like Yassib in *Keret*.

Baal is sometimes referred to as the son of El. Since El is considered the father of all human kind, then this epithet may be metaphorical.[81] Or it may be that in other versions of the myth, Baal *is* the son of El, and not of Dagon. On the other hand, the attack on Dagon by Samson may be the Israelite author's invention when adapting the myth as an Israelite story. He is attacking the Philistines, whose god is Dagon. It no longer matters that his heroic prototype was a son of Dagon.

Although I have not invented a hypothetical plot for these materials, I believe that when the storyteller brought the god down to earth and gave Samson an earthly form, he retained his Baal-like attributes.

Samson and the Solar Myth

That the story is a solar myth or was influenced by solar mythology is hardly a new idea, though in general it was discredited and displaced by interpreters in their search for history.[82] With the emergence of recent scholarship on the Ugaritic myths, however, we must consider this possibility anew.

If Samson is the Sun god, then the problem of the enmity between Samson and Dagon makes sense, for in the Middle East, the sun is a destroyer of fields of grain whom the farmer no doubt would like to control. "With Baal, *Sps* [the sun goddess] is a great blessing for the crops," writes Oldenburg, "and these two worked well together; but in the power of Mot, or literally 'in the hand of' (Ugaritic *byd*) Mot, *Sps* can destroy the field, burning the crops" (94). Though it was also within the rain god's power to withhold rain and thus burn the fields, the sun was the greater enemy.

In a long essay, "The Mythical Element in the Story of Samson" in his commentary on *Judges* (1903), C. F. Burney acknowledges that the story exhibits "strongly-marked traces of an ancient solar myth . . ." (339). Burney recounts Samson's similarity to Gilgamesh, tells in detail the journey of Gilgamesh and its correspondence to the journey of the sun, and lists the many ways in which Samson could be a solar hero.

Three of his conclusions, however, can be questioned. First, he called *Judges* an "artless" folktale, the product of storytellers. But as I have shown throughout this present study, *Judges* as anything but "artless." Second, he did not believe that the Israelite author of *Judges* was conscious that he was using a solar myth; rather, he thinks that "the original significance" of the story "had doubtless been forgotten when it was drawn upon to enrich the halo of the marvelous with which the popular imagination loved to surround the deeds of the tribal hero" (339). Possibly this is true; it would be hard to prove otherwise. But it is much more likely that the author was rescuing a myth valued by storytellers at a time when the Israelites still worshiped the sun, transforming it later when the Canaanite religion was being condemned by Yahwists. (Astral worship still existed in the time of Josiah, as shown in the long quote above from 2 Kg 23, *passim*).

Third, Burney did not find the mythic elements significant in comparison to the information which the story gives us about the simple village life of those times (339, 403). The information about village life is important, as I have shown elsewhere, but certainly it is not more important than other details of the story. Despite these reservations, Burney's suggestions about Samson are extremely perceptive—especially considering the period in which he wrote, many years before the discovery of the Ugaritic texts at Ras Shamra and the proliferation of scholarly articles about the literature of the Middle East.

It is surprising that recent commentaries on Samson either do not discuss the solar myth theory, or else dismiss it without discussion (Hooke 15). Theodor H. Gaster, for example, mentions the possibility of Samson representing the sun, only to repudiate the idea:

> In the light of Comparative Folklore, this interpretation can no longer be sustained. The incident of the foxes has, as we shall see, several parallels in other cultures, in all of which it possesses no symbolic significance, but can be readily explained as based either on a well-established ritual practice or an equally well-documented military stratagem. There are likewise plenty of analogues to the story of how a hero was enfeebled by the shearing of his locks, and in none of them does he bear a name which has anything whatsoever to do with the sun. What is more, we now know both from Mesopotamian and from Canaanite sources that Samson (or its equivalent) was in fact a not uncommon name among ordinary mortals.[83]

I question in particular that the fox story "possesses no symbolic significance." As I have shown elsewhere, the story shows Samson in his role as a consumer and destroyer, and equates him with the characteristics of a fox, as well as of a lion and a donkey in other parts of the story. These objections, in any case, do not nullify the existence of solar imagery in the Samson story. Even if the stratagem of the foxes has an origin in a real stratagem in the ancient world, this does not mean it cannot be used creatively in myth or story. Likewise the etymology of his name.

One difficulty in identifying Samson with the Sun God is that the Sun God in the Ugaritic texts is Shapash, a goddess. Since in other mythologies the Sun is depicted as male, however, the actual source of the Samson myth may have not been Ugaritic but some other ancient Near Eastern myth, but anyway, according to Walter Beyerlin, the sun god, Shamash, was male elsewhere in Palestine.[84]

Samson fits into the role of the Sun God for two reasons: first, his name and second, the fire imagery. Three consonants of Samson's name (שמשון) are the same as the consonants for the Hebrew word for *sun* (shemesh, שמש). And the story is set near the location of Beth-shemesh ("house," or "temple of the sun").[85] If, as Gaster says, his name was a common one, the author did not have to invent another name for him; it was undoubtedly theophoric, a likely reference to the sun god.

Second, sun and fire imagery plays an important role in the Samson story. (I am indebted to C. F. Burney for several of the following ideas.)

1) Samson's "hot anger," for example, is like the blaze of the sun.

2) Samson burns the fields of grain by tying torches on the tails of 300 foxes. Both Burney (393-394) and Gaster (435), among others, refer to the Roman custom on the feast of Ceres in April when foxes were released into their fields with lighted torches on their tails to prevent some type of fungus. If such a custom ever existed

(though it taxes one's imagination to believe they used foxes to do it), it reinforces the theory that the Samson story is a fertility myth, for Ceres, the Roman goddess of grain, is a counterpart to the Ugaritic Dagon. However it was done or why, we are to understand that fields of grain were burned.

But in addition to the fields of grain (produce of the earth), he also burned up the vineyards (fruit) and olive groves (olive) (15.5). This line seems *significantly comparable* to the following passage when Baal has been condemned to be swallowed by Mot:

> [Ba]al must enter his belly,
>
> down into his mouth he must go,
>
> since he scorched *the olive*,
>
> the *produce of the earth*,
>
> and the *fruit of the trees*. (1.5.ii.4-8, Wyatt, *Religious Texts*, 120)

The reference of the pronoun in the third line of the passage is ambiguous. Wyatt thinks it refers to Mot, but more likely it refers to Baal whose scorching of olive, produce (grain), and fruit (grape?) gives the reason why Mot swallowed him. The fact that these are the very crops that Samson burned is most significant.

3)   When Samson is bound, "the ropes which were on his arms became as flax that has caught *fire*, and his bonds *melted* off his hands" (15.14)—as one might expect the powerful sun to do. This happens again in the Delilah episode: "he snapped the bowstrings, as a string of tow snaps when it touches the *fire*" (16.9).

4)   His bursts of energy, as Burney mentions, are like that of the sun. In fact, no other character in *Judges* has such bursts or could be cited as analogous to the sun.

5)   His way of disappearing (to Timnah, to the vineyards, to the Rock of Etam, or to Lehi) is like the sun going temporarily under a cloud.

6)   Like the Sun, Samson is always in motion, always changing. The Sun can be regarded as having no rhyme or reason. Just as it burns and destroys and comes and goes willy nilly, so does Samson. When he is perceived as the Sun, his behavior is not so stupid as it would be for a human being acting like this.

7)   The scene at En Hakkore—where Samson asks Yhwh (El) for, and receives, a spring of water to slake his thirst (15.18)—also fits into the sun imagery. When the water came from the hollow place at Lehi, Samson "drank, his spirit returned, and he revived." In other words, as Burney suggests, like the sun at times he is "drawing water."

8)   Samson represents the heat of passion: he attempts to marry the Timnite, he sleeps with a harlot in Gaza, and he has a love affair with Delilah. "To the Akkadians, Samas [the Sun God], the moon god Sin, and the Venus Star Ishtar constituted a triad" (Oldenburg 92). A similar triad may have existed in Canaanite myth. One of these triads might have come into Israelite legend as Samson, the Timnite (or the harlot), and Delilah.

The sun imagery is especially apparent in the incident with the harlot, for after a night of pleasure, Samson gets up and like Apollo or Helios transporting the sun, also carries the gates—a heavy burden—from Gaza up to the top of the hill before Hebron. Burney's explanation is that "the sun, in rising, issues through a door with double gates on the extremity of the eastern horizon. Compare the representation of the Sun-god Samas passing through such gates, which are held open for him by attendants." Burney suggests further that "some particular hill to the east of Hebron may have acquired a name as the hill over which, from the Shephelah, the sun was regularly observed to rise" (407). Samson's carrying of the *gates* so many miles up to the top of a the hill has no explanation except as a feat of strength. But if Samson represents the rays of the sun, this feat makes sense.

9)   The sun loses its strength when its rays (locks) are removed. Samson's locks are removed by Delilah, who may represent Night. No satisfactory etymology has been found by Semitic scholars for the name "Delilah," as far as I know. Boling suggests that her name means "Flirtatious," while Soggin ventures "falling curl," or "be humble" (248), and Soggin thinks that her name might be related to that of Lilith, the demon (253). Delilah's name in Hebrew, however, contains the consonants for "Night," even though they are pointed differently. Daniel I. Block agrees.[86] This part of Samson's story represents a division between Sun (eyes) and Darkness (blindness). Day and Night are divine pairs in cosmogonic myths (Cross 40). Night is the one element that can conquer the sun, but it can do that only temporarily. For the next day, the sun will rise again in its might (5.31). It is one of the many binary opposites in the book: Night (no sun, Delilah) vs. Day (sun, Samson). Night wins temporarily, but then "the sun rises in its might."

10) Delilah (night) is being paid by the Philistines, or the "family of Dagon" (grain fields), to trap Samson (the sun).

The trap is the loom that Delilah has in her chamber. To our amusement and for our edification, she is weaving Samson into her tapestry, catching him in her web. The simple raison d'être for having the loom in the story is to give Delilah the tool with which she might capture Samson and thus to provide one of the author's many links between Jael and Delilah. Delilah uses the same tool (יתד) as Jael. Perhaps Delilah's room is another reference to the immoral houses in which the women were weaving "hangings" for Asherah in 2 Kg 23.7. The weaving and loom might signify that she was a cultic prostitute. Burney mentions the attempt of Ishtar to seduce Gilgamesh and connects Delilah's name with *"Dail-(ilu)-Istar,"* meaning "worshiper of Ishtar." He concludes that Delilah was "a sacred prostitute devoted to the service of the goddess" (407). Though these are interesting possibilities, they are not relevant to the solar myth theory, unless it is Night which does it. Then the weaving (i.e., capturing the sun) is relevant.

11) If Dagon is Samson's opponent, one must then ask: why would the sun god want to defeat the grain god, especially since the sun is necessary for the crops? The answer is that in reality, the sun often destroys crops and helps create droughts. And we can imagine the sun doing so angrily.

In the Ugaritic version of the Sun God, the goddess Shapash, is a fertility goddess: "*Sps* makes fruitful their branches and grapes" ("Birth of the Gods," UM 52:25-26. Quoted by Oldenburg 94). Sorek, the valley in which Delilah lives, is known for its grape production. This may be why the Philistines do not *kill* Samson (the sun); they only want to "overpower him," "bind him to subdue him," and "mock him" (16.5, 25). Control of the sun would have been desirable to the farmer to prevent it from destroying crops through its excessive heat.

Samson's punishment, when caught, is to have his eyes (his illumination) put out and be made *a slave to grain*. Samson at the mill, says Burney, may also represent the daily fixed routine of the sun which, though powerful, is powerless to alter its own course (408).

In adapting a Ugaritic myth for Israelite audiences, moreover, the author made the Philistines and their god Samson's enemies. In the Israelite story, he is no longer the son of Dagon.

12) As Burney points out, the collapse of the temple on Samson may represent the way the sun seems to be "pulling down the western pillars which were thought to support the vault of heaven" at night.[87] The collapse of the temple may represent folk wisdom: better leave nature alone, for in trying to control it, we may wreak our own destruction. As the ending shows, "those he killed at his death were more than those he had killed during his life" (16.30).

13) Samson is a *judge*, albeit an undignified and unlikely one, who is never depicted in an act of judging, and who we would guess would do it badly. Though all the gods in Ugaritic myth are *judges*, the Sun God may have had a greater connection with judgment than the other gods. In Mesopotamia, where "the worship of the sun god became very important," Samas (the Sun God) "was the god of righteousness, and it was he who gave to Hammurapi the laws of Babylonia. Samas and Adad [Baal Haddad] are often mentioned together as lords of divination and dispensers of judgment" (Oldenburg 92). Brought down to an earthly status, the storyteller did not retain the wisdom aspect of his character, but kept his title.

Samson is also a Danite, and the word *Dan*, in Hebrew, means *judge*. Burney believes that the original patron-deity of the tribe of Dan may have been the Sun God (392). (See above discussions of Dan and Asher in the sections about the term *judge* and the identification of Barak with Baal.)

The ultimate meaning of the myth seems to be that the two gods—Sun and Grain—are interdependent. The death of Samson (the sun) was not the Philistines' intention; they wanted only to harness the sun, to get it to work on their grain for them. In fact, Samson (the Sun) brings about his own death at the same time that he destroys Dagon. The story is another death-and-resurrection fertility myth, the cycle of which is seasonal. We know that neither the Sun nor Dagon will remain dead; in the spring, they will rise again.

The argument that Samson represents the sun is strong. Elsewhere in the Middle East, moreover, Baal Hadad himself was known as the Sun God. In the time of

Sanchuniathon, writes Oldenburg, "when Hadad has become the god above all other gods of the Syrian pantheon, he takes over the dominion and title of Samas and becomes Baal Samaiim," God of the Heavens, the Sun God (10, 94). Baal assumes control of both rain *and shine*. Possibly the Samson story represents this stage of the myth; he is the perfect candidate for both roles. We can combine the characteristics identified as those of Baal with the characteristics of the Sun God. And now we have a plot: the plot of the Samson story.

The theophany of the Samson story (Ch. 13) does not fit in with the solar myth theory, as far as extant information shows. No supernatural visitations were needed for the birth of a god. As already discussed, the theophany has other reasons for existence.

This hypothetical reconstruction of the Shamash/Baal/Dagon myth provides explanations for a number of odd details in the Samson story. Whatever else, it enables us to perceive the closeness of the Samson story to themes in the Ugaritic poems.

VII. Other Stories

Without a more thorough examination of other stories in *Judges* for mythic material, I can offer only a few observations about the influence of the myths on them.

Achsah (1.12-15)

The scene in *The Palace of Baal* where Athirat (Asherah) bids her servant to prepare an ass for her journey to her husband, El, recalls the scene where Achsah sets off on her ass to go to her father.

In the myth, Anat and Baal bribe Athirat with rich gifts, crafted by Kothar-and-Khasis, to help Athirat intercede with her consort El to give Baal permission to build a palace of his own. Her attendant is Qodesh-and-Amrur, a composite (male) deity whose name means *holiness* and *blessing* (Gibson 10 n. 4). Compare these names with Achsah's request from her father for a בְּרָכָה, which means *present* or *blessing* (1.15).

It is not clear in *Judges* who urged whom to ask for the *present*, whether Achsah urged Othniel, as in the MT, or Othniel urged Achsah as in the LXX (but the latter makes more sense).[88] Perhaps her husband rehearsed her on how to plead, just as someone (Baal) in the myth has urged Anat to instigate the mission and is lurking in the background (like Othniel), but does not go with her. Although it is El's *wife* who approaches El, El is called the "*father* of years," and she is going to ask *a boon*. The poem reads:

> [Hear, o Qodesh-]and-Amrur,
> '[o fisherman of dame] Athirat of the sea.
> '[Saddle a he-ass], yoke a donkey,
> '[put on harness of] silver,
> '[trappings] of gold,
> 'make ready the harness of [my] she-asses.'

Qodesh-and-Amrur heard,

he did saddle a he-ass, did yoke a donkey,

did put on harness of silver,

trappings of gold,

did make ready the harness of her she-asses.

Qodesh-and-Amrur put his arms around (her)

(and) set Athirat on the back of the he-ass,

on the easiest part of the back of the donkey.

Qodesh took a torch,

Amrur was like a star in front.

Behind (came) the virgin Anat,

but Baal did depart to the height(s) of Zephon.

Then indeed she set (her) face

towards El at the source(s) of the rivers,

amid the springs of the two oceans;

she penetrated the mountain(s) of El

and entered the massif of the king, father of years.

(*The Palace of Baal*, 4.iv.3-24, Gibson 59.)

(I do not know why there are asses of both gender, but I believe there must be a reason.) Like Athirat, Achsah rides on an ass.The counterpart in *Judges* reads:

When she came to him [Othniel], she urged him to ask her father for a field. As she dismounted from her donkey, Caleb said to her, "What do you wish?" She said to him, "Give me a present [blessing]; since you have set me in the land of the Negeb, give me also Gulloth-mayin" [basins of water]. So Caleb gave her the Upper Gulloth and Lower Gulloth (1.14-15).

In the myth, El receives Athirat joyously, snapping his fingers, and hinting that he hopes that she has come for love-making. But she has not.

She did homage at the feet of El and fell down,

she prostrated herself and did him honour.

Behold! El surely perceived her,

he opened wide the passage of (his) throat and laughed,

he placed his feet on the footstool

and snapped his fingers,

he lifted up his voice and cried:

'How (is it that) dame Athirat of the sea has arrived,

'how (is it that) the creatress of the gods has come?

'Are you very hungry, having journeyed afar?

'Or are you very thirsty, having travelled all night?'

(*Palace of Baal*, 4.iv.25-34, Gibson 59; de Moor 51-53)

In Soggin's translation of *Judges*, Achsah clapped her hands (1.14). El (called "Latipan kindly god") grants Athirat's request, and Caleb grants Achsah's. The mood of this exchange between Athirat and El is similar to that between Achsah and her father. Notice also that it is Achsah (Athirat) who goes to Caleb (El), not her husband Othniel, who like Baal disappears from the scene.

Ehud (3.15-30)

Ehud, a left-handed man, is similar to Pughat in *Aqhat* in his careful preparations for deceiving his victim, fashioning a two-edged sword and concealing it under his clothing on his right thigh, opposite to where a right-handed man carries his sword. Pughat too is wearing a disguise, dressed as a woman, but with her male (battle) clothing underneath. Whereas Ehud will appear to Eglon as a man who has secret knowledge of Yhwh, which he can disclose to Eglon only if they are alone, Pughat will appear to Yatpan as a seductress. Both of them carefully planned their disguises.

Jael Identified with Pughat

As we have seen, Anat is a prototype for Jael. Another prototype for Jael is Pughat in *Aqhat*. Again, it is a woman—this time a human being—motivated to murder in revenge for her beloved brother, Aqhat.

Anat has murdered Aqhat because she selfishly covets the priceless bow that the gods gave Aqhat. In a suggestively seductive scene, she offers Aqhat gold, silver, and immortality, if he will hand it over to her. He arrogantly rejects her offers, and taunts her contemptuously:

> The bow is a warrior's [weapon],
>> shall womenfolk now go hunting [with it]?"
> 'Anatu laughed [al]oud,
>> but in her heart she devised [a vicious plan].
> (*Aqhat*, I.vi.40-42, de Moor, 239)

A woman scorned, Anat rushes to get permission from El to kill Aqhat. She threatens to make El's blood run if he does not grant her request. El answers as he did before when she was wheedling him to grant Baal a palace:

> "I know you, my daughter, (I know) that you are like a man,
>> and that among goddesses your scorn is unequalled."

But he adds:

> "Depart, my daughter!
> [Execute] the vicious plan of [your] heart.
>> seize what is in your bosom,
>>> realize what is in your breast.
> Surely your opponent will be threshed . . . ."
> (*Aqhat*, II.i.16-20, de Moor 242)

(The word *thresh* in the last line might remind us of what Gideon did to the princes of Succoth in 8.7.)

Unlike Jael with Sisera, Anat does not kill Aqhat herself, but enlists her henchman Yatpan to do it. After Danel (Aqhat's father) and Pughat learn of the death of Aqhat, Pughat resolves on revenge. Apparently Danel is too old to perform this duty himself. Like Anat, who must receive permission from her father El, Pughat must also receive permission from her father. She pleads with Danel:

" . . . fortify me (that) I may go fortified!
I want to slay the slayer of my brother,
I want to destroy the destroyer of my kin!"
(*Aqhat*, III.iv.33-35, de Moor 263)

After receiving consent, she prepares a disguise (donning the dress of a woman over a man's battle suit),[89] and like Anat, she paints herself with murex:

she washed herself [and] roughed herself
with rouge from the shell of the [sea],
whose source is a thousand tracts away in the sea.
[Beneath] she put on the garments of a hero,
she put [ ] (in) its sheath,
put (her) sword in [its] scabbard,
and on top she put on the garments of a woman.
(*Aqhat*, 19.195-196, 203-208, Gibson 121; III.iv.41-46, de Moor 263-264)

Like Jael, whom Ackerman calls an "erotic assassin" (61), Pughat uses her womanly wiles to lure Yatpan into a feeling of security. Interestingly, Mata Hari is also said to have made herself up before being executed as a spy. To be sure, this is not quite the same as roughing oneself before going out to kill a man, but maybe Mata Hari did that, too. According to Wyatt, however, roughing is a masculine custom. Anat and Pughat do it because they are warriors.[90]

Like Ehud, she conceals her weapons, and gains access to Yatpan by a ruse, also violating hospitality in the process. She is a woman become man, clothed outwardly like a woman, but inwardly a killer.

In a scene parallel to the one above where Anat approaches Aqhat, Pughat enters Yatpan's tent with revenge for her brother's death in her heart: a woman in a tent, alone with a man, affecting to seduce him, and then assassinating him. Ackerman describes the scene:

A male military hero, unaccompanied by any of his warrior companions, sits eating and drinking inside a tent. The image initially seems a peaceful one, but the scene quickly turns to violence as the hero is murdered through the agency of a woman. In both cases, moreover, the murder is effected by a blow to the head (61).

Actually, it is not known if and how Pughat kills Yatpan. But Pughat's motivation is loyalty and love for a brother—a parallel to Anat's love for Baal, which impelled Anat to kill Yam. We assume it is also loyalty that led Jael, though not a sister to Barak in the Israelite story, to kill Sisera. The parallels in *Aqhat* between Anat and

Pughat, both killers, are designed to show the pettiness of Anat and the nobility of Pughat, while the parallel between Pughat and Jael may reinforce our respect for what the author sees as Jael's nobility in killing Sisera. After all, she is called "most blessed of women."

Pughat first plies Yatpan with drink—whether poisonous or soporific is not stated, but in any case, a drink meant to allay his suspicions:

> Pughat took (the cup) and served him drink,
>> She took the cup from his hand.
>>> (She took) the goblet from his right (hand).
> Then declared Ytpn, the Sutean warrior:
> 'From (this) wine shall drink ILA, god of the Suteans,
>> The god who created tent-camps.
> May the hand that smote Hero-Aqht
>> Smite the enemy of the Suteans by the thousands!'
> A double-couch (was) set up inside the tent;
>> And as his chest fi[lled up] (with wine) like a rivulet,
>>> His strength eb[bed level] with a snake.
> She served him spirits a second time,
>> She served him [the intoxicating] beverage.
>
> (*The Ugaritic Poem of Aqht*, lines 55-64, Margalit, 165-66. The lines about the double-couch and chest are not in Wyatt's *Religious Texts* or in Gibson.)

In Parker's and Wyatt's translations, it is a drink of "mixed wine" (Parker 78; Wyatt 312). In Gibson's translation, it is Yapan who gives *her* the drink, but in the translations of Margalit, de Moor, Parker, and Wyatt, Pughat is giving *Yatpan* the drink. It makes more sense if Yatpan is the one who is drunk. Nevertheless, "her heart (was) like a serpent's" (*Aqhat*, 19.iv.223, Gibson 122).

Jael also allays Sisera's suspicions by giving him a soothing drink:

> He asked water, and she gave him
>> milk,
>> she brought him curds in a lordly
>> bowl.
> She put her hand to the tent peg
>> and her right hand to the
>> workmen's mallet;
> she struck Sisera a blow,
>> she crushed his head,
>> she shattered and pierced his
>> temple.
> He sank, he fell,
>> he lay still at her feet;

at her feet he sank, he fell;

where he sank, there he fell dead.

(5.25-27 already partly quoted in the Jael/Anat identification).

No doubt, however, it is while Yatpan is under the influence of this drink that Pughat slays him. In the story, the drink Jael served Sisera may also have originally been *mixed wine*, but if so, was changed to *milk*, possibly to lend it an Israelite significance.

Yatpan is depicted as a ruthless slayer of his enemies. He killed Aqhat and boasts to Pughat (taking her to be Anat) that he "will kill thousands of the Lady's [Anat's] enemies yet here" (1.19.iv.59, Wyatt, ibid. 312). But, writes Ronald S. Hendel,

> he will be killed by a single enemy, a woman, the sister of Aqhat . . . . Pughat, like similar heroines in Israelite tradition (Jael, Judith), will kill the adversary after she has lulled him into submission with wine and her beauty . . . . She will kill her brother's killer; in order to do so she will dress in a warrior's garb, while dressed outwardly as a woman (93).

Like Jael, Pughat is fierce, a woman capable of anything. But whereas Anat is ferocious and treacherous, Hendel finds Pughat to be "wise, compassionate, loyal, and extremely courageous," and she kills not for the joy of it, like Anat, but out of just revenge.[91] To Margalit, she is the antithesis of the Raphaite (warrior) society which pays allegiance (like Yatpan) to the vicious and pitiless goddess Anat (ibid. 55).

Unfortunately, the ending of this poem is missing, and we do not know exactly what Pughat accomplished. But it can scarcely be doubted that she slew him, just as Jael slew Sisera. Anat is the model and the contrast for Pughat, and both she and Pughat are the models for Jael.

Gideon (Ch. 6-9)

A number of situations in the Gideon story are similar to situations in the myths. Outstanding is the dew-on-the-fleece test (6.36-40), which has an intriguing counterpart in *Aqhat*.

Pughat, Aqhat's sister, is a competent daughter who, we are told 3x, "carries water on her shoulder, wrings the dew from the fleece, and knows the courses of the stars" (Wyatt, *Religious Texts*, 297, 298, 309). She wrings the dew out of the fleece in the morning in order to get water during the drought (*Aqhat*, III.ii.2, 6; de Moor, 251, 251). When she checks the fleece and finds instead "[that the *fleece*] *on the threshing-floor was dry*" (I.19.i.30, Wyatt, ibid. 294), she interprets this as an omen that something dire has happened to her brother. This is very close to, if not exactly like, the incident of the fleece in the Gideon story (6.37-40). He too takes the result of the test as an omen.

As in the story of Keret, the size of Gideon's army after the first muster (6.34-35), before reducing it radically at Yhwh's command, is like Keret's—enormous. Every available person in *Keret* is conscripted, even the newly-wed and the widow. And the collecting of provisions is important in both stories:

Keret did come down [from] the roof;

he did *make ready corn* for the city,

w*heat* for Beth Khubur;

he *parched bread* (from grain) of the fifth,

r*ations (from grain* of) the sixth month.

A multitude was gathered and [went forth];

[a mighty] army was gathered;

[then the multitude went forth] together.

His army (was) *a [numerous] force, three hundred times ten thousand.*

They did go *by thousands (like) storm-cloud(s),*

and *by ten thousands* like the early rains.

After two two did go,

after three them all . . . .

   (*Keret*, 14.iv.171-184, Gibson 87; de Moor 199)

Mustering, calling up, gathering, and *assembly* are keywords in many of the stories in *Judges*—in Ehud, Deborah, Gideon, Jephthah, and in the civil war at the end. Rules were ultimately developed in Israel as to who could be called (Deut 20.5-8; 24.5; de Moor 196, n. 25). Keret likewise has rules he must observe, though on this occasion, to indicate his haste and desperation, he is released from some of them. So urgent is his need that he even drafts the blind man, the invalid, newly wedded man (forbidden in Deut.24.5), and the widow! True, Keret's mission is vastly different from Gideon's: he is on his way not to fight an enemy, but to besiege a city in an attempt to force the king into giving his daughter to Keret as wife. But his urgency is great. While Gideon started out with 32,000 men, Keret has "a million charioteers; mercenaries without number, archers beyond reckoning . . . in their thousands and in their ten thousands" (1.14.ii.35-40, Wyatt, *Religious Texts*, 190). The exaggeration of numbers here is like the hyperbole in *Judges*. Gideon, at the command of Yhwh of course, winnowed his enormous army down. But otherwise Gideon and Jephthah both march around the country much like Keret.

Keret mentions provisioning of the army as part of the preparations for his march. Provisions are also important in the Gideon story, but they serve a narrative purpose: they provide Gideon with the jars for his midnight raid. They are also part of the keyword system and foreshadow his need to beg for bread from two cities.

The many references in the Gideon story to food, in addition to provisions—seed, fields, harvest, threshing grain in a wine-press, flour, unleavened cakes, threshing floor, loaf of barley bread, and the bread denied by Succoth and Penuel, as well as the wine and water themes and the themes of locusts, thorns, and briers (plagues to any farmer)—emphasize the agricultural aspect of this story and bring it into the realm of fertility myth, which the Ugaritic myths are also assumed to be. Gideon trampling on (threshing) the flesh of the elders of Succoth (8.7) is reminiscent of the way Anat defeats Mot—flailing, winnowing, grinding, and sowing

Mot in the fields (Gibson *Baal and Mot* 6 ii 31-37, p. 77) and of what El says of her as she goes to kill Aqhat, "Surely your opponent will be threshed . . . ." (*Aqhat*, II.i.16-20, de Moor 242).

Fertility refers as well to the producing of progeny. When Keret loses many sons and becomes childless, his prayer to El brings more offspring. Like Keret, Gideon also has many sons and loses most of them, though after his death. Each man has one bad son (Abimelech and Yassib) who destroy the line of succession, or cause it to be destroyed.

The problem of Gideon's dual name is solved if the Gideon story had an Ugaritic origin. Then Gideon/Jerubbaal is like one of the many composite figures in the poem—like Kother-and-Khasis or Qodesh-and-Amrur or even the dual name of Prince Yam and Judge Nahar.

Or *Jerubbaal* may have been his Canaanite name, while *Gideon* was his name in the Israelite story, just as in Homeric myth, it is Odysseus in the Greek and Ulysses in the Roman. Or it is also possible that two independent stories were yoked together by the Israelite author by identifying the protagonist in the second story with Gideon.

The second story is about a king named Jerubbaal whose 70 sons were killed by another son named Abimelech. The Abimelech story can be interpreted as a theomachy like that between the family of El and the assembly of Baal. In this case, Jerubbaal would be El, and Abimelech would be an evil Baal (who eventually murders El's sons and becomes king)—an important identification.

Judges defines the name Jerubbaal as "Let Baal contend against him" (6.32), but it could be "Baal fights" (Graves and Patai 229). Then we have to ask, against whom is Baal fighting? We have to turn to the next story about Abimelech for the answer. The answer is: his brothers—like Baal in the myths. (Remarking on Gideon's Canaanite name, Soggin calls the story an "Israelite anti-Canaanite polemic" with "a sarcastic undertone" (125).[92] Again, Soggin's comment itself smacks of polemic.)

The presence of *locusts* in both the Gideon and Keret stories and in at least one other myth is worth noting. The fragment of a myth designated KTU 12 has to do with "an encounter in the desert between Baal-Haddad and some creatures called 'the devourers'" (quoted above in the section about Samson-as-Baal). Kapelrud thinks the encounter is "a ritual to guard against a locust plague" (Gibson 32), for Baal captures the locusts in a net before he falls into the marsh.

The following passage from *Keret* uses the simile of locusts to describe the enormous size of Keret's army, which will go by "the thousands and ten thousands" and spread through the land like locusts:

> 'Let them settle
> like locusts on the field,
> 'like hoppers on the fringe of the wilderness.'
> (*Keret.* 14.ii.104-105. See also iv. 192-193, Gibson 87; also I.ii.50-iii.1, de Moor 196; also
> 1.14.ii.50-i.1, Wyatt. *Religious Texts*, 192 and 1.3.ii.10-11, ibid. 73).

The Midianites in the Gideon story are likened twice to a plague of locusts who "encamped on their territory, destroying the produce of the land" and who, "when they fell upon a region . . . devastated it completely" (6.4, 5, Soggin's translation, 109). Of course, the simile of *locusts*, like the grains of sand on the seashore, may have been one of the common clichés of storytellers of those times.

Another reader may find more parallels than I have been able to identify.

Abimelech (Ch. 9)

The references in the Abimelech story to the temples of Baal-berith (9.4) and El-berith (9.46) in the city of Shechem and to "Hamor, Father of Shechem" (9.28, see Gen 34), as well as his own name and the name of his father (Jerubbaal) suggest a Canaanite origin. It is a story about choosing a ruler, and about avoiding the choice of the wrong one. From the very beginning, we see that Abimelech is the wrong one. The themes of fratricide, succession, treachery, and insurrection bear a strong resemblance to the problems of the theomachy in the Ugaritic myths. It is a story about the abuse of power. Abimelech is a submerged Baal, but this time, an evil Baal, as seen from the perspective of his opponents.

First, he is misnamed. His name means "My father the king," but his father, Jerubbaal (Gideon), had renounced kingship. Israel did not have a king at or before this time. But if Abimelech is Baal, then Gideon (who has 70 sons) *is* El (who was a king and had 77-88 sons), transformed into Jerubbaal when the story was reshaped into an earthly story.

Second, Abimelech killed his 70 brothers just as Baal killed the 77-88 sons of El and Athirat, who are called Baal's "brothers" in the following passage:

> Seven years the god was full [i.e. dead], even eight returning year cycles, because he [i.e. Baal] put on like a dress the blood of [his] bro[thers], like a garment the blood of his kinsmen; because he s[mote] the seventy-seven of his brothers, even the eighty-eight. (UM 75:II:45-50. Oldenburg 119.) (Cf. *KTU* VI.v.1-6, de Moor 94, quoted above in the section about Athirat/Sisera's mother.)

Third, Abimelech's steward's name is Zebul, an Ugaritic word meaning *prince.* We know that both Baal and Yam are called *princes,*[93] and the other sons of El probably are, too. In an Ugaritic tale about Abimelech, Zebul (i.e., a "prince") would be another brother, who escaped assassination, like Jotham, but who went to work for his evil brother Abimelech (Baal) instead of fleeing. Or maybe he is Abimelech's son.

Fourth, this scenario helps us decipher Jotham's fable about the danger of choosing the wrong king. The fable tells us that the excellent candidates for the job have the sense to refuse the position, because they know that the role they already have in life is the best one for them. Only the poorest candidate, the bramble, is willing to accept.

According to de Moor's theory, Jotham's fable originated among the polytheistic Canaanites at a time when Yahwists were promoting Yhwh to become the exclusive god. The author of the fable rejects this promotion and shows why Yhwh is a bad choice. In this interpretation, the first tree, the olive, is Baal, the second and third, the fig and vine, are female gods, and the fourth, the bramble, is Yhwh. Yhwh is a "thornbush," de Moor believes, because of Yhwh's appearance to Moses from the burning bush and because of the reference to Yhwh as a thornbush in Ps 58.10. The author of the fable is rejecting the claim that *any* gods could be the exclusive god; he is particularly opposed to the claim of Yhwh's superiority (*The Rise of Yahwism*, 391). This idea of the choosing of gods is supported by a line from *The Song*, "When *new gods were chosen*, then war was in the gates" (5.8). "Gods" are also mentioned in the fable. The "gods," says Jotham, are honored by the olive, and "wine which cheers both gods and men" (9.9, 13). Thus this fable appears to have been written not by a monotheist, but by a polytheist.

A better interpretation of the fable in my opinion is to construe it as a diatribe *against Baal*, who in the myths, after all, is determined to become king over all the gods: "I alone am the one who can be king over the gods, *who can fatten gods and men*, who can satisfy the multitudes of the earth" (KTU 1.4.vii.49-52 de Moor's trans. in *The Rise of Yahwism* 80, quoted above; my italics). In Jotham's fable, the other trees (that is, gods) who are invited to rule, demur, because they are already benefitting "gods and men" in their natural roles (9.9, 11, 13). When the fourth candidate (Baal) is invited, he answers that he will provide shade for them, but that if they *refuse* to elect him, he will *let fire shoot out and devour the greatest trees.* The *shade* originates from the clouds which Baal can cause to cover the land. And the fire would be Baal's *lightning*, which can destroy forests. The Ugaritic myth also goes on to prove why Baal would be a bad king: he has usurped the throne by assassinating his rivals. And he would be unreliable: he would bring about thunder, lightning, drought, and damaging rainstorms. Baal is incapable of ruling all the gods because, as Wyatt says, he produces chaos, alarm, destruction (*Religious Texts*, 140). (It should be remembered that, as stated above, Yhwh is an Israelite counterpart both to Baal and to El.)

Likewise, Abimelech is not qualified. As the story shows, he is a weak ruler who allows insurrection to arise, and ultimately loses the support of his people. Though he puts down the insurrection, he destroys his own people, and because he has sown salt there, nothing will ever grow in Shechem again. He has destroyed one tower by fire (using *branches of trees* to ignite the tower), as was prophesied by the fable, and is in the process of torching the second when he is killed. Someone has to put an end to his tyranny (just as the Judahites had to put an end to Samson's rampages). A woman does it—originally a goddess, no doubt, but we do not have enough information from the existing mythology to venture a guess as to who that would be. She would not be Anat or Athtart, but she would be an Amazon of sorts. As a story about the gods, we do not have to ask how the woman got the fairly heavy millstone up in the tower. Goddesses are capable of mighty acts.

If the fable is an attack on Baal and he is a bad candidate to be king, this still does not solve the problem of who is the *proper candidate*. Could there be a fifth candidate waiting in the wings? Yhwh? For this story may have been composed at a time when Yhwh existed along with other gods but had not yet risen to the top of the pantheon.

A minor situation in *Keret* that is similar to the Abimelech story is that a herald is told to go to the top of the mountain and shout out his message that Keret is ill (i.16.iv.16, Wyatt, *Religious Texts*, 234), just as Jotham shouts out his message from the top of a mountain.

Jephthah (Ch. 11-12)

The death of Jephthah's daughter might be compared with the death of Aqhat as both stories are possibly fertility myths. The women in *Judges* weep for the virgin maiden the way women weep in the Mesopotamian myth for Tammuz, a deity who also died too young (see Eze 8.14) or for Persephone in the Thesmophoria. The death of Aqhat (who was killed by Anat's henchman) is followed by a drought, symbolizing the grief of the whole land and brought about, Margalit thinks, by Baal, who sympathizes with the fallen youth (*The Ugaritic Poem of Aqht* 481), though we would expect his first sympathy to go to Anat.

In the Jephthah story, agricultural failure after the sacrifice of his daughter is lacking. The burnt offering and the commemoration of the loss by weeping women, however, are suggestive of a fertility rite. Though Aqhat was not sacrificed, he was the prized miracle child whose sudden unexpected death broke his father's heart, just as Jephthah's heart broke when he realized the identity of his victim.

Child sacrifice was an important part of the Canaanite and Phoenician religions. Diodorus Siculus observed

> that human sacrifice was limited to worship of . . . El, and [Diodorus Siculus] alludes to the myth of El's sacrifice of his own children. Sakkunyaton [Sanchuniathon] preserves the myth of El's sacrifice of Yadid and Mot . . ." (Oldenburg 26).

Whereas the Abraham-Isaac story seems to be a repudiation of the concept of human sacrifice, the Jephthah story seems to accept it as a grievous custom, perhaps extraordinary, but not totally alien. It seems to have been a tale which arose at a time when Israel had not yet denounced the custom of child-sacrifice, to judge from the fact that neither society itself nor Yhwh punished Jephthah for what he did.

In the myths, there is no sacrifice comparable to this one, but there are two ideal daughters in the Ugaritic stories to compare with Jephthah's: The first is Pughat in *Aqhat*, who tenderly assists her father when he gets on his ass to seek news of Aqhat and who also assumes the mission of avenging her beloved brother (with her father's blessing). The second is Thitmanat in *Keret*, who shows deep compassion, grief, and love for her father Keret in what seems to be his fatal illness. In her beautiful elegiac poem she cries:

> In your life, father, we rejoiced;
>
> in your immortality we took delight
>
> Like dogs shall we howl at you [*sic*] tomb,
>
> like curs at the entrance to your burial chamber.
>
> Yet father,
>
> how can you possibly die? etc.
>
> (1.16.ii. 37-49, Wyatt, *Religious Texts*, 230)

Jephthah's daughter also respects and loves her father. Readers in the past have struggled to transform the story of her sacrifice into one in which Jephthah is a hero and the daughter is not sacrificed. But maybe Jephthah is a Canaanite transplanted imperfectly into an Israelite story. Then our struggle is over.

Another parallel is the vow which Jephthah *keeps* (to his dismay)—to sacrifice his daughter—contrasted with the one which Keret *fails* to keep (to *his* dismay)—the vow to reward Athirat if Keret becomes a father. The morals are different. The *Keret* story warns us to fulfill our vows. The Jephthah story warns us not to make vows too recklessly.

The Jephthah story is a down-to-earth story like *Keret* and *Aqhat*, not a myth about the gods. Such a story might well have existed in Canaanite literature or storytelling and retold by the Israelites.

The childless couple in Samson, "Aqhat," and "Keret"

The story of the childless couple who miraculously receive an heir (also called the "barren wife" story) appears frequently in ancient literature. Robert Alter found four different conditions that must prevail in such a "type scene":

> the notice of the barrenness of the wife;
>
> the annunciation by the deity that the barrenness will be ended;
>
> the failure of perception by the person to whom it was announced; and
>
> the birth of the child, who in most cases will be an extraordinary man.[94]

Susan Ackerman shows that the Keret, Aqhat, and Samson stories all follow this formula, at least to a degree. But she adds two other components:

1) the near death of the child and
2) the survival of the child after the danger is over (185).

I find two other (ironic) features:

1) the child may fail to obey the ethical code, or fail to respect the gods or his parent and
2) the miracle child may ironically not bring the joy that the parents expected.

With this background we can now examine some of the ramifications of these similarities among the three stories. Several features in the two Ugaritic stories are also found in the Samson story. In *Aqhat*, the son is

1) put in danger and
2) does not survive to full manhood (Samson dies, but in full manhood).

In *Keret* (which Ackerman does not discuss) the miracle child Yassib is not threatened by anything until he attempts (unsuccessfully) to usurp his father's throne; then

1) he is put in danger from his father's curse, and
2) he is not likely to survive the effect of the curse. (The story breaks off before the conclusion.)

The aftermath of the miraculous beginnings is that the three characters make serious mistakes:

1) Aqhat spurns the goddess Anat.
2) Yassib does not honor his father.
3) And Samson violates his vow and consorts with foreign women. (The breaking of a vow entails a curse.)

The fathers' feelings about their sons vary in each story:

1) Danel grieves deeply over Aqhat's early death.
2) Keret comes to hate his son.
3) Samson remains a disappointment almost until the end.

We can conclude this about Samson from his parents' protest against the Timnite [14.2], as well as the many admonitions in the book against fraternization and intermarriage.

Whether or not the fate of the father is deserved also varies from story to story:

1) The miracle does not exempt Keret from his duty. Because he failed to keep his vow to Athirat, he deserved his punishments (his illness and his son's treachery).
2) But Danel does *not* deserve *his* misfortune—the treachery of his son.
3) Neither have Samson's parents done anything to cause, or make them deserve, their disappointment and then the loss of their son.

As for "extraordinary son" feature,

1) except for their births, the two Ugaritic sons, Aqhat and Yassib, are not extraordinary. They do not redeem themselves and are thus failed heroes.
2) Samson, however, is "extraordinary," as his subsequent fame proves. Some interpreters believe that his father was really the messenger-angel, not Manoah.[95]
3) Both Danel and Keret, however, have "extraordinary" daughters—Pughat in *Aqhat* and Thitmanat in *Keret*. These daughters and Anat can *love*.[96]
4) Jephthah's daughter is "extraordinary." She is noble and also loves her father, as we infer from her immediate response to his plight.

Death or near-death experiences can be found in all the stories.

1) Aqhat is murdered by Yatpan, Anat's henchman.
2) Yassib's near-death experience is the curse for Keret's failure to keep his vow.
3) Samson has many near-death experiences. He is finally taken prisoner, blinded, and mocked, and at the very last minute, in the nick of time, dies a

martyr's death. Ultimately he is successful in that he did what the "man of god" predicted: "begin to deliver Israel from the hand of the Philistines" (13.5).

How helpful are the gods through all this? The Ugaritians, like other believers, expected to receive divine help in time of need. In one of the rituals, the people pray to Baal to relieve them from a siege and vow to make a sacrifice to him if they are saved (*Ritual IV*, 1.119, 28-34, de Moor, 173-174).[97] *Aqhat* and *Keret* can be compared with the Samson story for the belief that the gods can help human beings:

1) Keret becomes ill, but El helps him to recover; thus he is not abandoned entirely. When last seen, however, he is cursing his son.

2) Danel, on the other hand, is apparently abandoned by the gods—unfairly, for Danel is a good man.

3) Yhwh allows Samson to be punished (probably for *hubris*) but never completely abandons him. Every time Samson calls on him, Yhwh comes to his aid.

The theophany in the Samson story might have been derived from the Ugaritic materials—not from a myth about Baal or El, but from a nonextant tale about a larger-than-life human being.

A fragment of another myth has a question similar to Manoah's question to the messenger-angel: "Now when your words come true, what is to be the boy's rule of life; what is he to do?" (13.12). The messenger-angel replies rather acidly: "Let the woman give heed to all that I said to her." Samson's mother has already been told that Samson's mission is to "begin to deliver Israel from the hand of the Philistines," (13.5), and the angel will waste no further words on Manoah.

The following situation in the Ugaritic fragment (discovered by F. C. Fensham and noted by Block) seems to be a parallel, where the parent is told to go to the "lord of the great gods" and ask about his child's future:

> When he arrives at the lord of the great gods with a gift, he must ask for a decision [mtpt] about the child.
>
> And your messenger will arrive with a gift; he will receive a decision [mtpt].[98]

The difference is that here, the lord of the great gods agrees to give the answer only after the parent's messenger goes away and returns with a gift. The fragment tells us no more than this.

Though the basic structures of the three stories are similar, the details make all the difference. In general, however, some of the patterns of the Samson story are similar to patterns set out in *Aqhat* and *Keret*. At the least, this type story was known in both cultures.

VIII. Ugaritic Poems and *Judges* Compared and Contrasted

Though the myths share many narrative elements with the stories of *Judges*, they also differ radically in many ways. The following table is a *tentative* list of comparisons and contrasts (mostly contrasts). Overlapping of items within the table is unavoidable.

Table II

UGARITIC POEMS   *JUDGES*

Style	
1. Lofty, exalted, often gently comic	1. Comic (black comedy, grotesque)
2. Poetry	2. Prose except *The Song*
3. Often beautiful, lyrical; emotion inherent. Some of the poetic effects may be due to the translations, however	3. Completely lacking in beauty (except for the Song of Deborah); terse, laconic
4. Many metaphors and similes; apparently some wordplay	4. Few metaphors and similes; much wordplay
5. Conventional word-pairs; binary opposites not noticeable	5. Similar pairs rare in *Judges*; plentiful use of binary opposites throughout
6. Frequent repetition of blocks of lines for mnemonic purposes; the duties of a son in Aqhat, for example (given 4x, with slight variations)	6. Repetition of lines used rarely (twice, at most), in order to underline the meaning of the episode or book
7. Certain categories of keywords used frequently but distributed randomly	7. Similar use of keywords, but many more categories and much more complex use; distributed evenly throughout
8. Characters have epithets	8. Epithets not used
9. Occasional irony	9. Many ironies
10. No apparent design in the structure of the corpus of texts nor in individual texts; texts do not constitute a cycle	10. Structural design of book intricate

11. Long leisurely dialogues	11. Laconic on the whole; short crisp dialogues; only one long one
12. Long stories; much leisurely action; dynamic action only in scenes of combat, usually involving Baal or Anat	12. Stories short, sometimes very short; action almost always dynamic, bizarre
13. Place names infrequent and either of distant exotic places like Memphis, or mythological like Mt. Zaphon; great distances involved	13. Geographical references are Israelite, but locations perplex modern interpreters; distances not mentioned
14. Myths take place in cosmic space; some stories take place on earth; supernatural elements throughout	14. Tales all take place on earth; supernatural elements confined to messenger-angels and responses to "inquiries" of Yhwh; stories otherwise realistic
Lifestyle	
1. The lifestyle, actions, and dialogue of the gods emphasized; two myths, however, concern human beings	1. No reference to the lifestyle of the god, only of what the god expects of human beings
2. References to silver, gold, precious jewels; no money mentioned; no common utensils; cups of precious metals	2. References to money in Samson and Micah stories; a few precious objects taken in plunder; otherwise, many common utensils and tools
3. Buildings: palaces and tents; minimum interest in architectural details	3. Tents, tent communities, houses in towns, temples, no palaces mentioned; strong interest in architectural details
4. Many banquets and feasts among the gods; gods eat like human beings; they consume huge quantities of meat; they show hospitality to other gods	4. Food important throughout; only one banquet; hospitality is a prevailing theme. Yhwh does not eat or drink; meals are served twice by humans to his divine messengers, but they do not eat them
5. Frequent consumption of enormous quantities of wine by the gods and people, customarily for 7 days at a time; drunkenness approved of and enjoyed by both gods and people; drunkenness may be part of religious rites	5. People probably drink for 7 days at Samson's banquet (משתה, which means *drinking bout*); in the story of the concubine, drinking occurs 5 days in a row. Excessive drinking of wine perhaps frowned upon, since bad things happen to those who we assume were drunk

Characters	
1. Gods called "judges"	1. Heroes called "judges"
2. Some myths are about the gods and concern only the gods; two myths concern human beings (*Keret* and *Aqhat*); the gods can be invoked and they interact with people (sometimes in a dream); some of the gods have consorts and families	2. The god Yhwh either appears himself or communicates with human beings through divine messengers and "inquiry"; he has an army (in *The Song*). We do not know anything about Yhwh's home life or companions; he has no consort, no family. The Midianite's dream mentioned in the Gideon story is thought to contain a prophecy
3. The people are elite–like the patriarchs of Genesis–not of the folk	3. All characters are ordinary men and women–the folk–except Kings Jabin and Eglon. Though king, Abimelech is not "kingly."
4. Baal and Anat, outstanding in character and different from the other gods; the other gods are not particularly distinguishable from each other; gods behave like human beings	4. Yhwh not shown as a character, once speaks to an individual (Gideon); otherwise has messenger-angels communicate with human beings. Human characters extraordinary, bizarre, unique; some represent "humors" or temperaments e.g., Jephthah = rashness; Gideon = cowardice; Abimelech = megalomania; Samson = impulsiveness, anger, lust
5. Some gods are treacherous; some capricious (Anat); some compassionate. The gods show interest in human beings, some interact with them (in *Keret* and *Aqhat*), but not frequently; Aqhat is killed by a goddess because he insulted her; Keret does not keep his vow to a goddess and is punished	5. Yhwh consistent; moved to anger and pity; loves his people; human beings often beseech Yhwh and get help; Yhwh brings misery only when the people are unfaithful, and he sometimes relents; Yhwh not capricious; Jephthah probably erred in making his vow; thus Yhwh does not intervene to save his daughter
6. El participates in human conception and birth; Keret and Danel receive children through intercession and intervention of the gods.	6. Yhwh sends a messengers to 1) Gideon to inspire him to fight (Yhwh talks to him himself) and to 2) Samson's parents to announce (and possibly bring about) conception
7. Intense love is shown by Anat for Baal and by Athirat for her children. El shows affection for Athirat. Love is shown between human beings, with Keret's daughter for her father and Danel's daughter for her father and brother	7. Love mentioned 3x only (in Samson story) but not demonstrated Love not shown for Yhwh Anger important throughout

8. Gods and human beings experience grief over the death of their loved ones People become ill and suffer (e.g. Keret). El is concerned with human illness and asks,"Who among the gods will remove the sickness?"	8. Grief over the dead is not shown except Jephthah's dismay when his daughter comes out of the house; Israelites as a whole weep and show misery when assailed by misfortune; illness not mentioned; people get wounded, but they are not shown with wounds (with exception of Eglon, Sisera, and Samson) or suffering
9. Equality seems to prevail among the gods, though El is their king; Yam, Mot, and Baal vie for power; not even El is all powerful; gods can die, but they are resurrected	9. Equality of people, except when Abimelech becomes king; all power is in the hands of Yhwh; no information about whether or not Yhwh can die or be resurrected
10. Society depends on kings. Females, both divine and human, have power and can act independently (Anat, Pughat); Anat kills both gods and people; the gods kill each other	10. Yhwh kills only in one battle. Society needs leaders in battle and in government; males are warriors and judges; one judge is female. Women are active and can be both saviors and destroyers; if destroyers, they are not Israelites
Themes	
1. Fertility themes; the gods personify forces of nature; plots concern the control of the natural elements; seasonal cycles ever changing and unreliable; myths possibly designed for ritual use	1. Fertility themes submerged; growth, consumption, and destruction of crops; water important; seasons, climate, rain/drought receive no attention; stories designed not only for entertainment, but also for ethical questioning. Enemy defeated in battle by Yhwh producing a storm
2. Nature responds to human tragedy. Drought is caused by the gods sometimes in response to human tragedy, like the death of Aqhat	2. Nature does not respond to human events; drought not mentioned
3. Universe run by the gods in a disorderly fashion	3. Universe apparently runs in an orderly fashion; ruler is Yhwh
4. Gods and people are self-centered; communal action between gods and human beings infrequent	4. Importance of heroes (successful warriors) and of communal action; the god sends angel-messengers to people
5. Resurrection themes; human beings, however, are not resurrected, as far as can be discerned	5. No resurrections except figuratively (Samson); the coming of the judge or savior to the stricken people might be considered a resurrection theme
6. Sexuality important and explicit; Gods engage in sex	6. Sexuality alluded to but not explicit; Yhwh is nonsexual

7. Gods vying for leadership; two plots with human beings concern succession; idea of "divine kingship" for human beings seems to be mocked in one story	7. Political themes important; succession important in one tale; questions of governance and of whether or not Yhwh alone should be king; rulers cannot always be trusted; but leadership is needed
8. Migration not referred to	8. Israelites have already migrated; one story concerns a later migration
9. Honor and revenge important to people and gods. Retribution exists for the people but not for the gods; revenge important on divine and human levels (Anat for Baal; Anat against Aqhat for his refusal to grant her his bow; Pughat for Aqhat)	9. Honor referred to (by Jotham), but not a main theme such as it is in the *Iliad*; revenge (including a feud) and retribution important; retribution follows bad behavior; usually it is Yhwh who brings about retribution; people can also bring it about
10. People have ethical concerns (e.g., the duties of a son to a father, the duties of a judge); people must respect the gods and one's father	10. Situations involve questions about ethical behavior; though the characters (except Jotham) do not seem concerned about it, the audience of the stories may interact and respond to ethical questions in the stories
11. Pessimistic in outlook; gods cannot be trusted; justice is not expected from gods but is important to human beings; some focus is on the failings of the gods; the gods are not necessarily "good"; they control the elements and life and death	11. People expected to work out their own destinies; people not always trustworthy or reliable; focus is on human failings; Yhwh is not looked upon as either "good" or "bad"; his saving them from slavery in Egypt is brought to their attention; Yhwh punishes them when they disobey his two important rules: to have no other gods besides him and to not intermarry with foreigners
War	
1. Wars among the gods; no wars in which gods are united against outsiders or human beings; Baal wages war against unidentified towns; on earth, peace; human beings go to war in one tale but not to exterminate an enemy	1. War tales; wars against outsiders and enemies; mainly defensive wars; one war for territory; peace lasts only for short intervals between wars; civil war
2. Gods attack each other; some are punished, but not for long	2. Yhwh participates in one battle (in the Deborah story); otherwise not seen as fighting
3. Single-combat fighting as a rule	3. Single encounters in Ehud and Samson stories

4. Entire armies not seen fighting, except a short incident of Baal's army and of Keret's when he musters an enormous army in order to procure a wife (but not to fight)	4. Many battles; huge armies fighting against outside enemies; the potential for civil war among the tribes increases through passage of time; civil war at end
5. No questions raised about right and wrong in combat	5. Questions (implied) about right and wrong methods of annihilating enemy, of child sacrifice in order to gain victory, of intermarriage with foreigners
6. Weapons of special power; also swords, clubs, mace, arrows	6. Swords the only traditional weapon; other traditional weapons not used; no arrows or lances; curious nontraditional weapons like household implements (knives, tent pegs, goads, etc.) used
7. Horse-drawn chariots; human transportation on foot; gods ride asses, walk, or fly	7. Most travel done on foot; some asses; Israelites have no horses, camels, chariots, or wheels; but the enemy of the Israelites has chariots, horses, and camels; no supernatural means of transportation shown

IX. Conclusion

The story of Deborah is the only story that I have found which could have been adapted wholly from the extant myths. The other stories in *Judges*, in particular the Abimelech and Samson stories, though not exact copies of anything in the Ugaritic corpus seem to make significant use of Canaanite mythology (transformed). The other stories have incidents which parallel the Ugaritic. The style of Judges is vastly different from the myths. The style of *Judges* was developed, I believe, for two reasons: first, the stories are only scenarios, not fully fleshed out until the time the storyteller was before an audience, and second, they are meant for dramatic and exciting live performances (see Chapter Six).

Some will believe that the similarities between the two corpora are not sources but exemplify structuralism—the similarities arising from that fact that the workings of the human brain and the creation of narratives always follow certain patterns, from culture to culture. And as we have seen in other parts of the Bible, what gives the appearance of being unalloyed Canaanite materials (like the killing of the dragon by Yhwh), has been explained away by some scholars as a means to prove the Israelites' superiority to the Canaanites. Craigie, for example, believed that the Ugaritic poetic imagery in *The Song* was used in order to achieve "a subtle effect"— for he found that the material "not only dramatizes Deborah's role in the war, but points ultimately to that power greater than any divine Canaanite power which resided in Yahweh and in his 'friends'" (*ZAW* 381). I myself do not see how this poem shows that the Israelite god is superior to the Canaanite gods. Craigie's statement seems apologetic.

The longer I study these materials, the more I see deliberate and conscious use of local Canaanite folk material about the gods, into which the storytellers wove information about their own folk heroes for literary, nationalistic, or entertainment purposes. The material they used would not necessarily be these identical myths, but variants.

The early storytellers were free to appropriate whatever they wanted from any literature they knew and adapt it to the current conditions, needs, and beliefs. When ideas about the mythic characters changed within their community, they would not likely abandon their favorite story supply immediately and create a new one. Nothing resembling the idea of plagiarism or copyright laws existed at that time. And the transfer of information may have been occurring gradually, when there was no clear line of demarcation between the two religions. The storytellers would keep using their favorite stories, modifying them here and there both consciously and unconsciously in response to the needs of their community. My theory of the process is something like the following:

1. Both storytellers and audience were familiar with, and liked, the Canaanite myths.
2. Some of the best possible available material were the Canaanite myths and stories.
3. The myths were first absorbed when the two religions overlapped and when El, Baal, and Yhwh were perhaps all worshiped simultaneously.
4. When Yhwism came to the fore, the characters were given Israelite names and the myths given earthly Israelite settings and problems. Direct references to the Canaanite gods were removed, and Yhwh substituted for El. As superstitions began to wane, the gods became "faded gods," and the characters were brought down to earth and became human.
5. As Yhwh began to dominate, the Canaanite folktales were purged of references that would be offensive to Yahwists, and only traces of their origin remained here and there in the Israelite stories.

When the Canaanite gods were submerged, the myths became Israelite.

Many aspects of the stories of *Judges* are mythic, and the myths they most resemble are the Ugaritic poems. The multiplicity and complexity of surface details, the intricate structure, and the chronicle-like character of the Israelite book obscure the mythic situations in *Judges* and cause readers to search in them for the "history" of Israel, when the stories are more likely describing something about the Canaanites.

The stories in *Judges* probably originated orally in the period of time in which they are set—that is, late Bronze Age or early Iron Age (1500-1000) and continued to be told among the Israelites over a long period of time, being transformed gradually to express the difficulties Israel had with other indigenous peoples, a time when the Israelites were trying to exterminate, drive out, or absorb groups with whom they could not live peacefully side by side. The stories probably reached their final form in a later period of time, perhaps as late as the Persian period or after.

The Song has always been regarded as very ancient and archaic. It does not give the impression of having been deliberately archaized or "antiqued" by a later poet; there would be no reason to "antique" one chapter of a book and not the rest of the book as well. The corruption of the Deborah text may be an indication that the language was not originally Hebrew but a dialect of Ugaritic or another "Canaanite" (Semitic) language. The prose version of the Deborah story may be a "translation" or adaptation of the myth (or variant myth) into a version that contemporary Israelites could relate to, or it was an alternate version of the story.

Both sets of stories—Ugaritic myths and Israelite tales—are archetypal and follow models discovered by the structuralists to be universal to all storytellers. Though their deep structures are similar, surface details of the two sets of tales are vastly different from each other.

Many of the stories in *Judges* seem to be Canaanite myths adapted for Israelite consumption through the process of syncretism. This hypothesis should continue to be investigated by readers and scholars. I have tried to establish a basis on which other scholars and literary critics can build.

Chapter Six

CONCLUSION: A BRIEF THEORY
OF EVERYTHING

Who is worthy to open the scroll and break its seals?   —Revelation 5:2

Information is beauty.   —Yuri Lotman

Entities should not be multiplied unnecessarily.
                    —*Ockham's Razor* by William of Ockham (1320)

Mundus vult decipi: the world wants to be deceived. The truth is too complex and
frightening; the taste for the truth is an acquired taste that few acquire.
                    —Walter Kaufmann, *Prologue to Martin Buber's I and Thou*

A good news/bad news joke: the good news is that our lives have purpose; the bad
news is that their purpose is to help some remote hacker estimate pi to nine jillion
decimal places.   —Edward Fredkin

Did the universe just happen?   —Robert Wright

The Work of Art

*J*udges is an anthology of ancient Israelite tales, perhaps of Canaanite origin,
composed for oral storytelling in some ancient period of time before the towns and
tribes united to become a nation. The stories proceed from episode to episode
anecdotally. Most of them are very short and seem to have been honed to minimum
essentials in the telling and retelling. But though the book has a minimalist
appearance, it has a maximalist effect.

Oral transmission might account for the apparent unevenness of the text and also
for its many anomalies. Upon closer inspection, however, none of its "defects" turns
out to be a flaw. Instead, we discover a work of art. The stories have been designed and
arranged in a formal structure consisting of carefully proportioned, symmetrical units.

Why should we prefer to identify *Judges* as art and as great art, rather than merely as history or chronicle or theology?—Because of its admirable perfections.

The reasons are comprised in the word *style*, those distinctive commendable features of the work, including this artist's imagination, creativity, and originality, which enable him not only to represent crucial information about his society in the form of memorable stories, but to do so in such a way that is immensely pleasurable, fascinating, and even exhilarating.

Already discussed at length in the body of my book,* the characteristics of *Judges style* include:

Structure, organization, design
- an ingenious, decorative, even beautiful, and carefully-designed multifaceted structure;
- a functional design with deliberately-fashioned symmetries, imposing order upon the unruly, disruptive, chaotic aspects of the life represented;
- many parallels and contrasts between stories and in the language (for example, binaries), which provide a meaning-filled inner intertextuality; of fathers/daughters. fathers/sons; and mothers/sons;

Language allowing minds of the listeners to roam in all directions
- economy of language (almost laconic) with no superfluous word or statement, but with every single word contributing essential meaning; language stripped of connotations but deriving connotative power from the juxtaposition of words in context;
- a complex ambiguity of meanings (belying the simplicity of the language) achieved through four systems:
  - 1) *wordplay* and other *linguistic games* which entertain and inform the reader or listener;
  - 2) abundant use of *binary opposites* to supplement meaning;
  - 3) a system of *keywords* in which numerous artifacts and appurtenances of daily life are distributed evenly throughout each story and throughout the book;
  - 4) two kinds of *intertextuality*, both a) between the stories in the book and b) between the stories of this book an those of other books of the Bible;

Narrative aspects
- a frame, with introduction, connecting stories to a prevailing theme;
- the frame consisting of a clever and unobtrusive table of contents of all the main themes;
- dramatic, dynamic, action-packed stories of violence, filled with excitement, suspense, and irony;
- stories in which theology or ideology never obstructs or slows down the action;
- a surprising, exciting and satisfying closure;

---

* All the preceding chapters contain information about style that cannot be repeated here for lack of space. Chapter 5, Sec. "IV. Ugaritic Myths Compared and Contrasted with *Judges*," and the table at the end of that chapter are important analyses of the style of *Judges* from a comparative point of view.

Characterization
- variety of perspectives, with links provided between stories pointing out comparisons and contrasts in character and action;
- variety of human relationships, representing a whole society—the folk—from which the characters emerge;
- strong individualistic characters (though weak in power), each one unique;
- strong individualistic tribes (as important as the characters) whose actions determine the most important message of the book—the decline of the nation through the lack of a strong leader;

Special effects
- large assemblage of graphic, memorable, and striking iconic poses of individuals or groups of characters in each episode—diverse tableaux which serve in lieu of drawings or photographs, and which because of the rapidity with which they are presented give a sense of rapidity and drama to the actions;
- each iconic scene, like a picture, does as much service as "ten thousand words";

Meaning of the narratives
- dramatic depictions of both internal and external problems confronting a society desperate to find living space and peace in a hostile environment;
- examples of the ingenuity with which otherwise powerless and vulnerable people (underdogs) try to solve their problems and meet their goals;
- Interactive nature of the narrative, inviting the audience to ponder situations in which some of the most profound philosophical, ethical, and legal problems of human behavior are depicted and the limits of evil and of good explored;
- because the text does not interpret itself, we must interpret the narratives, and through this very interactive process, we see why a system of law and ethics was needed and how it could eventually be developed;
- through exemplification of weak, defective, or bad leadership, we begin to learn what kind of a leader was needed;
- important—though often sometimes subliminal—information is being transmitted about the society, especially with respect to agriculture, food and drink, war, women, loyalty, hospitality, tribal and parental duties, and, of course, duties to Yhwh (to mention only a few of the areas examined);
- insight into the origins and history of attitudes toward outsiders, toward those with different beliefs, toward one's brother tribes;
- carefully-positioned, memorable but subtly-presented statements suggestive of the meaning of the book as a whole (3.19, 30 and 20.7);

Entertainment aspects
- games such as finding hidden objects, solving riddles. playing with the anomalies;;
- entertainment intended to inspire not only pity and fear, but also to evoke suspense, surprise, pleasure, and laughter;

- a little book of horrors—the "pulp fiction" of ancient literature—its horrors (as in dismemberments and mutilations) are offset by many pleasurable variations of comedy:
- and finally—and perhaps most importantly—a fantastic window on an ancient civilization.

Analysis of the author's use of Canaanite (or Ugaritic) materials sheds light on the creative process and also offers one more bit of evidence that these stories are not mere historical chronicles or theological treatises, but are a work of art. I have tried to give prominence to this creative aspect by putting the name of the book *Judges* in italics, like a title, and by continual reference to "the author." This work took effort and skill—nay, genius—to accomplish.

Harold Bloom in *Genius: A Mosaic of One Hundred Exemplary Creative Minds* (2001), uses the *Sefirot* (the center of the Kabbalah) to define ten categories of *genius*:

1) *Keter*, the crown. *Keter* paradoxically means "to be everything and nothing." (Shakespeare, whom Bloom calls "a kind of secular godhead," Lucretius, Virgil, Dante, and Chaucer);

2) *Hokmah*, wisdom (Socrates, Plato);

3) *Binah*, "intellect in a receptive mode . . . open to the power of wisdom" (Nietzsche, Kafka, Kierkegaard);

4) *Hesed*, the "bountiful covenant love that issues from God or from women and men" (John Donne, Lady Murasaki, the Bronte sisters);

5) *Din*, also called *Gevurah*, strict judgment with "the power that enables such rigor" (Emily Dickinson, Wallace Stevens, T. S. Eliot, Wordsworth);

6) *Tiferet*, beauty, or *Rahamin*, compassion (Pater, Hofmannsthal, Baudelaire, Rimbaud);

7) *Nazah*, "God's victory, or as the eternal endurance that cannot be defeated" (the epics; Homer, Hemingway Stendhal, Joyce);

8) *Hod*, "splendor or majesty that has prophetic force" (the poet-prophets like Whitman, George Eliot, Scott Fitzgerald);

9) *Yesod*, foundation, "a fathering force" (erotic narratives, Flaubert, Borges); and

10) *Malkhut*, the kingdom, or *Atarah*, the diadem, the "radiance of God" (male geniuses who transcend sexuality: Balzac, Yeats, Celan, Ellison) (xi-xiv).

Something of all of these kinds of genius can be found in *Judges*, with the possible exception of "radiance of God" in Item #10. The writers given as possible compatriots to the author of *Judges*, who might otherwise be considered a minor writer, are awesome company, but deserved. Some surely surpass him, but I believe he can comfortably hold his own small niche among them.

Excellence is marked by *decorum*; the artist's manner is appropriate to the matter, and is sustained throughout the work—without faltering, weakening, or boring the audience, but continuing throughout at the same high level until completion.

A great artist is one who has a unique ability in the sense that no other artist prior to him, nor subsequent to him, has done what he has done. As far as can be determined, he is inimitable in the sense that whatever epigones may follow, they have neither improved on, nor subtracted from, his achievement.

While some artists have the ability to create many different specimens of art and greatly influence artists who follow, the reputation of others (like Coleridge with *The Ancient Mariner* or Voltaire with *Candide*) may rest today on a single, unique, and incredible work. In the singular case of *Judges*, I do not know of any artist who has achieved the same aims with similar or different material. But that is perhaps because no one, until now, has analyzed the art of this author's masterpiece so that this template can be used by others. If artists today in almost any field knew of this design and what it accomplished, some of them would enjoy the challenge it poses: of using it with their own medium, the diversity of which might include paintings and sculpture, tapestries and rugs, music, opera, ballet, theater, cinema, photography, cartoons, storytelling, drama (comedy or tragedy), poetry, fiction, or video games—all of these and many more, in wide varieties of style. Artists set for themselves the challenge to extend the range of what art can do. Here is one more.

One of the supreme values of human civilization, art gives enjoyment and pleasure simply by being contemplated. The greatest of arts, to my mind, have a profound impact on viewers or listeners, teaching them something about life that they did not know, changing their own lives in the process.

All art has to be deciphered. We have to learn how to appreciate it. In our effort to see an art work, the longer it takes to analyze the nature of its wondrous components completely, the longer we can appreciate and enjoy it. As with the ceiling of the Sistine Chapel, one cannot just glance at it and believe one has seen it. Great art is inexhaustible; each time we turn back to it, the more it gives in return.

As I have shown throughout this book, the author of *Judges* is an accomplished artist in all these respects.

An Ancient Derrida

What is so strange about the language of *Judges* is that it is not connotational. It is spare, elemental. Words get their meanings almost solely from placement. They are like empty vessels, into which the reader puts meanings. Of course, through the ages, readers have wrapped many of the words with connotations, but we cannot be sure that all these are correct.

The foremost theory of our time describing how language gets its meaning was developed by the late Jacques Derrida, a theory which he discovered, not created. Derrida used the term "deconstruction" (not invented by himself) for the system and supplied a terminology for its parts. Examples of this system are plentiful in philosophy or any discipline that makes extreme demands on the reason, but in literature are more difficult to perceive. Perhaps no better specimen exists in literature than *Judges*.

The early theories of Derrida that are useful here have been discussed and exemplified thoroughly in the preceding chapters of this book but not identified as such, since it is only after we have reached our conclusions about the characteristics of the book that we can identify them as Derridean. They are closely related to each other, and often overlap:

1) There is no *presence*, no transcendental signified, no foundation. We cannot assume that the transcendental signified is God. Derrida's famous statement, "There is nothing outside the text,"[1] is controversial, but useful. Language does not refer directly to reality—it refers only to language. And this is certainly true of texts that are of a time or place for which we have no corroborating data.

We must try to focus solely on the Yhwh who is *in* the text, for example, not one who is *outside* it, for we cannot know the meaning of this text if we assume something to be there, that is not there. By referring to the god who is in the text, we can avoid the pitfall of injecting our own meanings into that word. Our own meaning for the name *Yhwh* may in fact conflict with the author's conception.

Conceptions of God vary from person to person. Though people may find God through their own experience, they cannot transfer this experience except through language or the arts. God may be stable, but the language used to describe God is not stable. Thus Ruth may have been mistaken when she said to Naomi, "Thy god will be my god." I would wager that my Derrida is not the reader's Derrida. Probably Derrida's Derrida is not anyone else's Derrida. We must tread carefully.

As for history, we do not have any documents relating to that period of time that can assure us that we have found any bedrock of history in *Judges*. Whether the tales refer to a reality outside of the book, or are an invented fiction, or whether these heroes had historical prototypes, we have no way of knowing. Because they have all the earmarks of fiction, and none of history, I myself think they are fiction. Whether the characters owe their origin to "real" people cannot be ascertained. This is not to disparage the text: those of us who work with literature of all kinds know that fiction often provides "truths" that "history" does not.

Perhaps we can say what the stories represent—to a degree. That is, they represent the author's own society, or one which his own experience enabled him to imagine.

As we have already seen, analyzing the keywords teaches us that this is an agricultural and pre-political, pre-technological society, an age of very small villages, isolated from each other, an age when there was no aristocracy, before the development of skilled crafts or commerce, a time when the religion was not strongly organized. The stories appeal for unity, strong leadership (monarchical), a religion that owes obedience to Yhwh and excludes all other gods and foreign idols; and indirectly, they are about a society looking for laws to replace the vigilante character of the society.

But we do not know that society firsthand. All we have is the text. That's what Derrida means by lack of *presence*.

2) Following Saussure, Derrida uses his neologism *différance* to describe this "systematic play of differences, of the traces of differences, of the *spacing* by means of

which elements are related to each other."[2] Words in themselves have no meaning except in context and in reference to, and by contrast with, other words. Texts refer only to texts. This is certainly true of our understanding of the words in the Bible. Words, furthermore, derive their meanings from *all* the texts, not just from a single one. Every definition refers to every other definition. Any kind of reference can be only to language itself. People and objects disappear once we have left their vicinity or the age or text in which they once existed, and afterwards exist only in our minds.

The problem for us is to try to keep within the author's language system. What other texts was he familiar with? Since we cannot know, we must stick mainly to the words in *Judges* and derive their meanings from within the text itself insofar as possible and not to stray too far from it, or at least not often, not even to other books of the Bible, which may have been written after *Judges*.

3)   *Différance* draws us into a *free play of signification* (*free play* is Derrida's term). Just as Kant and Schiller commend literature because it honors the free play of imagination and reason, Derrida not only finds, but acclaims, the free and endless play of signification within all texts. And so does *Judges*, to an extraordinary degree.

The word *play* is ambiguous: it signifies both how texts work (with freedom within parts) and the pleasure that they give us (as in games or diversions). Both of these meanings apply to *Judges*. *Free play* also means that we cannot put boundaries around meaning. *Judges* seethes with multiple meanings, and some of these meanings are subversive, some even threatening to dismantle the text, for the meanings of the words and stories cannot always be reconciled with each other.

4)   *Intertextuality* is basic to Derrida's thinking. A term invented by Kristeva, *intertextuality* refers to the way meaning depends upon, or is added to, a text by its reference to other texts, either consciously or unconsciously, and in the case of *Judges* the relationship of any one story to all the others in the group. When we cut the stories in *Judges* apart, lay them down side by side, we can read across the matrix, studying what we can learn from the innumerable comparisons and contrasts that have been devised. A better metaphor for the structure than *matrix* is that we should lay them down side by side in a circle and then erect them—something like the stelae at Stonehenge—and allow them to speak to each other in all directions across the intervening distances. (See Chapter I, **Table VII,** the symmetries in the four stories about Fathers & Daughters, two stories about Mothers & Sons, and three incidents about Fathers & Sons.)

Within the text, everything relates to everything else in the text. And there are also fifty or more relationships between *Judges* and other books of the Bible, from *Genesis* through *2 Samuel*, like the sacrifice of Isaac (compared with Jephthah's daughter) or the story of Lot (compared with the Levite's Concubine story). These are the only times we may venture out of the immediate text, and then we must remember that we do not know in what directions the meanings go—that is, the order of their precedence. We notice these parallels, but must be cautious about what meanings we bring back from those stories into *Judges*. Each text has its own niche within the language system. And with biblical Hebrew, we do not yet know precisely where those niches are. Purists may want to stick with just one text, *Judges*, and forget about the others elsewhere in the Bible, but in any language system, this is not really possible, especially when deliberate allusions are made. (See **Table X** in the Appendix of Chapter 1.) To this mix, we must confront the further distraction of the complex relationship of these stories to Ugaritic myths (see Chapter 5).

Judges is intertextual in still another way: the mad proliferation of translations and scholarly books and articles, a veritable torrent in recent years, about *Judges* and related material in the Bible—histories, archaeology, commentaries, discussions of language issues, etc.—have created a vast array of referents. For those of us who study the scholarship, the meaning is no longer only *in* the text; it is "out there," somewhere, in other people's minds. Meaning has been dispersed. It is hopeless to try to extract a definitive meaning of *Judges* from all this, though scholars (including myself) will not give up trying.

This perspective, like all the others, multiplies meanings still further.

5)   Because of *différance*, meaning is always *deferred* (Derrida's term). *Judges* is the repository of 10,000 words. When we examine and classify all of them—arranging a taxonomy of *keywords* as I have tried to do—we discover so many relationships that we have incalculable numbers to crunch, making it difficult, though not impossible, to reach any conclusions about them.

The keywords are distributed plentifully, evenly, and playfully throughout the stories, and all the categories appear, almost without exception, in each story (see Chapters 1 and 3).

One of the purposes the keywords in *Judges* serve may be that, like Homer's use of epic similes, they afford us glimpses of ordinary society, the lives of other people and animals—apart from the terrible deeds of war that are reported. "History" of sorts is found in these words. They also give us information about temperaments—about moods and fears. The stories are about war and warriors, but war is not everything. The keywords remind us that *life* is going on.

6)   The book is loaded with polarities—many pairs of *binary opposites* (a term important to Derrida). (See long list of them in Chapter 3.)

In any language or text, binary opposites (*différance*) establish meaning, and we cannot do away with them—even though Derrida tempts us to try. How can there be such a thing as "good," without its counterpart "evil"?—a vexing conundrum for theologians and ethicists to solve. Derrida makes much of the fact that in language, one half of any binary pair is "privileged" over the other. The author of *Judges* seems to give equal time to both extremes of many of these binary pairs. Women hold their ground with men, for example, and some even "become" men. There is a surprising amount of equity between other binary pairs. Yet there are also many intermediate terms between opposites—as between "good" and "evil" in *Judges*. This is the excluded middle that this author brings back into the system.

The situations in the book are both horrible and comic at one time—elaborately so. When we focus on the serious side, we cannot see the comic. When we focus on the comic, the horrible either fades into the oblivion or transforms itself into "black comedy." Most of us cannot focus on both simultaneously. We cannot resolve the cognitive dissonance (see Chapter 2). This too is part of *différance*.

7) Derrida uses the term *aporia*, meaning "wayless." What he means here is that from time to time, we reach an "impasse," the impossibility of getting to the center of a text because of its opposing or incompatible views. It is a "blocked path" or "blind spot." It is a space where a limitless number of interpretations are generated. The word *aporia* is related to *mise en abyme*, the abyss, or bottomless chasm. Encountering the book is like looking into a set of mirrors that keep on reflecting each image ad infinitum.

The aporias in *Judges* are innumerable, but do not despair, for the clashing ideas, as of behavior, for example, lead us in developing conclusions about such behavior, ultimately resulting in a legal or ethical system for the society.

In *Judges*, meaning is always being *deferred* because we can never get to the end of the possibilities of comprehending the comparisons and contrasts that have been set up for us. We are always finding new perspectives, new riddles, new dilemmas, new difficulties in making judgments. Should Jephthah, for example, keep his vow, or obey the commandment not to kill? How do you solve the dilemma when one ethic conflicts with another ethic? (See Chapter 4.) Antigone had her own solution; Creon another in Sophocles' play.

All the impasses in *Judges* could not have happened just by chance—not even by the proverbial monkey randomly tapping through infinity on the computer keyboard and eventually typing out *Judges*. Most of the impasses seem to be deliberate, created in order to make us think for ourselves. The author does not supply an answer key. That is left to each reader.

8) Derrida is fond of telling us that meaning in texts tries to "spill out"; that there is a *surplus* of meaning; that language is "always threatening to outrun and escape the sense which tries to contain it," as Terry Eagleton puts it.[3] What we discover is a vast network of relationships like the neural network of the human brain, a wiring problem with maybe trillions of connections.

Judges is what Barthes calls a "writerly text." Writerly texts are those that encourage the critic

> to carve them up, transpose them into different discourses, produce his or her semi-arbitrary play of meaning athwart the work itself. The reader or critic *shifts from the role of consumer to that of producer*. It is not exactly as though 'anything goes' in interpretation, for Barthes is careful to remark that *the work cannot be got to mean anything at all*; but literature is now less an object to which criticism must conform than a free space in which it can sport . . . (Italics mine. Eagleton 137-138).

We who once were New Critics thought that we could arrive eventually at what a text means. But if we could actually do that, why would there be so many different of interpretations of the Bible, in particular, and why so many different religious institutions emanating from it?

Readers of *Judges* may not even perceive that judgments can and ought to be made. They tend to wait for the author to tell them what to think. This will not happen with *Judges*. The best way to make judgments of any kind is to collaborate actively with other readers. We need a team, a jury. By oneself, one can understand only partially. Inactive readers, relying on "authorized" interpretations, remain passive and continue to regard the text as full of Israelite "heroes" or whatever they have been told to find. But as *the text does not interpret itself*, such readers may never know the difference. Perhaps none of us does.

9)   All of the above add up to *indeterminacy* or *undecidability*. The book is full of mirages, optical illusions that are so interrelated it is hard to keep them separate. In my opinion, at such times, the reader should cherish Keats' "negative capability"— which Keats explains as "when a man is capable of being in uncertainties, Mysteries, doubts, without any irritable reaching after fact & reason"[4]—a statement which could equally apply to postmodern art and to *Judges*.

Derrida's theories help explain why it is so difficult to get down to the hard core of that thing called *truth*, and try to agree on it—why we can never agree on it—and why an *endless stream of scholarly texts* has been generated to explain a mere 30 pages of this ancient manuscript. The book of *Judges must* contain an explanation. Yet we never seem to reach the end of its information, like the ancient pot of gruel. Derrida helps us understand why there is this surplus, and why there must be numberless critics and philosophers ad infinitum, and why we will never get out of the labyrinth or, luckily for us, never be out of our job of endlessly interpreting.

What Derrida taught is really nothing new. If you have difficulty reading Kant, you go to secondary sources. But what you discover there is not clarification, but a wide variety of opinions and arguments, an *entire* literature about what Kant *meant*. Was Kant simply a poor writer? Or is language slippery, elusive, intractable? It has always been so, though we would like to think otherwise.

Some readers will resist my connecting this book to Derrida and to certain aspects of postmodernism. The very words *postmodern* and *deconstruction* and the name *Derrida* have made certain people—like William G. Dever and A. O. Wilson of the consilience theory—hysterical. For them, it is a pejorative term, as the term *modernist* used to be in the 1920s. People feel threatened by new ideas; they detest the new terminology, which they suspect is used to shut them out. And they cannot understand what is being said. True enough, some theorists do not write intelligibly. But new terminology is always required for new ideas so that the old ideas will not leak into the new. And of the making of bad writers there is no end.

What some people do not understand is that first, there is no definitive meaning of the word *postmodern*, and second, postmodernism is not a *cause* of anything, nor an *advocate* of anything. As Stanley Fish wrote recently: "post-modernism is a series of arguments, not a way of life or a recipe for action."[5]

Conclusion: A Brief Theory of Everything

And by the way, deconstruction, like existentialism, is not really dead. It is not the fad anymore. In my opinion, although it could be forgotten (like the ability to read hieroglyphics or Linear B), it will never go away. Perhaps the reason why the ferment has subsided is that no one has anything more to say about it than has already been said. And so we are on to culture studies and globalization.

Why should we get angry with Derrida? Derrida is only *describing* how texts work— or do not work. And I find his terms of immense help in describing the uses to which the author of *Judges* put language. What word we apply to the system itself does not matter. The term *deconstruction* was not Derrida's term for the system he adumbrated.

The resistance to theory, Paul de Man believed, lies in the fact that we are resistant to the act of reading, a "resistance inherent in the theoretical enterprise itself"[6] because the enterprise is so demanding. We want things to be simpler than they are. We want to find clarity, coherence, and closure. The only way to find this in *Judges*, is to ignore the details—and this is what many biblical scholars do when they write about the book. They ignore or phase out the disturbing anomalies, which they think irrelevant, everything which interferes with their desperately-desired destination—closure.

De Man asks: "What is it about literary theory that is so threatening that it provokes such strong resistance and attacks?" His answer:

> *It upsets rooted ideologies* by revealing the mechanics of their workings; it goes against a powerful philosophical tradition of which aesthetics is a prominent part; it upsets the established canon of literary works and blurs the borderlines between literary and non-literary discourse (11, itals. mine).

We fear to upset the applecart of scholarship. Marvelous though biblical scholarship is, however, it is only an applecart.

This passage from de Man, incidentally, seems to show the influence of Thomas Kuhn's *Structure of Scientific Revolution*, written 24 years earlier. My study has attempted to account for all the so-called "irrelevant details"—the anomalies—and bring them back in from the margins.

De Man goes on to say:

> *Nothing can overcome the resistance to theory since theory* is *itself this resistance.* The loftier the aims and the better the methods of literary theory, the less possible it becomes. Yet literary theory is not in danger of going under; it cannot help but flourish, and the more it is resisted, the more it flourishes, since the language it speaks is the language of self-resistance. What remains impossible to decide is whether this flourishing is a triumph or a fall (19-20).

To me it is a triumph. For those of us who have taught literature for many years, our own theories have developed in our minds of their own accord, and we have become mesmerized by the desire to penetrate the secrets of communication.

One of my efforts has been to try to make "judgments" about individual behavior in *Judges*, by comparing each behavior with all the other behaviors in the book. The problem becomes immensely complex (See Chapter 4). It is dizzying, mentally exhausting. The choices are too many. The problem-solving is too demanding. We cry out for some outside authority to step in and relieve us of the chore of decision-making. Let someone else do it.

If we persist, we may reach what looks like a stopping place, only to learn that there is *always already* (another of Derrida's terms) one more specimen to bring under the microscope, one more (different) perspective from which to view the whole thing. A grand polyphony of ideas, a labyrinth from which there is no thread to get us out of it. There is no finality. New perspectives are always popping up. And that is why my book is so long. Possibly neither the ancient author who concocted the scheme and put it to work, nor any modern reader who has discovered his system can be aware of the extent to which this Pandora's box has been let loose on us. We feel like that remote hacker in the sky that Robert Wright mentioned in his article on Fredkin—like trying to "estimate pi to nine jillion decimal places." A limerick by George Gamow expresses my own plight:

> There was a young fellow from Trinity
>
> Who took the square root of infinity.
>
> But the number of digits
>
> Gave him the fidgets;
>
> He dropped Math and took up Divinity.[7]

It was not Ockham's razor that Delilah applied to Samson.

The critic looks at a picture on the wall and interprets it for us. We look back at the picture and try to see what the critic told us. We wonder if we are obtuse, or if what the critic sees is only in his imagination. Can the critic be right? We see something different. We leave the picture. It is still on the wall. But now it exists in our imagination, too, where it will remain until sooner or later it fades from our memory. No one is there to interpret what is still on the wall. The picture exists only when there is an interpreter of it—like the sound of the falling tree in the forest, heard only if someone is there to hear it.

What compels us to keep looking is that we sense that *Judges* is a wonderful mural on the wall, a meticulous work of art.

"Nobody knows how to look anymore," exclaims art critic Jed Perl.

> People have an idea that to look at art in a sophisticated and up-to-date way means that you do not look at it very long or very hard. What people are no longer prepared for is *seeing* as *an experience that takes place in time*. They have ceased to believe that a painting or sculpture is a structure with a *meaning that unfolds as we look*. This endangered experience is not a matter of imagining a narrative; it involves, rather, the more fundamental activity *of relating part to part*. We need to see the particular elements, and see that they add up in ways that become more complex—and sometimes simpler—as we look and look some more. *The essential aspect of all the art that I admire the most, both old and new, is that it makes me want to keep looking* (311-312) . . . . And then the surface

opens up, and effects multiply, and you see more and more. You enter into an intimate imaginative collaboration with an artist. [my emphasis]

And he concludes, "To look long is to feel free."[8]

Information Theory: the Dangerous Information

The process of deconstructing a book, according to Derrida, was likely to "dismantle" it (Derrida's term). My particular deconstruction of *Judges*, however, does not destroy anything; rather, it creates, it builds. But, as Derrida's anayses of other texts demonstrate, it does lay bare the subsurface or deep structure of the work, uncovering concealed meanings, teasing out conflicts of signification within the text, and subverting its surface meaning. The search for history and/or God here obscures the other meanings. Concentration solely on surface meanings blinds us to the murky underneath structure, for the surface is like the surface of a lake reflecting the sky: it conceals from the uninitiated the "dangerous" information that lies below.

What is this dangerous information? In *Judges* the surface meaning is the glorification of certain heroes who arose in Israel and by mysterious means and divine help conquered the enemy.[9] But the deep structure shows this book savagely attacking these same heroes for their pride, cowardice, megalomania, tyranny, brutality, and lust, transgression of all kinds of laws, commandments, and ethics, and the embodiment of the seven deadly sins. The reader or listener observing the ignorant, innocent victims floundering in this nightmarish landscape, at first is apt to call the black "white" and the wrong "right" until the comedy sets him straight (or sets him wrong). Gideon asks his messenger-angel the significant question that we are supposed to answer: "If Yhwh is with us, why then has all this happened to us? And where are all his wonderful deeds that our ancestors recounted to us?" (6.13).

As has been shown throughout my study, *Judges* attacks certain tribes—particularly the Ephraimites, Danites, Benjaminites, and Levites, and to a lesser extent, the Manassehites and Gileadites. The tribe of Judah, though kept in the background, is the only one which remains with its reputation nearly, though not completely, untarnished. The reader who does not pay attention to each mention of the tribes will miss the main message of the book.

Next to the Benjaminites, the *Ephraimites* are the most important tribe in this book. The name *Ephraim*, for example, is used 28x.[10] It is mentioned in all the stories except in the Abimelech and Samson stories. Ephraim is in the "hill country," which is part of its name 12x. Ehud was a brave lone Benjaminite who rid Israel of the tyrant Eglon and who called the Ephraimites to a successful battle against the Moabites. The Ephraimites then fight bravely in the Deborah story, but after the Deborah story, nothing good is said about them. In the Gideon story, though they are useful, they are quarrelsome. In the Jephthah story, they have become angry fellows and apparently refuse to come to the aid of Jephthah (and the Gileadites) against the Ammonites; they falsely insist that they had not been invited to come, and they use this "slight" as a pretext to taunt the Gileadites. Jephthah stops them flat, though with a comic ruse. Micah, an Ephraimite, is a breaker of commandments, a coward, and a defenseless victim defeated by bullies. The Levite in the last story is en route to his home in the hill country of Ephraim. The elderly host of the Levite in Gibeah also hails from Ephraim. A wine-bibber and a coward like the Levite, the Ephraimite host must share the Levite's guilt for forcing the Concubine out the door to become their scapegoat, the victim of the base Benjaminites (see Lev 16). Needless to say, the reports about the Ephraimites deteriorate from good to bad.

Manasseh is represented by the cowardice, boasting, and idolatry of Gideon and the treachery of Abimelech. Gideon seems to have been friendly with the repugnant city of Shechem and its carousing, Baal-worship, and civil unrest. Abimelech, with his fratricide, makes it his "capital" and then utterly destroys it before he himself is destroyed. Sic semper tyrannis.

Gilead (Gad) is represented by Jephthah, with his low birth, cowardice, hypocrisy, and cruelty. Are his bad traits offset by his valor in battle? It is for us to decide.

The *Danites* are represented by Samson who is strong but not intelligent and who does not direct his energies toward saving Israel until the last minute of his life, while in the Micah story, the Danites are idolaters, thieves, and bullies.

Whereas the *Benjaminites* of the first story are heroic (Ehud, representing them, is a Benjaminite), in the last story they are sodomites, rapists, and wild brutes.

And the *Levites* are false and untrustworthy (in the Micah story) and drunken, secular, and self-serving (in the story of the Levite's Concubine).

One cultic center is being attacked in this book—Shechem in the Abimelech story. Two other cultic centers, Shiloh (shortly to disappear) and Dan (in Ch. 18), are also under negative scrutiny. Thus in the subsurface meaning (underneath the black humor), the most important northern tribes, including the Levites—from Benjamin in the south to Dan in the north—as well as "all-Israel," in the last two chapters, are all discredited.

The Levite's Concubine, as noted in an earlier chapter, is none other than *Israel* herself, who is no longer even a full wife; she has been ravaged and destroyed and is now dead and childless, because of the negligence of Ephraim and the Levite, and because of the violence of Benjamin. Earlier avatars of Israel in the book may be Achsah (the proper wife, as in Proverbs 30),[11] Jael and Deborah (warriors for Israel), Jephthah's daughter (Israel sacrificed), and finally, the Concubine and the 600 virgins of Jabesh-Gilead and Shiloh (Israel raped and dismembered by Benjamin).[12] Saul, we may surmise, emerged from one of these unions and was acceptable perhaps only because he was not pure Benjaminite but was a mixture of Benjamin and either Ephraim or Gilead.[13]

The tribe of *Judah* has a curiously small place in this book. It acts in the narrative only twice. In the Achsah story, a Judahite (Othniel, the husband of Achsah) is a successful conqueror. In the Samson story the men of Judah bind up Samson as an effort to propitiate the Philistines. From one point of view, the Judahites are only trying to get their loose cannon back under control (see Chapter 4). From another point of view, the Judahites are treacherous in turning over Samson, one of their own, to the enemy

Though the Levite in the Micah story is from Judah, he is basically a Levite, not an authentic Judahite. That he left Judah, possibly abandoning Judah, may be a clue to the weakness of his character. He certainly deserted (betrayed) Micah.

Finally, the Concubine, though originally from Judah, was ill-matched with her husband (representing Ephraim and the Levites). In her, we also see the Judah female being torn apart by Benjamin and Ephraim.

"Which of us will go first?" is the question asked both at the beginning (1.1, go up against the Canaanites) and again at the end (20.18, go up against Benjamin). The answer both times is "Judah." The Joseph and Rachel tribes (Ephraim, Manasseh, and Benjamin) have sunk to their nadir. But into the vacuum *may arise* Judah. A signpost at the very beginning of the book announces this important possibility— prophecy about Judah, it may be intended to be—when Yhwh is said to declare, "Behold, I have delivered the land into his hand" (1.2), as was true until the Exile. That Judah combines with the other tribes against Benjamin, however, may be intended to explain why the Captivity happened, removing indeed the last tribe.

The book demonstrates the decline of Israel, a decline which it attributes to disobedience. But by not condemning the northern tribes more directly, the author left the story "open"—in case the north eventually returned to power.

The one clear religious function of the book was to command Israelites to remain loyal to Yhwh and not to revert to idolatry. That they were disloyal explains (to the readership) why Yhwh's chosen people could not defend themselves successfully against their enemies, Assyria and Babylon, but were in turn eventually conquered by them.

The author is depicting the deeply divisive feelings and disturbing actions that dissolved the prospects for tribal unity. The fact that in the last chapter the civil war has ended and the Benjaminites are recovering from total defeat does not mean that the internecine struggles are over and that unity has been achieved. The author hoped that a monarch might arise who would prevent eventual dissolution of tribal unity, but he also gave evidence why such a king might fail (like Abimelech), why Israel eventually split into two kingdoms, and why Judah did not escape captivity.

Near the beginning of the book, Yhwh declares, "I will not henceforth drive out before them any of the nations . . . , that by them I may *test Israel*, whether they will take care to walk in the way of Yhwh as their fathers did, or not" (2.20-22).

Did they pass The Test? One by one all the tribes failed.

Did the *Book of Judges* "Just Happen"?

Any literature is both the expression of the author's subjectivity and the product of it. It is the place where the author's observation of the external world and his imagination meet and are combined with his beliefs—conscious and unconscious.

What is most strange about *Judges* is that you will find no trace of this author's personality in it, or at least nothing that can be pinned down as of *this* man and no other. He is unknowable. Or maybe he is like Joyce's artist, who like God, "remains within or behind or beyond or above his handiwork, invisible, refined out of existence, indifferent, paring his fingernails."[14] This author effaces himself, represses himself completely. In fact, he is missing. The death of the author is not a new postmodern idea.

Yet the words and the ideas that we read on the page had once been filtered through a human mind. This mind had thousands of ideas, but a small space on which to express them. He invented a unique form for this purpose. Even though the vocabulary and sentence structure are like those of the alleged Deuteronomic writer, we cannot mistake this literary product for any other in the Bible. And that is because of the form. The form expresses the content. Form and content blend into one another.

The author gives us an abundance, even a plethora, of contours, both within and without. He is coming at us from all directions, from underneath in language, from the outside in allusions to other parts of the Bible, and from within in story-to-story parallels and contrasts which provoke the active reader to engage in the dialectical practice of arriving at the truth by the method of logical argument.

The form is almost visible, almost tactile or characterized by the illusion of tangibility. It is malleable. We can participate ourselves in molding it by changing our own perspective in the same way that the author changes his. We knead it like clay and work it.

It is protean. It is "always already" an emerging creation, growing, dynamic, kinetic, shaping itself, letting us shape it.

We are looking through a kaleidoscope at a pattern created by mirror fragments. Mirrors create illusions. One turn of the cylinder, and in a trice, a cataclysmic crash occurs, a nano-second shift in the pattern into something made up of the same elements yet altogether different.

The author has a theme: warfare and the salvation of Israel. Will warfare save Israel? We cannot be sure of the answer to that question. Maybe it will, maybe it won't. All was in question, perhaps until Assyria and Babylon answered it for the nonce. And all is still in question—to this day.

The author is not foisting off (imposing) on us an inflexible set of ethics. He is asking us to question ethics, to explore our own minds and imagination. It is a Socratic process. If we have a mentor and if our mentor asks the right questions, we should come to the right conclusion, the inevitable conclusion, the only one left after we have dispatched all the other possibilities through trial and error. Perhaps at the beginning of their study, the ancient readers would have had an enlightened teacher as guide, like Virgil to Dante. But who will be *our* mentor? If we choose a mentor, we also choose the answers, as the existentialist Sartre told us. This we know. This is why we must choose *all possible mentors*, not just one. Is the larger truth in our own minds, as Socrates and Emerson taught? How will we recognize it when we get there? Literature critics in the early days in my profession taught us we could. After teaching many years, we find that we cannot.

The author juxtaposes *opposites* both on the larger scale (story for story) and on the smaller scale (word for word): peace and war, order and chaos, love and death, the natural and the macabre, the appalling and the comical, the absurd and the credible, the realistic and the imagined, dignity and humiliation, the male and the female, and so on and on. Off/on, zero/one, left/right, up/down, matter/antimatter—bits of information. It is a digital system, in which the data are represented by measurable physical variables—electrical impulses, *ethical* impulses, as it were. The off/on button must blink continuously. If it does not, "off" might get into a loop and proliferate until darkness is all. In information theory, we are each but cells blinking on and off. Words in texts are blinking on and off. The configuration of bits is what is important. Information is the most fundamental stuff of the universe.[15]

The binary code is the starting principle of language. Contraries mingle. But there are more than three dimensions in superstring theory, as Edward Fredkin saw it. Take a piece of paper; it has three dimensions. Then you roll it up into a tube, then roll it ever more tightly until it becomes very tiny and coiled up. There are new curled dimensions in the tiny particles. Combine quantum theory (the microscopic) and relativity (the macrocosmic) and you get incredible explanatory power. (Are they irreconcilable?)[16] There is much more to the universe than we would expect (or suspect), no matter how hard we have tried to become aware of all of it.

Judges appears to be a most *objective* of books in that it does not reveal the *author's* subjectivity. But it is the *most subjective* of books in that it demands subjectivity of the *readers*. The author is not in touch with his own emerging creation, for he cannot be aware of how readers have been continually improvising on it, creating something different on their own.

We read the text to find out what is in ourselves. We reason with it; we argue. It is not a purely subjective process because we are analyzing *other* people and *their* actions throughout. In this book, we are trying to find rules to guide their and our behavior. We are constructing an ethical system. What could be better for our minds than the discovery of laws? (See Chapter 4.)

We are not dictators of the law, however; we may be creators of the law, but we are also discoverers of the law. Whether it is a narrow or a broad discovery depends on what we bring to the table—that is, our own experience and knowledge—to help us adjudicate. Unlike usual art forms, here it is not so much what is *on the paper*, but what is *in the reader's mind* that is most significant. It is our *observation* of the design that generates meaning.

The solutions to the readers' ethical dilemmas in *illo tempore* were probably to be found in the Commandments and the laws in the Pentateuch—that is, after they were written down. Readers of today, however, should not hesitate to go outside the Bible and compare the problems of these people with those of our own time. In the face of recent acts of terrorism in our own country and in Israel, for example, can we continue to accept the underdog philosophy proposed by a number of scholars of *Judges*—the philosophy by which the terrorist behaviors of these ancient heroes are shown to be justified? *It all depends on what side you are on.*

To exert ourselves in following the author's design is to discover not his beliefs, but our own. Maybe this is true of all great literature, provided that the reader not merely absorb what is on the printed page, but dialogues with it; not accept external authorities, but quarrels with them. The danger is that we might not find our better selves but some tyrant or madman or irrational zealot within.

I have used the words *interactive* and *dialogic* to describe the way the book functions, but those words are too vapid to describe how we are stimulated and excited by the possibilities in *Judges* once we have discovered them, how we can be goaded, spurred on, provoked, roused to heightened activity in search of our ever-elusive goal, the final meaning—the will o' the wisp that we can never attain.

The author is aggressive, extroverted, experimental. We are playing a game, a serious game. And we are the plaything.

A Theory of Composition

How did this artist make his decisions about placement of the keywords and other details in the stories—especially in an age where writing materials were scarce—how did he fashion the elaborate design of the book?

In theory, the book originated as a group of folktales with a common theme, passed along orally, perhaps having many audiences and many storytellers, the storytellers expanding and embellishing the scenarios as they had been taught to do, or improvising or reducing them as they thought fit.[17] One can also imagine that the storytellers would *mime* and *act out* the scenes and *make appropriate gestures* and *sounds* (such as the fighting, dancing, dropping the millstone, binding the foxes and lighting their tails, etc.). When the scenario depicts Jotham shouting out his fable from the top of a mountain, the storyteller would stand in a commanding position on another level and shout it out. When pots are broken and trumpets blare, the storyteller must reproduce these sound effects with whatever tools he has at hand, for he, like his characters, is an improviser—a *bricoleur*. Perhaps the torches will burn his fingers. When a man is stabbed in the belly or has his eyes gouged out, or when the stricken Concubine crawls on the ground to the threshold, the storyteller must act it all out, from silences, to whispers, to songs, to primal screams. The dynamic stories beg for a dynamic storyteller to portray them.

Perhaps we should think of storytelling as a performance art, and imagine the storytellers to have the gifts of Charlie Chaplin, Red Skelton, Bob Hope, Woody Allen, Steve Martin, or Jim Carrey—take your pick as to which wacky comedian would enact which character. It would make a difference whether Samson was portrayed by Jim Carrey or Arnold Schwartzenegger or by Victor Mature as in the Cecil B. De Mille film, or when sung by Placido Domingo in Camille Saint-Saens' opera, or painted by Rubens being shaved, or etched by James Tissot or Gustave Doré pushing against the great columns of a vast temple, or put into charming verse by Chaucer or noble poetry by Milton. What was Milton doing but fleshing out the skeleton scenario in his *Samson Agonistes*? Through this short list of wildly different versions of Samson as well as many others through the ages that we have encountered here and there, we can see endless possibilities. How we receive the stories depends on the storyteller's perspective, as well as on our own religious and literary background of information.

The stories would be beloved by the audience (probably of males), which would respond passionately and vociferously to each event and signal throughout its pleasure or displeasure, interacting without restraint. The audience loved the storytellers—because they were funny, with the kinds of comedy and horror that still give pleasure to audiences in entertainment today.

The comic vein was intrinsic and could not be eliminated without demolishing the stories, for if eliminated, its absence would turn the stories upside down. The comedy signifies that the author is mocking human beings, who, whatever their good intentions and achievements, are perpetually screwing up. The actions of "heroes" as comic bunglers have unintended consequences: they bring about events and meanings *beyond the hero's comprehension*, meanings which *are hidden from him or her*—just as meanings are always *hidden from us* in life.

Curiously, the interpretation is in the storyteller's hands. He can diminish or increase a man's evil or a woman's innocence. He can accentuate the humor, or raise the decibels of horror. He can make it tragic, or he can make our sides split with laughter.

The stories are an instrument. Each storyteller plays the instrument differently, and each audience listens differently. As with the Homeric stories, these tales were passed along orally from generation to generation.

Perhaps one single storyteller (our author) contrived the idea of stabilizing the sequence of the folktales he was narrating, little by little creating and expanding their similarities and contrasts, and eliminating what was inert. He gradually, mentally established the keyword categories one by one, and would tinker with his system each time he re-told the story to an audience. Each time new ideas would break into his mind, he would add them into the appropriate categories—door here, vineyard there, hammer here, blaze here, millstone there, thumbs and big toes here, mothers there, rape here, what have you—but without destroying the coherence of the work.

William of Ockham and Thoreau wanted us to simplify. But with *Judges*, we simply cannot. Though it is a small universe, it has innumerable details. If we want to understand this universe, we have to examine as many of its parts as possible. We must keep exploring as long as we can hold out.

Eventually the author had to stop adding words and ideas, had to decide that enough was enough, and let the whole thing go. Additions could pile up forever. The stories were passed along as he left them, and then written down by someone else.

"We murder to dissect," wrote Wordsworth. Now is the time to put all the pieces back together in their original form, and enjoy the book.

Now is time for us to stop adding to our scholarly text and just let it go. Not tinker forever.

Endnotes

Preface and Foreword

1. The quotation is from Conrad's *Heart of Darkness*, spoken by Mr. Kurtz, who was also trying to conquer a promised land.

2. "Lovis Corinth's *Blinded Samson*," *Biblical Interpretation*, 6 (1998): 410-423.

3. *The Body in Pain: The Making and Unmaking of the World* (New York: Oxford University Press, 1985), 4.

4. Seth Lerer, "Lecture One," *Comedy Through the Ages* (audio tapes; [Chantilly, Va.]: The Teaching Company, 2000).

5. *Rabelais and His World* (trans. Helene Iswolsky; Cambridge, Mass.: M.I.T. Press, 1965, 1968), passim.

6. Lillian Klein catches many of these ironies in *The Triumph of Irony in the Book of Judges* (Sheffield: The Almond Press, 1988), but more remain to be discovered, even more than I have added to her list.

7. Daniel N. Robinson, "Lecture One," *The Quest for Meaning: Value, Ethics, and the Modern Experience* (audio tapes; Chantilly, Va.: The Teaching Company, 1999).

8. David Noel Freedman, ed. *Eerdmans Dictionary of the Bible* (Grand Rapids Mich.: Eerdmans, 2000), 213-214.

Chapter One

1. "Exposition, Judges: Introduction and Exegesis," in *The Interpreter's Bible* (ed. Jacob M. Myers; New York and Nashville: Abingdon, 1973), II, 708, 711.

2. *The World of the Judges* (Englewood Cliffs, N.J.: Prentice-Hall, 1966), 157-158.

3. Robert Boling, *Judges: Introduction, Translation, and Commentary* (AB 6A; New York: Doubleday, 1975), 278-279, citing Julius Wellhausen, *Prolegomena* (trans. W. Robertson Smith [New York: Meridian 1957]), 235-237. Boling's excellent scholarship and perceptions have provided me with many clues, although I had to abandon Boling's historical perspective.

4. J. Gordon Harris, Cheryl A. Brown, and Michael S. Moore, *Joshua, Judges, Ruth* (ed. J. Gordon Harris; New International Biblical Commentary; Peabody, Mass.: Hendrickson Publishers, 2000), 124-125. Brown's commentary on *Judges* is excellent.

5. Brown does at least see that Samson was destroyed because he became like other men. Just so Israel, which "wanted to be like other nations" (260). It would be disastrous for Israel to become so.

6. According to Boling, the skill of the stories points to "a guild of professional storytellers in premonarchic Israel" (Boling 33). Writes Block, citing Boling: "The turmoil within Israel following the fall of Jerusalem in 586 is reflected in the tragic-comic framework consisting of a new introduction (chap. 1) and a new conclusion (chaps. 19-21). According to Boling the final Deuteronomistic editor counters the disillusionment of the exile with comedy as an escape not from the reality but from the despair the reality evokes . . . . " Daniel I. Block, *Judges, Ruth* (vol. 6; The New American Commentary; Nashville: Broadman, 1999), 47.

7. *Judges: A Commentary* (trans. John S. Bowden; Philadelphia: Westminster, 1981), 92. This is an excellent commentary.

8. Throughout this book, I have referred to the author as "he." I see no reason for thinking the author is female; it is a "macho" book in every way. When forced to refer to the reader with a pronoun, I use the male pronoun so as to avoid cumbersome locutions like "he or she." While there may originally have been multiple authors, at the end, I believe, a single author was in charge of the text as we have it now. This will be discussed later.

9. Wolfgang Richter, *Die Bearbeitungen des "Retterbuches" in Deuteronomischer Epoche* (Bonn: Hanstein, 1964), passim. Barry G. Webb, *The Book of the Judges: An Integrated Reading* (JSOTSup 46; Sheffield: JSOT Press, 1987), 20-23.

10. *The Book of Judges* (London: Routledge, 2002), passim. See pp. 104, 107, 110, 112.

11. Webb writes, for example: " . . . Judges as a whole is . . . a coherent literary work with thematic focus on the one hand and richness of meaning on the other" (76). Klein calls the book "a structured entity," the unity of which is manifested through the author's use of irony. *The Triumph of Irony in the Book of Judges* (Sheffield: The Almond Press, 1988), 11. Schneider, *Judges* (Berit Olam Studies in Hebrew Narrative and Poetry; Collegeville, Minn.: Liturgical Press, 2000), xii, xiii.

12. *Eerdmans Dictionary of the Bible* (ed. David Noel Freedman; Grand Rapids, Mich.: William B. Eerdmans, 2000), 752, partially quoted below.

13. This excellent Introduction appears as Chapter 3, "The Literary Character of the Bible," in Robert Alter, *The World of Biblical Literature* ([New York:] Basic Books, 1992).

14. I met Alter in the Bible as Literature seminar at the University of Indiana 1979 and heard him discuss the Bible as literature and also lecture on Stendhal. Yet I did not have the benefit of Alter's criticism until after I had developed my own ideas fully. I only read his books recently, within the last year, in fact.

    My own ideas were relatively complete by 1983, as is substantiated by papers I read at SBL meetings and distributed to a number of prominent scholars. I came to appreciate his innovations, insights, and brilliance much more after reading his words late, than I ever would have, had I read him earlier, when I was not so familiar with the Bible and with the work of many other scholars in the field, with whom I can now compare Alter's achievements. He has truly been a joy to read.

15. *The World of Biblical Literature,* 128.

16. *The Art of Biblical Narrative* (New York: Basic Books, 1981), 12.

17. *Missing Persons and Mistaken Identities: Women and Gender in Ancient Israel* (Minneapolis: Fortress, 1997), 13-14, 45.

18. *Fragmented Women: Feminist (Sub)versions of Biblical Narratives* (JSOTSup 163; Sheffield: Sheffield Academic Press, 1993), 32.

19. "Feminist Criticism and Biblical Studies on the Verge of the Twenty-First Century," in *A Feminist Companion to Reading the Bible: Approaches, Methods and Strategies* (eds. Athalya Brenner and Carole Fontaine; Sheffield: Sheffield Academic Press, 1997), 31.

20. I am a feminist, but in this book I am doing literary criticism, not feminist criticism.

21. Exum says that there is a "plurality of interpretive possibilities that feminist reading permits." Ibid., 12.

22. In Sue Halpern, "City People," rev. of Temple Grandin, *Thinking in Pictures*, in *New York Review of Books* (May 13, 2004): 14.

23. Or as Locke put it, "Beasts abstract not." Whether or not the author of *Judges* was autistic, I decline to guess. What is plain is that he abstracts not. He thinks in pictures.

24. T. S. Kuhn, *The Structure of Scientific Revolutions* (Chicago: University of Chicago Press, 1962), 52, 111.

25. Soggin, 196-200, 206-207, discusses the roles of the minor judges and Jephthah.

26. Except for Gideon, Jephthah, and the minor judges, we are not told much about descendants in *Judges*. Ehud and Deborah (we do not know), Sisera's mother (at least had one son, who was killed), Gideon (70 or 72 sons, 70 of whom are murdered by Abimelech except Abimelech and Jotham), Jephthah (one, and then none), Samson (we do not know, but suspect that he had none), Micah (had at least one son), and the Levite's Concubine (do not know, probably none).

27. For an episode or character to be "parallel" is not to say that the episodes are exactly alike, or the same length, or with the same components, as Marc Brettler seems to think they must be (59 et passim). Length has no bearing on parallelisms, and differences are just as important as similarities, as they provoke thought.

28. Johannes C. de Moor notes the close relationship of *The Song* with Ps 68 and believes that Ps 68 "fits a time close to the texts of Ugarit . . . " He believes this Psalm is older than *The Song*. *The Rise of Yahwism: The Roots of Israelite Monotheism* (rev. and enl. ed; Leuven: Leuven University Press, 1997), 185, 183.

29. See the chart at the end of Cedric Whitman's *Homer and the Heroic Tradition* (Cambridge, Mass.: Harvard University Press, 1958).

30. Unless otherwise stated, quotations from the Bible are from the New Standard Revised Edition, Copyrighted 1989 by the Division of Christian Education of the National Council of the Churches of Christ in the United State of America (copied from *BibleWorks for Windows 5.0* on CD Rom. Big Fork, Mont.: Hermeneutika Bible Research Software, 2001).

31. *The New Interpreter's Bible* (vol. II; Nashville: Abingdon Press, 1998), 762.

32. Though called גבור החיל, "mighty men of valor," the main characters, thinks Block, are not what we supposed "charismatic" leaders to be: "Othniel is not a native Israelite; as left-handed, Ehud is considered handicapped; Barak is unmanly; Gideon is a skeptic; Jephthah is a brigand.

Samson also falls short . . ." (35). Ehud is treacherous and brutal; Barak "weak-willed and indecisive"; Gideon "cynical," "resistant," "brutal," and "imperial"; Jephthah "ambitious" and "abusive" to his daughter (and abusive to a tribe, though Block does not say this); and Samson "fritters away his high calling with illicit philandering with pagan women" (40). Far from being spiritual, Block finds that the deliverers showed repeatedly that they were part of the problem rather than a solution.

A number of times throughout his book Block ascribes this behavior to the bad influence of the Canaanites: "The theme of the book is the *Canaanization of Israelite society during the period of settlement"* (58). And "Like Ehud's assassination of Eglon . . . , the account of [Jael's] behavior seems to have been lifted from a Canaanite notebook" (208). He calls the lex talionis "a Canaanite ethic, which the Israelites adopted after their arrival (91). But it is an Israelite ethic (Exod. 21.23). Since virtually nothing is known of Canaanite society—except what we glean from the Bible—we cannot know who influenced whom—except what we learn from the Bible. Perhaps Canaanite ethics were the same as Israelite ethics. Ozwald Loretz thinks that the Israelites, in fact, derived their ethics from Canaanite culture. *Ugarit und Die Bibel: Kanaanaische Götter und Religion im Alten Testament* (Darmstadt: Wissenschaftliche Buchegesellschaft, 1990), 232. He cites N. P. Lemche, *Early Israel* (VTSup 37; Leiden: Brill, 1985), 434. Finally, the book itself is blaming the Israelites, not the Canaanites.

33.   Boling's translation of אנשים ריקים ופחזי (9.4) merely as "mercenaries" is misleading (171) as it removes the pejorative connotation of Abimelech's men as *empty* and *reckless*.

34.   *After Virtue* (Notre Dame, Ind.: Notre Dame Press, 1981), 117.

35.   If these were originally Canaanite stories, the idols would not have been regarded as evil (see Chapter 5). The author does not make a judgment on the idols. We know that they are evil because of the "downward slope" of virtue to vice. And the later audiences of the stories would regard them as evil.

36.   Boling has noted some of the parallels, especially the honey and the torches (230, 235). "The frequency with which so many narrative elements from earlier stories reappear in inverted relationship in the Samson stories is indeed striking" (230). "The Samson stories swarm with reminiscences and allusions to virtually all of the great protagonists from Deborah to Jephthah. . . . This can scarcely be accidental" (232).

Likewise, he writes: "There is in fact a number of indicators, to be noted below, which point to a narrative relationship between this story of the honorable honorary judge Deborah early in the book and dishonorable divinely appointed judge Samson late in the book" (94). And "A number of similarities to the traditions of chs. 4 and 5 . . . suggest that the narrator believes that Samson as a judge was several cuts below Deborah . . . " (226).

37.   Ch. 13, with its focus on the barren wife conceiving through divine intervention, contrasts sharply with the sexual aberrations of this son. She is the model for what Samson should have become but did not.

38.   *Social World of Ancient Israel 1250-587 BCE* (Peabody, Mass.: Hendrickson, 1993), 91.

39.   Susan Niditch, "Eroticism and Death in the Tale of Jael," in *Women in the Hebrew Bible* (ed. Alice Bach; New York: Routledge, 1999), 43-57.

40. There are many parallels to Greek mythology. In this respect, *Judges* is mythic. To investigate all the parallels is beyond the aim of my study.

41. "Dealing/With/Women: Daughters in the Book of Judges," in *The Book and the Text: The Bible and Literary Theory* (ed. Regina Schwartz; Oxford: Basil Blackwell, 1990), 20.

42. *Tragedy and Biblical Narrative: Arrows of the Almighty* (Cambridge: Cambridge University Press, 1992), 66. See also Esther Fuchs, "Marginalization, Ambiguity, Silencing the Story of Jephthah's Daughter" in *A Feminist Companion to Judges* (ed. Athalya Brenner; Sheffield: JSOT Press, 1993), 116-130. Fuchs thinks that the author is "covering up" the crime, whitewashing the father. See also Exum, "On Judges 11," in Brenner 142.

43. Likewise, had Jephthah really had faith, would not Yhwh have saved his daughter, as Isaac was saved in Genesis 22.12? One way of interpreting both the Concubine story and the Jephthah story is that they tell us that if we push our wife out to rapists or sacrifice our daughter, neither the angel nor the Lord will save those poor creatures. Or perhaps this author is implying that the stories of Genesis are not models of realistic behavior.

44. Israel Finkelstein and Neil Asher Silberman argue for the composition of the Deuteronomistic History in the time of Josiah (late 7th century BCE). *The Bible Unearthed: Archaeology's New Vision of Ancient Israel and the Origin of Its Sacred Texts* (New York: The Free Press, 2001), 14. John Van Seters at the 1999 annual meeting of SBL puts the writing of the laws *not* in the 8th century but in the time Jeremiah and Ezekiel (early 6th century BCE).

    John C. H. Laughlin writes: "The Bible, as we know it, is a product of the post-exilic period, written primarily by relatively few *literati* (Dever 1995 a: 73) . . . . " *Archaeology and the Bible* (London and New York: Routledge. 2000), 74-5, 120. Others have argued for an even later Hellenistic period. See Laughlin 90-92 concerning the lack of archaeological evidence concerning the Exodus. "However, the contemporary dogma now accepted in some scholarly circles that there is no historical validity in the Bible prior to the post-exilic period seems to me as extreme as it is unwarranted" (Laughlin, 120). The question as to what is valid and what is not valid has not so far been answered definitively.

45. Juan Pablo Vita, "Ch. XI. The Society of Ugarit," in *Handbook of Ugaritic Studies* (eds. Wilfred G. E. Watson and Nicolas Wyatt; Cologne: Brill, 1999), 498. Robert Drews, however, writes that "nowhere in the ancient world, at any period, are ironplated chariots attested" and that in fact chariots were not used for battle after about 1200 BCE. Iron tires were in use "as early as the reign of Sennacherib." Drews dates the writing of the stories in *Joshua* and *Judges* during the Persian Period. "The 'Chariots of Iron' of Joshua and Judges," *JSOT* 45 (1989): 18-20. As the texts in Ugarit show, chariots were in use in the 12th C. BCE. The word *iron* could have been added in the Persian period. The chariots of the Hittites were not ironplated, but were very light in weight. The warriors, however, used iron armor and weapons. [www.allempires.com/empires/hittites/hittites1.htm]

46. In *The Song*, Sisera's mother is waiting with other women for Sisera's return (from battle); these women are "her wise noble ladies" (שָׂרוֹתֶיהָ חַכְמוֹת). שָׂרוֹתֶיהָ is the fem. pl. of שַׂר, meaning *commander* (5.29). As already mentioned, some commentators call Sisera's mother a "queen." But Sisera is only a "noble" or "commander of his army," that is, of Jabin's army

(שַׂר־צָבָא, 4.2). Susan Ackerman, for example, assumes that Sisera is one of the kings mentioned in 5.19. And then she extrapolates from ancient middle eastern cultures, information about queen mothers and their power. But there is no evidence that Sisera was a king and that his mother was a "queen mother." Nor can we conclude that just because his mother is looking out of a window that she represents the cult of Asherah, as Ackerman thinks. *Warrior, Dancer, Seductress, Queen: Women in Judges and Biblical Israel* [New York: Doubleday, 1998], 3, 130-131. Boling says that Sisera's mother is waiting in the "Canaanite court" (119), but he calls Sisera a mere "captain." "The woman at the window" is a well-known icon, but nothing in this story allows us to infer anything about the religious beliefs of the mother other than that she was a Canaanite and for that reason probably worshiped Asherah.

47. Cf. *Keret*, 16, vi, 33-35, for example. Vita, *idem.*

48. Hess examined a fragmentary text containing Judg 6:2-6 and 11-13 and found that verses 7-12 (the prophecy) are missing from the scroll. Thus it seems likely that they were a later insertion, as has long been considered possible. "The Dead Sea Scrolls and Higher Criticism of the Hebrew Bible: The Case of 4QJud[a]," in *The Scrolls and the Scriptures* (eds. S. E. Porter and C. A. Evans; RILP, 3; JSPSup, 26, Sheffield: Sheffield Academic Press, 1997), 122-128, passim.

49. These could have been family deities, like what the people of Ugarit had and like the *teraphim* Rachel stole from her father in *Genesis*. Micah's idols included *teraphim.*

50. Janet B. Tollington argues that Ch. 19 and Chs. 20-21 "could not have been joined prior to the exile," that the two halves together testify to the "degeneracy of life among the tribes of Israel prior to the formation of the nation and the monarchy" and that the "pro-Judean slant . . . prevents their use by any who wanted to assert that the northern kingdom had not been entirely to blame. Consequently . . . an appropriate context for the compilation of the epilogue is among a community seeking the restoration of the monarchy in the post-exilic period." "The Book of Judges: the Result of Post-Exilic Exegesis?" in *Intertextuality in Ugarit and Israel* (ed. Johannes C. de Moor; Leiden: Brill, 1998), 195.

51. The first Levite is from Judah and goes to Dan; the second is from Ephraim, goes to Judah, and returns to Ephraim. The author seems to be saying that whatever their origin (whether from a "good" or a "bad" tribe), the Levites are not to be trusted. Tollington thinks the sub-text of the second story is that "the northern kingdom [is] a danger to Judah's continued existence" 193.

52. "In the Ruins of the Future: Reflections on Terror and Loss in the Shadow of September," *Harper's Magazine* (December 2001): 34.

Chapter Two

1. Yhwh is always to be considered a character in the author's mind. The author's Yhwh must be kept separate from other conceptions about the god of the Hebrew Bible. We cannot learn how the author of *Judges* perceives his god if we invest Yhwh with meanings that are not in the book.

2. (New York: Oxford University Press, 1985), 89, 19, et passim.

3. *Judges: Introduction, Translation, and Commentary* (AB 6A; Garden City, N.Y.: Doubleday, 1975), 54-55. Boling is trying to make the numbers reasonable. Phillip J. King and Lawrence E. Stager think that "a thousand" means a *clan* (מִשְׁפָּחָה). *Life in Biblical Israel*

(Louisville, London: Westminster John Knox Press, 2001), 240-241. Baruch Halpern thinks that a large number indicates that at least some men (several or a few) were involved. *David's Secret Demons: Messiah, Murderer, Traitor, King* (Grand Rapids, Mich: William B. Eerdmans, 2004), 126 ff. In my opinion, the numbers in this kind of story are supposed to be enormous.

4. J. Alberto Soggin, *Judges: A Commentary* (trans. John S. Bowden; Philadelphia: Westminster, 1981), 293-294.

5. According to 20.15, the Benjaminites had 26,000 men, and 700 more from Gibeah, making 26,700 in all; [700 of them were sling shooters, not necessarily those from Gibeah (20.16)]. Soggin thinks that two accounts of one battle are given, joined rather crudely together (294). Either there were 50,000 more Benjaminites than reported in 20.15, or there is a triplication of casualties. I did not include the extra 50,000 in the total casualties.

6. John C. H. Laughlin, *Archaeology and the Bible* (London and New York: Routledge, 2000), 117. According to Israel Finkelstein and Neil Asher Silberman: "The early Israelite settlement began around 1200 BCE. . . . Like its predecessors, it commenced with mainly small, rural communities with an initial population of approximately 45,000 in 250 sites." Population grew gradually so that not until the eighth century was it anything like the size given in *Judges*. At that time, Finkelstein and Silberman estimate that there were "over five hundred sites, with a population of about 160,000." That would give the cities on the average a population of 320 each, three or four centuries after the supposed time of *Judges*. *The Bible Unearthed: Archaeology's New Vision of Ancient Israel and the Origin of Its Sacred Texts* (New York: The Free Press, 2001), 115. I mention these figures to give a perspective on the size of the towns and population of this alleged historical period.

7. Hermann Michell Niemann argues that instead of being located originally in the south, Dan was originally located in the north, and moved south in about 720 BCE and Danaized the local legends about Samson. "Zorah, Eshtaol, Beth-Shemesh and Dan's Migration to the South: a Region and its Traditions in the Late Bronze and Iron Ages," *JSOT* 86 (1999): 47.

8. *Rabelais and His World* (trans. Helene Iswolsky; Cambridge, Mass.: MIT, 1965, 1968), 19-20.

9. This is about "spin." Scarry has an excellent discussion of the distancing effect of language during wartime (64-81).

10. See Endnote 22, Chapter 3 for data taken from the reporting on the war with Iraq by the news in the last week of April 2004, all of which confirms Elaine Scarry's discussion of the use of torture, war, and how these are reported by the media.

11. *Judges, Ruth* (vol. 6; The New American Commentary; Nashville: Broadman & Homes, 1999), 582, n. 408.

12. Moshe Weinfeld, *The Promise of the Land* (Los Angeles, Ca.: University of California, 1993), 83.

13. Tony W. Cartledge, *Vows in the Hebrew Bible and the Ancient Near East* (JSOTSup147; Sheffield: Sheffield Academic Press, 1992), 14.

14. *On the Way to the Postmodern: Old Testament Essays 1967-1998* (vol. 1; JSOTSup 292; Sheffield: Sheffield Academic Press, 1998), 153, 156.

15. Juan Pablo Vita, "Ch. XI. The Society of Ugarit," in *Handbook of Ugaritic Studies* (eds. Wilfred G. E. Watson and Nicolas Wyatt; Cologne: Brill, 1999), 491 et passim.

16. Improvised weapons are still being used today, still by the underdog. In the Iraqi War, our military even has an acronym for them: IEDs or Improvised Explosive Devices. Today's IEDs are usually missiles or bombs, but they can also be airplanes used as missiles to destroy buildings.

17. Two critics who note the interplay of the tragic and comic in the Samson story are J. Cheryl Exum and J. William Whedbee: "This interplay . . . is essential to the vitality of these visions, for without the tempering of a comic perspective, tragedy moves into the realm of melodrama, while comedy without a recognition of tragic potential becomes farce (cf. Frye, 1965:50). . . ." "Isaac, Samson, and Saul: Reflections on the Comic and Tragic Visions," *On Humour and the Comic in the Hebrew Bible* (ed. Yehuda Radday and Athalya Brenner; Sheffield: Almond Press, 1990), 135. See also Exum, *Tragedy and Biblical Narrative: Arrows of the Almighty* (Cambridge: Cambridge UP, 1992), ch. 2 et passim. William J. Whedbee's full-length book, *The Bible and the Comic Vision* does not analyze humor in *Judges*. (Cambridge University Press, 1998. Repr.: Minneapolis: Fortress Press, 2002).

18. "None So Blind: Perceptual blindness experiments challenge the validity of eyewitness testimony," *Scientific American* (March 2004): 42.

19. The Super Computer is enabled to function in diverse ways simultaneously. The example given is of the atom, which is spinning. You would think it was spinning either clockwise or counterclockwise, but if you hit it with a pulse of light, it will spin in both directions at once. Jim Holt, "Quantum Weirdness," rev. George Johnson, *A Shortcut Through Time: The Path to the Quantum Computer, New York Times Book Review* (April 6, 2003): 12.

20. Daniel Boyne, "Portrait of a Woman as a Young Boxer," *The Atlantic* (December 2001): 122.

21. Harry Levin, *Playboys and Killjoys: An Essay on the Theory and Practice of Comedy* (New York, Oxford: Oxford University Press, 1987), 191.

22. *Dictionnaire universalle de la langue française* by Johann Josef Schmidlin (1771), in Wolfgang Kayser, *The Grotesque in Art and Literature* (trans. Ulrich Weisstein; Bloomington, Ind.: Indiana University Press, 1957, 1963), 28.

23. "Lecture One," *Comedy Through the Ages* (audio tapes; [Chantilly, Va.:] The Teaching Company, 2000).

24. "Taking Humor Seriously: George Meyer, the Funniest Man in TV," *The New Yorker* (March 13, 2000): 70. Another excellent recent article on humor is Tad Friend, "What's So Funny: A scientific attempt to discover why we laugh," *The New Yorker* (November 11, 2002), 78-93.

25. Contemporary film noir is characterized by "the moral ambivalence, the criminality, the complex contradictions in motives and events," according to Raymond Borde and Étienne Chaumeton in "Towards a Definition of Film Noir," in A. Silver and J. Ursini, eds., *Film Noir Reader* (New York: Limelight Editions, 1996), 25, and quoted by Eric S. Christianson, "The Big Sleep: Strategic Ambiguity in Judges 4-5 and in Classic 'Film Noir,'" *The SBL Forum,* v. 3, no. 4 (April 2005).

26. Daniel Mendelsohn, "Double Take: *The Producers,* a musical at the St. James Theatre, New York City," *The New York Review of Books,* 48 (June 21, 2001): 14.

27. Writes Terry Castle:

> "It is true that the ruling visual motif of *Don Quixote* could be said to be the bruise. Once off on their sallies, Quixote and Sancho are repeatedly punched, flogged, tripped,

unhorsed, poked, pulled along by their beards, clobbered on the pate. . . . Quixote loses part of an ear: Sancho gets tossed in a blanket by rambunctious peasants, both characters tumble into holes and caves with some regularity.

"The injuriousness of this fictional world might be explained, of course, by slapstick convention. Comic blows, we surmise, don't really hurt. The Quixotean buffoon can slip, fall, crash into walls—but he immediately gets up again, perhaps grimacing but essentially unscathed. Nabokov was right to say that Cervantes lays special emphasis on bodily affliction. He makes us linger on his characters' physical vulnerability—gives it new specificity . . . .

"Yet surely this emphasis on a sort of banal, nonheroic suffering—contra Nabokov— is something other than authorial sadism. *I take it as another emblem, perhaps the most tangible one, of Cervantes's revolutionary interest in the individual. No writer before him (not even Chaucer or Boccaccio) registered the physical life of the ordinary human being in quite the palpable way that he did . . . .*

"This attention to physical detail—to the sensation of lived experience—is everywhere in *Don Quixote*."

"High Plains Drifter: *Don Quixote*, a masterpiece of comic seriousness, gets a new and 'virtually twee-free' translation," *Atlantic* (Jan./Feb., 2004): 187-188.

28. There are many instances of beheadings, dismemberment, mutilation, and desecration of bodies in *1* and *2 Samuel*, but these acts are not combined with comedy; they are simply grisly.

29. In *Text and Tradition: The Hebrew Bible and Folklore* (ed. Susan Niditch; Atlanta, Ga.: Scholars Press, 1990), 47-56, passim.

30. (Sheffield: Almond, 1988). See also Edwin M. Good, *Irony in the Old Testament* (1965; Bible and Literature 3; Sheffield: Almond; repr.1981). Daniel I. Block also mentions a number of ironies. For example, Barak, the son of Abinoam, is commanded to "take captive his own captives," reversing the present situation in which Israel is held hostage by the Canaanites and ironically inverting the expectation of Sisera's mother in v. 30 (231). In the beginning of the Gideon story, Ophrah is the scene of clan idolatry (6:24-32); in the end Ophrah is the focus of national idolatry (8:27) (250). In the Samson story, the Timnite was trying to avoid being burnt up by the wedding guests; but as a result of her disclosing the secret, Samson leaves, she is given away to another man, Samson gets mad and destroys things, and the Philistine guests burn her up anyway (433). It is ironic also that once the Philistines discover the secret of Samson's strength, he loses the strength (452). "With delightful irony, the despised Danites serve as agents of judgment upon this most representative [Micah] of the high and mighty Ephraimites" (490). It is ironic that Delilah accuses Samson of deception, while she is deceiving him (459).

31. Quoted by H. Sjursen, "Excess of Sorrow Laughs," in *The Masks of Comedy* (ed. Ann Boaden; Rock Island, Ill.: Augustana College Library, 1980), 87.

32. *Micropaedia*, X, 119.

33. Paul Radin, *The Trickster: A Study in American Indian Mythology* (New York: Schocken, 1956, 1972), 206.

34. Quoted by Edith Kern, *The Absolute Comic* (New York: Columbia University Press, 1980), 190-191.

35. Kern, 155.

36. F. Michael Krause, *Milton's Samson and the Christian Tradition* (Princeton: Princeton University Press, 1949), 40-44.

37. Henri Bergson, "Laughter" [1900] (trans. Cloudesley Brereton and Fred Rothwell) in *Comedy* (ed. Wylie Sypher; New York: Doubleday, 1956), 63.

38. B. F. Skinner, *Verbal Behavior* (New York, Appleton-Century, 1957), 232-233.

39. Lowell K. Handy points out the contrast between the "canny" Ehud and the "stupid" Eglon. The Samson story is an inverse parallel, with the character traits reversed, the Israelites being negative in the Samson story and the Philistines positive. "Uneasy Laughter: Ehud and Eglon as Ethnic Humor," *Scandinavian Journal of the Old Testament*, 6 (1992): 233-246, passim. I do not see the Philistines as "positive," however.

40. Aristotle, *The Poetics* (trans. S. H. Butcher), in *Criticism: Major Statements* (3rd ed.; eds. Charles Kaplan and William Anderson; New York: St. Martin's, 1991), 45.

41. How about the Al-Qaeda terrorists? Are they not "underdogs"? Here is another example of the importance of both perspective in making judgments and also the problematic morality of the theological defense of the Conquest. See also the important essay by David J. Chalcraft, "Deviance and Legitimate Action in the Book of Judges," in *The Bible in Three Dimensions: Essays in Celebration of Forty Years of Biblical Studies in the University of Sheffield* (ed. David A. Clines, et al.; JSOTSup 87; Sheffield: Sheffield Academic Press, 1990), 177-201. Chalcraft's theory is discussed in Chapters 3 and 4.

42. Baruch Halpern, *The First Historians* (San Francisco: Harper & Row, 1988), 58.

43. Freema Gottlieb, "Three Mothers [Deborah, Jael, Sisera's Mother]," *Judaism*, 30 (Sept. 1981): 104-203.

44. The word for hammer in Ch. 4 is מקבת, (4.21 hammer), while in Ch.5 it is הלמות (5.26, workman's hammer (BDB 666, 240).

45. Some critics call pitching and striking the tent "woman's business" (e.g., Johanna Bos) and that therefore this is a "woman's tool." The truth is, we haven't the foggiest notion who pitched and struck the tents *in illo tempore*. In any case, the entire scene is in stark contrast to the way women are viewed both in the Bible, and elsewhere in literature, as indeed Bos admits. "Out of the Shadows: Genesis 38; Judges 4:17-22; Ruth 3," *Semeia 42* (Atlanta, Ga.: SBL, 1988), 55.

46. When I was asked "Is there a better comparison than Tyson, who is considered an odious person by most?" my answer was that for the purpose of comparison, I wanted a great champion who lacked self-control, mouthed off continually, was brutal to an extreme, was an outright womanizer, was a repeat offender, had been in jail, and would provide a great spectator sport. "So they called Samson out of the prison, and he performed for them" (16.25). Tyson's last bout, for which one had to pay $2500 a seat to see, is the kind of "entertainment" (ושמש הראים בשחוק [16.27]) that Samson may have provided to the Philistines. (Tyson lost.)

     I could not use Ali because he is like Samson in only *one* respect: Ali is a great champion. In all else, it is an unfair comparison—unfair to Ali. Suggesting both Tyson and Ali shows how the characterization really depends on the perspective of the reader or storyteller.

47. King and Stager cite John Macdonald, who thinks that the reason Jether did not strike Zebah and Zalmunna was that he "was not of sufficient rank to slay kings" (46). However, boys went

to war in ancient times with their elders in order to learn the art of war. The implication of the text is that it was not his insufficient rank, but that Jether was not mature enough to do the slaying.

48. Though this is one of the rules of warfare (Deut 30.8), I doubt that it was intended to release ⅔ of an army. The author is using this rule ironically. Almost everyone is afraid in this story.

49. Actually the trumpets and jars are provided for in the text. When Gideon sent all the thousands home, he kept their trumpets and provisions (presumably in jars) (7.8). Still, 300 jars and torches and trumpets are a serious logistical problem.

50. Block *is* anxious about whether or not the story is "true to life": "Delilah's success in neutralizing Samson's strength raises serious questions about the realism of the story, particularly the soundness of Samson's sleep in the last two episodes." *Judges, Ruth* (The New American Commentary; vol. 6; Nashville: Broadman, 1999), 460. Because this incident stretches his ability to take the Bible literally, he must conclude that the sleep was "divinely induced" (461). His God is a kind of *deus ex machina.*

   David M. Gunn suggests that Samson may have hoped Delilah was playing some kind of love game and was not really "out to get him." Samson was also "in a classic state of vulnerability" because of his "unrequited love." "Samson of Sorrows: An Isaianic Gloss on Judges 13-16," in *Reading Between Texts* (ed. Danna Nolan Fewell; Louisville, Ky.: Westminster, 1990), 244.

51. Matthew Winston, "Black Humor: To Weep with Laughing," in *Comedy, New Perspectives* (ed. Maurice Charney; New York: Literary Forum, 1978), 42.

52. Lecture Sixteen, *Comedy Through the Ages* ([Chantilly, Va.:] The Teaching Company, 2000).

53. "Humor as a Tool for Biblical Exegesis" in *On Humour and the Comic in the Hebrew Bible* (ed. Yehuda Radday and Athalya Brenner; Sheffield: Almond Press, 1990), 104, 103.

54. David Marcus classifies Jephthah "with the fools who do not distinguish between various kinds of vows. . . . God does not intervene with a fitting conclusion. . . . Hence the angry deity punished him by having his daughter fulfill the promise of the vow: 'What did the Lord do? He answered him unfittingly and prepared his daughter for him.'" *Jephthah and His Vow* (Lubbock, Tex.: Texas Tech, 1986) 55.

55. W. H. Auden, "Notes on the Comic," *Thought* 27 (1952): 60.

56. Thomas C. Römer mentions the Greek festival at Brauron, which was somehow bound with the myth of Iphigenia and which probably marked the onset of puberty for females. He thinks the author of *Judges* "wanted to present Jephthah's daughter as a Hebrew Iphigenia." The festival is paralleled, he says, with the festival of the dead Josiah in 2 Chron 35.25. "Why Would the Deuteronomists Tell About the Sacrifice of Jephthah's Daughter?" *JSOT* 77 (1998), 32, 35, 36.

57. Soggin, 248. Perhaps there is some connection between these two festivals and the scene in *Judges.*

58. *Myth, Legend, and Custom in the Old Testament* (New York: Harper and Row, 1969), 434-35.

59. According to Soggin, it was a distance of 60 kilometers and a climb of almost 1000 meters (253).

60. I point this out in my analysis of Samson's many body parts in Chapter 3.

61. In addition to numbers already mentioned above, Alter writes: "30 wedding guests and 30 garments are translated by Samson into 300 dead Philistines, after which he is confronted by

3,000 men of Judah, who deliver him to the Philistines, of whom he slays 1,000 . . . the reduction by 300% . . . [and in the temple of Dagon] there will be 3,000 Philistine men and women . . . ," "Samson Without Folklore," 48-49.

[62.] Erich Segal, *The Death of Comedy* (Cambridge, Ma.: Harvard University Press, 2001), 45-46.

[63.] Why the numbers should be divided this way between the towns, I do not know, but I believe the author had a reason. Perhaps it is merely that Jabesh-Gilead was known to be a bigger town than Shiloh. The 600 Benjaminites have their counterpart in the 600 heavily armed Danites in Ch. 18. More important, they are part of the Chiasmus, balancing the 600 Philistines killed by Shamgar in 3.31. (See Appendix 1, Chapter 1.) As to the virgins, I do not know whether raping a virgin was considered worse than raping a concubine. Perhaps it was, especially since the fathers had not given their consent.

[64.] (Washington, D.C., University Press of America, 1977), 38.

[65.] "Under the Influence: Trust and Risk in Biblical Family Drinking," *JSOT* 90 (2000): 13-29.

[66.] Cf. Moshe Garsiel, "Homiletic Name-Derivations as a Literary Device in the Gideon Narrative: Judges VI-VIII," *VT* (1993): 302-317. Two important sources that I was not able to use are Moshe Garsiel, *Biblical Names: A Literary Study of Midrashic Name Derivations and Puns* (Ramat-Gan, 1991) and R. T. Cherry, *Paronomasia and Proper Names in the OT: Rhetorical Function and Literary Effect* (diss. 1988; Ann Arbor, Mich.: 1990).

[67.] Block, 390.

[68.] Garsiel, "Homiletic Name-Derivations," 304.

[69.] Boling, 56.

[70.] Yehuda T. Radday, "Humour in Names" in *On Humour and the Comic in the Hebrew Bible*, 63.

[71.] Block, 417 n. 292.

[72.] May relate to Samson's blindness and fit in with the motif of light and darkness.

[73.] "The Rabbi said, 'she diminished (Heb *delilah*) his strength'" (Radday 67).

[74.] Block 455. Block says that we do not know the meaning of this Philistine name.

[75.] Soggin, 248.

[76.] Boling, 235; however, he questions this translation.

[77.] Block points out the similarity of the name *Gaal* to the word *go'el* meaning "kinsman," "redeemer," 325.

[78.] Judith M. Hadley, "The Fertility of the Flock? The De-Personalization of Astarte in the Old Testament," in *On Reading Prophetic Texts: Gender-Specific and Related Studies in Memory of Fokkelien van Dijk-Hemmes* (eds. Bob Becking and Meindert Dijkstra; Leiden: Brill, 1996), 130.

[79.] Ellen Van Wolde, "Deborah and Ya'el in Judges 4," in *On Reading Prophetic Texts*, 291.

[80.] As Block points out, the name signifies the belief of the parent, not necessarily of the offspring, 351.

[81.] Same spelling as "bowstrings," BDB 451.

[82.] Stanislav Segert, *OT Abstracts*, 8 (Jun 1985): 162. Marc Brettler says that the true etymology of the name is unknown. *The Book of Judges* (London: Routledge, 2002), 48.

[83.] Block 417, n. 292. "This is rejected by Fowler in *Theophoric Names*, 167."

84. *The New Oxford Annotated Edition*, ed. Michael Coogan (Oxford, New York: Oxford University Pres), 368, v. 5 footnote. (NRSV.)

85. In Ras Shamra texts, Baal and Yam are called *zblym* (*princes*).

Chapter Three

1. Johan Huizinga, *Homo Ludens: a Study of the Play Element in Culture* (trans. R. F. C. Hull; Boston: The Beacon Press, 1950, 1955). Also useful are David L. Miller, *Gods and Games: Toward a Theology of Play* (New York: World Publishing Company, 1970); Steven J. Brams, *Biblical Games: A Strategic Analysis of Stories in the Old Testament* (Cambridge, Mass.: MIT, 1980) (this is an application of game theory to stories in the Bible); and Peter Hutchinson, *Games Authors Play* (New York: World Publishing Company, 1970). These studies show how in the most serious of pursuits, a person may also be playing games. Only Brams refers to *Judges* (Jephthah's daughter and Samson's revenge).

2. Jim Holt, "Quantum Weirdness," rev. George Johnson, *A Shortcut Through Time: The Path to the Quantum Computer, New York Times Book Review* (April 6, 2003) 12.

3. I learned about these Ugaritic categories at a conference at the University of Michigan in the 1980s in a paper given by H. Van Dyke Parunak. I have not found any other papers on the subject, though they may exist.

4. "Samson's Dry Bones: A Structural Reading of Judges 13-16," in *Literary Interpretations of Biblical Narratives* (vol. 2; eds. Kenneth R. R. Gros Louis with James S. Ackerman; Nashville: Abingdon, 1982), 149.

5. M. H. Abrams, *A Glossary of Literary Terms*, (7th ed.; Fort Worth: Harcourt Brace, 1999), 197.

6. George Lakoff and Mark Johnson, *Metaphors We Live By* (Chicago: University of Chicago Press, 1980), passim.

7. To pass over, or cross over (עבר) is an important word in this text, as it is in *1* and *2 Samuel*, as pointed out by Robert Alter, *The David Story: A Translation with Commentary of 1 and 2 Samuel* (New York, London: W. W. Norton & Company, 1999), passim. I do not take time to deal with this as a category, though I refer to the word several times in passing.

8. When I first began my project, my chief tool in compiling these lists was *An Analytical Linguistic Key-Word-in-Context Concordance to the Book of Judges* by Y. T. Radday, G. M. Leb, and L. Natzitz (vol. XI of The Computer Bible, ed. Arthur Baird and David Noel Freedman; Wooster, Ohio: Biblical Associates, 1977). I discovered it in the early 1980s, long before any CD Rom was produced. I am extremely grateful to Radday, et al., as most of my analysis was done with the help of this work.

Since November 1997 I have used BibleWorks 3.5, 4.0, and 5.0 on CD Rom (Big Fork, Mont.: Hermeneutika, 1999; 5.0 is dated 2001). This is carefully and lovingly supported and updated on the Internet on a daily basis by its compilers, Michael Bushnell, et al. BibleWorks has helped me check and improve my results. Without it, publication of this book would have been delayed many years. It is, in my opinion, indispensable software for biblical scholars today. (It is no longer associated with Hermeneutika.)

9.   *Judges: A Commentary* (trans. John S. Bowden; Philadelphia: Westminster, 1981), 277.

10. Israel Finkelstein and Neil Asher Silberman, *The Bible Unearthed: Archaeology's New Vision of Ancient Israel and the Origin of Its Sacred Texts* (New York: Free Press, 2001), 115. John C. H. Laughlin, *Archaeology and the Bible* (London and New York: Routledge. 2000), 79 et passim.

11. *David's Secret Dreams: Messiah, Murderer, Traitor, King* (Grand Rapids, Mich.: William B. Eerdmans, 2001), 126.

12. Othniel, son of Kenaz, Caleb's younger brother. Kenaz is thought to be the nephew of Caleb; therefore, Othniel would be a grandnephew. *Eerdmans Dictionary of the Bible* (ed. David Noel Freedman; Grand Rapids: Eerdmans, 2000), 995.

13. Alter, *The David Story*, 204, 280.

14. It has been conjectured that Jephthah's mother is not a *prostitute* (זֹנָה) but a "secondary wife," one who lives in her father's house, rather than her husband's house. Naomi Steinberg. "The Problem of Human Sacrifice in War: An Analysis of Judges 11," in *On the Way to Nineveh*, (ed. Stephen L. Cook and S. C. Winter; ASOR Books, Vol. 4; Atlanta, Ga.: Scholars Press, 1999), 124, following P. Bird and others. In my opinion, the author's intention is to make Jephthah out to be a man of low birth, an unlikely person to become the leader of his tribe. The word זֹנָה is the same one applied to Samson's prostitute (16.1), to the Concubine (19.2), and to the Israelites, who *go whoring* after other gods (2.17, 8.27, 33). To make Jephthah's mother a "secondary wife" may be just another attempt to sanitize Jephthah.

15. *Judges: An Introduction, Translation, and Commentary* (AB 6A; Garden City: Doubleday, 1975), 211-212.

16. Daniel I. Block suggests an interesting inversion. First the Ephrimites taunt the Gileadites as being *fugitives*; then *the Ephrimites* themselves become fugitives from the Gileadites. *Judges, Ruth* (vol. 6; The New American Commentary; Nashville: Broadman, 1999), 383.

17. "Ch. XI. The Society of Ugarit," *Handbook of Ugaritic Studies* (eds. Wilfred G. E. Watson and Nicolas Wyatt; Cologne: Brill, 1999), 467.

18. The author uses *sense impressions* in a few places: we have the sense of touch here and later when Samson *feels* the pillars, and when Gideon's men drink water from their hands. Hearing is important (see Appendix 1 of this chapter). I have not tried to list other sense impressions.

19. *The Book of Judges: the Art of Editing* (Leiden: Brill, 1999), 265.

20. Johannes C. de Moor, *An Anthology of Religious Texts from Ugarit* (Leiden: E. J. Brill, 1987).

21. *Religious Texts from Ugarit: The Words of Ilimilku and his Colleagues* (Sheffield: Sheffield Academic Press: 1998), 43 n.23.

22. (See references to Elaine Scarry in Chapter 2.) In the recent war with Iraq, a hullabaloo occurred in the media about the exhibiting of the flag-draped coffins of the dead being transported home to Dover by air and also about the reading aloud of the 700 names of the American dead, with their pictures and information about their home city, their rank, and age by Ted Koppel on *Nightline* (April 2004). This was assailed by the supporters of the war as "political" and "unpatriotic." That same week, the brutal abuse (a form of torture) of Iraqi prisoners by American military and civilian guards was exposed by the media and deplored as highly unusual and criminal, soon to be punished. But the airing of the photographs of this abuse was seen by the supporters of war as "political" and "unpatriotic." At the same time the Democratic presidential candidate was assailed by the opposition

for his lack of patriotism for protesting against the Vietnam War 30 years earlier and exposing at the time that war creates barbaric brutes out of ordinary men—though he had volunteered twice to serve and though he had been honorably discharged with a number of medals attesting to his courage. Ironically, or not so ironically, in the *NY Times Magazine* that same week (May 2, 2004), Michael Ignatieff had an article in which he discussed the issue of the use of torture by American military, not so much about whether it should be used as policy but *how* it should be used and limited in the media. This problem has not yet been solved. The administrators of war, no matter on which political side, do not want this kind of truth exposed to the public. The author of *Judges* gives the statistics about the dead, but not the gory reality of war. We cannot know exactly why. One reason may have to do with these horrors being also a comedy, but his other reasons might be the same as ours today.

23. *Life in Biblical Israel* (Louisville, London: Westminster John Knox Press, 2001), 31.

24. In mountain warfare, horses were not useful. "In the hills, where cavalry did not operate (David takes no horses from highlanders), the light infantry are at a premium—slingers in particular." Halpern, 303.

25. Cullen Murphy writes that "Camels are not as fast as racehorses, but they have a lot more stamina—they start out at about forty miles an hour, and can hold a pace of twenty miles an hour for more than half an hour. They have been known to run at ten miles an hour for eighteen hours . . . . It can go two weeks without drinking water, and when it does drink, it can tolerate salts and poisons that would kill a human being." "Lulu, Queen of the Camels," *The Atlantic*, 284 (October 1999): 74, 77.

26. *Hayyei shimshon* (Jerusalem: Magnes Press, 1982), 230-31, cited in *The Hebrew Bible in Literary Criticism* (eds. Alex Preminger and Edward L. Greenstein; New York: Ungar, 1986), 555-56. In the Ugaritic myths, the goddess Anat may have seduced Aqhat, but I do not recall a male god trying to seduce a mortal woman.

27. Think of how Iraq, Afghanistan, and Lebanon look at the present time (2006).

28. Laughlin, 79, 74-5, 115, 117.

29. The conjecture is probably based on the fact that she has attendants.

30. Laughlin, 69. "If indeed it was a temple, it is the largest yet discovered in Palestine. Originally constructed during the MBA . . . , this building measured some 70 x 86 feet with walls 16 feet thick. Going through several phases, it was used throughout the LBA and on into Iron Age I [1550-1200 BCE]. The excavator, G. E. Wright, suggested that this building was the temple of El Berith . . . mentioned in . . . Judges 9:46-49 . . . " (82).

31. Pillar houses have been excavated, but Laughlin says nothing about a pillar temple (106), but recent excavations by T. Dotham and S. Gitan have uncovered "a magnificent temple with a pillared forecourt" (7th C. BCE). King and Stager, 336.

32. Robert Alter, *The Art of Biblical Narrative* (New York: Basic, 1981), 38-41. Marc Z. Brettler, *The Creation of History in Ancient Israel* (London and New York: Routledge, 1995), 82. Each of them emphasizes the sexual references in the story. The encounter between Ehud and Eglon is both a rape and a slaughtering of an animal for sacrifice (Eglon's name being "fatted calf").

33. Pughat in the Ugaritic story *Aqhat* also wrings the fleece to obtain water.

34. Alter 39. Brettler 81.

35. "Under the Influence: Trust and Risk in Biblical Family Drinking," *JSOT* 90 (2000): 13-29.

36. *Aqhat* (trans. Simon B. Parker) in *Ugaritic Narrative Poetry* (ed. Simon B. Parker; Atlanta, Ga.: Scholars Press,1997), 56.

37. J. C. L. Gibson, *Canaanite Myths and Legends* 2nd ed. (Edinburgh: T & T Clark Ltd., 1978), 46.

38. Nicolas Wyatt, *Space and Time in the Religious Life of the Near East* (Sheffield: Sheffield Academic Press, 2001), 227. See also 1.3.i.10-17, Wyatt, *Religious Texts*, 70-71.

39. Marjo C. A. Korpel, "Exegesis in the Work of Ilimilku of Ugarit," in *Intertextuality in Ugarit and Israel* (ed. Johannes C. de Moor; Leiden: Brill, 1998), 91.

40. Victor Matthews has written an article about hospitality—"Hospitality and Hostility in Genesis 19 and Judges 19," *Biblical Theology Bulletin*, 22 (1992): 3-11—and given a "protocol" of hospitality in his commentary, *Judges and Ruth* (Cambridge, Eng.: Cambridge University Press, 2004), 68-74 et passim. His information is derived from a study of hospitality of nomad tribes and biblical and anthropological sources. It is difficult to say how many of the rules of the protocol were known and observed by the characters of *Judges* or the author or editor. Many of them are not represented in the stories. I have tried to derive my information solely from what can be inferred from *Judges*.

41. (Notre Dame, Ind.: Notre Dame Press, 1981), 116-17.

42. I have not included sexual relations as an independent category, but this would be an important addition at a future date.

43. See Chalcraft's important essay, "Deviance and Legitimate Action in the Book of Judges," in *The Bible in Three Dimensions: Essays in Celebration of Forty Years of Biblical Studies in the University of Sheffield* (ed. David A. Clines, et al.; JSOTSup 87; Sheffield: Sheffield Academic Press, 1990), 183, 184, 177-201, et passim. Chalcraft's theory is also discussed in my Chapter 4.

44. T. R. Hobbs cites William Robertson Smith, *Lectures on the Religion of the Semites: Fundamental Institutions* (3rd ed.; London: A. & C. Black, 1927), 27, who says that "to harm a guest or to refuse him hospitality, is an offence against honor, which covers the perpetrator with indelible shame." "Hospitality in the First Testament and the 'Teleological Fallacy,'" *JSOT* 95 (2001): 3.

45. Hobbs cites Janzen that "no sacrifice is too high for a host on behalf of his guest" (6). W. Janzen, *Old Testament Ethics: A Paradigmatic Approach* (Louisville, Ky.: Westminster/John Knox Press, 1994), 44.

46. "Lecture 21," *Comedy Through the Ages* (audio tapes) ([Chantilly, Va.:] The Teaching Company, 2000.)

47. "Incomparable Naturalism: Only an artificer of the highest skill could have produced so seamless an illusion of reality," rev. of Ronald Hingley, *Translations of Anton Chekhov* (Oxford University Press, 2001), *The Atlantic*, 289 (January 2002): 128-29.

48. Samson is naturally using his hands when in 15.1 he comes bearing a kid as a present for his wife.

49. Freeman, 147.

50. See Robert Alter, Ch. 5, "Allusion and Literary Expression," *The World of Biblical Literature* ([New York:] Basic Books, 1992), 107-130.

51. Alter gives many examples of this in *The World of Biblical Literature*.

52. Mieke Bal, *Death and Dissymmetry: the Politics of Coherence in the Book of Judges* (Chicago: University of Chicago Press, 1988), 74.

Chapter Four

1. Elizabeth Vandiver, "Lecture Five," *The "Iliad" of Homer* (audio tapes) (Chantilly, Va.: The Teaching Company, 1999).

2. "Lecture One," *The Great Ideas of Philosophy* (Chantilly, Va.: The Teaching Company, 1997). Professor Robinson teaches both psychology and philosophy at Georgetown University.

3. As T. R. Hobbs notes, we must also guard against the "teleological fallacy" of using "ancient documents as 'a springboard for a modern polemic.'" "Hospitality in the First Testament and the 'Teleological Fallacy,'" JSOT 95 (2001), 5. He is quoting W. Janzen, *Old Testament Ethics* (Grand Rapids, Mich.: Zondervan, 1983), 43.

4. John D. Caputo, ed., *Deconstruction in a Nutshell* (New York: Fordham University Press, 1977), 17-18.

5. John Rawls, *A Theory of Justice* (Cambridge, Mass.: Harvard University Press, 1971).

6. "Deviance and Legitimate Action in the Book of Judges" in *The Bible in Three Dimensions: Essays in Celebration of Forty Years of Biblical Studies in the University of Sheffield* (ed. David A. Clines, et al.; JSOTSup 87; Sheffield: Sheffield Academic Press, 1990), 178.

7. *The Elementary Forms of the Religious Life* (trans. Joseph Ward Swain, New York and London: The Free Press, 1912, 1982 ed.), 129.

8. *After Virtue: A Study in Moral Theory* (Notre Dame, Ind.: Notre Dame Press, 1981), 147.

9. The stories may have originated in a period when the laws were not known, but written down when they were known. John Van Seters at the 1999 annual meeting of SBL put the writing of the laws *not* in the 8th Century but in the time of Jeremiah and Ezekiel. John H. C. Laughlin puts the writing of the Hebrew Bible in the post-exilic period. *Archaeology and the Bible* (London and New York: Routledge, 2000), 74-75, 120.

   Laws from Deuteronomy and Leviticus have been inserted occasionally by me as points of reference only. No matter when the laws and the stories were written, a great deal of "natural" or "traditional" law was in existence in some form or another. Readers of *Judges* must try to deduce the laws from the text, not impose laws from some outside source on the text. This entails detective work.

10. *Representation in Old Testament Narrative Texts* (Leiden: Brill, 1998), 113.

11. Idols may have been in common use in the period before Yhwism won out against Baalism, or against any other indigenous religion of Canaan. The idols may have represented Yhwh or one of the Canaanite gods, or they may simply have been "household gods," such as the Roman penates. Laban in Gen 31.30 referred to the teraphim as his "gods." They may have been consulted for divination. Karel van der Toorn, *Family Religion in Babylonia, Syria and Israel: Continuity and Change in the Form of Religious Life* (Leiden: Brill, 1996), 219, 221, 222, 224.

12. The rise of Yhwism and monotheism are discussed in Chapter 5.

13. This comment was perhaps the source of Latimer's cry in 1555 to his fellow victim, as they were burning on the stake: "Be of good faith, Master Ridley, and *play the man.* We shall this day light such a candle, by God's grace, in England, as I trust shall never be put out."

14. Steve A. Wiggins, *A Reassessment of 'Asherah'* (Neukirchen-Vluyn: Neukirchener Verlag, 1993), 22.

15. J. C. de Moor, *An Anthology of Religious Texts from Ugarit* (Leiden: Brill, 1987), 222.

16.   "The Legend of Keret," in *Handbook of Ugaritic Studies* (eds. Wilfred G. E. Watson and Nicolas Wyatt; Cologne: Brill, 1999), 213.

17.   *Judges and Ruth* (The New Cambridge Bible Commentary; Cambridge, Eng.: Cambridge University Press, 2004), 171, n. 395.

18.   *On the Way to the Postmodern: OT Essays* (vol. 1; JSOT #292; Sheffield: Sheffield Academic Press, 1998), 17.

19.   Ben Witherington III, "From Hesed to Agape: what's love got to do with it?" *Bible Review* (December 2003): 10.

20.   "The people of Laish were living in a land with *nothing lacking* and they possessed *prosperity*" (אֵין־מַכְלִים דָּבָר בָּאָרֶץ יוֹרֵשׁ עֶצֶר) (18.7). The text of 18.7 is corrupt. It means either "there is no lack of anything" or "there is no one to restrain us from anything." For מַכְלִים, see BDB 483-484 and for עֶצֶר, see BDB 783.

21.   Translated from the Chinese with Introduction and Critical Notes by Lionel Giles, M.A. Assistant in the Department of Oriental Printed Books and MSS. in the British Museum (1910). Worldwide Web Virtual Library www.clas.ufl.edu/users/gthursby/taoism/suntext.htm 2002.

22.   Robert G. Boling, *Judges: An Introduction, Translation, and Commentary* (AB 6A; Garden City: Doubleday,1975), 51, 56., 18.

23.   James A. Freeman, "Samson's Dry Bones: A Structural Reading of Judges 13-16." In *Literary Interpretations of Biblical Narratives* (vol. 2; ed. Kenneth R. R. Gros Louis with James S. Ackerman; Nashville: Abingdon, 1982), 149.

24.   *The David Story: A Translation with Commentary of 1 and 2 Samuel* (New York: W. W. Norton, 1999), 289.

25.   *Vows in the Hebrew Bible and the Ancient Near East* (JSOT, Supplement Series 14; Sheffield: Sheffield Academic Press, 1992), 14. Cartledge's book is a useful review of the background materials and of the distinction between "vowing" and "swearing."

26.   Steven L. McKenzie believes that David did not marry Michal until after Saul's death. *King David: a Biography* (New York: Oxford University Press, 2000), 119.

27.   *The Pre-Biblical Narrative Tradition: Essays on the Ugaritic Poems "Keret" and "Aqhat"* (SBL Resources for Biblical Study 24; Atlanta, Ga.: Scholars Press, 1989), 86.

28.   Allan Rosengren Petersen remarks that "the Old Testament came into being in the Persian era as a kind of identity-creating survival literature" and may not be a historically-valid document. Thus "we cannot use the ideology contained in it to describe the way of thinking of the ancient semites in general. What we perhaps *can* say is how the authors of the Old Testament wished them to think." *The Royal God: Enthronement Festivals in Ancient Israel and Ugarit?* (JSOT Sup 259; Sheffield: Sheffield Academic Press, 1998), 102, 1044. It is a distinction we should always keep in mind.

29.   In Aeschylus, Iphigenia *had* to be sacrificed; otherwise, the Greeks believed that they could not sail to Troy. Agamemnon reaps a terrible retribution for what he did. In *Judges*, nothing, so far as we know, hinges on the sacrifice, as we are told that Jephthah had already received the Spirit before he made the vow. It is clear from both stories, however, that in previous societies, people were tempted to sacrifice something in order to obtain victory. In *Judges*, this custom is being put in question.

30. *Yahweh and the Gods and Goddesses of Canaan* (JSOTSup 265; Sheffield: Sheffield Academic Press, 2000), 211.

31. The story of the Moabite king seems to be a deliberate parallel to the Jephthah story. Both men wanted to *win*. Both sacrificed a precious child, their successor. Both won. And the purpose of the parallel may be to show that if the Moabite king was wrong (as he was), Jephthah was also wrong.

32. "The Problem of Human Sacrifice in War: An Analysis of Judges 11," in *On the Way to Nineveh* (eds. Stephen L. Cook and S. C. Winter; ASOR Books, vol. 4; Atlanta, Ga.: Scholars Press, 1999), 125.

33. It is quite possible that the prototype for the Jephthah story—the real person behind this legend, if there was one—made the sacrifice *before* going to war and that the Israelite author gave Jephthah the benefit of "ignorance" about who or what he was sacrificing in order to reduce the degree of his criminality.

34. H. Hubert and M. Mauss, *Sacrifice: Its Nature and Function* (1st ed. 1898; Chicago: University of Chicago, 1964), 101-102, as discussed by Steinberg, 117-118.

35. Toronto, November 21, 2002. In response to a question about whether or not Abraham and Mohammed Atta, who master-minded the plot to destroy the World Trade Center on 9/11, were criminals, Derrida answered: "Each time we have to make a choice. The choice against life is not justifiable in any way. Abraham remains a criminal and Mohammed Atta also."

36. Exum says that since there is no historical evidence that there was such a festival (celebrating female puberty), then there cannot have been one. However, the story in *Judges* says there *was* a festival.

    Thomas C. Römer thinks the sacrifice part of the story is a late interpolation by someone who knew Euripides' *Iphigenia in Taurus*. He also mentions the Greek festival at Brauron, given every fourth year, that "marked the end of the girls' status as virgins in the sense that they became nubile women." "Why Would the Deuteronomists tell about the sacrifice of Jephthah's Daughter?" JSOT 77 (1998), 34-36.

37. I take this term from W. H. Auden who made a number of references to, and wrote an essay about, the Truly Great Man. Spender's poem, "I think of those who are truly great" gets its inspiration from Auden.

38. W. H. Auden, "Notes on the Comic," *Thought* 27 (1952): 60.

39. "Did Jephthah Kill his Daughter?" *Bible Review* 7 (1991): 28-31, 42.

40. Saul M. Olyan, *Asherah and the Cult of Yahweh in Israel* (Atlanta, Ga.: Scholars Press, 1988). "The cult of human sacrifice is closely associated with El in extant texts from the first millennium. According to Sanchuniathon, El sacrificed his 'only' son or *yadid*, 'beloved.' . . . It seems quite evident that human sacrifices to Yahweh were an indigenous practice in certain Israelite circles" (11, n. 33; 12, n. 34).

41. Hermann-Josef Stipp believes that Ch. 13 was a late addition (6th or 5th centuries BCE) meant to provide information that Samson's hair was not cut by his own volition, that the prohibition of touching dead bodies did not include animal bodies, and that only his mother, not Samson, was forbidden to drink alcoholic drinks. "Simson, der Nasiräer," *VT* 45 (1995): 335-69, passim.

42. See Endnote 11.

43. An *exemplum* is "a brief story used to make a point in an argument or to illustrate a moral truth"—*American Heritage Dictionary*.

44. Definitions are taken in part from *The American Heritage Dictionary*, in part from Webster's *Third International Dictionary*, and in part from the *OED*.

45. Daniel I. Block, *Judges, Ruth. The New American Commentary* (vol. 6; Nashville: Broadman & Homes, 1999), 91, 443.

46. *Wild Justice: The Evolution of Revenge* (New York: Harper & Row, 1983), 129.

47. *Law and Literature* (rev. and enl. ed.; Cambridge, Mass.: Harvard University Press, 1998), 52, 50, 51.

48. Some of my ideas on retaliation are derived from "Crime and Punishment," under Justice.4 and Justice.5 in *The Encyclopedia Britannica Online*. Accessed August 20, 1999.

49. We have some very good words coined, it might seem, to describe Samson: *amok, berserk* and *mayhem*. The word *amok* comes from the Malay. It is "a sudden rage in which an otherwise normal person goes berserk, sometimes killing all those in his path." Lawrence Osborne "Regional Disturbances," *New York Times Magazine* (May 8, 2001), 100. Or as found in *Webster's Third International Dictionary*, "possessed with a murderous or violently uncontrollable frenzy."

    The word *berserk* comes from the Old Norse word "*berserkr*, 'a wild warrior or champion.' Such warriors wore hides of bears, which explains the probable origins of *berserkr* as a compound of *bera*, 'bear,' and *serkr*, 'shirt, coat.' These *berserkers* became frenzied in battle, howling like animals, foaming at the mouth, and biting the edges of their iron shields. *Berserker* is first recorded in English in the early 19th century, long after these wild warriors ceased to exist." *American Heritage Dictionary*. The second definition for *berserker* in *Webster's Third International Dictionary* is "one whose actions are marked by a headstrong intractable spirit or by reckless defiance . . . ."

    Mayhem is defined in *Webster's Third International Dictionary* as "1 a : the malicious and permanent deprivation of another of the use of a member of his body resulting in impairment of his fighting ability and constituting a grave felony under English common law. b : the malicious and permanent crippling, mutilation, or disfiguring of another constituting a grave felony under modern statutes but in some jurisdictions requiring a specific intent as distinguished from general malice 2 : needless or willful damage."

    These words describe Samson and his actions well. *Mayhem* describes what the Philistines did to Samson, the second part of the definition what Samson did to the Philistines.

50. In *Biblical Games: A Strategic Analysis of Stories in the Old Testament* (Cambridge, Mass.: MIT, 1980), Steven J. Brams applies game theory to several stories from the Hebrew Bible. From *Judges* he selects Jephthah's sacrifice of his daughter (11.30-37) and Samson's revenge (14:25-20; 16: 9-29). The three other books that I have used for game theory are those of Ridley, Axelrod, and Pinker (409-414), cited later in the text.

51. Matt Ridley, *The Origins of Virtue: Human Instincts and the Evolution of Cooperation* (New York: Penguin, 1997), 77-78.

52. Paraphrase from the Lehrer Report broadcast on PBS, March 5, 2002.

53. Remarking on the Palestinian/Israeli conflict today, Nobel Prize Winner Thomas J. Aumann (an American with dual citizenship in Israel) remarked that it had been going on for 80 years,

and probably would continue another 80 years. In my opinion, it has been going on a lot longer than that. The hope is that through understanding of game theory, both sides will come to their senses. But can one teach game theory to madmen?

54. Roger Axelrod, *The Evolution of Cooperation* ([NP]: Basic Books, 1984), 15.

55. Ridley, 120.

56. Ridley, Ch. 8 passim.

57. Richard Dawkins coined the term in his book *The Selfish Gene* (1976). Robert Frank in Ridley 132-33.

58. Steven Pinker, *How the Mind Works* (New York: Norton, 1997), 510-12 passim.

59. Ira R. Buchler and Henry A. Selby, *A Formal Study of Myth* (Monograph Series No. I; Austin: The University of Texas, 1968), 117.

60. From the documentary by Errol Morris, "The Fog of War" (2003).

61. (Oxford: Oxford University Press, 1992), 310.

Chapter Five

1. "*Canaan*" is what the Israelites in the Hebrew Bible called the "other" people in the land now occupied by Lebanon, Syria, Israel, the Transjordan, and the Sinai. *Canaanite* refers to such people and literatures as the Akkadian, Sumerian, Hurrian, Hittite, and Aramean. The Amarna letters were written by "Canaanites."

2. Mark S. Smith, *The Origins of Biblical Monotheism: Israel's Polytheistic Background and the Ugaritic Texts* (Oxford: Oxford University Press, 2001), 72.

3. Itamar Singer, "A Political History of Ugarit," in *Handbook of Ugaritic Studies* (ed. Wilfred G. Watson and Nicolas Wyatt; Cologne: Brill, 1999), 733.

4. "The Hebrew Bible and Canaanite Literature," in *The Literary Guide to the Bible* (eds. R. Alter and F. Kermode; Cambridge, Mass.: The Belnap Press of the Harvard University Press, 1987), 545. Information and quotation from Greenfield were cited by Mark S. Smith on p. 10 of his handout, "The Whole and Its Parts: A Review of Ziony Zevit, *The Religions of Ancient Israel*," at the Hebrew Bible, History and Archaeology Section of SBL, Nov. 22, 2004.

5. "The 'Cluster' in Biblical Poetry," *Maarav* 5-6 (1990) =*Sopher Mahir: Northwest Semitic Studies Presented to Stanislav Segert* (ed. E.M. Cook; Santa Monica, Calif.: Western Academic Pres, 1990), 167. Quoted in Smith's handout.

6. *The Ugaritic Poem of Aqht* (Berlin and New York: De Gruyter, 1989), 487.

7. Ulf Oldenburg, *The Conflict Between El and Ba'al in Canaanite Religion* (Leiden: E. J. Brill, 1969), 4-6. See also J. L. C. Gibson, ed. and trans., *Canaanite Myths and Legends* (Edinburgh: T. & T. Clark, 1977), 6, n. 3.

8. Marjo C. A. Korpel, "Exegesis in the Work of Ilimilku of Ugarit," in *Intertextuality in Ugarit and Israel* (ed. Johannes C. de Moor; Leiden: Brill, 1998), 87, 91, 105, et passim.

9. Johannes C. de Moor, *An Anthology of Religious Texts from Ugarit* (Leiden: Brill, 1987), 225, n. 5. References to de Moor hereafter will be from this anthology unless otherwise noted.

10. J. David Schloen explains the discrepancy of Baal's being the son of both Dagon and El. The story comes from Philo of Byblos, who got it from Sanchuniathon: Ouranos (Heaven) and Ge (Earth) had four sons, including El (Kronos) and Dagon. Baal was born of one of the mistresses

of Ouranos and was a half brother of El and Dagon. The pregnant mistress was married to Dagon. When El overthrew Ouranos, Dagon departed from the scene. Baal and his half-brothers became bitter rivals. *The House of the Father as Fact and Symbol: Patrimonialism in Ugarit and the Ancient Near East* (Winona Lake, Ind.: Eisenbrauns, 2001), 354.

11. John Day, *Yahweh and the Gods and Goddesses of Canaan* (JSOTSup 265; Sheffield: Sheffield Academic Press, 2000), 107.

12. Dagon-Baal/El may signify the merging of two cultures, the Amorite with the Canaanite. Gregorio del Olmo Lete, *Canaanite Religion according to the Liturgical Texts of Ugarit* (rev. ed.; Bethesda, Md.: CDL Press, 1999), 49.

13. "Anat is not really a virgin in the modern sense of the word, for she had "some sort of intercourse with her husband Ba'lu . . . . The term . . . designates a 'young woman who did not yet bring forth male offspring'" (de Moor 7, n. 33).

14. Mark S. Smith, trans., "The Baal Cycle" in *Ugaritic Narrative Poetry* (ed. Simon B. Parker; [N.P.:] Scholars Press, 1987), 93. References to Parker hereafter are to this anthology unless otherwise noted.

15. N. Wyatt, *Religious Texts from Ugarit: the Words of Ilimilku and His Colleagues* (Sheffield: Sheffield Academic Press, 1998) 73, n. 17.

16. *Eerdmans Dictionary of the Bible* (ed. David Noel Freedman; Grand Rapids, Mich.: Eerdmans 2000), 59. J. C. De Moor thinks Anat is Baal's consort, *The Rise of Yahwism: The Roots of Israelite Monotheism* (rev. and enl. ed.; Leuven: Leuven University Press, 1997), 73, 74, 79. Smith says that "The ritual texts do not clarify the identity of Baal's spouse," *Origins* 44.

17. The titles I have used for these myths are taken from Gibson.

18. Wayne T. Pitard, "The *RPUM* Texts" in *Handbook of Ugaritic Studies*, 265. Or they may be "an elite group of chariot warriors who had strong connections with the king" (267).

19. "Keret," in *Handbook of Ugaritic Studies*, 206. See also his "The Geographical Setting of the Aqhat Story and Its Ramifications," in *Ugarit in Retrospect: Fifty Years of Ugarit and Ugaritic* (ed. D. G. Young; Winona Lake, Ind.: Eisenbrauns, 1981), 206, 405.

20. John C. H. Laughlin, *Archaeology and the Bible* (London: Routledge, 2000), 87 et passim. Karel van der Toorn, *Family Religion in Babylonia, Syria and Israel: Continuity and Change in the Form of Religious Life* (Leiden: Brill, 1996), 183. See also Israel Finkelstein and Neil Asher Silberman, *The Bible Unearthed: Archaeology's New Vision of Ancient Israel and the Origin of Its Sacred Texts* (New York: The Free Press, 2001); and Lester L. Grabbe, ed., *Can a 'History of Israel' Be Written?* (JSOTSup 245; Sheffield: Sheffield Academic Press, 1999).

21. Van der Toorn, 186, 187.

22. According to Manfried Dietrich and Oswald Loretz, "the Proto-Ugaritic ruling class must have originated in the south of Canaan, possibly in the Edomite part of Transjordan" and moved to the Levant around the middle of the second millennium BCE, about the same time as the Proto-Israelites moved north from southern Palestine. (Cited by Johannes C. de Moor, *The Rise of Yahwism*, 196, 206. De Moor concurs.)

23. Ibid. 315.

24. *The Royal God: Enthronement Festivals in Ancient Israel and Ugarit?* (JSOT Sup 259; Sheffield: Sheffield Academic Press, 1998), 102.

25. *Early History of the Israelite People From the Written and Archaeological Sources* (Studies in the History and Culture of the Ancient Near East, 4; Leiden: Brill, 1992), 421, 422, quoted by Petersen, 102-103.

26. *The Early History of God: Yahweh and the Other Deities in Ancient Israel* (2nd. Ed.; Grand Rapids, Mich.: Eerdmans, 2002), 3, 11.

27. *Canaanite Myth and Hebrew Epic: Essays in the History of the Religion of Israel* (Cambridge, Mass.: Harvard University Press, 1973), 147.

28. *The Religion of Ancient Israel* (Louisville, Ky.: Westminster John Knox Press, 2000), 24, 25.

29. De Moor puts Ps 68 at late 13th century, which may be the date of the Ugaritic writings *(The Rise of Yahwism* 181, 185). Ps 68 contains a number of parallels with (1) *The Song of Deborah*, which de Moor thinks was written after Ps 68 (183) in about 1100 BCE (292), and (2) Hab 3 (203ff); all three have with significant parallels to the Ugaritic myths.

30. Smith, *Origins*, 48-49.

31. Nicolas Wyatt, *Space and Time in the Religious Life of the Near East* (Sheffield: Sheffield Academic Press, 2001), 58.

32. *Chaoskampf* is the term Wyatt uses. Wyatt, "Arms and the King," in *'Und Mose schrieb dieses Lied auf . . . .' Studie zum Alten Testament und zum Alten Orient. Festschrift für O. Loretz zur Vollendung seines 70. Lebensjahres mit Beiträgen von Freunden, Schülern und Kollegen*, AOAT 250 (ed. M. Dietrich and I. Kottsieper; Münster: Ugarit-Verlag, 1998), 861.

33. Cited by Ozwald Loretz, *Ugarit und die Bibel: Kanaanaische Götter und Religion im Alten Testament* (Darmstadt: Wissenschaftliche Buchegesellschaft, 1990), 92.

34. Hugh Rowland Page, *The Myth of Cosmic Rebellion: A Study of Its Reflexes in Ugaritic and Biblical Literature* (Leiden: Brill, 1996), 64-201 passim.

35. "Tracking Observance of the Aniconic tradition through Numismatics," *The Triumph of Elohim: From Yahwisms to Judaisms* (ed. D. V. Edelmam, Grand Rapids, Mich.: Eerdmans, 1996), 185-225, cited by Smith *Origins* 142.

36. *The Ras Shamra Discoveries and the Old Testament* (Oxford: Basil Blackwell, 1965), 34.

37. Loretz, 234-236 passim.

38. Miller, 24, 25, drawing on Frank Moore Cross, 6, 12, 42ff.

39. *Asherah and the Cult of Yahweh in Israel* (Atlanta, Ga.: Scholars Press, 1988), 38.

40. It is significant that the Yahwists at Elephantine, Egypt, worshiped Anat (the warrior goddess) until the 5th century BCE, as is attested in the Papyri.

41. Susan Ackerman, *Women in Judges and Biblical Israel: Warrior, Dancer, Seductress, Queen* (New York: Doubleday, 1998), 149.

42. Of the Judean kings: Ma'acah, the Queen Mother and grandmother of Asa, had erected a statue of Asherah, probably in the temple. Asa (913-873 BCE) hated her. He deposed her and destroyed the statue, but it was replaced after Asa died (1 Kg 15.2, 9-13). Hezekiah (715-687) removed an asherah from Jerusalem (2 Kg 18.4). Manasseh (687-642) erected an asherah in the temple. This was destroyed by Josiah (2 Kg 23.6). (From Ackerman, 143 ff.)

43. *The Religions of Ancient Israel: a Synthesis of Parallactic Approaches* (London and New York: Continuum, 2001), 688, 690.

44. W. G. E. Watson, "Ugaritic Poetry," in *Handbook of Ugaritic Studies*, 169-191. Also Simon B. Parker, *The Pre-Biblical Narrative Tradition: Essays on the Ugaritic Poems "Keret" and "Aqhat"* (SBL Resources for Biblical Study 24; Atlanta, Ga.: Scholars Press, 1989), Ch. 1, passim. Other references to Parker are to his *Ugaritic Narrative Poetry* unless otherwise noted.

45. Baruch Margalit writes: "'Tent-dwelling' implies temporary settlement and is usually associated with 'nomadism'. . . . the notable exception is El, who resides in a royal QRS (*qrs. mlk.*) . . . . But this is a parade example of the exception which proves the rule. For El's tent-residence is to be understood in traditio-historical terms as a fossilized residue of an earlier era in 'Ugaritic' religion, the equivalent of the 'patriarchal age' in Israel and the MAR.DU era of the early West-Semitic dynasties in Mesopotamia, 'when kings dwelt in tents'" (*The Ugaritic Poem of Aqht*, 296).

    Johannes C. de Moor translates *tent* as *encampment*. He says that "encampment" is a metaphor for "territory" and "tent" a metaphor for "dwelling" (14).

46. Ronald S. Hendel, *The Epic of the Patriarch: The Jacob Cycle and the Narrative Traditions of Canaan and Israel* (HSM 42; Atlanta, Ga.: Scholar's Press 1987), 93.

47. De Moor thinks he may have been called *judge* because "the deceased were thought to be judged on the bank of the River of Death" (*Rise of Yahwism*, 30 n. 127), but this does not explain why Baal is also called *judge*. El is called *judge* because he does judge.

48. Herman Michell Niemann argues that Dan was originally located in the north, not central Israel. "Zorah, Eshtaol, Beth-Shemesh and Dan's Migration to the South: a Region and its Traditions in the Late Bronze and Iron Ages," *JSOT* 86 (1999): 47. After migrating south, their migration north in Judg 18 would have been a return to their original settlement.

49. Robert Graves and Raphael Patai, *Hebrew Myths: The Book of Genesis* (New York: McGraw Hill, 1964), 104.

50. *Eerdmans Dictionary of the Bible*, 311.

51. *The Pre-Biblical Narrative Tradition*, 201.

52. Ackerman is following Dempster's "Mythology and History in the Song of Deborah," WTJ 41 (1978), 33-53. I developed the same idea independently in papers I delivered to SBL meetings in early 1980s. Ackerman's discussion of the relationship of *The Song* to Ugaritic myth is valuable.

53. *The Rise of Yahwism*, 185.

54. J. Alberto Soggin, *Judges: A Commentary* (trans. John S. Bowden; Philadelphia: Westminster, 1981), 92.

55. Peter C. Craigie, "Three Ugaritic Notes on The Song of Deborah," *JSOT*, 2 (1977): 35-37.

56. Peter C. Craigie, "Deborah and Anat: A Study of Poetic Imagery (*Judges* 5)," *ZAW* (1978): 376.

57. According to Victor H. Matthews, " . . . ben Anath was a common name used by the 'Apiru/Habiru mercenaries employed by the Egyptians during the twelfth-tenth centuries BCE. They took on the name of the Canaanite goddess of war to mark both their ferocity in battle and their membership in a military cadre." *Judges and Ruth* (Cambridge, Eng.: Cambridge University Press: 2004), 62, citing Nili Shupak, "New Light on Shamgar ben 'Anath," *Bib* 70 (1989): 517-25.

58. In the Bible, the smashers of heads are Yhwh and the king (Ps 110.5-6). Wyatt, "Arms and the King," 865, 867. Horonu is the "God of black magic, master of evil demons" (de Moor 30, n. 128).

59. Glen Taylor, "The Song of Deborah and Two Canaanite Goddesses," *JSOT* 23 (1982): 101.

60. "The Fertility of the Flock? The De-Personalization of Astarte in the Old Testament," in *On Reading Prophetic Texts: Gender-Specific and Related Studies in Memory of Folkkelien van Dijk-Hemmes* (eds. Bob Becking and Meindert Dijkstra; Leiden: Brill, 1996), 130.

61. Mark S. Smith, remarks, "The bloody battle represented in Ugaritic tradition by the goddess Anat, may provide an insight into the mythos behind the biblical ban (BH *herem*; Ugaritic **hrm*) utilized by Iron Age Levantine monarchies (Israel, Judah, and Moab). The same root applies to Anat's warfare in CAT 1.13:

    Destroy under the ban (*hrm*) for two days,

    Sh[ed blood (?)] for three days,

    go, kill for fo[ur] days . . . ! (*Origins* 162)

62. Peter C. Craigie, *Ugarit and the Old Testament* (Grand Rapids: Eerdmans, 1983), 65.

63. Mark S. Smith, in Parker, 89. De Moor translates this passage differently, with no mention of milk (3).

64. Freema Gottlieb, "Three Mothers [Deborah, Jael, Sisera's Mother]," *Judaism*, 30 (Sept. 1981): 200.

65. A cow bears the offspring, in Parker, "Baal Fathers a Bull," 10.III.20-36, 184-186. And Baal and Anat have intercourse in 11.V.17-19, 147-148. (See also KTU 1.11.1-8, de Moor 116).

66. Was there a sexual encounter between Anat and Aqhat? Wyatt thinks not. *Handbook of Ugaritic Studies*, 248. But judging from all the other information, it is entirely possible.

67. *Social World of Ancient Israel 1250-587 BCE* (Peabody, Mass.: Hendrickson, 1993), 91.

68. *The Ugaritic Poem of Aqht*, 92; also 73, 333.

69. Eusebius, *Preparatio evangelica* 1.10.31, in H. W. Attridge and R. A. Oden, *Philo of Byblos: The Phoenician History: an Introduction, Critical Text, Translation Notes* (CBQMS 9: Washington, DC: Catholic Biblical Association of America, 1981), 54-55. Cited by Smith *Origins*, 74.

70. Helmer Ringgren, *Religions of the Ancient Near East* (trans. John Sturdy; Philadelphia: Westminster, 1973), 141.

71. Robert Boling, *Judges* (Anchor Bible, 6A; Garden City, NY: Doubleday, 1975), 95.

72. Hilliger, cited by C. F. Burney, *The Book of Judges with Introduction and Notes* (London: Rivingtons, 1902, 1918; repr., New York: KTAV, 1970), 85. Burney, however, calls the combination of Lappidoth and Barak a "precarious suggestion."

73. In Wyatt's translation, Athirat is not doing the laundry, but her clothes are made of the sea (*Religious Texts*, 93).

74. What Ackerman says about queen mothers and their power (Ch. 4) seems to me to be irrelevant to the situation in *Judges*. First, Ackerman's evidence comes from a much later period and cannot be applied to *Judges*. Second, Sisera is not a king. Thus in my opinion, his mother is not a "queen mother."

75. That Israelite writers were aware of these wise women Gibson thought was attested by an allusion to them in Ps 68.7 (Gibson 31, n. 6). בכושרות in Ps 68.7 (the sole use in the Bible) is translated by BDB as *in prosperity*, but it is related to the word *skill*. The Kotharat in the Ugaritic poems are skilled (idem, 24, n. 4).

76. Gideon's spoil includes embroidered cloth, but not captive maidens.

77. "On the River Kishon," *VT* 40 (1990): 429, 430, 434.

78. *The Ugaritic Poem of Aqht*, 405, 420. See also his "The Geographical Setting of the Aqhat Story and Its Ramifications," 140-141.

79. Margalit writes that it is bizarre that *Keret* deals "with a mythic ritual alleged to transpire in Bashan [Transjordan], a region several hundred kilometers away" from Ugarit (*Ugarit in Retrospect* 153).

80. Dagon was possibly a new god; this may be why myths about him are lacking. See also endnotes 10 and 12.

81. See endnote 10.

82. S. H. Hooke, *Middle Eastern Mythology* (Middlesex: Harmondsworth, 1963), 15.

83. *Myth, Legend, and Custom in the Old Testament* (New York: Harper and Row, 1969), 434.

84. *Near Eastern Religious Texts Relating to the Old Testament* (Philadelphia: Westminster, [1978]), 188.

85. It may be significant that the word *sun* (שמש) is used only once in *Judges* as a direct reference to the sun (5.31). Otherwise it is used to represent time (sunset or sunrise, 4x) and for direction in the expression of "to the east" (toward the rising of the sun, 1x). Another word for *sun*, Heres (חרס), is a place name and is used 2x. Beth-Shemesh (1.33) is in, or near, the territory of Dan after migration but is not mentioned in this story. If Samson is about a solar god, why is the word *sun* not referred to more often? The answer is that the sun *is* being referred to, for Samson is the sun.

86. But he adds that it could simply be a Philistine name (454).

87. Burney (idem) cites Smythe Palmer Ch. XV.

88. See Soggin's discussion of this (22).

89. "An Egyptian mythological passage characterizes [Anat] as 'a woman acting (as) a warrior, clad as a male and girt as a female.'" Ackerman, 52.

90. *Religious Texts*, 186, n. 44.

91. Hendel was citing D. R. Hillers, "Bow of Aqhat: The Meaning of a Mythological Theme," in *Orient and Occident. Essays Presented to C. H. Gordon* (ed. H. A. Hoffner, Jr.; AOAT 22, Neukirchen-Vluyn: Neukirchener, 1973), 90, 71-80.

92. Notice again that the explanation is not that Jerubbaal is an evil Baal-worshiping Israelite, but that the story is an "anti-Canaanite polemic." In my opinion, this is a fanciful rationalization.

93. *Baal Zebul*, meaning *Baal the prince*, is the source of the name of *Baalzebub*, the *Lord of the Flies*. *Eerdmans Dictionary of the Bible*, 136-137. Though loyal to Baal (Abimelech), Zebul serves an evil master; this (or something like it) explains the origin of Beelzebub.

94. *The Art of Biblical Narrative* (New York: Basic Books, 1981), 47-62, 81-87 as summarized by Ackerman, 186-94, passim.

95. For example, Marc Brettler, *The Book of Judges* (London: Routledge, 2002), 45. See also Endnote 9, Chapter 6.

96. This daughter is called Thitmanat (16.i.29, Gibson 95), Thitmanit (1.16.29, Greenstein, in Parker, 33), "the lyre-player" (1.16.i.29, Wyatt, *Religious Texts*, 223), and Octavia (because she is the 8th child) (Margalit, "Keret" in *Handbook of Ugaritic Studies*, 224).

97. Cited by Parker, *The Pre-Biblical Narrative Tradition*, 71.

98. "The Ugaritic Root *špt*," *JNSL* 12 (1984): 68. Quoted by Block 408-409.

Chapter Six

1. Jacques Derrida, *Of Grammatology* (trans. Gayatri Chakravorty Spivak; Baltimore and London: Johns Hopkins Press, 1976), 158.

2. *Positions* (trans. Alan Bass; Chicago: University of Chicago Press, 198), 23.

3. *Literary Theory: An Introduction.* (2nd ed.; Minneapolis, Minn.: University of Minnesota Press, 1983, 1996), 116.

4. Letter of December 1917. Quoted in M. H. Abrams, *A Glossary of Literary Terms* (6th ed.; New York: Harcourt Brace College Publishers, 1993), 124.

5. "Postmodern Warfare: The Ignorance of our Warrior Intellectuals," *Atlantic* (July 2002): 34.

6. *The Resistance to Theory* (Theory and History of Literature, Vol. 33; Minneapolis, Minn.: University of Minnesota Press, 1986), 12.

7. Quoted by Michael Shermer, "Digits and Fidgets; Is the universe fine-tuned for life?" *Scientific American*, 288 (January 2003), 35.

8. *Eyewitness: Reports from an Art World in Crisis* (New York: Basic Books, A New Republic Book, 2000), 330.

9. The heroes are, however, mythic. Quoting Alex Preminger and Edward L. Greenstein: "Lord Raglan complied a comparative study of . . . stories from different cultures (Oedipus, Zeus, Hercules, Romulus, Theseus, Moses, Elijah, King Arthur, etc.) Every one of these heroes earned 'points' according to the number of 'pure type' elements that appear in his biography. The type has implications for the degree of historicity of these traditions: As the character hews more to the type, we subtract from the historical credibility of the traditions concerning him. In the Samson story he cites numbers 3, 4, 5, 11, 12, 13, 16, 18, 20 as being like those listed by Lord Raglan. Among them is no. 5: The hero is reckoned as a son of a god (this point does not appear in the Bible because the story has been adapted to a monotheistic belief, but in the birth account we have uncovered a process of demythologization whose origin so it seems, is in a story in which the wife is impregnated by a god). . . . the classic paradigm could not be kept because of the need to tailor the traditions both to the religion of Israel and to the sociopolitical framework of the period of the Judges. Therefore it is not said that he was a son of God, an attempt by his father to slay him is not depicted, he is not king, his wife is not a princess, and so on." Preminger and Greenstein, eds. *The Hebrew Bible in Literary Criticism* (New York: Ungar, 1986), 555, citing Yair Zakovitch, *Hayyei shimshon* (Jerusalem: Magnes Press, 1982), 230-31.

10. Including "Ephrathite." (12.5, BDB 68).

11. Othniel's bride, Achsah, who represents both faith and fertility and symbolizes Israel as "bride to Yahweh" in contrast with the Concubine (chapter 19), who symbolizes "dishonored Israel." Lillian R. Klein, *The Triumph of Irony in the Book of Judges.* (Sheffield: The Almond Press, 1988), 34, et passim, in Barnabas Lindars, *Judges 1-5: A New Translation and Commentary* (ed. A. D. H. Mayes.; Edinburgh: T & T Clark, 1995), 173.

12. Other scholars have found other allegories. For example, Alex Preminger, citing Kenneth R. R. Gros Louis, writes that "Samson in a sense epitomizes the judges," while Edward L. Greenstein writes that "Samson *is* Israel. . . . What appears to be Samson is the people

Israel; what appears as the Naziriteship of Samson is the Israelite covenant." Preminger and Greenstein, 553, 554.

13. Barry G. Webb writes, "for all we know [the rapists of Gibeah] could have been among the six hundred survivors." *The Book of the Judges: An Integrated Reading* (JSOTSup 46. Sheffield: JSOT Press, 1987), 197. Very likely—as it increases the irony.

14. James Joyce, *A Portrait of the Artist as a Young Man* [1916], Ch. 5.

15. The metaphor is from Edward Fredkin, as quoted by Robert Wright, "Did the universe just happen?" *Atlantic* (April 1988), 29-44.

16. Fredkin, quoted by Wright.

17. According to Boling, the skill of the stories points to "a guild of professional storytellers in premonarchic Israel" (Boling 33).

Abbreviations

AB	Anchor Bible
AOAT	*Alter Orient und Altes Testament*
ASOR	American Schools of Oriental Research
BASOR	*Bulletin of American Schools of Oriental Research*
BAR	*Biblical Archeology Review*
BDB	*Hebrew and English Dictionary of the Old Testament* by Brown, Driver, and Briggs
Bib	*Biblica*
Bib Not	*Biblische Notizen*
BJRL	*Bulletin of the John Rylands University Library of Manchester*
BR	*Bible Review*
BS	*Bibliotecha Sacra*
BT	*Bible Today*
CBQ	*Catholic Biblical Quarterly*
EB	*Encyclopaedia Britannica*
EBM	*Encyclopaedia Britannica* Micropaedia
HAR	*Harvard Annual Review*
HSM	Harvard Semitic Monographs
HTR	*Harvard Theological Review*
JAAR	*Journal of the American Academy of Religion*
JBL	*Journal of Biblical Literature*
JJS	*Journal of Jewish Studies*
JNES	*Journal of Near Eastern Studies*
JNSL	*Journal of Northwest Semitic Languages*
JSOT	*Journal for the Study of the Old Testament*
JSP	*Journal for the Study of the Pseudepigrapha*
JSS	*Journal of Semitic Studies*
JTS	*Journal Theological Studies,*
NEB	*New English Bible*
NRS	*New Revised Standard Version*
NYRB	*New York Review of Books*
SBL	Society of Biblical Literature
Semeia	*Semeia Studies*
SJOT	*Scandinavian Journal of the Old Testament*

SJOT	*Scandinavian Journal of the Old Testament*
TE	*Theologica Evangelgoodica*
TBT	*The Bible Today*
TNR	*The New Republic*
UBL	Ugaritisch-biblische Literatur [in Korpel citation]
UF	*Ugarit-Forschungen*
USQR	*Union Seminary Quarterly Review*
VT	*Vetus Testamentum*
WTJ	*Westminster Theological Journal*
ZAW	*Zeitschrift für die altestamentliche Wissenschaft*

Bibliography

Abrams, M. H. *A Glossary of Literary Terms.* 7th ed. Fort Worth: Harcourt Brace, 1999.

Ackerman, J. S. "Prophecy and Warfare in Early Israel: A Study of the Deborah-Barak Story." *BASOR,* 220 (1975): 5-12.

Ackerman, Susan. *Women in Judges and Biblical Israel: Warrior, Dancer, Seductress, Queen.* New York: Doubleday, 1998.

Adam, A. K. M., ed. *Handbook of Postmodern Biblical Interpretation.* St. Louis, Mo.: The Chalice Press, 2000.

_____. *Postmodern Interpretations of the Bible—a Reader.* St. Louis, Mo.: The Chalice Press, 2001.

Adams, Hazard and Leroy Searle. *Critical Theory Since 1965.* Tallahassee: University of Florida, 1986.

Ahlström, G. W. "Judges 5:20f. and History." *JNES,* 36 (1977): 287-88.

Aichele, George et al., eds. *The Postmodern Bible.* The Bible and Culture Collective: George Aichele, Fred W. Burnett, Elizabeth A. Castelli, ed., Robert M. Fowler, David Jobling, Stephen D. Moore, ed., Gary A. Phillips, ed., Tina Pippin, Regina M. Schwartz, ed., and Wilhelm Wuellner. New Haven and London: Yale University Press, 1995.

Albertz, R. *The History of Israelite Religion in the Old Testament Period.* Vol. I: *From the Beginnings to the End of the Monarchy.* Translated by J. Bowden. Louisville: Westminster John Knox, 1994.

Alonso-Schökel, Luis. "Arte Narrativa en Josue-Jueces-Samuel-Reyes." *Estudios Biblicos,* 48 (1990): 145-69.

_____. "Erzählkunst im Buche der Richter." *Bib* 42 (1961): 143-72.

Alter, Robert. *The Art of Biblical Narrative.* New York: Basic Books, 1981.

_____. *The David Story: A Translation with Commentary of 1 and 2 Samuel.* New York, London: W. W. Norton & Company, 1999.

_____. "Samson without Folklore." Pages 47-56 in *Text and Tradition: The Hebrew Bible and Folklore.* Edited by Susan Niditch. Atlanta, Ga.: Scholars Press, 1990.

_____. "Sodom as Nexus: The Web of Design in Biblical Narrative." Pages 146-160, in *The Book and the Text: The Bible and Literary Theory.* Edited by Regina Schwartz. Oxford: Basil Blackwell, 1990.

_____. *The World of Biblical Narrative.* [New York:] Basic Books, 1992.

_____ and Frank Kermode, eds. *The Literary Guide to the Bible.* Cambridge, Mass.: Harvard, 1987.

Altick, Richard D. "Symphonic Imagery in *Richard II.*" Pages 199-144 in William Shakespeare, *The Tragedy of Richard II.* Edited by Kenneth Muir. New York: The New American Library, 1963.

Amit, Yairah. *The Book of Judges: the Art of Editing.* Translated from the Hebrew by Jonathan Chipman. Leiden: Brill, 1999.

———. "Hidden Polemic in the Conquest of Dan: Judges 17-18." *VT* 40 (1990): 4-20.

———. "Judges 4: Its Contents and Form." *JSOT* 39 (1987): 89-111.

———. "Literature in the Service of Polemics: Studies in Judges 19-21." Pages 28-40 in *Politics and Theopolitics in the Bible and Postbiblical Literature.* Edited by Henning Graf Reventlow et al. JSOTSup 171. Sheffield: JSOT Press, 1994.

———. "'Manoah Promptly Followed His Wife' (Judges 13.11): On the Place of the Woman in Birth Narratives." Pages 146-56 in *A Feminist Companion to Judges.* Edited by Athalya Brenner. Sheffield: JSOT Press, 1993.

———. "The Story of Ehud (Judges 3:12-30): The Form and the Message." Pages 97-123 in *Signs and Wonders: Biblical Texts in Literary Focus.* Edited by J. Cheryl Exum. Decatur, Ga.: Scholars Press, 1989.

Anderson, Jeff S. "The Social Function of Curses in the Hebrew Bible." *ZAW* 110 (1998): 223-37.

Anonymous. "Irony." *EBM* V (1979) 432.

Aristotle. *Aristotle's Theory of Poetry and Fine Art with a Critical Text and Translation of "The Poetics."* Translated by S. H. Butcher. 4th ed. New York: Dover, 1951.

———. "Poetics." Pages 47-66 in *Critical Theory Since Plato.* Edited by Hazard Adams. [Tallahassee: University of Florida,] New York, 1971.

Arnold, P. M. *Gibeah: The Search for a Biblical City.* JSOTSup 79. Sheffield: JSOT Press, 1990.

Aschkenasy, Nehama. *Eve's Journey: Feminine Images in Hebraic Literary Tradition.* Philadelphia: University of Pennsylvania Press, 1986.

———. *Woman at the Window: Biblical Tales of Oppression and Escape.* Detroit: Wayne State, 1998.

Atkins, G. Douglas and Laura Morrow, eds. *Contemporary Literary Theory.* Amherst: University of Massachusetts Press, 1989.

Auden, W. H. "Notes on the Comic." *Thought* 27 (1952): 57-71.

Auld, A. Graeme. "Gideon: Hacking at the Heart of the Old Testament." *VT* 39 (1989): 257-67.

———. "Judges I and History: A Reconsideration." *VT* 25 (1975): 261-85.

———, ed. *Understanding Poets and Prophets: Essays in Honour of George Wishart Anderson.* JSOTSup 12. Sheffield:JSOT Press, 1993.

Avishur, Yitschak and Joshua Blau, eds. *Studies in Bible and the Ancient Near East: Presented to Samuel E. Loewenstamm on His Seventieth Birthday.* Jerusalem: E. Rubinstein's Publishing House, 1978.

Axelrod, Robert. *The Evolution of Cooperation.* [NP:] Basic Books, 1984.

Bach, Alice, ed. *The Pleasure of Her Text: Feminist Literary Readings of Biblical and Historical Texts.* Bloomington: Indiana University Press, 1990.

_____. "Rereading the Body Politic: Women and Violence in Judges 21." Pages 389-401 in *Women in the Hebrew Bible*. Edited by Alice Bach. New York: Routledge, 1999.

_____, ed. *Women in the Hebrew Bible*. New York: Routledge, 1999.

Baker, Cynthia. "Pseudo-Philo and the Transformation of Jephthah's Daughter." Pages 195-209 in *Anti-Covenant: Counter-Reading Women's Lives in the Hebrew Bible*. Edited by Mieke Bal. Sheffield: Almond Press, 1989.

Bakhtin, Mikhail. *Rabelais and His World*. Translated by Helene Iswolsky. Cambridge, Mass.: M.I.T. Press, 1965, 1968.

Bal, Mieke. "A Body of Writing: Judges 19." Pages 208-30 in *A Feminist Companion to Judges*. Edited by Athalya Brenner. Sheffield: JSOT Press, 1993.

_____, ed. *Anti-Covenant: Counter-Reading Women's Lives in the Hebrew Bible*. Sheffield: Almond Press, 1989.

_____. "Dealing with Women: Daughters in the Book of Judges." Pages 317-333 in *Women in the Hebrew Bible*. Edited by Alice Bach. New York: Routledge, 1999.

_____. *Death and Dissymmetry: the Politics of Coherence in the Book of Judges*. Chicago, Ill.: University of Chicago Press, 1988.

_____. *Lethal Love: Feminist Literary Readings of Biblical Love Stories*. Bloomington: Indiana University Press, 1987.

_____. *Murder and Difference: Gender, Genre, and Scholarship on Sisera's Death*. Translated by Matthew Gumpert. Bloomington: Indiana University Press, 1988.

_____. "The Rhetoric of Subjectivity." *Poetics Today* 5 (1984): 337-76.

_____. "Toward a Feminist Philology." Pages 211-31 in *Anti-Covenant: Counter-Reading Women's Lives in the Hebrew Bible*. Edited by Mieke Bal. Sheffield: Almond Press, 1989.

Barr, James. "Mythical Monarch Unmasked? Mysterious Doings of Debir King of Eglon." *JSOT* 48 (1990): 55-68.

Barré, Michael l. "The Meaning of PRŠDN in Judges III 22." *JSOT* 41 (1991): 1-11.

Barstead, Hans M. "History and the Hebrew Bible." Pages 36-64 in *Can a 'History of Israel' Be Written?* Edited by Lester L. Grabbe. JSOTSup 245. Sheffield: JSOT Press, 1999.

Bartlett, John R. ed. *Archaeology and Biblical Interpretation*. London: Routledge, 1997.

_____. "The Conquest of Sihon's Kingdom: A Literary Reexamination." *JBL* 97 (1978): 347-51.

Baudelaire, Charles. "On the Essence of Laughter." Pages 47-165 in *The Painter of Modern Art and Other Essays*. Translated and edited by Jonathan Maybe. London: Phaidon (1955).

Bauer, Uwe E. "Judges 18 as an Anti-Spy Story in the Context of an Anti-Conquest Story: The Creative Usage of Literary Genres." JSOT 88 (2000): 55-65.

Becking, Bob, "Inscribed Seals as Evidence for Biblical Israel? Jeremiah 40.7-41.15 *Par Exemple*." Pages 65-83 in *Can a 'History of Israel' Be Written?* Edited by Lester L. Grabbe. JSOTSup 245. Sheffield: Sheffield Academic Press, 1999.

Becking, Bob and Meindert Dijkstra, eds. *On Reading Prophetic Texts: Gender-Specific and Related Studies in Memory of Fokkelien van Dijk-Hemmes.* Leiden: Brill, 1996.

Beekman, John and John Callow. *Translating the Word of God.* Dallas: Summer Inst. of Linguistics, 1986.

Bergson, Henri. "Laughter" [1900]. Translated by Cloudesley Brereton and Fred Rothwell. In *Comedy.* Edited by Wylie Sypher. New York: Doubleday, 1956. [Also *Le Rire, Essai sur la Signification du Comique.* Paris: Presses Universitaires de France, 1958.]

Berichto, Herbert C. *The Problem of "Curse" in the Hebrew Bible.* JBL Monograph 13, 1963.

Berman, Art. *From the New Criticism to Deconstruction: The Reception of Structuralism and Post-Structuralism.* Urbana and Chicago: University of Illinois Press, 1988.

Beyerlin, Walter. *Near Eastern Religious Texts Relating to the Old Testament.* Philadelphia: Westminster, 1978.

BibleWorks for Windows 5.0 (on CD Rom). Big Fork, Mont.: Hermeneutika Bible Research Software, 2001.

Bird, Phyllis A. Review of Tilde Birger, *Asherah: Goddesses in Ugarit, Israel, and the Old Testament. JBL* 118 (Summer 1999): 333-35.

_____. "To Play the Harlot: An Inquiry Into an Old Testament Metaphor." Pages 75-94 in *Gender and Difference in Ancient Israel.* Edited by Peggy L. Day. Minneapolis: Fortress, 1989.

_____. *Missing Persons and Mistaken Identities: Women and Gender in Ancient Israel.* Minneapolis: Fortress, 1997.

Bledstein, Adrien Janis. "Is Judges a Woman's Satire of Men Who Play God?" Pages 34-54 in *A Feminist Companion to Judges.* Edited by Athalya Brenner. Sheffield: JSOT Press, 1993.

Blenkinsopp, Joseph. *The Pentateuch: An Introduction to the First Five Books of the Bible.* New York: Doubleday, 1992.

_____. "Some Notes on the Saga of Samson and the Heroid Milieu." *Scripture* 11 (1959): 81-9.

_____. "Structure and Style in Judges 13-16." *JBL* 82 (1963): 65-76.

Block, Ariel A. "The Cedar and the Palm Tree: A Paired Male/Female Symbol in Hebrew and Aramean." Pages 15-17 in *Solving Riddles and Untying Knots: Biblical Epigraphic and Semitic Studies in Honor of J. C. Greenfield.* Edited by Z. Zevit et al. Winona Lake, Ind.: Eisenbrauns, 1995.

Block, Daniel I. "Echo Narrative Technique in Hebrew Literature: A Study in Judges 19." *WTJ* 52 (1990): 325-41.

_____. "Deborah among the Judges: The Perspective of the Hebrew Historian." Pages 229-53 in *Faith, Tradition, and History: Old Testament Historiography in the Near Eastern Context.* Edited by A. R. Millard et al. Winona Lake, Ind.: Eisenbrauns, 1994.

_____. *Judges, Ruth.* The New American Commentary. Vol. 6. Nashville: Broadman, 1999.

Bloom, Harold. *Genius: A Mosaic of One Hudnred Exemplary Creative Minds.* New York: Warner Books, 2002.

Boaden, Ann, ed. *The Masks of Comedy*. Rock Island, Ill.: Augustana College Library, 1980.

Bodine, W. R. *The Greek Text of Judges: Recensional Developments* (Harvard Semitic Studies). Chico, Calif.: Scholars Press, 1980.

Bodner, Keith. *National Insecurity: A Primer on the First Book of Samuel*. Toronto: Clements Publishing, 2003.

_____. *Power Play: A Primer on the Second Book of Samuel*. Toronto: Clements Publishing, 2004.

Boling, Robert. "For the Birth of a New People: The Books of Joshua and Judges." *TBT*, 104 (Nov. 1979): 2159-67.

_____. "In Those Days There Was No King in Israel. Pages 33-48 in *A Light Unto My Path: Old Testament Studies in Honor of Jacob M. Myers*. Edited by H. N. Bream, R. Heim, and C. Moore. Philadelphia: Temple University Press, 1974.

_____. *Joshua*. A *New Translation with Notes and Commentary*. Garden City, N.Y.: Doubleday, 1982.

_____. *Judges: Introduction, Translation, and Commentary*. Anchor Bible 6A. Garden City, N.Y.: Doubleday, 1975.

Bohmbach, Karla G. "Conventions/Contraventions: The Meanings of Public and Private for the Judges 19 Concubine." *JSOT* 83 (1999): 83-98.

Boogaart, T. A. "Stone for Stone: Retribution in the Story of Abimelech and Shechem." *JSOT* 32 (1985): 45-56.

Bos, Johanna W. H. "Out of the Shadows: Genesis 38; Judges 4:17-22; Ruth 3." *Semeia*, 42 (1988): 37-67.

Bowman, Richard G. "Narrative Criticism of Judges: Human Purpose in Conflict with Divine Presence." Pages 17-44 in *Judges and Method: New Approaches in Biblical Studies*. Edited by Gale A. Yee, Minneapolis: Fortress, 1995.

Bowman, Richard G. and Richard W. Swanson "Samson and the Son of God, or Dead Heroes and Dead Goats: Ethical Readings of Narrative Violence in Judges and Matthew." *Semeia* 77 (1997): 59-73.

Boyarin, Daniel. "History Becomes Parable: A Reading of the Midrashic *Mashal*." Pages 54-71 in *Mappings of the Biblical Terrain*. Edited by V. Tollers, V. and J. Maier. Lewisberg, Pa.: Bucknell University Press, 1990.

Boyne, Daniel. "Portrait of a Woman as a Young Boxer." *Atlantic* (December 2001): 122.

Brams, Steven J. *Biblical Games: A Strategic Analysis of Stories in the Old Testament*. Cambridge, Mass.: MIT, 1980.

Branham, R. Bracht, ed. *Bakhtin and the Classics*. Evanston, Ill.: Northwestern University Press, 2002.

Bream, H. N., R. Heim, and C. Moore, eds. *A Light Unto My Path: Old Testament Studies in Honor of Jacob M. Myers*. Philadelphia: Temple University Press, 1974.

Brenner, Athalya, ed. *A Feminist Companion to Judges*. Sheffield: JSOT Press, 1993.

_____. "Afterword." Pages 231-35 in *A Feminist Companion to Judges*. Edited by Athalya Brenner. Sheffield: JSOT Press, 1993.

_____. *The Israelite Woman: Social Role and Literary Type in Biblical Narrative*. Sheffield: JSOT Press, 1985.

_____. "A Triangle and a Rhombus in Narrative Structure: A Proposed Integrative Reading of Judges IV and V." Pages 98-109 in *A Feminist Companion to Judges*. Edited by Athalya Brenner. Sheffield: JSOT Press, 1993. [Also in *VT* 40 (1990): 129-38.]

_____. "Who's Afraid of Feminist Criticism? Who's Afraid of Biblical Humor? The Case of the Obtuse Ruler in the Hebrew Bible." *JSOT* 63 (1994): 38-55.

Brenner, Athalya and Carole Fontaine, eds. *A Feminist Companion to Reading the Bible: Approaches, Methods and Strategies*. Sheffield: Sheffield Academic Press, 1997.

Brenner, Athalya and Fokkelien Van Dijk-Hemmes. *On Gendering Texts: Female and Male Voices in the Hebrew Bible*. Leiden: E. J. Brill, 1993.

Brettler, Marc Zvi. *The Book of Judges*. London and New York: Routledge, 2002.

_____. *The Creation of History in Ancient Israel*. London and New York: Routledge, 1995.

_____. "Jud 1,1-2,19: From Appendix to Prologue." *ZAW* 101 (1989): 433-35.

_____. "The Book of Judges: Literature as Politics." *JBL* 108 (1989): 395-418.

_____. "Never the Twain Shall Meet? The Ehud Story as History and Literature." *Hebrew Union College Annual* 62 (1991).

Bronner, Leila Leah, "Valorized or Vilified? The Women of Judges in Midrashic Sources." Pages 72-95 in *A Feminist Companion to Judges*. Edited by Athalya Brenner. Sheffield: JSOT Press, 1993.

Brooks, Simcha Shalom. "Saul and the Samson Narrative." *JSOT* 71 (1996): 19-25.

Brown, F., S. R. Driver, and C. S. Briggs, eds. *A Hebrew and English Lexicon of the Old Testament*. Oxford: Clarendon, 1907 and reprints.

Buchler, Ira R. and Henry A. Selby. *A Formal Study of Myth*. Monograph Series No. I. Austin: The University of Texas, 1968.

Burney, C. F. *The Book of Judges with Introduction and Notes*. London: Rivingtons, 1903, 1918. Reprinted, New York: Ktav, 1970.

Bynum, David E. "Samson as a Biblical φὴρ ὀρεδκῷοζ." Pages 57-73 in *Text and Tradition: The Hebrew Bible and Folklore*. Edited by Susan Niditch. Atlanta, Ga.: Scholars Press, 1990. [A response to Alter's "Samson Without Folklore."]

Cahill, P. J. "Hermeneutical Implications of Typology." *CBQ* 44 (Apr 82): 266-81.

Camp, Claudia V. "Wise and Strange: An Interpretation of the Female Imagery in Proverbs in Light of Trickster Mythology." Pages 14-36 in *Reasoning with the Foxes: Female Within a World of Male Power*. Edited by J. Cheryl Exum and Johanna W. H. Bos. *Semeia* 42. Atlanta, Ga.: Scholars Press, 1988.

_____ and Carole R. Fontaine. "The Words of the Wise and Their Riddles." Pages 128-51 in *Text and Tradition: The Hebrew Bible and Folklore*. Edited by Susan Niditch. Atlanta, Ga.: Scholars Press, 1990.

Caquot, Andre. *The Goddess Anath: Canaanite Epics of the Patriarchal Age. Texts, Hebrew Translation, Commentary and Introduction.* Translated by Israel Abrahams. Jerusalem: The Magnes Press, The Hebrew University, 1951.

————. "Les Tribus d'Israël dans le Cantique de Debora (Juges 5, 13-17). *Semitica* 36 (1986): 47-70.

————. and Maurice Sznycer. *Ugaritic Religion.* Leiden: E. J. Brill, 1980.

Carden, Michael. "Homophobia and Rape in Sodom and Gibeah: A Response to Ken Stone." *JSOT* 82 (1999): 83-96.

Carroll, Robert P. "Madonna of the Silences: Clio and the Bible." Pages 84-103 in *Can a 'History of Israel' Be Written?* Edited by Lester L. Grabbe. JSOTSup 245. Sheffield: Sheffield Academic Press, 1999.

Cartledge, Tony W. *Vows in the Hebrew Bible and the Ancient Near East.* JSOTSup 147. Sheffield: Sheffield Academic Press, 1992.

Cassuto, U., ed. *Biblical and Oriental Studies.* Translated by. Israel Abrahams. Vol. II Bible and Ancient Oriental Texts. Jerusalem: The Magnes Press, The Hebrew University, 1975.

Chalcraft, David J. "Deviance and Legitimate Action in the Book of Judges." Pages 177-201 in *The Bible in Three Dimensions: Essays in Celebration of Forty Years of Biblical Studies in the University of Sheffield.* Edited by David A. Clines, et al. JSOTSup 87. Sheffield, 1990.

Charney, Maurice, ed. *Comedy High and Low: An Introduction to the Experience of Comedy.* New York: Oxford University Press, 1978.

Clements, R. E., ed. *The World of Ancient Israel: Sociological, Anthropological and Political Perspectives.* Cambridge: Cambridge University Press, 1989.

Clines, David A. *The Bible and the Modern World.* (Biblical Seminar 41). Sheffield: Sheffield Academic Press 1997.

————. et al., eds. *The Bible in Three Dimensions: Essays in Celebration of Forty Years of Biblical Studies in the University of Sheffield.* JSOTSup 87. Sheffield: Sheffield Academic Press, 1990.

————. *Interested Parties: The Ideology of Writers and Readers of the Hebrew Bible.* JSOTSup; GCT, 1. Sheffield: Sheffield Academic Press, 1995.

————. *On the Way to the Postmodern:OT Essays.* 2 vols. Sheffield: JSOT Sup292. Sheffield: Sheffield Academic Press, 1998, Vol. I.

Collins, Adela Yarbro, ed. *Feminist Perspectives on Biblical Scholarship.* Chico, Calif.: Scholars Press, 1985.

Collins, John J. and George W. E. Nickelsburg, eds. *Ideal Figures in Ancient Judaism: Profiles and Paradigms.* Chico, Calif: Scholars Press, 1980.

Cohen, A. *Joshua and Judges.* Translated with Introduction and Commentary. London: Soncino, 1950.

Coogan, Michael David. *The Oxford History of the Biblical World.* Oxford: Oxford University Press, 1998.

Coogan, Michael David, trans. *Stories from Ancient Canaan*. Louisville, Ky.: Westminster, 1978.

———. "Canaanite Origins and Lineage: Reflections on the Religion of Ancient Israel." Pages 115-24 in *Ancient Israelite Religion: Essays in Honor of Frank Moore Cross*. Edited by Patrick D. Miller, Jr., Paul D. Hanson, and S. Dean McBride. Philadelphia: Augsburg Fortress, 1987.

———. "A Structural and Literary Analysis of the Song of Deborah." *CBQ* 40 (1978): 143-66.

Corrigan, Robert W., ed. *Comedy: Meaning and Form*. 2nd ed. New York: Harper and Row, 1981.

Couturier, Guy. "Débora: une autorité politico-religieuse aux origines d'Israël." *Studies in Religion/Sciences Religieuses*. 18 (1989): 213-28.

Craigie, Peter C. "The Comparison of Hebrew Poetry: Psalm 104 in the Light of Egyptian and Ugaritic Poetry." *Semitics* 5 (1977): 10-21.

———. "Deborah and Anat: A Study in Poetic Imagery (Judges 5)." *ZAW* 90 (1978): 374-81.

———. "Three Ugaritic Notes on the Song of Deborah." *JSOT* 2 (1977): 33-49.

———. "Ugarit and the Bible: Progress and Regress in 50 Years of Literary Study." Pages 99-100 in *Ugarit in Retrospect: Fifty Years of Ugarit and Ugaritic*. Edited by D. G. Young. Winona Lake, Ind.: Eisenbrauns, 1981.

———. *Ugarit and the Old Testament*. Grand Rapids, Mich.: Eerdmans, 1983.

Crenshaw, James L. "The Samson Saga: Filial Devotion or Erotic Attachment?" *ZAW* 86 (1974): 470-504.

———. *Samson: a Secret Betrayal, A Vow Ignored*. Atlanta, Ga.: John Knox Press, 1978.

Cross, Frank Moore. *Canaanite Myth and Hebrew Epic: Essays in the History of the Religion of Israel*. Cambridge, Mass.: Harvard University Press, 1973.

Crown, A. D. "A Reinterpretation of Judges IX in the Light of Its Humor." *Abr-Nahrain* 3 (1961-62): 90-98.

Cudden, J. A. *A Dictionary of Literary Terms*. London: Andre Deutsch, 1977.

Culler, Jonathan. *The Pursuit of Signs: Semiotics, Literature, Deconstruction*. London: Routledge and Kegan Paul, 1981.

Culley, Robert C. *Studies in the Structure of Hebrew Narrative*. Philadelphia: Fortress, 1976.

Curtis, Adrian. *Ugarit*. Grand Rapids, Mich.: Eerdmans, 1985.

Dahood, Mitchell S. J. "Ugaritic-Hebrew Parallel Pairs." In *Ras Shamra Parallels*. Edited by Loren I. Fisher. Roma: Pontificium Institutum Biblicum. I (1972), II (1975).

———. *Ugaritic and the Old Testament*. Bruges: Édition J. Duculot, 1968.

Davies, G. I. Rev. of S. Wiggins, *A Reassessment of 'Asherah': A Study According to the Textual Sources of the First Two Millennia BCE*. 574-576.

Davies, Philip R. *In Search of 'Ancient Israel.'* *JSOT* 148. Sheffield: Sheffield Academic Press, 1992.

————. "Method and Madness: Some Remarks on Doing History with the Bible." *JBL* 114 (Winter 1995): 699-705.

————. *Scribes and Schools: The Canonization of the Hebrew Scriptures.* Louisville, Ky.: Westminster John Knox Press, 1998.

————. "Whose History? Whose Israel? Whose Bible? Biblical Histories, Ancient and Modern." Pages 104-22 in *Can a 'History of Israel' Be Written?* Edited by Lester L. Grabbe. JSOTSup 245. Sheffield: Sheffield Academic Press, 1999.

Day, John. "Asherah in the Hebrew Bible and Northwest Semitic Literature." *JBL* 105 (1986): 385-408.

————. *God's Conflict with the Dragon and the Sea, Echoes of a Canaanite Myth in the Old Testament.* (University of Cambridge Oriental Publications 35.) Cambridge: Cambridge University Press, 1985.

————. *Yahweh and the Gods and Goddesses of Canaan.* JSOTSup 265. Sheffield: Sheffield Academic Press, 2000.

Day, Peggy L., "From the Child Is Born the Woman: the Story of Jephthah's Daughter." Pages 58-74 in *Gender and Difference in Ancient Israel.* Edited by Peggy L. Day. Minneapolis: Fortress Press, 1989.

————, ed. *Gender and Difference in Ancient Israel.* Minneapolis: Fortress Press, 1989.

————. "Why Is Anat A Warrior and Hunter?" Pages 141-46 in *The Bible and the Politics of Exegesis.* Edited by David Jobling, Peggy Day, and Gerald Sheppard. Cleveland: Pilgrim Press, 1991.

Delaney, Carol. "The Legacy of Abraham." Pages 27-41 in *Anti-Covenant: Counter-Reading Women's Lives in the Hebrew Bible.* Edited by Mieke Bal. Sheffield: Almond Press, 1989.

De Man, Paul. *The Resistance to Theory.* Theory and History of Literature, Vol. 33. Minneapolis: University of Minnesota Press, 1986.

Derrida, Jacques. *Of Grammatology.* Translated by Gayatri Chakravorty Spivak. Baltimore and London: Johns Hopkins Press, 1976.

Dershowitz, Alan M. *The Genesis of Justice: Ten Stories of Biblical Injustice that Led to the Ten Commandments and Modern Law.* New York: Warner Books, 2000.

Detienne, Marcel. *The Gardens of Adonis: Spices in Greek Mythology.* Translated by. J. Lloyd. Harvester Press, 1977.

Dever, William G. "Archaeology, Material Culture and the Early Monarchical Period in Israel." Pages 103-15 in *The Fabric of History: Text, Artifact and Israel's Past.* Edited by Diana Vikander Edelman. JSOTSup 127. Sheffield: Sheffield Academic Press, 1991.

————. "The Contribution of Archaeology to the Study of Canaanite and Early Israelite Religion." Pages 209-47 in *Ancient Israelite Religion: Essays in Honor of Frank Moore Cross.* Edited by Patrick D. Miller, Jr. Paul D. Hanson, and S. D. McBride. Philadelphia: Augsburg Fortress, 1987.

Dietrich, M. and I. Kottsieper, eds. *'Und Mose schrieb dieses Lied auf . . . '. Studie zum Alten Testament und zum Alten Orient. Festschrift für O. Loretz zur Vollendung seines 70.*

Lebensjahres mit Beiträgen von Freunden, Schülern und Kollegen. AOAT 250, Münster: Ugarit-Verlag, 1998.

Dietrich, Walter. "The 'Ban' in the Age of the Early Kings." Pages 196-210 in *The Origins of the Ancient Israelite States.* Edited by Fritz Volkmar and Philip R. Davies. JSOTSup 228. Sheffield: Sheffield Academic Press, 1996.

Dijkstra, Meindert. "Goddesses, Gods, Men and Women." Pages 99-111 in *On Reading Prophetic Texts : Gender-Specific and Related Studies in Memory of Fokkelien van Dijk-Hemmes.* Edited by Bob Becking and Meindert Dijkstra. Leiden: Brill, 1996.

Dion, Paul E. "YHWH as Storm-god and Sun-god: The Double Legacy of Egypt and Canaan as Reflected in Psalm 104." *ZAW* 103 (1991): 43-73.

Dragga, Sam. "In the Shadow of the Judges: The Failure of Saul." *JSOT* 38 (1987): 39-46.

Drews, Robert. "Canaanites and Philistines." *JSOT* 81 (1998): 29-61.

Driver, Godfrey. *Canaanite Myths and Legends.* Edinburgh: T. & T. Clark, 1956.

Driver, G. R. "Problems in Judges Newly Discussed." *Annual of Leeds University Oriental Society,* Leiden. 4 (1962/63): 6-25.

Dumbrell, W. J. "'In Those Days There Was No King in Israel; Every Man Did What Was Right in His Own Eyes': The Purpose of the Book of Judges Reconsidered." *JSOT* 25 (1983): 23-33.

Durkheim, Emile. *The Elementary Forms of the Religious Life,* 1982.

Eagleton, Terry. *Against the Grain: Essays 1975-1985.* London: Verso, 1986.

———. *Literary Theory: An Introduction.* 2nd ed. Minneapolis: University of Minn Press, 1983, 1996.

Edelman, Diana Vikander, ed. *The Fabric of History: Text, Artifact and Israel's Past.* JSOTSup 127. Sheffield: Sheffield Academic Press, 1991.

———. "Saul ben Kish in History and Tradition." Pages 142-60 in *The Origins of the Ancient Israelite States.* Edited by Fritz Volkmar and Philip R. Davies. JSOTSup 228. Sheffield: Sheffield Academic Press, 1996.

Edwards, Anthony T. "Historicizing the Popular Grotesque: Bakhtin's *Rabelais and His World* and Old Attic Comedy." Pages 27-55 in *Bakhtin and the Classics.* Edited by R. Bracht Branham. Evanston, Ill.: Northwestern University Press, 2002.

Ehrmann, Jacques, ed. *Game, Play, Literature.* Boston: Beacon Press, 1968, 1971.

Elliott, Phillips P. "Exposition," in "Judges: Introduction and Exegesis." Pages 708-11 in *The Interpreter's Bible.* Vol. II. Edited by Jacob M. Myers. New York and Nashville: Abingdon, 1973.

Emerson, Caryl. "Coming to Terms with Bakhtin's Carnival: Ancient, Modern, sub Specie Aeternitatis." Pages 5-26 in *Bakhtin and the Classics.* Edited by R. Bracht Branham. Evanston, Ill.: Northwestern University Press, 2002.

Emerton, J. A., ed. *Studies in the Historical Books of the Old Testament* (SVT 30, ed.). Leiden: Brill, 1979.

———. "'Yahweh and his Asherah': The Goddess or Her Symbol?" *VT* 49 (1999) 315-337.

Exum, J. Cheryl. "Aspects of Symmetry and Balance in the Samson Saga." *JSOT* 19 (1981): 3-29.

_____. "The Centre Cannot Hold: Thematic and Textual Instabilities in Judges." *CBQ* 52 (1990): 410-31.

_____. "Feminist Criticism: Whose Interests Are Being Served?" Pages 65-90 in *Judges and Method: New Approaches in Biblical Studies.* Edited by Gale A. Yee, Minneapolis: Fortress Press, 1995.

_____. *Fragmented Women: Feminist (Sub)versions of Biblical Narratives.* JSOTSup 153. Sheffield: JSOT Press, 1993.

_____. "Murder They Wrote: Ideology and the Manipulation of Female Presence in Biblical Narrative." *Union Seminary Quarterly Review,* 43 (1989): 19-39. [Also in her *Fragmented Women: Feminist (Sub)versions of Biblical Narratives.* JSOTSup 153. Sheffield: JSOT Press, 1993.]

_____. "On Judges 11." Pages 131-44 in *A Feminist Companion to Judges.* Edited by Athalya Brenner. Sheffield: JSOT Press, 1993.

_____. *Plotted, Shot, and Painted: Cultural Representations of Biblical Women.* JSOTSup 215. Sheffield: Sheffield Academic Press, 1996.

_____. "Promise and Fulfillment: Narrative Art in Judges 13." *JBL* 99 (1980): 43-59.

_____. "Raped by the Pen." Pages 178-94 in *Fragmented Women: Feminist (Sub)versions of Biblical Narratives.* Edited by J. C. Exum. JSOTSup 163. Sheffield: JSOT Press, 1992.

_____, ed. *Signs and Wonders: Biblical Texts in Literary Focus.* Decatur, Ga.: Scholars Press, 1989.

_____. "The Theological Dimension of the Samson Saga." *VT* 33 (1983): 30-45.

_____. *Tragedy and Biblical Narrative: Arrows of the Almighty.* Cambridge: Cambridge University Press, 1992.

Exum, J. Cheryl and J. William Whedbee. "Isaac, Samson, and Saul: Reflections on the Comic and Tragic Visions." Pages 117-59 in *On Humour and the Comic in the Hebrew Bible.* Edited by Yehuda Radday and Athalya Brenner. Sheffield: Almond Press, 1990. [Originally published as "Isaac, Samson, and Saul: On the Comic and Tragic Visions." *Semeia* 32 (1984).]

Exum J. Cheryl and Johanna W. H. Bos, eds. *Reasoning with the Foxes: Female Within a World of Male Power. Semeia* 42. Atlanta, Ga.: Scholars Press, 1988.

Fensham, F. Charles. "The Son of a Handmaid in Northwest Semitic." *VT* 19 (July 1969): 312-21.

Fewell, Danna Nolan. "Deconstructive Criticism: Achsah and the (E)razed City of Writing." Pages 119-145 in *Judges and Method: New Approaches in Biblical Studies.* Edited by Gale A. Yee, Minneapolis: Fortress Press, 1995.

_____. "Feminist Reading of the Hebrew Bible: Affirmation, Resistance and Transformation." *JSOT* 39 (1987): 77-87.

_____. "Judges." Pages 67-77 in *The Women's Bible Commentary.* Edited by C. A. Newsom and S. H. Ringe. Louisville, Ky.: Westminster John Knox Press, 1992.

_____, ed. *Reading Between Texts: Intertextuality and the Hebrew Bible.* Louisville, Ky: Westminster, 1990.

Fewell, Danna Nolan and David M. Gunn. "Controlling Desires: Women, Men and the Authority of Violence in Judges 4 and 5." *JAAR*, 48 (1990): 389-411.

_____. *Gender, Power, and Promise. The Subject of the Bible's First Story*. Nashville: Abingdon Press, 1993.

Finkelstein, Israel and Neil Asher Silberman. *The Bible Unearthed: Archaeology's New Vision of Ancient Israel and the Origin of Its Sacred Texts*. New York: The Free Press, 2001.

Fisher, Loren R., ed. *Ras Shamra Parallels*. Roma: Pontificium Institutum Biblicum, I (1972), II (1975).

Fisher, Michael. *Does Deconstruction Make Any Difference? Poststructuralism and the Defense of Poetry in Modern Criticism*. Bloomington: Indiana University Press, 1985.

Fitzpatrick-McKinley, Anne. *The Transformation of Torah from Scribal Advice to Law*. JSOTSup 287. Sheffield: Sheffield Academic Press, 1999.

Fontaine, Carol R. "The Abusive Bible: On the Use of Feminist Method in Pastoral Contexts." Pages 84-113 in *A Feminist Companion to Reading the Bible: Approaches, Methods and Strategies*. Edited by Athlaya Brenner and Carole Fontaine. Sheffield: Sheffield Academic Press, 1997.

_____. "A Heifer from Thy Stable: On Goddesses and the Status of Women in the Ancient Near East." Pages 159-78 in *Women in the Hebrew Bible*. Edited by Alice Bach. New York: Routledge, 1999.

Freedman, David Noel, ed. *Eerdmans Dictionary of the Bible*. Grand Rapids, Mich.: Eerdmans, 2000.

Freeman, James A. "Samson's Dry Bones: A Structural Reading of Judges 13-16." Pages 145-60 in *Literary Interpretations of Biblical Narratives*. Edited by Kenneth R. R. Gros Louis with James S. Ackerman. Vol. II. Nashville: Abingdon, 1982.

Friend, Tad. "What's So Funny: A scientific attempt to discover why we laugh." *The New Yorker* (November 11, 2002), 78-93.

_____ and Philip R. Davies, eds. *The Origins of the Ancient Israelite States*. JSOTSup 228. Sheffield: Sheffield Academic Press, 1996.

Frymer-Kensky, Tikva. *In the Wake of the Goddesses: Women, Culture, and the Biblical Transformation of Pagan Myth*. New York: Free Press, 1992.

Fuchs, Esther. "The Literary Characterization of Mothers and Sexual Politics in the Hebrew Bible." *Semeia* 46 (1989): 151-66. [Also in *Feminist Perspectives on Biblical Scholarship*. Edited by Adela Yarbro Collins. Chico, Calif.: Scholars Press, 1985.]

_____. "Marginalization, Ambiguity, Silencing: The Story of Jephthah's Daughter." *Journal of Feminist Studies in Religion*, 5 (1989): 35-45. Also pages 116-30 in *A Feminist Companion to Judges*. Edited by Athalya Brenner. Sheffield: JSOT Press, 1993.

Gaines, Janet Howard. *Music in the Old Bones: Jezebel Through the Ages*. Carbondale and Edwardsville: Southern Illinois University Press, 1999.

Garbini, G. "*Parson* 'Iron' in the Song of Deborah." *JSS* 23 (1978): 23-24.

Garsiel, Moshe. "Homiletic Name-Derivations as a Literary Device in the Gideon Narrative: Judges VI-VIII." *VT* 43 (1993) 302-317.

_____. *The First Book of Samuel: A Literary Study of Comparative Structures, Analogies and Parallels.* Translated by Phyllis Hackett. Ramat-Gan, Israel: 1983, 1985.

Gaster, Theodor H. *Myth, Legend, and Custom in the Old Testament.* New York: Harper and Row, 1969.

_____. *Thespis: Ritual, Myth and Drama in the Ancient Near East.* New York: Schuman, 1950.

Gernet, Jean-Pierre Vernant, and Pierre Vidal-Naquet. *Myth, Religion, and Society: Structuralist Essays.* Edited by R. L. Gordon. Cambridge University Press, 1981.

Gibson, J. L. C., ed. and tr. *Canaanite Myths and Legends.* 2nd ed. (Originally edited by G. R. Driver.) Edinburgh: T. & T. Clark, 1977.

Gibson, John. "The Mythological Texts." Pages 193-202 in *Handbook of Ugaritic Studies.* Edited by Wilfred G. E. Watson and Nicolas Wyatt. Cologne: Brill, 1999.

Globe, Alexander. "The Literary Structure and Unity of the Song of Deborah." *JBL* 93 (1974): 493-512.

_____. "Judges V 27." *VT* 25 (1975): 362-67.

Golb, Norman. *Who Wrote the Dead Sea Scrolls?* New York: Scribner's, 1995.

Good, Edwin M. *Irony in the Old Testament,* 1965. 2nd ed. Sheffield: Almond Press, 1981.

Gooding, D. W. "The Composition of the Book of Judges." *Eretz-Israel* 16 (1982): 70-79.

Gordon, C.H. *Ugarit and Minoan Greek.* New York: W. W. Norton, 1966.

_____. *Ugaritic Textbook: Texts in Transliteration,* Cuneiform Selections, Glossary, Grammar. Rome: Pontifical Biblical Institute, 1965.

Gottlieb, Freema. "Three Mothers [Deborah, Jael, Sisera's Mother]." *Judaism,* 30 (Sept. 1981): 104-203.

Gottwald, Norman. *The Tribes of Yahweh.* Maryknoll, N.Y.: Orbis, 1979.

Grabbe, Lester L., ed. *Can a 'History of Israel' Be Written?* JSOTSup 245. Sheffield: Sheffield Academic Press, 1999. "Reflections on the Discussion," 188-196.

Granot, M. "Anonymous Prophecy in Judges." *Beth Mikra* 25 (1980): 256-58.

Graves, Robert and Raphael Patai. *Hebrew Myths: The Book of Genesis.* New York: McGraw Hill, 1964.

Gray, John. *Joshua, Judges, Ruth.* (New Century Biblical Commentary.) Rev. ed. Grand Rapids, Mich.: Eerdmans, 1986.

_____. *The KRT Text in the Literature of Ras Shamra.* Leiden: E. J. Brill, 1955.

Greenbaum, Sidney. *Oxford English Grammar,* Oxford: Oxford University Press, 1992.

Greenspahn, Frederick E. "An Egyptian Parallel to Judg 17:6 and 21:25." *JBL* 101 (1982): 129-30.

Greenstein, Edward L. "The Riddle of Samson." *Prooftexts* 1 (1981): 237-60.

_____. "Theory and Argument in Biblical Criticism." *Hebrew Annual Review* 10 (1986): 77-93.

Grimm, Dieter. "Der Name des Gottesboten in Richter 13." *Biblica,* 62 (1981): 92-98.

Grønbaek, Jakob H. "Baal's Battle with Yam—a Canaanite Creation Fight." *JSOT* 33 (1985): 27-44.

Gros Louis, Kenneth R. R. with James S. Ackerman, eds. *Literary Interpretations of Biblical Narratives.* Vol. II. Nashville: Abingdon, 1982.

Grote, David. *The Sit-Com and the Comedic Tradition.* Hamden, Conn.: Archon, 1983.

Guerin, Wilfred L. et al., *A Handbook of Critical Approaches to Literature,* 4th ed. (New York: Oxford, 1999).

Guest, P. Deryn. "Can Judges Survive Without Sources? Challenging the Consensus." *JSOT* 78 (1998): 43-61.

Gunn, David M. "Joshua and Judges." Pages 102-21 in *The Literary Guide to the Bible.* Edited by Robert Alter and Frank Kermode. Cambridge, Mass.: Harvard, 1987.

_____."Narrative Patterns and Oral Tradition in Judges and Samuel." *VT* 24 (1974) 286-317.

_____. "Samson of Sorrows: An Isaianic Gloss on Judges 13-16." Pages 225-53 in *Reading Between Texts: Intertextuality and the Hebrew Bible.* Edited by Danna Nolan Fewell. Louisville, Ky.: Westminster, 1990.

_____. "'Threading the Labyrinth': A Response to Albert B. Lord." Pages 19-23 in *Text and Tradition: The Hebrew Bible and Folklore.* Edited by Susan Niditch. Atlanta, Ga.: Scholars Press, 1990.

Gunneweg, Antonius. *Leviten und Priester.* Göttingen: Vanderhoeck & Ruprecht, 1965.

Gutwirth, Michael. *Laughing Matter: An Essay on the Comic.* Ithaca and London: Cornell University Press, 1993.

Hackett, Jo Ann. "Religious Traditions in Israelite Transjordan." Pages 125-36 in *Ancient Israelite Religion: Essays in Honor of Frank Moore Cross.* Edited by Patrick D. Miller, Jr., Paul D. Hanson, and S. Dean McBride. Philadelphia: Augsburg Fortress, 1987.

Hadley, Judith, M. "The Fertility of the Flock? The De-personalization of Astarte in the Old Testament." Pages 115-33 in *On Reading Prophetic Texts: Gender-Specific and Related Studies in Memory of Fokkelien van Dijk-Hemmes.* Edited by Bob Becking and Meindert Dijkstra. Leiden: Brill, 1996.

Halpern, Baruch. "The Assassination of Eglon—The First Locked Room Murder Mystery." *BR* 4 (1988): 32-41, 44. [Also in Halpern, *The First Historians,* 40-69.]

_____. *David's Secret Demons: Messiah, Murderer, Traitor, King.* Grand Rapids, Mich.: Eerdmans, 2001.

_____. "Erasing History." *BR* (December 1995): 26-47.

_____. *The First Historians: The Hebrew Bible and History.* San Francisco: Harper and Row, 1988.

_____. "The Resourceful Israelite Historian: the Song of Deborah and Israelite Historiography." *HTR,* 76 (1983): 379-402.

_____. "The Rise of Abimelech Ben-Jerubbaal." *HAR,* 2 (1978): 79-100.

Handy, Lowell K. "Uneasy Laughter: Ehud and Eglon as Ethnic Humor."*SJOT,* 6 (1992): 233-246.

Hanselman, Stephen W. "Narrative Theory, Ideology, and Transformation in Judges

4." Pages 94-112 in *Anti-Covenant: Counter-Reading Women's Lives in the Hebrew Bible*. Edited by Mieke Bal. Sheffield: Almond Press, 1989.

Harris, J. Gordon, Cheryl A. Brown, and Michael S. Moore. *Joshua, Judges, Ruth* (New International Biblical Commentary). Peabody, Mass.: Hendrickson, 2000.

Hauer, Chris, Jr. "David and the Levites." *JSOT* 23 (1982): 33-54.

Hauser, Alan J. "The Minor Judges: A Re-Evaluation." *JBL* 94 (1975): 190-200.

Heimerdinger, Jean-Marc. *Topic, Focus and Foreground in Hebrew Narratives*. JSOTSup 295. Sheffield: Sheffield Academic Press, 1999.

Heltzer, M. "New Light from Emar on Genesis 31." Pages 357-362 in *'Und Mose schrieb dieses Lied auf . . . ' Studie zum Alten Testament und zum Alten Orient. Festschrift für O. Loretz zur Vollendung seines 70. Lebensjahres mit Beiträgen von Freunden, Schülern und Kollegen*. Edited by M. Dietrich and I. Kottsieper. AOAT 250, Münster: Ugarit-Verlag, 1998.

Hendel, Ronald S. *The Epic of the Patriarch: The Jacob Cycle and the Narrative Traditions of Canaan and Israel*. HSM 42, Atlanta, Ga.: Scholar's Press,1987.

Hess, Richard S. "The Dead Sea Scrolls and Higher Criticism of the Hebrew Bible: The Case of 4QJud[a]." Pages 122-128 in *The Scrolls and the Scriptures*. Edited by S. E. Porter and C. A. Evans; RILP, 3; JSPSup, 26; Sheffield: Sheffield Academic Press, 1997.

Higgs, Liz Curtis. *Really Bad Girls of the Bible: More Lessons from Less-Than-Perfect Women*. Colorado Springs, Colo.: Waterbrook Press, 2000.

Hillers, I. R. "A Note on Judges 5, 8a." *CBQ* 27 (1965): 124-26.

Hobbs, T. R. "Hospitality in the First Testament and the 'Teleological Fallacy.'" JSOT 95 (2001): 3-33.

Hoerth, Alfred J. *Archaeology and the Old Testament*. Grand Rapids: Basic Books, 1998.

Holman, C. Hugh. *A Handbook to Literature*. 3rd ed. Indianapolis and New York: Odyssey, 1972.

Hooke, S. H. *Middle Eastern Mythology*. Middlesex: Harmondsworth, 1963.

Houston, Walter J. "Murder and Midrash: The Prose Appropriation of Poetic Material in the Hebrew Bible (Part II)." *ZAW* 109 (1997): 534-48.

Hoy, Cyrus H. "Comedy." *EBM* IV (1979) 958-967. "Irony." *EBM* V, 432.

Hudson, Don Michael. "Living in a Land of Epithets: Anonymity in Judges 19-21." *JSOT* 62 (1994): 49-66.

Hübner, Ulrich. "Mord auf dem Abort? Überlegungen zu Humor, Gewaltdarstellung und Realienkunde in Richter 3,12-30." *BN* 40 (1987): 130-40.

Huizinga, Johan. *Homo Ludens: a Study of the Play Element in Culture*. Translated by R. F. C. Hull. Boston: The Beacon Press, 1950, 1955.

Humphreys, W. L. "The Story of Jephthah and the Tragic Vision: A Response to J. Cheryl Exum." Pages 85-96 in *Signs and Wonders: Biblical Texts in Literary Focus*. Edited by J. Cheryl Exum. Decatur, Ga.: Scholars Press, 1989.

Hutchinson, Peter. *Games Authors Play*. London and New York: Methuen, 1983.

Hvidberg, Flemming Friis. *Weeping and Laughter in the Old Testament: A Study of Canaanite-Israelite Religion.* Leiden: E. J. Brill, 1962.

Irvin, Dorothy. *Mytharion: The Comparison of Tales from the Old Testament and the Ancient Near East.* Kevelaer: Butzon and Bercker, 1978.

Ishida, Tomoo. *History and Historical Writing in Ancient Israel: Studies in Biblical Historiography.* Leiden: Brill, 1999.

Jacoby, Susan. *Wild Justice: The Evolution of Revenge.* New York: Harper & Row, 1983.

James, William. "Good as the Satisfaction of Demands," from *The Will to Believe and Other Essays in Popular Philosophy.* New York: Longmans Green, 1899, 189-205. [First published in 1891.] In Singer, Peter, ed. *Ethics.* Oxford: Oxford University Press, 1994., 205-211.

Janzen, J. Gerald. "A Certain Woman in the Rhetoric of Judges 9." *JSOT* 38 (1987): 33-37.

Jobling, David. *The Sense of Biblical Narrative: Structural Analysis in the Hebrew Bible.* JSOTSup 37. Sheffield: JSOT Press, vol. 2, 1986.

————. "Structuralist Criticism: The Text's World of Meaning." Pages 91-118 in *Judges and Method: New Approaches in Biblical Studies.* Edited by Gale A. Yee, Minneapolis: Fortress Press, 1995.

Jobling, David, Peggy Day, and Gerald Sheppard, eds. *The Bible and the Politics of Exegesis.* Cleveland: Pilgrim Press, 1991.

Jobling, William Jeffree. *Canaan, Ugarit and the Old Testament.* Thesis. Sydney University, 1974.

Jones, G. H. "The Concept of Holy War." Pages 299-321 in *The World of Ancient Israel: Sociological, Anthropological and Political Perspectives.* Edited by R. E. Clements. Cambridge: Cambridge University Press, 1989.

Jones-Warsaw, Koala. "Toward a Womanist Hermeneutic: A Reading of Judges 19-21." Pages 172-86 in *A Feminist Companion to Judges.* Edited by Athalya Brenner. Sheffield: JSOT Press, 1993.

Jull, Tom A. "מקדרה in Judges 3: A Scatological Reading." *JSOT* 81 (1998): 63-75.

Jung, C. J. "On the Psychology of the Trickster Figure" (1956). Pages 195-211 in *The Trickster: A Study in American Indian Mythology.* Edited by Paul Radin. New York: Schocken Books, 1956, 1972.

Jüngling, Hans-Winfried. "Richter 19—Ein Plädoyer für das Königtum. Stilistische Analyse der Tendenzerzählung Ri 19,1-30a; 21,25." (*Analecta Biblica,* 84.) Rome: Biblical Institute Press, 1981.

Kahn, Coppélia. "Travesties and the Importance of Being Stoppard." In *Comedy High and Low: An Introduction to the Experience of Comedy.* Edited by Maurice Charney. New York: Oxford University Press, 1978.

Kaiser, Walter C., Jr. *Toward Old Testament Ethics.* Grand Rapids, Mich.: Academic Books, 1093.

Kamuf, Peggy. "Author of a Crime." Pages 187-207 in *A Feminist Companion to Judges.* Edited by Athalya Brenner. Sheffield: JSOT Press, 1993.

Kane, Robert H. *The Quest for Meaning: Value, Ethics, and the Modern Experience.* (Audio tapes.) Springfield, Va.: The Teaching Company, 1999.

Kapelrud, Arvid. *The Ras Shamra Discoveries and the Old Testament.* Oxford: Basil Blackwell, 1965.

———. *The Violent Goddess.* Oslo: Universitetsforlaget 1969.

Kayser, Wolfgang. *The Grotesque in Art and Literature.* Translated by Ulrich Weisstein. Bloomington, Ind.: Indiana University Press, 1957, 1963.

Keel, Othmar and Christoph Uehlinger. *Gods, Goddesses, and Images of God in Ancient Israel.* Minneapolis: Fortress Press, 1998.

Kel, C. F. and Delitzsch, F. *Commentary on the Old Testament.* Vol. 2. Grand Rapids, Mich.: Eerdmans. [1978] (Reprint.)

Kerényi, Karl. "The Trickster in Relation to Greek Mythology" (1956). Pages 173-91 *The Trickster: A Study in American Indian Mythology.* Edited by Paul Radin. New York: Schocken Books, 1956, 1972.

Kermode, Frank. *Genesis of Secrecy.* Cambridge, Mass.: Harvard University Press, 1979.

Kern, Edith. *The Absolute Comic.* New York: Columbia University Press, 1980.

Khanjian, John. "Wisdom." In *Ras Shamra Parallels.* Edited by Loren I. Fisher. Roma: Pontificium Institutum Biblicum. I (1972), II (1975).

Kirk, G. S. *Myth: Its Meaning and Functions in Ancient and Other Cultures.* Cambridge: Cambridge University Press, 1970.

Klein, Lillian R. "The Book of Judges: Paradigm and Deviation in Images of Women." Pages 54-71 in *A Feminist Companion to Judges.* Edited by Athalya Brenner. Sheffield: JSOT Press, 1993.

———. *The Triumph of Irony in the Book of Judges.* Sheffield: The Almond Press, 1988.

Knauf, Ernst Axel. "Eglon and Ophrah: Two Toponymic Notes on the Book of Judges." *JSOT* 51 (1991): 25-44.

Knox, Bernard. "Greece à la Française." *NYRB* 30 (Mar 3, 1983): 26-30.

Koestler, Arthur. "Humor and Wit." *EBM* IX (1979) 5-11.

Kohlenberger, John R., ed. *The NIV Interlinear Hebrew-English Old Testament.* Vol. II Joshua-2 Kings. Grand Rapids, Mich.: Zondervan, 1979.

van der Kooij, Arie. "'And I Said': A New Interpretation of Judges II 3." *VT* 45 (1995) 194-306.

———. "On Male and Female Views in Judges 4 and 5." Pages 153-152 in *On Reading Prophetic Texts: Gender-Specific and Related Studies in Memory of Fokkelien van Dijk-Hemmes.* Edited by Bob Becking and Meindert Dijkstra. Leiden: Brill, 1996.

Korpel, M. C. A. *A Rift in the Clouds: Ugaritic and Hebrew Descriptions of the Divine.* UBL 8. Münster: Ugarit-Verlag, 1990.

———. "Exegesis in the Work of Ilimilku of Ugarit." Pages 86-111 in *Intertextuality in Ugarit and Israel.* Edited by Johannes C. de Moor. Leiden: Brill, 1998.

Kuhn, T. S. *The Structure of Scientific Revolutions.* Chicago: University of Chicago Press, 1962.

La Belle, Maurice Marc. *Alfred Jarry: Nihilism and the Theater of the Absurd.* New York: New York University Press, 1980.

Lakoff, George, and Mark Johnson. *Metaphors We Live By.* Chicago: University of Chicago Press, 1980.

Landers, Solomon. "Did Jephthah Kill His Daughter?"*BR* 7 (April 1991): 28-31, 42.

Landy, Francis. "Humor as a Tool for Biblical Exegesis." Pages 100-15 in *On Humour and the Comic in the Hebrew Bible.* Edited by Yehuda Radday and Athalya Brenner. Sheffield: Almond Press, 1990. [Originally published under the title "Humour,' *Jewish Quarterly* 28.1 (1980): 13-19.]

Langer, Susanne. "The Comic Rhythm. Pages 67-83 in *Comedy: Meaning and Form.* Edited by Robert W. Corrigan. 2nd ed. New York: Harper and Row, 1981.

Larmore, Charles. "The Visible Hand" (review of Charles L. Griswold Jr., *Adam Smith and the Virtues of Enlightenment).TNR* (Oct. 18, 1999): 42-45.

Lasine, Stuart. "Guest and Host in Judges 19: Lot's Hospitality in an Inverted World." *JSOT* 29 (1984): 37-59.

Laughlin, John C. H. *Archaeology and the Bible.* London and New York: Routledge, 2000.

Lemche, Niels Peter. "From Patronage Society to Patronage Society." Pages 106-20 in *The Origins of the Ancient Israelite States.* Edited by Fritz Volkmar and Philip R. Davies. JSOTSup 228. Sheffield: Sheffield Academic Press, 1996.

_____. *Ancient Israel: A New History of Israelite Society.* The Biblical Seminar, 5. Sheffield: Sheffield Academic Press, 1988.

_____. *The Canaanites and Their Land: The Tradition of the Canaanites.* JSOTSup 110. Sheffield: Sheffield Academic Press, 1991.

_____. "Clio is Also among the Muses! K. W. Whitelam and the History of Palestine: A Review and a Commentary," SJOT 10 (1996): 88-119. [Also pages 124-51 in *Can a 'History of Israel' Be Written?* Edited by Lester L. Grabbe. JSOTSup 245. Sheffield: Sheffield Academic Press, 1999.]

_____. *The Israelites in History and Tradition.* Louisville, Ky.: Westminster John Knox Press, 1998.

Lerer, Seth. *Comedy Through the Ages* (Audio Tapes). [Chantilly, Va.:] The Teaching Company, 2000.

Levin, Harry. *Playboys and Killjoys: An Essay on the Theory and Practice of Comedy.* New York, Oxford: Oxford University Press, 1987.

Levin, M. Z. "A Protest Against Rape in the Story of Deborah." *Beth Mikra* 25 (1979): 83-84. [in Hebrew]

Lewis, Theodore J. "The Identity and Function of El/Baal Berith." *JBL* 115 (1996): 401-23.

Lindars, Barnabas. "Deborah's Song: Women in the Old Testament." *BJRL* 65 (1983): 158-75.

_____. *Judges 1-5: A New Translation and Commentary.* Edited by A. D. H. Mayes. Edinburgh: T & T Clark, 1995.

————. "The Israelite Tribes in Judges." Pages 95-112 in *Studies in the Historical Books of the Old Testament* (SVT 30, ed.). Edited by A. Emerton. Leiden: Brill, 1979.

Long, G. O., ed. *Images of Man and God: Old Testament Short Stories in Literary Focus.* Sheffield: Almond Press, 1981.

Loretz, Ozwald. *Ugarit und Die Bibel: Kanaanaische Gotter und Religion im Alten Testament.* Darmstadt: Wissenschaftliche Buchegesellschaft, 1990.

Löwenstamm, Samuel E. "Ugarit and The Bible, Pt. 1." *Bib* 56, 1 (1975): 103-19.

————. "Ugarit and The Bible, Pt. 2." *Bib* 59, 1 (1978): 100-22.

McGinn, Colin. Review of T. M. Scanlon, *What We Owe to Each Other* (Harvard University Press, 1999). *TNR* (May 24, 1999): 34-38.

Macintosh, A. A. "The Meaning of *Mklym* in Judges XVIII 7." *VT* 35 (1985): 68-77.

MacIntyre, Alasdair. *After Virtue: A Study in Moral Theory.* Notre Dame, Ind.: University of Notre Dame Press, 1981.

McKay, Heather A. "On the Future of Feminist Biblical Criticism." Pages 61-83 in *A Feminist Companion to Reading the Bible: Approaches, Methods and Strategies.* Edited by Athlaya Brenner and Carole Fontaine. Sheffield: Sheffield Academic Press, 1997.

McKenzie, John L. *The World of the Judges.* Englewood Cliffs, N.J.: Prentice-Hall, 1966.

McKenzie, Stephen L. *King David: A Biography.* New York: Oxford University Press, 2000.

————. and M. Patrick Graham, eds. *The Hebrew Bible Today: An Introduction to Critical Issues.* Louisville, Ky.: Westminster John Knox Press, 2000.

————. *The History of Israel's Traditions: The Heritage of Martin Noth.* JSOTSup 182. Sheffield: Sheffield Academic Press, 1994.

Maier, Walter A., III. *'Ašerah: Extrabiblical Evidence.* HSM 37. Atlanta, Ga.: Scholars Press, 1986.

Malamat, Abraham. "Ch. 7 Charismatic Leadership in the Book of Judges." Pages 153-168 in *Magnalia Dei: The Mighty Acts of God. Studies . . . G. E. Wright.* Edited by Frank M. Cross et al. Garden City, N.Y.: Doubleday (1976). [Also pages 151-170 in Abraham Malamat, *History of Bliblical Israel: Major Problems and Minor Issues.* Leiden: Brill, 2001.]

————. *History of Bliblical Israel: Major Problems and Minor Issues.* Leiden: Brill, 2001. [All the essays in this book were written from the 1950s through the 1970s.]

Marais, Jacobus. *Representation in Old Testament Narrative Texts.* Leiden: Brill, 1998.

Marcus, David. *Jephthah and His Vow.* Lubbock, Tex.: Texas Tech, 1986.

————. "The Legal Dispute Between Jephthah and the Elders." *Hebrew Annual Review* 12 (1990): 105-14.

Margalit, Baruch. "The Geographical Setting of the Aqhat Story and Its Ramifications." Pages 131-58 in *Ugarit in Retrospect: Fifty Years of Ugarit and Ugaritic.* Edited by D. G. Young. Winona Lake, Ind.: Eisenbrauns, 1981.

————. "The Legend of Keret." Pages 203-233 in *Handbook of Ugaritic Studies.* Edited by Wilfred G. E. Watson and Nicolas Wyatt. Cologne: Brill, 1999.

———. "The Meaning and Significance of Asherah." *VT* (1990): 264-97.

———. "Observations on the Jael-Sisera Story (Judges 4-5)." Pages 629-41 in *Shechem: The Biography of a Biblical City.* Edited by Ernest G. Wright. New York: McGraw-Hill, 1965.

———. *The Ugaritic Poem of AQHT: Text, Translation, Commentary.* Berlin: De Gruyter, 1989.

Margalith, Othniel. "The Legends of Samson/Heracles." *VT* 37 (1987): 63-70.

———. "More Samson Legends." *VT* 36 (1986): 397-405.

———. "Samson's Foxes." *VT* 35 (1985): 224-29.

———. "Samson's Riddle and Samson's Magic Locks." *VT* 36 (1986): 225-34.

Margulis [Margalit], B. "An Exegesis of Judges V 8a." *VT* 15 (1965): 66-72.

Markos, Louis. *From Plato to Postmodernism: Understanding the Essence of Literature and the Role of the Author.* (Audio Tapes.) Springfield, Va.: The Teaching Company, 1999.

Marks, J. H. and R. M. Good, eds. *Love and Death in the Ancient Near East: Essays in Honor of Marvin H. Pope.* Guilford, Conn.: Four Quarters, 1987.

Martin, James D. *The Book of Judges* (commentary with NEB translation). New York: Cambridge University Press, 1975.

Mason, Wyatt. "Flying Up and Flying Down: The rise and fall of the American superhero." Review of Sean Howe, ed., *Give Our Regards to the Atomsmashers! Writers on Comics* (Pantheon, 2003); Arler Schumer *The Silver Age of Comic Book Art* (Collectors Press, 2003); and Chip Kidd and Geoff Spear, *Mythology: The DC Comics Art of Alex Ross (Pantheon, 2003). Harper's* (August 2004), 77-83.

Matthews, Victor H. "Freedom and Entrapment in the Samson Narrative: A Literary Analysis." *Perspectives in Religious Studies,* 15-16 (1988-1989): 245-57.

———. "Hospitality and Hostility in Genesis 19 and Judges 19." *Biblical Theology Bulletin,* 22 (1992): 3-11.

———. "Hospitality and Hostility in Judges 4." *BTB,* 21 (1991): 13-21.

———. "Jael: Host or Judge?" *BT* 30 (1992), 291-296.

———. *Judges and Ruth.* Cambridge, Eng.: Cambridge University Press, 2004.

Matthews, Victor H. and Don C. Benjamin.*Old Testament Parallels: Laws and Stories from the Ancient Near East.* Rev. and expanded 2nd ed. New York: Paulist Press, 1997.

———. *Social World of Ancient Israel 1250-587 BCE.* Peabody, Mass.: Hendrickson, 1993.

van der Meer, W. and J. C. de Moor, eds. *The Structural Analysis of Biblical and Canaanite Poetry.* JSOTSup 74. Sheffield: Sheffield Academic Press, 1988.

Megill, Allan. *Prophets of Extremity: Nietzsche, Heidegger, Foucault, Derrida.* Berkeley: U. of CA Press, 1985.

Mendelsohn, Daniel. "Double Take: *The Producers,* a musical at the St. James Theatre, New York City," NYRB 48 (June 21, 2001): 14.

Merideth, Betsy. "Desire and Danger: The Drama of Betrayal in Judges and Judith." Pages 63-78 in *Anti-Covenant: Counter-Reading Women's Lives in the Hebrew Bible.* Edited by Mieke Bal. Sheffield: Almond Press, 1989.

Miles, Jack. Review of Stephen L. McKenzie, *King David: A Biography*. *NYTBR* (June 18, 2000): 11.

Millard, A. R. et al., eds. *Faith, Tradition, and History: Old Testament Historiography in the Near Eastern Context*. Winona Lake, Ind.: Eisenbrauns, 1994.

Miller, David L. *Gods and Games: Toward a Theology of Play*. New York: World Publishing Company, 1970.

Miller, Patrick D. "The Absence of the Goddess in Israelite Religion." *HAR* 10 (1986): 239-48.

————. "Aspects of the Religion of Ugarit." In *Ancient Israelite Religion: Essays in Honor of Frank Moore Cross*. Edited by Patrick D. Miller, Jr. Paul D., and S. Dean McBride. Philadelphia: Augsburg Fortress Press, 1987.

————. *The Religion of Ancient Israel*. Louisville, Ky.: Westminster John Knox Press, 2000.

Miller, Patrick D. Jr., Paul D. Hanson, and S. Dean McBride, eds. *Ancient Israelite Religion: Essays in Honor of Frank Moore Cross*. Philadelphia: Augsburg Fortress, 1987.

Milne, Paula J. "Toward Feminist Companionship: The Future of Feminist Biblical Studies and Feminism. Pages 39-60 in *A Feminist Companion to Reading the Bible: Approaches, Methods and Strategies*. Edited by Athlaya Brenner and Carole Fontaine. Sheffield: Sheffield Academic Press, 1997.

Minkoff, Harvey. "Coarse Language in the Bible?" *BR* (April 1989): 22-27, 44.

Mobley, Gregory. "The Wild Man in the Bible and the Ancient Near East." *JBL* (1997): 217-33.

Mohamed, Feisal G. "Confronting Religious Violence: Milton's *Samson Agonistes*. *PMLA* (March 2005): 327-340.

de Moor, Johannes C. *An Anthology of Religious Texts from Ugarit*. Leiden: Brill, 1987.

————. ed. *Intertextuality in Ugarit and Israel*. Leiden: Brill, 1998.

————. *The Rise of Yahwism: The Roots of Israelite Monotheism*. Rev. and Enlarged Ed. Leuven: Leuven University Press, 1997.

————. *The Seasonal Pattern in the Ugaritic Myth of Ba'lu According to the Version of Ilimilku*. Kevelaer: Verlag Butzon and Bercker, 1971.

————. "Seventy! Pages 199-203 in *'Und Mose schrieb dieses Lied auf . . . '. Studie zum Alten Testament und zum Alten Orient. Festschrift für O. Loretz zur Vollendung seines 70. Lebensjahres mit Beiträgen von Freunden, Schülern und Kollegen*. Edited by M. Dietrich and I. Kottsieper. AOAT 250, Münster: Ugarit-Verlag, 1998.

————. "The Twelve Tribes in the Song of Deborah." *VT* 43 (1993) 483-93.

————. "Ugarit and Israelite Origins." Pages 295-338 in *Intertextuality in Ugarit and Israel*. Edited by Johannes C. de Moor. Leiden: Brill, 1998.

Morson, Gary Saul. "Contingency and the Literature of Process."Pages 250-172 in *Bakhtin and the Classics*. Edited by R. Bracht Branham. Northwestern University Press: Evanston, Ill., 2002.

Mullen, E. Theodore, Jr. "The 'Minor Judges': Some Literary and Historical Considerations." *CBQ* 44 (Apr 1982): 185-201.

Murphy, Cullen. "Lulu, Queen of Camels." *Atlantic*, 284 (Oct. 1999): 72-82.

Murray, D. F. "The Deborah-Barak Story." Pages 155-189 in *Studies in the Historical Books of the Old Testament* (SVT 30, ed.). Edited by A. Emerton. Leiden: Brill, 1979.

———. "Narrative Structure and Technique in the Deborah-Barak Story (Judges IV 4-22)." Pages 155-89 in *Studies in the Historical Books of the Old Testament* (SVT 30, ed.). Edited by A. Emerton. Leiden: Brill, 1979.

Murray, Patrick. *Literary Criticism, a Glossary of Major Terms.* Dublin: Longmans, 1978.

Myers, Jacob M., ed. "Judges: Introduction and Exegesis." *The Interpreter's Bible*, II. New York and Nashville: Abingdon, 1973.

Na'aman, Nadav. "Sources and Composition in the History of David." Pages 170-86 in *The Origins of the Ancient Israelite States.* Edited by Fritz Volkmar and Philip R. Davies. JSOTSup 228. Sheffield: Sheffield Academic Press, 1996.

———. "Literary and Topographical Notes on the Battle of Kishon (Judges IV-V)." *VT* 40 (1990): 423-36.

Neef, Heinz-Dieter. "Der Sieg Deboras und Baraks über Sisera (Jdc 4,1-24)." *ZAW* 101 (1989): 28-49.

Newsom, C. A. and S. H. Ringe. *The Women's Bible Commentary.* Louisville, Ky.: Westminster John Knox Press, 1992.

Niditch, Susan. *Ancient Israelite Religion.* New York: Oxford, 1997.

———. "Eroticism and Death in the Tale of Jael." Pages 305-15 in *Women in the Hebrew Bible.* Edited by Alice Bach. New York: Routledge, 1999. [Also in Peggy Day, ed., 43-57.]

———. *Folklore and the Hebrew Bible.* Guide to Biblical Scholarship: Old Testament Series. Minneapolis: Fortress Press, 1993.

———. "Samson as Culture Hero, Trickster, and Bandit: The Empowerment of the Weak." *CBQ* 52 (1990): 608-24.

———. "The 'Sodomite' Theme in Judges 19-20: Family, Community and Social Disintegration." *CBQ* 44 (1982): 365-78.

———, ed. *Text and Tradition: The Hebrew Bible and Folklore.* Atlanta, Ga.: Scholars Press, 1990.

———. *War in the Hebrew Bible.* New York: Oxford, 1993.

Niemann, Hermann Michell. "Zorah, Eshtaol, Beth-Shemesh and Dan's Migration to the South: a Region and its Traditions in the Late Bronze and Iron Ages." *JSOT* 86 (1999): 25-48.

O'Brien, Mark. "Judges and the Deuteronomic History." Pages 235-59 in *The History of Israel's Traditions: The Heritage of Martin Noth.* Edited by Stephen L. McKenzie and M. Patrick Graham. JSOTSup 182. Sheffield: Sheffield Academic Press, 1994.

O'Connell, Robert H. "Proverbs VII 16-17: A Case of Fatal Deception in a 'Woman and the Window' Type-Scene." VT 41 (1991): 235-41.

O'Connor, M. "The Women in the Book of Judges."*HAR* 10 (1986): 277-94.

_____. *The Rhetoric of the Book of Judges*. Leiden: E. J. Brill, 1996.

Oldenburg, Ulf. *The Conflict Between El and Ba'al in Canaanite Religion*. Leiden: E. J. Brill, 1969.

del Olmo Lete, Gregorio. *Canaanite Religion according to the Liturgical Texts of Ugarit*. Revised ed. of 1992. Bethesda, Md.: CDL Press, 1999.

Olsen, Dennis T. "Dialogues of Life and Monologues of Death: Jephthah and Jephthah's Daughter in Judges 10:6-12:7." Pages 43-54 in *Postmodern Interpretations of the Bible—a Reader*. Edited by A. K. M. Adam. St. Louis, Mo.: The Chalice Press, 2001.

Olyan, Saul M. *Asherah and the Cult of Yahweh in Israel*. Scholars Press: Atlanta, Ga. 1988.

Oren, E. "The Samson Stories." *Beth Mikra*, 25 (1980): 259-62 [Hebrew].

Otzen, Benedikt, Hans Gottlieb, and Knud Jeppersen. *Myths in the Old Testament*. Translated by Frederick Cryer. London: SCM Press, 1980.

Owen, David. "Taking Humor Seriously: George Meyer, the Funniest Man on TV." *The New Yorker*, March 13, 2000, 64-74.

Owen, David I. "Ugarit, Canaan, and Egypt: Some New Epigraphic Evidence from Tel Aphek in Israel." Pages 52-53 in *Ugarit in Retrospect: Fifty Years of Ugarit and Ugaritic*. Edited by D. G. Young. Winona Lake, Ind.: Eisenbrauns, 1981.

Pachet, Pierre. [Article on Vidal-Naquet.] *Esprit* (March 1982): 213-30.

Page, Hugh Rowland. *The Myth of Cosmic Rebellion: A Study of its Reflexes in Ugaritic and Biblical Literature*. Leiden: Brill, 1996.

Parker, Simon B. *The Pre-Biblical Narrative Tradition: Essays on the Ugaritic Poems "Keret" and "Aqhat."* SBL Resources for Biblical Study 24. Atlanta, Ga.: Scholars Press, 1989.

_____, ed. *Ugaritic Narrative Poetry*. Translated by Mark S. Smith, Simon B. Parker, Edward L. Greenstein, Theodore J. Lewis, and David Marcus. Atlanta, Ga.: Scholars,1997.

_____. "The Vow in Ugaritic and Israelite Narrative Literature." *UF*, 11 (1980): 693-700.

Payne, J. B. *"Judges." The New Bible Dictionary*. London (1965): 676-79.

Penchansky, David. "Staying the Night: Intertextuality in Genesis and Judges." Pages 77-97 in *Reading Between Texts: Intertextuality and the Hebrew Bible*. Edited by Danna Nolan Fewell. Louisville, Ky: Westminster, 1990.

_____. "Up for Grabs: A Tentative Proposal for Doing Ideological Criticism." *Semeia* 59 (1992): 35-42.

Petersen, Allan Rosengren. *The Royal God: Enthronement Festivals in Ancient Israel and Ugarit?* JSOTSup 259. Sheffield: Sheffield Academic Press, 1998.

Petr, Pavel, David Roberts, and Philip Thomson. *Comic Relations: Studies in the Comic, Satire and Parody*. Frankfurt: Peter Lang, 1985.

Pinker, Steven. *How the Mind Works*. New York: Norton,1997.

Plato, "The Ion." Pages 937-949 in *Plato: Complete Works*. Edited by John M. Cooper. Indianapolis/Cambridge: Hackett Publishing Company, 1997.

Polliack, Meira. Review of Yair Amit, *The Book of Judges: the Art of Editing* (1992). *VT* 45 (1995): 392-98.

Polzin, Robert. *Moses and the Deuteronomist: A Literary Study of the Deuteronomic History, Part One: Deuteronomy, Joshua, Judges*. New York: Seabury, 1980.

Pope, Marvin H. "The Cult of the Dead at Ugarit." Pages 139-79 in *Ugarit in Retrospect: Fifty Years of Ugarit and Ugaritic*. Edited by D. G. Young. Winona Lake, Ind.: Eisenbrauns, 1981.

———. "The Status of El at Ugarit." *UF*, 19 (1987): 219-30.

Porter, J. "Samson's Riddle: Judges XIV, 14, 18." *JTS* 13 (1962): 106-09.

Porter, S. E. and C. A. Evans, eds. *The Scrolls and the Scriptures*. RILP, 3; JSPSup, 26; Sheffield: Sheffield Academic Press, 1997.

Posner, Richard A. *Law and Literature*. Rev. and Enlarged Edition. Cambridge, Mass.: Harvard University Press, 1998.

Power, E. S. I. "'He Asked for Water, Milk She Gave,' (Iud. 5,25)." *Bib* 9 (1928): 47.

Pratt, Alan R., ed. *Black Humor: Critical Essays*. New York and London: Garland Press, 1993.

Preminger, Alex and Edward L. Greenstein, eds. *The Hebrew Bible in Literary Criticism*. New York: Ungar, 1986.

Prouser, O. Horn. "The Truth about Women and Lying." *JSOT* 61 (1994): 15-28.

Provan, Iain W. "Ideologies, Literary and Critical: Reflections on Recent Writing on the History of Israel." *JBL* 114 (Winter 1995): 585-606.

Rabin, Chaim. "Judges V, 2 and the 'Ideology' of Deborah's War." *JJS* (London) 6 (1955): 125-34.

Radday, Yehuda T., et al. "The Book of Judges Examined by Statistical Linguistics." *Bib* 58 (1977): 469-99.

———. "Humour in Names." Pages 59-97 in *On Humour and the Comic in the Hebrew Bible*. Edited by Yehuda T. Radday and Athalya Brenner. Sheffield: Almond Press, 1990.

———. "On Missing the Humour in the Bible: an Introduction." Pages 21-38 in *On Humour and the Comic in the Hebrew Bible*. Edited by Yehuda T. Radday and Athalya Brenner. Sheffield: Almond Press, 1990.

——— and Athalya Brenner, eds. *On Humour and the Comic in the Hebrew Bible*. Sheffield: Almond Press, 1990.

——— and Athalya Brenner. "Isaac, Samson, and Saul: On the Comic and Tragic Visions." *Semeia* 32 (1984): 117-59.

———. G.M. Leb, and L. Natzitz. *An Analytical Linguistic Key-Word-in-Context Concordance to the Book of Judges*. [n.p.:] Biblical Research Associates, 1977.

Radin, Paul. *The Trickster: A Study in American Indian Mythology*. New York: Schocken Books, 1956, 1972.

Rasmussen, Rachel C. "Deborah the Woman Warrior." Pages 79-93 in *Anti-Covenant: Counter-Reading Women's Lives in the Hebrew Bible*. Edited by Mieke Bal. Sheffield: Almond Press, 1989.

Rauber, D. F. "Literary Value in the Bible: The Book of Ruth." *JBL* 89 (1975): 27-37.

Reinhartz, Adele. "Feminist Criticism and Biblical Studies on the Verge of the Twenty-First Century." Pages 30-38 in *A Feminist Companion to Reading the Bible: Approaches, Methods and Strategies*. Edited by Athlaya Brenner and Carole Fontaine. Sheffield: Sheffield Academic Press, 1997.

————. "Samson's Mother: An Unnamed Protagonist." *JSOT* 55 (1992): 25-37. Also pages 157-70 in *A Feminist Companion to Judges*. Edited by Athalya Brenner. Sheffield: JSOT Press, 1993.

Revell, E. J. "The Battle with Benjamin (Judges XX 29-48) and Hebrew Narrative Technique." *VT* 35 (1985): 417-33.

Reventlow, Henning Graf et al., eds. *Politics and Theopolitics in the Bible and Postbiblical Literature*. JSOTSup 171. Sheffield: JSOT Press, 1994.

Richter, Wolfgang. *Die Bearbeitungen des "Retterbuches" in der Deuteronomischer Epoche*. Bonn: P. Hanstein, 1964.

————. *Traditionsgeschichtliche Undersuchungen zum Richterbuch*. Bonn: P. Hanstein, 1963.

Ricoeur, Paul. *Paul Ricoeur on Biblical Hermeneutics*. *Semeia* 4. Scholars Press, 1975.

Ridley, Matt, *The Origins of Virtue: Human Instincts and the Evolution of Cooperation*, New York: Penguin, 1997.

Ringgren, Helmer. *Religions of the Ancient Near East*. Translated by John Sturdy. Philadelphia: Westminster, 1973.

Robinson, Daniel N. "Roman, the Stoics, and the Rule of Law," in *The Great Ideas of Philosophy*, Part II, Lecture 15. (Audio tapes.) Springfield, Va.: The Teaching Company, Ltd., 1997.

Römer, Thomas C. "The Book of Deuteronomy." Pages 178-212 in *The History of Israel's Traditions: The Heritage of Martin Noth*. Edited by Stephen L. McKenzie and M. Patrick Graham. JSOTSup 182. Sheffield: Sheffield Academic Press, 1994.

————. "Why Would the Deuteronomists Tell About the Sacrifice of Jephthah's Daughter?" *JSOT* 77 (1998): 27-38.

Rose, Margaret A. *Parody//Meta-Fiction: an Analysis of Parody as a Critical Mirror to the Writing and Reception of Fiction*. London: Croom Helm, 1979.

Rösel, Hartmut N. "Jephthah und das Problem der Richter." *Bib* 61 (1980): 251-55.

————. "Überlegungen zu Abimelech und Sichem im Jdc. ix."*VT* 33 (1982): 500-3.

Rosenbaum, Ron. "Degrees of Evil: Some thoughts on Hitler, bin Laden, and the hierarchy of wickedness." *Atlantic*, 289 (February 2002): 66.

Sasson, Jack M. "Flora, Fauna, and Minerals." Pages 353-482 in *Ras Shamra Parallels*. Edited by Loren I. Fisher. Roma: Pontificium Institutum Biblicum. I (1972), II (1975).

————. "Literary Criticism, Folklore Scholarship, and Ugaritic Literature" Pages 81-98 in *Ugarit in Retrospect: Fifty Years of Ugarit and Ugaritic*. Edited by D. G. Young. Winona Lake, Ind.: Eisenbrauns, 1981.

————. *Ruth. A New Translation with Philological Commentary and a Formalist-Folklorist Interpretation*. Baltimore: Johns Hopkins, 1979.

Satterthwaite, P. E. "Narrative Artistry in the Composition of Judges XX 29ff." *VT* 42 (1992): 80-89.

Sawyer, John F. A. "From Heaven Fought the Stars (Judges 20)." *VT* 31 (1981): 87-89.

Scarry, Elaine. *The Body in Pain: The Making and Unmaking of the World.* New York: Oxford University Press, 1985.

Schaafsma, Roberta. "A Model for Israel." *BT* 31 (1993): 208-212

Schäfer-Lichtenberger, Christa. "Sociological and Biblical Views of the Early State." Pages 78-105 in *The Origins of the Ancient Israelite States.* Edited by Fritz Volkmar and Philip R. Davies. JSOTSup 228. Sheffield: Sheffield Academic Press, 1996.

Schiltknecht, Hans R. "Ehud der Linnkshänder." *Reformatio,* 30 (Nov-Dec 1981): 637-40.

Schley, D. G. *Shiloh: A Biblical City in Tradition and History.* JSOTSup 63 Sheffield: Sheffield Academic Press, 1989.

Schloen, J. David. "Caravans, Kenites, and *Casus belli*: Enmity and Alliance in the Song of Deborah." *CBQ* 55 (1991): 18-38.

_____. *The House of the Father as Fact and Symbol: Patrimonialism in Ugarit and the Ancient Near East.* Winona Lake, Ind: Eisenbrauns, 2001.

Schneidau, H. N. *Biblical Narrative and Modern Consciousness.* Pages 132-150 in *The Bible and the Narrative Tradition.* Edited by F. McConnell. New York: Oxford University Press, 1986.

Schneider, Tammi J. *Judges.* (Berit Olam: Studies in Hebrew Narrative & Poetry.) Collegeville, MN: The Liturgical Press, 2000.

Schwartz, Regina, ed. *The Book and the Text: The Bible and Literary Theory.* Oxford: Basil Blackwell, 1990.

Segal, Erich. *The Death of Comedy.* Cambridge, Mass.: Harvard University Press, 2001.

Segert, Stanislav. "Paronomasia in the Samson Narrative in Judges XIII-XVI." *VT* 34 (1984): 454-61.

Shershow, Scott. *Laughing Matters.* Amherst: University of Massachusetts Press, 1986.

Shupak, Nili. "New Light on Shamgar ben 'Anath." *Bib* 70 (1989): 517-25.

Singer, Peter, ed. *Ethics.* Oxford: Oxford University Press, 1994.

Sjursen, H. "Excess of Sorrow Laughs." Pages 82-102 in *The Masks of Comedy.* Edited by Ann Boaden. Rock Island, Ill.: Augustana College Library, 1980.

Skinner, B. F. *Verbal Behavior.* New York, Appleton-Century, 1957.

Slotkin, Edgar. "Response to Professors Fontaine and Camp." Pages 153-59 in *Text and Tradition: The Hebrew Bible and Folklore.* Edited by Susan Niditch. Atlanta, Ga.: Scholars Press, 1990.

Smith, Carol. "Biblical Perspectives." JSOT 93 (2001): 93-110.

_____. "Challenged by the Text: Interpreting Two Stories of Incest in the Hebrew Bible." Pages 114-135 in *A Feminist Companion to Reading the Bible: Approaches, Methods and Strategies.* Edited by Athlaya Brenner and Carole Fontaine. Sheffield: Sheffield Academic Press, 1997.

_____. "Samson and Delilah: A Parable of Power?" *JSOT* 76 (1997): 45-57.

Smith, Mark S. "Baal's Cosmic Secret." *UF* 16 (1984): 295-98.

————. *The Early History of God: Yahweh and the Other Deities in Ancient Israel.* 2nd ed. Grand Rapids, Mich.: Eerdmans, 2002.

————. "The God Athtar in the Ancient Near East and His Place in KTU 1.6.I." Pages 627-640 in *Solving Riddles and Untying Knots: Biblical Epigraphic and Semitic Studies in Honor of J. C. Greenfield.* Edited by Z. Zevit et al. Winona Lake, Ind.: Eisenbrauns, 1995.

————. "Interpreting the Baal Cycle." *UF*, 18 (1986): 313-39.

————. *The Origins of Biblical Monotheism: Israel's Polytheistic Background and the Ugaritic Texts.* Oxford: Oxford University Press, 2001.

————. *The Ugaritic Baal Cycle.* Vol. 1, SVT, 55. Leiden: Brill, 1994.

Snaith, N. H. "The Altar at Gilgal: Joshua xxii 23-29." *VT* 28 (1978): 330-35.

Soggin, J. Alberto. *An Introduction to the History of Israel und Judah.* London: SCM Press, 1993.

————. "Ehud und Eglon: Bemerkungen zu Richter III 11b-31." *VT* 39 (1989): 95-100.

————. *Judges: A Commentary.* Translated by John S. Bowden. Philadelphia: Westminster Press, 1981.

Spina, Frank Anthony. "The Dan Story Historically Reconsidered." *JSOT* 4 (1977): 60-71.

Stager, Lawrence E. "The Song of Deborah: Why Some Tribes Answered the Call and Others Did Not." *BAR* (1989): 51-64.

Steinberg, Naomi. "The Problem of Human Sacrifice in War: An Analysis of Judges 11." Pages 114-135 in *On the Way to Nineveh,* edited by Stephen L. Cook and S. C. Winter. ASOR Books, Vol. 4. Atlanta, Ga.: Scholars Press, 1999.

————. "Social Scientific Criticism." Pages 45-64 in *Judges and Method: New Approaches in Biblical Studies.* Edited by Gale A. Yee, Minneapolis: Fortress Press, 1995.

Sternberg, Meir. *The Poetics of Biblical Narrative.* Bloomington, Ind.: Indiana University Press, 1987.

Stewart, Susan. *Nonsense: Aspects of Intertextuality in Folklore and Literature.* Baltimore: Johns Hopkins, 1979.

Steyn, J. "Simson in Gasa (Rigters 16:1-3)." *TE* 11 (1978): 13-21.

Stipp, Hermann-Josef. "Simson, der Nasiräer." *VT* 45 (1995): 335-69.

Stone, Ken. "Gender and Homosexuality in Judges 19: Subject-Honor, Object-Shame." *JSOT* 67 (1995): 87-107.

Stuhlmueller, Carroll. "Joshua and the great annual festival at Gilgal." *BT* 104 (Nov. 1979).

Sweeney, M. A. "Davidic Polemics in the Book of Judges." *VT* 47 (1997).

Sypher, Wylie, ed. *Comedy.* New York: Doubleday, 1956.

Tanner, J. Paul. "The Gideon Narrative as the Focal Point of Judges." *BS* 149 (1992): 146-61.

Tapp, Anne-Michele. "An Ideology of Expendability: Virgin Daughters Sacrifice in Genesis 19.1-11, Judges 11.30-30 and 19.22-26." Pages 155-74 in *Anti-Covenant: Counter-Reading Women's Lives in the Hebrew Bible.* Edited by Mieke Bal. Sheffield: Almond Press, 1989.

Taylor, Glen. "The Song of Deborah and Two Canaanite Goddesses." *JSOT* 23 (1982): 99-108.

Taylor, Joan E. "The Asherah, the Menorah and the Sacred Tree." *JSOT* 66 (1995): 29-54.

_____. *Yahweh and the Sun: The Biblical and Archaeological Evidence for Sun Worship in Ancient Israel.* JSOTSup 111. Sheffield: Sheffield Academic Press, 19.

Thompson, Thomas L. *Early History of the Israelite People From the Written and Archaeological Sources.* (Studies in the History and Culture of the Ancient Near East, 4.) Leiden: Brill, 1992.

_____. "Historiography of Ancient Palestine and Early Jewish Historiography: W. G. Dever and the Not-So New Biblical Archaeology." Pages 26-43 in *The Origins of the Ancient Israelite States.* Edited by Fritz Volkmar and Philip R. Davies. JSOTSup 228. Sheffield: Sheffield Academic Press, 1996.

_____. "A Neo-Albrightean School in History and Biblical Scholarship?" *JBL* 114 (Winter 1995): 683-98.

_____. "Text, Context and Referent in Israelite Historiography." Pages 65-92 in *The Fabric of History: Text, Artifact and Israel's Past.* Edited by Diana Vikander Edelman. JSOTSup 127. Sheffield: Sheffield Academic Press, 1991.

Thomson, Philip. *The Grotesque (The Critical Idiom).* London: Methuen, 1972.

Tolbert, Mary Anne. "Gender." Pages 100-105 in *Handbook of Postmodern Biblical Interpretation.* Edited by A. K. M. Adam. St. Louis, Mo: The Chalice Press, 2000.

Tollers, V. and J. Maier, eds. *Mappings of the Biblical Terrain,* Lewisberg, Pa.: Bucknell University Press, 1990.

Tollington, Janet E. "The Book of Judges: the Result of Post-Exilic Exegesis?" Pages 186-96 in *Intertextuality in Ugarit and Israel.* Edited by Johannes C. de Moor. Leiden: Brill, 1998.

Toombs, Lawrence E. "Baal, Lord of the Earth: The Ugaritic Baal Epic." Pages 613-623 in *Archaeology and Biblical Interpretation.* Edited by John R. Bartlett. London: Routledge, 1997.

van der Toorn, Karel. *Family Religion in Babylonia, Syria and Israel: Continuity and Change in the Form of Religious Life.* Leiden: Brill, 1996.

_____. "Judges XVI 21 In the Light of the Akkadian Sources." *VT* 36 (1986): 248-51.

Tov, Emmanuel. "The Textual History of the Song of Deborah in the A Text of the LXX." *VT* 28 (1978): 224-32.

Trible, Phyllis. "A Meditation in Mourning—The Sacrifice of the Daughter of Jephthah." *USQR* 36 (1981): 59-73.

_____. *Texts of Terror: Literary-Feminist Readings of Biblical Narratives.* Philadelphia: Fortress Press, 1984.

"Trickster." *EBM* X, 119.

Tsevant, M. "A Window for Baal's House; the Maturing of a God." Pages 151-61 in *Studies in Bible and the Ancient Near East: Presented to Samuel E. Loewenstamm on His Seventieth Birthday.* Edited by Yitschak Avishur and Joshua Blau. Jerusalem: E. Rubinstein's Publishing House, 1978.

Van Dijk-Hemmes, Fokkelien. "Mothers and a Mediator in the Song of Deborah." Pages 110-114 in *A Feminist Companion to Judges*. Edited by Athalya Brenner. Sheffield: JSOT Press, 1993.

Vandiver, Elizabeth. *The "Iliad' of Homer*. (Audio Tapes.) Chantilly, Va.: The Teaching Company, 1999.

van Selms, A. "Judge Shamgar." *VT* 14 (1964): 294-309.

Van Seters, John. *In Search of History: Historiography in the Ancient World and the Origins of Biblical History*. New Haven: Yale University Press, 1983.

Van Wolde, Ellen, "Deborah and Ya'el in Judges 4." Pages 283-295 in *On Reading Prophetic Texts: Gender-Specific and Related Studies in Memory of Fokkelien van Dijk-Hemmes*. Edited by Bob Becking and Meindert Dijkstra. Leiden: Brill, 1996.

Vernant, Jean-Pierre. *The Anthropology of Ancient Greece*. Translated by John Hamilton and Blaise Nagy. Baltimore: Johns Hopkins University Press, 1981.

————. *Tragedy and Myth in Ancient Greece*. Humanities Press, 1981.

Vickery, J. B. "In Strange Ways: The Story of Samson." Pages 58-73 in *Images of Man and God: Old Testament Short Sories in Literary Focus*. Edited by G. O. Long. Sheffield: Almond Press, 1981.

Vidal-Naquet, Jean-Pierre. *Le Chasseur noir: Formes de pensée et forms de société dans le monde grec*. Paris: Maspero, 1982.

Vita, Juan Pablo, "Ch. XI. The Society of Ugarit." Pages 435-498 in *Handbook of Ugaritic Studies*. Edited by Wilfred G. E. Watson and Nicolas Wyatt. Cologne: Brill, 1999.

Volkmar, Fritz. "Abimelech und Sichem in Jdc. IX." *VT* 32 (1982): 129-44.

————. "Monarchy and Re-Urbanization: A New Look at Solomon's Kingdom." Pages 187-95 in *The Origins of the Ancient Israelite States*. Edited by Fritz Volkmar and Philip R. Davies. JSOTSup 228. Sheffield: Sheffield Academic Press, 1996.

———— and Philip R. Davies, ed. *The Origins of the Ancient Israelite States*. JSOTSup 228. Sheffield: Sheffield Academic Press, 1996.

Waldman, Nahum M. "Concealment and Irony in the Samson Story. *Dor le Dor*, 13 (1984/85): 71-80.

Walls, Neal H. *The Goddess Anat in Ugaritic Myth*. SBL Dissertation Series 135. Atlanta, Ga.: Scholars Press, 1992.

Walsh, Carey Ellen. "Under the Influence: Trust and Risk in Biblical Family Drinking." JSOT 90 (2000): 13-29.

Warner, Sean M. "The Dating of the Period of the Judges." *VT* 28 (1978): 455-63.

Washburn, David L. "The Chronology of Judges: Another Look." *BS* 147 (1990): 414-25.

Watson, Wilfred G. E. and Nicolas Wyatt, eds. *Handbook of Ugaritic Studies*. Cologne: Brill, 1999.

Webb, Barry G. *The Book of the Judges: An Integrated Reading*. JSOTSup 46. Sheffield: JSOT Press 1987.

Weinfeld, Moshe. "Judges 1.1-2.5: The Conquest under the Leadership of the House of Judah." Pages 388-400 in *Understanding Poets and Prophets: Essays in Honour of*

George Wishart Anderson. Edited by A. Graeme Auld. JSOTSup 12. Sheffield: Sheffield Academic Press, 1993.

————. *The Promise of the Land*. Los Angeles: University of California Press, 1993.

Weinsheimer, Joel. "Hermeneutics." Pages 117-36 in *Contemporary Literary Theory*. Edited by G. Douglas Atkins and Laura Morrow. Amherst: University of Massachusetts Press, 1989.

Weisman, Ze'ev. *Political Satire in the Bible*. Atlanta, Ga.: Scholars Press, 1998.

West, James King. *Introduction to the Old Testament*. New York: Macmillan, 1971.

Whedbee, J. William. *The Bible and the Comic Vision*. [N.p.:] Cambridge University Press, 1998. Repr., Minneapolis: Fortress Press, 2002.

White, Kenneth Steel. *Savage Comedy since King Ubu: A Tangent to 'Absurd.'* Washington, D.C.: University Press of America, 1977.

Whitelam, Keith W. *The Invention of Ancient Israel: The Silencing of Palestinian History*. London: Routledge, 1996.

Wiencek, Henry. "Yale and the Price of Slavery." Op. ed. column, *New York Times*, August 18, 2001.

Wifall, Walter. "El Shaddai or El of the Fields." *ZAW* 92 (1980): 24-32.

Wiggins, S.A. *A Reassessment of 'Asherah.'* Kevelaer: Butzon and Bercker, Neukirchen-Vluyn, Neukirchener Verlag, 1993.

Williams, Jay G. "The Structure of Judges 2.6-16.31." *JSOT* 49 (1991): 77-85.

Willis, Timothy M. "The Nature of Jephthah's Authority." *CBQ* 59 (1997): 33-44.

Wilson, R. R. "The Death of the King of Tyre: The Editorial History of Ezekiel 28." Pages 211-218 in *Love and Death in the Ancient Near East: Essays in Honor of Marvin H. Pope*. Edited by J. H. Marks and R. M. Good. Guilford, Conn.: Four Quarters, 1987.

Winston, Mathew. "Black Humor: To Weep with Laughing." Pages 42ff. in *Comedy High and Low: An Introduction to the Experience of Comedy*. Edited by Maurice Charney. New York: Oxford University Press, 1978.

Wright, Ernest G. "The Sacred Area of Shechem in Early Biblical Tradition." Pages 123-38 in *Shechem: The Biography of a Biblical City*. Edited by Ernest G. Wright. New York: McGraw-Hill, 1965.

————. *Shechem: The Biography of a Biblical City*. New York: McGraw-Hill, 1965.

Wright, Robert. "Did the Universe Just Happen?" *Atlantic* (April 1988), 29-44.

Würthwein, Ernst. *The Text of the Old Testament: An Introduction to the Biblia Hebraica*. Grand Rapids, Eerdmans, Mich.: 1979.

Wyatt, Nicolas. "The 'Anat Stela from Ugarit and its Ramifications." *UF* 16 (1984): 327-37.

————: "Arms and the King." Pages 833-882 in *'Und Mose schrieb dieses Lied auf . . . '. Studie zum Alten Testament und zum Alten Orient. Festschrift für O. Loretz zur Vollendung seines 70. Lebensjahres mit Beiträgen von Freunden, Schülern und Kollegen*. Edited by M. Dietrich and I. Kottsieper. AOAT 250, Münster: Ugarit-Verlag, 1998.

_____. *Religious Texts from Ugarit: The Words of Ilimilku and His Colleagues.* Biblical Seminar 53. Sheffield: Sheffield Academic Press, 1998.

_____. *Space and Time in the Religious Life of the Near East.* Sheffield: Sheffield Academic Press, 2001.

_____. "The Story of Aqhat." Pages 234-258 in *Handbook of Ugaritic Studies.* Edited by Wilfred G. E. Watson and Nicolas Wyatt. Cologne: Brill, 1999.

_____, W. G. E. Watson, and J. S. Lloyd eds. *Ugarit, Religion and Culture: Proceedings of the International Colloquium on Ugarit, Religion and Culture, Edinburgh, July 1994, Festschrift J. C. L. Gibson.* UBL 12, Munster: Ugarit-Verlag, 1996.

Yadin, Yigael. "Is the Biblical Account of the Israelite Conquest of Canaan Historically Reliable?" *BAR* 8, No. 2 (Mar-Apr 1982): 16-23.

Yee, Gale A., ed. *Judges and Method: New Approaches in Biblical Studies.* Minneapolis: Fortress Press, 1995.

_____. "By the Hand of a Woman: The Metaphor of the Woman Warrior in Judges 4." In *Women, War, and Metaphor: Language and Society in the Study of the Hebrew Bible.* Edited by C. V. Camp and C. R. Fontaine. *Semeia* 61 (1993): 99-132.

Young, D. G., ed. *Ugarit in Retrospect: Fifty Years of Ugarit and Ugaritic.* Winona Lake, Ind.: Eisenbrauns, 1981.

Younger, K. Lawson, Jr. "Judges 1 in Its Near Eastern Literary Context." Pages 207-27 in *Faith, Tradition, and History: Old Testament Historiography in the Near Eastern Context.* Edited by R. Millard et al. Winona Lake, Ind.: Eisenbrauns, 1994.

_____. "The Configuring of Judicial Preliminaries: Judges 1.1-2.5 and Its Dependence on the Book of Joshua." *JSOT* 68 (1995): 75-92.

Zakovitch, Yair. "Humor and Theology or the Successful Failure of Israelite Intelligence: A Literary Folkloric Approach to Joshua 2." Pages 75-98 in *Text and Tradition: The Hebrew Bible and Folklore.* Edited by Susan Niditch. Atlanta, Ga.: Scholars Press, 1990.

_____. "Sisseras Töd." *ZAW* 93 (1981): 364-74.

Zevit, Ziony. *The Religions of Ancient Israel: a Synthesis of Parallactic Approaches.* London and New York: Continuum, 2001.

_____, et al., eds. *Solving Riddles and Untying Knots: Biblical Epigraphic and Semitic Studies in Honor of J. C. Greenfield.* Winona Lake, Ind.: Eisenbrauns, 1995.

Index

Index to Style, Features, Comedy

NOTE: The Table of Contents is also an excellent index for stylistic features.

1. Judges, style, features

alienation technique, strangeness. viii, 1, 18, 74, 93, 94, 121

alternate way of reading, vi-xiii, 1-4, 9, 154-155, 211-215, 358-362

ambushes (see hiding)

anomalies, curious details, hidden objects, strangeness, v, vii, ix, x, 6, 18-19, 24, 89-93, 95, 99, 100, 115-118, 147, 154, 172, 184, 211, 223, 353-356

"appendices" so-called, additions or epilogues of, 7, 23, 303

ark, xxxi, 58, 66, 67, 70, 176

art of, design, vi, ix, xiii, 13-14, 18-19, 23, 54, 61, 93, 146-147, 151, 206, 211-215, 303, 353-357, 361, 364, 369

the arts in Israel, 55-56, 178, 346

authorship of (see also storytelling), vi, vii, 7, 24-25, 54, 61, 357, 368-369, 374, 375

barren wife, 69, 160, 174, 342, 376

binary opposites, x, xii, 94, 149-151, 170, 184, 187, 207, 209, 211, 216, 222, 243, 345, 360, 369

bribe, bribery, xxvii, 79, 113, 123, 132, 133, 163, 229, 238, 250, 251, 255, 256, 270, 312, 321

the bricoleur, improvisation, 40, 90, 91, 98, 104, 106, 111, 179, 370, 380

brothers, xxvii, xxviii, 14, 15, 18, 29, 30, 32, 34, 55, 62, 63, 65, 67, 68, 76, 78, 80, 84, 116, 117, 123, 135, 137, 157, 158, 163, 164, 166, 167, 183, 191, 192, 195, 212, 217, 223, 241, 266, 267, 268-269, 270, 273, 288, 303, 309, 310, 311, 318, 333, 334, 336, 338, 339, 341, 347, 386, 394

burnt offering (see offerings)

camels, 55, 90, 95,113, 116, 168, 179, 180, 181, 185, 192, 350, 387

cause and effect, conditional statements, 203, 262, 263, 282-284

chariots, x, xxviii, 29, 42, 55, 179, 181, 225, 232, 291, 300, 306, 316, 318, 332, 350, 377, 394

chiasmus, 14, 15, 26, 31, 62-64, 82, 214, 384

commandments, apodictic law, Deuteronomic law, 10, 28, 30, 45, 131, 132, 133, 134, 218, 222, 229, 246-248, 253, 254, 259, 261, 264, 278, 298, 361, 365, 366, 370

comparisons and contrasts (see also parallels), vi, vii, xii, 6, 25, 28, 31, 36-38, 40, 42, 47, 48, 49, 56, 111, 119, 140-143, 146, 151, 152, 159, 173, 195, 202,

109, 110, 111, 113, 119, 121, 122, 124, 126, 129, 130, 132, 133, 135, 137, 149, 169, 170, 175, 183, 202, 226, 229, 233, 273, 307, 308, 320, 342, 345, 354, 373, 374, 381, 383, 400

madness, folly, 47, 100, 106, 127

paradox, 39, 86, 111, 129, 136, 137, 174, 257

parody, travesty, burlesque, 99, 100, 115, 123, 126, 131, 132, 133, 135, 373, 389

preposterous actions, ix, 115-118, 122, 128, 136, 191, 383

riddles, puzzles, viii, x, xxviii, 9, 40, 41, 61, 91, 101, 102, 108, 109, 110, 115, 118, 127, 135-136, 147, 149, 154, 180, 188, 194, 196, 200, 201, 212, 222, 227, 238, 242-243, 259, 271, 275, 284, 307, 324, 361

satire, 17, 34, 101, 126, 127, 133

suspension of normal rules, 99, 100

topsy-turvy world, viii, 98, 100, 107, 110, 112, 131, 136

trickster, trick (see also treachery, above), ix, xi, xxvi, 5, 30, 50, 74, 91, 99, 104-106, 108, 110, 112, 114, 116, 117, 119, 122, 125, 126, 128, 129, 130-131, 132, 136, 137, 204, 220, 226, 236, 257, 271, 273

weapons, strange, 74, 100, 121, 131

Index to Characters, Mythological Figures, and Place Names

NOTE: Characters in *Judges* and the Ugaritic myths are not given here. See the main entries about them in the Table of Contents.

Index to Scholars, Literary Critics, Artists, Author, Literary Works

3251594

Made in the USA